Satellite Newsgathering

Satellite Newsgathering

Second Edition

Jonathan Higgins

ELSEVIER

AMSTERDAM • BOSTON • HEIDELBERG • LONDON • NEW YORK • OXFORD •
PARIS • SAN DIEGO • SAN FRANCISCO • SINGAPORE • SYDNEY • TOKYO

Focal Press is an imprint of Elsevier

Focal Press

Acquisitions Editor: Angelina Ward
Publishing Services Manager: George Morrison
Project Manager: Kathryn Liston
Assistant Editor: Doug Shults
Marketing Manager: Christine Degon Veroulis
Cover Design: Eric DeCicco

Focal Press is an imprint of Elsevier
30 Corporate Drive, Suite 400, Burlington, MA 01803, USA
Linacre House, Jordan Hill, Oxford OX2 8DP, UK

♾ Recognizing the importance of preserving what has been written, Elsevier prints its books
on acid-free paper whenever possible.

Library of Congress Cataloging-in-Publication Data
Higgins, Jonathan.
    Satellite newsgathering / Jonathan Higgins. — 2nd ed.
      p. cm.
    Includes bibliographical references and index.
    ISBN-13: 978-0-240-51973-9 (pbk.)
    ISBN-10: 0-240-51973-6 (pbk.)
  1. Artificial satellites in telecommunication. 2. Electronic news gathering. I. Title.
    TK5104.H54 2007
    384.5'1—dc22

                                                                        2007008806

British Library Cataloguing in Publication Data
A catalogue record for this book is available from the British Library.

ISBN: 978-0-240-51973-9

For information on all Focal Press publications
visit our website at www.book.elsevier.com

Typeset by Charon Tec Ltd (A Macmillan Company), Chennai, India
www.charontec.com

07   08   09   10   11   10 9 8 7 6 5 4 3 2 1

Printed in the United States of America

Working together to grow
libraries in developing countries

www.elsevier.com | www.bookaid.org | www.sabre.org

ELSEVIER   BOOK AID International   Sabre Foundation

Contents

Preface

There have been a number of developments in satellite newsgathering (SNG) since the first edition of this book was published in 2000, but nothing has fundamentally changed the impact of SNG as the vital process that delivers 'live' and 'breaking' news to the viewer and listener as it unfolds. It is the most powerful tool of cutting-edge newsgathering, and when used effectively, stunning in the way a situation can be so vividly conveyed to an audience.

As an intrinsic part of most news bulletins, whether on television or radio, the use of SNG is taken for granted in a world of 24/7 rolling news channels. The process of newsgathering is not a subject that most audiences consider as they take in a television newscast, an Internet news page or a radio news bulletin. Yet an increasingly higher proportion of the global population now obtain their 'fix' of daily news from radio, television or the Internet than from newspapers, and consequently rely on the processes of electronic newsgathering (ENG) to deliver information from the scene. SNG is one of the core tools used, involving the use of very advanced technology in sometimes the most primitive of conditions.

The way in which a war or some other disaster virtually anywhere in the world can be brought 'live' as it happens onto the television screen in the living room only became possible less than 30 years ago. Before 1980, film cameras were still largely the key tools of television newsgathering, as ENG cameras were still not commonplace, except in certain markets such as the USA. Conventional electronic outside broadcast cameras were too large and heavy for newsgathering operations. There were reports from the scene of a story on occasions, but because they were on film, there was a delay due to the transportation, processing and editing involved.

Arthur C. Clarke, the famous science fiction author, first proposed the concept of artificial communications satellites in 1945. Through the 1950s and early 1960s, a race ensued between the USA and Russia to develop rocket technology to offer improved military capability, and in addition to attempt to place the first man on the Moon – though this second objective was more political than military. The development of communications satellites occurred in parallel, and as part of the overall scheme to exploit space for the 'betterment of mankind'. (Incidentally, the word 'satellite' comes from the Latin word *satelles*, meaning 'an attendant'.)

The use of satellites alone to deliver news material back to the major news networks really began with the Vietnam War in the late 1960s – Vietnam was dubbed the first 'TV war'. The US networks needed a way to obtain video from overseas that was faster than by air transportation, and the relatively new communications satellites provided the means for doing so – though the stories were still at least a day old before they were reported on television with pictures. The first significant use of satellite technology for news occurred in 1968 during the Tet offensive in the Vietnam War. But the passage of time does not always improve matters, as the Falkland Islands conflict between Britain and Argentina of 1982 illustrates – it was not well reported in television news terms. There were no satellite links available, and due to other hindrances imposed by the British government, many of the stories were covered on television with visual background until film pictures arrived, typically up to 48 hours or more later. The Persian Gulf conflict in 1990 and the ensuing First Gulf War in 1991 changed that forever. SNG was 'made' by the situation in the Gulf, and no major conflict has since occurred without the use of SNG to bring it to our screens.

The change crept up on the public almost unnoticed. Today's television news bulletins are a complex weave of studio material, sophisticated computer graphics, video (from tape or computer 'server') and live reports delivered by terrestrial microwave links and satellite uplinks from innumerable scenes of news stories. Radio bulletins are similarly a complex mix of different sources, put together to recreate the situation in the listeners' mind, and convey the key information of the story.

But the focus of this book is the use of satellite uplinks for newsgathering, and although that typically means television news, we will not be restricting our discussion to television only, but also considering the part that satellite delivery systems from the field play in radio news reporting. Radio has had the advantage of the availability of the telephone since the advent of reports from the scene; though in the early days of radio news, it was common to merely read news items from newspapers or news agency wire services. Even now, radio reports from difficult locations are delivered via telephone – either a mobile phone or often a satellite phone.

I wrote the first edition of this book over seven years ago, and in the intervening years both little and much has changed. The process of satellite transmission is essentially that of a transmitter transmitting a beam to an artificial satellite orbiting the Earth, which in turn transmits another beam back to a receiver at a different point on the Earth's surface. This basic concept remains the same, but over the last seven years we have seen the virtual extinction of the use of analog technology in SNG equipment, the introduction of the use of Internet-based technologies, the emergence of new digital compression technologies, more types of SNG terminals from a wider range of manufacturers with reductions in size and cost, greater use of SNG technology by broadcast organizations of all sizes – and so the list goes on. However, the process of SNG goes beyond solely how the equipment works and is used in the operation of communication satellites in orbit to regulatory affairs, transportation, safety and logistics. Not least, it is about working in a wide range of environments, from city streets to battlefields or areas of devastation following some natural disaster, in all climates and where time is of the essence.

This is all reflected in this new edition, yet even for those involved in the broadcast news business, it can still be bewildering to find out about many of the aspects of the use of SNG equipment, and the challenges posed for those who are responsible, either directly or indirectly, for its deployment or operation in the field. The difficulty I had in writing this new edition (and the first edition as well) was to decide how far and how deep to go into any particular topic or aspect, yet still try to convey the principles of a subject to a reasonable depth to satisfy the wide audience this book is aimed at.

The writing of the first edition was triggered by the realization of a need for a primer that could be used by anyone wanting to know more about SNG, since no such comprehensive text existed. In this book, those interested in this subject will gain a solid basis in the technical and practical considerations in understanding, specifying and operating these systems around the world, and an insight into both the sense of achievement in doing so successfully as well as the challenges occasionally faced. It is intended to give a practical treatment of this specific application of satellite communications engineering, and the use of scary mathematics has been virtually restricted to the appendices for those that are interested.

A note of caution – the term 'SNG' is often used erroneously in a generic sense to describe any mobile satellite uplink that may be used for coverage of a sports fixture, a local or national event, or an international event such as the Olympic Games. This book is specifically about using mobile satellite uplinks for the gathering of news, and nothing else. Throughout the focus remains on newsgathering, and the use of satellite technology in the field to serve this purpose.

I have treated the whole subject of SNG in a 'holistic' fashion, as there is a flow and intertwining of the different themes in the following chapters that put this subject beyond a strictly technical treatise on satellite communications engineering (of which there are numerous in print). This book covers a range of issues and hopefully can continue to act (as it did with the first edition) as a handbook for both professionals working in the field as well as those with an incidental interest. The most expert people in the use of SNG have strong editorial, technical and logistical skills – be they an uplink technician, producer or reporter – and so this book covers the subject in a similarly multi-disciplined approach.

Finally, I want to express gratitude to the many colleagues and friends across the industry, who freely gave their time for both the first and the second editions to discuss issues, look at drafts of chapters, make suggestions, supply information, provide images, and generally encouraged me in this endeavor. I also want to thank all at Focal Press, particularly Joanne Tracy, who patiently waited for the manuscript while several deadlines passed.

Not least, I thank my wife Annie, who has constantly supported and encouraged me from the very beginning when I first decided to launch into a writing career, and has endured countless lost evenings, weekends (and occasionally holidays!) throughout without question.

Jonathan Higgins
April 2007

Acknowledgments

My deepest thanks to all my colleagues who supplied information, debated issues and generally aided me in the writing of this book. In particular I would like to acknowledge the following for their contributions – Tim Barrow, Peter Beardow, Marco Franken, Wes Gordon, A.R. Lewis, Professor Steven Livingston, Neil McSparron, Professor Gérard Maral, Steve McGuiness, Richard Penman, Derek Tam, Dick Tauber, Ian Trow, Richard Wolf and Andy Woodhouse.

To the following I would like to express my appreciation for allowing their valuable photographs taken on location to be included – Simon Atkinson, Martin Cheshire, Jack Raup, Paul Szeless, Leo Tucker-Brown and Steve Williams.

I also wish to record my thanks to the following companies and organizations that kindly supplied images and information:

7E Communications, Advent Communications, Agilent Technologies, Alcatel Space, Arianespace, AvL Technologies, BBC Training & Development, Boeing Network & Space Systems, CPI Satcom, EDAK, E2V, Envivio, Eutelsat, Frontline Communications, Glensound Electronics, Holkirk Communications, Inmarsat, Intelsat, Livewire, New Delhi TV, Newtec, Nexred, Norsat, NSSL, Peak Communications, Radyne, Research Concepts, Sat-Comm, Scopus Technologies, SES New Skies, SISLink, Swedish Microwave, Swe-Dish Satellite Systems, Tandberg Television, Telecast Fiber Systems, Thrane & Thrane, Vocality International, Wolf Coach, and Xicom Technology.

Finally, I am honored by the encouragement given to me by Sir Arthur C. Clarke after the publication of the first edition.

1

From the beat of the distant drum ...

It was January of 1991, and in the hotel conference room in Dharhan, Saudi Arabia, the US general turned away from the overhead projection screen, completing the briefing to the assembled international media and inviting questions. Across the world, millions of people watching and listening via satellite had been drawn into the story told by the general's words and the pictures projected onto the screen from the on-board 'smart bomb' cameras. The world had seen graphic pictures illustrating the latest round of sorties of Operation Desert Storm on Iraq, which had taken place only hours before. This briefing in the Persian Gulf conflict was yet another example of satellite newsgathering giving audiences across the world the sense of 'being there' – and this power had also become a political force. Scenes like this occurred on numerous occasions in early 1991, with 'live' coverage from Riyadh and other Iraqi targets in the Middle East of attacking Scud missiles (Figure 1.1).

Now we fast forward 12 years to the spring of 2003, and almost eerily we see almost the same scenario, only this time from the US Central Command's headquarters and main media center, Camp As Sayliyah

Figure 1.1   Satellite dish farm on the crazy golf course at the hotel in Dharhan, Saudi Arabia, 1991

in Doha, in the Gulf sate of Qatar. But instead of using a hotel conference room, the US Department of Defense (DOD) has converted one of the warehouses on the base into a huge US$1.5 million media center, dominated by a US$250,000 briefing stage designed by a top Hollywood art director, in front of a 11.5 m (38 ft) wide world map, with seven plasma screens, two podiums, and digital clocks showing six time zones, including Baghdad time. From the tentative show-and-tell flirtation with the media over a decade previously, the US military had learned to put on a show for the media – and therefore for the viewer.

The Second Gulf War is underway with Operation Iraqi Freedom, only this time the use of satellite newsgathering has mushroomed, with satellite uplinks not only in use at Command HQ but on the battlefield itself, with some broadcasters even transmitting live from the backs of military vehicles on the move as they advance with the Allied forces.

The use of satellite newsgathering is now so powerful that no one can be in any doubt that war is sometimes fought as much on television as on the battlefield – the political impact of which has been dubbed the 'CNN effect'.[1,2] It was for this reason that the Iraqi government wanted the Western media present in Baghdad during both conflicts to bring to the world live coverage of the night-time Allied attacks. As a tool of the media, satellite newsgathering (SNG) is of such significance and immediacy that no major international conflict can ever now be reported without its use. While SNG brings everything from reports on the pile-up on the local freeway, to live 'vox-pops' on the street, to national political events, it is in the arena of major international news events that its remarkable power to evoke the sense to the audience of 'being there' is felt the most. It brings these news events into the home and the workplace, delivering the impression to audiences that they are viewing through a 'window on the world'. The development and use of SNG is the culmination of a long history of gathering and distributing news and, to put SNG into context, we are going to take a journey through the history of telecommunications, from the early methods of communicating news to today's sophisticated electronic newsgathering process.

1.1 News by drum, horn, shout, fire and smoke

The early communication of news is naturally closely linked with the development of spoken language over 100 000 years ago. Spoken news sent by messenger was essential for the survival of early peoples – by warning of attack or flood, informing of the whereabouts of sources of food, or the proclamation of the birth and death of leaders.

The earliest technologies used to send news over distances (without sending a human messenger) revolved around the use of drums, horns, birds, shouting, beacon fires, mirrors and smoke. In the sixth century BC the Persians could send news from the capital of the Persian Empire to the provinces by means of a line of men shouting one to another, positioned on hills. This kind of transmission was up to 30 times faster than using messengers. In the first century BC, the Gauls could call all their warriors to war in just 3 days using only the human voice in a similar manner.

However, in many societies the drum and the horn were the quickest and easiest way of relaying information by sound waves, by using a string of local 'repeaters' to cover large distances. (It is interesting to consider the parallel with modern telecommunications, which still relies on 'repeaters' and 'waves', although at a much higher frequency than sound.)

The recording and sending of complex messages is tied to the development of writing. Telegraphy (from the Greek 'writing in the distance') describes a communication system able to convey signals that represent coded letters, numbers and signs of writing, and has very ancient origins. The use of hieroglyphics and symbols on clay tablets brought the ability to send more complex information by messenger, and the first alphabet appeared around 1500 BC. In 105 AD T'sai Lun (China) first developed paper, and the use of paper spread across Asia to Egypt in the third and fourth centuries AD.

The beginning of the development of a technological telegraph system came in the late eighteenth century. In 1791, Claude Chappe (France) invented the optical telegraph – the 'tachygraphe' – which was a mechanical semaphore system based on towers. In 1792, he showed his invention to the French Legislative Assembly, which adopted it officially, and in 1794 the first message sent via this semaphore system brought news of French victory over the Austrians. In 1798 its name was changed to the 'telegraphe' by order of the French government. Napoleon was reported to have been impressed by this, and soon semaphore systems were established between most of the cities of France, followed by prominent cities in Italy, Germany, Russia and the US, and many remained in use until the 1860s, when they were superseded by the electric telegraph.

1.2   Dots and dashes

The true revolution in telegraphy came in the eighteenth and early nineteenth centuries with the discovery of electricity. The work on electricity at various times over this period of Stephen Gray (UK), Pieter van Musschenbroek (Holland), Ewald Georg von Kleist (Germany), Luigi Galvani (Italy), Alessandro Volta (Italy), Andre Ampere (France), Christian Oersted (Denmark) and Michael Faraday (UK) all contributed to the development of the electric telegraph.

The invention of the electric telegraph was the first significant technological leap in the conveyance of news. As with so many inventions, a number of people were working on the same idea at the same time (as we shall also see later with both the telephone and television), and came up with various types of equipment – these included Soemmering (Bavaria), Ronalds (UK) and Oersted (Denmark). In 1830, Joseph Henry (US) transmitted the first practical electrical signal, and in 1832 Pawel Schilling (Russia) had constructed the needle telegraph in St. Petersburg, in which electricity flowed through a magnetic spool and moved a magnetic needle, thus demonstrating the first working electromagnetic telegraph.

In 1835 William Cooke (UK) and Charles Wheatstone (UK) demonstrated an electric telegraph system, based on Cooke's observation of a demonstration of Schilling's system which he had seen a few years earlier. Their system used electric currents to deflect needles that pointed to letters of the alphabet laid out on a grid. They developed their system and built a telegraph line from London to Slough in 1843. In 1845, their telegraph system made history when it aided the capture of a murder suspect, who was seen boarding the train for London. Police used the telegraph to send details to Paddington railway station in London, and the police captured the suspect as he got off the train.

However, the first practical electric telegraph that was widely adopted was based on a relatively simple design, developed by Samuel Morse (US) in 1837. Morse had seen Cooke and Wheatstone's telegraph demonstrated in London. His system used a key (a switch) to make or break the electrical circuit, a pair of wires joining one telegraph station to another distant station, and an electromagnetic receiver or sounder that, upon being turned on and off, produced a buzzing noise. These electrical impulses were received as a series of dots and dashes that could be translated into letters and hence words – thus came the invention of the Morse code. Morse patented his telegraph system in 1840.

In 1844 Morse demonstrated the use of the telegraph to send a news story over his first long-distance telegraph circuit under construction alongside the railway line from Baltimore in Maryland to Washington, DC, a distance of about 60 km (37 miles). A telegraph operator at Annapolis Junction, Maryland, heard news of the announcement of the presidential nominee for the Whig party at a convention in Baltimore from a messenger on a Washington-bound train passing through Annapolis Junction. The telegraph line did not yet extend the full distance from Washington to Baltimore, but the telegraph operator was able to signal the news to Morse in Washington – the message via the train arrived in

Washington an hour later. A few weeks later, on completion of the telegraph line, Morse sent the famous words from the Bible, 'What hath God wrought!' on his telegraph from the Supreme Court chamber in the US Capitol Building in Washington to the Mount Clare railroad depot in Baltimore.

This was completely revolutionary, and newspapers in the US and Europe quickly seized upon the idea of using the telegraph as a means of gathering news from distant locations. Telegraph lines sprung up alongside railway tracks – for these provided a convenient path across the country – so that by 1852 there were 37 000 km (23 000 miles) of lines across the USA. By 1867 the Western Union Telegraph (which had an almost monopolistic position in the US) had over 74 000 km (46 000 miles) of lines, and by 1895 over 300 000 km (189 000 miles).

In 1865, twenty participating countries signed the first International Telegraph Convention, and thus the International Telegraph Union (ITU) was established. (The birth and significance of the ITU is examined in Chapter 6.) However, up until around 1880, the land-line telegraph was mostly used for short-distance metropolitan communication.

1.2.1   Wiring the world

To really take advantage of its potential, the telegraph needed to reach around the world. In 1866, after 11 years of attempts to lay a cable across the Atlantic, the first submarine cable between Newfoundland and Ireland came into service. By 1879, there was a combination of routes, both overland and under the sea, linking London with India, China, Java and Australia. By 1890, Brazil was linked by submarine cable with the US and Europe. In 1880 a cable linking the east coast of Africa was completed, linking the Yemen in the Arabian Gulf via Mozambique to South Africa, and by the late 1880s Europe was linked to the west coast of Africa via Portugal. By 1892, there were ten transoceanic telegraph links. In 1902, the first transpacific telegraph cable began operating, stretching from Vancouver, British Columbia, through the Fiji Islands and Norfolk Islands to Australia, before landing in New Zealand.

1.2.2   The news and the telegraph

The use of the telegraph for newsgathering grew, as the following few examples illustrate. The telegraph played an important role in disseminating news from the battlefronts during the American Civil War, feeding detailed reports to the newspapers. The telegraph was instrumental in disseminating news of Abraham Lincoln's assassination, for within 12 hours of his shooting in 1865, newspapers in every major American city had printed the story. In an article entitled 'The Intellectual Effects of Electricity' in *The Spectator*, London, November 9, 1889, the following observation was made:

> 'With the recording of every event, and especially every crime, everywhere without perceptible interval of time the world is for purposes of intelligence reduced to a village … All men are compelled to think of all things, at the same time, on imperfect information, and with too little interval for reflection … The constant diffusion of statements in snippets, the constant excitements of feeling unjustified by fact, the constant forma-tion of hasty or erroneous opinions, must, in the end, one would think, deteriorate the intelligence of all to whom the telegraph appeals.'

Some areas of the press were obviously not as impressed by this new tool for newsgathering as others. Even after the invention of the telephone, the telegraph remained the predominant method of long-distance communication for some considerable time, because of the extensive network that had become established and the relatively low cost of sending messages. The use of Morse code, of course, was essential to the early development of radio.

1.3   Bell ringing

The development of the telephone began soon after the invention of the electric telegraph, and although attributed to Alexander Graham Bell (US), others also had a hand in its development. In 1854, Charles Bourseul (France) wrote about transmitting speech electrically and, in 1861, Philip Reis (Germany) devised a telephone system, which unfortunately, although tantalizingly close to reproducing speech, only poorly conveyed certain sounds.

However, it was Bell who filed a patent for a telephone on February 14, 1876, only hours before another inventor, Elisha Gray (US), also filed his patent for a telephone system. Even though neither man had actually built a working telephone, Bell made his telephone operate 3 weeks later using ideas outlined in Gray's patent and not described in his own patent – an issue of some dispute at the time. Bell was heavily dependent on the electrical knowledge of his assistant, Thomas Watson (US). On March 10, 1876, the first complete sentence was heard on the telephone when Watson was waiting in another room to receive the call. Bell was setting up his equipment when he accidentally spilled battery acid on his trousers and called to his assistant, 'Mr. Watson, come here. I need you.' These were the first words transmitted by telephone.

Bell's invention used a continuously varying (analog) electrical signal to transmit a person's voice over a line, unlike the telegraph's 'dots' and 'dashes'. As a transmitter, the telephone converts sound waves into analog signals by reacting to variations in air density caused by the sound waves. These variations in air density are converted into an electrical current of varying force and, at the receiver, the sequence is reversed whereby the analog signals are converted back into sound waves.

Telephones were developed as personal communication devices, as usually only one person transmitted and received messages with one other person at a time; so from the point of view of newsgathering, the telephone did not offer a significant advantage over the telegraph. Although the messages could be instantly understood, without the need for decoding Morse, the use of the telephone for newsgathering lagged behind the telegraph until well into the first part of the twentieth century. However, for messages to be telegraphed or telephoned in the late nineteenth century, a physical link had to be established and maintained between the points of communication. Remove the need for the physical link, and the potential for communication expanded greatly.

1.4   Without wires

In 1894, Guglielmo Marconi (Italy) began to investigate the laws of electricity and magnetism determined by previous experimenters. He built upon the work of Heinrich Hertz, who in 1887 produced radio waves, and the other work on radio waves by Oliver Lodge (UK) and Edouard Branly (France).

Specifically, Marconi believed that there was a way to use electromagnetic waves for the purpose of communication, and he began to conduct his own experiments to test these ideas. These experiments led to the first elementary radio set.

In 1894, Marconi's first radio transmissions traveled only a few hundred meters. Marconi successfully sent the Morse code letter 'S' to a farmer who owned the adjacent property through the use of a basic transmitter and receiver. He noted that ground obstacles such as vegetation and hills weakened the signal slightly, but otherwise the experiment was a huge success. For the following 18 months, Marconi continued to experiment in seeking to improve upon his previous successes, during which time he successfully demonstrated the sending of a telegram by radio wave over 20 km (13 miles). Marconi obtained his first patent for his radio device in 1896 and, from then on, worked to improve and to commercialize his design. The Marconi Wireless Telegraph Company was formed in 1898, backed by British investors, to develop Marconi's system for maritime applications and to continue experimentation, and in 1899, Marconi wireless systems were fitted to three British battleships and two US battleships.

Marconi's wireless telegraph helped make the headlines in 1899 when he placed transmitters on two steamships in New York harbor and telegraph operators aboard reported the progress of an international yacht race. The ship-to-shore signals were received at stations in New York and then relayed across the US and the Atlantic by land-line telegraph. This was the first use of wireless telegraphy (radiotelegraphy) to cover 'breaking' news.

On December 12, 1901, Marconi achieved his furthest radio transmission to date – across the Atlantic Ocean, from St. Johns in Newfoundland to Poldhu in Cornwall. This advancement was of great impact to worldwide communications, as the potential for transmitting information and news across the world instantaneously was realized.

Over the following 20 years, the Marconi Wireless Telegraph Company established such a dominance in marine communications, and conducted its business in such a manner, that considerable problems were caused which began to encroach on what a number of countries regarded as issues of sovereignty. In both the US and the UK, in the years up to and during the First World War, wireless became the preserve of the respective navy departments of government. After 1912 (directly as a result of the sinking of the ocean liner *Titanic*), a number of countries, including the UK and the US, made it a condition that all vessels had to be fitted with wireless telegraphy equipment. The particular details of this aspect of wireless are not relevant to our exploration of the development of broadcast news, save to say that in the US it eventually led to the establishment of a company who became dominant in US broadcasting – RCA.

American Telephone & Telegraph (AT&T), Westinghouse Electric, Western Electric Company, Marconi Wireless of America and General Electric were all US companies who were crucial to the war effort in their manufacture of wireless telegraphy equipment for the Allies. However, because of US government concern over the dominant position of the Marconi Company (due to its foreign roots), there was a determination to end the grip of the Marconi Company on US radiotelegraphy. This led to encouragement by the US government to form a consortium of US companies in order to challenge the dominance of the Marconi Company in the US.

In this aspect of the development of wireless in the US, one name is prominent – David Sarnoff (US). Sarnoff was not an inventor, but he was a visionary and an entrepreneur. He started working for Marconi Wireless of America in 1906, and there is an apocryphal story that in 1912, while on duty working as a wireless telegraphy operator, he picked up the signals from the ships near to the doomed *Titanic* and relayed news of survivors to waiting relatives for the following 72 hours. Another story is that he wrote a memo to his boss, E.J. Nally, in 1916: 'I have in mind a plan of development that would make radio a "household utility" in the same sense as the piano or phonograph. The idea is to bring music into the house by wireless.' Nally is said to have rejected Sarnoff's idea.

In 1919, General Electric bought out Marconi Wireless of America to form the Radio Corporation of America (RCA), with the aim of developing the US market for radio equipment. McNally, the President of Marconi America, and Sarnoff, by then the General Manager, transferred to the same positions in RCA. Within 2 years, RCA had taken significant holdings in AT&T and Westinghouse, to become the dominant commercial force in the US broadcasting industry. Sarnoff, the ultimate broadcasting marketeer, later became President of RCA in 1930.

The development of wireless was the subject of innumerable patent wrangles (and similar patent-ownership struggles continued on in the development in television up until 1939), but with the formation of RCA, combining a 'patent-pool' of all the important technologies, the issues were largely resolved.

1.5   Radio is born

Marconi's wireless relied on the use of Morse code, but voice transmission over the airwaves had been a dream of many, including Reginald Fessenden (Canada). Marconi did not believe there was much future in voice wireless, preferring to concentrate on improving radiotelegraphy. (The last maritime transmission of Morse code was on January 31, 1997.)

Fessenden believed that electromagnetic waves could be altered with the voice superimposed, using the same principles that made Bell's telephone work, and in 1900 he first proved that it was possible. Fessenden succeeded in being the first to broadcast a voice message, on Christmas Eve 1906, from Massachusetts, US, when radio operators on ships in the Atlantic were startled to hear a human voice emitting from their Morse telegraph equipment. Many operators heard Fessenden make a short speech, play a record and give a rendition of 'O Holy Night' on his violin. Radio broadcasting was born.

The technique of voice transmission that Fessenden had developed lacked power and amplification, and in 1906 Lee De Forest (US) patented the 'Audion' amplifier (the triode electron tube) which was an improvement on the thermionic valve (vacuum tube) invented by John Ambrose Fleming (UK) in 1904. De Forest, like many other pioneers of radio, was a controversial figure, and in 1910 he attempted (unsuccessfully) the first live broadcast of an opera, sung by Caruso, from the Metropolitan Opera House in New York. On the night of the US presidential election in 1916, De Forest also transmitted the returns of the elections. (Unfortunately, he announced the wrong candidate as the winner, as he closed down at 11 p.m. before the final results were in.) This transmission arguably made him the first broadcast journalist.

Although Fessenden's work and De Forest's invention made voice radio possible and practicable, it was not until after the First World War that public and commercial broadcasting began. Throughout this period, radio was still seen primarily as point-to-point communication – a 'wireless' telephone. The notion of 'broadcasting' to a large audience of listeners was not seen as practical or of much interest. Radio at that time was used mostly for commercial shipping purposes, but land-based amateur operators began to appear as electronic technology developed, 'broadcasting' to other enthusiasts listening on crystal radio sets. Most of these operations were very tentative affairs – just single operators transmitting recordings and talking – but in 1920 in the US alone it is estimated that radio experimenters spent over US$2 million on radio parts. In many other countries, groups of amateur enthusiasts were communicating with each other, and laying the foundations for the establishment of radio broadcasting in their respective countries.

The beginning of true public broadcasting is generally attributed to station KDKA in Pittsburgh, Pennsylvania, US. It is still a matter of historical debate as to whether it was KDKA or one of a number of other stations in the US which was first in broadcasting, and much turns on the definition of 'broadcasting'. An amateur enthusiast, Frank Conrad (US), who worked for Westinghouse Electric, built a transmitting station in his garage at his home in East Pittsburgh, Pennsylvania. In his experimental 'broadcasts' in 1919, he read items from the newspapers but discovered that when he substituted a phonograph for his microphone, a large number of listeners (who had built their own crystal radio sets) wrote or telephoned requests for more music. When Conrad became swamped with these requests, he decided to broadcast a regular program to satisfy his listeners. Having exhausted his own collection of records, he borrowed records from a local music store in exchange for mentioning the store on the air – the first radio advertisement. All of these concepts of broadcasting – the station, the audience, the programs and a means to pay for the programs – came about through Conrad's experiments. A local department store promoted Conrad's broadcasts in one of their newspaper advertisements to sell radios, and promptly sold out of them. As a direct result, Westinghouse took notice and, seeing the potential of broadcasting for selling radios they could manufacture, decided to set up its own station and use its defunct war radio manufacturing facilities to produce simple receivers.

On November 2, 1920, station KDKA went on air for the first time with a 4-hour news program – bringing the returns of the US elections relayed over the telephone from the wire service of the local newspaper, culminating in the announcement that Harding had been elected as US President. This is generally considered as marking the birth of the broadcasting industry. (Shortly after this, Westinghouse merged its radio interests with RCA.)

During the latter part of the 1920s, networks of affiliated radio stations were formed in the US, as part of the natural growth of a new industry. In 1926 at RCA, Sarnoff established the National Broadcasting Company (NBC), and in 1928, William Paley formed the Columbia Broadcasting System (CBS) from the struggling United Independent Broadcasters company. In 1943, the independent Blue Network Company was formed from the Blue Network of NBC (one of its two networks) as a result of a federal anti-trust ruling against the dominance of NBC. The Blue Network Company changed its name in 1945 to the American Broadcasting Company (ABC). Other networks, such as the Mutual Broadcasting System (1934), the DuMont Network (1946) and the Liberty Broadcasting System (1949), were all formed but were eventually overwhelmed by the dominance of the 'Big Three' networks and their well-established network of affiliate stations.

A large number of stations around the world began broadcasting through the 1920s, many using wireless equipment developed during the First World War. In 1920, in Chelmsford in the UK, the Marconi Company's station 2MT famously transmitted an experimental broadcast of a concert by the opera singer Nellie Melba. In 1922, 2MT went on air with scheduled broadcasts, followed by the British Broadcasting Company's station, 2LO, in London later that year. The Marconi station became integrated into the BBC, who bought Marconi transmitters. In 1927, the British Broadcasting Company became the British Broadcasting Corporation, and by 1930 covered most of the populated areas of the UK with their broadcasts.

As a vast continent as well as a nation, Australia was a natural market for radio. The first 'broadcast' in Australia in 1919 was by AWA (Amalgamated Wireless Australasia, an amalgamation of Marconi and Telefunken in 1913), when the Australian National Anthem was broadcast. Radio station 2SB in Sydney was the first to go on air with scheduled programs in 1923. A string of other stations went on air through the 1920s, and in 1929 the Australian Broadcasting Company (ABC) was formed. By 1932, there were 55 stations across the country.

1.5.1 Early news bulletins

Through the 1920s in the UK, the BBC developed its programming of entertainment and music, but news was only broadcast after 7 p.m. to avoid upsetting the newspapers. Radio news bulletins consisted of announcers (in full evening dress) reading brief items of news, usually from the newspapers or prepared from news agency wire services. There was little or no 'actuality' (news from the scene itself) and the amount of news conveyed was roughly equivalent to brief headlines. Nevertheless, the newspapers were increasingly hostile to radio news, and the BBC held off objections from the press by beginning its evening news bulletins with the statement[3]: 'Here is the last news bulletin for today. General situation section. The following items of news indicate the general situation in the country. Copyright in these items is reserved outside the British Isles.'

This awkward relationship with the press was repeated in other countries as radio quickly established itself as the predominant medium, with the newspapers continually fighting rearguard actions as they jealously fought to hold on to their monopoly of news before it was heard on the radio. The newspapers considered that they had the primary right to disseminate news, and many newspaper groups sought to control the situation by buying up radio stations.

In the US, radio stations, as in other places, rarely had their own systems of newsgathering, but produced news bulletins from news agency wire services or newspapers. Disputes raged when radio stations not owned by local newspapers used material from newspapers. This developed into the 'press-radio wars' from around 1931 to 1935, when the news agency wire services were forced to stop providing news material to radio stations that threatened sales of newspapers. Obviously, radio could broadcast prime news agency wire service stories before the newspapers could print them.

CBS is of particular interest, as from the beginning it established a stronger interest in news than NBC. It later developed the 'eyewitness news' concept, with the emphasis on a report from the scene, either from a reporter in the studio who had just returned from the scene or, where possible, a live report by whatever means (telephone or radio).

In response to the embargo of the news agencies, the networks developed their own newsgathering systems, bypassing the news agencies, even covering major stories overseas as the following example illustrates. In 1936, the Spanish Civil War was raging, and an NBC news correspondent was caught in the middle of a battle. He and an engineer established a telephone line at an abandoned farmhouse between the Loyalist and Rebel armies, and reported while sounds of artillery shells exploding could be heard during the live broadcasts, which were relayed to the US by short-wave radio.

Occasionally the 'live' broadcasting of news events in the US occurred as well. The first famous instance was in 1925, when a Chicago radio station transmitted live coverage of the Scopes 'monkey' trial from Dayton, Tennessee, where a teacher named Scopes had been charged with breaking a Tennessee state law prohibiting the teaching of the Darwinian Theory of Evolution. Dayton was 800 km (500 miles) from Chicago, and the broadcasts were carried using 'open' telephone lines. In 1930, a Colombus, Ohio, station transmitted very dramatic live reports of a fire at the Ohio State Penitentiary, with the sounds of the fire and the screams of three hundred inmates dying in the background. But such reporting of major news stories was unusual. Newsgathering was not the first priority of the mainly entertainment-oriented radio networks, though they did provide coverage of important speeches, political conventions and election results (as we have seen).

The battle for disseminating news between the newspaper publishers on one side and the broadcasters on the other, continued in several countries until the Second World War. Meanwhile, in the UK, the BBC generally avoided the same type of confrontation with the newspapers. Live reporting from the scene of a story happened only very occasionally for special events, such as at the funeral of King George V (1936), and the Coronation of King Edward VIII later that year (which, incidentally, was the first 'live' television transmission on the BBC's experimental TV service). The abdication speech of Edward VIII on December 11, 1936 was also carried 'live' by radio from Windsor Castle.

One of the more hilarious incidents of early BBC 'live' reporting of a news event was the Review of the Fleet, one evening in 1937. The commentator had plainly enjoyed the spirit of the occasion too much before he went on air – the broadcast was a shambles as the commentator incoherently stumbled on, while no one in London seemed to have the courage to pull the plug!

1.5.2 Getting the story back

From the 1920s radio stations relied on telephone lines, mobile transmitters and, later on, short-wave radio transmissions from abroad, to receive reports from remote locations. In the US, the networks, with more money to invest in new technology, started using hand-held portable high-frequency (microwave) transmitters for such events as party conventions. This gave the reporters increased mobility to roam the convention floors, and their comments and interviews, picked up by temporary control rooms set up at the convention centers, were then relayed by telephone lines to the network. For many years, neither NBC nor CBS allowed recorded material in their news bulletins or entertainment programs, as they took pride in their live presentations, believing audiences would otherwise object. In any case, recording breaking news was impossible with the technology available in the 1920s.

Recording in the field became possible when the technology had developed further. The arrival of a recorder using steel tape, the 'Blattnerphone', in 1931 meant that material could now be recorded – but the equipment was large, heavy and impractical for newsgathering in the field. Editing metal tape required more the skills of a welder than a radio technician. From 1933 onwards, both the BBC in the UK and the US networks pursued the use of acetate disk recorders, but the machines were still not very practical for use in the field. Meanwhile, the Germans were developing the use of cellulose acetate tape impregnated with magnetic particles with the 'Magnetophon' system. In 1937, a disk recording made by a reporter sent to cover the arrival of the German airship the *Hindenburg* in New Jersey, and its destruction in the subsequent terrible explosion, was both the first time a recording had been broadcast on a radio network and also the first transatlantic broadcast from the US to Europe.

An example of how the BBC responded to a major UK news story in 1937 was the appalling East Anglian floods in which many died, where a BBC correspondent was sent to report on the disaster. His reports were not to be transmitted live, but instead a mobile recording team in a truck was also sent, who recorded the correspondent's words and the location sounds onto acetate disks, and then sent the disk recordings back via the guard on the London train.

1.5.3   The Second World War

During the Second World War, radio was the focus as a disseminator of news on both sides. Leaders on all sides used radio to make speeches to rally morale, and radio was considered vital by all sides as a way of ensuring that the war effort was sustained. The use of radio in such a political manner, of course, was fitting for the time. Listeners in the US and the UK kept abreast of the war listening to live-on-the-scene reports from Europe, North Africa and the Far East. The BBC developed the use of portable 'midget' disk recorders, weighing under 15 kg (30 lb), for recording reports from the battlefield, which were then flown back to London for transmission to give an element of 'actuality'. The Americans used wire recorders, using steel wire with a magnetic coating, which although more portable than the traditional disk recorders, still weighed over 22 kg (50 lb). They were still too large to be moved easily from one location to another, and some American correspondents jealously eyed the midget disk recorders used by the BBC correspondents. However, whatever the type of recorder used, without them many reports and sounds of the war would not have been heard by radio listeners, because military censors (and practical considerations) prohibited live broadcasts from the battlefield. After the war, continuing development work by the Americans using the acetate tape system pioneered by the Germans, led to the development of 6 mm (1/4 in.) 'reel-to-reel' tape recorders in the late 1940s. This recording format remained in common use until the development of the professional 'compact cassette' units in the 1990s.

1.5.4   The threat of television

From 1920 until the late 1940s, radio broadcasting enjoyed an explosive growth. But by the 1950s, with the development of television, radio stations found themselves fighting a similar battle for survival as the newspapers had decades earlier. Unfortunately for radio in the US, television was fast becoming the dominant medium as advertisers and audiences were drawn away from radio. The caliber of programming on radio had reached a peak, but many foresaw the demise of radio in the face of the 'trivialities' of television.

1.6   Television

Television (from the Greek 'seeing at distance') was a concept that, as with the history of radio, had seriously been discussed since the middle of the nineteenth century, and had some overlap with the development of wireless. The roots of television can be traced back to 1817, with the discovery of the light-sensitive element selenium by Jons Berzelius (Sweden). The first development was in 1839, when Edmond Becquerel (France) discovered a relationship between the voltage of a metal–acid battery and exposure to light. In 1878 Willoughby Smith (UK) showed that current flowing through selenium crystals changed with fluctuations in light falling on the crystals. In 1880 Alexander Graham Bell (US) developed the forerunner to the fax machine with his invention, the 'Photophone', based on a selenium cell, which could transmit still images over a telephone line. This led to the development of technology that enabled the news agency wire services to transmit photographs back via a telephone line.

1.6.1 *The beginnings of television*

In 1884 Paul Nipkow (Germany) took out a patent on his 'electric telescope'. This early conception of television used a mechanical scanning system with motors and large rotating disks, and consisted of a perforated disk with a spiral of holes, spinning in front of a selenium cell, which could produce images with scanning rates of up to 30 times per second. There is no evidence that Nipkow ever demonstrated his idea, as it was impossible with the technology available at the time, particularly to achieve the amplification or synchronization of the receiver to the transmitter.

In 1908, Alan Campbell-Swinton (UK) proposed the concept of electronic television in an article in a British science magazine, describing the principles of scanning, synchronization and display.

As with some other inventions, who can precisely be described as the inventor of television is still a subject of debate, even over 75 years later. The three principal claimants to the title are Philo Farnsworth (US), Vladimir Zworykin (US) and John Logie Baird (UK). Other contenders include Jenkins (US), Takayanagi (Japan), Rosing (Russia), Belin (France), Barthelemy (France), Karolus (Germany) and von Mihaly (Hungary). What is certain is that many small inventions and discoveries all contributed to the phenomena of television.

Of the other contenders listed above, Charles Jenkin (US) is of note because he actually produced a television service in the late 1920s and 1930s. In 1925, Jenkins demonstrated his development of the Nipkow system, which he called 'radiovision'. By 1928, Jenkins was transmitting 'radiomovies' on short-wave frequencies, but his audience was restricted to principally radio amateurs. Nevertheless, it kept interest in television alive in the US until NBC (part of RCA) launched an electronic television service in 1939.

Farnsworth conceived his idea of how to produce an electronic television system in 1922, and demonstrated it in 1927 when he transmitted a 60-line image of a dollar sign. Farnsworth patented a complete electronic television system in 1927, based on an 'image dissector' used to scan the image for wireless transmission. At the receiver, an 'oscillite' tube reproduced the picture, and an electron multiplier tube, a 'multipactor', increased the sensitivity of the image dissector. Engaged in time-consuming patent litigation with RCA for over 10 years, Farnsworth finally signed a cross-patent agreement with RCA in 1939, opening the way for electronic television in the US.

Zworykin, who worked at Westinghouse with Conrad, invented the 'Iconoscope' (patenting it in 1923) and the 'Kinescope', which were the forerunners of today's television camera and picture tubes. He developed an electronic scanning television system using his inventions, and demonstrated a working system in 1929. Sarnoff tempted him away from Westinghouse in 1929 to develop an electronic television system at RCA.

Baird refined Nipkow's spinning disk system to demonstrate successfully a mechanical television system in 1925. It has been said that Baird only pursued mechanical scanning to get a television system working as quickly as possible, as he lacked the expertise to develop an electronic system. Baird's 'Televisor' used a 16-line scanning disk camera and receiver, with a neon tube as a light source at each end. However, this produced a picture only about 12 mm (1 in.) square. By 1926 he had further developed the system to 30 lines of scanning with a larger screen size. In 1928, Baird achieved the first transatlantic television transmission, and shortly afterwards the first demonstration of color television. The BBC experimented with Baird's mechanical 30-line system via radio transmissions between 1929 and 1935, starting a regular broadcast service in 1932, while Baird tried to further improve his mechanical system. From 1930, with BBC transmissions underway, Baird launched his system onto the market, and by 1936 his system produced 240 lines of scanning. But by 1935, the BBC decided to switch to the 405-line electronic system developed by EMI in the UK, based on a derivative of Zworykin's Iconoscope from RCA. EMI was associated with RCA from the days when the London companies, Victor Talking Machine Company in Camden and Gramophone Company in Hayes (from which EMI was born), were related.

Throughout the 1920s and 1930s, a number of countries experimented with various mechanical and electronic methods of television, and there are many claims made as to who was first with a true television system or service.

It is acknowledged, however, that in 1935, the Nazi government in Germany inaugurated the world's first public television broadcasting service (using the Farnsworth system) and, on the opening night, broadcast speeches by Hitler and other senior party officials. It also broadcast the 1936 Olympics in Berlin. The BBC officially launched its public electronic television service in 1936, but transmissions were suspended in September 1939 at the outbreak of the Second World War, when it is estimated that 20 000 television receivers had been sold to the public, and the service did not resume until 1946.

In the US, NBC began work on developing a television service in 1935 and launched its television service in 1939. At the World Fair in New York in 1939, Franklin Roosevelt made a speech that was transmitted by NBC on their inaugural service – this transmission was the first use of television by a US president. In 1931, CBS put an experimental TV station on the air in New York and transmitted programs for more than a year before becoming disillusioned with the commercial aspects of the new medium. Following NBC, CBS began development of a commercial television system in 1937, with a public service beginning in 1941.

1.6.2   Early television news

Local experimental stations in the US began 'newscasts' during the 1930s, though they were restricted to announcers reading news headlines. At least one station is reputed to have begun showing 'newsreels' sometime in the mid-1930s. Newsreels were produced by motion picture studios and shown in cinemas as part of their entertainment schedules, and when the television experimenters wanted to show moving pictures in their newscasts, they used the newsreels.

Covering breaking news was a challenge for television because it was an expensive and awkward proposition to equip vehicles for remote broadcasts with the heavy, bulky cameras and transmitting equipment. In 1939 in New York, NBC developed the ability to undertake 'remotes' (outside broadcasts) with two vehicles – one transporting the transmitter for the link to the studio, the other carrying the camera and production equipment. The BBC did not attempt any remote television news coverage until well after the end of the Second World War.

1.7   Television news after the War

In the UK, the BBC started television transmissions again in 1946, and for the next 8 years ran cinema newsreels alone as the sole source of news. In the US, NBC and CBS launched their first regularly scheduled newscasts, but the programs only went out once or twice a week. As in the UK, the principal diet of moving pictures from outside the studio came from newsreels. These contained feature material rather than hard 'news', compiled by the news agencies and the motion picture studios, and they were the equivalent of a weekly magazine (the most famous newsreels were MGM/Hearst Metrotone, Paramount, Movietone and Pathé). As a result, the newsreels tended to cover planned events and timeless features, edited with titles, music and commentary, so that viewers saw a lot of departures and arrivals of politicians, dignitaries and celebrities, fashion shows, news conferences, and ship arrivals and departures.

In the UK, it was not until 1953, after the sudden rise in popularity of television with the coverage of the Coronation of Queen Elizabeth II, that the BBC established a dedicated television news department. In 1954, the BBC showed their first television news bulletins, but they were visually uninspiring.

On both sides of the Atlantic when breaking news occurred, the audience were offered only a few studio visual aids such as still pictures, charts and maps, or perhaps an on-the-scene report filed by a reporter using the telephone, to accompany stories that were read by the announcer. Because live video from the scene could not be delivered instantly, except in rare situations, television offered little more than radio when immediacy counted, and so these programs were little more than radio news bulletins combined with still pictures and some newsreel footage.

In the UK, Independent Television News (ITN) was launched in 1955, a dedicated television news company supplying news bulletins to the UK's Independent Television (ITV) commercial channel, and this forced the BBC to further develop its television news output with its own dedicated news film camera crews.

1.7.1 'Film at eleven'

In the US, with newsgathering for television based on film cameras, local stations starting using the 'film at eleven' ruse to encourage viewers to watch a later newscast, by which time the filmed report of a news event would be ready. Having pictures to show in a newscast was highly desirable, as was creating a sense of immediacy. Some stations, as early as the 1950s, began pushing 'eyewitness' formats, based on CBS's idea. For instance, the anchor would introduce the reporter in the studio who had returned after covering a big news story. The reporter would then provide a live 'eyewitness' account of the event and introduce the film report shot at the scene. It was a compromise that worked, as the audience had not come to expect anything more immediate.

1.8 Newsgathering technology before ENG

The technology of newsgathering for television was based on film cameras, and there was the problem of recording the sound and lighting the scene as well. The cameras first used were derivatives of 35 mm cinema film cameras and were, therefore, bulky and heavy, and required considerable electrical power. Fred Friendly, a producer working with the famous CBS correspondent Edward R. Murrow in the Korean War in 1952 (the first time television cameras had covered a war), famously described their 35mm film camera as the "thousand pound pencil". (How apt this will seem when we look later at the logistics of SNG!)

By the late 1950s, smaller and lighter 16 mm cameras were developed, weighing under 10 kg (22 lb). Sound was recorded onto a magnetic track striped on the film itself and two-man crews were needed to shoot the film and record the sound, with a lighting electrician required where shooting was to occur in poor or difficult lighting conditions. Once the film was shot, there were problems in preparing the film for transmission. It had to be physically transported back to the studio, usually by road by the film crew themselves, or by use of other methods of transportation. Back at the studio, there was at least a 40-minute delay while the film was processed before it could even be edited. The whole process was lengthy, even with the fastest and most skilled technicians.

Television networks did cover news events live from remote locations, but they required considerable notice and pre-planning. Bulky, awkward equipment had to be transported and multiple telephone circuits ordered to set up remote broadcasts. In the US, the audience draw of the political party conventions was a strong influence in establishing the infrastructure required. By 1952, the US networks were linked east to west with coast-to-coast coaxial cable circuits, which provided a nationwide audience for the political parties and their nominees. In the early 1950s, US Senate hearings into organized crime, the Eisenhower presidential inauguration and the McCarthy hearings all offered opportunities for television to deliver news as it happened, and were treated as special coverage. But in each case, arrangements to cover these events were made well in advance.

In the UK in 1953, the BBC in co-operation with the Post Office, had arranged for a coaxial cable ring to be set up around central London (called the 'LoCo') with spurs to various important venues in time for the Coronation. This network was further developed and widely used, only finally disappearing in 1997. The use of cable circuits was not universal – as a result of the radar technology developed during the war, microwave transmitters and receivers had been developed and were used from the 1950s onwards. However, this early transmission equipment was bulky and not particularly reliable, although the development of solid-state electronics (as opposed to the use of vacuum tubes) through the 1960s established terrestrial microwave link technology for coverage of remote events.

Live coverage of breaking news events during regularly scheduled news bulletins was difficult to arrange in those days, because television lacked the technology for speed and mobility. In both the UK and the US, dependence on newsreels ended in the mid-1950s as television stations assembled their own film crews, but delays in showing news pictures were still a problem because of the time required to transport, process and edit film.

In the US, the networks established permanently leased 'wideband' telephone circuits that linked the network centers in New York to their affiliate stations. Edited material could be transmitted over these circuits, making same-day coverage of news events possible, as long as the film crews had enough time to complete their shoot, drive to the nearest affiliate with connectivity to New York, and then process and edit the film before sending it. Only significant stories were sent by this method, because of the very high cost of transmission. Normally the film was flown to New York for processing and editing, and would typically not be broadcast until the next day.

To cover foreign stories during this era, the only reliable way of moving pictures from one part of the world to another was by air, meaning there was a heavy reliance on scheduled airline flights, which were much less frequent than today. This was a very slow way of bringing 'breaking' news to the television screen. To tackle the problem of quickly getting pictures from the US, the BBC used the 'Cablefilm' system, developed during the 1950s. With this process, film pictures had to be obtained (to cope with the use of the different TV standard in the US) which were then converted to electronic pictures and transmitted by a 'slow scan' process while being recorded on film in the UK. The resulting pictures were jerky and of poor quality, and the only transmission of note was the coverage of the arrival of Queen Elizabeth in New York on a state visit in 1958. The process was abandoned shortly afterwards because of the poor results.

In 1962, to try to speed up newsgathering on film, the BBC started experimenting with mobile film processing. The Mobile Film Processing Unit consisted of three vans – nicknamed the 'three ring circus' – which could travel to the scene of a major news story. There was a processing truck, an editing truck and a telecine (film projection-to-television conversion) truck, so the pictures could then be connected to a terrestrial microwave links truck to transmit the pictures back to the studio. However, the system was cumbersome and not particularly successful, and the Unit was dismantled in 1966.

It was clear that an alternative to the use of film was required. Videotape recording was invented during the 1950s, based on 50 mm (2 in.) wide tape, but it was of no use to newsgathering in the field, as the machines were large and designed to be bolted to the floor!

It was not until the advent of electronic newsgathering (ENG) in the 1970s that the solution to the problem of transmitting news as quickly as possible was found. This solution was rapidly developed in the US, where television news was then (and still is) a very aggressive area of the broadcast industry. In a revolutionary development, over approximately a 5-year period, the problems of shooting, recording and editing in the field were solved.

1.9   Electronic newsgathering

The rise of the electronics industry in Japan through the 1950s and 1960s, along with the invention of the transistor and the beginning of progress in miniaturization, led to the development of ENG. The first problem was the recording medium, and the solution of that problem coincided with the development of compact portable electronic cameras.

As mentioned earlier, 2 in. ('quadruplex') videotape was the standard broadcast television tape format (and remained so until the early 1980s). In Japan, Germany and the US, television video recorder manufacturers worked on producing a smaller tape format for a number of reasons, newsgathering being only one, but the result would be smaller and more portable video recorders. The standard that finally became predominant was the Sony U-matic 3/4 in. (19 mm) standard, which remained dominant until it was superseded by the Sony 'Beta' 1/2 in. (12 mm) format in the mid-1980s. Subsequently there was a battle between digital 12 and 6 mm formats, but the future is 'tapeless', with the use of magneto-optical disks and hard drive packs as storage medium, increasing operational flexibility, capacity and reducing running costs.

Soon after the resolution of tape formats was becoming clear, the camera manufacturers were working on reducing the size and weight of the television camera, with RCA (US) and Ikegami (Japan) each leading with compact models. The result was that, by the late 1970s, film was rapidly disappearing as the standard medium for newsgathering, to be replaced by the compact camera and recorder. In the mid-1980s, the first one-piece camcorder appeared, based on the Sony 'Betacam' standard.

Now that the pictures were in electronic format in the field, and the tape recorders and players were smaller, portable editing equipment for field use was now practicable. All the equipment could be transported easily in one small truck that was customized for field use and equipped with a portable microwave transmission system. Television stations now had the technology to record on-site, or broadcast live, electronic pictures from a remote location.

In the US the network-owned stations were the first to be equipped with the new ENG equipment. A Los Angeles station provided one of the first dramatic examples of live ENG reporting. The station broadcast 'live' a police shoot-out with a radical group calling itself the Symbionese Liberation Army. For 2 hours the station had live coverage of the gun battle, though the live pictures stopped before the shoot-out ended because the camera batteries in operation went flat.

ENG was the biggest change in newsgathering since the invention of wireless. The next big development was the use of satellites.

1.10   Satellites and newsgathering

The development of satellite communications technology was the next leap forward in newsgathering, overlapping with the development of ENG. The technological drive to develop satellite technology came, of course, from the military, but news organizations (and television and radio audiences) ultimately bene-fited as well. In the 1950s, with the Cold War at its peak, the 'race to space' between the US and Russia was intense. The successful launch of the SPUTNIK satellite by the former USSR in October 1957 was a bitter blow to the US, who were thus spurred on even more. Explorer 1 was launched just a few months after SPUTNIK in January 1958.

TELSTAR 1, launched for AT&T in 1962, was the first communications satellite, but it had limited use because tracking stations were necessary to follow its non-geosynchronous orbit. The following year another satellite, SYNCOM II, was put into a geosynchronous orbit at an altitude of 36 000 km (22 500 miles). At this height, the satellite moved in synchronicity with the Earth's rotation, thereby remaining sta-tionary relative to the Earth's surface (see Chapter 2). The first commercial communications satellite in geosynchronous orbit, INTELSAT I ('EARLY BIRD') was launched in 1965 (see Chapter 7). As the num-ber of communications satellites increased, more opportunities were available to deliver news from distant locations.

1.10.1   In the US

For the US networks, the Vietnam War helped promote the use of satellite technology as a newsgather-ing tool. The networks needed a way to obtain video from overseas that was less time consuming than by air, and satellites provided the means. This was achievable between fixed earth stations, but was not possible in the mobile environment.

In the 1970s, the only transportable satellite earth stations were large and expensive 'C-band' vehicle- or trailer-mounted uplinks, which could be used for major events. However, they could not easily be used at short notice because of the FCC requirement for site surveys before a permit to transmit could be issued, due to the restrictions on the use of C-band (see Chapter 6). Hence, these uplinks were used for events such as sports or for political party conventions in the run-up to presidential elections that were going to be carried by the networks.

Widespread use came with the availability of 'Ku-band' satellite capacity in the early 1980s. Operation on Ku-band capacity was not subject to FCC restrictions, making it more suitable for news, and the uplinks could use cheaper, smaller antennas and systems than those typically used for C-band.

In 1984 Stanley Hubbard, the owner of a television station in St. Paul, Minneapolis, organized the 'Conus' satellite news co-operative for local television stations to share news material by satellite. At the same time, he encouraged stations to buy vehicles customized for satellite newsgathering, manufactured by another of his companies in Florida, Hubbard Communications. The Conus News Service was closed down in 2002, and the Conus Communications satellite uplink business was bought out by its employees in 2003 to form Arctek Satellite Productions.

The Conus satellite news co-operative spurred many local stations to invest in SNG. Many early sys-tems were constructed by adapting larger, fixed earth station antennas (known as 'cutting') and utilizing other components designed for fixed earth stations. Many stations built their own trucks rather than com-missioning construction by bespoke vehicle builders. In these early days there were a few other vehicle manufacturers apart from Hubbard Communications, such as Dalsat and Encom (now long gone).

Nevertheless, through the 1980s a number of companies became established in this area of the broad-cast vehicle market, and the current principal companies in the US (and the rest of the world) involved in building SNG systems are listed in Appendix J.

1.10.2   In Europe

The development of SNG in the UK stemmed from the work of the Independent Broadcast Authority (IBA) and GEC McMichael in the late 1970s and early 1980s on trailer-mounted satellite communication uplinks. The IBA was the broadcasting authority for independent television in the UK and, along with the BBC, was very interested in the development of SNG. In 1978, the IBA built a trailer-mounted Ku-band satellite uplink system with a 2.5 m antenna which it was using to experiment with the OTS-2 satellite, with a view to developing a system that could be used for newsgathering.

GEC McMichael was a company with many diverse interests, including fiber-optic technology, television monitors, video-conferencing and television standards conversion, and its strategic position within the GEC group of companies was to act as the conduit for transferring relevant research and development in its defence activities into commercial applications. (These diverse applications may seem at first sight strange bedfellows but, on closer examination, it can be seen that satellite communications, video-conferencing and television standards conversion did have a common linking thread.)

McMichael's position was also unusual within the rigid GEC group in that the philosophy of the McMichael company was to be more liberal, encouraging imaginative thinking from its engineers in order to create new commercial products as a spin-off from military development work.

In 1979, GEC McMichael began to work on developing a transportable satellite system aimed at the news and special events market, with the assistance of engineers from Marconi Space & Defence, another company within the GEC group whose prime business was military satellite communications. One of the biggest challenges was to design an antenna that could meet the rigorous new specification for 2° spacing of satellites required by EUTELSAT, and subsequently adopted by INTELSAT and the US FCC (see Chapters 2 and 6). These new specifications were enforced by EUTELSAT in Europe, but neither INTELSAT nor the FCC actually insisted on these requirements being met for a number of years (partly because there were no satellites in the geostationary arc yet spaced at 2°), much to the relief of US satellite system manufacturers. However, this did prevent most US antenna manufacturers from being able to sell their products into Europe until they could achieve the required performance specification. In 1981 the BBC followed suit and built their own trailer-mount satellite uplink system.

By 1983, GEC McMichael had, like the IBA and the BBC also developed a Ku-band transportable uplink on a trailer, which could be used for either analog or digital transmissions. It was used to demonstrate *digital* video conferencing at the annual defence systems exhibition at Farnborough in 1983 – this was over 10 years before Digital Satellite Newsgathering (DSNG) became a reality.

The next objective was to develop the first transportable flyaway SNG uplink that could meet the rigorous 2° satellite spacing requirements. Another company in the GEC group, EEV, was brought in to develop compact high-power amplifiers required for the new flyaway. By 1984 the prototype flyaway was produced and rigorously tested to meet the EUTELSAT specification, and the GEC McMichael 'Newshawk' flyaway was launched at NAB in 1985 – the first SNG flyaway able to meet the 2° spacing specification (Figure 1.2). The US company Comsat General also exhibited their first Ku-band SNG flyaway system, but they did so more as a design concept rather than a commercial product.

The Newshawk flyaway, with its flat elliptical antenna and relatively lightweight, compact construction created a great deal of interest. In 1985, two systems were sold, one to CBS in the US and one to ITN in the UK. Both systems saw their first serious outing in 1986 to cover the Reagan-Gorbachev Summit in Reykjavik in Iceland, and they remained in service with both companies for over 10 years.

But by the end of 1985, GEC had decided to dissolve the McMichael company and absorb the various activities back into the other companies within the GEC group. Three engineers who had moved to GEC McMichael in 1980 from Marconi Space & Defence to work on the original transportable satellite uplink project, and who were at the heart of the development of the Newshawk, decided to leave GEC and set up their own company to manufacture SNG flyaways. This company became Advent Communications, which had developed its 1.5 m Mantis flyaway system by 1986 and sold its first system to the BBC in 1987, and went on to become the byword globally for SNG flyaways for nearly 10 years.

Figure 1.2 GEC McMichael Newshawk (ITN) in Kumming, China (for the state visit of Queen Elizabeth II, 1986)

Advent produced their first SNG trucks in 1989, building four 7.5 tonne (16 500 lb) trucks with uplink systems based on their 1.9 m Mantis flyaway product, swiftly followed by a number of 3.5 tonne (7700 lb) vehicles also based on the 1.9 m Mantis flyaway. The company now produces a range of systems based on various vehicle sizes, in addition to their range of flyaway products.

Across the rest of Europe, the uptake of SNG was slow, due both to the very high cost of the equipment and because the use of temporary terrestrial microwave links was well established. The distances to be covered in any one country were not on the same scale as in the US, and therefore there was not the same impetus. However, through the 1990s, other companies in the UK and Europe started producing SNG trucks and flyaways.

1.10.3   Digital SNG

The development of digital SNG in 1994 in Europe heralded the second era in SNG. The cost of the equipment in Europe came very close to matching that of analog systems and the antenna size reduced, opening up the possibility of using smaller vehicles than the typical 2 m analog SNG antenna allowed. Most importantly, the lack of ad hoc analog capacity, combined with the lower cost of digital capacity, could more than offset the slightly higher capital cost of DSNG systems. In Europe, DSNG grew quickly, primarily because of this lack of analog capacity (particularly ad hoc), as the economic demands on bandwidth meant that more channels could be carried on a satellite, and because a viable digital compression system – the ETSI 8 Mbps derivative – became widely used. The EBU Eurovision News network adopted this compression standard for DSNG in 1995. In fact, the speed of the demise of analog SNG was surprising, and in Europe, by 1997, DSNG had become the norm rather than the exception. This coincided with the introduction onto the market of the first MPEG-2 digital compression encoders, which rapidly became the de facto standard for DSNG.

It was not until 1998 that DSNG started to take a hold in the US. This has been attributed to a number of factors:

- There was not the same pressure on capacity until the loss of the satellites Telstar 401 in early 1997 and Galaxy IV in 1998; for, although these particular satellites carried Direct-to-Home (DTH) traffic, their disappearance created a squeeze as the DTH traffic was shifted to other satellites.
- The cost of MPEG-2 compression equipment began to fall (the US was never interested in pursuing the European ETSI digital compression standard), and through 1999 there was a significant drop in the cost of encoders from some manufacturers.
- The thrust by the CBS network, including its affiliate stations, toward digital domestic contribution.
- The prospect of all television production processes moving into the digital domain with the introduction of HDTV.

(This last factor is perhaps not as significant as it might first seem, as no major US network had committed to newsgathering in high definition by the end of 2006.)

But, whatever the reasons for the delay, there is no doubt that the US has now embraced DSNG. As analog SNG has virtually disappeared, we will no longer make a distinction between 'SNG' and 'DSNG', and from now on any reference to SNG is to its digital form.

1.10.4   Ultra portable SNG

The third era of SNG was ushered in with the launch of the first 'ultra portable' SNG terminal – the Swe-Dish IPT (IP Terminal) in late 2001, manufactured by Swe-Dish Satellite Systems (Sweden). Al Jazeera, NHK (Japan), and a number of other global newsgatherers used the Swe-Dish IPT extensively during the 2003 Gulf conflict.

Norsat (Canada) also developed a unit – the NewsLink. The Norsat NewsLink was used in 2003 by CBS and Fox News to great effect with news teams 'embedded' with frontline US Army units, enabling them to move rapidly with the troops.

With the further developments in digital signal compression, the newer generation of satellites being capable of handling lower-power signals, the rapid spread of the use of the Internet, and the pressure from both military and media users for much more compact equipment, led to a number of companies developing systems that are considerably smaller in size and weight as well as being significantly easier to set up and use.

The greater mobility and freedom of non-technical staff to operate these types of terminal has led to a further broadening of the scope of use of SNG, and we will examine this in more detail later.

1.10.5 The videophone

The phrase 'videophone' is a ubiquitous term now heard on almost every TV newscast containing some foreign reporting. The first use of a compact 'videophone style' technology was the introduction of the TOKO VAST-p in 1994, manufactured in Japan by TOKO. VAST-p was an acronym for 'Video and Audio Storage and Transmission – portable'. It provided two-way video and audio for video conferencing as well as store and forward application, transmitting at data rates from 2.4 kbps to 2 Mbps – although it was generally most widely used in a store and forward mode. The video-coding algorithm was proprietary, based on MPEG-1/H.261/JPEG, so transmissions could only be received and decoded by another TOKO VAST-p unit. It had simplified coding rate selections and a user-friendly menu-driven control panel requiring few key presses for quick 'plug and go' operation. The video and audio are also sent as two separate segments, so an incomplete transmission may result in a full complement of video pictures, but only part of the audio. It was a very rugged unit, designed with the government market in mind, and weighed only 6.5 kg (14 lb) in a shock-resistant shipping case weighing a further 5.5 kg (12 lb), so that the whole unit, ready for shipping, weighed only 13 kg (26 lb), which for the time, was a dramatic decrease in size and weight for equipment for this purpose.

While some other manufacturers followed suit during the latter part of the 1990s with various offerings, the next significant development was 7E Communications' 'Talking Head' videophone, a product developed from standard COTS (Commercial Off The Shelf) video-conferencing equipment. Its impact on live news cannot be underestimated, and in particular its use along with other similar types of compact SNG systems covering the invasion of Iraq in 2003 shaped the news agenda of coverage of that conflict.

The videophone was conceived in 1998 by the BBC and 7E Communications – a UK technology company deeply involved in Inmarsat technology (see Chapter 6) – but it was not physically born until early 2000. The Talking Head videophone was designed to be used with the then newly developed compact digital satellite phone – the Inmarsat GAN (or M4) 'satphone' – to provide a compact two-box solution to live newsgathering. Since then a further version has been produced to work with the new BGAN service from Inmarsat.

Its first use was in February 2000 for a live interview with the Dalai Lama from his home in Tibet via the BBC News website, and throughout that year the BBC continued to use the Talking Head unit, while other organizations such as CNN also bought units. The 'Talking Head' unit really came to prominence when CNN used one to cover the return of the 24 captured aircrew of a US Navy EP-3 plane (a signals intelligence reconnaissance aircraft) at Hainan Island, China, in April 2001. The Chinese government had no idea it was being used, and were appalled that live pictures originating from their territory without their control were being shown on CNN around the world – it was even seen 'live' on-air being confiscated by Chinese security personnel.

Following this, the Talking Head videophones rapidly became a 'must-have' item for all the US networks as well as the TV news agencies and other broadcasters, and the list of major news events at which it has made a significant contribution are now too many to list here, but include coverage from central New York on 9/11 when a good deal of central Manhattan infrastructure was destroyed or severely disrupted; the invasion of Iraq in 2003 and the continuing conflict; a number of natural disasters including the earthquake in Bam, Iran in 2003, and the Indonesian tsunami disaster in December 2004.

1.10.6 High definition (HD) TV

HDTV services are now available in North America, Japan, South Korea, Australia and parts of Europe. At the end of 2004, it was estimated that there were 20 million HDTV receivers worldwide, and various industry forecasts put the number of HDTV sets at 200 million by 2010.

Throughout the development of television, the characterization of high definition has altered. High definition TV (HDTV), as it is spoken of today, is obviously a development on what is currently referred to as standard definition (SD) television – the 525- and 625-line standards we are familiar with.

On the other hand, it should not be forgotten that while in the 1930s, Baird's 240-line system was deemed to be high definition compared to the original 30-line system, the subsequent transition to 405-line TV in UK, and 525-line in US, was also deemed to be high definition. However, it was the French who led in the early days, with their 819-line monochrome system launched in 1948 (though it was later superseded by the European 625-line color system).

In today's sense however research into higher definition television systems began in Japan in the 1960s, and carried on through the 1970s, resulting in the announcement of the first real high definition television by NHK of Japan in 1983. The system – called MUSE (Multiple Sub-Nyquist Encoding) – was an 1125-line compressed analog system that was launched as a public service branded as Hi-Vision in Japan in 1990. However, it never really took off primarily because of the high cost of the TV receivers, and there have never been more than 1 000 000 sets in use. The service has been superseded by ISDB-S (Integrated Services Digital Broadcasting – Satellite), a digital standard based on 1080-line transmission which started in Japan in late 2000.

In the US, CBS had developed a 1050-line HDTV system by the early 1980s, and in 1982 the Advanced Television Systems Committee (ATSC), a private organization developing voluntary standards for advanced television, was formed by a group of manufacturers and other interested parties. But it was not until the late 1980s (with the challenge from Japan's high definition standard potentially threatening their domestic TV manufacturing industry) that the US seriously organized efforts to decide on an HDTV system with the establishment of the Advisory Committee on Advanced Television Service (ACATS) under the auspices of the US Federal Communications Commission (FCC).

By 1993, the advocates of a digital rather than an analog solution (AT&T, Philips, General Instrument, Thomson, MIT and Sarnoff Research Labs) came together as the 'Grand Alliance' to create a set of Advanced TV (ATV) standards. ACATS worked closely with the ATSC, subsequently recommending the adoption of the ATSC standards before its dissolution in 1996. However, with such a widespread group of interests, instead of a single HDTV standard, the US ended up with a total of six different standards – but even fewer are in use.

Meanwhile in Europe in the 1980s, work was also underway on an HDTV standard under the umbrella of the Eureka project – a European consortium of broadcasters, network operators, consumer electronic industries and research institutes. In 1987 it announced the development of Eureka 95/HD-MAC system. These developments in the US and Europe thwarted Japanese efforts to have their system adopted worldwide.

Throughout the latter part of the 1990s until the beginning of this decade, Europe largely chose to ignore the development of HDTV. However, from 2004, with the increasing influence of HDTV in the US, the Europeans again began to explore the development of a European HDTV standard and services launched in 2006 on a number of satellites.

1.10.7 High definition (HD) TV and SNG

At the time of writing, the use of HDTV in SNG is as yet very limited. NHK of Japan have been routinely operating HD SNG uplinks since 2002, but otherwise major news organizations have shied away from using HD acquisition as yet because of the cost of the equipment, the additional bandwidth requirements, and the different operational techniques required for shooting in HD – all of which can prove cumbersome for a slick newsgathering operation.

1.11 Impact of SNG

As we mentioned earlier, television coverage of the Vietnam War saw the US developing the use of satellites to bring news from the war faster to the viewer. The delivery of graphic pictures that brought the reality of war closer than ever before into the living rooms of millions (with no censorship from the US military) is said by some to have reversed US public opinion on the war within a few years. Transportation time of news film from Vietnam to New York was about 20 hours, although this decreased dramatically with the availability of satellite connections later in the war. Although the coverage was not live, the impact of the use of satellite technology was emerging, and was to become unstoppable.

As the use of SNG grew through the 1980s, the number of SNG uplinks increased as they were used to cover the major international news events. Such events included: the TWA hostage hijack in the Mediterranean in 1985; the Reagan-Gorbachev Summit in Iceland in 1986; the PanAm airliner disaster in Lockerbie, Scotland in 1988; the Tianamen Square crisis in Beijing, China, along with the fall of the Berlin Wall in 1989; and the release of Nelson Mandela from prison in South Africa in 1990.

Without doubt, the event that brought SNG to the fore in newsgathering, as well as having an enormous impact on the public, was the conflict in the Persian Gulf in 1990/1991. It began in August 1990 when Iraq invaded Kuwait, culminating in the 6 weeks of fighting after the Allied attack in early 1991.

All the major newsgathering organizations had a presence across the Middle East, particularly in Baghdad where they were invited by the Iraqi President Saddam Hussein from the beginning in 1990 to witness the effects of 'Western aggression'.

In the US, the CNN news channel was heralded as the star of news organizations for its early coverage of the Gulf War. CNN was alone in providing live and continuous coverage throughout the first night of the Allied attack on Baghdad on 17 January 1991 (though the coverage was by voice only, on CNN's 'four-wire' communications channel). The other US networks lost their telephone connections from Iraq during the initial shelling, but their correspondents were able to report live from Saudi Arabia and Israel, which faced possible Iraqi Scud missile attacks. All around the world, on any channel carrying the news, correspondents could be seen donning gas masks to prepare for Scud attacks, repeated night after night. Audiences felt a sense of 'being there' as the correspondents in Saudi Arabia, Baghdad and Israel provided the drama, rather than combat troops, who were seen less often. The correspondents under fire from Iraqi Scud attacks provided an illusion of audience participation in the drama of the war and, for the US, the fact that the TV personalities could actually be hit involved the audience in a new kind of live drama. The combined coverage of ABC, CBS, CNN and NBC attracted nearly 90 million viewers in the US on the first night of the war.[4]

Since then, the list of major and minor events covered by use of SNG – be it from an SNG truck, a conventional SNG flyway, an ultra-portable suitcase terminal, or a videophone – runs into countless numbers, and it has become as vital to the newsgathering process as the camera itself.

1.11.1 The 'CNN effect': Witness or instrument of foreign policy?

Finally, we must briefly cover a phenomenon widely referred to as the 'CNN effect' – though it is now applicable to all major global 24-hour television news outlets – which is directly attributable to the rapid growth in influence and effect of satellite newsgathering. The term was coined after the first Gulf War, and it was based on the perceived effect from the supposed dramatic impact of CNN news broadcasts. This effect was said to be evident in US government decision-making in times of war or economic crisis because of the immediacy of the media coverage. For instance, it is widely acknowledged that the US went into Somalia and Rwanda partly because of this influence, and the CNN effect is alleged to have heavily influenced overall US foreign policy.[5] The US military operation in Somalia in November 1992 in particular is said to have been set up with coverage by the US networks primarily in mind, and its disastrous consequences ending with the humiliating withdrawal of the US military still haunts US policy-makers.

Furthermore, the CNN effect is believed to be exerted by global television media in general, influencing other governments to take actions that will be widely reported by the global newsgathering organizations. It is said that these organizations have no respect for political boundaries, and pressure is put on governments to act because of their population's emotional responses to televised images. Governments feel compelled by television-generated public opinion to intervene in overseas conflicts, creating situations that would otherwise may not occur. Particularly in times of war, there is a debate as to the role of the media, and questions have been raised as to whether media coverage is forcing policy-makers to alter their approach.

This whole subject of the role of mass media shaping political policy is an area of wide academic and journalistic study, and is beyond the scope of this book to fully explore. However, there is a debate that has been running for more than a decade over the influence that news media in general – and 'live' television specifically – has over national government policy-making process. While some observers argue that there have been numerous examples of a direct link (either for better or for worse), others question claims that the media have any impact at all.[6–9] There is evidence for both sides of the argument, so the reality probably lies somewhere between these polarized positions, and changes depending on the nature of the event.

What cannot be denied is that extensive television coverage of events of international interest certainly informs governments faster than their own resources often permit, and so probably accelerates the decision-making process. The issue is whether the decisions reached are affected as a result of the coverage, or whether the same decisions would have been reached anyway, given time.

Government spokesmen – and even government leaders such as George W. Bush – use 24-hour news channels to directly address the world on breaking news issues; while terrorists use channels to deliver their messages – for example, Al Q'aeda's exclusive funneling of information to Al Jazeera to publicize their position to the Muslim world. This is an example of the question of whether a broadcaster is being used by a malevolent force to further its own ends, or is simply acting in the public interest to inform and present a balanced perspective (Al Jazeera's motto is "Opinion – and the other opinion").

The media's political influence is mentioned here mainly because it underscores the dramatic rise in the significance of satellite newsgathering in delivering rolling news coverage, not only in terms of audience ratings for network television, but also in the way it has extended media influence into international politics.[8]

1.11.2   Media: Neutral or target?

Traditionally, the media has enjoyed a position of relative neutrality, and this had unquestionably been the case up until the 1990s. In the first Iraq conflict, Saddam Hussein's government was always keen to see the Western media presence in Baghdad – even though they had to operate under severe restrictions. Even when Baghdad was under attack by US and European forces in 1991, the journalists of those countries were not in danger from the Iraqis – the greater hazard in reality was from 'friendly fire'.

On the other hand, in the Kosovo conflict, the Serbian government became positively hostile toward newsgathering organizations from NATO-aligned countries remaining in Belgrade, and a number of organizations had staff temporarily imprisoned and SNG uplink equipment confiscated – an action not seen in any other conflict up until that time.

Perhaps one of the most contentious episodes was the US bombing – whether accidental or deliberate – of Al Jazeera's Baghdad offices in April 2003, when one of Al Jazeera's foremost correspondents was killed. Five other journalists, including three from Reuters, were also injured when a US tank fired a round at the Palestine Hotel in Baghdad where at least 200 international correspondents, including Al Jazeera staff, were based. There has been a vigorous debate as to whether this was a crude attempt by the US military to silence some international media critical of their actions, and lends credence to the view that the media now exert a crucial influence on public opinion, to the extent that they themselves have become 'legitimate military targets'. To illustrate this, 89 journalists have been killed in Iraq in 2003–2006 (and year-on-year these figures are rising), compared to 66 journalists killed during the entire 20-year conflict in Vietnam.

The politicization of the media extends to the 'embedding' of TV broadcasters with the military, dating back to the Vietnam War, though at that time it was not administered in a systematic manner. Following this unfettered access, which undermined the US military and effectively accelerated the US withdrawal from Vietnam, it was re-born on a very minor scale in the First Gulf War, when the BBC and two of the US networks were allowed to be relatively close to the frontline. After the First Gulf War, the media in general complained that they had little chance to witness the battles for themselves and had to rely on official briefings which were widely criticized for tightly controlling what the media saw.

By the time of the Second Gulf War in 2003, the US and UK governments were determined to take advantage of controlled media access to assist them in their publicity campaigns – almost as important as the military ones in the case of this particular conflict. The embedding of almost 700 journalists with military units brought the media closest to battlefield warfare since Second World War, when correspondents were even given officer rank (although this certainly also applied to all the members of the BBC news team, including the two SNG uplink engineers, embedded with the UK army during the First Gulf War).

The shift in the position of the media from neutrality to target, thus exposing them to the same risks as combatants, is a worrying development and has led to a new safety culture within the industry. The creeping politicization of media working in the field (including the issue of 'embedding' news crews within military units), and the risks thus imposed, will be examined in more detail in Chapter 9 where we look at issues of safety on location.

1.11.3   Military SNG

As a demonstration of how governments themselves acknowledge the power of rapid newsgathering and the impact on their own domestic audiences, the US government have now moved into using SNG for their public relations activities.

Seeking to provide US local stations with access to video footage they otherwise would find hard to obtain, the US military has to equipped their public affairs units in Iraq, Kuwait and Afghanistan with much of the same newsgathering equipment that reporters embedded with military units used to gather and transmit reports from the frontlines of the Iraq War. Called the Digital Video and Imagery Distribution System (DVIDS), the US military have their own news crews equipped with portable newsgathering technology, including compact SNG terminals.

1.12   Conclusion

Satellite newsgathering has evolved from the technological seed of the electric telegraph in just over a century and a half and there are several interesting parallels between the telegraph and digital SNG in particular. Both involve a compressed method of coding, both revolutionized newsgathering, and both have had a lasting effect on the impact of news.

If television bulletins of only 30 or 40 years ago are viewed today, the difference is startling, and one is left marveling at what we are served today. From the stiff and visually boring bulletins of the 1950s, we have progressed to the visually and aurally stimulating style of the twenty-first century, which on some digital channels even feature viewer interactivity. Over this period, an increasing amount of national and international news has been customized down to local station level. Live interaction between news anchors and on-the-scene correspondents has become an everyday occurrence – the norm rather than unusual – and is achieved with ease by the fluid interconnectivity that SNG allows, whether from the end of your street or the other side of the world.

Such was the impact of the 1991 Persian Gulf War coverage that virtually no major international crisis or conflict since has escaped being covered by the use of SNG uplinks in some form, either by an SNG fly-away or a 'videophone'. Whether in conflicts in Bosnia, Somalia, Rwanda, Kosovo, East Timor, Iraq and Sudan; or natural disasters in Iran, Indonesia, Thailand, the December 2004 Indonesian tsunami, and even Hurricane Katrina in the First World country of the United States in 2005; they have all featured on news agendas around the world, and it is unimaginable that they would have received such prominence if there had not been such instant availability of live or 'near-live' reports.[10,11]

It is important to understand that SNG is about the use of satellites to enable 'contribution' to news broadcasts, while the use of satellites to deliver programs to the consumer audience (Direct-to-Home) is the 'distribution' end of the process.

In the following chapters, we will look at how the technology in the sky and the equipment on the ground are used together, and the processes involved in getting news from out there to the audience at home by the quickest means.

References

1. Gowing, N. (1994) *Real-time television coverage of armed conflicts and diplomatic crises: does it pressure or distort foreign policy decisions?* Working Paper 94-1, Shorenstein Center on the Press, Politics and Public Policy, John F. Kennedy School of Government, Harvard University.
2. Dunsmore, B. (1996) *The next war: live?* discussion Paper D-22, Shorenstein Center on the Press, Politics and Public Policy, John F. Kennedy School of Government, Harvard University.
3. Barnard, P. and Humphrys, J. (1999) *We Interrupt this Programme.* BBC Consumer Publishing.
4. Nielsen Media Research.
5. Livingston, S. (1997) *Clarifying the CNN effect: an examination of media effects according to type of military intervention.* Research Paper R-18, Shorenstein Center on the Press, Politics and Public Policy, John F. Kennedy School of Government, Harvard University.
6. Strobel, W. (1997) *Late Breaking Foreign Policy: The News Media's Influence on Peace Operations.* US Institute of Peace Press.
7. Livingston, S. and Eachus, T. (1995) *Humanitarian crises and US foreign policy: Somalia and the CNN effect reconsidered.* George Washington University, Political Communication, **12**, 413–429.
8. Gowing, N. (1997) *Media Coverage: Help or Hindrance in Conflict Prevention.* Carnegie Commission on Preventing Deadly Conflict.

9. Gilboa, E. (2002) *The global news networks and US policymaking in defense and foreign affairs.* Shorenstein Center on the Press, Politics and Public Policy, John F. Kennedy School of Government, Harvard University.

10. Livingston, S. (1997) *Beyond the "CNN Effect": The Media-Foreign Policy Dynamic,* Politics and the Press: The News Media and Their Influences, Lynne Rienner, pp. 291–318.

11. Livingston, S. and Van Belle, D. (2005) *The Effects of Satellite Technology on Newsgathering from Remote Locations.* Political Communication, Taylor & Francis Inc.

2

From launch to transmission: satellite communication theory and SNG

2.1 The birth of an idea

In October 1945, the then unknown (but now famous science fiction author) Arthur C. Clarke, who was at that time an RAF technical officer working on radar and a member of the British Interplanetary Society, wrote an article that was published in the British radio enthusiasts' magazine *Wireless World*. In this article, he put forward an idea about how the coverage of television transmissions could be improved by using radio 'relays' situated above the ionosphere.[1] Clarke had been working for some time on this concept, which was an astonishing proposal for the time and of such breathtaking prescience that, even now, as one reads the original article, it is uncanny how closely today's satellite communications systems mirror his prediction. Currently (2006), there are around 340 satellites in 'geostationary orbit' and in total over 3000 operational artificial satellites in various types of orbit around the Earth, not only serving commercial telecommunications needs, but also experimental, scientific observation, meteorological and military purposes.[2]

In his article (Figure 2.1), Clarke extrapolated the developments that the Germans had made in rocket technology, witnessed in the V1 and V2 rocket attacks on south-east England during the war, and proposed that a rocket of sufficient power could be launched from the Earth's surface into a high orbit.

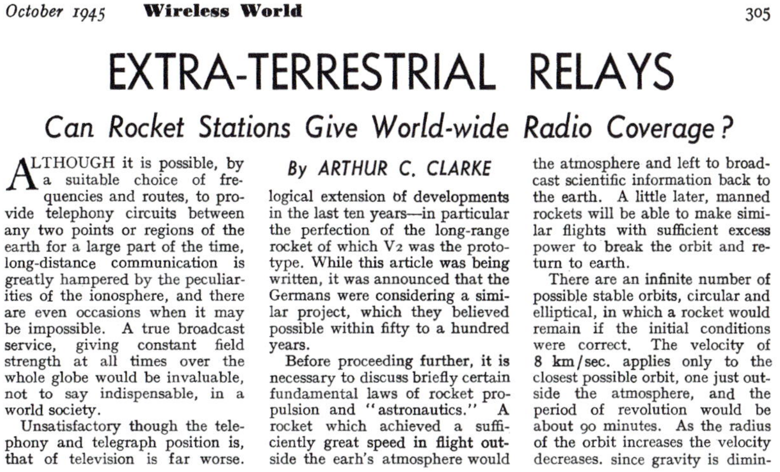

October 1945   **Wireless World**   305

EXTRA-TERRESTRIAL RELAYS

Can Rocket Stations Give World-wide Radio Coverage?

By ARTHUR C. CLARKE

ALTHOUGH it is possible, by a suitable choice of frequencies and routes, to provide telephony circuits between any two points or regions of the earth for a large part of the time, long-distance communication is greatly hampered by the peculiarities of the ionosphere, and there are even occasions when it may be impossible. A true broadcast service, giving constant field strength at all times over the whole globe would be invaluable, not to say indispensable, in a world society.

Unsatisfactory though the telephony and telegraph position is, that of television is far worse.

logical extension of developments in the last ten years—in particular the perfection of the long-range rocket of which V2 was the prototype. While this article was being written, it was announced that the Germans were considering a similar project, which they believed possible within fifty to a hundred years.

Before proceeding further, it is necessary to discuss briefly certain fundamental laws of rocket propulsion and "astronautics." A rocket which achieved a sufficiently great speed in flight outside the earth's atmosphere would

the atmosphere and left to broadcast scientific information back to the earth. A little later, manned rockets will be able to make similar flights with sufficient excess power to break the orbit and return to earth.

There are an infinite number of possible stable orbits, circular and elliptical, in which a rocket would remain if the initial conditions were correct. The velocity of 8 km/sec. applies only to the closest possible orbit, one just outside the atmosphere, and the period of revolution would be about 90 minutes. As the radius of the orbit increases the velocity decreases. since gravity is dimin-

Figure 2.1   Clarke's seminal article (*Wireless World*, October 1945)

It would be steered on its way by radio control into an orbit that exactly matched the speed of the Earth's rotation – this orbit is approximately 42 000 km (26 250 miles) from the center of the Earth (or 36 000 km [22 500 miles] from the surface). In this way the rocket would become a 'space station', and antennas on the space station could receive a signal from a transmitter on the Earth's surface and re-transmit it back to a wide area. At that time it was not known if signals from the Earth's surface could penetrate the Earth's atmosphere and reach space but, postulating that this would be possible, Clarke calculated the theoretical downlink power from the space station to cover the Earth's surface with enough signal to enable television reception. Clarke also predicted that three satellites placed at three longitudinal positions around the Earth (30°E, 150°E and 90°W) and above the Equator (i.e. at latitude 0°) would provide global coverage (Figure 2.2) – three satellites in geostationary orbit can cover 95% of the Earth's surface (the remaining 5% is above the Arctic Circle). The relationship between the Earth and the geostationary orbits, relative to the orbit of the Moon around the Earth, is shown in Figure 2.3.

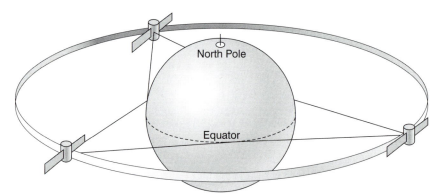

Figure 2.2 Principle of Clarke's theory of covering the Earth

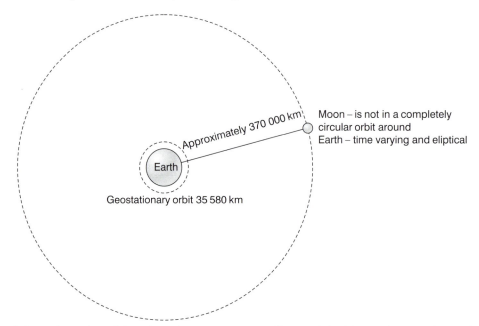

Figure 2.3 Relationship of the orbits of geostationary satellites and the Moon relative to the Earth

In his honor, the orbit that he proposed – which we now know as a 'geostationary Earth orbit' (GEO) – is named the 'Clarke belt'. Clarke never claimed to have invented the geostationary orbit, stating that he simply made a natural deduction from the laws of Newton and Kepler, and his article also makes reference to an article written in 1928 by Hermann Nordung (the pseudonym of an Austrian military officer named Potocnik) referring to the concept of satellites in 'geosynchronous Earth orbit'. There are other types of orbit as well – low Earth orbit (LEO) used by some satellite phone systems as well as for meteorological and scientific satellite observation; medium Earth orbit (MEO) used for Earth observation and by global positioning system (GPS) satellites – but the geostationary orbit is the one currently utilized for satellite newsgathering. Thus, this is the starting point for our discussion in this chapter.

Although it is not necessary to have knowledge of how the satellite arrives in orbit ready for use, and the actions that take place on the satellite during its life, it is useful background for an understanding of the process of satellite newsgathering.

2.2 Geostationary orbit

2.2.1 Principles

The Earth turns about its polar axis one revolution every 24 hours. (Strictly speaking, it actually rotates in 23 hours 56 minutes and 4.2 seconds – this is referred to as the 'sidereal' cycle, which equals one sidereal day.) It can be calculated that, at a specific distance from the Earth, a satellite in a circular orbit around the Earth will rotate at the same speed and direction as the Earth's rotation. This will be essentially in an orbit where the centrifugal force of the satellite's orbit is matched by the gravitational pull of the Earth, as shown in Figure 2.4. The effect of varying the distance from the Earth and the resulting effect on the period of the orbit is shown in Figure 2.5.

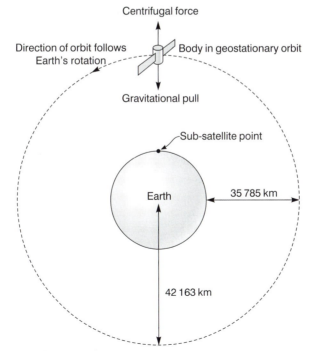

Figure 2.4   Geostationary orbit principle

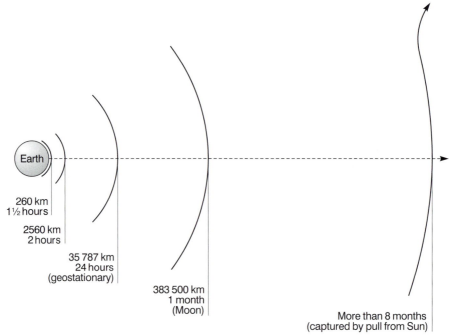

Figure 2.5 Differing orbits in time period and distance from the Earth

This satellite orbit is measured from the center of the Earth, and is called a 'geosynchronous' orbit. If that satellite orbit is above the Equator, then the satellite is said to be in 'geostationary' orbit. The geostationary orbit is calculated to be at a distance of 42 163 km measured from the center of the Earth, and the Earth's radius is calculated as 6378 km at the Equator. Therefore, the satellite is calculated to be 35 785 km (see Appendix B) above the Earth's surface at any point on the Equator, traveling at an orbital speed of about 11 000 kmh, in a west to east direction in synchronism with the Earth. The point on the Equator below the satellite is termed the 'sub-satellite' point and is at the latitude of 0°.

2.2.2 Longitude and latitude

For those of you who only have a hazy memory of geography, let us briefly look at the principles of longitude and latitude, as this is implicit in understanding how we refer to points on the Earth's surface.

Imaginary symmetrical lines of reference run from the North to the South Poles – these are called lines of longitude ('meridians'), some of which are shown in Figure 2.6. The line that runs through Greenwich in London, UK, is termed the Greenwich Meridian, and is the 0° longitude reference point. Lines run North to South around the complete 360° circumference of the Earth. Any point can be referred to as being at a certain point °E or °W, depending in which direction around the Earth the point is being referenced. (Satellite orbital positions in the geostationary arc are also referred to in the same way.)

Similarly, there are parallel lines that run in rings around the Earth from the North to the South Poles – these are lines of latitude ('parallels'), some of which are also shown in Figure 2.6. The line that runs around the Earth at its middle is the Equator and is the 0° latitude reference point. Lines of latitude run from 0° to 90° running North (Northern Hemisphere), and similarly 0° to 90° from the Equator to the South (Southern Hemisphere). Any point is referred to as being at a certain point °N or °S, depending on whether it is in the Northern or Southern Hemispheres, respectively.

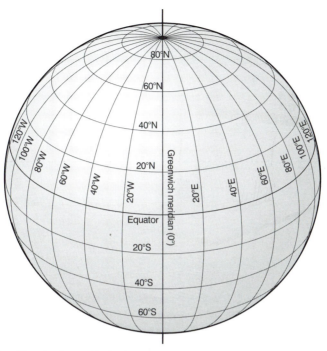

Figure 2.6 Principle of longitude and latitude

2.3 From launch to orbital position

2.3.1 Into orbit

The satellite is placed into a geostationary orbit by use of a rocket launch vehicle. Ideally, the launch vehicle would lift the satellite straight from the Earth's surface to the destination orbital position. However, the amount of force and hence power required are far beyond current capabilities, and the centrifugal force of the Earth's rotation has to be used in combination with the rocket's motors to catapult the satellite, in stages, into the correct orbit.

The ideal launch site is at or near the Equator, to be as close to the final orbital plane as possible. Also at the Equator, the Earth itself is rotating from west to east at 1675 kmh (1041 mph), so if the satellite is launched in the same direction as the Earth is rotating, it benefits from harnessing the 'sling effect' of the Earth's rotation.

In a geostationary orbit mission, there are essentially three phases: the launch, the transfer orbit and the final geostationary orbit positioning, as shown in Figure 2.7. There are a number of different types of launch vehicle used for the launch of commercial satellites, varying in size and range depending on customer choice and the payload (the satellite), and types include Delta (US), Atlas (US), Sea Launch (US), Ariane (European Space Agency or ESA), Proton (USSR) and Long March (China). Commercial satellites are made by companies such as Boeing Satellite Systems (US), Space Systems/Loral (US), Lockheed Martin (US) and Alcatel Space (France).

Typical costs to place a satellite into a geostationary orbit are US$100 million for construction of the satellite, and a further US$100 million for the launch, and US$40 million for insurance – a total of US$240 million. On average, the failure rate of launches and in-orbit satellites is over 10% and has risen steeply in the last 15 years (though admittedly the number of launches has also increased significantly

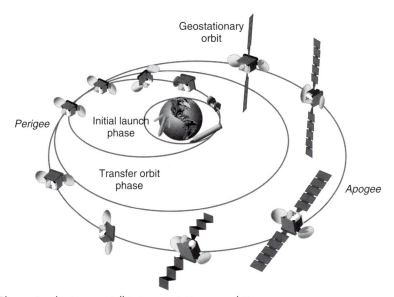

Figure 2.7 Phases in placing a satellite in geostationary orbit

in this period); hence the high cost of insurance. The rate of launch failure has not been distributed evenly across the industry – higher on US launches than on Russian.

The satellite, carried in the nose cone of the rocket launch vehicle, is very small relative to the size of the rocket. Primary launch sites for commercial satellites are near to the Equator and include Cape Canaveral, Florida, US; Kourou, French Guiana; Baikonur, Kazakhstan; and Xichang, China. In addition, Sea Launch provides a launch service from a marine platform normally sited for launches at 154° West on the Equator, near to Christmas Island in the Pacific.

The launch vehicle is composed of a 'payload' module, containing either one or a number of satellites depending on the size of the satellites and the launch vehicle, and a multi-stage set of motors. Typically, there are three motor stages, which detach from the vehicle in sequence as each one burns out during the launch phase, and the first stage may carry additional strapped-on boosters to increase the launch thrust.

To illustrate the whole process, we can examine a launch from Kourou, French Guiana, which was used to put Eutelsat's Atlantic Bird 2 satellite into orbit on September 25, 2001. Atlantic Bird 2 is a Spacebus 3000 series satellite built by Alcatel Space (France). Its body dimensions are 3.4 × 2.9 m and it was 4.7 m tall at launch, reaching a span of 29 m with the solar panels deployed (Figure 2.8). It weighed 3150 kg at launch, but its mass on reaching the beginning of its life in geostationary orbit reduces due to the burning of fuel by its thruster motors – most of the satellite's fuel is burnt in the initial phase of its life. It has a predicted life of 12 years, and its orbital position is at 8°W, serving North America and Europe providing television and radio connectivity, as well as Internet and multimedia streaming services. The launch process described is typical for most types of commercial geostationary satellite.

This launch used an Ariane-44P launch vehicle, which was 56 m high and weighed approximately 358 tonnes at launch, which included 43 tonnes for the launch vehicle itself and 312 tonnes of fuel, as well as the 3.15 tonnes for the satellite (Figure 2.9). The launch example is simplified for the sake of brevity (and to avoid the complex mathematics).

The timing of the launch and the weather conditions – particularly wind speed at both ground level and at high altitude – are critical. At launch, the rocket is on a near vertical trajectory, the angle of which

(a)

(b)

Figure 2.8 (a) Eutelsat Atlantic Bird 2 satellite (b) Alcatel Spacebus 3000 satellite (courtesy of Alcatel Space)

Figure 2.9   (a) Launch of Atlantic Bird 2 on Ariane Flight 144 (courtesy of Arianespace)

will be close to the latitude angle of the launch site due to the curvature of the Earth's surface. In the case of Kourou, French Guiana, the trajectory angle is at 7° to the Equator, as shown in Figure 2.10. The angle of trajectory then changes within the first minute to 40°, and the trajectory angle will be 90° (i.e. horizontal) on reaching entry into the transfer orbit. For safety reasons, for a launch to be initiated, wind speed is critical and has to be below 17 m/s at ground level, with both the wind speeds on the ground and at high altitude (between 10 and 20 km) being taken into account.

After launch, the rocket leaves the ground and carries the satellite to a position typically 300 km above the Earth's surface, which it reaches approximately 23 minutes after launch. These are the steps:

- Just under 5 seconds after the first stage engines have ignited, the launch vehicle leaves the ground, and in the first 3½ minutes the first stage burns 266 tonnes of fuel to reach 60 km altitude, reaching a velocity of 3 km/s.
- The first stage is then jettisoned and the second stage fires for just over 2 minutes using 34 tonnes of fuel to reach just over 150 km altitude at a velocity of 5 km/s.

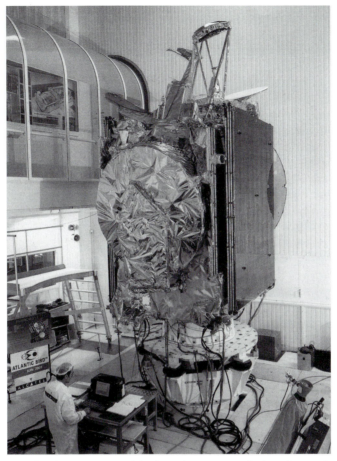

Figure 2.9 (b) AB2: satellite being prepared for launch (courtesy of Alcatel Space)

● The second stage is then falls away and the third stage is fired for 12 minutes using 12 tonnes of fuel to reach 300 km altitude at a velocity 10 km/s to launch it into the highly elliptical transfer orbit. Thus, 312 tonnes of fuel is burnt in just over 20 minutes.

The satellite is now in the elliptical transfer orbit at a velocity of 10 km/s – equivalent to 36 000 kph (22 500 mph). It weighed 3150 kg at launch, and due to burning of fuel this reduces to approximately 2000 kg on final positioning in geostationary orbit.

The highly elliptical transfer orbit – referred to as the 'injection orbit' or 'geostationary transfer orbit' (GTO) – has two points that define the degree of ellipticity in relation to the Earth: the 'perigee' and the 'apogee'. The perigee is the point of the orbit when the satellite is closest to the Earth's surface and is usually the same as the height of the initial entry into the transfer orbit. The apogee is the point of the orbit when the satellite is furthest away from the Earth. Thus the perigee of the transfer orbit is 300 km, and the apogee is equivalent to the geostationary orbit distance, i.e. 35 785 km in this example, and to reach the perigee of the orbit, the satellite fired its apogee motors four times. As it is an elliptical orbit,

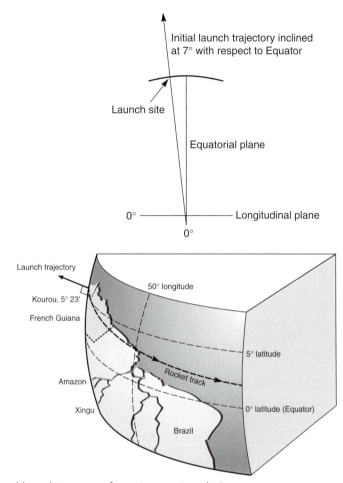

Figure 2.10 Typical launch trajectory from Kourou, French Guiana

the velocity of the spacecraft varies through the orbit. Typically, the perigee velocity of a spacecraft in GTO is around 10 km/s while the apogee velocity is around 2 km/s.

The key to the transfer, positioning and 'station-keeping' of the satellite is ensuring all the maneuvres in the life of a satellite can be achieved with the minimum expenditure of fuel. Essentially, fuel capacity defines the life of a satellite, as this obviously cannot be replenished despite the systems on the spacecraft potentially having a much longer life. The on-board fuel is used for both early orbit maneuvres and station-keeping for the rest of its operational life.

Both the perigee and the apogee have to be above the line of the Equator, and this is the reason for the need for complicated maneuvres in accomplishing the transfer orbit, where the launch is from a location not on the Equator. It has to be remembered that the Earth is not static during orbital maneuvres, and its movement has to be taken into consideration. For instance, when the satellite has reached the apogee of the transfer orbit, the Earth rotates 15° for each orbit of the satellite. This, combined with the movement of the satellite, means that there are extremely complex calculations and subsequent maneuvres to ensure the satellite is on the right course, at the correct inclination and at the correct orbital position by the end of the final phase. It is analogous to a soccer player kicking the ball from the middle of the pitch toward the goal, but as soon as the ball leaves the boot of the player, the pitch begins to rotate and the ball has to be steered toward the changing position of the goal to score – literally 'moving the goal-posts'!

The process of correcting the inclination to 0° with respect to the Equator is incrementally progressed throughout the process of the transfer orbit and the final positioning of the satellite. Assuming the typical transfer orbit, where the apogee is at or close to 35 900 km (near to the nominal geostationary orbit distance), then the period of this orbit is initially approximately 10 hours. The Earth rotates 150° in every 10-hour orbit. After four orbits, the first apogee motor firing will occur for about 40 minutes, increasing the perigee to 5500 km and the orbital period to 12 hours. The Earth rotates a further 180° in every 12-hour orbit.

After another two orbits, the second apogee motor burn occurs, lasting 1¼ hours, which brings the satellite into a practically circular orbit, raising the perigee to approximately 30 000 km. The orbital period will now be over 22 hours, and the Earth rotates a further 330° in every 22-hour orbit.

After a further two orbits, the third firing of the apogee motor occurs at the point of apogee to move the satellite into geostationary orbit where it will orbit the Earth almost in synchronism. The whole process has so far taken 5–6 days, though the satellite will not yet be at its precise longitude, but 4–5° away. The third burn also ensures that the satellite will move extremely slowly to its final location and place the satellite into a circular orbit. Although the apogee motor may be fired again, the natural forces of centrifugal force and gravity are used as much as possible to conserve fuel, and the satellite is 'drifted' toward its final orbital position, using a series of precise East–West maneuvres to decrease its advance and finally halt its drift.

At near final positioning in its orbit, the satellite's solar arrays and antennas are deployed. These enable the satellite to be fully powered-up and pass communication signals to and from the spacecraft. Then, using on-board infrared Earth sensors, which sense the heat of the Earth against the cold of space, 'earthlock' is achieved, and the spacecraft antenna are orientated toward Earth.

Finally the solar array is fully unfolded, ranging signals are sent up from the ground to determine the exact location of the satellite so that the thrusters can be fired to gently place the satellite in its final orbital slot, and the solar panels are set to track to follow the path of the Sun.

This whole process, from launch to final positioning, takes approximately 10 days. There is constant monitoring from a number of ground-based Tracking, Telemetry and Control (or command) (TT&C) stations, and the various sub-systems are now methodically activated, tested and monitored. In Orbit Test (IOT) is a period of exhaustive performance testing to ensure each sub-system of the spacecraft is performing correctly. The time taken to bring the satellite online usually needs to be kept to a minimum, as the customer – the satellite system operator – will want to commence telecommunications and control system testing leading to commercial operations, as soon as possible. For the satellite payload IOT, the satellite system operator checks out the satellite's transmission capabilities, including the command and telemetry links, the uplink sensitivity, transponders, and downlink power. The full IOT program typically lasts up to 4 weeks. A compromise must be reached between the time required for a full test program and the shortest time to full commercial service.

2.4 In orbit

2.4.1 Station-keeping

The satellite, once in orbit, has to be maintained in a constant position to meet the geostationary requirement. This process is termed 'station-keeping'. It could be inferred from what has been said so far that the orbital position will be maintained purely naturally. However, there are a number of forces that can cause disturbances in the orbital path. If these are uncorrected, the satellite position will not comply with the ITU definition of 'geostationary'. (For the role of the International Telecommunications Union, see Chapter 7.) Generally satellites have to be station-kept to within 0.05°.

The orbit is generally considered circular, but it is in fact slightly elliptical as the Earth 'bulges' at the Equator at longitude 15°W and 165°E. This causes a slight circular oscillation of the satellite orbit and, more significantly, a shift in the gravitational pull that appears to be slightly off-center from the center of the Earth. If uncorrected, the force from the uneven gravitational field would cause satellites to move slowly to positions 90° away from each of these points (105°W and 75°E) where the gravitational pull is more stable. (These positions correspond to the eastern Pacific and Indian Ocean, respectively.)

At the end of their operational life, satellites are recommended to be finally drifted further out into space from the geostationary arc (termed 'de-orbiting') into what is known as the 'graveyard' orbit (245–435 km beyond the geostationary arc, depending on the area-to-mass ratio of the spacecraft[3]). But these recommendations are not internationally binding character and are left to be fulfilled by the satellite operators voluntarily. Thus, not all dead satellites have been de-orbited, and it is estimated that at least 30% of defunct satellites still remain in geostationary orbit.

The advantage of collecting what is effectively 'space junk' in graveyard orbit is that this orbit can be closely monitored to ensure that there is minimal risk of this space debris damaging any active spacecraft. Space surveillance, using radar and optical telescopes, provides information on what is orbiting Earth, and this information includes each object's orbital parameters, size and shape, and other data useful for determining its purpose. Only a small fraction represents defunct satellites; the remainder is the consequence of over 40 years of payload and rocket fragmentation.

These objects are a hazard for future space missions due to the increasing probability of an impact with satellites or spacecraft. Active and inactive satellites, along with space debris such as boosters, shrouds and other objects are tracked; the smallest object that can be tracked is about 1 cm in diameter. Over 11 000 objects are actively tracked,[4] and the population of particles between 1 and 10 cm in diameter is estimated at over 100 000 (typically, tracked low Earth orbit objects at 1000 km distant from the Earth's surface are as small as 1 cm, and 60 cm at geostationary orbit distances – the tracked size varies with their altitude). The number of particles smaller than 1 cm probably exceeds tens of millions. Objects over 10 cm in size that are not tracked could seriously damage an operational spacecraft. At geostationary orbits, the ability to detect orbital debris is limited, but studies indicate that the orbital debris population at geostationary orbits is probably less severe than in low Earth orbit.

There are further effects on the satellite's orbit. The Earth is not completely circular as the Poles are slightly 'flattened' (termed 'oblate'), and this causes a distortion in the Earth's gravitational field. Add to this the disturbances from both lunar and solar forces, and all this accounts for the distorting effects on the ideal geostationary orbit. If uncorrected, the satellite would oscillate both on its 'North–South' axis and its 'East–West' axis over a 24-hour period (one rotation of the Earth) and the orbit would thus be described as 'inclined'. This is sometimes described as having a 'figure-of-eight' orbit. However, this description of the shape is exaggerated, as the true shape of the oscillation of a satellite in inclined orbit is very much more elongated on the North–South axis than the East–West axis, resulting in a very stretched 'figure-of-eight' shape, as shown in Figure 2.11. If uncorrected, this would cause an increase in the inclination of the satellite orbit by an average of 0.8° per annum, and cause increasing difficulties on the ground in maintaining tracking of the satellite by earth station antennas. This inclination leads to the apparent North/South and East/West oscillation as viewed from the Earth.

The distorting effects on the satellite's orbit create the need for station-keeping maneuvres on the satellite. The nominal spacing for satellites in the geostationary arc is 2°, as defined by the agreement of the principal satellite authorities and some national administrations (see Chapter 7). If the 0.8° average drift per annum were allowed to go unchecked, there would be a serious risk of multiple illumination of

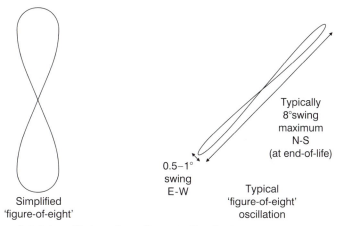

Figure 2.11 'Figure-of-eight' oscillation of satellite in inclined orbit

adjacent satellites from uplink signals where there is common frequency band usage. It would also cause problems for the large antenna of a fixed land earth station (LES or 'ground station') in trying to track the satellite. It should also be noted that there are often a number of satellites co-located at the same orbital position – this is particularly used for DTH (Direct-To-Home) services so that consumers need only have an antenna pointed at one orbital position for multiple services. For example, in Europe, there are four DTH satellites in the Hotbird series co-located at 13° E at the time of writing. This particularly increases pressure to maintain accurate station-keeping on Eutelsat, the Paris-based operator of the Hotbird series.

The relationships between all the parameters of the geostationary orbit are shown in Figure 2.12a. The area in which the satellite has to be maintained while in station-kept geostationary orbit is termed the 'box' (Figure 2.12b), and the satellite operator has to maintain the satellite above the sub-satellite point to within ±0.05° in the vertical (longitude) and horizontal (latitude) planes. The sub-satellite point is the point of the Earth's surface that is directly below the satellite's nominal position. This therefore translates to a cube of space ('box'), the dimensions of which are typically 75 km high × 75 km wide × 35 km deep.

To give an idea of the scale, the beam transmitted from a Ku-band 1.5 m SNG uplink antenna will have spread to approximately 750 km wide by the time it reaches the satellite at the geostationary arc. The centers of the 2° spaced 'boxes' are approximately 1500 km apart. Larger antennas have narrower beams (as we will see later) and therefore the spread is smaller.

There are two principal types of station-keeping, East–West and North–South, and the process is controlled by an integral attitude control system on the satellite. There are typically two types of attitude control on satellite, spin-stabilized and three-axis stabilization. Most modern geostationary satellites used for commercial telecommunications traffic use three-axis stabilization control, so we will concentrate on describing this system.

The aim of the attitude control system is to always keep the satellite in the correct position or 'attitude', with the antennas pointing toward the Earth, and the solar panel array pointing toward the Sun (earthlock). In a three-axis stabilization system, a gyroscope in each of the three planes is used to control the satellite attitude (see Figure 2.13).

Station-keeping is achieved by use of small rocket booster motors called 'thrusters'. A three-axis stabilized satellite typically has five sets of thrusters to correct the movements in orbit (roll, pitch, yaw, East–West and North–South). These are regularly fired under control from the main TT&C station that is receiving information on the satellite's attitude back from the satellite's on-board sensors. The satellite's rate of drift is relatively slow, and so adjustments are typically made on a weekly basis.

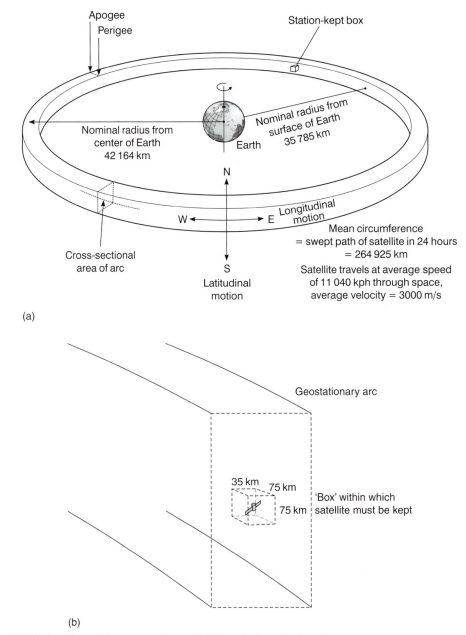

Apogee
Perigee

Station-kept box

Nominal radius from
surface of Earth
35 785 km

Nominal radius from
center of Earth
42 164 km

Earth

N

W ← → E   Longitudinal
motion

Cross-sectional
area of arc

S
Latitudinal
motion

Mean circumference
= swept path of satellite in 24 hours
= 264 925 km

Satellite travels at average speed
of 11 040 kph through space,
average velocity = 3000 m/s

(a)

Geostationary arc

35 km   75 km

'Box' within which
75 km   satellite must be kept

(b)

Figure 2.12   (a) Geostationary satellite arc (b) Detail of station-kept box

As described in Chapter 7, satellites are maintained in a station-kept state for as long as is possible. At some point near the end of the operational life of the satellite, the North–South station-keeping maneuvres are virtually abandoned to extend the operational life of the satellite (though there are some occasional minor adjustments to support the East–West station-keeping). This makes the satellite only usable for certain services and this can include SNG operations. When the North–South inclination

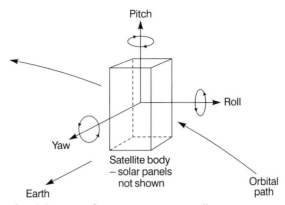

Figure 2.13   Three axes of stabilization of a geostationary satellite

exceeds a swing of 7–8° daily, the decision is usually taken to end the operational life of the satellite, and it is moved to a 'graveyard' orbit.

2.4.2   Locating the satellite from the Earth

The satellite has to be 'seen' from the Earth by any transmitter or receiver that is going to work through it. The transmitter is referred to as the 'uplink' and the receiver as the 'downlink'. Both the uplink and the downlink have to be accurately pointed at the satellite, and the 'azimuth' and 'elevation' of alignment to the satellite have to be calculated. Azimuth is the compass bearing direction to the satellite in the horizontal plane from a point on the Earth's surface, and elevation is the angle of the satellite above the horizon from that location. Both of these parameters vary according to the longitude and latitude of the location on the Earth's surface and define the 'look angle' of the uplink or the downlink toward the satellite (Figure 2.14).

The calculation can be found in Appendix B, and it is a relatively simple one to program into a spreadsheet on a PDA or laptop computer for use in the field for SNG.

The theoretical calculation produces an azimuth value that relates to the True North Pole, expressed in degrees East of True North (°ETN), which is a geographical designation at 90°N latitude, 0° longitude. The 'True' value is the theoretical position of the North Pole, where all the lines of longitude meet at the top of the Earth and the axis about which the Earth rotates – a point some 750 km north of Greenland. However, it is the 'magnetic' bearing in degrees East of Magnetic North that is actually required (°EMN) as it is the Magnetic North Pole toward which a compass needle will point, and is actually further south than the True North Pole. (It is currently about 500 km NW of Resolute Bay in Canada in the Arctic Sea and moves northward on average 10 km/year – it can vary up to 80 km each day from its average position.)

There are maps that provide a correction value for any point on the Earth's surface which when added to the True value will give the Magnetic value, which can then be used with a compass to find the azimuth on which the satellite lies. A magnetic variation of 5–10° from True North is not unusual, and this variation is significant when trying to locate a satellite and must therefore be factored into the compass bearings used.

2.4.3   Telemetry, Tracking and Control (TT&C)

It is briefly worth describing the principal functions of Telemetry, Tracking and Control (TT&C), as this is a background management that operates 'behind the scenes' so far as users of satellites are concerned.

The satellite contains a complex system of sensors and control mechanisms, which are all remotely controlled from TT&C ground stations around the globe operated by the satellite operator. These play a role in

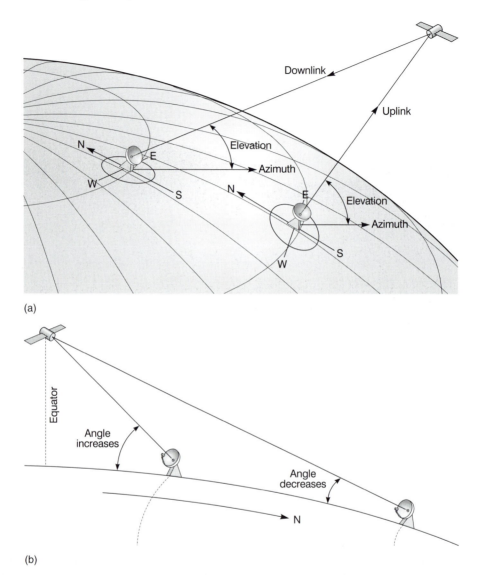

Figure 2.14 (a) Change of azimuth and elevation with change of longitude and latitude (b) Change of elevation angle with change of latitude in Northern hemisphere (reversed in Southern hemisphere)

both the launch and throughout the whole life of the satellite, and these ground stations are the crucial control centers that sustain the operation of the satellite. The following primary functions are carried out:

- Orbit and attitude control, including solar panel pointing for optimum power.
- Configuration of satellite and back-up switching (such as which transponder, or channel, is connected to which satellite 'beam', 'footprint' steering and adjustment of transponder amplification).
- Monitoring of external and internal parameters.

Figure 2.14 (c) The evaluation angle on this uplink antenna in Rwanda, which is very close to the Equator, is almost 90° (courtesy of Paul Szeless)

Typically, the control and monitoring channels between the satellite and the TT&C ground station operate on frequencies well away from the telecommunications channels. There is usually a basic TT&C system used in the transfer orbit phases, operating in the L-band (see Appendix A), while the main TT&C system operates during the rest of the operational life of the satellite in the C- or Ku-band. Many of the primary satellite functions are transmitted as part of the 'beacon' signal, a special signal transmitted from the satellite, which is normally in the same frequency band as the telecommunications channels, as it also serves as a unique identifier for the satellite users on the ground.

The satellite management activity is, for obvious reasons, regarded as a security issue for satellite operators, and there is no specific information officially put into the public domain. A satellite is an extremely costly and valuable asset, and a satellite operator must use highly complex and secure control systems to ensure that the satellite remains protected from accidental or malicious interference. In many satellite organizations, there is almost a 'wall' between the TT&C operation and the commercial payload operation of the satellite. It is useful, however, to be aware of the existence of the TT&C operation.

2.4.4 Solar eclipses and outages

Before moving on to describe the telecommunication principles of satellites, we need briefly to discuss the phenomena of solar eclipses of satellites and the effects of solar outages. Both these types of event can cause disruption to satellite transmission and reception, respectively, and can therefore impact on SNG operations.

The Earth revolves around the Sun once every 365 days while rotating once every 24 hours on its own axis. The Earth spins on its axis at a tilt of 23.5° from a line perpendicular to its own orbital path around

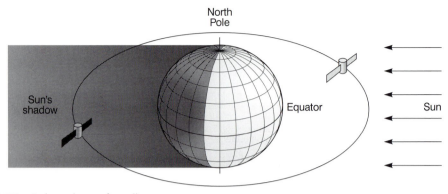

Figure 2.15   Solar eclipse of satellite

the Sun, resulting in the North Pole always pointing in the same direction in space, and it is this tilting of the Earth's axis that causes the seasons. Thus in June the Northern Hemisphere is tipped slightly toward the Sun increasing the length of daylight (summer), and the Southern Hemisphere slightly away from the Sun decreasing the length of daylight (winter). In December the opposite is true. In March and September (the spring and autumnal equinoxes) both hemispheres are equally exposed to the Sun.

For most of the year, the orbit of the satellite keeps the satellite in view of the Sun. However, the satellite is out of view of the Sun for a few days around midnight at the time of the spring and autumn equinoxes at the sub-equatorial position, when the Earth moves between the satellite and the Sun. This causes a solar eclipse of the satellite, as shown in Figure 2.15. These do not occur during the summer and winter equinoxes, as the satellite is in view of the Sun at all times.

During the eclipse, the Sun's energy is obscured from the satellite solar panels that provide the primary electrical power on the satellite. The satellite has batteries on board which are charged by the solar panels, and during the period of an eclipse the satellite is switched to use the stored energy in these batteries to maintain operation. Satellite operation should therefore normally be unaffected despite the temporary loss of solar power.

Solar outages (or 'Sun-outs') occur during the equinoxes when the satellite is on that part of its orbit where it comes between the Sun and the Earth. The result of this is that a downlink antenna receiving the satellite signals is 'blinded' as the Sun passes behind the satellite, as shown in Figure 2.16. This is not due to the visible light from the Sun, but to the invisible electromagnetic 'noise' that is also radiated from the Sun, which swamps the signal from the satellite. The Sun has a surface temperature typically in excess of 6000°C, and this level of radiation is produced across the rest of the electromagnetic spectrum – effectively a very high-intensity microwave noise source aimed directly at the antenna during the period in question. The outage may last several minutes over a number of days both before and after the peak day and the smaller the antenna, the longer the outage (related to the beamwidth of the antenna). Outages will occur at roughly the same time each day on a daily basis for a week or so.

Figure 2.16b shows the effect of an outage viewed at an antenna in Jerusalem, where the Sun's rays are directly focused from the parabolic antenna onto the 'feedhorn'. The reception of signals from the satellite toward which the antenna is pointing is impossible under these conditions, and therefore care needs to be taken in the timing of the booking of satellite feeds at this time. Satellite operators typically give customers due warning, and the effects can be obviated by using alternative satellites during this time, thus avoiding a particular critical alignment of Sun – satellite – antenna.

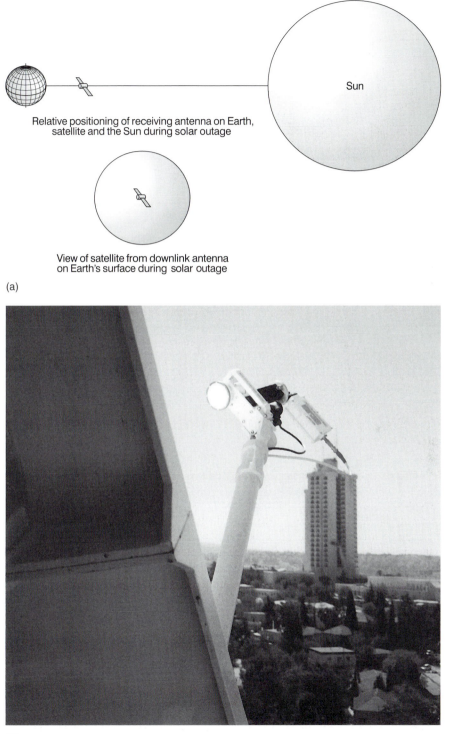

Relative positioning of receiving antenna on Earth,
satellite and the Sun during solar outage

Sun

View of satellite from downlink antenna
on Earth's surface during solar outage

(a)

(b)

Figure 2.16   (a) Solar outage (b) Solar outage of satellite in Jerusalem (courtesy of Paul Szeless)

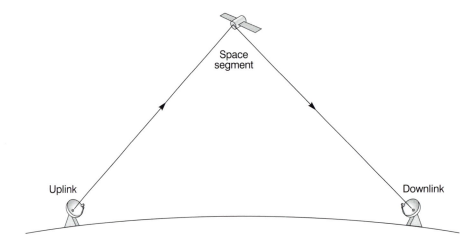

Figure 2.17   Overview of uplink–downlink system

2.5   Communication theory

As Arthur C. Clarke originally envisioned, satellites are effectively 'radio mirrors' in the sky. A satellite receives a signal from a ground transmitter – the uplink – and re-transmits ('reflects') the signal to a ground receiver – the downlink. A satellite can be considered to have a number of these 'radio mirrors' – termed 'transponders' – and these transponders can be dynamically configured by ground control (TT&C) for particular applications or services. The part of the system in the sky is generically termed 'space segment'. The concept of the transmission system is shown in Figure 2.17. Because the uplink is of most interest to us we will be concentrating on describing this part of the system, although we will briefly cover the other elements. However, there are few basic concepts to be dealt with before we examine the uplink system.

2.5.1   Analog and digital signals

The words 'analog' and 'digital' are in everyday parlance, and before we can begin to cover the principles of satellite transmissions, we need to cover the concept of analog and digital – with the minimum of maths. Those readers who already understand these principles can skip to Section 2.6.

In telecommunications there are two types of transmission, analog and digital, which describe the nature of the signal and the method used to convey the video and audio program information. For historical reasons it is necessary to briefly look at analog theory, as up until the mid-1990s analog SNG was widespread, but as digital technology developed, analog use had virtually disappeared in terms of SNG by the end of the decade. It is not necessary for you to have a deep understanding, but the basic concepts need to be appreciated.

2.5.2   Analog

An analog signal is a 'wave' signal that carries information by the continuous varying of its amplitude (size) and frequency (period), as shown in Figure 2.18. The concept is analogous to two people, each holding the end of a rope, and standing some distance apart. One person acts as the 'transmitter' and one as the 'receiver'. The 'transmitter' flicks the end of the rope up and down, creating a wave shape that passes down the rope to the 'receiver'. The harder the rope is flicked, the greater the amplitude of the wave, and the more frequently it is flicked, the faster the waves are created and the faster the rope oscillates. This demonstrates the two fundamental properties of an analog signal – amplitude and frequency.

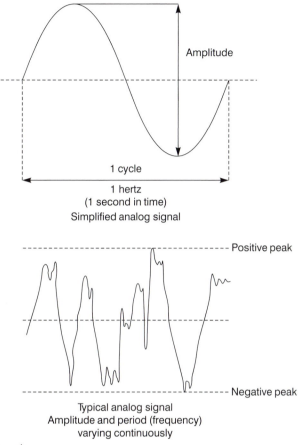

Figure 2.18 Analog signals

Table 2.1 Greek prefixes and the multipliers

Greek prefix	Multiplier/scaling factor	Scientific notation
micro	0.000001 (1/1 000 000)	10^{-6}
milli	0.001 (1/100 000)	10^{-3}
kilo	1000	10^{3}
mega	1 000 000	10^{6}
giga	1 000 000 000	10^{9}

One complete wave (as shown in Figure 2.18) is equal to one cycle in a one second period, or 1 Hertz (Hz). The essential difference between an analog signal and a digital signal, as we shall see shortly, is that the analog signal amplitude can be *any* value between pre-defined limits.

Because we measure frequency across a wide range – in this book, for example, we span from 1 hertz to tens of thousands of millions hertz (10 000 000 000 Hz), we have to use a shorthand to show the magnitude of a signal instead of writing strings of numbers. We use the term kilohertz (kHz) for 1 thousand Hz, megahertz for 1 million hertz and so on. Based on Greek terminology, Table 2.1 shows the terms used and their scale. Note that we also use very small numbers – when measuring power, one thousandth of a watt is a milliwatt, for example.

This is how many electrical signals are conveyed, such as those reproduced by hi-fi systems. In terms of audio, the amplitude is the 'loudness', and the period is the frequency or 'pitch' of the program signal. The human ear has a range of approximately 50–20 000 Hz. Loud, high-pitched sound signals correspond to large and closely spaced waves, and quiet, low-pitched signals to small and widely spaced waves. Obviously, these two components vary independently to create a wide spectrum of sounds.

A radio transmitter is a device that converts this type of 'message' signal (often termed the 'baseband' signal) to a signal at a much higher frequency and power that can travel over a distance (often termed the 'carrier' signal). Although it is at a much higher frequency, the amplitude and the frequency of the original signal can be received at the distant point. The process of converting this signal to a much higher frequency to become a radio signal is called 'modulation', and the inverse process of recreating the original baseband message signal, 'demodulation'.

There are several ways of modulating a carrier with a baseband analog signal, but the two most common methods are amplitude modulation (AM) and frequency modulation (FM). Amplitude modulation is the process where a baseband message signal modulates (alters) the amplitude and frequency of a high-frequency carrier signal, which is at a nominally fixed frequency, so that the carrier signal varies in amplitude. If this signal is analyzed, it can now be seen to contain the original carrier signal plus lower and upper 'sidebands' of frequencies. The entire modulated carrier now occupies a frequency range termed the 'RF bandwidth' (where RF is an abbreviation for radio frequency). AM is commonly used in radio broadcasts as amplitude modulation has the advantage of carrying great distances with a relatively moderate amount of power from the transmitter.

Frequency modulation is of interest as it was used for analog SNG transmissions. The principle of frequency modulation is based on a carrier that shifts up and down in frequency ('deviates') from its 'at rest' (center) frequency in direct relationship to the amplitude of the baseband signal, though its amplitude remains the same, as shown in Figure 2.19. The maximum deviation (shift) of the frequency is equal above and below the center frequency, and is usually referred to as the 'peak-to-peak' frequency deviation, and equates to the lowest and highest input signal amplitudes being conveyed.

In an FM signal, the instantaneous frequency of the baseband signal is represented by the instantaneous rate of change (speed of change) of the carrier frequency. If the modulated signal 'waveform' is viewed on an electronic measurement instrument such as an oscilloscope or a spectrum analyzer, the relationship appears much more complex than in amplitude modulation, and it is difficult to see exactly what is occurring.

However, the advantage of frequency modulation is that the signal has significantly greater immunity from random effects ('noise') than AM, and is much more effective than AM at the very high carrier

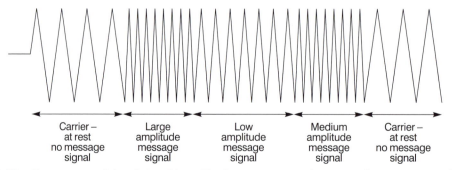

| Carrier –
at rest
no message
signal | Large
amplitude
message
signal | Low
amplitude
message
signal | Medium
amplitude
message
signal | Carrier –
at rest
no message
signal |

Figure 2.19   Frequency-modulated signal (simplified): constant input frequency, but varying amplitude

frequencies used for satellite transmissions. FM is spectrally very inefficient, i.e. the amount of bandwidth required to transmit a message signal is greater, but if the right conditions are met, it produces a much higher-quality signal compared to AM. Satellite communications have traditionally been power limited rather than bandwidth limited, so the spectral inefficiency has not been an issue.

The principles of modulation, and in particular frequency modulation, are difficult concepts to grasp, so you need not be unduly concerned if you don't fully understand. There are innumerable communications engineering textbooks that cover the subject in considerable depth (and which require a good grounding in mathematics!), but let this description suffice, alongside accepting that frequency modulation was the preferred method for analog SNG transmissions.

2.5.3   Digital

Of much greater interest to us is the use of digital techniques. A digital signal can convey information as a signal containing a series of 'on' and 'off' states, which can be thought of as corresponding to numbers 1 and 0 based on the binary number system (Figure 2.20). In a stream of 1s and 0s, each 1 and each 0 is termed a 'bit', and a digital signal is defined by the parameter of 'bits'. For instance, the signal is transmitted at a certain speed or 'bit-rate', measured in bits per second (bps). (There is a more detailed discussion of binary arithmetic in Chapter 5.)

The analog signal can be converted to a digital signal (using the processes of 'sampling', 'quantizing' and 'coding', discussed in Chapter 4), and the digital signal can then be transmitted. However, most current broadcast video equipment can directly output a digital signal. The advantage of a digital signal, particularly in relation to satellite transmissions, and after it has been processed, is that the amount of power required to transmit it successfully can be significantly lower than the power required for analog transmission. This is because, in general, the signals are more easily recovered from the background 'noise' and interference – more on this shortly.

If digital signals were used in direct replacement for the same analog information, the resultant bit-rate at which the information would have to be transmitted would be very high. This would use much more bandwidth (frequency spectrum) than an equivalent analog transmission, and is therefore not very efficient (i.e. 36 MHz for analog FM video and up to 270 MHz for digital video). There is a need to strip out the redundant and insignificant information in the signal, and this process of data rate reduction, or 'compression' as it is more commonly referred to, is dealt with in more detail in Chapter 4. The important point to grasp is that the use of digital technology is now the norm for SNG transmissions.

Analog transmissions require significantly greater power and bandwidth than compressed digital transmissions, but the quality of the signal recovered can be very high. This greater power can only be delivered by a larger transmitting amplifier and/or a larger antenna than is required for a digital transmission.

Digital transmissions are always compressed for SNG, thus achieving savings in power and bandwidth. Although the quality of the signal can look very good at first glance, there are particular picture degradations (termed 'compression artifacts'; see Chapter 4) that can be objectionable for certain types

Figure 2.20   Digital signal

of picture content. However, as the cost of satellite capacity and the size of the SNG equipment are often primary considerations, these artifacts are tolerated as the compromise for the financial savings. The compression process also increases the overall delay of the signal, as the processing involved in compressing and decompressing the signal takes an appreciable time. This is in addition to the delay that the signal suffers in traveling from the Earth to the satellite and back to Earth, as we shall see later – note that any delay can be problematical in conducting 'live' interviews.

The issues of gain and bandwidth crop up frequently in discussions on satellite communications. Having identified the two types of analog transmission, we can now move on to look at the digital transmission system. Because we will be dealing with specific components in the system, we need to look briefly at the frequencies used for the transmission and reception of signals.

2.6   Frequency bands

There are two principal frequency bands used for satellite transmissions for television, including those used for SNG (Appendix A). The band in the frequency range of approximately 4–6 GHz is called the C-band, and the frequency band between approximately 10–18 GHz is called the Ku-band (1 GHz is equal to 1 000 000 000 Hz or 1×10^9 Hz). The use of terms such as 'L', 'C' and 'Ku' for frequency bands dates from the development of radar in the Second World War, when engineers and scientists wanted to discuss these matters without anyone else knowing what they were talking about (so not much different from now!).

2.6.1   C-band

The C-band is the frequency band that has been used for telecommunication transmissions since the 1960s (see Chapter 3). The 'transmit' frequency is typically in the range 5.9–6.4 GHz and the 'receive' frequency is 3.7–4.2 GHz; and, as far as SNG is concerned, C-band is used predominantly for digital transmissions. In 1994, Intelsat began promoting the use of C-band for digital SNG as there was an increasing amount of their C-band capacity becoming available, and many parts of the world lacked adequate Ku-band coverage. However, the use of C-band SNG does have some limitations from a regulatory aspect (see Chapter 7), and the use of C-band for SNG has declined in recent years as the geographical and commercial availability of Ku-band has spread. It is however still widely used in equatorial regions of Asia, South America and Africa where the propagation characteristics of being less affected by rainfall make it essential.

2.6.2   Ku-band

The Ku-band is the frequency band (10–18 GHz) that is now, in many parts of the world, the predominant band for TV signals (particularly DTH services) and has been the dominant frequency band for SNG since the early 1980s. The 'transmit' frequency is typically in the range 14.0–14.50 GHz and the 'receive' frequency is 10.7–12.75 GHz. The 'K' comes from the German '*kurz*' meaning short (referring to the wavelength), and the letter 'u' refers to '*über*' meaning 'under'. The K-band covers the frequency range 18.0–26.5 GHz, and so Ku is the band below this. It should be noted that the band 13.75–14.0 GHz is widely used in the Middle East for SNG, and is also starting to be used in Europe for SNG.

2.6.3   Other frequency bands

Either in our discussions through the book, or heard generally in the area of satellite communications, there are several other frequency bands the reader should be aware of (see Appendix A).

L-band (1000–2000 MHz) is used in two ways in the context of SNG. It is the transmission band used by satellite phones (see Chapter 6), and it is also referred to as an intermediate frequency (IF) band. The term 'intermediate' is used as it lies between the baseband frequency range of the originating signal and the final transmission frequency (and vice versa), and is found being used between pieces of equipment at both the uplink and the downlink.

The Ka-band (the letter 'a' refers to 'above' – a mixing of languages!) extends from around 26–40 GHz, but there are different interpretations as to exactly what constitutes Ka-band depending on the application. In SNG, reference to Ka-band generally refers to the transmit band of 27.5–31.0 GHz, and the receive bands of 18.3–18.8 and 19.7–20.2 GHz. While at present the Ka-band is not used for SNG, there is discussion from time to time of its use in the future (we will discuss this in Chapter 10). In the mid to late 1990s, some satellite operators foresaw a shortage of Ku-band capacity, and so equipped some new satellites with Ka-band payloads (remembering that it can take 3–5 years from planning a satellite to it being in operational orbit). Unfortunately for these operators, their Ka-band capacity is largely under-utilized, although attempts are being made to use it for Internet access services.

The DBS (Direct Broadcasting Service) band is used for DTH services for distribution of programming. In the US, DirecTV and EchoStar both transmit in the DBS band, and in the Middle East, both Arabsat and Nilesat DTH services use this band for uplinking programming. The transmit band is 17.3–18.4 GHz, while the downlink used is the middle part of the Ku-band receive frequency band at 11.7–12.0 GHz. The DBS band is only for DTH, and mention is made of it here only because it is a satellite frequency band used for TV viewing at home.

What is common with all these frequency bands (except for L-band) is the necessity to use highly directional antennas in order to both transmit to and receive from the satellite. The directivity increases with the frequency. We will look at the types of antenna used later in this chapter. Bearing in mind what we have noted about the C- and Ka-bands and their use for SNG, we will mostly focus our discussion on the Ku-band.

2.6.4 Polarization

The transmission signals to and from satellites in any frequency band have a property termed 'polarization', and this relates to the geometric plane in which the electromagnetic waves are transmitted or received. There are two types of polarization, circular and linear, and the signal is transmitted and received via the 'feedhorn' – the assembly on the end of the arm extending out from the antenna. This either delivers the signal to the 'focus' of the transmit antenna on an uplink or satellite, or receives the signal at the focus of the receive antenna on a downlink or satellite (remembering that the satellite both receives and transmits signals).

As with many other aspects of satellite transmission, you need not be overly concerned with the technical detail, but for the purpose of discussion here, you need simply be aware of the property of polarization, as it is one of the defining parameters for a satellite transmission. Polarization is described in more detail later in this chapter in the discussion of uplink antennas. Suffice to say that, in general, circular polarization is used in transmissions in C-band and linear polarization is used in the Ku-band.

What is the reason for having different polarizations? Principally, the use of polarization allows the maximum utilization of frequency bandwidth on the satellite, as it allows the re-use of a frequency on a different polarization on the satellite. An antenna switched to one particular polarization will not detect or be subject to interference from signals on the opposite polarization, even though they may be at an identical frequency.

In general, a signal transmitted (uplinked) on a particular polarization is received (downlinked) on the opposite polarization. The uplink and the downlink antennas have operationally adjustable polarization, but the polarization of the receive and transmit antennas on the satellite is fixed. We will come back to polarization later in this chapter.

2.6.5 Decibels and signal to noise

Before we move on to look at the transmission system, we need to look at the fundamental way of measuring signals that is widely used and implicit in any discussion of overall satellite link quality – although this measurement method is used not only for RF link quality but also for other qualitative measurements of video and audio.

In any system we are always looking at the ratio between 'wanted' signals and 'unwanted' signals. The unwanted signals come from various sources, and can loosely be described as 'interference' but are normally referred to as 'noise'. The wanted signal – the original message signal – should always be much greater than the noise. This is often referred to as the signal-to-noise (S/N) ratio or the carrier-to-noise (C/N) ratio. We have referred to noise frequently, so let's examine it a little more closely, as it is critical in any communications system.

Imagine a crowded room – a party, say – where everyone is talking at once and there's music playing. At the beginning of the party everyone is talking quietly, and the music is playing very quietly in the background. If you wanted to speak to your friend across the room it would be relatively easy to make yourself understood. The message is easily conveyed across the room, as the background is relatively quite low and you can speak at your normal voice level. This means your 'message' is conveyed with a good signal-to-noise ratio. Then the party begins to liven up – more people arrive, the conversation level increase, the music gets louder. Now you want to send another message to your friend across the room – instead of speaking, you have to raise your voice to make yourself understood (increase your transmit power) but the background noise is relatively higher than before. So your signal-to-noise ratio is getting worse.

Finally, the background noise is deafening, and you are yelling at your friend across the room (maximum transmit power). Your friend has cupped their hands around their ears to try to hear what you're saying (maximum receive sensitivity). You are shouting so loud it is difficult to understand what you are saying even if someone is standing next to you (distortion); your friend knows you are saying something, but can't make out what it is, and so misses the many of the words (errors). The signal-to-noise ratio is now so bad, your 'message' is lost and communication has ceased.

So the signal-to-noise ratio is exactly what it says – the ratio of the (wanted) signal against the (unwanted) background noise. It is a measurement of relative power, but instead of being expressed as a straightforward ratio (e.g. 1000:1), which is not that easy to use in calculations, it is expressed in decibels (dB). The convenience of using decibel units is that multiplication and division of elements (some of which are very large numbers) can be performed by simply adding or subtracting values in dBs. The decibel is widely used in electronic engineering, and it is also a logarithmic unit – that is to say, 2 dB does not represent twice the power that 1 dB does (in fact, 3 dB is twice the power). Both the human ear and eye are 'logarithmic', i.e. non-linear, in their response to differing levels of stimuli, which is another reason why we use a logarithmic measurement unit.

Mathematically, a ratio expressed as decibels is:

$$X\,(\mathrm{dB}) = 10 \times \log_{10}(Y)$$

where X is the value in dB and Y is the original numerical value. The '$\log_{10}$' may terrify some readers as it may bring back memories of grappling with logarithms at school, but don't worry, we will limit reference to them only to here, so that you may appreciate why we use the decibel.

So, for instance, if we wanted to know how many dB represents an increase by 1000 (or a ratio of 1000:1), the calculation looks like this:

$$X = 10 \times \log_{10}(1000)$$

The logarithm (to base 10) of 1000 is 3, and thus:

$$= 10 \times 3$$
$$= 30\,\text{dB}$$

Returning to S/N, which is a ratio, it is expressed as:

$$\text{S/N} = \frac{P^{\text{signal}}}{P^{\text{noise}}}\,\text{dB}$$

where P is the power.

So an S/N ratio of 30 dB is where the signal power (level) is 1000 times greater than the power (level) of the noise.

As an easy to understand example of the use of dBs, in terms of audio, an S/N ratio of 30 dB is not very good. Hi-fi audio quality is generally considered to be in excess of 60 dB (1 000 000:1), and an audio CD is generally reckoned to have an S/N ratio in excess of 90 dB (1 000 000 000:1).

2.7 The transmission system

As we look at the functions within a complete satellite transmission system, there are certain elements that are part of the uplink and the downlink which, in principle, will be seen to be common, as the signal is modulated or demodulated, amplified, and converted up or down in frequency. There are also similarities in some of the processes on-board the satellite. Although the actual components vary in construction, as they are built for the environment in which they will be operating, they essentially fulfill the same functions.

The uplink is primarily composed of an 'encoder' – the compression device – a 'modulator', an 'upconverter' and a 'high-power amplifier' (HPA), which is connected to an antenna ('dish'). This is shown in overview in Figure 2.21a. Some form of monitoring of the uplinked signal would also be implemented.

The downlink has an antenna, a 'downconverter' (LNB), a 'demodulator' and a 'decoder' for the digitally compressed signal. This is shown in overview in Figure 2.21b. There would also be a sophisticated monitoring system able to measure all the parameters of the received signal. Typically the downlink antenna will be significantly larger than the SNG uplink antenna (from 3 to 13 m in diameter) and a cluster of antennas at one location is termed a 'teleport'. National PTTs, PTOs, satellite operators, individual broadcasters and private enterprises operate teleports.

2.7.1 Delay

As we have seen earlier in this chapter, the signal path from the uplink to the satellite is approximately 35 800 km above the Earth. The signal therefore travels a 'roundtrip' distance of 71 600 km, and as radio signals travel at the speed of light, this is calculated to take around 240 ms if both the uplink and the

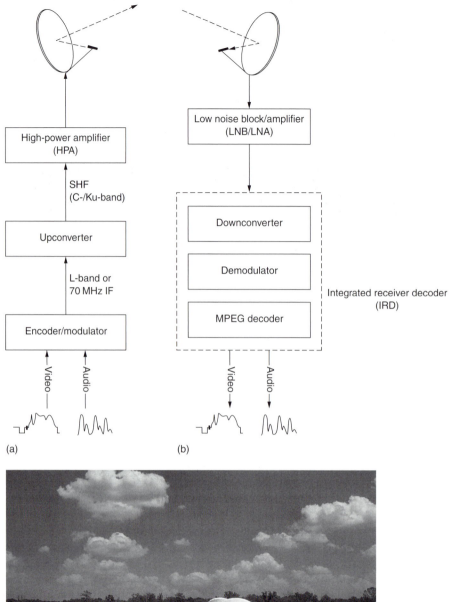

(a)

(b)

(c)

Figure 2.21   (a) Uplink overview (b) Downlink overview (c) Intelsat Teleport, Atlanta, US (courtesy of Intelsat)

Figure 2.21 (d) Intelsat Teleport Control Center, Atlanta, US (courtesy of Intelsat)

downlink are on the Equator (the sub-satellite point). If either (or both) are at a location distant from the Equator, this delay will increase as the path length increases. The maximum delay would be 277 ms, and so the delay is generally approximated to 250 ms.

Each Earth–Satellite–Earth path is termed a 'hop', and care has to be taken to allow for the multi-hop delay if a signal has to traverse several satellite links from the point of origination to the final destination. This delay causes unnatural pauses or hesitations if a 'live' two-way conversation is attempted, and this delay can be further exacerbated by digital coding and decoding caused by the compression process on a digital link (see Chapter 4).

2.8 The digital uplink

As uplinks are clearly the focus of attention in this book, this section will be the most descriptive. Where possible, we will give some idea of the size of each of the pieces of equipment in the uplink, expressed in terms of how much space is occupied in equipment racks. An 'equipment rack' is case or unit that conforms to certain dimensional standards, and equipment that fits into such a rack are measured in terms of height in 'rack-height units' (RU), where 1 RU is equal to 1.75 in. (44.5 mm) height (see Table 3.1).

The processes used in digital SNG for adaptation of the source signal to the transmission medium includes the compression, error correction and modulation processes, as well as various kinds of format conversion and filtering. The uplink has a baseband video and audio signal as its input, and from the antenna it produces a high-power radio signal directed toward the satellite. For the purposes of describing the process, we will use a Ku-band signal as it is the most common band used for SNG. Figure 2.22 shows the digital uplink 'chain' in more detail – note the uplink transmission chain is often referred to as a 'thread'.

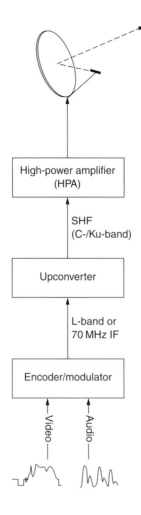

Figure 2.22 Digital uplink chain

Before we look at the equipment in the uplink chain, we need to look at the principle of phase modulation and error correction.

2.8.1 Phase modulation

Earlier we dealt with frequency modulation, and a further derivative of frequency modulation called 'digital phase modulation' is used for digital signals. Historically, digital phase modulation has been referred to as 'phase shift key' (PSK) modulation, and there are a number of different forms.

Before we can describe the process of PSK modulation, we must first explain the concept of phase. Any signal can be described as having parameters of amplitude, frequency and, in addition, 'phase'. In Figure 2.18 we saw a simplified analog signal, which was in fact a sine wave. If we consider that the point where the sine wave begins is 0°, and that by the time it has gone through one cycle it has reached a value of 360°, we have given the sine wave the properties of a circle, i.e. it describes 360° (Figure 2.23).

If we consider this as our 'reference' signal then, if we compare it to another sine wave that is running slightly later, the difference can be measured as a 'phase shift' in degrees. In Figure 2.24 we can see two

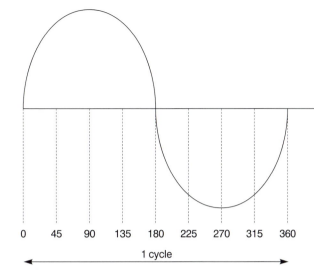

0   45   90   135   180   225   270   315   360

1 cycle

Figure 2.23   Properties of phase

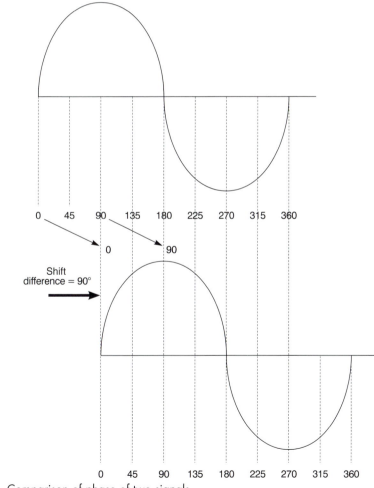

Figure 2.24   Comparison of phase of two signals

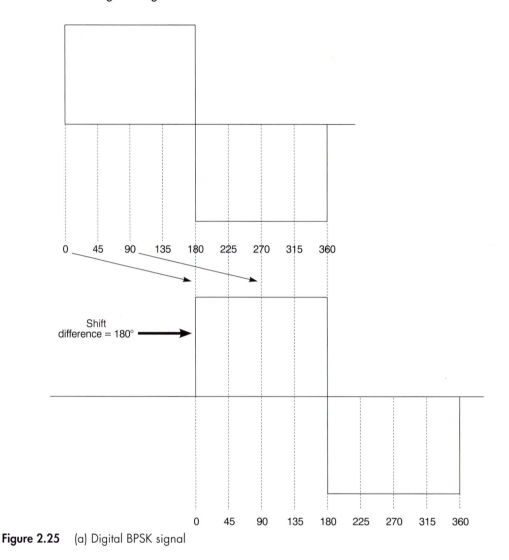

Figure 2.25 (a) Digital BPSK signal

signals, where the bottom signal is 90° phase shifted with respect to the top signal. By using the property of phase, we can modulate a signal in different phases in relation to a reference signal, and so convey information.

If we use the same phase property with a digital signal we can send a signal composed of bits that have one of two phases, 0° and 180°. This is called a two-state or binary phase shift key (BPSK) signal (Figure 2.25a), but because it is not efficient in its use of bandwidth, a further derivation is more commonly used.

If we generate two streams of BPSK signals, with one stream phase shifted by 90° with respect to the other, and then add these together, we can have any one of four phases of signal, and have created four-state or quadrature phase shift key (QPSK) modulation. One BPSK stream has bits with a phase value of either 0° or 180°; the other BPSK stream has bits with a phase value of either 90° or 270° (Figure 2.25b). Therefore, the combined signal effectively has one of four phases, i.e. 0°, 90°, 180° and 270°,

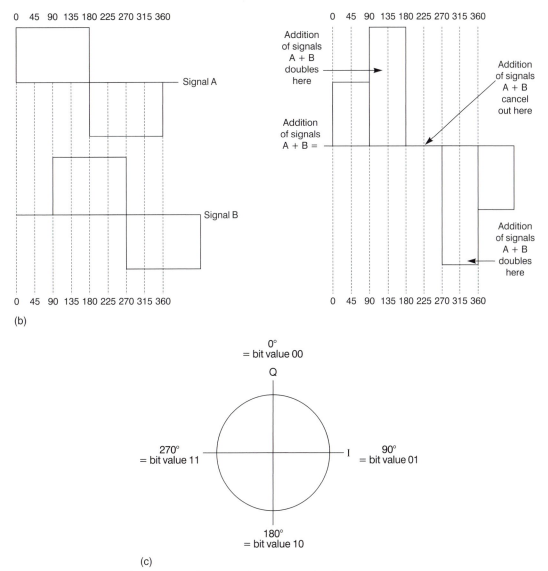

Figure 2.25 (b) Digital QPSK signal (c) Digital QPSK signal values

and so 2 bits can be transmitted at the same time (Figure 2.25c). 'I' is the Incidental or In-phase axis, while 'Q' is the Quadrature axis (90° to I). Both I and Q are at the same frequency and amplitude but the phase is modulated. Therefore, twice the amount of information can be communicated in the same bandwidth for the same data rate as BPSK requires.

The term 'symbol' is often used in connection with the transmitted bits, and all this means is that in a BPSK signal each bit represents a 'symbol', and also that in a QPSK signal, each pair of bits also represents a 'symbol'. Therefore, a symbol in a QPSK signal carries twice the information that a BPSK symbol does in the same bandwidth. The symbol rate is measured in symbols per second, historically referred to as the 'baud rate'.

The process of combining bit-streams with phase differences can be further extended, and there are satellite modems on the market that offer the facility of 8-PSK (8-phase shift key), where each symbol now contains 3 bits of information. The total number of symbols is now $2 \times 2 \times 2 = 8 \; (= 2^3)$; hence 8-PSK. By doing this we seem to be getting 'something for nothing', but the problem is that the quality of the received signal has to increase significantly with each step up in the number of phases modulated. This can typically only be achieved by increasing the amount of power to improve the S/N ratio – a concept we covered earlier. Increasing power means a larger HPA and/or antenna, and this increases cost, and this has to be evaluated against the savings in bandwidth over the life of the equipment.

As a modulation scheme, 8-PSK is starting to be used by a small but slowly growing number of uplink operators, because as indicated, the increase in bandwidth efficiency necessitates a doubling of uplink power to achieve the same performance as QPSK.

It should be noted that no reference signal is actually transmitted – the demodulator at the downlink has to generate its own reference signal by examining the incoming bit-stream. If the reference signal cannot be correctly generated or it becomes 'out-of-sync' with the incoming bit-stream, the incoming signal cannot be decoded and a period of time will pass while the demodulator tries to recreate the correct reference signal. In short, to generate the reference signal (termed the 'clock') and decode the incoming data stream, the incoming signal needs to be as 'clean' as possible – the risk here is interference and noise. Later, when we look at link budgets, we will see the effect of noise and how we measure the quality of the received signal.

QPSK is currently the typical modulation scheme used for SNG, but the other types of modulation, as well as 8-PSK, include 16-QAM (16-state Quadrature Amplitude Modulation), 16-APSK (16-state Asymmetric Phase Shift Key) and 64-QAM (64-state Quadrature Amplitude Modulation). Quadrature amplitude modulation is a scheme where both the amplitude and the phase are used to convey information – increasing the number of signal states that can be transmitted – but as the different signal states are much closer together, it is far more difficult to distinguish between the small differences in phase and amplitude. Therefore, as has already been said, more power is required to improve the S/N ratio. As the number of signal states increase, the signal is more susceptible to interference and noise for the same power, and the only way of combating this is to increase the power level, effectively doubling the power for each step up in modulation complexity. Asymmetric phase shift key is a variation of QAM which gives a distribution of signal states that are more resilient to noise and interference.

It is beyond the scope of this book to further describe these processes, and as QPSK is most widely used we will focus on the use of this modulation scheme in our further discussion of SNG.

2.8.2 Error correction

We talked earlier of the concept of noise, and how it can potentially swamp the wanted baseband signal. In the analog world, if we have increased noise, we are still able to discriminate between the wanted signal and the background noise – think of when you are tuning an analog signal on your TV when you first set it up. Where you get a clear picture, you can tune on either side of the strongest point of reception, and still make out the picture, albeit that it is covered in 'snow' and the sound may come and go.

With a digital signal, the pictures are either perfect or not there at all. Digital signals suffer from what is known as the 'cliff-edge' effect, i.e. either perfect results or nothing, since a bit is either at '1' or '0', and if it is not clearly at its 'defined state', then it is 'in error'.

Therefore, there is an absolute divide between complete success and total failure. Although this statement is technically correct, we will see that by the use of a technique called 'error correction', just as the signal approaches the threshold of going over the edge, there is a zone where errors are generated in between bursts of clear signal, but these errors can be compensated for by some intelligent signal processing.

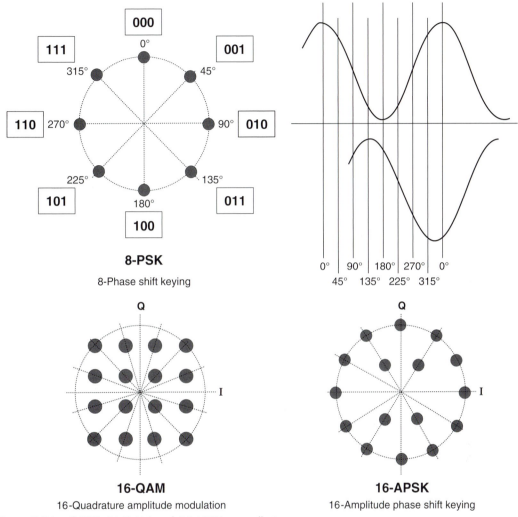

Figure 2.26 8-PSK, 16-QAM and 16-APSK constellations

Bits are added in the modulation of a digital signal before transmission to correct for errors introduced over the transmission channel, and therefore able to correct the errors at the receiver – this is 'forward error correction' or FEC. Note the convention that a block of 8 bits forms a 'byte', and within the transmission stream the signal is made up of 'packets' of bytes (see Chapter 5).

Since the signal is inevitably degraded in transmission due to the effects of noise and interference, then to compensate for this inevitable consequence 'check' bytes are added to the bit-stream in the modulator to enable errors to be detected at the demodulator at the downlink. Although error correction coding reduces the transmission power required, as the error correction can tolerate higher levels of noise, the demand for bandwidth increases because of the increased overall amount of data being transmitted.

Simply put, to minimize the incidence of errors, either transmit high power in a smaller bandwidth or lower power in a wider bandwidth.

There are two levels of error correction coding, an 'outer' code and an 'inner' code, applied to a satellite signal – including an SNG signal – before (typically QPSK) modulation. It is considered desirable to add an 'energy dispersal' signal to the data stream from the compression encoder before the error correction is added.

There are a number of different types of outer code, but a typical type conventionally used in SNG is 'Reed–Solomon' (RS) code, named after the mathematicians (Irving Reed and Gustave Solomon) who devised it in the early 1960s (before the hardware existed to implement it!).

The outer code adds a number of parity (check) bytes to blocks of data, while the inner code (typically what is described as a 'convolutional' code) is applied after the outer code. The inner convolutional coding used in SNG is typically referred to as forward error correction (FEC), although strictly speaking both the outer RS coding and the inner convolutional codes are types of FEC.

Outer code: RS

In Reed–Solomon code, for each given number of symbols forming the information data 'packet', an additional parity check 'block' of data is added to make up a complete packet of data termed a 'codeword'. This additional parity block is to compensate for any bursts of errors that the signal may suffer on its passage from the transmitter to the receiver.

So, for instance, in a typical data stream used in an SNG uplink, the Reed–Solomon code is defined as (204,188), meaning that a codeword is 204 bytes long but actually has only 188 bytes, and a parity block of 16 bytes is added (188 + 16 = 204). By adding 16 bytes, up to eight errors in that codeword can be corrected at the decoder. Therefore, the size of the data block has grown from 188 to 204 – an increase of some 8.5%. The numbers involved in this calculation are derived from the mathematics of the Reed–Solomon theory.

Inner code: FEC

The inner FEC is the 'convolutional' type of code that adds bits in a pre-determined pattern. This is decoded at the receiver (using a decoding algorithm called 'Viterbi') to detect any loss of information bits and attempt to reconstruct the missing ones. The number of bits added by this process defines the FEC ratio for the signal, and is typically 3/4; in other words, for each 3 bits, 1 extra bit has been added. Other FEC rates that can be used are 1/2, 2/3, 7/8, 5/6, 8/9 and 15/16, but the current standard SNG rate is generally 3/4 or 5/6.

As mentioned above, however, the bandwidth demand is increased, so that a 1/2 FEC QPSK-coded signal requires the same amount of bandwidth as a BPSK-coded signal with no FEC. Table 2.2 shows the effect of varying the FEC on occupied bandwidth for an 8.448 Mbps QPSK-coded signal. The

Table 2.2   Effect of varying FEC on occupied bandwidth
[8.448 Mbps, QPSK, RS (204,188)]

FEC	Occupied BW (MHz)
1/2	12.4
2/3	9.3
3/4	8.3
5/6	7.4
7/8	7
15/16	6.6

greater the degree of FEC applied, the more rugged the signal will become – thus requiring less power – but the occupied bandwidth will need to increase to cope with the error correction overhead. So why use QPSK with FEC rather than BPSK? Because it is still the case that more information can be carried in the same bandwidth.

In between these two processes the signals are 'interleaved' – this is where consecutive bits leaving the outer RS coding stage are spread over a certain period of time before the resulting bit-stream is then further protected by the inner FEC coding stage. This further decreases the risk of damaging corruption of the data stream in the transmission process.

The process of interleaving is relatively simple to understand. Consider the following message:

This is a sample message

If interleaved, it might look like:

eTsh aais mgis mea espl

Should an error occur and say wipe out the 'mgis' part of the message, the de-interleaved message will now read:

Thi* *s a sa*ple messa*e

As a result, only single characters are missing from the groups of letters in the message (shown here as *), rather than an entire word missing in the case of non-interleaved data, and it is relatively easy to reconstruct the phrase as it was meant. The key is constructing the interleaving pattern key, and the decoder having the interleaving pattern key.

The fundamental point to remember about error correction is that the aim is protect the signal from errors in its transmission from point A to point B while balancing the amount of bandwidth and power used. Because Reed–Solomon coding is still the most commonly used FEC used at the time of writing, we will base our discussion on transmission and symbol rates using conventional Reed–Solomon coding. However before we can move onto that topic, we will briefly look at a recent development in modulation coding – Turbo coding.

2.8.3   Turbo code

The problem with traditional FEC coding is that it is not as efficient as is theoretically possible in carrying the maximum amount of information. The new modulation standard DVB-S2, which we will discuss in Chapter 4, and uses a technique called LDPC, is likely to be the future modulation standard used in SNG. During the evolution of DVB-S2 it was thought that Turbo coding would be used to help achieve the improved performance in terms of error correction, but at a relatively late stage the DVB group contentiously selected LDPC (Low-Density Parity Block) coding instead.

Because LDPC is very complex, and beyond the scope of this book to describe, we are going to briefly look at Turbo coding as an example of a higher-order modulation scheme (and has similarities to LDPC). Turbo code is available in some satellite modulators, and gives a significant improvement in the efficiency of transmission.

Conventional error correction coding uses a 'serial' process, in adding the correction at the encoding stage and conversely at the decoding stage. Turbo coding makes use of fast digital signal processing technology and performs the encoding process in as a parallel process at both the encoding and decoding stage. The result is an improvement in the transmission power required of about 3 dB over conventional Reed–Solomon coding, i.e. around half the transmission power is theoretically possible.

The Turbo process distributes the codeword to be transmitted to two encoders (Figure 2.28) the first encoder uses a convolutional code on the codeword and calculates parity bits from it. The second

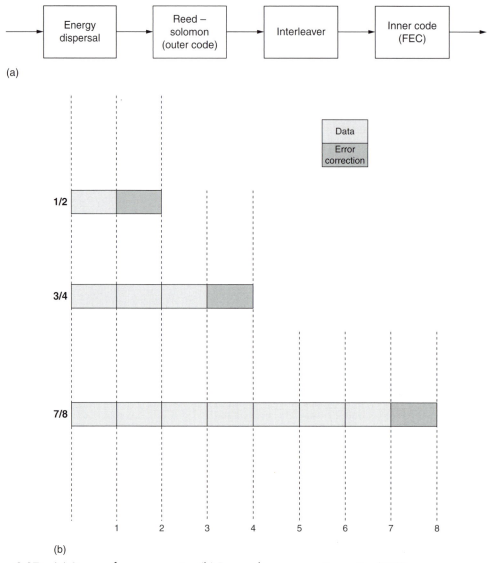

Figure 2.27 (a) Stages of error correction (b) Forward error correction ratios (FEC)

encoder gets the original codeword with the bits scrambled by an interleaver, and then uses an identical convolutional code as the first encoder.

Finally, the output summing stage uses the original codeword and sends it, along with the two strings of parity bits derived from the two encoders, to the next stage (which would normally be modulation).

At the receiving end there are two decoders working in parallel, and the role of each decoder is to interpret the codeword, which might have been corrupted by noise over the link, and decide which is the more likely value (0 or 1) for each individual bit.

Each Turbo decoder also counts on 'clues' that help it guess whether a received bit is a 0 or a 1. Firstly, it inspects the analog signal level of the received bits and creates a value on based on confidence

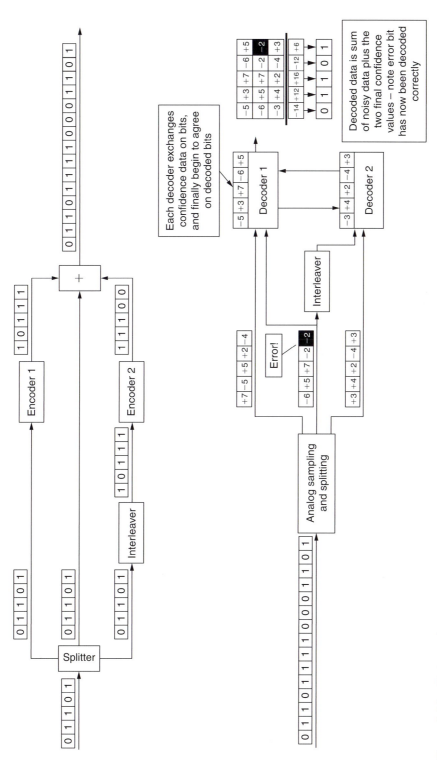

Figure 2.28 Turbo-coding process

that a bit is 0 or 1. In addition, the decoder looks at its parity bits, which tell it whether the received data seems intact or has errors. The result of this analysis is essentially an informed guess for each bit. These bit reliabilities are expressed as numbers, which can vary, for instance, between -127 and $+127$. A value of $+127$ means the decoder is positive the bit is 1, whereas a value of, for example, -90 means the decoder decides the bit is 0 but is not absolutely certain.

Even though the signal level and parity checks are helpful clues, a single decoder still can't always make correct decisions on the transmitted bits and often will come up with an incorrect codeword. But the reliability of information of one decoder is useful to the other and vice versa, because the two strings of parity bits refer to the very same codeword, but the bits are arranged in a different order. The two decoders are trying to solve the same problem but looking at it from different perspectives.

The two decoders, then, can exchange reliability information in an iterative way to improve their own decoding. Before swapping 'reliability' strings, a decoder arranges the codeword content in the order the other decoder needs. So a bit that was strongly detected as a 1 in one decoder, for example, influences the other decoder's decision on the corresponding bit.

2.8.4 Transmission and symbol rates

The aggregate data rate, including RS, convolutional encoding and the information rate (and, strictly speaking, overhead framing as well), is termed the transmission rate.

There are two ways of sending the information signal: as a 'variable bit-rate' (VBR) signal or as a 'constant bit-rate' (CBR) signal. A variable bit-rate signal has a data rate that varies according to the information content – when there is a lot of movement in the picture, the bit-rate will rise, while if it is a sequence where there is little action, the bit-rate will be low. Therefore, VBR coding encodes the video content to maintain a defined constant quality, resulting in an often quite widely varying range of data rates over a period of time. VBR signals are used when multiplexed together with other VBR signals in a DTH transmission, as the bit saving from the VBR encoder along with the multiplexing efficiency improvement from an intelligent multiplexer can be used to increase the number of video programs within a fixed transmission bandwidth. With SCPC (such as is common in SNG), not using a multiplexer causes a constant fluctuation in the occupied bandwidth – undesirable from the satellite operator's point of view.

On the other hand, a CBR signal has a data rate that is normally set at, or just higher than, the acceptable data rate for the more complex scenes likely to be found in the video stream. Therefore by definition it has periods where the video data rate is lower than the maximum rate. This may mean that in scenes where there is little activity, additional 'null' packets of data are used to pack out the data stream to maintain a constant bit-rate, and this is carried out as part of the compression/modulation process. In SNG, the video and audio stream is always sent as a CBR signal.

So now we can calculate the actual transmitted symbol rate – this is an important defining parameter for a digital signal. We are going to base the following calculation on a conventional 8 Mbps SNG signal, though as we will see later in this book, SNG data rates are falling.

So a typical SNG signal has traditionally been an 8 Mbps information rate signal, and this has an actual bit-rate of 8.448 Mbps – a standard data rate in the digital 'hierarchy'.

The data stream is QPSK modulated, so the information symbol rate is 4.224 Msps – with QPSK we have 2 bits per symbol, therefore 8.448 divided by 2 equals 4.224.

The information symbol rate (S^{info}) is now multiplied by 4/3, to account for the inner convolutional code:

$$S^{info} = 4.224 \times 1.333 = 5.632 \, \text{Msps}$$

This now gives us the symbol rate including the FEC rate (S^{FEC}), but excluding Reed–Solomon coding.

The actual transmitted rate (S^t) is the FEC symbol rate (S^{FEC}) with the Reed–Solomon code added:

$$S^t = S^{FEC} \times 204/188$$
$$= 5.632 \times \frac{204}{188}$$
$$= 6.1113\,\text{Msps}$$

Therefore, the 8 Mbps SNG signal is expressed as an 8.448 Mbps signal transmitted with QPSK modulation at 3/4 FEC inner rate, and 204,188 Reed–Solomon outer coding, giving a modulated symbol rate (modulation rate) of 6.1113 Msps. Sometimes the transmitted symbol rate is expressed as before RS coding, i.e. 5.632 Msps. There is a specification for the encoding of the audio in such a signal, but as it is part of the compression process, it is described in Chapter 4.

The RF bandwidth required is approximately the modulation rate multiplied by a factor to allow for protecting signals on either side. This is termed the 'roll-off' factor, and is commonly a factor of either traditionally 35% added to the required bandwidth or more recently 25% is sometimes used. Thus this signal will fit within a 9 MHz channel; it will actually occupy just over 8 MHz with 35% roll-off, but there is an extra 'guard-band' allowed, minimizing any potential interference with signals in adjacent channels on the satellite.

The 9 MHz channel was a nominal standard for SNG signals in most satellite operators' systems, and in 1994 this modulation scheme became a standard – DVB-S – and is discussed further in Chapter 4. There is now more flexibility with many satellite operators, and capacity may be used typically from 4 MHz upward, with 5 Mbps being a typical SNG signal data rate.

2.8.5 Encoder

Since around 1994, digital SNG uplinks have been made possible by the development of low bit-rate digital compression encoders. Digital links had been possible for some time, but the development of a new generation of digital compression encoders that could run at bit-rates as low as 8 Mbps created an opportunity for use in SNG. The advantage was lower-power uplinks and narrower bandwidth channels on the satellite, offering the possibility of smaller, lower cost uplinks and lower satellite charges.

A digital encoder essentially converts full bandwidth (uncompressed) video and audio to a compressed digital signal, and then presents it in a form suitable for the process of modulation and upconversion on the output of the encoder. Indeed, it is now increasingly common in SNG applications for the encoder to include the modulator together in a single unit. Note that in compression, reference is often made to a 'codec' (from enCOder/DECoder), which describes the compression/decompression process.

The process of digital compression is covered in detail in Chapter 4. The most common type of digital compression used for SNG is still MPEG-2 (although as will see in Chapter 4, there are other new compression technologies emerging), so let us assume that an MPEG-2 encoder is being used for an uplink. The encoder, which is typically 1 or 2 RU in height, has an analog and/or serial digital video input, and up to four analog or digital audio inputs, with some degree of input level control (see Figure 2.29).

The reason for having up to four audio inputs is that at least two channels are required for stereo, and although not necessarily applicable to many SNG operations, the ability to handle a second stereo language stream is often desirable.

There are also front-panel controls for setting a number of digital parameters such as bit-rate, symbol rate, 'horizontal' and 'vertical' resolution, and 'delay mode' – some of these terms are dealt with later in Chapter 4. Although the typical information bit-rate for SNG has traditionally been 8 Mbps, lower rates are increasingly used due to the improvements in compression technology.

Figure 2.29   MPEG-2 encoder (courtesy of Tandberg Television)

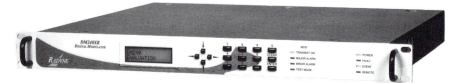

Figure 2.30   Modulator (courtesy of Radyne Corporation)

The output is produced as a multiplexed video and audio 'DVB-compliant' signal referred to as the transport stream (TS), and is an ASI (asynchronous serial interface) signal that can then be fed to the modulator. DVB refers to the Digital Video Broadcasting standards (see Chapter 4).

However, with the development of IP (Internet Protocol), the transport stream may be in IP format rather than ASI. We will look at this in more detail in Chapter 5.

2.8.6   Modulator (modem)

The modulator in a digital SNG system is often referred to as a 'modem'. It is a digital device, and in digital and computer terminology, a modem is a modulator/demodulator (hence MOdulator/DEModulator), which implies a bi-directional process. However, this is not necessarily the case in an SNG system, so do not necessarily assume that the 'modem' is capable of demodulating, for instance, for 'off-air check' purposes. To differentiate between a digital modulator used for satellite transmissions and any other type of modulator or modem, it is often referred to as a 'satellite' modulator or modem, and the unit is typically 1 or 2 RU in height (see Figure 2.30), or is commonly integrated into the encoder.

The purpose of the modulator is to convert the data stream (ASI or IP) from the encoder into a modulated RF signal. Where the modulator is combined with the encoder in a single unit, it is called (unsurprisingly) an encoder/modulator. The RF carrier frequency of the modulator output is either at nominally 70 MHz or, more often nowadays, at L-band (950–1450 MHz). This is referred to as an intermediate frequency (IF) signal. The term 'intermediate' is used as it lies between the baseband frequency range and the final transmission frequency.

The modulator can be referred to as a DVB modulator, if it requires a DVB ASI standard input, with the incoming signal containing the compressed multiplexed video and audio program information. Alternatively, it may be an IP modulator (modem) if the input stream is in IP format.

The output is produced as a signal modulated onto an IF carrier signal as described previously, while some digital satellite modulators offer C- or Ku-band outputs for direct input to the HPA, without any further upconversion being necessary. However, it is most common for the modulator output IF to be at L-band.

Key to the operation of a digital modulator is error correction, which as we saw earlier, is applied before the modulation. As mentioned before, an 'energy dispersal' signal is added to the DVB stream from the compression encoder before the error correction. This is based on a pseudo-random 'noise' signal to distribute any constant peaks of energy in the spectrum of the digital bit-stream, and this process is carried out in the DVB modulator. The averaging of the energy is advantageous as it makes the signal co-exist with other signals on the satellite in a more benign manner, minimizing the possibility of interference (i.e. contributing to the noise component of adjacent signals).

The modulator will typically have the following front-panel controls:

- Modulation scheme: QPSK, 8PSK, 16QAM
- FEC
- Output carrier frequency: either in the range 50–90 MHz (70 MHz band) or more typically 950–2000 MHz (L-band)
- Carrier on/off
- Output level control

The Reed–Solomon outer code settings are factory set (204,188) and are therefore not user-configurable. As previously mentioned, the compression and modulation stages are now often contained within one unit specifically for SNG.

2.8.7   The upconverter

The function of the upconverter is to transform the modulated IF signal from the modulator up to the desired Ku-band frequency by a process of frequency shifting or 'conversion'. This is sometimes performed in two discrete steps: from 70 MHz to L-band, then L-band to Ku-band (obviously only the latter step is necessary if the modulator output is in the L-band). However, any process of upconversion has a number of smaller steps of frequency shifting within it.

The reason for using the 70 MHz standard IF is largely historical, but as the output frequency can only be varied over a range of around 45 MHz, it lacks the flexibility of an L-band IF which typically has a range of 500 MHz, giving increased flexibility.

Increasingly, with developments in digital signal processing, the upconversion is now part of the encoder/modulator, and a number of manufacturers produce MPEG encoder/modulators that now have all three stages – compression, modulation and upconversion – in one box. It is also now more common to find L-band is used as the output IF – there used to be a significant price difference between modulators of 70 MHz IF and L-band IF, but this has now largely disappeared. Therefore, a number of stages are required to arrive at the final modulated transmission frequency. Assuming we already have an L-band modulated frequency from the modulator, this is now upconverted to the final SHF (Super High Frequency) modulated transmission frequency – in the Ku-band, which as we said earlier was going to be our focus (rather than the C- or Ka-band).

An obvious question might be 'why is the baseband signal not directly modulated onto a 14 GHz carrier?' One reason is the order of magnitude between the baseband signal and the Ku-band frequency. If we assume that the digitally compressed signal is, say, 9 MHz, and the Ku-band frequency is 14 000 MHz (which is another way of expressing 14 GHz), then the transmission frequency is 1550 times greater than

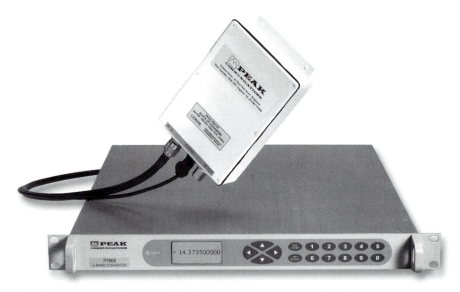

Figure 2.31   Upconverter with separate block upconverter (courtesy of Peak Communications)

the baseband frequency. The transmission frequency stability has to be maintained within very precise limits, and a direct single stage upconversion that meets the required tolerance at this very high frequency is not achievable in one step.

The upconverter, typically 1 RU high (see Figure 2.31), usually has few controls on it, the most significant of which is the upconverter output frequency. Assuming the next stage of upconversion is a fixed frequency transition, then this frequency control is usually calibrated in the final Ku-band frequency. Therefore, this is effectively the equipment on which the operator 'dials-up' the actual transmit frequency.

The output of this first stage of upconversion then passes to the fixed (block) upconverter. This unit may either be rack-mounted or, if mounted as near as possible to the HPA to minimize losses, is normally contained within a small weather-proofed box (as seen in Figure 2.31). The final upconverter produces a low-level Ku-band 'drive' signal that is applied to the HPA, which then amplifies this to the desired transmit level.

Because digital transmission involves phase modulation, the upconverter has to be very stable in terms of frequency and phase stability and has to be maintained within very close tolerances.

The satellite operator Intelsat has issued reference documents as 'Intelsat Earth Station Standards' (IESS) that define minimum performance specifications for digital modulation in satellite systems – IESS-308[5], IESS-309[6] and IESS-310[7]. IESS-308 covers the modulation standard for digital QPSK modulation, and IESS-309 and IESS-310 cover the phase requirements for higher-order modulation and error correction schemes. Although each of these documents defines standards for users of the Intelsat system, they are the de facto standards for each type of modulation for the whole of the satellite industry.

An upconverter to at least IESS-308 specification is essential for digital SNG transmissions, as a small error in its operation will destroy the transmission. This is because the upconverter has to carry out a number of stages of frequency multiplication, maintaining not only a high accuracy in frequency but, more critically, phase stability and accuracy. Bearing in mind the rigors of the environment in which this equipment has to operate, it is perhaps not surprising that this delicate electronic process can be susceptible to failure in the field. Incidentally, the modulator and upconverter stages are sometimes generically referred to together as the 'exciter' – a term which dates from the days of analog operation.

2.8.8 The high-power amplifier (HPA)

High-power amplifiers for digital SNG uplink system range in maximum output power from 50 to 350 W, with typically a 125 to 175 W HPA being used in conjunction with a 1.2–1.8 m antenna. The bigger units are generally relatively large and heavy pieces of equipment, and the HPA is typically one of the two most expensive components in the uplink, the other being the antenna and mount.

The function of the HPA is to amplify the low-level signal from the upconverter to a very large power that is then fed to the antenna. At the heart of the HPA is typically a device called a traveling wave tube (TWT), and such an amplifier is also known as a TWTA (traveling wave tube amplifier). It is beyond the scope of this book to describe the operation of a TWT, but essentially it is a very powerful amplifying vacuum tube. Relatively fragile, it requires sophisticated control electronics and a power supply unit – some of the voltages are extremely high, in the range of several thousand volts.

Although the output power of the HPA is measured in watts, it is often expressed in decibel watts or 'dBW'. The expression dBW means decibels greater or less than 1 W (0 dBW) – indicated by a '+' or '−' sign. Earlier in the chapter we referred to the measurement unit of a dB, and the convenience of using decibels in measurements is that power calculations can be achieved by simply adding values in dBs together. The power used in satellite transmissions produces large numbers, resulting in unwieldy calculations, so by using decibels the calculations are more manageable. As we shall see later in calculating 'link budgets', the standardization of all the factors into a single unit of measurement – the dB – eases overall calculations. So, for instance, an HPA used for SNG transmissions might have an output power of 300 W, or +25 dBW in dB notation: the '+' shows that the signal is 25 dB greater than 1 W (in ratio terms, this is an amplification of over 300:1).

The TWT device is generally non-linear in amplifying a signal; in other words, an increase in input signal level is not matched by a directly proportional increase in output power. The input-to-output relationship – termed the 'power transfer characteristic' – is shown in Figure 2.32. This non-linearity might not be seen to matter, but in fact operation of the TWT in the non-linear or 'saturated' part of the 'transfer curve' results in spurious frequencies being produced in addition to the desired signal at the output of the HPA. This type of spurious signal, called an 'intermodulation product' or IP (not to be confused with Internet Protocol, which we cover later in this book!), is a form of distortion, causing interference to other adjacent signals, and are therefore undesirable. In addition, the operation of the TWT into the non-linear part of the transfer curve can result in distortion and phase disturbances of the wanted transmission – seen as 'shoulders' on either side of the main transmitted signal when viewed on a spectrum analyzer (see Figure 2.32c). But in the lower part of the power transfer curve, the relationship is linear (Figure 2.32b). Figure 2.32d shows the HPA driven into fully saturated condition. Therefore, in operation, the input signal to the HPA is 'backed-off' so that the TWT is operating on the linear part of the transfer curve. This is often called 'input back-off' (IBO) and is defined in dB. For a given value in dB of input back-off, a number of dBs of 'output back-off' (OBO) results, and as TWTs are also used in satellite transponders, this term is often heard in reference to the operation of a transponder.

Because of the nature of the digital signal, it is particularly critical that the HPA is operated in the linear part of its transfer characteristic to avoid increased bit errors introduced from intermodulation products (IPs) generated 'in-band', i.e. within the bandwidth of the transponder. Therefore, the HPA is not usually operated at anywhere near its maximum rated output power, and on a Ku-band uplink it is 'backed-off' typically by at least 4–6 dB from saturated power output. If there are a number of digital carriers being combined, care has to be taken in achieving the correct power balance. Therefore, the power output back-off has to be increased to approximately 7 dB for two carriers and by 9–10 dB for three carriers. A device called a 'linearizer' can be included in the HPA design (at significant financial cost), which effectively compensates for the non-linearity near the top of the power transfer characteristic – but this is not offered by all HPA manufacturers. Alternatively, a separate discrete linearizer can be used.

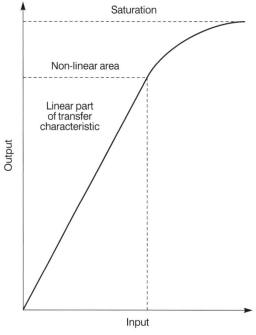

(a)

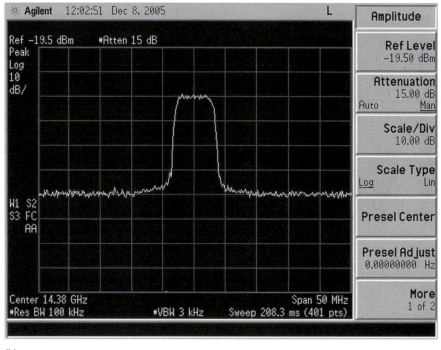

(b)

Figure 2.32 (a) HPA power transfer characteristic (b) Spectrum analyzer display: HPA linear operation (5.632 Msps QPSK signal) (courtesy of Richard Penman (BBC Training & Development))

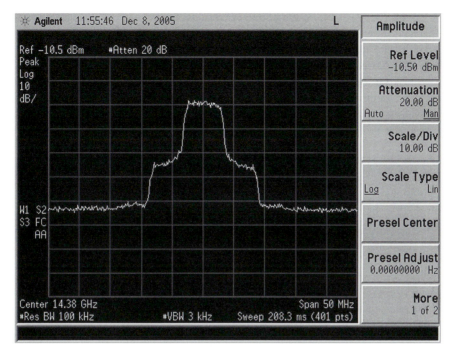

(c)

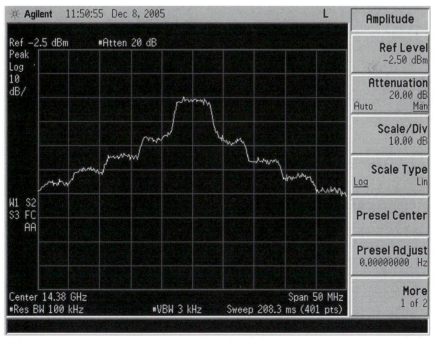

(d)

Figure 2.32   (c) Spectrum analyzer display: HPA starting to saturate (5.632 Msps QPSK signal) (courtesy of Richard Penman (BBC Training & Development)) (d) Spectrum analyzer display: HPA fully saturated (5.632 Msps QPSK signal)

particularly suited for compact SNG flyaway systems. The hub-mounted HPA is mounted either very close to or on the antenna assembly itself (hence the name). The advantage of mounting it in such a fashion is that the power losses in the waveguide connection between the HPA output flange and the antenna feedhorn are minimized because of the short physical distance involved. The rack-mounted HPA is, as the name suggests, mounted more remotely from the antenna in an equipment rack, in either a flyaway or a vehicle installation, and is offered in a wider range of output powers. These increased powers are often required typically for the transmission of a high data rate HDTV signal or for multiple carriers per channel (MCPC) operation.

2.8.9   The solid-state power amplifier (SSPA)

It is possible to use a solid-state power amplifier (SSPA), rather than a TWT-based HPA, which has high-power semiconductors – field effect transistors (FETs) – as opposed to a vacuum tube device as the amplifying element, and where the output power demand is not very large (typically no greater than 200 W). With the new generation of satellites launched from the mid-1990s onward, uplink power has dropped as bandwidth requirements have also decreased, due to increases in the efficiency of digital compression. In SNG use, SSPAs are in the sub-100 W range.

Typically an SSPA consists of an amplifier made up of a number of small discrete amplifiers arranged in both series and parallel configurations to amplify the incoming signal to a higher power. Because of this arrangement of series and parallel amplifying stages, the SSPA has a feature that is not found in TWTAs. In a TWTA – which has a TWT vacuum tube as its single amplifying element – if the tube fails, all output is lost. However with a typical SSPA design, if an FET amplifier fails, the output power is reduced, but the unit still functions to a degree (how effectively depends on the individual design).

Because an SSPA commonly has an upconverter at the input, it can take a 70 MHz or L-band input signal, and then upconvert and amplify the input signal. It is often referred to as a 'block upconverter' (BUC).

SSPAs require less back-off because they do not suffer from the non-linearity of the TWT device. A smaller SSPA may replace a larger TWT HPA for the same given level of linear power. So, for instance, we have said that a TWT HPA may require typical back-off of 7 dB. An SSPA will require only 1–2 dB of back-off to achieve equivalent performance – at least 5 dB better performance.

With an SSPA, the power output is often quoted at what is commonly referred to as the 'P1' or 'P1dB' point, which is the power at 1 dB below the point where the amplifier goes into saturation (also referred to as the '1 dB gain compression point'). This is different to the way output power of a TWTA is assessed. SSPAs are typically operated below the P1 point, so because of this difference in the naming convention for rated power for the two types of amplifiers, engineers cannot specify linearity at a specified output back-off alone to determine which amplifier to use.

To do so would result in comparing distortion of the TWTA at an output power 3 dB higher than the SSPA. Remember the TWTA was developed in the analog era, where operating the amplifier at near saturation was common and acceptable – but now in the digital world, as has been discussed previously, the TWTA has to be backed-off by at least 3 dB to avoid the non-linearity close to saturation point.

So, to put it simply, the performance of an SSPA with a P1 point of 150 W is approximately equivalent to a TWTA with a rated output power of 300 W (this is the power at saturation), which would need to be backed-off by at least 3 dB (i.e. half the power) to operate linearly. This is an over-simplification, as there are a number of other factors related to distortion that have to be taken into account, and this demonstrates the difficulties in determining equivalent performances between the two types of amplifier.

SSPA units come in a range of sizes from 2–200 W, and in the past the significant drawback in their use is the amount of primary (mains/line input) power that is required. TWTAs have about 50–60% efficiency compared to SSPAs with 25–30% efficiency. So an SSPA is typically 50–70% less efficient in terms of input-to-output power than a TWT-based HPA. Historically, SSPAs have had a reputation for 15–20% lower reliability than TWT-based HPAs.

In part this unreliability has been due to the fact that SSPAs generate a much greater amount of heat compared to a TWTA – a design often aims to keep the heart of the SSPA below 150°C! However, there is a new generation of SSPAs now available that offer excellent performance with greater reliability in a smaller package, and the minimization of the generation of heat and maximization of the dissipation of heat generated has been key to these latest designs.

Finally, a note about power measurement. Sometimes – and in particularly with SSPAs – output power is expressed in 'dBm', which means decibels greater or less than 1 mW (0 dBm), where the 'm' is 'milli', i.e. 1/1000. So a signal of 0 dBW equals +30 dBm or 1 W. To convert between the two units of measurement, remember to add 30 to the dBW figure for the equivalent dBm figure, or subtract 30 from the dBm figure to get the dBW figure (Table 2.3).

2.8.10 Phase combiner

A 'phase combiner' is a device that combines two HPA outputs together – and these can be used with TWTA or SSPA units. It is essentially an 'adding' device that operates at microwave frequencies,

Figure 2.35 (a) Solid-state power amplifier (SSPA) – 60 W (courtesy of Xicom Technology)

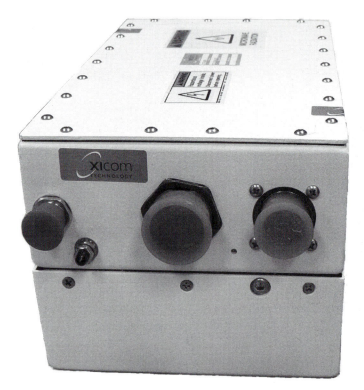

Figure 2.35   (b) Solid State Power Amplifier (SSPA) – 25W (courtesy of Xicom Technology)

Table 2.3   dBW/dBm/watt conversion for amplifier power

dBW	*dBm*	*W*
−10	20	0.01
−5	25	0.316
0	30	1
5	35	3.16
10	40	10
15	45	31.6
20	50	100

located between the HPAs and the antenna, and is often referred to as a 'variable phase combiner' (VPC). This can be used for either or both of the following:

● to produce higher power in the antenna to increase the overall uplink power
● to provide immediate redundancy in the event of failure of one of the HPAs

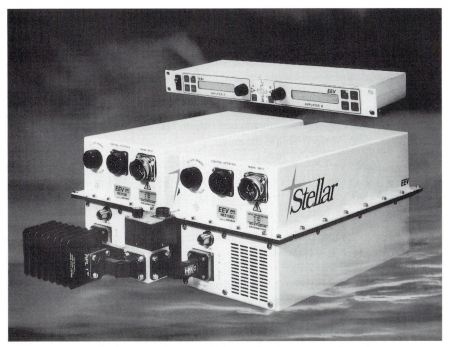

Figure 2.36 Two HPAs with phase combiner and dummy load (courtesy of E2V)

The system typically consists of a VPC unit with a remote control panel, which provides manual or automatic switching and combining of two HPAs used in any satellite earth station uplink, including SNG uplinks (see Figure 2.36). The remote control unit monitors both HPAs and controls the switching or combining in either 'single thread' or phase combined modes through the VPC. In the 'hot standby' mode, if a fault is detected from the 'online' HPA, the VPC switches in the backup HPA to maintain the transmit signal to the satellite. Alternatively, the two outputs from the HPAs can be combined to provide increased power. The phase combiner is designed to ensure that the individual outputs from each of the HPAs are combined together so that they are added 'in-phase' – the concept of phase is described more fully later. The 'variable' in the name VPC is because the output of one HPA has to be adjusted to match the phase of the other HPA, as an 'out-of-phase' addition would result in a reduction in power and wasted energy. The phase combiner will usually allow the output of one or both HPAs to be fed to the antenna, or one or both HPAs to be switched into 'dummy load'. Note that if both HPAs are switched to the dummy load, there will still be a small degree of leakage into the antenna, and the antenna will, therefore, still be radiating.

A dummy load is a device that will absorb most of the power from the HPAs safely, and enables the uplink to be tested at full power as if it was transmitting to the satellite. The huge amounts of energy are dissipated as heat, and it is a routine procedure to test the uplink by running it up to full transmit power into the dummy load. Because of the small amount of leakage of the antenna, it should be 'skyed' (pointed in the opposite azimuth to the geostationary arc – North when in the Northern Hemisphere and South in the Southern Hemisphere) with no risk of directing the small leakage power toward people.

The phase combiner does attenuate the combined signal to a small degree; it has a 'through' loss of around 1 dB and this loss has to be subtracted from the gain of adding the outputs of two HPAs. For example, if two 300 W HPAs are combined, the power output from the phase combiner would be equivalent

There are a few SNG antennas based on using the dual-offset (dual-optics) type (classically described as Gregorian), where the offset feedhorn is focused in conjunction with a sub-reflector (Figure 2.39a). The use of a sub-reflector allows the beam to be more accurately shaped to match the antenna reflector, and the feed arm also becomes shorter – particularly advantageous on compact (ultra-portable) systems, such as the one shown in Figure 2.39b. Dual optics can have higher aperture efficiency due to the shaping

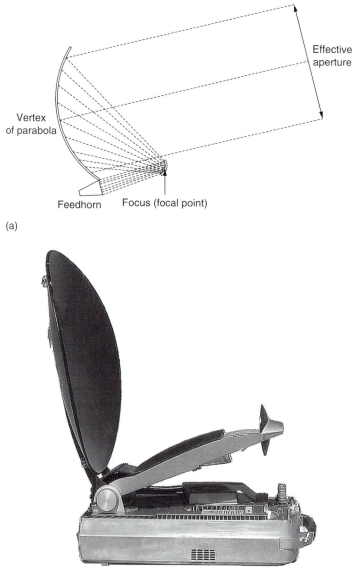

(a)

(b)

Figure 2.39 (a) Dual-offset (Gregorian) antenna (b) Dual-offset (Gregorian) antenna (courtesy of SweDish Satellite Systems)

of the sub- and main reflectors. Shaping is the process of altering the true parabolic shape in order to control key characteristics of the aperture field of the main reflector.

A parabolic antenna is fundamentally described by two parameters. The physical diameter of the antenna is expressed in meters (or centimeters) and the amplification factor ('gain') of the antenna is measured in 'dBi'. The two are interrelated, as the gain of the antenna is a function of its diameter and frequency of operation.

The measurement 'dBi' means dBs with reference to the gain of an 'isotropic' antenna (the 'i' in dBi). An isotropic antenna is a theoretically ideal antenna that radiates equal electromagnetic power in all directions (the Sun is an optical isotropic radiator because it emits the same amount of light in all directions), and therefore the gain of an isotropic antenna is 0 dBi. The gain figure of a parabolic antenna is a measure of the increase of power over an isotropic antenna radiating the same power, in a particular direction defined by the focus of the antenna. The direction of maximum gain is often referred to as the 'boresight'.

A characteristic of a parabolic antenna is that as its diameter increases, the 'beamwidth' decreases. Beamwidth describes the angle or conical shape of the beam that the antenna projects into space. This offers two principal advantages – gain and directivity – and these are important both for the uplink and the downlink.

The equations used to calculate beamwidth are complex and based on the theoretical assumption of even and uniform illumination of the reflector to obtain maximum gain. However, in reality, with a manufactured antenna the 'illumination' is never uniform, and the precise performance depends on the type of feed being used. This leads to the concept of the effective area or aperture of an antenna system, which translates to maximum signal power being transmitted or received from the center area of the dish and tapers off nearing the outside edge. The 'wasted' or under-utilized aperture area can be considered as a shield against ground noise, i.e. rejection of unwanted signals bouncing from the surrounding Earth into the antenna. In fact, the design process involves a balancing of the illumination of the antenna – and hence the size of the side lobes – with the desire to achieve optimum gain.

In terms of the uplink, by using a large parabola the focused beam is more powerful and is thus projected at a higher gain, which means that it may be possible to use a smaller amplifier (ignoring issues that a larger antenna creates when assembling a transportable system – see Chapter 3). Thus increasing the size of the antenna is cheaper than increasing the power of the HPA. Antenna gain only results with a reduction of the beamwidth of the main lobe (i.e. an example of the 'conservation of energy' law). Additionally, because the beam is much narrower, it is much less likely to interfere with satellites adjacent to the target satellite.

From the point of view of a downlink, the increased gain of a larger antenna is particularly desirable as it enables lower-power signals to be received with improved C/N performance. As with the uplink, the narrower beam also gives greater selectivity, and less likelihood that satellites adjacent to the desired satellite will cause interference to the desired signal.

It should be noted that as beamwidth is a function of wavelength (and hence frequency), there is a variation between receive and transmit beamwidths for a given antenna size. Table 2.4 illustrates this – note that the beamwidth is measured at the antenna's −3 dB point (half power) point, and the frequencies chosen are in the middle of each of their respective bands.

The construction of the antenna varies according to the application, depending on whether it is to be used in a flyaway or is mounted on a vehicle (see Chapter 3). Irrespective of what type of application it is designed for, antennas have to meet the requirement of being able to operate to satellites spaced only 2° apart in the geostationary arc (see Chapter 7). The reason for the demand for 2° spacing is that in the 1980s it was anticipated that the number of satellites was going to increase steadily, with a resulting need to move satellites closer together to increase capacity in the geostationary arc.

Table 2.4   Antenna size versus beamwidth

Antenna diameter (m)	TX beamwidth (14.25 GHz)	RX beamwidth (11.75 GHz)
0.9	1.75	2.13
1.2	1.31	1.59
1.5	1.05	1.28
1.9	0.83	1.00
2.4	0.66	0.80
3.7	0.43	0.52

Figure 2.40   Illustration of main lobes and sidelobes

This means not interfering with adjacent satellites to the intended one, and therefore the radiation pattern from the antenna has to be accurately defined. Due to the relative difference between the wavelength of satellite frequencies and the typical range of antenna sizes, no parabolic antenna can be manufactured to produce a completely perfect radiation pattern, which would be a single focused beam, but always has a main 'lobe' (centered on the boresight) and a number of 'sidelobes' radiating out from the antenna, as shown in Figure 2.40. The sidelobes can potentially interfere with adjacent signals on the satellite, and one of the aims of good antenna design is to seek to minimize the sidelobes while maximizing the main lobe. Typically, up to 70% of the signal energy will be on boresight – this is a measure of the efficiency of the antenna. Too much energy in the sidelobes will reduce energy in the main lobe signal and will interfere with signals on adjacent satellites. Hence, the requirement to meet a performance target based on 2° satellite spacing.

The characteristic to meet the 2° spacing requirement is defined in ITU Recommendation 580[8] by the mathematical expression of gain (dBi) $= 29 - 25 \log_{10}\theta$, where the sidelobes must not (in theory) exceed this mathematical 'mask' or 'envelope'. The Greek letter theta (θ) is the angle in degrees away from the foresight.

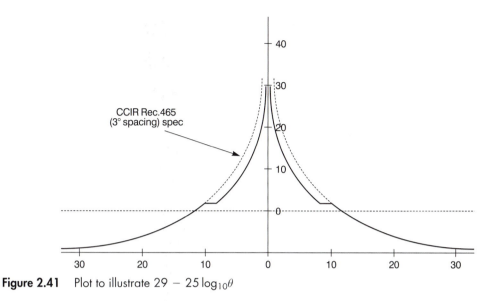

Figure 2.41 Plot to illustrate $29 - 25\log_{10}\theta$

The $29 - 25\log_{10}\theta$ characteristic is shown in Figure 2.41 where the distance in degrees away from the boresight in each direction is shown along the horizontal axis, and the relative signal level is shown on the vertical axis. This pattern will vary with frequency and, as part of proving the performance of an antenna (see Chapter 6), the manufacturer will have to produce a number of plots of this type across the range of frequencies the antenna is intended to operate. In practice, the specification is generally relaxed slightly as it is very difficult to produce antennas commercially that can exactly meet the specification, due to the variance that can occur in production.

Manufacturers frequently seek 'type approval' for particular models of their antennas from the major satellite operators (normally Intelsat and Eutelsat). This is a process which smoothes the path for obtaining uplink registration (and is covered in more detail in Chapter 7).

As we have said, no antenna is 100% efficient, i.e. it does not radiate all the power on boresight. This is deliberately due to reducing the illumination toward the edges of the antenna (to reduce sidelobes) and blockage of the beam. This is particularly true of in-line fed prime focus dishes, where the feedhorn is directly in front of the antenna (see Figures 2.42 and 2.43). This type of feed is typically used on larger SNG antennas where the amount of RF 'shadowing' is a small proportion of the whole antenna surface area. Even with a perfectly smooth parabolic surface, the beam spreads out due to diffraction, and so it is not perfectly parallel in any case. Efficiency therefore has to be taken into account when calculating the gain of an antenna. Most high-grade parabolic antennas have efficiencies ranging from 55% to 70%. A typical SNG antenna of 1.5 m diameter and 60% efficiency has a gain of around 45 dBi at 14.25 GHz.

Offset fed antennas have significantly improved efficiency as the feedhorn – which on smaller diameter antennas can be significant in mass in proportion to the overall antenna size – does not obstruct the signal.

The gain figure is the single most important descriptor of the antenna, as together with the power output rating of the HPA, the total system power is defined in the 'effective isotropic radiated power' (EIRP). This figure is calculated by adding the HPA dBW figure to the dBi figure from the antenna. Hence, we have quoted 25 dBW for a 300 W HPA and 45 dBi for a 1.5 m antenna, and by adding these two figures together we have a system EIRP of 70 dBW – a typical minimum uplink power requirement for a Ku-band analog SNG system. For a digital system, using the same 1.5 m antenna, an EIRP of 60 dBW would be adequate, and so an amplifier producing 15 dBW would be required – this can be achieved with a 50 W unit.

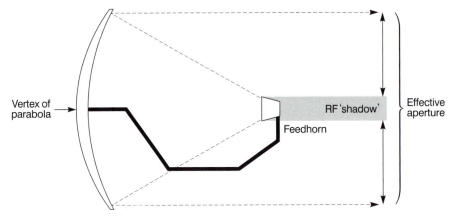

Figure 2.42 In-line fed prime focus antenna

Figure 2.43 In-line fed prime focus antenna (courtesy of Advent Communications)

2.9.3 Feedhorn polarization

Earlier in this chapter, we discussed the property of polarization. The two types of polarization – linear and circular – are each further subdivided and determine how the signal is transmitted (and received) from the feedhorn.

Linear polarization is subdivided into horizontal (X) and vertical (Y) polarization, and a signal uplinked on one particular polarization is typically downlinked on the opposite polarization. Both circular and linear polarizations are shown in Figure 2.44, noting that C-band transmissions are always circularly polarized on Intelsat, but are often linearly polarized on other operators' satellites (e.g. US domestic capacity). Ku-band signals are generally linearly polarized (exceptions are some DTH services and services for Russia).

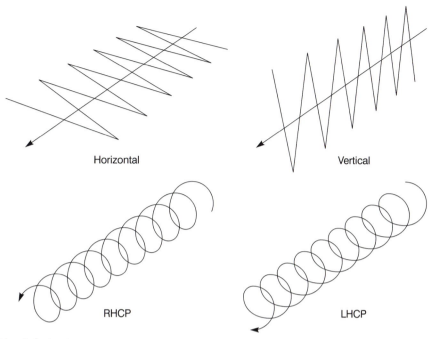

Figure 2.44 Polarization

Circular polarization can either be clockwise (left-hand circular polarization or LHCP) or counter-clockwise (right-hand circular polarization or RHCP). Note that the sense of the direction of rotation is always looking away from the transmitter. The C-band polarization depends on whether talking about transmitting to or receiving from a satellite, and is sometimes referred to by the Intelsat terms of 'A-polarization' or 'B-polarization'. If transmitting to the satellite in LHCP, A-polarization, then the signal would be received in RHCP, A-pol. Alternatively, transmit to the satellite in RHCP, B-pol, and the signal would be received in LHCP, B-pol. Thus, the satellite converts or changes the 'direction' of the signal polarization from left-hand to right-hand, or from right-hand to left-hand, so as not to interfere with transponder inbound and outbound signals at the same frequency.

Note that if a linearly polarized feedhorn receives a circularly polarized signal, the signal can be received on both X and Y polarizations, though at −3 dB (half power) compared to a correctly adjusted circularly polarized feedhorn.

Although the polarization configuration of the waveguide determines the polarization of the transmitted or received signal, on both the uplink and the downlink, the waveguide also has to be rotated to compensate for the angular difference between the antenna position on the Earth's surface and the satellite position. This is referred to as 'polarization skew', and the degree of skew can be calculated from the latitude and longitude of the uplink (or downlink). Particularly for linear polarization, it is critical in achieving a good transmission or reception of a signal that the polarization skew is correctly applied to the antenna orientation. It is typical for a satellite operator[9] to require polarization to be set to within 1–2° accuracy.

It is also important that any receive antenna is as 'blind' as possible to signals on the opposite polarization – this is termed 'cross-polar discrimination' (XPD) – so that any potential interference from a signal on the same frequency but opposite polarization is minimized. 'Good' cross-polar discrimination is at least 30 dB (and nearer to 35–40 dB), and professional-grade transmit-capable uplink antennas must at least match this to comply with the major satellite operators' technical specifications for using their satellites.

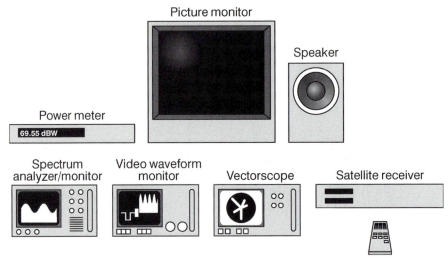

Figure 2.45 Typical array of monitoring equipment

2.10 Monitoring

In addition to any baseband monitoring, an uplink has to have some form of monitoring for the radio frequency signal processing, and this is achieved by the use of a 'spectrum analyzer'.

The array of monitoring equipment typically required is shown in Figure 2.45. A spectrum analyzer can directly measure the high-frequency signals that are transmitted, but a good-quality spectrum analyzer typically costs from US$7000 upward, depending on whether the frequencies being measured are in the IF band (70 MHz/L-band) or in the transmission band (Ku- or C-band).

Alternatively, a simple 'spectrum monitor' can be used, but if a problem occurs with the uplink and the operator is expected to venture beyond simple signal monitoring to fault detection and analysis, then a spectrum analyzer is required.

2.10.1 Spectrum analyzer

A spectrum analyzer is a very complex piece of equipment. Fundamentally, it is a radio receiver which can repeatedly and automatically tune across a selected band of electromagnetic spectrum, displaying the amplitude (voltage) of signals present in that band on a visual display (Figures 2.46 and 2.47).

A signal is fed into the analyzer and as the analyzer rapidly and repeatedly tunes (scans) across a specified frequency range, the display sweeps from left to right across the screen and individual signals are displayed as a voltage signal. Although there are spectrum analyzers available that can work at Ku- or C-band frequencies, it is common to use one that works within the L-band range (typically up to around 2 GHz). This is because spectrum analyzers that, for instance, can work in the Ku-band range typically cost around US$40 000, whereas an L-band analyzer typically costs less than a quarter of this. Because the operation of a spectrum analyzer is crucial to the correct operation of an SNG uplink (and the downlink as well), Appendix D describes the typical steps in its operation.

On the HPA there is a connection called the 'sample' or 'sniffer' port, which the analyzer can be connected to measure the output signal (provided it works in the direct frequency range, i.e. at Ku- or C-band). However, more typically the spectrum analyzer is connected to the output of the modulator as here it can operate in the IF band of either 70 MHz or L-band.

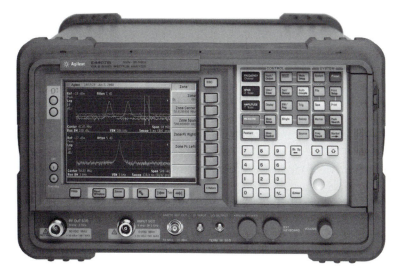

Figure 2.46 Spectrum analyzer (courtesy of Agilent Technologies)

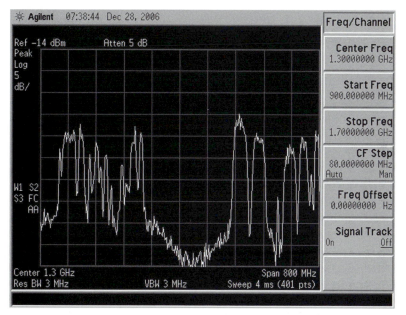

Figure 2.47 Typical display from a satellite seen on a spectrum analyzer

To be able to view the signal coming back from the satellite, an 'orthogonal-mode transducer' (OMT) is fitted to the back of the feedhorn. An OMT is a small, multi-port (but typically in SNG two-port) microwave device that allows the transmission of signals on one polarization to be combined with the reception of signals on the opposite polarization (remembering that the downlinked signal is normally on the opposite polarization) (Figure 2.48).

The OMT is also connected via a combined amplifier and downconverter called a low noise block converter (LNB), so that the uplink operator is able to view signals received from the satellite either on

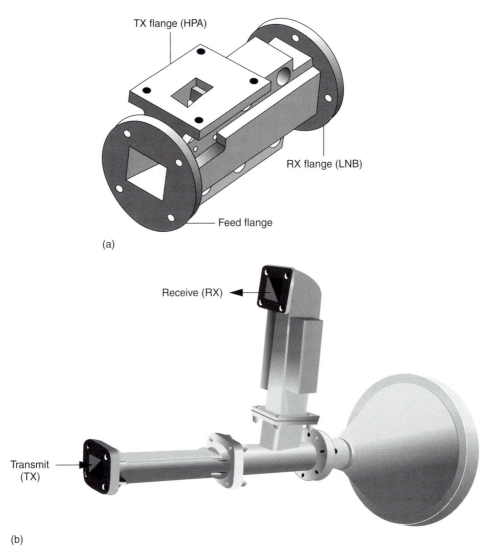

TX flange (HPA)

RX flange (LNB)

Feed flange

(a)

Receive (RX)

Transmit
(TX)

(b)

Figure 2.48 (a) Orthogonal-mode transducer (OMT) (b) OMT with feedhorn attached

an L-band spectrum analyzer or a satellite receiver. Often the uplink is monitored by observing its own signal coming back on the downlink from the satellite (assuming the location of the uplink is within the downlink pattern of the satellite on which it is working), though this does depend on the strength of the uplink signal and the size of the uplink antenna (which affects the receive performance).

2.10.2 The LNB

The 'low noise block converter' (LNB) connected to the OMT both amplifies the weak signal from the satellite and frequency shifts it down from Ku-band (or C-band) to L-band, as required at the input to the satellite receiver. The 'block' referred to is because it amplifies and downconverts a whole frequency band or 'block'. The signal received through the OMT is extremely weak, and so the front-end

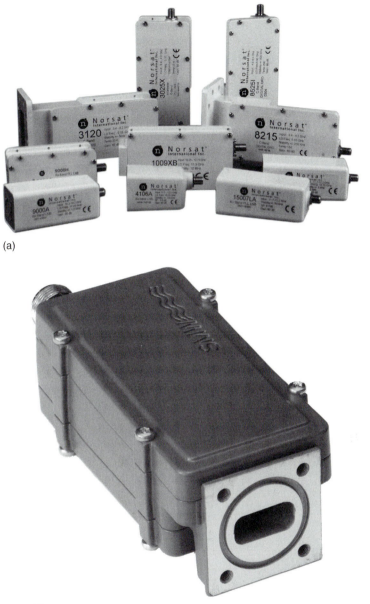

(a)

(b)

Figure 2.49 (a) A selection of C- and Ku-bands low noise block downconverters (LNB) (courtesy of Norsat) (b) Close-up of a Ku-band LNB (courtesy of Swedish Microwave)

of an LNB will amplify the signal by typically 60 dB (i.e. a million times greater). Referring back to the analogy of signal-to-noise ratio and the crowded party, the output of the LNB is like a soft whisper in the noisy party (Figure 2.49).

We saw earlier in this chapter that the Ku-band, for instance, has a receive frequency band of 10.7–12.75 GHz. Professional-grade LNBs typically have one of three downlink frequency ranges – the

Figure 2.50   Integrated receiver decoder (IRD) (courtesy of Tandberg Television)

lower band of 10.7 or 10.95–11.7 GHz, the middle band of 11.7–12.2 GHz and the upper band of 12.2–12.75 GHz. The correct LNB is required to receive a particular frequency band, though there are now some LNBs available that enable the range the whole band to be covered with two rather than three LNBs. It is possible to use two LNBs that are selected via a special waveguide switch to cover the required part of the band for a particular transmission.

The LNB produces an L-band signal, and this is accomplished by frequency shifting the transmit frequency down by using a 'local oscillator' within the device. The frequency of this local oscillator is an important parameter to be familiar with as it is used in the setting of the L-band spectrum analyzer to display the signal. This significance of this is covered in Appendix D.

2.10.3   The satellite receiver (integrated receiver decoder)

The satellite receiver is useful for identifying TV programs (sometimes referred to as 'traffic') on a satellite, which can aid the uplink operator in correctly identifying satellites. The digital satellite receiver will also include an integrated MPEG-2 compression decoder, and so it is referred to as an Integrated Receiver Decoder (IRD) (Figure 2.50). It will allow the uplink operator to directly monitor the uplink signal directly back from the satellite, subject to the following:

- uplink being in the downlink footprint as well as the uplink footprint of the satellite (which is not necessarily always the case)
- the uplink is transmitting adequate power to be received on the same antenna
- there is enough power radiated from the satellite being used in the part of the footprint the uplink is situated in

It is not always the case that the antenna has enough gain adequately to receive and decode the uplink signal, but the satellite receiver can still be used as an aid to identify satellites if they carry DTH TV programs.

Nevertheless, even if the digital signal cannot be demodulated or decoded at the uplink, it can still often (but not always) be monitored on the spectrum analyzer. The only time when this might not be possible (apart from the issue of not being within the downlink footprint as mentioned before) is that with some very small antennas – typically below 1.2 m – the transmit gain and the receive gain of the antenna is so low that it cannot distinguish the relatively low-power uplinked signal.

It is quite common for a second (smaller) satellite antenna to be used for monitoring 'off-air' DTH pictures from the studio, which might not be available on the satellite that the SNG antenna is pointed at. This can be either mounted on the roof of the SNG van or provided via a small domestic transportable

Figure 2.51 SNG truck with second antenna at the rear for receiving off-air broadcasts (courtesy of Sat-Comm)

system in a case used alongside the main antenna, and picks up the off-air signal from whichever satellite carries the broadcast signal. This signal is not only useful for monitoring the SNG uplink's transmission if it is live to air, but also can be used by the reporter to take 'off-air cues' and see any pre-recorded edited packages being played out from the studio as part of the reporter's item (Figure 2.51).

2.10.4 The power meter

There is one additional piece of measurement equipment that may be used by some uplink operators. This is a power meter, which can be connected directly to the sample port of the HPA to give a constant readout of the power being produced from the HPA. Power meters can either have an analog or digital display. Measurement of absolute power output is possible with a spectrum analyzer, but power control is much easier and sometimes more accurate with a digital power meter, as often the uplink (particularly for digital operation) may be operating at low to medium power. The uplink operator can make both absolute and relative measurement of HPA power in either watts or decibels. However, it is another expensive piece of equipment, and another box to carry – though it should be borne in mind that some satellite operators[10] theoretically require the uplink EIRP to be measured and set by the uplink operator to an accuracy of ± 0.5 dB.

2.11 The studio-to-remote communications system

Before we leave looking at the uplink, we need briefly to look at the subject of studio–remote communications. Communications with the studio is a vital component of an SNG uplink, and with the development of the digital uplink came the possibility of easily integrating a digital transmit and receive carrier for the 'comms'. The comms system involves principally audio circuits that provide both 'talk-back' and a feed of the studio audio output to the remote site. This is so that the reporter can hear instructions from the studio and is able to conduct a two-way dialog with the studio presenter, which requires the reporter to hear the questions from the studio. There is also a talkback circuit from the remote location to the studio, and as the talkback circuit is a bi-directional path, the uplink system has to have both a transmit and a receive 'side-chain' to handle the bi-directional signals.

The feed of the studio output is known by a number of names, but the most common is IFB – the various definitions are dealt with in more detail in Chapter 3. Other communication circuits will typically include phone lines (usually directly interfaced into the PBX at the broadcast center) and an IP connection with the newsroom computer system; and these can all be provided via an additional transmit/receive side-chain on the satellite uplink. The comms is uplinked as a separate carrier in the same frequency band as the main program uplink channel, and is typically at a data rate of 64 kbps – hence it is common to talk of comms 'channels' in terms of 64 kbps slots. The combining of the comms transmit signal with the main program signal can be carried out at any one of three points:

- At a lower IF of 70 MHz
- At the upper IF in the L-band
- At C-/Ku-band before or after the HPA (but this is not common in the case of a comms carrier)

Mixing the comms carrier with the main program signal at the 70 MHz IF has historically had the advantage that it can be achieved generally at a relatively low cost. The disadvantage is that the degree of frequency 'agility' of the comms carrier, relative to the main program carrier, is limited to the maximum offset from the 70 MHz available in the comms modem. The uplink operator also has to calculate this offset and adjust the comms modem each time a new main program and comms channel allocation is given by the satellite operator – this can lead to operational confusion.

To see this problem, we will assume that we have a system with a 70 MHz IF comms modem. If the modem has an output carrier frequency in the range 50–90 MHz, the maximum that the comms carrier can be offset from the main program signal is 20 MHz (as that is the maximum offset up or down from 70 MHz). It may not be possible for the satellite operator to allocate a comms carrier slot this close to the main program, and therefore it can be operationally limiting to configure the system in this way.

In the last few years the cost of L-band modems has fallen, and therefore the advantage of carrying out the combining at L-band is that:

- There is full frequency agility by the addition of a separate comms up or down converter within the frequency range of the satellite (typically 500 MHz)
- The C-/Ku-band transmit and receive frequencies can be 'dialed up' directly on the up or down converter (which is performing a fixed frequency shift), making it easier for the uplink operator

Combining at C-/Ku-band at a point before the HPA can be achieved using a simple combiner, but the disadvantage is that the overall signal level will be reduced by 3 dB (i.e. halved) because of the loss through the combiner. Combining at high power after the HPAs is rarely seen on an SNG uplink, as the power levels are so high that large components are required which can dissipate large amounts of heat. However, combining at this level does minimize the generation of IPs, and is carried out on large fixed Earth stations. In general, on an SNG uplink the addition of a comms carrier is now carried out at L-band.

The comms carrier does not need to be transmitted at as high a power level as the main program signal, because of the much smaller bandwidth requirement of the data carrier of the comms. At whichever level the two carriers are combined (assuming it is before the HPA), the HPA will need to be backed-off to prevent the generation of IPs and to achieve satisfactory power balancing of the two signals. One also has to be wary where the satellite transponder is being operated at or near saturation of an effect called 'small signal suppression', when mixing the relatively low-power comms carrier with the high-power program carrier. Observed on the downlink, as the level of the higher-power carrier increases, the low-power carrier is reduced in level. This is caused by non-linear effects in the TWT amplification stages on the satellite. It can be seen in a transponder where there is a mixture of high-power signals with low-power signals – usually satellite operators try to avoid this scenario because of these effects.

Figure 2.51 shows a comms system with a digital uplink where the combining is carried out at L-band, and Figure 2.52 shows the detail of combining at 70 MHz IF. If it is a simple comms system, with just a single audio 'go' and 'return' for IFB, then the signals can be sent and received via a comms modem with an integral ITU-T G.722 codec fitted.

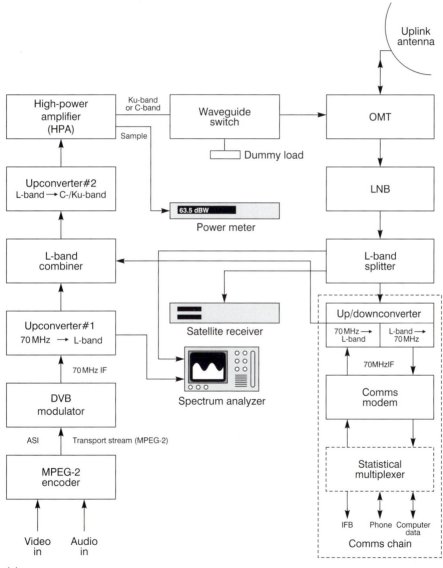

(a)

Figure 2.52 (a) SNG uplink with L-band comms system

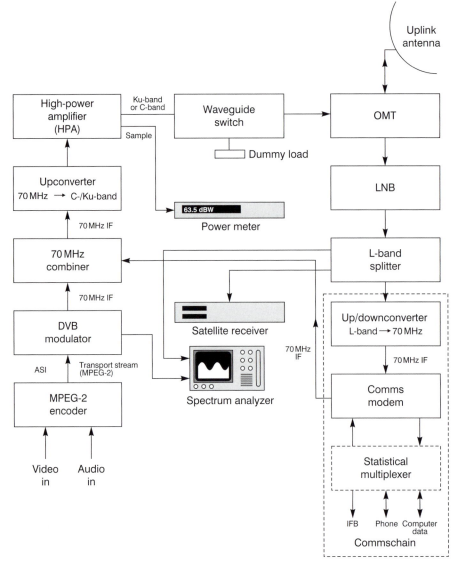

Figure 2.52 (b) SNG uplink with 70 MHz IF comms system

2.11.1 *Statistical multiplexing*

It is increasingly common nowadays to use a more complex system based on a 'statistical' data multiplexer to maximize effective bandwidth usage. The 'statmux' varies the bandwidth allocation of the relatively narrow data bandwidth of each of the audio channels according to the wider simultaneous bandwidth demand of a number of circuits. This means that a carrier with a data rate lower than the sum of all the included channels can be used, based on the statistical probability that not all of the channels will be in use at the same time. It is also worth noting that this bandwidth calculation is carried out on a near-instantaneous basis, so that gaps in speech between words are freed up to be used by other channels. The multiplexer efficiently allocates the bandwidth of the link by detecting silence periods in the speech and suppressing the sending of speech information at these times to preserve bandwidth.

It is usual to include the IP connection in this 'bandwidth pool', and because is a classed as a 'non-real-time' application, it has does not have priority over voice traffic. For instance, if the IP traffic were given equal or higher priority than voice traffic, one could end up with the audio channels being chopped by bursts of IP data, resulting in breaks in the audio. The brain is very sensitive to this, so voice traffic always has the highest priority.

Channels on the statistical multiplexer can be programmed with different priorities, and it is also common to be able to reconfigure one end from the other if necessary.

The use of an integrated communications system with the uplink is highly advantageous from both a cost and convenience point of view, as the bandwidth and power requirements of the comms carriers on the transponder are much lower than for the main program channel. Hence, satellite operators, even on ad hoc occasional capacity, will typically make only a modest charge for the use of this bandwidth; often the comms carriers can be squeezed between main program channel 'guard-bands', with no noticeable degradation to either signal. There is further discussion of the studio–remote communications system in Chapter 3.

2.12 The satellite

We will briefly look at the processes on board the satellite itself. The satellite has a receive antenna and, for each transponder, a frequency translator (converter), an input multiplexer, a switching matrix, an HPA, an output multiplexer and a transmit antenna. This is shown in Figure 2.53. A switching matrix is a router which, under remote control from the ground, can connect different source inputs to different destination outputs. A multiplexer combines a number of separate signals into one signal. As we are primarily concerned with the processes on Earth, it is not proposed to go into any further detail about the signal processing on board a satellite (Figure 2.54).

The satellite has a defined area of coverage, both for the uplink and the downlink, and the satellite operator defines these in planning a service from a satellite before it has even been launched. The individual beam patterns are published by the satellite operator in the form of 'footprints', which show the geographical coverage of each of the uplink and the downlink beams from the satellite; an example of a beam patterns for Intelsat 10-02 is shown in Figure 2.55a.

Each transponder on the satellite has a frequency plan defined for it. In fact, a transponder can have a number of frequency plans defined, and depending on the mode or type of service the satellite operator wishes to offer, a suitable frequency plan is put into operation. In general, frequency plans are infrequently changed on most satellites and transponders, but the satellite operator may choose to have more flexibility on some transponders to be able to respond to differing demands. A typical transponder frequency plan is given in Figure 2.55b, and it shows the center frequencies of the channels within the transponder, the size of the channels and the beacon frequency that is used as a unique identifier of the satellite. This information is obviously important for both the uplink operator and the downlink, and both footprints and frequency plans published by satellite operators are frequently referred to.

2.13 The downlink

2.13.1 Background

The function of the downlink is to capture enough of the transmitted signal from the satellite to at least attain, or more preferably exceed, the 'threshold' of operation. A digital receive system will fail abruptly

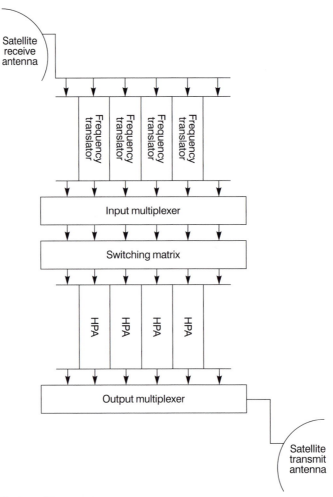

Figure 2.53   Simplified satellite overview

with either a 'frozen' or black picture when the input signal fails (depending on how the decoder has been set up).

The system at the downlink is essentially the reverse of the uplink process, and fixed downlink Earth stations are typically large sophisticated installations. We will only briefly describe the processes involved, as this is not the focus of the present book.

A typical downlink chain is essentially composed of an antenna, an LNA (or LNB), a downconverter and a demodulator. This was shown in overview earlier in this chapter in Figure 2.21b. As with the uplink, for a digital system there would also be a 'decoder'. As we shall see later, a critical factor in downlink design is the need to minimize 'system noise power', as this will potentially reduce the quality of the link.

For a fixed continuous point-to-point link application, the other critical factor is the percentage of time that the given link will be received successfully ('availability'); a typical target is in excess of 99.7%. In other words, the link will fail (termed 'outage') for no longer than an aggregated total of just over 26 hours in a year. However, this is more applicable to fixed Earth stations, whereas SNG uplinks by their very nature are only in one place on a temporary basis, and therefore a calculation of availability is academic.

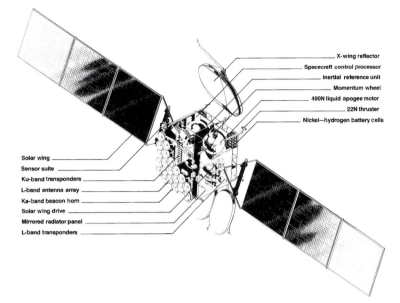

Figure 2.54   Boeing 601 satellite (courtesy of Boeing Network & Space Systems)

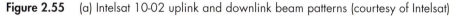

(a)

Figure 2.55   (a) Intelsat 10-02 uplink and downlink beam patterns (courtesy of Intelsat)

2.13.2   The antenna

On a fixed Earth station, the receiving antennas are usually 2–13 m in diameter, and there are typically two to four antennas on a small Earth station teleport (Figure 2.56) and possibly in excess of thirty antennas at a major teleport, as shown in Figures 2.21d (these are sometimes referred to as 'dish farms',

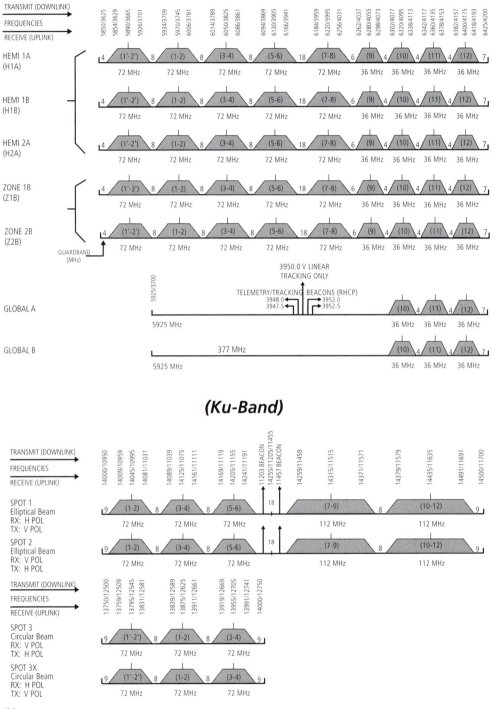

Figure 2.55 (b) Intelsat 10-02 transponder plan (courtesy of Intelsat)

Figure 2.56   Small teleport (courtesy of BeaconSeek)

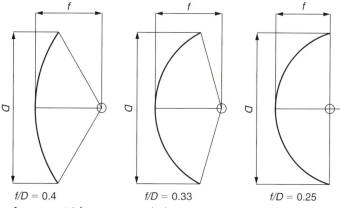

f/D = 0.4   f/D = 0.33   f/D = 0.25

Figure 2.57   Effect of varying *F/d* ratio on parabolic antenna

for obvious reasons). Antennas may either be fixed on one particular satellite or be agile and able to be freely moved from one satellite to another as required. The control mechanisms to achieve this are complex and beyond the scope of this book to describe.

As we have seen, an antenna has gain, and this is true for both directions of signal travel, i.e. both transmit and receive. The deeper the parabola, the greater the rejection of unwanted signals on receive, but the receive gain of the antenna reduces. The depth of the parabola is described as the *f/D* ratio (Figure 2.57) – the *f/D* ratio is the focal distance of the antenna (*f*) divided by the diameter (*D*). The gain of an antenna in receive mode is measured in dBi. The downlink also has to have some measure of its performance and this is termed its 'figure of merit'. The figure of merit of a downlink station depends on the antenna's receive gain (in dBi) as well as the amount of receiving system noise, which can be expressed

Figure 2.58 Downconverter (courtesy of Peak Communications)

as a temperature in degrees Kelvin (K). This figure of merit is called the 'G/T' and is expressed in units of dB/K. The larger and more positive this figure is, the more sensitive the receiving system.

2.13.3 LNA

As mentioned previously, the uplink uses an LNB as part of the satellite receiver chain. The LNB is relatively simple and inexpensive, but on a large fixed downlink earth station, a high-performance low noise amplifier (LNA) is used to receive the signal – and one antenna may have a number of these. The unit is relatively large, as to meet the performance required it needs to achieve a low 'noise temperature', and this is an important factor in link budgets. The signal from the satellite is very weak and once received it has to be amplified without adding noise. The signal is typically amplified by at least 60 dB.

2.13.4 The downconverter

The process of downconversion is generally the direct inverse of the upconversion at the uplink, and signals may travel 'cross-site' at an Earth station at L-band or 70 MHz (or even 140 MHz, a historical value often used on fixed Earth station installations) between stages of downconversion. An example of a downconverter is shown in Figure 2.58. Again the design of the downconverter would minimize as much as possible the system noise power, and for digital operation the phase noise characteristics are most important.

2.13.5 The receiver/decoder

Fixed earth stations generally have a large number of receivers that can be switched to different antennas, and this switching forms part of the whole control system. The receivers are to a high specification and offer a number of configurable facilities that are not available on domestic-grade satellite receivers.

The essential process within the receiver is to filter the incoming signal to eliminate unwanted signals outside of the frequency to which the receiver is tuned, demodulate the carrier to recover the transmitted video and audio information, and reproduce a stable, 'clean' version of the transmitted picture and sound.

For digital systems the signal has to be digitally demodulated, and digital receivers may either have inbuilt digital decoders or are directly connected to separate digital decoders. The decoders take an incoming compressed digital data stream received from the satellite and produce a baseband video signal in either digital or analog form as required. An integrated MPEG-2 digital receiver (which combines a downconverter and a demodulator, as well as a compression decoder) is commonly referred to as an integrated receiver decoder (IRD). An example of such an IRD is shown in Figure 2.59.

Figure 2.59   Integrated receiver decoder (IRD) (courtesy of Scopus Technologies)

2.14   Overall system performance

2.14.1   Background

The fundamental basis for assessing whether a satellite communication link will work is the calculation of the link budget. This determines whether the threshold level of the signal will be achieved – and hopefully exceeded, to give some degree of margin for factors that could not be included at the time of the calculation of the link budget. In this section, the principal elements that contribute to the link budget will be described, although the actual calculations of a sample link budget are in Appendix B for the benefit of engineers.

2.14.2   Factors to be considered

We need to consider what elements have to be included. These are:

- Uplink power
- Type of modulation
- Atmospheric losses (on both the uplink and the downlink)
- Satellite gain
- Downlink gain
- Noise and interference

We have already looked at the factors of uplink power and downlink gain (or 'sensitivity'), and will shortly consider the key satellite factors and examine the losses that affect overall system performance.

What are we trying to measure with the calculation of a link budget? Fundamentally, we are determining whether enough signal transmitted from the uplink can be received at the downlink to convey the information carried accurately. This encompasses the uplink and downlink equipment, and the uplink and the downlink paths, as well as the effects of the transition through the satellite. The link budget is a 'relative' power calculation that looks at ratios of lost or gained power, and the end result is, in fact, a set of ratios.

The link budget is similar to a financial budget, with contributions (income) and deductions (expenditure) which define the overall performance, and where the 'currency' is the decibel (dB). Because the dB is the fundamental unit of currency in the link budget, we need briefly to remind ourselves why we use this unit of measurement; otherwise the contributions (and deductions) of the link budget will not carry the weight or meaning required to understand its significance.

The convenience of using decibels is that multiplication and division of elements (some of which are very large numbers) can be performed by simply adding or subtracting values in dBs, as all the factors in a link budget can be expressed in dBs. As we saw earlier with the HPA, gain is expressed with a '+' and therefore losses are expressed with a '−'.

As with a financial budget calculation, depending on the level of detail, the link budget can be a relatively simple one, involving perhaps only a page of calculations, or it can be extremely detailed and spread over a number of pages. The link budget in Appendix B is a simple one.

Analog link budgets are relatively straightforward, but digital link budgets are more complex, as the potential effects of interference from both adjacent (co-polar) carriers, carriers on opposite (cross-polar) polarizations, IPs etc. are potentially much more damaging to a digital signal than an analog one. When these factors are included in the link budget, the calculations can become very complex. Link budgets are normally performed using either spreadsheets or specific application software, as the process of calculating and including each of the individual elements is very tedious if carried out manually.

The significant results of the link budget will be a ratio that is a measure of the predicted quality of the link, so in a digital link this is the energy per bit (E_b) to noise density (N_0) ratio (E_b/N_0) (or the RF signal carrier-to-noise ratio (C/N) in the case of an analog link). In a digital link, we are also concerned with the bit error rate (BER), i.e. the ratio of 'failed' bits to successfully received bits.

The RF signal carrier-to-noise ratio can be calculated for both analog as well as digital links. For analog links, this is then converted into video and audio baseband signal-to-noise ratio (S/N). However, we cannot use the concept of S/N for digital video or audio signals, as these are essentially noise-free. The imperfections on the video signal are 'glitches' or 'artifacts' (see Chapter 4) which (although they should not be present in theory) result from defects either in the compression or transmission processes. Audio signals would suffer from random clicks. A better measure of digital signal quality is the energy per bit received (E_b) relative to the noise power spectral density (N_0), expressed as the E_b/N_0 ratio in dB.

This can then be converted into bit error rate (BER), which is the number of bits received in error compared to the total number of bits sent in a given time period, and varies inversely with the E_b/N_0 ratio. If the E_b/N_0 is too low (and hence the BER is too high) the decoder will stop working, giving a frozen or black picture. By increasing the FEC rate, the BER can be improved, and Figure 2.60[11] shows a QPSK demodulated signal with no error correction, and the E_b/N_0 required to achieve a certain BER, and how adding Viterbi and Reed–Solomon coding can reduce the E_b/N_0 to achieve the same BER. These are referred to as 'waterfall curves' E_b/N_0.

QPSK demodulation, Viterbi and Reed–Solomon decoding

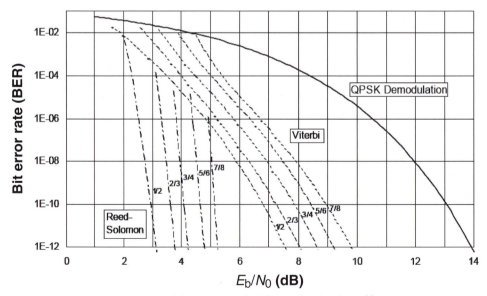

Figure 2.60   Bit error rate (BER waterfall) curves with differing levels of FEC[11]

At the critical threshold of crossover between a working and a failing link, the pictures will go 'blocky', i.e. exhibit severe artifacts and the audio may break up or disappear altogether. So, in practice, the results will be disappointing if:

- the uplink does not produce enough power
- the satellite does not have a sensitive receive or powerful transmit characteristics
- the downlink antenna is not large enough (i.e. does not have enough gain)
- there is more noise and interference than expected

In the case of an analog SNG link, this can result in either a 'noisy' picture with a lot of interference (which can still be used if the editorial value is overriding) or no picture at all. In the case of a digital link, anything apart from total success results in just no picture at all. Digital signals suffer from what is known as the 'cliff-edge' effect, i.e. either perfect results or nothing – there is almost an absolute divide between complete success and total failure, though as we've just seen there is a critical narrow margin where the pictures and audio will break up.

What prevents the signal being clearly received? Assuming that the uplink and downlink equipment are working correctly, then it is predominantly the factors involved in interference, noise and losses, such as the dispersal of the signal in its passage through space and the atmosphere, on both the uplink and the downlink paths.

As signals travel through space and through the Earth's atmosphere, natural factors such as noise from space (galactic noise) and the Sun (solar noise), atmospheric absorption and refraction affect them. In addition, particularly for the downlink, artificial sources of interference from terrestrial radio frequency transmissions are a potential problem. The effects vary somewhat depending on whether the link is in the C- or Ku-band.

2.14.3 The satellite

The sensitivity of the satellite is defined by the 'input power flux density' (IPFD) needed to 'saturate' the transponder on the satellite. This is, in effect, a measure of the 'illumination' required from the uplink and is measured in dBW/m^2. An uplink must produce enough power to achieve a specified IPFD at the satellite, allowing for the location of the uplink on the satellite's receive G/T contour ('footprint') projected onto the Earth's surface. Note that, as with the downlink, the receive antenna of the satellite has a figure of merit, G/T. The satellite operator will quote figures for the IPFD of a particular transponder and this varies according to the gain setting ('gain step') of that transponder. This is not based on saturating the transponder, but on the fact that the transponder channel is 'backed-off' by a number of dBs.

As the signal is transmitted from the uplink antenna, the signal spreads out to cover a very wide area. However, as the signal spreads out, it gets weaker the greater the distance from the antenna. This is analogous to a stone being dropped into the middle of a pond and, as the ripples spread out from where the stone fell into the water, they get smaller and weaker. In engineering terms, this is termed the 'inverse-square law'.

Energy lost as a result of the distance the electromagnetic wave travels is known as 'spreading loss'. As the distance from the source (the uplink) increases, the energy spreads out to cover a larger area, thus decreasing the amount of energy (intensity) per unit area.

Because of the distances involved, this 'spreading loss' is a significant and constant loss in satellite transmissions, and has to be calculated to derive the amount of uplink power required to achieve the specified IPFD at the satellite. It is therefore an absolute measurement of power loss, rather than a relative power calculation that is used in the link budget. Spreading loss is not frequency dependent and is a function of the path distance between the uplink and the satellite.

On its transmission side, the satellite also produces an IPFD toward the Earth, which is a measure of its 'illumination' of the Earth's surface, and this varies according to the transmit footprint of the satellite. Again, the satellite operator publishes information relating to the IPFD, which in turn determines both the location and the size of receive antenna required to produce the correct level of input signal to the receiver.

2.15 Losses

2.15.1 Free space loss

As the signal travels through space, it suffers attenuation. The ratio of the attenuation of the signal transmitted to the amount of signal received at an antenna is termed 'free space loss' (FSL) or 'free space attenuation' (FSA). The path between the Earth station and the satellite is termed the 'slant range', and as the latitudinal position of the Earth station increases, the elevation angle to the satellite decreases, thus increasing the slant range. Thus, as the slant range lengthens, the loss increases. Free space loss is frequency dependent, increasing at higher frequencies, and affecting both the uplink and the downlink path losses.

At elevation angles less than 5°, a significant part of the path will pass through the Earth's atmosphere and will therefore be subject to terrestrial interference and more noise picked up from the 'hot' surface of the Earth compared to the 'cold' background of space. This increases the attenuation of the signal. In addition, at such a low angle of elevation, the link may be subjected to 'scintillation'; this is a rapid fluctuation in amplitude and phase caused by the signal traveling a longer path through the atmosphere and ionosphere.

2.15.2 Atmospheric absorption

At the frequencies used for satellite transmissions, electromagnetic waves interact with gas molecules in the atmosphere causing attenuation of the signal. The effects are minimal and usually the signals suffer no more than 1 dB of attenuation, which would only be of significance if the link budget looked marginal.

2.15.3 Precipitation loss

In the Ku-band, rain is a significant factor in attenuating the signal, further dispersing the signal as it passes through water drops. Rain rather than clouds cause the problem, as even the direction of fall and shape of the water drops affect the signal. As frequency increases, the effect of rain increases – which is why at Ku-band, the effects are far greater than at C-band (and are even greater in the Ka-band). The detrimental effects of rain also vary depending on the polarization of the signal.

To aid in calculating the effect of rain the world is divided into 'precipitation zones' or 'rain climatic zones', each of which has a numerical value that is used in the calculation of a link budget. These zone values are defined by the ITU (International Telecommunications Union; see Chapter 7) and are a statistical analysis based on the frequency of rainstorms, the amount of rainfall in a year and even the type of rain. They are published in the form of tables with a letter identifying each zone, with various values depending on the percentage of time in the year when there is rainfall of a certain rate (mm/hour).

It is important to note that is not the *amount* of rain that falls in a year that is significant so much as the *rate* at which it can fall. Areas that have high rainfall values – tropical zones, for instance – have a value that effectively increases the free space loss, and vice versa for arid zones. In detailed link budget calculations, rain is accounted for on both up- and downlinks, but it is generally ignored for an SNG uplink (because of the relatively temporary nature of the transmissions). The exception is when it is located in a high precipitation zone, where there would then be a high risk of outage even during the relatively brief period it is transmitting.

2.15.4 Pointing loss

It should be clear by now that if an uplink is aiming to 'hit' a satellite with a signal, the pointing accuracy has to be very high. We have seen that the satellite is station-kept to within 0.1° of its nominal orbital slot, and therefore the uplink and the downlink have to be steered to within the same accuracy. In theory, if the boresights of the earth station antennas are aligned exactly with the boresights of the antennas on the satellite, then the 'pointing loss' is zero. In practice, partly due to movement of the satellite (within the nominal 'box'), and partly allowing for some error in maintaining absolute pointing accuracy at the uplink and downlink, there is a small amount of pointing loss. This equates to some signal not reaching the satellite from the uplink, or from the satellite to the downlink. Typically, a value of 0.3 dB of pointing loss is allowed for in a link budget for a manually panned antenna at the SNG uplink, and 0.1 dB for an auto-tracking antenna at the fixed downlink.

2.15.5 Waveguide loss

At both the uplink and the downlink, there are lengths of waveguides connecting different parts of the systems together. These waveguides introduce some attenuation to the signal and, in addition, with each waveguide joint there will also be some losses. These are calculated in a link budget collectively as 'waveguide loss', and typically account for 0.5–1 dB of loss in the uplink, and varying figures at the downlink depending on the length of the 'cross-site' distances.

2.16 Noise

Having dealt with the various losses encountered that have to be included in a link budget, the concept of noise has briefly to be examined. Noise is present on the uplink signal received by the satellite and is further added on the downlink signal. As such, noise on the up- and downlinks affects overall performance. If noise added to the uplink path signal dominates the overall performance of the system, the system is described as 'uplink limited'. Conversely, if the noise on the downlink path dominates, the system is termed 'downlink limited'.

Earlier in this chapter, we looked at the concept of noise in terms of an audio signal, and this same principle applies to the satellite link. The main sources of noise are antenna noise, made up of sky and, to a lesser extent, galactic noise, and system noise from receiver thermal noism, waveguide noise and other component noise, and intermodulation noise through the whole system.

System noise is typically measured in Kelvin (K), which is a unit of measurement of temperature used in engineering calculations. At microwave frequencies, everything with a physical temperature above 0 K generates electrical noise in the receiver. As the decibel is used as the primary unit of 'currency' in link budgets, noise expressed as Kelvin can be converted to 'system noise power', measured in dBW.

The calculations involved in calculating noise powers can be lengthy and complex, and here it will suffice to say that every component in a receive downlink chain introduces some noise into the system. The aim of good downlink design is therefore to minimize these noise powers as they effectively make the downlink less sensitive. The signal being transmitted from the satellite is traveling a great distance and, as we have seen, suffers losses on its passage. The signal is therefore extremely weak when it arrives at the antenna and the addition of noise power reduces the C/N ratio, as it 'lifts' the noise 'floor'. Therefore, if the downlink design cannot minimize the noise power to a small enough degree, compensation can only be made by increasing the size of the antenna.

However, because of the nature of digital modulation and signals, noise is less of an issue, and as long as the noise remains below the threshold of the receiver, the output of the receiver and decoder will produce perfect pictures. As soon as the noise level rises to match or exceed the threshold level, the digital signal quickly breaks up and no usable pictures are produced from the decoder. As mentioned earlier in this chapter, digital modulation and demodulation processes are particularly sensitive to 'phase noise' (most likely generated in the equipment), which has disastrous effects on the signal. Therefore in particular the downlink chain in a digital system has to minimize the amount of phase noise.

2.16.1 Interference

Interference can come from a number of sources, and where the interference is above a certain level it needs to be included in the link budget calculations. Interference can come from signals in the same transponder (IPs), adjacent satellites and transponders on the same satellite, and signals at similar frequencies but on the opposite polarization, i.e. cross-polar interference (XPI), related to XPD.

As we have already seen, the ratio of signal to noise is expressed as an E_b/N_0 figure, and so for a digital link, E_b/I_0 and $E_b/(N_0 + I_0)$ figures can be derived.

It is not proposed to go into the details of all the effects of interference here, and the impact on digital links has already been covered.

2.16.2 Link budget numbers

Having taken into account all the losses, the effects of noise power and interference, what is the scale of the numbers we would like to see from a link budget as a measure of the received signal? There will be some variation as to what is perceived to be 'good' depending on where in the world the signal is being received and what the expectations are, taking into account the parameters of the uplink, the satellite and the downlink.

In the case of a digital link, the energy per bit to noise density ratio (E_b/N_0) is one of two significant factors, the other being the bit error rate (BER). Generally, in a low precipitation zone, a satisfactory 8 Mbps digital SNG link (either C- or Ku-band) needs to have an E_b/N_0 of 8–15 dB. At the input to the MPEG-2 decompression process (i.e. after RS error correction), there needs to be a BER of at least 10^{-9} – this means there must be less than 1 bit error in every one thousand million bits. The BER is largely dependent on the E_b/N_0, as the nearer the carrier level is to the noise floor, the greater the likelihood of bit errors that cannot be recovered by the error correction process. This should allow some 'fade margin' to allow for some adverse weather or other unforeseen effects causing the signal to be degraded. Again, margins need to be increased in high precipitation zones. In tropical areas, this fade margin will have to be greater to allow for extremely heavy rainstorms.

The E_b/N_0 figure for the digital link must have a high enough fade margin above the threshold level of the link to ensure reliable operation. Separate figures for the uplink and the downlink paths are calculated, which can then give an overall C/N or E_b/N_0.

Link budgets are not calculated before every transmission. Back in the 1980s, when satellites were very much lower in power and SNG systems were often operated at their limit to achieve a usable analog signal, the calculation of link budgets was a frequent necessity. Nowadays, link budgets tend only to be produced either during the exploratory period of securing a suitable satellite lease, or where it is anticipated that operation of an SNG uplink on a particular satellite is likely to be marginal. This may be either due to the uplink's specification or its location on the satellite's footprint. Current generations of satellites are much higher power and because, in particular for digital transmissions, the power requirement from both the satellite and the uplink is lower.

Finally, a note of caution regarding link budgets. A link budget is only a theoretical calculation and it is only as good as the quality of the data used. In practice, the link can behave quite differently from the prediction. A small error in one small element of the budget can result in a significantly different answer from that expected.

A link budget can also be manipulated to produce a 'desired' figure and it should be regarded with caution if it has been prepared by someone else. On the other hand, link budgets prepared by satellite operators can often be very pessimistic, usually when satellite 'end-of-life' data is used (when the satellite will be at the bottom end of its performance), so minimizing the exposure of commercial risk to the satellite operator. The satellite operator may wish to minimize the risk of link failure being attributed to the satellite performance, and shift the onus of failure onto the uplink and/or downlink performance which is probably not within their control, but in that of the customer.

2.17　Conclusion

In this chapter we have covered every aspect of satellite theory that affects the SNG uplink operator, and have hopefully clarified a number of issues that are not always easily understood in isolation but need to be considered in conjunction with other issues. In particular, it is hoped that the explanation of how satellites are placed in orbit gives some insight into the 'behind the scenes' aspects of satellite operation that are not necessarily obvious to users of satellites as a newsgathering tool.

We have shown that the technical parameters of digital transmission present the opportunity to access the space segment at a much lower cost, hence opening up the opportunity of using SNG to those who previously had viewed SNG as too expensive an operation. It must be borne in mind that it is likely that the operating costs of an SNG uplink (i.e. the space segment costs) will, in the long term, far outstrip the initial capital cost of purchasing a system.

The deliberate minimization of the use of scary mathematics has also hopefully helped the non-technical reader, while Appendix B will help clarify many of the link budget calculations for the technically inclined.

References

1. Clarke, A.C. (1945) Extra-terrestrial relays – can rocket stations give world-wide radio coverage? *Wireless World*, October, 305–308.
2. http://celestrak.com
3. Inter-Agency Space Debris Coordination Committee.
4. NASA Orbital Debris Program Office.
5. Intelsat (1998) IESS-308, Performance characteristics for intermediate data rate (IDR) digital carriers using convolutional encoding/viterbi decoding and QPSK modulation.
6. Intelsat (1998) IESS-309, Performance characteristics for Intelsat Business Services (IBS).
7. Intelsat (1998) IESS-310, Performance characteristics for intermediate data rate digital carriers using rate 2/3 TCM/8PSK and Reed–Solomon outer coding.
8. ITU-R Recommendation 580: radiation diagrams for use as design objectives for antennas of Earth stations operating with geostationary satellites.
9. Eutelsat EESS 400 issue 12 Rev. 0 (2006) – Standard L – minimum technical and operational requirements for Earth stations transmitting to leased capacity in the Eutelsat space segment transmitting to leased capacity in the EUTELSAT space segment – Standard L.
10. Eutelsat (2005) Issue 1.1: Eutelsat Systems Operations Guide (ESOG), Television Handbook, Volume II, Module 210.
11. ETSI TR 101 290 V1.2.1 (2001–05) Digital Video Broadcasting (DVB): measurement guidelines for DVB systems.

3

Boxes or wheels: types of systems

3.1 Where to begin. . .

How do you choose an SNG system? For new users, this can be a bewildering decision with a large array of specifications and features to consider. Apart from the obvious requirement for digital operation, the other major defining parameters are whether it should be a 'suitcase' compact terminal, 'traditional' fly-away or a vehicle-based system, and whether C- or Ku-band. With development of 'compact' newsgathering terminals, there is also the option of choosing an Inmarsat system, which is particularly appropriate for a certain type of newsgathering. Although only briefly discussed in this chapter, Inmarsat systems are fully covered in Chapter 6.

Potential customers for any type of system have to assess its capabilities against their own operational needs. It is important to clearly identify these needs in the beginning so that an informed purchase can be made, as it will be a considerable financial investment. In this chapter, different configurations for each type of operation are examined to help the new user to decide on the best system for their needs. However, as well as careful consideration of the requirements, thorough research of the market by any prospective purchaser is vital.

In addition, the signals that are to be fed to the SNG uplink have to be considered. An SNG uplink system on its own is not going to be sufficient to provide all the elements of a news field operation. There is a considerable amount of extra equipment required in addition to the basic uplink to provide all the facilities to enable 'live stand-ups' and tape feeds to be accomplished. These configurations will be examined later in this chapter.

3.2 The basics

An SNG uplink system consists of the following primary component parts:

- antenna with mounting support
- high-power amplifier(s) (HPA)
- upconverter
- modulator
- compression encoder
- signal monitoring
- baseband signal processing

The physical transmission components of an uplink are typically referred to collectively as the 'chain' or 'thread'. A chain typically consists of a single transmission 'path' that has one of each of the primary transmission components, i.e. modulator, upconverter and HPA. An SNG system may have some or all of its constituent components duplicated. Two or more chains can be combined to feed via a single antenna, using a 'phase combiner'. This may be to give a degree of 'redundancy' and provide immediate back-up in the event of failure; that is to say, protection against failure of either a part or the whole of the system which would make the entire system inoperable. An extra HPA may be added to increase the uplink power. Alternatively (or additionally), it may be that the system has to provide more than one transmission 'path' where there is a requirement to uplink more than one program signal simultaneously, combining two program signals into a single signal applied to the antenna. A single transmission chain could also achieve this by using cascaded digital encoders.

Some system variants are shown in Figure 3.1. This figure is by no means exhaustive, as there are various permutations possible. No matter what the configuration, in news operations the factors of speed and reliability are significant issues, and the component parts have to be rugged, reliable and quick to set up and operate.

However, since a system can be configured in a variety of ways, the operational use of the system and the purchasing budget must strongly influence the choice of system. The characteristics of an SNG system are defined by:

● Type of packaging (i.e. flyaway, ultra-compact ('suitcase'), vehicle based)
● Antenna size
● Type of compression (i.e. MPEG-2, MPEG-4, VC-1)
● Frequency band of operation (i.e. C- or Ku-band)
● Level of redundancy (i.e. none, partial or full)
● Number of 'paths' (i.e. one or several)

3.3 Specifying a system

The type of system is crucial to successful operation. For instance, where an SNG uplink system is going to be used in city or urban areas local to the operating base, it should be considered that physical space and access are often restricted in busy streets. Flyaway systems have to be transported in a dismantled state and then re-assembled before use. A safe zone has to be created in front of the antenna, and it is desirable to provide some weatherproof protection such as a tent for the uplink operators as well as the equipment. It is therefore difficult for a flyaway to be operated quickly and easily in busy street environments, with frequent rigging and de-rigging. If transporting the system by air is unlikely to be a frequent requirement, then vehicle systems are the best choice for a restricted operating range in areas well served by road.

Buying a system of any type requires a very exact set of criteria to be examined and addressed, and these criteria need to be clarified as early as possible. It is very important to establish the operational function of the completed system and the form of the system that the manufacturer expects to deliver. The best constructors welcome a precise specification. There is a higher risk of failure when a customer simply says 'Build me an SNG system', as the constructor may never be completely sure what the customer means. This has happened on numerous occasions to SNG manufacturers and system integrators, and a contract entered into on this basis is more likely to be problematic on both sides. Stories are heard from both manufacturers and purchasers about misunderstandings, prefaced by 'I assumed they knew. . .', which often result in bad feeling on both sides. A customer is much more likely to be satisfied if both the technical and the operational specifications are as precise as possible. It is important that the manufacturer understands exactly how the system is intended to be used by the customer, as then the manufacturer may be able to use their experience of having built other customers' systems to satisfy the requirements. The complexity of an SNG system is such that it cannot be treated as a single article of equipment. It is unlikely that a customer would go to a manufacturer and ask for a small studio without

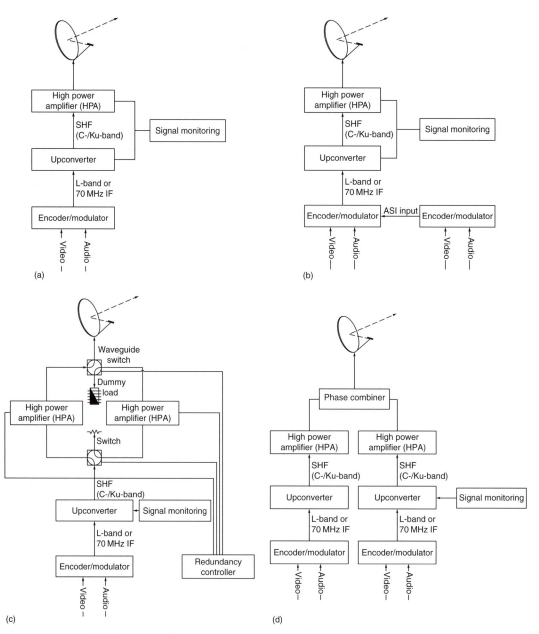

Figure 3.1   (a) Block diagrams of SNG system configurations – Single thread (b) Dual path digital/single thread (c) RF redundancy/dual thread (d) Fully redundant dual thread

specifying a number of key parameters. In the field, an SNG system can form a mini-studio environment, so similarly these key parameters need to be established.

How long should a specification be and how detailed? Well, the answer is as long and as detailed as possible. In fact, the maximum amount of time should be spent on deciding and writing the specification. It should state the type of operations the system is expected to cover and the key components must be identified. For instance, the specification may define particular regulatory parameters that have to be met. It may be a requirement for the manufacturer to obtain the final system registrations with satellite system operators (e.g. Intelsat or Eutelsat), so that the system can be used as soon as it is delivered to the customer. There may be a need for particular equipment to be integrated into the system, both bought and installed by the SNG system provider, or equipment may be 'free-issued' to the constructor by the customer to integrate as part of the project. Therefore, the basic rule is the more detail the better.

In choosing a supplier, market research is obviously very important. As well as visiting the manufacturer and inspecting the product, ask for a client list so that independent views from other customers can be obtained. The quality of build on an SNG vehicle, for instance, can be crucial to both the safety of the vehicle and its longevity. It is important to look at the finished examples of the constructor's range, and checking for even the most minor details – a sharp edge here, loose or poorly fixed cabling there – can tell a lot about the standard the constructor typically builds to. It may be convenient for a constructor to promote the color and finish of the interior trim, in the hope that the customer might not notice the fundamental flaws. Another good idea is to look at a customer's vehicle that has been in service for at least 1 to 2 years; this will give a good indication of the quality of build.

Another very pertinent way of gauging the quality of product and service from the constructor is to ask how much repeat business is placed with them: it is easy to sell something to someone once but harder to sell a second time. It is also important to measure the after-sales support. Does the constructor have 24-hour, 7 days-a-week technical support? This is particularly crucial when the system may often be operational in a different time zone to that of the constructor. Systems rarely fail Monday to Friday during office hours. Have they a process in place to ship replacement units to the location rapidly? Do they have replacement units 'on the shelf'? A helpful, knowledgeable voice on the telephone is important, but not much use if a replacement unit can only be supplied within 28 days – it's highly likely to be needed now!

Once the system is specified and ordered, the customer would be unwise to let the constructor proceed with building a system without checks and progress meetings along the way. It is highly inadvisable to change the specification during construction, as this can increase cost, delay the project, and can leave the purchaser open to accusations by the constructor if any problems crop up during or after the project is completed. This reinforces the importance of being clear about the requirements before placing a contract with a supplier.

Many customers may not have the very critical skills of project management and the time to closely monitor the project as it progresses. Budget permitting: it is well worth considering engaging the services of a professional project manager, who will closely monitor that the constructor is adhering to the specification, as well as dealing with any disputes over interpretation of the contract. The cost of using the services of a good project manager is not usually cheap and could perhaps amount to 5–10% of the total project cost. It can be regarded as a type of insurance; though, like many types of insurance, its value is only realized when needed!

3.3.1 Packaging for a purpose

By their very nature, SNG systems cannot be fixed permanently as the essential requirement is to be able to move quickly and operate in response to a breaking news story. SNG systems therefore have to be packaged in a way that allows them to be easily transported and then rapidly set up on location.

Systems are constructed in one of the following ways.

- Flyaways: As indicated by the term, flyaway systems are designed to be broken down to fit into a number of equipment cases for easy transportation by air and then re-assembled on location.
- Ultra-portables: These are systems which are effectively 'mini-flyaways', small enough for virtually one or two persons to carry, and also come in fly-drive configuration for occasional vehicle use.
- Vehicle based: Here the SNG uplink is built into a vehicle (e.g. a car, van, SUV, truck or trailer) as a permanent installation. The system can then be driven to the news event and rapidly put into operation at the desired location.

3.4 Flyaways

Flyaway systems can potentially offer the lowest cost SNG uplink. They are therefore very appealing as an entry-level system. However, the flyaway fulfills a primary requirement for a system that can easily be transported by air and re-assembled at location typically in under an hour. Therefore, to gain the full benefit of operation of a flyaway, it should be routinely deployed in this manner. A flyaway can also be rigged and operated out of the back of a vehicle, and this is often satisfactory on a short-term basis. However, if vehicle-mounted operation is a regular requirement, the drawbacks of operating in this fashion will soon become apparent. Flyaway antennas range in size from 0.9 to 3.7 m, though for SNG use the typical size used is 0.9–2 m.

Their flexibility in terms of ease of transportation is of critical value to international newsgatherers, who regularly fly all over the world with such equipment in a variety of aircraft of different types and sizes. The key factors are total weight and number of cases, as news crews frequently transport these systems on scheduled commercial flights as excess baggage. Costs consequently increase greatly in direct proportion to weight and volume.

The design of a flyaway involves diametrically opposed demands. Strength has to be achieved with minimum mass while also sustaining stability. Precision and adherence to close mechanical tolerances have to be met, while all components have to be rugged. Overall size has to be minimized while also achieving maximum uplink power. The individual component parts have to be in an easily assembled form for both minimum rigging time and reliable operation – a challenging objective in view of the inherently delicate nature of some of the parts. Figure 3.2 shows a typical flyaway system.

Either the antenna is transported in a single piece or it is broken down into a number of segments or 'petals' (as can be seen if you look carefully at the antenna in Figure 3.2). It can then be mechanically re-assembled on-site onto the support or mount system (see Figure 3.3), a reconstruction that has to be achieved to a very high tolerance. The mechanical integrity of the antenna system is crucial to its correct operation in maintaining the correct pointing toward the satellite – being 'on-station'. This integrity has to be carefully monitored throughout the operational life of a flyaway antenna because of the vulnerability to damage in transportation as well as the repeated assembly and disassembly. Permanent vehicle-mounted antennas are plainly not so vulnerable.

The mount for the flyaway antenna is where wide differences can often be seen between the manufacturers, but the objective is common to all. The antenna has to be mounted so that it can easily be steered to align to the satellite correctly. At the same time, the mount has to provide maximum rigidity and stability to maintain pointing accuracy up to the satellite during operation even in poor weather. However, this physical rigidity has to be achieved while keeping the mass (and therefore weight) of both the mount and the antenna to the minimum. Nowadays the use of carbon fiber and aluminum alloys is common to achieve this design aim.

Figure 3.2   SNG flyaway system (courtesy of Jack Raup)

Figure 3.3   Assembling antenna petals (Photo courtesy of Harvey Watson)

The control of the antenna is a very precise engineering requirement. Domestic DTH antennas use a very simple low-cost mounting system called a 'polar' mount, which offsets the antenna elevation by a fixed amount to take account of its position on the Earth's surface as it is moved from east to west, tracing the arc of the satellites across the sky. It uses a single motor to achieve this through a special mounting mechanism. Professional antennas need to be individually adjusted using two motors in both azimuth and

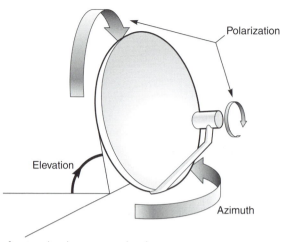

Figure 3.4   Properties of azimuth, elevation and polarization on an antenna system

elevation in order to ensure absolute pointing accuracy. In addition, there is often a third motor to adjust the polarization of the antenna.

The flyaway antenna has to be able to be finely adjusted in three axes, as shown in Figure 3.4: azimuth (the rotational position), elevation (the angle of tilt) and polarization (the circular orientation of the beam, achieved either by rotating the whole antenna or the feedhorn itself), all of which have to be controlled to within fractions of a degree. There are typically both coarse and fine adjustment controls provided on the mount to achieve this. Movement on all these axes has to be as fluid as possible to ensure swift and accurate alignment of the antenna. The coarse controls allow rapid movement of the antenna on the mount to a point very close to the desired position, while the fine controls allow precise final alignment of the antenna toward the satellite.

When the antenna has been aligned it is critically important that the antenna remains on-station, and this is where the manufacturer's quality in the design of the mechanical locks on the azimuth and elevation controls is critically tested. Once the antenna is correctly positioned, it must be positively locked in position so that it cannot be knocked off alignment inadvertently or by wind. These locks are often difficult to design, as they are subject to the relatively large mechanical leverage force of the antenna. Yet, even at the instant the locks are applied, the actual locking process must not move the antenna even a fraction of a degree off alignment. The locks are repeatedly used in operation and so it can be seen just how important precision engineering is, and in what may seem to be a minor detail. It is as important here as in the other key aspects of the antenna and mount design.

The overall stability of the mount and antenna design is another area that has to be considered carefully. Manufacturers use different techniques, based around simple tripods, complex stabilizing frames and legs, or even interlocking the antenna and mount to equipment cases to increase the ground 'footprint' of the system. Each of these methods has its strengths and weaknesses, and it is very much up to each potential user to decide which they prefer.

The antenna must also be capable of being positioned on uneven ground and retaining pointing accuracy under quite severe weather conditions such as high winds. In aerodynamic terms, the antenna represents a sailplane, so that it is common to quote two different figures as a measurement of stability in windy conditions. One measurement is the maximum wind speed for the survival of the system (i.e. before parts may disintegrate under the wind's force). The other figure is the maximum wind speed at which the antenna will stay on-station as it faces into the wind. Side winds are less of an issue as the side profile of the antenna has low wind resistance.

3.4.1 Antennas

The antenna itself in a flyaway system is typically between 0.9 and 2.2 m and, as previously mentioned, it is also usually segmented to allow easy transportation. Only the very smallest antennas (1 m or under) can usually be shipped as a single-piece assembly. The antenna shape also varies between manufacturers and each design has individual merits, but are generally either circular or diamond shaped. Diamond-shaped antennas offer improved gain through a more effective radiation area, though sometimes at the expense of sidelobe performance. In fact, circular antennas are usually manufactured to be very slightly elliptical in the horizontal plane to improve sidelobe performance.

The relationship between the antenna and the feedhorn is crucial as this fundamentally determines the RF performance characteristics of the antenna in defining the focus and radiation pattern. The feedhorn has to be correctly positioned so as to correctly illuminate the antenna, and typically SNG antennas (Figure 3.5) are either 'prime focus fed' or 'offset fed prime focus' in type, although one manufacturer uses dual focus (dual reflector) configuration (see Figure 3.6).

The use of an in-line fed prime focus is generally found on larger SNG antennas. The design of the feed arm with the antenna therefore has to ensure repeatable and mechanically precise assembly. In addition, the feed arm has to allow quick and easy connection of the RF feed from the HPA, by interconnection with a length of flexible waveguide.

3.4.2 Flight-cases

The remainder of the system consists of a number of cases of electronic equipment where the equipment is grouped in a manner set out to keep the number of cases to a minimum but also allow easy manual handling. Typically, the electronic equipment is fitted into flight-cases, although a few manufacturers have broken out of the strictures of the conventional rack-mount flight-case and produced small modular units which can be easily transported in soft bags or in lightweight plastic transit cases.

The equipment grouping also has to adhere to the functionality of the system, so that component parts that directly electrically interconnect are also physically co-located, particularly for high-power RF signals.

Historically, flight-cases were developed primarily for the military and scientific exploration industries, where expensive and delicate instrumentation has to be transported and operated in rugged environments. When SNG systems were developed, in particular by companies that were already involved in these other fields, it was natural that they should use these flight-cases for a similar requirement.

There are commonly three types of flight-case used in SNG systems. Firstly there is the type into which the antenna and mount can be dismantled and fitted into as a number of sub-systems. In this, the case acts purely as a protective shell for transportation. The second type is a case into which the electronics of the system can be fitted and also operated with the equipment in situ. The third type is the small 'half-rack' width modular equipment unit which does not necessarily fit into a larger case for operation, but is carried in soft bags or stowed inside the antenna cases.

A conventional flight-case is essentially a case that has an outer skin of (usually) metal while the contents are in some way protected against mechanical shock. This shock protection is high-density foam for the antenna and mount elements, and sprung-mounted frames for the electronics.

In addition to protecting the equipment, the other essential requirement is that cases conform to the sizes and dimensions as outlined in International Air Transport Association (IATA) regulations. IATA recommendations on the carriage of passenger hold baggage changed in 2004, and gradually all airlines

Figure 3.5 A range of SNG antennas (courtesy of Jack Raup)

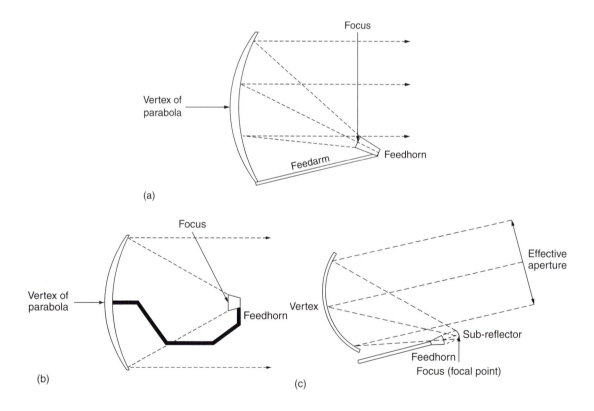

Figure 3.6 Types of SNG antenna (a) Offset prime focus antenna (b) In-line prime focus antenna (c) Dual offset antenna

have implemented the recommendations. The general regulation is that any single piece of checked baggage weighs no more than 32 kg (70 lb), and that the dimensions of each piece of checked baggage must not exceed 158 cm (62 in.) calculated on the sum of the length, height and width. However, in 2005, a number of airlines announced that they were intending to apply a lower limit of 23 kg (51 lb) to any single piece of checked hold baggage.

In 2006 one major international carrier announced they would enforce an absolute limit of 23 kg per individual piece of checked baggage from early 2007, although some arrangements could be made 24 hours in advance or at time of booking – not very convenient for rapidly deploying for a breaking news story. This is posing a considerable challenge both to SNG operators and to SNG antenna equipment manufacturers.

Cases are typically designed for military use and are therefore constructed to an extremely high standard. However, correspondingly the cost of the case is greatly increased over a standard transit case, and typically run into thousands of US dollars per case. This may seem very high until the cost of the equipment it is designed to protect is taken into account, which can be typically 10 times the cost of the case. Figure 3.7 shows a case of typical construction.

An equipment flight-case has an internal shockproof-mounted frame into which the electronics are fitted in such a way as to allow quick and easy set-up for operation at the destination. The removable front cover allows access to the front control panel, and typically has neoprene seals to protect against ingress of water and dirt during transit. The rear of the case may also be removable to allow access to rear panel connectors and controls.

The case is constructed in a manner that allows the outer skin to act as a crumple zone for the equipment inside. In addition, there is usually a pressure relief valve fitted to the body of the case to allow equalization of possible differential air pressure between the inside and outside of the case. This is typically caused by transportation in the unpressurized hold of an aircraft. If no valve was fitted, there is the potential for a partial vacuum to be created inside the case, which would make removing the end caps very difficult!

The shock mounts are typically blocks of very dense rubber, which will allow some movement under force but effectively absorb any shocks that the equipment fitted into the frame is subjected to. The frame is usually a standard 19 in. rack frame, to reflect the international mounting standard dimension for professional electronic equipment. Equipment modules that fit into such a frame are measured in terms of height in 'rack-height units' (RU), where 1 RU is equal to 1.75 in. (44.5 mm) (see Table 3.1). There is no standard for the depth of units.

The case is usually made from aluminum alloy or sometimes polypropylene, and must be able to withstand a drop test that is usually defined at 2 m. It typically has proprietary dimples or ridges on the top and bottom of the case, which mechanically locate with corresponding recesses on the top or bottom of other cases. This is so that, when piling up a number of cases, both for operation but also in transportation, it is possible to form an interlocked stack that has a degree of stability. The corners of the case are either rounded or have some kind of protection to minimize damage if dropped on a corner, which would potentially distort the case or more importantly the internal frame.

The case also has to be able to allow the electronic equipment contained within to operate satisfactorily in extremes of temperature, high humidity, driving rain or standing in shallow puddles. Some cases are also designed to minimize the effects of any external electromagnetic interference (EMI). Taking into account all these factors, it is easy to see why the cases are so expensive, and it is a cost that has to be borne for the repeatedly reliable operation that is expected for newsgathering.

Nonetheless, the fact that the cases are so rugged does not mean that the usual standards of care in handling delicate electronic equipment can be neglected. If care is taken in handling as well as the use of these cases, the equipment should be fully operational when it reaches its destination. Military personnel have marveled that SNG equipment works reliably on arrival at location, while their equipment transported in

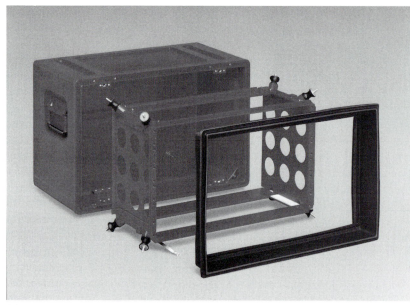

(a)

(b)

Figure 3.7 (a) Typical construction of flight-case (Photo courtesy of EDAK) (b) Flight-cased SNG flyaway system (courtesy of GigaSat)

Table 3.1   Standard 19 in. equipment rack-height units (RU)

Units	Inches	Millimeters
1	1.75	44.5
2	3.5	89.0
3	5.25	133.4
4	7.0	177.8
5	8.75	222.3
6	10.5	266.7
8	14.0	355.6
10	17.5	444.5

similar flight-cases does not. This is probably because there is an assumption that equipment in flight-cases can tolerate anything, but in fact care in the handling and loading of the equipment cannot be neglected.

The baseband equipment provided with an SNG uplink, either flyaway or vehicle based, can vary widely, from simple monitoring of the incoming video to providing a small outside broadcast facility. This may include vision switcher, routing matrix, one or more equipped camera positions and comprehensive studio-remote communications.

3.4.3   Typical flyaway operation

Because there is such a wide variation for a flyway operation it is perhaps the most useful to look at one particular scenario, from which other configurations can be imagined.

Basic set-up
The most common requirement is to be able to do stand-up 'lives' (also called 'live-shots') and replay tape material. This means providing a live camera position, with studio-remote communications and some audio mixing for the reporter and perhaps a guest contributor, and also a videotape recorder (VTR) or disk storage (from a laptop PC or disk-based camcorder) to play in material live or feed back to the studio for later transmission. There needs to be a small routing switcher, able to 'synchronously' switch between the output of the camera and the VTR, and some vision and sound monitoring.

Electrical power
Of course, mains power may not be available or, if it is, it may not be very reliable, so a power generator is required as well. Because some of the live-shots may take place at night or in bright sun, either of which will require additional lighting for the live stand-up position, the generator will need to be capable of delivering suitable levels of power. The uplink system itself may require quite a significant amount of power, so that the generator (or generators) will need to supply typically somewhere between 5 and 20 kW, depending on the overall demand. It is also desirable to have some capacity in hand, as it is not very beneficial for the generator(s) to be running at maximum output. For more sophisticated setups, a powering system similar to that used for vehicles may be utilized (see Section 3.6.2).

The whole issue of electrical power generators and SNG uplinks is fraught with difficulties. Generators are one of the most common reasons for failures in the operation of SNG uplink systems. There is a maxim that every generator will fail at some point – a situation not helped by the less than ideal conditions they are often operated in. Manufacturers' servicing schedules should be rigorously adhered to – ignore them at your peril!

Studio-remote communications

Communications with the studio usually involve a bundle of circuits. Of vital interest are the audio circuits that provide both an audio feed of the studio output and talkback to the remote site. This is so that the reporter can hear the studio presenter's 'link' into the live piece, listen to cues from the studio control room, and also be able to conduct a two-way dialog with the studio presenter, which requires the reporter to hear the questions from the studio. There is also often a talkback circuit from the remote site to the studio, so that information can be communicated back to the studio control room – this is often referred to as a '4-wire'.

The feed of the studio output is known by a number of names, and the functions vary slightly. Examples are 'cleanfeed', 'mix-minus', 'reverse audio', 'return audio' and 'interrupted foldback' (IFB), and what is actually carried on is that the circuit varies slightly according to the term used. Cleanfeed, mix-minus or reverse/return audio is usually a mix of the studio output without the audio contribution from the remote location. IFB is this same mix but with talkback superimposed on top. Switched talkback can sometimes be superimposed on the cleanfeed type of circuit as well. The exact configuration varies from broadcaster to broadcaster with local variations.

Other communication circuits will include a number of telephone lines and a data connection with the newsroom computer system. These can all be provided via either an additional transmit/receive side-chain on the satellite uplink, an Inmarsat satphone or any available telephone landlines. The most desirable method of delivery is via the satellite uplink, as this usually provides the most direct paths to and from the studio. The circuits can be fed directly to the side-chain. They can also be fed via a statistical data multiplexer that can vary the allocation of a relatively narrow data bandwidth according to the wider simultaneous bandwidth demand of several circuits. Figure 3.8 shows a typical configuration of studio-to-remote communications, and three types of statistical multiplexers are shown in Figure 3.9.

As an example of the sophistication that can be achieved with statistical multiplexers, one specialist statistical multiplexer manufacturer has developed a centralized management facility which allows broadcasters the ability to centrally manage the configurations of their comms and networks across their fleet of vehicles and flyaways, with automatic reconfiguration of third party or affiliate operator's equipment to make it compatible with their own. This deskilling of the remote unit is in line with other organizations who are aiming to reduce the need for training field operators. This same manufacturer also has one of its compact statistical multiplexers integrated into one of the MPEG-2 encoder manufacturer's principal SNG models, thus demonstrating the need and demand for this type of ancillary service as part of the SNG process.

More than ever, the connection to the newsroom computer system and providing multiple telephone circuits are proving critical. The integration of the newsroom computer system into the overall news production process means that it acts as the heart of both the newsgathering and the news output operation. Information regarding contacts, running orders, news agency 'wire' information and background information to the story are all controlled and produced by the newsroom computer system, as well as it by providing rapid messaging between editorial staff and the field staff. It is also a truism that there can never be too many telephones.

No matter how simple the operation, however, this aspect of the news broadcasting chain is vital. Many operations have failed not for lack of program pictures and sound, but because the studio-remote communications have not been working correctly.

Video editing

In addition, it might be necessary to provide a video editing facility, and if this edit suite is required to be a source to the routing switcher as well, then this will further complicate the system. The format of

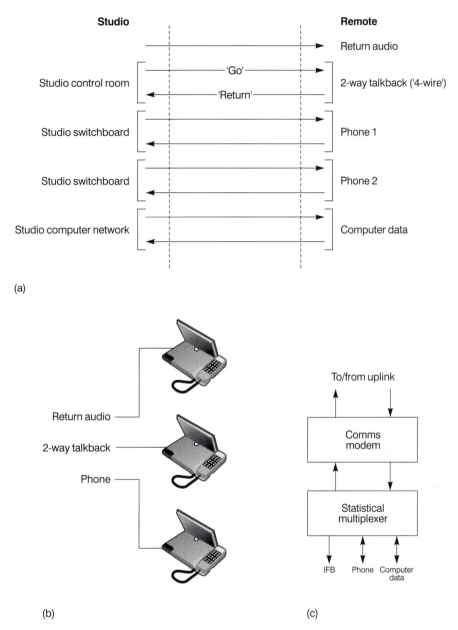

Figure 3.8 Comms system configurations (a) Typical studio-remote communications overview (b) Simple comms configuration using Inmarsat satphones (c) Comms as part of SNG uplink

the video editing in the field can obviously vary according to the organization – Sony BetaSP was originally the almost universal format, but now there is a wide variety of formats, some proprietary, some common – encompassing Panasonic DVCPro25 and DVCPro50, and Sony DigiBeta, BetacamSX, DV, DVCam, IMX and XDCam that have now largely replaced BetaSP. Each organization will have its

Figure 3.9 Statistical multiplexers (Photo courtesy of Vocality International)

preferred format, or not, as the case may be. Consider also the beginning of newsgathering in HD (High Definition), which has its own formats – HDV and DVCProHD.

The appeal of the digital formats in the field is both the availability of high-quality camcorders with sophisticated features and the compact laptop editors, weighing under 7 kg – a considerable reduction on the average 150 kg of equipment that traditionally made up the elements of a BetaSP edit pack back in the mid-1990s.

Almost all of the above formats are tape based (except XDCam, which is opto-magnetic disk based). Increasingly in the field Non-Linear Editing (NLE) systems are becoming commonplace, and these are based on disc-based editing on a high-spec laptop PC – typically Avid Xpress Pro (Windows) or Final Cut Pro (Mac) are the software packages of choice.

Whatever the format of the video editing, it is common to try to provide the ability to connect the editing as an 'online' facility to the rest of the rig. This is so that an edited piece (a 'cut package') that has just been finished can be immediately played out on the satellite uplink, without the need to take the tape to a separate VTR for play out.

Interconnections and layouts

The cabling requirements are quite considerable, particularly if there is a significant physical separation between the stand-up live camera position, the edit suite, the switching/monitoring point and the satellite uplink. Typically, such an operation might take place at a hotel; this scenario is shown in Figure 3.10a. If it can be imagined that this system is rigged at a hotel, then the uplink will probably be on the roof with a power generator (see Figure 3.10b – the power generator is out-of-shot). The edit suite can be several floors below in a room, and the 'live' position may also be on the roof (Figure 3.10c) or on a room balcony, to give a visual background statement of the location of the story. The switching/monitoring point is likely to be in another hotel room which often doubles up as a production office (Figure 3.10d). All too quickly, the cabling and interconnection requirements can rise to the extent that there may be perhaps over 100 kg of cable alone to be transported to cover hundreds of meters of multiple interconnects (Figure 3.11).

It is possible to greatly reduce the weight of cable carried by using fiber-optic 'cable', which provides an impressive number of circuits down a 6 mm diameter fiber optic cable, compared to a traditional 'copper' 15 mm diameter multi-core cable. The initial high cost of a fiber-optic system, which has a small unit of active electronics to convert and multiplex/de-multiplex the electrical signals to/from light signals at each end of the fiber, can be rapidly recouped in the savings on shipping weights. A typical fiber-optic system used for SNG can carry three video channels and eight program audio channels, as well as a

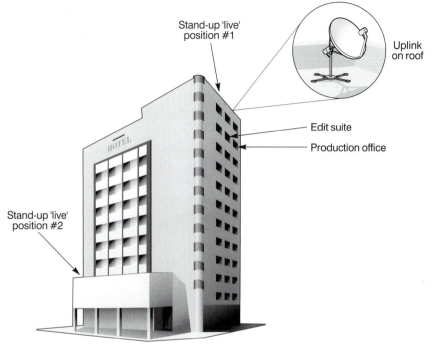

(a)

(b)

Figure 3.10 (a) Typical operation at a hotel (b) Uplink on roof (Photo courtesy of Simon Atkinson)

(c)

(d)

Figure 3.10 (c) Live position (Photo courtesy of Simon Atkinson) (d) Switching/monitoring point (Photo courtesy of Paul Szeless)

Figure 3.11 Flyaway 'spaghetti'

number of data channels for camera control and intercom channels for the cameraman. Figure 3.12 shows a typical fiber-optic system for field use, with a drum of fiber holding around 300 m of cable and weighing approximately 20 kg – less than a tenth of the equivalent capacity of multi-core copper cable.

The final picture

This whole system has to be built, tested and be operational in typically about 12 hours from arrival on location, and that doesn't include getting through the Customs formalities and traveling from the airport!

All these elements mean that the total number of cases that make up the entire system as described will probably double or triple the number of SNG uplink cases alone. This is an aspect of using SNG that is often only appreciated by those directly involved in actual deployments. However, the impression often given by SNG flyaway manufacturers is that the relatively few cases that make up their particular flyaway system is all the equipment that is required to accomplish a news assignment. If only that were true! The truth is that to mount an operation as described above, there is likely to be a total of 40 to 50 cases, and the total weight of the cases between 1000 and 1500 kg (see Figure 3.13).

With the new 'lightweight' DSNG systems (see Figure 3.14), this shipped weight can be reduced, but perhaps not as dramatically as might be assumed. Although there are complete lightweight SNG flyaway systems that claim to have a shipping weight near to 100 kg, production demands can quickly increase this weight. Developments in broadcast technology are reducing the size of the equipment, but the demands on many newsgatherers now mean that the levels of service required on location are that much higher to meet the demands of continuous news provision. This in turn can mean that the system described above has to be expanded to meet this greater demand, and the net result can be that just as much equipment has to be provided.

However, it is possible with determination – both technical and editorial – to 'travel light' and to keep the amount of equipment required to under 600 kg, and on certain stories this may be essential for logistical and safety reasons.

(a)

(b)

Figure 3.12 (a) Fiber-optic system – electronics (courtesy of Telecast Fiber Systems) (b) Fiber-optic system – fiber drum (courtesy of Telecast Fiber Systems)

Figure 3.13 Typical SNG flyaway system in cases!

Figure 3.14 Lightweight flyaway (Photo courtesy of Harvey Watson)

3.5 Ultra-portable systems

There are three types of ultra-portable system: Inmarsat, 'suitcase' and 'fly-drive'. Each one has increasingly become an important part of the newsgathering armory, and as costs have fallen in relative terms, their popularity continues to increase, as shown by more versions coming onto the market.

For Ku-band systems, the reason why it's possible to use this ultra-portable size of system compared to the more conventional sized flyaway is due to a number of factors – digital operation, the improvement in compression, miniaturization, lighter materials and a higher-power generation of satellites which requires less uplink power.

Firstly we will look at the type of terminal that has always been smaller than the conventional flyaway, and is today the smallest sized satellite terminal that can be used for newsgathering.

3.5.1 Inmarsat systems

Inmarsat satellite telephones can easily be used for the transmission of pictures and sound for television, as well as high-quality audio for radio. Inmarsat systems are particularly of interest for use in parts of the world where traditional means of getting material back is very difficult, or where logistics or some local political sensitivity lead to local difficulties. They are frequently used in civil war zones, or where there is no national telecommunications infrastructure that will enable material to be broadcast back to the studio.

The use of land mobile Inmarsat systems for SNG has been developing since the first portable satellite telephones became available. These MESs (mobile earth stations) were the satellite equivalent of the cellular telephone but offering near-global coverage operating in the L-band. Broadcasters could use the satellite technology to send back reports by using a compact satellite telephone – the 'satphone' as it has became commonly known – and the terminals were comparatively easy to set up because antenna pointing in L-band is far less critical than in higher-frequency bands.

For a number of years, these satphones were used purely for radio SNG. Further developments led to the transmission of high-quality video over an high-speed data circuit. By 1994 compact new equipment designed specifically for newsgathering applications enabled the transmission of television news pictures, albeit not in real time. A handful of companies developed digital video compression units for television newsgathering that could transmit video and audio over HSD channels in store and forward mode.

The videophone was conceived in 1998 and called the 'Talking Head', and was designed to be used with a compact satellite phone – the Inmarsat GAN 'satphone' – to provide a compact two-box solution to live newsgathering.

There is now a new type of Inmarsat system that uses just a high-spec laptop PC and the Inmarsat terminal itself – BGAN (see Chapter 6). The laptop has all the processing necessary to edit and file a story, or transmit the story live with the camera connected to the laptop directly. The editing (video and audio) is carried through the use of one of a number of software applications available for laptop PCs.

Inmarsat meets the need for an SNG system that is particularly suitable for use in areas where it would be logistically or politically unfeasible to use a flyaway system. Inmarsat systems are fully discussed in Chapter 6.

3.5.2 Suitcase SNG systems

So-called because their compact packaging resembles a suitcase, these systems were originally developed for military applications requiring a high-speed IP (Internet) connection. The characteristics of a suitcase system can be summarized as follows:

- small antenna around 1 m
- Ku-band operation (though one system works at L-band)
- small HPA – typically 25–40 W
- MPEG-2 or IP (MPEG-4) transmission
- total system weight less than 50 kg
- automated or semi-automated for non-technical operation

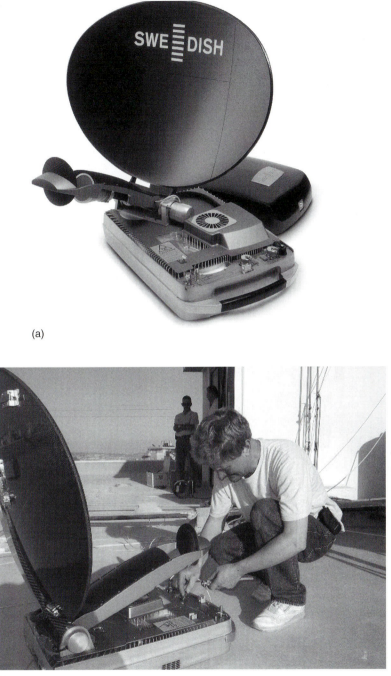

(a)

(b)

Figure 3.15 (a) Swe-Dish IPT (courtesy of Swe-Dish Satellite Systems) (b) Swe-Dish IPT in use in Ramallah, Palestine (courtesy of Swe-Dish Satellite Systems)

(c)

(d)

Figure 3.15 (c) Norsat Newslink (courtesy of Norsat) (d) Norsat Newslink deployed on Israel/Palestine border (courtesy of Steve Williams)

(e)

(f)

Figure 3.15 (e) Norsat GlobeTrekker (courtesy of Norsat) (f) Norsat GlobeTrekker backpack (courtesy of Norsat)

(g)

Figure 3.15   (g) AvL iSNG carry-on flyaway antenna (courtesy of AvL Technologies)

The newest systems have even be developed to be carried conveniently in a 'backpack' configuration, with the system split into two cases. One case typically carries the antenna assembly, while the second case contains the bulk of the electronics.

Manufacturers are continually pushing the laws of physics to try and achieve the smallest and lightest packaging – an example is shown in Figure 3.15g, where the unit has been designed to try and meet most airline requirements for cabin 'carry-on' hand luggage, while still including full motorization with a very small single button controller.

3.5.3   Fly-drive

A new type of flyaway has been developed over the last few years which is classed as a 'fly-drive' system. This type of system is designed to have a total system weight of well below 100 kg (220 lb) and be easily assembled by one person.

The fly-drive system is compact enough to be easily flown as checked baggage in its transit cases. The antenna can either be operated on the ground like a conventional flyaway, or it can easily be mounted onto the roof rails of a car, SUV or other similarly compact vehicle which can be hired once the operator has arrived at the location. The system can be fitted without any modification to the vehicle itself being necessary, and can be driven around with all the equipment in situ. As shown in Figure 3.16, the antenna is usually either mounted on its transit case for ground operation, or removed and attached to vehicle roof bars using spars that extend out from the front and rear.

Fly-drive systems are available in all the typical range of configurations as a conventional size flyaway, with antenna sizes typically around 1.0–1.2 m.

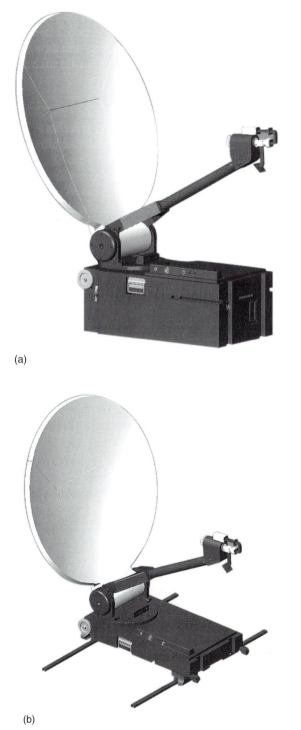

(a)

(b)

Figure 3.16 (a) Fly-drive concept – ground operation (courtesy of Advent Communications) (b) Fly-drive concept – roof bar operation (courtesy of Advent Communications)

(c)

 (d)

Figure 3.16 (c) Fly-drive system mounted on an MPV (courtesy of Holkirk Communications) (d) Fly-drive system operated on the ground (courtesy of SISLink)

3.6   Vehicles

SNG vehicles can be built on a variety of types of base vehicles such as towed trailers, estate cars, SUVs, MPVs, pick-up vehicles, panel vans, box-body vehicles and even combined tractor units for towing production trailers. The majority of SNG vehicles are constructed on a vehicle or van between 3500 and 7500 kg (7700 and 16 500 lb) GVW (gross vehicle weight) in Europe, and up to 26 000 lb in the US, though as can be seen in Figure 3.17, systems are often fitted to smaller vehicles.

(a)

(b)

Figure 3.17   (a) Estate car (courtesy of Swedish Satellite Systems) (b) Four-wheel drive (SUV)

(c)

(d)

Figure 3.17 (c) Pick-up truck (courtesy of New Delhi TV) (d) European King Cab (courtesy of Sat-Comm)

It is common (and desirable) to have an antenna that is mounted high up on the vehicle, typically on the roof. This will place a requirement on the SNG vehicle constructor to ensure that the support structure for the antenna is appropriate for the load of the antenna and its mount.

There are two types of SNG vehicle constructors. There are those who manufacture the satellite uplink system and combine it with the rest of the vehicle system that they will build, literally as a platform for their product. The other type are those constructors who do not manufacture satellite equipment, but buy in the components of the satellite uplink system from other suppliers and integrate them along with

(e)

(f)

Figure 3.17 (e) Compact European SNG van (courtesy of Sat-Comm) (f) Typical European SNG truck (courtesy of Sat-Comm)

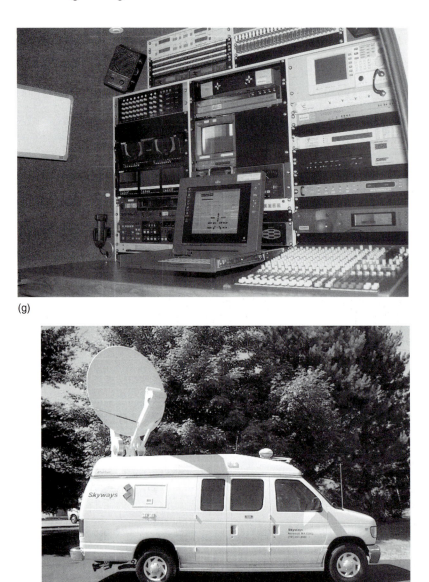

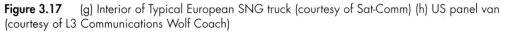

Figure 3.17 (g) Interior of Typical European SNG truck (courtesy of Sat-Comm) (h) US panel van (courtesy of L3 Communications Wolf Coach)

the rest of the systems of the vehicle; these are referred to as 'integrators'. Either type of constructor may have their own in-house coach-building facilities, or sub-contract this aspect of the work out to specialist coachbuilders.

The primary purpose of an SNG vehicle is to allow operational deployment to be accomplished more quickly than with a flyaway, and to have a number of additional facilities built-in so that they are also rapidly available once on-site. These facilities typically include an on-board generator to provide electrical power, production facilities, signal routing and bi-directional studio-remote communications. One of the

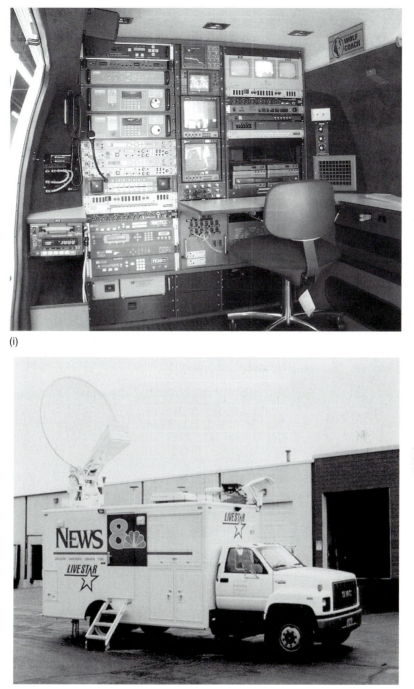

(i)

(j)

Figure 3.17 (i) US panel van – interior (courtesy of L3 Communications Wolf Coach) (j) US truck – medium size (courtesy of L3 Communications Wolf Coach)

(k)

(l)

Figure 3.17 (k) US truck – medium size – interior (courtesy of L3 Communications Wolf Coach) (l) US truck – large size (courtesy of Frontline Communications)

principal characteristics of achieving fast deployment is, of course, having the antenna already mounted on the vehicle. The antenna is motorized so that it can be controlled from the convenience of the interior of the vehicle, and typically uses GPS and an electronic compass to direct it to the desired position.

When it is motorized, the system has an antenna remote controller unit (see Figure 3.18), and it is now typical for this type of system to have an integrated GPS unit and electronic compass to give fully

(m)

Figure 3.17 (m) US truck – large size – interior (courtesy of Frontline Communications)

Figure 3.18 Antenna controller (courtesy of Research Concepts)

automated deployment of the system. This easy-to-operate technology, available from a number of manufacturers and system integrators, offers single button auto-deploy and auto-locate capabilities to get over the single most tricky part of operating any SNG uplink – locating the satellite.

In deciding what can be fitted onto the vehicle, it is crucial that a weight budget is calculated and maintained in parallel with the financial budget. Numerous SNG vehicles have suddenly been discovered to be overweight just as they are near completion, or even when they are delivered to the customer, resulting in a vehicle which is both unsafe and illegal to use on the road. The weight budget has to be calculated as a theoretical model beforehand, and then updated as each step of coachwork is carried out and as cabling and equipment are actually installed in the vehicle.

It is also vital to ensure that a more than adequate standard of documentation is supplied with the vehicle. The vehicle may well be intended to have a life exceeding 10 years, and it is unlikely that the engineers who will maintain it at the beginning will be the same as those maintaining it toward the end of its life. The documentation must include maintenance information on all the systems and sub-systems, from the RF transmission path to the air-conditioning unit.

Figure 3.19   European-style SNG panel van (courtesy of Sat-Comm)

3.6.1   Choice of chassis

SNG systems can be built on a wide choice of vehicles. Trailers and estate cars are, of course, options but the majority of SNG vehicles are based on vans and customized vehicles. Within this group there is a choice between panel vans and using chassis-cabs with purpose-built bodies on the back.

The advantages and disadvantages are as follows:

- Panel vans are cheaper but the construction of the SNG vehicle is constrained by the manufacturer's model dimensions of the load space. The GVW range is limited at the top end to around 7500 kg (16 500 lb) in Europe and 10 000 lb (4500 kg) in the US, restricting the size of SNG vehicle that can be constructed. In Europe, panel vans that have a GVW of less than 3500 kg are regulated by the same speed limits as cars, which is attractive if a particularly fast operation is required. In some countries in the EU (e.g. Germany), however, this may be limited to vehicles that have a GVW of less than 2800 kg. There are usually few driver licence restrictions in this weight class (Figure 3.19).
- Chassis-cab bodies are generally more expensive to build, but the load space can be dimensioned to suit. They are the only option where a large vehicle is required, as chassis-cab vehicles range in size from a medium to very large chassis. Additionally, the life of the vehicle can be extended because the part that usually wears out is the vehicle itself. The custom box body can be constructed so that it can be lifted off and put onto a new chassis-cab, thereby extending the overall life of the system.
- Estate cars/MPVs/SUVs are suitable for some small systems and often look very attractive, but in reality trying to carry out repeated rapid news operations in them can be difficult because of restrictions on space.
- Less popular than they used to be, trailers can offer more flexibility by not being tied to any particular vehicle. However, it should be remembered that maneuvering a vehicle with a trailer attached can be problematic, and the trailer will need to be fairly large if it is to include an operational area as well as the actual satellite uplink.

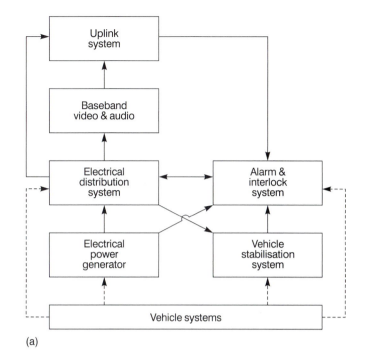

(a)

(b)

Figure 3.20 (a) Outline systems diagram of a European SNG vehicle (b) European panel van-based SNG vehicle under construction

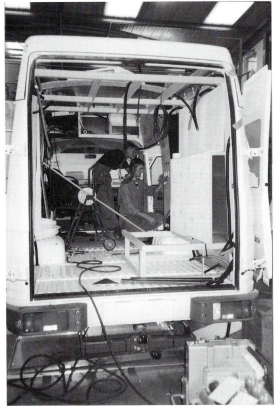

(c)

Figure 3.20 (c) European panel van-based SNG vehicle under construction

It should be noted that if the choice of vehicle is a panel van, as opposed to a chassis-cab, any modifications made by the SNG vehicle constructor to the base vehicle have to be made strictly in accordance with the vehicle constructor's recommendations. Most modern vans are of monocoque construction, and cutting into the vehicle structure can both invalidate the vehicle warranty and compromise the safety and integrity of the vehicle if not done in accordance with the vehicle manufacturer (Figure 3.20).

The choice of a vehicle base depends on the following:

- what is available on the market
- budget
- payload required
- facilities required
- driver licensing requirements
- typical usage (e.g. off-road or on-road)

Because there is a wide range of vehicles on which a satellite uplink system can be built, one type of vehicle will be considered for illustrative purposes. A particular type of vehicle that is currently popular in Europe and the US (and increasingly available in other markets), the Mercedes Sprinter panel van, has been selected as an example to illustrate the implementation of a system in more detail. The system shown could just as easily be found on other vehicles, and either expanded or reduced according to both the payload of the particular vehicle and the financial budget.

The SNG vehicle has a number of sub-systems fitted to it. Obviously, it has a satellite uplink system but in addition it usually has the following installed:

- electrical power system (AC)
- electrical power distribution
- stabilizing jacking system
- racking and wiring for broadcast equipment
- broadcast equipment

3.6.2 Electrical power system

Depending on the size of the vehicle, the power generator system can be usually one (but sometimes two) of four types:

- Self-contained generators driven by a separate engine to the vehicle road engine
- Inverter/UPS systems, where the road engine drives a 12/24 V DC alternator which then supplies 115/230 V AC via an inverter and a UPS (Uninterruptible Power Supply)
- Power take-off systems (PTO) where the road engine drives a generator either via a belt or indirectly via a specially equipped vehicle gearbox
- Battery operation, where a bank of high capacity but compact batteries are kept charged from the road engine, allowing silent operation while stationary

As with powering flyaways, it should be noted that whichever type of power system is used, the whole area of electrical power on location is fraught with difficulties. The power supply to the uplink from whatever type of generating system is in use is likely to fail at some point, and some (wise) uplink operators have taken to having two sources available on a vehicle, with one acting as a standby emergency source. The reason for the likelihood of failure is that generators are notoriously unreliable, probably because of the less than ideal conditions they are often operated in, and their routine maintenance is often overlooked.

Self-contained systems

The generator set, which consists of an electrical alternator and an engine, is installed in the vehicle in an enclosure to separate it from the rest of the vehicle for both acoustic and fire safety reasons. Typically a water-cooled unit (air-cooled units are inherently more noisy), the radiator-cooling unit for the generator engine, which may be fueled by either petrol or diesel, is either within the generator enclosure or separated off in another part of the vehicle where there is improved airflow. For example, the radiator can be mounted on the vehicle roof either at the front or rear, or less desirable, underneath the rear of the vehicle. Alternatively, it may be within the enclosure and draw cooling air through the side or rear of the vehicle via vents in the bodywork.

The alternator that produces AC may be either frequency or voltage regulated; voltage regulation is preferable, as broadcast equipment is usually more sensitive to voltage fluctuations than frequency fluctuations. The generator system needs to be in an acoustically isolated enclosure, and particular attention needs to be paid to the mounting of the generator engine itself to minimize vibration through the rest of the vehicle. Vibration at 50/60 Hz can be particularly uncomfortable for the vehicle occupants during extended periods of generator running.

The fuel for the generator can be drawn from the road engine tank, a separate tank or a tank that has a connection to the road engine tank to enable prolonged running. However, if the last option is chosen, the connection must not be at too low a point, otherwise there is a risk that the generator can run the main tank dry, thereby leaving no fuel for the road engine. Where there is a separate tank, and the generator uses a different fuel to the road engine, there must be clear signage on each tank-filling inlet to avoid wrong fuel being put into a tank. In fact, it is preferable to try to avoid having a mix of fuels on a vehicle, as it is a recipe for disaster. Sooner or later, probably while tired or under operational pressure, someone will forget and put the wrong fuel in the wrong tank.

Generators need regular servicing. If they are not serviced regularly in accordance with manufacturers' recommendations, the likelihood of failure increases by a factor of 10. Ignore servicing schedules at your peril. (If you think you've read this comment before, you have, earlier in this chapter. It's very important.)

Inverter/UPS systems

This is a very popular option on the smallest SNG vehicles where the power demands are modest, say up to 5 kVA. The road engine drives a 12 or 24 V DC alternator, which charges an additional number of high-capacity batteries to the vehicle battery. This separate battery bank then provides a 115 or 230 V AC supply via an electronic 'inverter' to the broadcast equipment – the inverter converts the low voltage DC supply to a higher AC voltage supply. This is called a UPS (Uninterruptible Power Supply), and is also now found in many computer and other critical equipment installations in buildings where the incoming mains supply is used to keep a bank of batteries charged to maintain mission-critical systems for a short period in the event of a loss of mains power.

It is possible to use the vehicle battery to supply the inverter, but a considerably larger battery needs to be fitted. Either two separate alternators can be used – one for the vehicle, one for the inverter system – or one large output alternator can be used for both. As a powering system it is compact, relatively reliable, very cost-effective and space saving. Particular design considerations are that the required output should be easily within the maximum output of the inverter, and particular care must be taken in 'split-charging' with the vehicle battery (i.e. where one alternator is charging two batteries). There should be a properly installed split-charging device to prevent either battery from being overcharged. If a battery is overcharged there is a serious risk of fire due to expansion and overheating of the electrolyte.

Power take-off (PTO) systems

Such systems are often used on vehicles that have four-wheel drive, as the vehicle gearbox sometimes has a power take-off drive as a standard feature. The PTO drive is a special selection on the vehicle gearbox while it is in neutral, where the road engine power is directed to a separate drive shaft for auxiliary devices rather than the vehicle road wheels. There is also usually an engine control system to regulate the speed of the road engine so that it runs at a speed fast enough to provide the required power. The disadvantage of this system is that, although compact and cost-effective, it is not necessarily designed to run for extended periods. Vehicle manufacturers do not usually recommend that the road engine should be operated in PTO mode beyond a certain period. There is a serious risk that both the road engine and the gearbox will overheat (even with an oil cooler) if run continuously for longer than the recommended period. It is also possible for PTO to be derived via a belt driving a supply alternator directly off the engine (as opposed to a low-voltage generator as with the inverter system). Again, this is suitable where power requirements are no more than 5 kVA, and there has to be close control of engine speed to prevent damage or the risk of fire.

Battery systems

With recent developments in battery technologies, compact high-power batteries are now available which have a gel electrolyte, making them suitable for use for battery-only operation. Use of this type of power

Figure 3.21   Battery-operated SNG vehicle (courtesy of Sat-Comm)

system lends itself to operational conditions where the cycle of use is relatively predictable – although these types of systems always allow the vehicle's road engine to be run to 'top-up' the battery charge if it is near depletion (Figure 3.21).

3.6.3   Electrical power distribution

By whatever means the power has been produced, it has to supply all the different systems within the vehicle. Electrical power has to be provided with over-current, short-circuit and ground/earth leakage current protection. Safety is of paramount importance, as there are particularly lethal voltages derived in the uplink HPA. Cabling has to be of the highest standard and no compromises can be permitted. It is normal to feed the power produced from the generator to a power distribution unit (PDU), which splits the power into separate feeds to each equipment rack or sub-system in the vehicle. Figure 3.22 shows a simplified power distribution system for an SNG vehicle.

Protection against over-current is provided within the PDU with the use of MCBs (miniature circuit breakers). An MCB is a resettable device that breaks the circuit under over-current conditions. It fulfills the same purpose as a fuse, but reacts much faster and is convenient because it can be reset with the push of a button. It is also highly desirable to provide protection against any part of the metal work of the vehicle becoming 'live'. This is best done by use of a residual current device (RCD), which monitors the balance of current flow in both the live and neutral supply conductors.

In an AC circuit, the same amount of current should flow to the equipment from the live supply conductor as flows back via the neutral supply conductor. If there is a difference in the current flow between the two supply conductors, a short circuit to earth (or to a person!) is assumed, and the RCD trips. An RCD operates by sensing when the current in the phase (live) and neutral conductors within an installation are not equal and opposite. Any imbalance would imply that an additional path existed for the flow

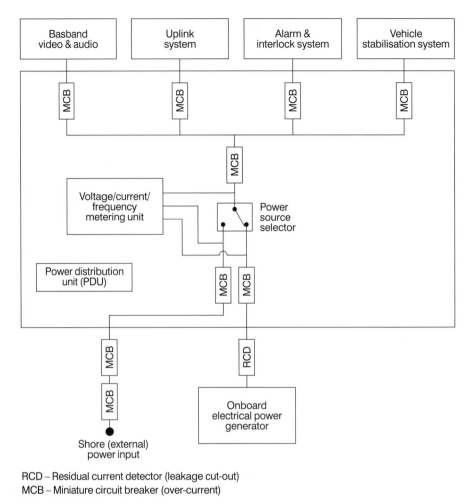

RCD – Residual current detector (leakage cut-out)
MCB – Miniature circuit breaker (over-current)

Figure 3.22   *Simplified power distribution system for an SNG vehicle*

of current, invariably through the earth due to excessive leakage and/or a fault situation. Devices of this type are referred to by a variety of different names, such as RCCB (residual current circuit breaker), ELCB (earth leakage circuit breaker), GFI (ground fault interrupt) and GFCI (ground fault circuit interrupter). They do not all work in exactly the same manner, as some directly measure leakage of current to the earth or ground, but the objective is the same – to protect from electrocution. Specifically an RCD-type device has a particular advantage in that it does not rely on any earth or ground wire connection being present.

There is also a potential safety issue where power is provided from an external input instead of from the on-board generator – often referred to as 'shore power'. The condition of the incoming supply cannot be necessarily known, and it is advisable to provide protection by both indication of potential phase reversal and use of an RCD (Figure 3.23). These must be at the entry point to the vehicle. It is arguable that for ultimate protection, you should use an RCD at the point where the shore power is connected to the vehicle cable, as well as at the point of entry into the vehicle's electrical system.

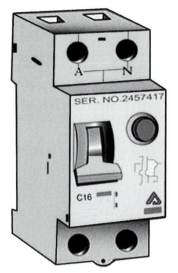

Figure 3.23   Residual Current Device (RCD)

The power, no matter where it is derived from, may need some 'conditioning' (filtering and smoothing) on the input to the uplink system, particularly the HPA, as the supply has to be very 'clean'. That is to say, there must no 'spikes' or irregularities in the supply waveform as this may, in particular, damage the HPA. Usually the HPA will have some kind of internal power conditioning and sensing which will shut down the HPA in the event of it being supplied power which cannot be coped with by the conditioning.

3.6.4   Stabilizing jacking system

The vehicle usually requires a stabilizing jacking system to ensure that the antenna stays on-station, as any movement of the vehicle could result in movement of the antenna. Movement of the vehicle can result from either people getting in and out or wind rocking the vehicle (particularly if the wind is coming broadside onto the vehicle or from other vehicles passing by at high speed). It is common to provide either a two- or four-point stabilizing system, with two jacks at each rear corner of the vehicle, or two at the middle of the vehicle on each side, or four jacks, one at each corner. The jacks can be manually, electrically or hydraulically operated. The most sophisticated stabilizing systems have computer-controlled stabilizing of the vehicle, with an on-board sensor feeding back the status of the vehicle's 'attitude' (high/low at the front/back).

Manual systems are usually fitted to smaller vehicles, and although some weight and cost is saved, the time taken to prepare the vehicle for operation is slower. It is possible on some vehicles not to need any stabilization if the antenna is small, as the wider beamwidth compared to larger antennas means that a slight movement of the antenna will not move it off-station. The choice of whether to use hydraulic or electrical drive for the jacks is a matter of preference. Hydraulic jacking systems generally use a single central pump driving the hydraulic rams on each jack in turn, via hydraulic piping and valves, and can often be heavy. Electrical screw jacking systems are lighter but can increase the demand for electrical power. Either type of set-up can use the sophisticated control system described, or rely on simple manual controls to achieve stability.

The aim of the jacking system is to take the movement out of the vehicle suspension system, rather than achieve absolute leveling. It is possible, particularly due to the significant power of hydraulic jacking systems, to lift the vehicle wheels off the ground, and this is undesirable for two reasons. Firstly, if the vehicle is lifted asymmetrically, i.e. one wheel is lifted clear of the ground while the other wheel stays on the ground, it is likely that the vehicle chassis will twist and be permanently damaged. This could seriously affect the road-handling of the vehicle. Secondly, if the vehicle is lifted either wholly or partly clear of the ground while parked on an incline, it is possible for the vehicle either to slide down the incline or topple to one side. This is a particular risk if the surface on which it is parked is icy or slippery.

3.6.5   Racking and wiring for broadcast plant

Another important sub-system of the SNG vehicle is the equipment racking in which the broadcast equipment is to be installed. There must obviously be enough rack space to take all the equipment required and so, at the start of the project, there has to be a calculation of the amount of rack space for the equipment needed. This underlines the need for clarity in the specification from the start, and it is one of the principal reasons why the specification should not change during the construction of the SNG vehicle.

The decisions with respect to the broadcast equipment that needs to be installed are very much a matter of preference, and there is certainly no 'standard' type of configuration. Requirements vary from user to user, and country to country, so it is beyond the scope of this book to deal with this area in detail. Suffice to say that, in pursuing the requirement to provide the satellite uplink, the broadcast function should not be overlooked. As mentioned earlier in this chapter with reference to flyaways, the SNG vehicle should also contain all the equipment that is required to accomplish a news assignment.

There also has to be careful design to fit all the required equipment into the vehicle. Constructors can be very adept at making use of every last inch of space inside a vehicle, and the racking often has to be constructed to custom specification to fit into a particular model of vehicle. The equipment racks should be as light as possible, as standard racks designed for studio installations are not usually built with weight saving in mind. Some firms construct the racking and wire the racks outside the vehicle, as space inside the vehicle is often very cramped. The completed racks and wiring looms are then transferred into the vehicle in the final stages of build. This also allows parallel construction operations to be carried out. For instance, the uplink can be installed into the vehicle at the same time as the equipment racks are being wired outside the vehicle.

3.6.6   Weight

At this point mention must be made again of the weight budget, as it must not only allow for all the fixed equipment but also the 'loose' load. The loose load is the ancillary equipment, cable and other sundry items that can be found in the back of every SNG vehicle, which slowly get added to for the 'just in case' situations. The weight budget must account for all the installed and loose load equipment. This then has to be balanced against both the gross vehicle payload and the individual gross axle loadings.

In addition, the center of gravity of the vehicle must be calculated and monitored throughout the construction. It is inevitable with installing broadcast equipment, the uplink chain and the antenna assembly that weight is going to be added into the upper part of the vehicle. This will raise the center of gravity of the vehicle, which may result in the vehicle becoming unstable and adversely affecting the vehicle while it is being driven. It is a fine balance to maintain the functionality of the vehicle while not adversely affecting the handling of the vehicle.

It is an almost unavoidable fact that SNG vehicles are generally at or very close to their maximum GVW, and will be running constantly near to fully laden over their life. This can be very wearing on the engine, transmission, steering, suspension and brakes. Running this close to the maximum GVW can shorten the life of the vehicle and vehicles need to be regularly checked for wear on all these components, as they are fundamental to safety.

3.6.7 *Method of construction*

There are broadly four approaches to building SNG vehicles:

- turnkey
- self-build
- part-build by a manufacturer, part-build by user
- sub-contracting

Turnkey

For customers who have the budgetary resources to contract a fully functioning vehicle from a constructor – manufacturer or integrator – the turnkey route is plainly the most obvious and attractive. However, it may still involve some allocation of the customer's own engineering resources to achieve the desired end product. It is however by far the best option for the first-time customer in the SNG vehicle market. Even if the customer is an experienced user of flyaway systems, the problems and challenges of building an SNG vehicle are different, as we have discussed.

Self-build

This approach is particularly attractive as it can potentially deliver the lowest-cost vehicle. However, it should only be attempted where the user has significant engineering resources. The elements involved in the construction of a vehicle are diverse and encompass not only coachbuilding and the consequent safety issues, but also the successful specification, purchase, installation and integration of a range of equipment. The challenge faced in doing this must not be underestimated, and it is sometimes questionable as to whether the end result is as cost-effective as it might seem on first inspection. However, local circumstances may dictate this approach, or it may suit the user who is mature in the use of SNG systems and who has particular ideas on how a system should be constructed in a vehicle. It should be borne in mind though that there are few examples of vehicles built in this way that compare with the best examples from the premier constructors. In addition, the issues of warranties and regulatory approvals must be carefully considered, as should the inherent risk of a safety incident that calls into question the method of construction, and the litigation that could follow.

Part-build by a manufacturer, part-build by user

The appeal of this approach is that a specialist manufacturer handles the satellite system, coachbuilding and vehicle infrastructure, and this includes the electrical generator and the vehicle stabilization system. The user (assumed here to be expert in broadcast engineering) can then install the broadcasting equipment and communication systems, completing the project. This can work very successfully. It can be seen as a middle way between self-build and turnkey that can deliver significant cost benefits. However, the issue of project management raises its head here, as a considerable amount of hands-on management of the project is required. The successful integration of the diverse elements of the system that come from different sources can be potentially problematic. This can be virtually a full-time job, and needs careful consideration of how it is to be achieved before the project is started. If the user is able to commit to this level of project involvement, then this can be a cost-effective way of building an SNG vehicle. Alternatively, the services of a professional project manager could be used.

Sub-contracting

A variation on part-build by a constructor is that the different elements of the whole project are subcontracted out to separate companies, each with a specialist contribution to the vehicle. For instance, one company can undertake the coachbuilding. Another company can carry out the electrical generator installation. The specialist company may not necessarily be expert on the construction of SNG vehicles. The above observations on project management are even more pertinent here.

3.7 Type of compression

Currently, in the latter part of the first decade of the new millennium, the decision as to which digital compression to choose is changing.

From 1995 onwards, the transition from predominantly analog SNG to digital SNG in many parts of the world was accelerated by the widespread adoption of MPEG-2 digital compression, and it is still the most widely used compression standard in almost all parts of the television broadcast process. From MPEG-2 coding in cameras to MPEG-2 manipulation, transmission and distribution through the broadcasting chain to delivery to the viewers TV, it was natural that the SNG uplink would mirror these developments.

In the 1990s, work began on a new standard for video compression – MPEG-4 – and this was finally ratified as a standard in late 1999. Originally intended for very low-bit rate applications, it is nevertheless applicable to broadcast use. The first generation of MPEG-4 – often referred to as MPEG-4 ASP (Advanced Simple Profile) – was not particularly suitable for broadcast use, but the development of the second generation – MPEG-4 AVC (Advanced Video Compression) – has broken through the broadcast barrier.

Meanwhile, Microsoft were working on their own media compression format. Windows Media Player had evolved through the 1990s in step with the evolution of the Windows operating system. Since version 7 (WMV1), Microsoft has used its own non-standard version of MPEG-4, and the latest version, WMV9 (Windows Media 9) now approved as SMPTE VC-1 standard, is challenging MPEG-4 AVC.

MPEG-2 will be largely replaced by these two compression formats by the end of the decade, but although it looks that MPEG-4 AVC is likely to be more widespread than WMV9, at this stage it is only a guess. MPEG-2 will last for some time because:

- It is a proven standard, widely deployed and has good track record
- Improvements are still being made to the encoders
- The encoders are relatively low cost
- Decoders are widespread

No matter which compression format is chosen, the most important characteristics that have to be considered are as follows:

- picture quality
- delay
- artifacts
- bandwidth
- cost

For new installations, then the choice will probably lie with either MPEG-4 or WMV9. We will look at all the compression formats in Chapter 4 in more detail. But for the purposes of distilling the choice for an SNG system, we will look at each of them briefly.

3.7.1 MPEG-2

It is now likely that for new projects, the selection of MPEG-2 is no longer automatic for the reasons outlined above. Where the uplink is adding to an existing station infrastructure, then the choice of compression will be dictated by whatever is already in use (i.e. probably MPEG-2).

The terms '4:2:2' and '4:2:0' are often seen in reference to MPEG-2 encoding; we will explain these in Chapter 4, but for our purposes here, if considering MPEG-2 encoding, you should opt for a 4:2:2 encoder, as it gives maximum flexibility because it will include the 4:2:0 mode as well. DTH transmissions are in 4:2:0 mode.

MPEG-2 encoding is well understood by the professionals in the business, and its idiosyncrasies have become accepted and adapted to. Picture quality is by and large very acceptable (as far as any compression format can be), as you can judge for yourself if you view any DTH program transmitted digitally either via satellite or terrestrially – it will almost certainly have been encoded in MPEG-2. Delay is down to an acceptable level, and as already mentioned, the cost of encoders is relatively low – a good quality encoder/modulator can be bought for less than $25 000.

3.7.2   MPEG-4 AVC

There are only a few encoders suitable for DSNG use on the market at the time of writing, though undoubtedly more will appear. The advantage of MPEG-4 AVC is bandwidth saving, and as a rough rule of thumb, the equivalent quality for a given data rate in MPEG-2 can be achieved at half the data rate with MPEG-4. The typical example is a contribution feed that would be transmitted at 4 Mbps in MPEG-2 can probably be squeezed into less than 2 Mbps with MPEG-4.

For HD (High Definition) newsgathering, then the choice will probably have to be either MPEG-4 or VC-1, as this is the principal target for these formats – the HD distribution market, i.e. delivery of HD programming to the consumer. MPEG-2 can be used for HD, but the data rates have to be relatively high – over 20 Mbps, and possibly more than 40 Mbps for the highest quality.

MPEG-4 AVC can also often be referred to (though not always correctly) as any the following:

- MPEG-4 Chapter 10/Part 10
- JVT codec
- H.264
- H.26L
- ISO/IEC 14496-10

Some of these are now historical, and we should use MPEG-4 AVC when discussing this compression algorithm. The biggest issue with MPEG-4 AVC at time of writing is processing delay – it is in the order of 1 s (compared to typically less than 200 ms for MPEG-2, ignoring satellite path delay) at data rates of around 2 Mbps.

3.7.3   VC-1 (Windows Media Video 9)

Windows Media Video 9 is Microsoft's venture into the professional broadcast community with a compression codec. As with any newcomer into an established market, and particularly with Microsoft's reputation for aggressive marketing, there has been some adverse comments on their attempt to enter this market. However, it would be foolish to disregard this format, and although it has not (at time of writing) been used for SNG, there will undoubtedly come a day when it will be used.

Microsoft submitted the WMV9 format to the Society of Motion Picture and Television Engineers (SMPTE) for approval and it became the VC-1 standard in 2006. Although VC-1 and WMV9 refer to the same codec technology, VC-1 is actually a superset of WMV9, containing coding structures not found in the original WMV9 codec.

The decision on which compression standard to use on an uplink is dictated by a number of factors, a few of which have been outlined in this section. Some organizations may adopt a particular standard as a policy, while others will use different standards in different parts of the chain. The subject of compression is dealt with in greater depth in Chapter 4.

3.8 Frequency band of operation

In specifying a system, be it for a flyaway or a vehicle, a key parameter has traditionally been the frequency band of operation. However, nowadays the choice is mostly confined to Ku-band, as C-band is only used for very specific reasons.

As described in Chapter 2, the transmit frequency of C-band for SNG is around 6 GHz, and the receive frequency is around 4 GHz. This compares with 14 and 12 GHz, respectively for Ku-band.

Why are there two different frequency bands used for SNG? C-band was the original frequency band for satellite transmissions because of the limitations of the technology. The 1977 ITU conference WARC-77 extended the frequency bands for satellite operation to the much higher frequencies of Ku-band. WARC-77 also defined the regions of the world where these frequency bands can be used (see Chapter 7). At that time the technology for working in the Ku-band was still in its infancy, but it was recognized that with the existing satellite services in C-band there would be ever-increasing congestion. Frequency congestion was widely predicted both on the ground and in space, and experimental transmissions in the Ku-band were undertaken in both the US and in Europe during the late 1970s and into the early 1980s. It was seen that Ku-band offered a number of advantages over operating in the C-band, principally smaller antennas and HPAs. Ku-band transmissions became common for SNG, overtaking C-band transmissions in the US through the 1980s, and in Europe SNG began in the Ku-band.

However, C-band has the benefit of being a more 'rugged' frequency band in terms of RF propagation, with less critical performance required of equipment and therefore a lower cost. It is little affected by rain, unlike Ku-band where rain has a particularly detrimental effect on the signal. With the advent of new digital coding techniques and the now rapidly increasing congestion in the Ku-band, the opportunity for using C-band for digital transmissions in a spectrally efficient manner has emerged. As identified below, digital C-band transmissions are of special interest in certain parts of the world.

3.8.1 C-band
The use of C-band for SNG transmissions is not permitted in Europe and many other areas of the world (see Chapter 7). However, it can be used in most of Africa, Asia and South America, and indeed in some of these regions it is unwise to use Ku-band because of the adverse affect of heavy equatorial rainfall on signal transmission.

The issue in some parts of the world is that C-band is widely used for terrestrial fixed microwave links. The potential for interference from what is essentially a temporary transmission from an SNG uplink is very high. Fixed networks are fundamental to the telecommunications infrastructure of a highly-developed country, and SNG transmissions will not be permitted to interfere with this. Typically, a C-band uplink for a fixed application has to be 'cleared' for interference for a radius of up to 1200 km, and this can obviously take some time as international co-ordination may be required for its use.

On the other hand, the attraction of C-band for SNG transmissions is that in many parts of the world there is no ad-hoc (occasional use) satellite transponder capacity in the Ku-band available for SNG usage. Coincidentally, often in these same areas there is not the sophisticated telecommunications infrastructure to limit C-band SNG transmissions. C-band can be used for analog transmissions, but requires large uplink powers resulting in the requirement for large antennas and HPAs. Hence, it is preferable to use C-band for lower power digital transmissions, with antennas and HPAs similar in size to those used in Ku-band systems. Indeed, in the latter part of the 1990s, INTELSAT in particular was keen to promote the use of C-band digital uplinks. This is because the spectral efficiency of this type of transmission matched the increasing amount of C-band capacity that INTELSAT had available in general, resulting in many more channels available for digital SNG.

3.8.2 Ku-band

The Ku-band is the most common frequency band used for SNG around the world and this is due to a number of factors. In the areas of the world where there is a developed telecommunications infrastructure, such as the US and Europe, Ku-band SNG is the norm. The antennas are small and the uplink powers required, particularly on the latest generation satellites, are relatively modest. This minimizes the risk of interference to fixed terrestrial link networks, and also allows very compact SNG systems to be assembled and easily transported between locations.

3.8.3 Dual band

By 1995 a number of manufacturers were offering 'dual-band' systems. They are termed dual band as the RF section of the system spans both the C- and Ku-bands. (Strictly speaking, they are triple band as they also cover the X-band – see Appendix A – which is used for military telecomms.) The operational advantage is obvious for flyaways, as with a single system the user has the comfort of traveling to a location with the option of operating in either frequency band. The principal global newsgatherers have often found these systems flexible. It can be decided before departure in which band the system is going to operate, or it can be left until arrival at the destination if the choice of available space segment cannot be made at the time of deployment. The additional components to enable the system to operate in both bands are relatively minor. The HPA is typically a wideband type, capable of operating in either band, and it is simply a matter of making a normally front panel selection on the HPA to change bands. This typically switches in a different set of filters for monitoring purposes. The only other components that are different are the feed capsule (containing the OMT specific for that frequency band) and LNB that fit onto the antenna. The same antenna is used, though the specification of the system will change depending on the frequency band of operation.

The only disadvantage of a dual-band system is the increased cost, as a separate feed capsule and LNB for each frequency band have to be purchased, and a wideband HPA is generally more expensive. However, with the increasing availability of high power Ku-band spot beams in many parts of the world, the attraction of dual-band systems has diminished, though if Ka-band were to become used for SNG, it is conceivable that triple-band systems (C-, Ku- and Ka-band) could be used. This would give maximum flexibility, although at a significant price difference to a conventional single band flyaway system.

3.9   Level of redundancy

Redundancy gives protection against failure of part of the system, and is an important factor to consider if the system is being used to cover an important event or story. An SNG system may have part or all of its electronic equipment duplicated to give a degree of redundancy. Normally it is not necessary to duplicate any of the mechanical components, save for perhaps having a spare length of flexible waveguide.

The level of redundancy can be varied according to the requirement. On a system, it might perhaps be sufficient to add a second HPA and upconverter – this would give partial redundancy. To achieve full redundancy another encoder/modulator should be added. The additional HPA can either be combined with the primary HPA via a phase combiner, or made available as a 'hot spare' via a waveguide switch. A hot spare is a part of the system that is switched on and in a fully operational state ready for rapid changeover in the event of a failure; conversely, a 'cold spare' is not switched on but still ready for a quick swap over!

The elements most likely to fail are the power supply within the HPA because of the high voltages generated and the amount of power produced, and the upconverter because of the frequency stability required. The upconverter is a particularly vulnerable unit in a digital system, as the both frequency and phase have to be tightly controlled to maintain system stability and operation. However the most recent designs have improved reliability over their predecessors.

The decision as to what level of redundancy is required or desired is not an easy one. In such a complex array of equipment as in an SNG system, failures are inevitable at some point during the system's life, and even full redundancy can never remove that risk totally – it simply minimizes it. Companies that provide their SNG systems to third parties on a commercial basis regard higher levels of redundancy as a priority so that the exposure of risk of failure to their clients is minimized. Other organizations, including a few of the global broadcasters who are primarily servicing their own outlets, prefer to reduce the capital cost, size and weight of the system and work single-threaded. They are willing to take the risk of an occasional failure in return for a lower capital cost and reduced operating costs in shipping smaller flyaway systems around the world.

3.10   Multiple program paths

It is an increasingly common requirement to be able to provide more than one program path from a single SNG uplink. This may be to provide differing sources of material to the destination simultaneously, either off-tape or 'live', or to service different destinations simultaneously.

For whatever reason, there are two methods of providing multiple paths. One is to provide two separate uplink chains that are combined just before the input to the antenna – this is the 'RF solution'. It has the added bonus of offering a degree of redundancy if the uplink is in a remote and not easily accessible location. The second method is more common nowadays with digital uplinks, and this is to 'multiplex' two or more program paths (or 'streams') in the digital domain by cascading a number of compression encoders together to provide a single digital data stream to the uplink chain. This is termed 'multiple channels per carrier' (MCPC). In an SNG system there are numerous permutations possible by using a combination of both of these methods, such that it is possible to have two RF chains, each fed by a number of digital compression coders. In the US, there are commonly SNG vehicles that have up to six paths available, via two RF chains each with three digital compression coders. This enables a vehicle to service both mainstream 'network' output as well as 'affiliate' station requirements on a big story.

3.11   Automatic systems

Automation has entered the broadcast process in all areas to varying degrees, and SNG is no exception. This may sound a little odd, considering the unpredictable way in which SNG systems are set up and used – after all, it is not like automating a process in a broadcast center. But in these days of constant downward pressure of costs, combined with the element of multi-skilling that has increased in many areas, there is a natural attraction toward the use of automated processes if it saves money.

So some automation is possible for vehicle, flyaway and ultra-portable systems, and there are two principal types of process that can be automated: acquisition of the satellite and remote operation of the system.

3.11.1   Automated acquisition of the satellite

The most difficult task in the operation of any SNG system, which by its very nature is never in one place for very long, is finding the satellite – 'acquiring the bird'. The satellite can be an elusive object to identify at times for even the most experienced operators, but the process can be relatively easily automated.

A satellite occupies a position in space that is defined by two parameters in relation to a particular location: its azimuth and elevation. By the co-ordinated usage of two (and sometimes three) devices, an automated system can be devised to find a satellite.

The two common devices are a Global Positioning System (GPS) unit and an electronic 'flux-gate' compass. The third unit can be either a beacon receiver or an integral DVB receiver inside the antenna controller. These components are then used in conjunction with a microprocessor control system in the antenna controller, within which satellite orbital positions have been programmed. This control system can then drive a motorized antenna to the correct azimuth and elevation for the required satellite, and even on some versions be capable of tracking a satellite in inclined orbit.

GPS

The Global Positioning System (GPS) was developed in the 1970s by the US Department of Defense to provide highly accurate location data, using the US military NavStar fleet of 24 satellites. The first GPS satellite was launched in 1978 and the constellation of 24 was completed in 1993. These satellites operate in a medium earth orbit (MEO) of 20 200 km (13 750 miles) in 6 orbital planes (each satellite has a 12-hour orbital period), providing global coverage 24 hours per day. From any point on the Earth's surface, a minimum of 6 satellites will be in view at any time.

The GPS concept of operation is based upon satellite ranging. A constant stream of timing and position information generated from a highly accurate atomic clock on each satellite is broadcast, and on the ground a GPS receiver can receive and read this information from at least three, and often four, satellites. By comparing the signal from each satellite with the time of its own local clock, the GPS receiver calculates the distance to each satellite it receives, and then uses 'trilateration' techniques from the information to calculate its location, providing a position accurate to within centimeters for military use. This is the technology behind the ability to provide the military with the exact positional information required for modern warfare, including the precision required by 'smart' bombs and missiles.

Commercial manufacturers of GPS equipment are permitted to manufacture units with an accuracy typically to within 2 m, or even less if using 'differential' GPS techniques (as is used on military grade units). The satellites transmit signals in the L-band, which a receiver locks onto and determines its position. The receiver needs to receive signals from at least three different satellites in the system to be able to accurately determine its position, and a signal from a fourth to determine its altitude. These receivers are available in many countries at very economical prices (from around US$200), and often sold as satellite navigation ('satnav') units – increasingly found in cars and trucks.

GPS technology is widely used for all forms of air, marine and terrestrial navigation. It is also used in automated satellite acquisition systems to provide the longitude and latitude information to determine the 'look angle' of the required satellite for antenna positioning. The GPS receiver is connected directly to the antenna controller for this purpose.

Flux-gate compass

The flux-gate compass provides an accurate bearing ('heading') and this is referenced to a nominal 'set' direction – the direction the antenna is pointing. The flux-gate compass works on the following principle.

When a magnetic field is generated in a material using an electric current, eventually the material becomes 'full' and can accommodate no more magnetic flux (magnetic flux is an expression of the magnetic field strength within a given area). If the electromagnetic coil wound around the material is formed into a ring – termed a toroid – this then forms a toroidal magnetic core. On one side of the ring, the external magnetic field – the Earth's magnetic field in the form of the magnetic force from the North Pole – 'lines up' with the internal field, increasing the overall electromagnetic field. On the other side of the toroid it lines up in reverse with respect to the internal field, decreasing the overall electromagnetic field. Thus, one side of the ring becomes 'full' of flux before the other as the internal field is increased and this difference can be sensed. It is then possible to determine which part of the ring the effect takes place in, and so the direction of the external field (North Pole) as well as its strength can be measured.

Hence, the flux-gate compass is a very accurate electromagnetic compass that has an electrical signal output giving orientation information that can be fed to the antenna controller to be combined with the absolute positional information from the GPS unit. Unfortunately, it is a relatively expensive component compared to the GPS unit.

Alternatively, it is possible to use a GPS compass to determine the magnetic heading. The GPS compass works by measuring the time difference between the arrival of signals from three to five GPS satellites at two antennas, using only the carrier wave from the satellite without decoding the navigation information contained in the carrier signal. The antennas of the GPS compass must be separated by a distance greater than the wavelength of the received signal – fortunately the wavelength of the L-band GPS signal is less than 200 mm, so the unit can be relatively compact.

Beacon receiver

Satellite beacon signals were discussed in Chapter 2, and a beacon receiver is a satellite receiver that is optimized to receive the narrow-band beacon signals continuously transmitted by the satellite. Beacon signals, amongst other things, uniquely identify a particular satellite, as they are transmitted on a specific frequency and polarization, available from the satellite operator. The output of the beacon receiver is fed to the antenna controller, or it may even be integrated within the antenna controller.

DVB receiver

Instead of using a beacon receiver, which is a relatively expensive component, a recent feature of some antenna controllers is the integration of a DVB receiver card within the unit. In Chapter 2 we referred to the DVB standard, and it is covered in more detail in Chapter 4. The antenna controller uses the signal from one of a number of 'reference' satellites that transmit DTH TV signals. Typically within many MPEG transport streams a satellite network ID is transmitted which can be used to identify the satellite being used.

Having found a reference satellite, the DVB receiver in the antenna controller identifies a particular MPEG-2 stream coming from that satellite, and from this, the antenna controller can calculate the relative position of the desired satellite, and then move the antenna to that position. The advantages of this type of system is that implementing a DVB receiver within the controller is relatively low cost, and by using the MPEG-2 stream from a known satellite it is simple processing to calculate the correct azimuth and elevation. Some systems even forgo the use of GPS and an electronic compass, and instead the approximate position of the uplink is fed into the antenna controller, which then scans the sky to find a reference satellite.

3.11.2   Operation

On arriving at site, the SNG uplink is readied for transmission. The required satellite is selected from a 'menu' list on the antenna controller (which may be either driven directly by front panel control or via

Figure 3.24 GPS satellite constellation

software on a laptop PC), and the GPS and the compass feed the positional information of the uplink antenna to the controller. From this information the controller can calculate the required antenna azimuth and elevation for the selected satellite.

Under the control of the automated acquisition system, which is activated by a single button press, the antenna is raised from its lowered ('stow') position, to a predetermined nominal elevation and azimuth ('deploy') position. It then rotates to the satellite's 'target azimuth' and raises to the 'target elevation' angle. In the case of beacon receiver control, the beacon receiver now starts tuning, scanning about a predefined frequency of the satellite (but within a very narrow range) 'looking' for the satellite's beacon. On finding the beacon signal, the controller system fine-tunes the antenna, 'stepping' in small increments in azimuth and elevation to optimize the signal level from the beacon receiver, to ensure that the antenna is accurately aligned.

In the case of DVB control, the antenna controller firstly moves the antenna toward one of a number of reference satellites that transmit DTH TV signals (which will vary according to where the uplink is in the world). Having found a reference satellite, the DVB receiver in the antenna controller identifies the MPEG-2 stream coming from that satellite, and verifies it is the correct reference satellite. From this, the antenna controller can then calculate the relative position of the desired satellite, and then move the antenna to that position. Finally, the antenna controller typically then attempts to

Figure 3.25 Fully automated acquisition and control SNG vehicle system (courtesy of SISLink)

'peak' the total RF signal level coming from the satellite to ensure that the antenna is pointed as finely as possible.

3.11.3   Fully remote operation

This is an extension of the automated acquisition system to a level where the entire uplink is remotely controlled. It has been implemented both on vehicles and on flyaway systems, where remote control can be used either where the antenna has been aligned manually or with some additional 'pointing aids' for the non-technical operator.

The remote control package allows control of all the key operational parameters by a separate communications channel. This return control channel is typically provided using a separate satellite channel that is activated via the antenna once it is correctly aligned.

The level of control can be relatively sophisticated, but as a basic minimum it will provide the following.

- Encoder control: Bit-rate, horizontal and vertical resolution, input audio and video parameters, MPEG-2 mode (4:2:2/4:2:0 – see Chapter 4)
- Modem: Bit-rate, modulation type, FEC, carrier on/off
- Upconverter: Frequency
- HPA mode: standby/transmit

However, as with the automatic acquisition systems, a failure of the system can be due to any number of reasons, and therefore there is a compromise that has to be accepted if opting for this mode of operation.

3.11.4 Advantages and disadvantages of automation

Automation has the undeniable advantage that technology can replace the highly tuned skills of a good uplink operator in finding the satellite. Staff with lesser technical skills are just as able to press the button to set the system in motion. This, combined with other technical functions that could be automated or pre-programmed in the operation of an uplink, allows the use of journalists or any other member of the team to operate the uplink.

However, one must consider that the typical SNG system is an already sophisticated set of equipment, and the addition of an automated system for 'finding the bird' is 'just another thing to go wrong'. If the system fails to find the satellite, it could be any one of a number of processes that have failed. If such a system is used by an experienced uplink operator to save time then, if it fails, the satellite can still be found by manual methods and the antenna correctly aligned. But in the hands of an unskilled operator, the transmission will be lost.

The limitations of its use therefore need to be fully appreciated. It is all too easy to overlook the limitation of its potential failure in unskilled hands, where a single small issue, which would be quickly resolved by an experienced technician, could outwit a journalist, cameraman, or producer who is already under a number of other pressures on a breaking story.

Its use is perhaps best on a small, journalist-operated uplink, which has relatively simple function and usage. Not many news organizations would want to deploy a highly automated system in the hands of non-technical operators on a major story.

It may seem here that we are debating whether someone whose primary job is not a technical one – e.g. a journalist – is capable of operating an SNG uplink with the different automated controls described. That is not the issue – it is more a question of whether, if (for example) a journalist is trying to do other jobs as well as their own, something will suffer. Newsgathering is not a serial process, i.e. the jobs and tasks that have to be done do not concatenate neatly together. There are task overlaps on the time-line of reporting a story, and some even run directly in parallel.

At times, it is not a matter of 'many hands make light work', but that 'many hands make it happen' – on-air and on time. On most stories, the journalist is busy simply keeping up with the story. Rapidly breaking events with the requirement repeatedly to 'go live' for a string of different outlets can mean that the journalist is no longer effectively reporting the story as it develops and unfolds, as they are still stuck in front of the camera reporting what has become 'old' news. Automation involving a journalist can make this worse. This directly impacts on competitive advantage, something close to the heart of every news network.

There is nothing wrong with automation so long as decision-makers understand fully not only the commercial advantages of such systems, but also the operational limitations they may pose.

3.12 Conclusion

From the discussion in this chapter, it should be clear that the fundamental choice of type of system should be straightforward once the requirement has been tightly defined. It is the implementation that often causes the problems, either due to financial constraints (which are always present) or physical parameters. In particular the IATA rules on checked baggage size and weight limits have had a dramatic effect on the design of new SNG systems. Carriers will refuse to load any piece of baggage that exceeds these dimensions, and so some SNG systems will have to be air-freighted rather than carried as checked baggage.

Clarity on what the system is expected to do and how it is to be actually used in the field is crucial before talking to any manufacturers and integrators. Is it a simple uplink or an integrated production facility that happens to have an uplink attached to it? Where will it be operated and who is expected to operate it? By being clear on these fundamental questions at the beginning of the project, there is a very good chance that you will end up with a system that does not disappoint.

4

Squeezing through the pipe: digital compression

4.1 Introduction

Around the world the use of digital compression is an essential characteristic of not only of satellite newsgathering itself, but also of the whole newsgathering process, so in this chapter we will look at types of compression used for both video and audio.

It should also be made clear at this point that we will primarily be dealing with 'standard definition' (SD) television – the TV service that most countries utilize. Modern 'high-definition' (HD) television is spreading from its roots in Japan and the US to other parts of the world, and we will look at its use in SNG later in this chapter.

Compression is a highly complex subject and far beyond the scope of this chapter (or this book) to explain fully in detail, and as in other chapters the use of mathematics will be kept to a minimum. For those who require a more theoretical explanation of the processes, there are a large number of books and papers on the subject, a few of which are listed in the bibliography at the end of the book.

So to begin with, why do we want to compress a signal? The answer is that, in an ideal world, we don't! If we had unlimited bandwidth available to us, then there would be no need for compression, for digital compression is essentially about squeezing large bandwidth signals into the typically narrower available bandwidth (frequency spectrum). On wideband fiber-optic routes there is the available bandwidth to send uncompressed video and audio signals at lower cost than using satellite. But as we have seen in Chapter 2, satellite communication revolves around the issues of power and bandwidth, and by digitizing and compressing the signal, we can reduce demand for both power and bandwidth – and hence minimize cost.

If digital signals were used in direct replacement for the same analog information, the resultant bit-rate at which the information would have to be transmitted would be very high, using more bandwidth than an equivalent analog transmission, and therefore not very efficient. Hence, there is a need to strip out the redundant and insignificant information in the signal, creating a compressed signal.

A common analogy that illustrates the underlying concept of compression is concentrated orange juice. Consider orange juice that you can buy in a supermarket. Freshly squeezed juice is the uncompressed version of our orange juice, and indeed you can just put it in a bottle, transport it to the supermarket and sell it to the customers. There is price premium to pay – because the cost of transportation is higher per liter, the method of transportation would probably have to be different and faster to make sure that the juice was still consumable before it naturally deteriorates, and perhaps you could not transport it to just anywhere.

This is the same as sending uncompressed video – it could be more expensive to sell because you would either use more bandwidth on the satellite (probably at an uneconomic price), maybe such an amount of bandwidth is not even available, or you would have to send it over a fiber-optic route, which might not be available everywhere.

But if we go back to the original process of producing the freshly squeezed juice, we can see that the process began with squeezing oranges to produce the juice, of which the major constituent is water. The water is removed to produce a concentrate that can be put into a small carton and transported to the shop for sale. The customer buys the orange juice concentrate, takes it home and reconstitutes the orange juice by adding water back in. Effectively, the orange juice is 'compressed' (just like the signal), so that a comparatively large volume can be transported in a small carton (or bandwidth), and then the juice is reformed by adding the equivalent volume of water back in that was removed in the first place (decompressed).

What is the advantage of this to the consumer? The cost of the orange juice concentrate is much less than the freshly squeezed juice and is therefore much more affordable, and the juice can be transported to just about anywhere without being degraded.

'Ah, but it doesn't taste the same as freshly squeezed juice' – and that inevitably is the result of the compression processes we will be looking at. The signal at the end of the signal compression and decompression process is never the same as the original signal; something is lost along the way that cannot be regained, just as with the orange juice. However, it costs less in the end and is a reasonable facsimile of the original for most people. But there should never be any doubt or misunderstanding that a signal that has been compressed, transported and decompressed (reconstituted) can never be as good as the original uncompressed video and audio we started with.

So compression is a necessity if we wish to reduce the amount of power and bandwidth used on the satellite, and hence reduce the cost of the space segment. The use of digital signals is a 'given', for although analog compression has been used historically in television to a degree, digital compression is now far more efficient and cost-effective as it uses technology developed in the computer industry with all the associated efficiencies of scale.

An inevitable result of compression is delay, due to the amount of processing carried out in both the compression and decompression stages. Delay through a compression process is termed 'latency', and latency is of particular concern in SNG, as it can have significant effect on air if not understood and compensated for.

It is at this point that some readers may choose to leave the subject of compression, before we get into some of the scary mathematically based theory. The orange juice analogy serves us well in explaining the concept of compression, and gives everyone the basic understanding of why we need to compress signals in order to transport them. Readers particularly concerned about latency may care to move forward to the section that covers methods of dealing with this. But for those who want to understand more, we move on to the subjects of algorithms, sampling and quantization, types of compression, and how it all works together.

4.2   The language of compression

The word 'algorithm' is often heard in discussion about compression, and this refers to the computational code used to compress or decompress the signal. Any technical discussion of the difference between types of compression (both video and audio) often centers around the algorithms being used. Methods of compression are often referred to as 'compression schemes', and reference is often made to a 'codec' (from enCOder/DECoder), which describes the compression/decompression process.

Let us just review how analog television works. The analog TV signal is made up of lines and fields, which form the scanned elements of the pictures. The number of lines varies according to the TV standard, and is either 625 lines per picture in the standard definition (SD) PAL color TV standard found in Europe, Australia, much of Asia, Africa and South America, or 525 lines in the NTSC standard (used in North America and Japan). A picture is referred to as a 'frame', and there are 2 'fields' in every frame. The field rate also varies, and is either 50 fields per second (25 frames per second) or 60 fields per second (30 frames per second). Although these rates are not necessarily tied exclusively to either PAL or NTSC color standards, the line/field rates are generally 625/50 for PAL and 525/60 for NTSC. The analog TV signal has timing pulses that occur at the start of every line and every field, and these are included in lines that are 'inactive' (i.e. they do not carry any picture information). The number of 'active' picture lines varies according to the standard – 486 of the 525 in NTSC, and 576 of the 625 for PAL.

In digital video compression, each frame of the television picture can be considered as being made up of a number of 'pixels', where a pixel is the smallest element that is discernible (quantified) in a picture (think of a pixel as a single tiny tile in a large mosaic). Each pixel is 'sampled', with a 'sample' being an instantaneous measurement of the picture at a particular point in time. With each frame of an SD television picture made up of 525 or 625 lines (depending on the standard used), a picture can be divided up horizontally and vertically into a number of pixels; in a television picture, the vertical pixels correspond with the lines of the television picture. The number of pixels defines the 'resolution' or sharpness of the picture. This is the same as the way a photograph in a newspaper is made up of individual dots of ink – the more dots per millimeter, the greater the resolution or detail of the picture. If a video picture is 'progressively' scanned, each line is scanned in sequence in the frame. If the picture has an 'interlaced' structure, where each pair of television fields is divided into odd- and even-numbered lines for sending in alternate sequence (a historical method of reducing flicker, and also of saving bandwidth), then each row of pixels will be offset by half a pixel width. Figure 4.1 shows the principle of scanning and how the pixel structure in a video picture differs between progressive and interlaced scanning.

Hence, if the picture is broken up into, say, 400 × 300 pixels, the picture would have a 'blocky' look to it. If the picture was to be divided up into double the number of pixels, i.e. 800 × 600 pixels, it would look a lot smoother and sharper. (In fact, 800 × 600 pixels is a common standard for a PC monitor picture.)

Compression processes are also described as being 'symmetrical' or 'asymmetrical'. A symmetrical compression process is where the decompression process is a direct inverse of the compression process in terms of the type and number of stages. There is therefore equal complexity at each end and equal time taken to process the signal. An asymmetrical process is where one part of the process (e.g. the encoding compression process in MPEG-2) is more complex than the decoding decompression process, and hence takes longer. MPEG-4 (particularly AVC) is not currently nearly as asymmetrical as the complexity of the decoder is still approaching the complexity of the encoder.

As we mentioned earlier, the inevitable result of compression, whether video or audio, is latency. There are a series of complex computations carried out in both the compression and decompression processes, and high order compression algorithms such as MPEG-2 and MPEG-4 take longer to be completed than more simple coding algorithms.

4.3   Principles of compression

4.3.1   Digital sampling

A digital signal conveys information as a series of 'on' and 'off' states (analogous to a switch turning a light on and off) which are represented as the numbers '1' and '0', based on the binary number system (Figure 4.2). In a stream of 1 s and 0 s, each 1 and each 0 is termed a 'bit', and a digital signal is defined by the parameter of 'bits'. For instance, as shown in Chapter 2, the signal is transmitted at a certain

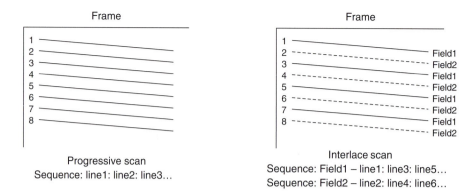

Progressive scan
Sequence: line1: line2: line3…

Interlace scan
Sequence: Field1 – line1: line3: line5…
Sequence: Field2 – line2: line4: line6…

Line structure exaggerated for the purpose of illustration

(a)

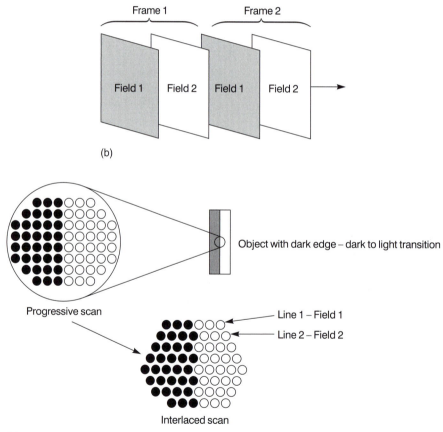

(b)

Object with dark edge – dark to light transition

Progressive scan

Line 1 – Field 1
Line 2 – Field 2

Interlaced scan

(c)

Figure 4.1 (a) Progressive and interlace scan principle (b) interlaced field sequence and (c) pixel structure

Figure 4.2 Binary digital signal

Table 4.1 Relationship between bits and values that can be measured

Bits	Number of steps that can be measured (quantization levels)
1	2
2	4
3	8
4	16
8	256
10	1024
12	4096
14	16 384
16	65 536

speed or 'bit-rate', measured in bits per second (bps). The analog signal is converted to a digital signal by a process called 'sampling'. Sampling is where a signal is instantaneously measured and the value of the signal at that instant is typically converted to a binary number.

The process of sampling is crucial to the quality of the signal that can be conveyed, as the more accurately the binary number obtained from each sample reflects the value of the signal at that instant, the more accurately the original signal can be reproduced.

Therefore, if a signal is sampled at 1 bit per sample, it can only be represented as either nothing or maximum signal, because the sample is either 0 (no signal) or 1 (maximum signal), which cannot accurately represent the signal.

As there is no gradation of the signal between zero and maximum, and as an analog signal can have a very wide range of values between minimum and maximum, more steps are required. Hence, using more bits per sample gives greater accuracy or 'resolution' of the value at the instant of sampling. Table 4.1 shows the relationship between bits and values that can be measured. In Figure 4.3 the process of sampling is shown with 1 bit, 4 bits and 8 bits, and it can be seen that, as the number of bits per sample is increased, the more precise the instantaneous value of the signal becomes.

If 4 bits are used, then a number between 0 and 15 can represent any point on the signal. If 8 bits per sample are used, then it can be represented by a number of steps between 0 and 255. If 10 bits per sample are used, the range is extended to between 0 and 1023 – remembering that the value of '0' counts as 1 step, hence giving us 1024 steps. A step is also referred to as a 'quantization level'.

The other key factor in sampling is how often the sample is taken – termed the 'sampling frequency'. If the signal is sampled at too low a frequency, the samples might be accurate at a particular instant but

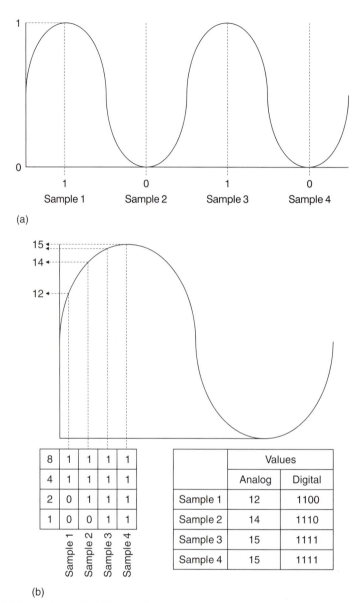

Figure 4.3   (a) 1-bit sampling (b) 4-bit sampling

are not taken closely enough together to be able to accurately reconstruct the signal at the other end of the process. This can lead to the 'blocky' look of a picture, for instance. On the other hand, if the signal is sampled too frequently, the data rate will rise to demand a large amount of bandwidth.

There is therefore a compromise to be made between the minimum number of samples required to convey the information to the brain and the data bandwidth available. The minimum rate is defined by Nyquist's theorem, which states that if a signal is sampled at a rate of just over twice the highest frequency component sine wave contained within, the accumulation of samples thus obtained are sufficient information to reconstruct the signal. If the highest frequency component for a given analog signal

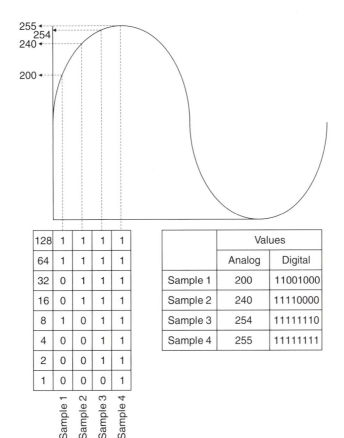

		Values	
		Analog	Digital
Sample 1		200	11001000
Sample 2		240	11110000
Sample 3		254	11111110
Sample 4		255	11111111

(c)

Figure 4.3   (c) 8-bit sampling

is F_{MAX}, then according to Nyquist's theorem, the sampling rate must be at least $2 \times F_{\text{MAX}}$ – or twice the highest analog frequency component.

Once a signal has been digitized, the signal is a bit-stream at a given overall data rate. Within that data stream there will inevitably be sets of data that are repeated, and the repeated sections represent 'redundancy' in the signal. There is also 'irrelevancy' in the data stream; that is data that should be transmitted but does not need to be because it cannot be seen by the human eye or heard by the human ear under normal viewing and listening conditions.

Therefore the aim of any compression system is to remove the *redundancy* and *irrelevancy* in the information signal to minimize the bandwidth or data rate required. There are a number of mathematical analyses of a signal that can be made to determine the redundancy and irrelevancy, depending on the compression process.

4.3.2   *Information reduction*

Before we delve into the relative complexities of compression, mention must be made of an important step that is carried out before any compression process – information reduction. In any information stream, there will be inherently some information that we do not need – information that doesn't need to be compressed because the receiver cannot reproduce it, information that is too 'verbose', or information that was never in the source signal but has been collected along the way – in other words, 'noise', which we covered in Chapter 2.

Of particular concern is noise, which has often crept in through the stages up until compression. Noise (and some interference) is by its very nature random, and as compression processes depend on the signal having degrees of predictability, processing energy is wasted if it is trying to compress noise which is inherently incompressible – so it's best removed at the very beginning. This is achieved by careful filtering of the signal before it enters the compression encoding process, ranging from removing signals that are 'out of band' i.e. beyond the frequency range of the core video and audio frequencies, to noise introduced in dark areas of the picture or silent parts of the audio. There are usually other filtering processes as well – these are just the obvious elements that need to be removed – and applies to elements introduced before analog to digital conversion as well as noise introduced in the digital stages.

The 'cleaner' the signal before compression, the more effectively the compression process can operate, and this follows on to the decompression process as well. Random and unwanted signals are the enemies of compression.

4.3.3   Types of compression

Lossless compression
Fundamentally there are two types of compression, namely 'lossless' and 'lossy'. Lossless compression creates a perfect copy of the original signal when it is decompressed at the end of the signal chain. This type of compression is commonly used in computers to achieve data compression, particularly where even the loss of a single bit would irretrievably corrupt the whole set of data. Hence it is a system that relies on removing as much *redundant* information as possible. Using lossless compression, the maximum data compression ratio that can be achieved for a digital video signal is around 3:1, which is far from the 33:1 or more that is required. Therefore we will concentrate on lossy compression, as this is the method used in SNG (and digital television in general).

Lossy compression
Lossy compression is used in the most prominent video and audio compression schemes, and relies on the fact that the human eye and ear can tolerate some loss of information yet still perceive that a picture or sound is of good or adequate quality – hence it is a system that relies on removing as much *irrelevant* information as possible. For example, PAL, NTSC and SECAM analog television systems are different variations of lossy analog compression, as compromises are made in the amount of color (chrominance) signal transmitted. In addition, the historical practice of 'interlacing' each pair of television fields into a single picture frame is also a method of reducing bandwidth. Each field carries half the information of each frame, so only half the bandwidth of the total picture is required when using interlacing. The reconstruction of each frame of video by combining the two fields back together again in the television receiver relies on a human psycho-visual effect, the persistence of vision. This is further enhanced by the type of device tube used where, once scanned with a field of video, the light output from the 'emitters' which make up the screen takes a while to decay. This applies to traditional CRT (cathode ray tube) displays but to a lesser extent to the latest TFT (Thin Film Transistor) and plasma devices.

Lossy compression depends on human psycho-visual and psycho-acoustic models that describe human sensory perception of sight and sound. Hence, lossy compression is also referred to as 'perceptive' compression, as the result is a picture or a sound that 'tricks' the brain into thinking it sounds and looks like the original. Referring back to the orange juice analogy, we can see that the reconstituted juice is 'perceptively' close to the original.

With the orange juice, we removed the redundant component (water) to achieve the compression. That is the essence of video and audio compression – to remove the redundancy and irrelevancy in the signal. So how do we identify which are the redundant and which are the irrelevant parts of the signal? In any frame of a television picture there are parts of the image that have the same values of brightness and color in particular areas. So, instead of sending a repeating string of numbers that represent individual values of brightness and color in these areas, one string of numbers can be sent that represents the brightness and color of part of an image that is the same.

In 1948, the mathematician Claude Shannon, an expert in information theory, proposed that signals will always have some degree of predictability, and data compression commonly uses the principle of statistical analysis of a signal to predict changes.

Here we step sideways into foreign territory, certainly for many broadcast engineers, the fringes of philosophy and pure mathematics (closely related disciplines). In information theory (a huge subject in its own right), it is said that the degree of unpredictability in a message can be used as a measure of information carried in the message – or in other words, a perfectly predictable message carries no useful information. If we know what the message is going to tell us, we are no better informed once we have received it. A still picture gives us information – send the same still picture again, and we still know no more. But with moving pictures (which is in essence a fast-moving sequence of still frames), after we have received the first picture, the following picture shows us something has changed – we have received useful information that we might not have predicted (this is not strictly true, as we shall see later). The next picture is again different, and again we see that something has changed, and so on...

So it is the unpredictable information in the message that increases our knowledge once we have received it, and this is fundamental to understanding how a message signal that has been compressed, transmitted and decompressed still gives us information (i.e. moving pictures and sound at the receiver). The key is to keep just the right amount of unpredictable information content in the signal, while discarding parts that our brains not really need.

The random or unpredictable information content of a signal is described in Shannon's Theory as 'entropy'- but the author dislikes this word as it is difficult to interpret, therefore instead will generally refer to 'entropy' as 'unpredictability'.

Hence in a lossless compression scheme all the unpredictability is maintained within the compressed signal. In a lossy compression scheme, some of the unpredictability is lost to gain further reductions in data rate and bandwidth, and the system relies on the fallibility of the human senses not to notice the loss.

We will look at the fundamentals of video compression and audio compression separately, as although some of the techniques used are common, it is easier to understand the different processes if we treat them separately. The standards used in SNG signal compression integrate both the audio and video into a single multiplexed signal.

4.4 Video compression

Compression schemes are devised for much wider application than simply that of data transmission through communications channels. Therefore, although a certain type of compression scheme could be used, for example, for SNG, it might not be suitable for picture manipulation. Due to the economies of scale in commercial manufacturing, the most flexible type of compression standard, which can be used for the greatest number of applications, is the one that will gain the widest acceptance.

The simplest form of compression would consist of simply looking at the difference between two frames and then sending only the information that describes the difference. This is called 'differential' coding. The disadvantage of this would be that if the first frame is lost, or the sequence is interrupted in any way, the signal is irrecoverable, as the very first frame is the reference frame and without that, no sense could be made of the following frames. Another disadvantage of differential compression is that it cannot be easily edited, which is a frequent requirement in manipulating compressed video signals for broadcast. Therefore, there has to be a more sophisticated way of compressing the video information.

The next form of compression would be simply looking for redundancy within each single frame and sending such frames in a continuous sequence. Two kinds of redundancy, spectral and spatial, can be handled inside each frame without reference to any other frame. Compression techniques based on these types of redundancy are therefore called 'intra-frame coding'. Intra-frame coding techniques can be applied to a single frame of a moving picture (or to a single still image).

The higher forms of compression use the most complex algorithms, which also attempt closely to predict data for any objects that have moved between one frame and the next. This is called 'motion estimation' and is the most taxing aspect of video compression, as it demands the greatest computational power. Video compression uses inter-coding (between frame), intra-coding (within frame) or a combination of both, depending on the standard.

We will initially focus on the compression algorithm based on what is known as the Discrete Cosine Transform (DCT) method – this is used in MPEG-1, MPEG-2, MPEG-4 and VC-1 but there are other compression algorithms being utilized for video and audio, including methods based on 'wavelets'.

There are currently five principal compression standards that can be used in SNG, although as said earlier, MPEG-2 is still currently the pre-eminent standard. The standards are:

- ITU (International Telecommunications Union – see Chapter 6) H.261/H.263/H.263+
- MPEG-2 (H.262)
- MPEG-4
- MPEG-4 AVC/H.264
- Windows Media Video 9 (VC-1)

These standards are interrelated, with methods and technologies elaborately intertwined, as historically MPEG-1 (the forerunner to MPEG-2) was derived from H.261. H.263 then followed, based on H.261 and MPEG-1, and then adding some enhancements of its own (H.263+). On the other hand, MPEG has some enhancements not found in H.261 or H.263. MPEG-4 is a further derivative of MPEG-2.

MPEG supports a range of frame sizes and frame rates, though in some standards e.g. MPEG-2 the most common standard definition is 720×486 pixels at 30 fps (720×576 pixels at 25 fps), while in others e.g. MPEG-4 there is as yet no common commonly used definitions.

Video-conferencing using H.261 supports Quarter Common Intermediate Format (QCIF) at 176×144 pixels and Common Intermediate Format (CIF) at 352×240 pixels, at frame rates of 7.5–30 fps. H.263 adds a smaller size (128×96 pixels) and larger sizes (704×576 and 1408×1152 pixels).

In case you wondered what happened to MPEG-3, it was originally intended to cover high-definition (HD) video standards, but MPEG-2 was found to be perfectly adequate at the time after some further development. The MPEG-3 project was subsequently abandoned, but the early work became part of the subsequent MPEG-4, originally developed primarily for very low bit-rate devices, but subsequently adapted to meet the demands of HD.

Although in this chapter we will look at some of the standards listed above, we have largely focused on MPEG-2, as this has now become the de facto standard for the vast majority of SNG transmissions.

4.5   MPEG: a brief history

The acronym MPEG stands for Motion Picture Experts Group, established in 1988, again under the auspices of the ISO (International Standards Organization) and the IEC (International Electotechnical Commission), to develop digital compression standards for video and audio material. Its work is not exclusively within the field of broadcasting – its remit is much wider than that, and works on standards that can be used with mobile phones to the Internet to HDTV.

The first project for MPEG was the development of a compression standard that could be used with new computer storage media such as CD-ROM and interactive CD (CD-i) formats, and was published in 1993 as the MPEG-1 standard.[8] This allowed video and audio compression coding up to around 1.5 Mbps, with a video data rate of approximately 1.3 Mbps and audio typically at less than 0.3 Mbps; and in terms of overall quality it approximated to pictures on the VHS tape format.

MPEG-1 was originally optimized to work at video resolutions of 352×240 pixels at 30 fps (NTSC) and 352×288 pixels at 25 fps (PAL). This is referred to as 'source input format' (SIF) and is comparable to the CIF standard used in video-conferencing (see Chapter 6). MPEG-1 has no direct provision for interlaced video applications, such as those used in broadcast television, and its use with interlaced television signals was contingent on a certain amount of pre-processing.

As a computer standard, MPEG-1 suffered slow acceptance because at the time it was introduced the PCs that were available were not fast enough to decode the 25 or 30 frames per second display rate. Once processors for PCs became fast enough to cope with this demand, MPEG-1 was used for a multitude of applications, from Internet video streaming to use in satellite newsgathering via Inmarsat (see Chapter 6).

MPEG standards, and particularly MPEG-2, are truly global standards, used in a very wide variety of applications from computers to HDTV, with a range of bit-rates from 2 to 80 Mbps. MPEG-2 has an architecture to support this range, as we shall see later.

The MPEG standards define the way the audio and video are compressed and then interleaved for playback – and this is the key point. MPEG standards do not define how the signal should be encoded, but how the signal must be decoded. This is a subtle shift in the normal process of standardization, where the defining standard normally sets the originating process, which then dictates how a signal is subsequently dealt with.

Up until the introduction of MPEG-4, MPEG streams were backward-compatible, i.e. a valid MPEG-1 bit-stream is also a valid MPEG-2 bit-stream. Particular characteristics of all MPEG bit-streams are that they are variable bit-rate and randomly accessible (this second factor is particularly important in post-production, as an MPEG bit-stream can begin playing at any point). However, as noted in Chapter 2, we will focus on constant bit-rate (CBR) signals as these are universally used in SNG.

All MPEG specifications are split into at least four parts: systems, video, audio and conformance testing. We will focus only on video and audio, which are Parts 2 and 3 respectively of the MPEG standards (in MPEG-4, Part 2 is referred to as Visual).

Although much of the rest of this chapter relates to MPEG-2, the concepts covered are also relevant to MPEG-4 and VC-1, which will eventually replace MPEG-2 for SNG (contribution) and DTH (distribution) transmissions generally.

4.6   MPEG-2

4.6.1   The MPEG-2 standard

Work on MPEG-2 began in 1991, with the MPEG-2 standard finally published in 1995 by ISO/IEC, and it was intended for the new era of digital television broadcasting. Later the same year the ITU both adopted the standard,[10] and hence MPEG-2 equipment began to be developed and manufactured. Within a few years it became the de facto standard for the delivery of broadcast video and audio programs.

In contribution it succeeded the now defunct '8 Mbps ETSI' standard originally used in Europe for digital SNG from 1994. MPEG-2 is a multi-part standard, consisting of a 'toolbox' of 10 sections, with different services for different applications.

MPEG-2 deals with issues not covered by MPEG-1 – in particular the efficient coding of interlaced video and the principle of 'scalability'. As already mentioned, MPEG-2 has an architecture to support a wide range of picture quality and data rates, which we will look at in more detail later in the chapter.

It is important to note that the MPEG-2 standard only defines the decoding process and the syntax and structure of the received data stream. This has given manufacturers great scope to develop encoding algorithms which can be optimized to perform particular tasks very well, and other not so well. So while one encoder may be optimized to handle pictures with minimum delay, another may be optimized to deal with high data rates for HDTV.

Unlike MPEG-1, which only has non-interlaced frames, MPEG-2 can deal with interlaced video frames. As we discussed earlier in the chapter, interlacing the frames has the effect of splitting each frame into two fields, such that half the picture is displayed at a time. Thus, 25/30 frames per second is displayed as 50/60 fields per second. MPEG-2 processes fields and performs all the functions on each field rather than each frame as in MPEG-1.

The concepts described are not unique to MPEG-2, and apply to a number of compression systems. The reason why video compression works so well is that there is a high level of redundancy and irrelevancy with respect to the video data, due to the way the human psycho-visual system operates. There are three types of redundancy in video: spectral, spatial and temporal.

4.6.2 Spectral redundancy

The analog SD television signal that is transmitted to the viewer is termed 'composite', as it combines the luminance, color and timing (synchronization) signals into one combined signal. The synchronization signals are required to ensure that the receiver displays the lines and fields that make up the whole picture correctly (historically this was particularly important for analog television receivers that used CRT displays). However, if the luminance and color information in the signal is processed separately, before being combined into a composite signal, there is greater opportunity to exploit the redundancy of information in the color elements of the signal.

Earlier we mentioned the ability to fool the human brain into thinking it is seeing a true representation of the original picture. This extends to how the brain is able to distinguish the brightness (luminance) and color (chrominance) detail of a picture. The human eye, as the visual sensory receptor of the brain, is much better able to distinguish brightness differences than color differences. This can be used to advantage in conveying color information, as there is less precision required – a higher level of precision would be 'wasted' as the brain is unable to make use of the additional information and distinguish the difference. When digitizing a video signal, fewer samples are required to convey the color information, and fewer samples means less bandwidth. Typically, for every two luminance samples there is only one chrominance sample required.

Let's just briefly look at the way the luminance and chrominance information is conveyed to the brain. The eye registers the amount of light coming from a scene, and visible light is made up of differing amounts of the three primary colors of red, green and blue. In terms of television, white is made up of 30% red signal, 59% green and 11% blue.

As with many aspects of television technology, the method of transmitting a color signal is a compromise. Back in the 1950s and 1960s when color television was being introduced, both the American

(NTSC) and European (PAL) color systems had to be able to produce a satisfactory monochrome signal on the existing monochrome television sets. Therefore, both color systems derive a composite luminance signal from 'matrixing' the red, blue and green signals. The matrix also produces color 'difference' signals, which when transmitted are disregarded by the monochrome receivers, but form the color components in color television receivers by re-matrixing with the luminance signal.

Why produce color difference signals? Why not simply transmit the red, green and blue signals individually? Again, this is a demonstration of the earlier use of compression in the analog domain. Individual color signals would each require full bandwidth and as a video signal requires 5 MHz of bandwidth, the three color signals would require 15 MHz in total.

On the other hand, by relying on the relatively poor color perception of the human brain, the color signals could be reduced in bandwidth so that the entire luminance and chrominance signal would fit into 5 MHz of bandwidth – a reduction of 3:1. This was achieved by the use of color difference signals – known as the 'red difference' signal (C_r) and the 'blue difference' signal (C_b) – which were essentially signals representing the difference in brightness between the luminance and the respective color signal. The eye is more sensitive to changes in luminance than in chrominance, i.e. it can more easily see an error when a pixel is too bright or too dark, rather than if it has too much red, blue or green.

Bright pixels tend to be bright in all three colors, red, green and blue, and therefore there is said to be 'spectral' redundancy (relating to the similarity between color values at any one point in the picture). Therefore, the difference in levels of the red and blue signals will be relatively small, so sending only the difference between the color signals and the luminance signal saves some data. The green signal can be reconstructed by deduction from the values of luminance and the color difference signals.

Hence video presented as three separate signals – a luminance and two color difference signals – is termed 'component' video, as opposed to composite video which has all the luminance and chrominance information combined into a single signal (along with the picture synchronization information).

So for historical reasons we have ended up with this convention of conveying chrominance separately from the luminance information, and this was compression in the analog domain. This efficiency can also be used in the digital domain. Having maximized the compression by determining the redundancy in the chrominance signal (and processing the chrominance components to remove spectral redundancy is often referred to as 'sub-sampling'), the signal has to be checked for further redundant information that can be removed to reduce the data rate drastically.

Spectral redundancy is already a feature of analog television, so in the digital domain the removal of further redundant information is carried out in two dimensions within each frame of picture, described as 'spatial' redundancy, and between successive frames, described as 'temporal' redundancy.

4.6.3 Spatial redundancy

Spatial redundancy is the relationship each pixel has with the neighboring pixels: more often than not, two neighboring pixels will have very nearly the same luminance and chrominance values. If they do not, then this represents fine detail (high spatial frequency).

Consider one frame of a picture signal. Suppose that within this frame there is a notable area of the picture that has either the same color or brightness content, or both. The samples of luminance and/or chrominance would sequentially be the same across this area, and therefore instead of sending the same numbers for each sample, one number could be identified as applying to a number of sample points in an area where the information content remains the same. Hence we have found some spatial redundancy, and this reduces the amount of data that has to be sent. Spatial redundancy can therefore be exploited by using 'intra' ('within') coding, where compression is achieved by reducing within a single frame the amount of information that needs to be sent. Because intra coding happens within each single frame, with no reference to what has come before or what follows, it is used as the basis for compression of still pictures.

4.6.4 Temporal redundancy

Temporal redundancy is the relationship between video frames. If consecutive video frames were not similar to the previous frames, there would be no sense of motion. Having said that, objects that move between one frame and the next often do not significantly change shape, for example, so there is some redundancy in the data from one frame to the next that can be removed.

Consider two frames of a picture signal. In the first frame, there is an object that is also present in the second frame; for example, let us presume that the first frame has a building in it. Unless there is a shot change or a rapid camera pan, the building will be present in the next frame (though not necessarily in the same position if the camera has moved slightly). The data block that contained the information on the building in the first frame could therefore be repeated in the second frame. This is termed 'temporal redundancy'. In fact, most pictures shot in a single sequence are remarkably similar from one frame to the next, even in a moderately quickly moving sequence – only 1/25 (PAL) or 1/30 (NTSC) second has elapsed. Therefore there is a significant scope for data reduction by simply re-using sets of data sent for the previous frame, albeit that the blocks of data may have to be mapped to a different position in the frame. Coding in this manner is described as 'inter' ('between') coding, and is dependent on what has occurred before to make use of the redundancy.

4.6.5 Sampling rates

Broadcast video is typically sampled at 8 or 10 bit accuracy, meaning that each sample can have a value of up to 255 or 1023 respectively, depending on the amplitude of the analog signal at that instant. As each sample represents a pixel, there are separate streams of samples for the luminance and for each of the chrominance difference signals.

The original standard for digital video was published as the European standard CCIR Recommendation 601. This now defunct CCIR standard was subsequently adopted by the ITU as Recommendation ITU-R BT.601 and a further standard dealing with digital video interfacing, Recommendation ITU-R BT.656, was published. These were also published in the US as SMPTE 125M[3] and SMPTE 259M[4] respectively. In general, 'standard definition' (SD) digital video at broadcast quality is loosely referred to as '601' video. In ITU-601, an uncompressed digital video signal has a data rate of 216 Mbps (sampled at 8 bits per sample) or 270 Mbps (sampled at 10 bits per sample). The choice between using 8 or 10 bits depends on the application; the original recommendation for ITU-601 was only for 8 bits, but some production systems required higher resolution for picture manipulation, and ITU-601 was subsequently revised to include 10-bit sampling. Readers should note that sometimes this standard is incorrectly referred to as 'D1', after the uncompressed tape format developed by Sony in the 1980s. The ITU-601 signal at 270 Mbps is over 33 times the data rate of the typical 8 Mbps SNG signal. A data rate of 270 Mbps, modulated in the same way as the typical 8 Mbps SNG signal, would require over 250 MHz of bandwidth. It is not feasible to allocate this amount of bandwidth on commercial satellite systems (although this capacity is available on wideband fiber-optic routes at a price).

The data rates are derived as shown in Appendix C. The specification of the number of pixels and hence the sampling rates is based on the use of multiples of a fundamental frequency of 3.375 MHz (which represents '1' in the sampling rates), which is based on a commonality of certain fundamental frequencies between 525 and 625-line systems. Notice that there is one luminance signal and two chrominance signals in the result. The chrominance signals are sampled at half the rate of the luminance

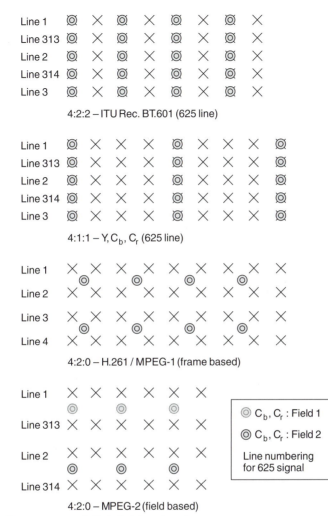

Figure 4.4 Sampling structure of digital video signals

signal; so for every four luminance samples, there are two red difference signal samples and two blue difference samples i.e. C_b and C_r are sampled only on odd-numbered pixel columns. This is termed a '4:2:2' signal and is shown in Figure 4.4.

In 4:2:2 the chrominance signals have been sampled at half the luminance rate in the horizontal (line) dimension, but vertically they have been sampled at the same rate. Because of what we said earlier about the brain's poor ability to discern detailed changes in chrominance, in a compression environment additional saving in bandwidth can be achieved by sampling the chrominance at only half the rate in the vertical dimension as well as the horizontal. Because a picture is made up of two fields, the chrominance samples can occur at half the vertical rate on each field. As each field is offset by a line (a feature of interlace), the chrominance samples 'lineup' when viewed over the period of two fields, i.e. a whole frame. This creates a picture that has chrominance sampled at half the rate relative to luminance in both the horizontal and vertical dimensions i.e. chrominance sampling is averaged over two fields. When the signal is sampled in this way, it is termed a '4:2:0' signal (Figure 4.4), and this is commonly the mode for digital TV broadcasts, whether by satellite or terrestrially.

We have shown how the data rate for video is 270 Mbps. In fact, because we do not need to fully digitize the complex analog timing and synchronization information (the 'verbose' information referred to earlier), the actual active video data rate is lower. The active video is the part of the video signal that describes the image, in other words it is the video signal excluding the 'vertical blanking interval' and the 'horizontal blanking interval', which contain the timing and synchronization information for the television display. For modern TV receivers, which are fundamentally digital processing devices, the timing information required is much simplified and hence requires far fewer bits.

Consequently, as shown in Appendix C, the actual active video data rate is lower – 166 or 168 Mbps according to the standard. However, the reduction in the data rate to 166/168 Mbps by only encoding the active picture is still not enough (over 20:1), and the need for compression obviously still exists. (The same is true of 4:2:0 coding at 124/126 Mbps.)

4.6.6   Discrete Cosine Transform (DCT)

As we said earlier, we are going to focus on DCT as it is the compression algorithm used in MPEG-2, MPEG-4, and VC-1, the three main broadcast video compression processes at the time of writing. DCT is a complex subject, and as with many other topics covered in the book, the following is a simplified explanation to give the reader a broad basic understanding. For those who want to delve more deeply into the mathematical basis, there are a wide range of textbooks on the subject.

In general, adjacent pixels within an image tend to be similar and this can be exploited to eliminate redundancy. There are a number of mathematical analyses of a signal that can be made to determine the redundancy, but the one most commonly used in video compression is the discrete cosine transform (DCT). DCT is a specific implementation of a mathematical process called a Fourier transform, in which a signal is represented as a sum of a number of different frequency sinusoidal waves. The discrete cosine transform expresses an image block as a weighted sum of 'basis functions' that represent various horizontal and vertical spatial frequencies.

According to Fourier's theorem, any complex signal can be broken down into a number of parts of sine waves of different frequencies. Any cycle of the target signal can be selected and considered to be one cycle of a periodic (repeating) waveform where the fundamental frequency is represented by a sine wave of that wavelength. If the selected cycle is not itself a sine wave, then there are other sine waves making up the sum, which are all multiples of the fundamental frequency.

The intra-frame coding technique that takes advantage of spatial redundancy is based on DCT, which represents a waveform as a sequence of numbers.

Mathematically speaking, the image is transformed from its spatial representation to its 'frequential' (frequency) equivalent. In other words, instead of looking at the image as a freeze-frame of a scene within a space, the image is analyzed by looking at how individual objects appear in terms of their detail, or frequency. Each element in the picture is represented by certain frequency 'coefficients'. A coefficient is a mathematical term for a number with a particular algebraic significance. Any number of coefficients can be used, but it has been determined that using a block of 64 coefficients, as shown in Figure 4.5, most picture information can be adequately analyzed in both the horizontal and vertical planes. As the sequence becomes closer to an actual cosine wave, then a single coefficient becomes very large and the remainder of the coefficients becomes smaller.

Most of the energy in an image is contained in the low-frequency coefficients: these are objects with large surfaces such as sky, walls or expanses of ground, and are the parts of the image that the human eye focuses primarily on, because of the energy concentrated in this area. Detail in an image is

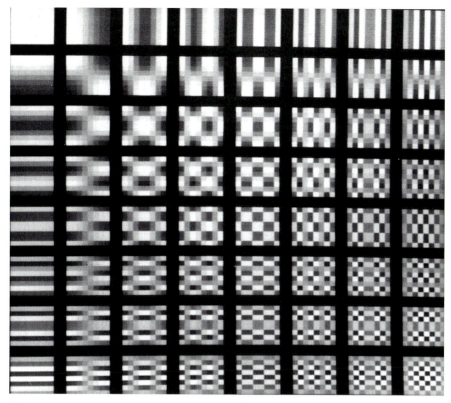

(a)

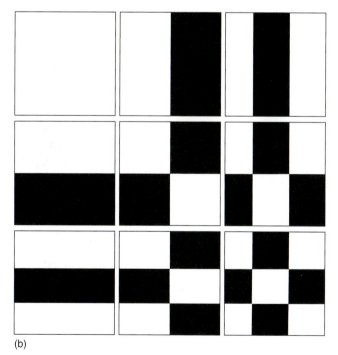

(b)

Figure 4.5 (a) DCT frequency Coefficients (Reproduced with permission from Watkinson, J. (1999) MPEG-2 Focal Press) (b) Simplified DCT coefficients

expressed by the high-frequency coefficients: these are objects with fine detail, such as hair, grass, leaves and tree branches. Interestingly, the low-frequency coefficients contain more information (unpredictability) than the high-frequency ones.

Each pixel has a value describing the 'amount' of horizontal and vertical frequencies corresponding to one of these 64 steps. In the DCT process, blocks of 8 pixels horizontally by 8 pixels vertically are converted to a set of frequency coefficients that describe that block. The block can be 'decomposed' into a set of coefficients from the 64 'basis functions', each of which contain 'pure' signals of specific horizontal and vertical spatial frequencies. The function of the DCT is to describe how much of each basis function is present in the block. From this is obtained the resulting multipliers for each basis function, known as DCT coefficients.

As a sequence becomes closer to an actual cosine wave, then a single coefficient becomes very large and the remainder of the coefficients have smaller values. Thus each 8×8 pixel data block can be described by an amount of each of the 64 frequency coefficients (as shown in Figure 4.5). The very first value in the top left, which is the most important, describes the average brightness of the whole 8×8 pixel block (widely termed the 'DC coefficient', but perhaps better described as the 'zero-spatial-frequency coefficient'). It is important to remember that this is a value for the *average* brightness of the whole block.

The coefficients to the right of the DC coefficient (or reference point) are the increasingly higher horizontal spatial frequencies. The coefficients that are below the DC reference point are increasingly higher vertical spatial frequencies, and therefore looking below and to the right see increasingly higher coefficients (sometimes referred to as the AC coefficients) in each of the horizontal and vertical planes. Each pixel's DCT coefficient is calculated from all other pixel values in the block, so using an 8×8 block saves time, and the smaller the difference between one pixel and its adjacent pixels, the smaller its DCT value. The larger coefficient values describe the lower-frequency elements of the 8×8 pixel block, because of the importance to the brain of low-frequency information. The high-frequency coefficients tend to have values towards zero, as there is usually less information at these frequencies in most frames, and this information is least useful to the brain.

It is important to note that the DCT process (and the following quantization process) is carried out separately on 8×8 pixel blocks in the luminance (Y), red difference (Cr) and the blue difference signals (Cb), producing blocks of samples for each.

At the decoder, an inverse DCT process is applied and the actual DCT process is essentially lossless. However, there is information loss because of the quantization stage that occurs next. The complexity of the DCT process is such that we cannot further describe it here without delving deeper into mathematics, but hopefully you have grasped the basic principles.

4.6.7 Quantization

It is in the quantization stage that the significant part of the compression process occurs. As we have seen, the signal has been digitized into a series of samples, and the DCT process has converted this stream of samples into a set of frequency coefficients. Quantization is used to assign a specific number of bits (resolution) to each frequency coefficient it rounds the transform coefficients to the appropriate precision.

Each 8×8 pixel data block is compressed by assigning fewer bits to the high-frequency coefficients (remembering that we have said that higher-frequency information is less obvious to the viewer). This process does discernibly affect the overall quality of the picture and it is a lossy process, i.e. the information that is lost cannot be reconstructed at a later stage. There may also be a decision-making process within the encoder that reduces the high-frequency (near-zero) coefficients to zero – this is one of the characteristics that can differentiate between one manufacturer's encoder and another.

Some blocks of pixels need to be coded more accurately than others. For example, blocks with smooth intensity gradients need accurate coding to avoid visible block boundaries. This is termed de-blocking filtering. To deal with this inequality between blocks, the algorithm may allow the amount of quantization to be modified for certain blocks of pixels.

4.6.8   Variable length coding

Following quantization, there is a final process of manipulation of the bit-stream called 'variable length coding' (VLC), where further efficiencies are used to reduce the amount of data transmitted while maintaining the level of information. To use a fixed length code in which small numbers are prefixed with many zeros is not desirable, so with variable length coding, the aim is to send the minimum number of bits. Variable length codes are thus devised such that the source values that need to be sent most often use fewer bits in transmission, and values that are sent on only a few occasions use codes that have many bits.

To help understand this principle, let us recall from Chapter 1 the achievements of Samuel Morse with his invention of 1837. Morse code is a classic example of variable length coding, with sequences of dots and dashes making up each word depending on the letters in the word, and the number of dots and dashes for each letter depending on how common the letter is in the English language. Incidentally, Morse code is the only digital modulation system designed to be easily read by humans without a computer.

Morse looked at each letter of the English alphabet, and calculated how often each letter occurred in common pieces of text that would be sent as messages. Not surprisingly, he found the letter e is the most common in the English language, so he gave it just one 'dot' (1 bit) – which is very brief. The next most common letter was the letter 't', so he gave that one 'dash' (1 bit) – also brief, but clearly distinguishable from a dot. The whole alphabet is thus reduced sequences of dots and dashes, the length of each sequence depending on how commonly the letter occurs in English. The longest codes are for punctuation, which have six 'bits', but then these occur very infrequently in the average message. Therefore the length of the transmitted string makes the most economic use of the operator's time in sending it.

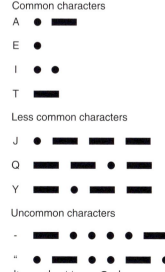

Figure 4.6   Early variable length coding – the Morse Code

Variable length coding therefore distinguishes between short runs of zeros, which are more likely than long ones, and small coefficient values, which are more likely than large values. 'Code words' are allocated which have different lengths depending upon the probability with which they are expected to occur. The values are looked up in a fixed table of 'variable length codes', where the most probable (frequent) occurrence of coefficient values is given in a relatively short 'code word', and the least probable (infrequent) occurrence is given a relatively long code word. The process is also known as 'entropy coding' – 'unpredictability coding' in our sense.

So returning to our sequence of quantized DCT frequency coefficients, the very first value read out is the DC coefficient (the average brightness of the whole block). The rest of the coefficients describe the amount of horizontal and vertical, and coarse and fine detail in the block. The resulting block has groupings of coefficient values interspersed with zero values, many of which often tend to have a predictable pattern. These are re-ordered into a form that is easier to manipulate. Starting with the first coefficient, which has the largest value (as it represents the average brightness of the whole frame), the coefficients are 'read out' out of the 8 × 8 pixel data block in a zig-zag sequence, as shown in Figure 4.6. When only zeros are left to be sent, an 'end of block' code is sent instead that includes a single number that gives the count of the zeros in the sequence instead of listing them. The aim is to maximize the likelihood of a run of zeros or a run of low-value coefficients – this is termed 'run length coding'.

There are therefore two types of data compression occurring in variable length coding. Firstly, the translation of patterns of the significant value coefficients (i.e. those that describe low-frequency information and which have some predictability) have been converted into short codes, which achieves a saving in the amount of data sent. Secondly, the sequence of zeros has been shortened to a single number describing how many zero values there are, rather than sending a string of consecutive zero values.

As with the DCT process, this has been much simplified to enable you to gain some insight into the process, and any further explanation would take us deeper into the realms of mathematics. As we shall see later, a typical frame is sampled in 4:2:2 SD broadcast quality video as 720 × 576 pixel resolution. In either 1/25 or 1/30 of a second, this results in 6480 of these 8 × 8 pixel blocks being processed for luminance, and 3240 pixel blocks for each of the two chrominance signals (as these are at half the resolution and therefore sampled at half-rate). There is a total of around 830 000 samples per frame with 4:2:2 sampling, to which the DCT, quantization and variable length coding processes are applied between 25 and 30 times per second. This plainly takes a phenomenal amount of processing speed and power.

4.6.9 Composition of the bit-stream

The composition of the bit-stream has a hierarchy, which occurs in the following order (Figure 4.7):

- Group of pictures: a particular sequence of pictures
- Picture: a frame of information of a particular type (I, P or B)
- Slice: a string of 'macroblocks' across the picture
- Macroblock: made up of a group of blocks
- Block: made up of a group of pixels

In digital video compression, using three types of information frames within a sequence reduces redundancy. The sequence forms the 'group of pictures' (GOP).

I-frames (Intra-coded frames) must be used at the beginning of any video sequence. An I-frame completely describes the picture and only has compression applied within (intra) the frame, and has no dependence on any frames before or after. I-frames are essential at the beginning of a GOP, and must occur regularly, otherwise errors occurring in a predicted frame will progressively worsen. For the

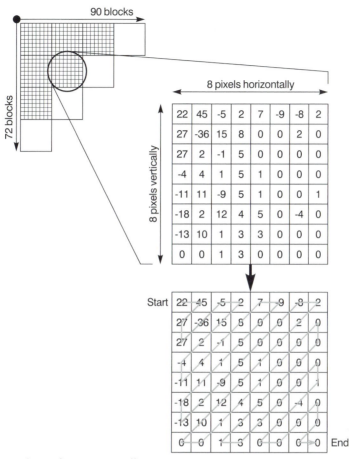

Figure 4.7 Quantized DCT frequency coefficients and processing

purpose of production processes, the I-frame also allows random access, but in a transmission chain, such as an SNG path, this is not of any significance. The I-frame can also constitute a reference frame, necessary for acting as an 'anchor' in the sequence used to predict B-frames.

P-frame (Predicted frame) is encoded using forward motion prediction. The P-frame is calculated by applying motion prediction to a previous frame (which has been stored in the encoder) and deriving a difference signal (inter-coding). From this it can be seen that an MPEG encoder contains internal decoders as it performs an iterative process to derive data for processing. A P-frame is forward predicted from the last I-frame or P-frame, i.e. it is impossible to reconstruct it without the data of another I- or P-frame. The P-frame is also an anchor frame, necessary for acting as a reference frame to predict B-frames.

B-frame (Bi-directional [predicted] frame) is encoded as a combination of forward and backward motion prediction information. Therefore, the use of B-frames implies out-of-order encoding, as the encoder can only encode a B-frame after encoding the requisite previous and future frames. We will consider this shortly when we examine the coding and transmission ordering of frames (Figure 4.8).

A B-frame can be considered as the average of two P-frames – one which has already been encoded and sent (i.e. in the past) and one that has been encoded but not yet sent (i.e. in the future) – used as predictors for the current input frame to be processed. B-frames are useful, for instance, when objects in a

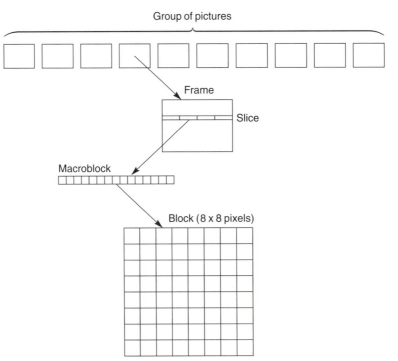

Figure 4.8 Bit stream hierarchy

picture alter during a sequence. A B-frame yields much better compression than a P-frame which, in turn, yields much better compression than an I-frame. This is because B-frames take advantage of maximum temporal redundancy, while I-frames cannot take advantage of any temporal redundancy. Generally speaking in terms of data, a B-frame can be about one-third the size of a P-frame.

Quality can also be improved in the case of moving objects that reveal hidden areas within a video sequence. Backward prediction in this case allows the encoder to make decisions that are more 'intelligent' on how to encode the video within these areas. Also, since B-frames are not used to predict future frames, errors generated will not be propagated further within the sequence. B-frames, while enabling the highest level of compression, have the disadvantage that a future frame must be decoded before the present frame, a process that introduces further delay.

4.6.10 GOP sequences

A Group of Picture (GOP) sequence contains a combination of I-, B- and P-frames. Some compression algorithms (e.g. MPEG) enable the encoder to choose the frequency and location of I-frames. This choice is based on the application's need for random accessibility and the location of scene cuts in the video sequence. For instance, in post-production where random access is important, I-pictures are typically every frame. The number of B-pictures between any pair of reference (I- or P-) frames can also vary. For example, many scenes have two B-frames separating successive reference frames (I,B,B,P,B,B,P).

An example of a typical GOP is shown in Figure 4.9, where there is a repeating sequence of 12 frames, beginning with the I-frame. The sequence runs I,B,B,P,B,B,P,B,B,P,B,B and then repeats with the next I-frame. We have already seen that a B-frame is encoded as a combination of forward and backward motion prediction information, but it is difficult to see from the above sequence how use can be

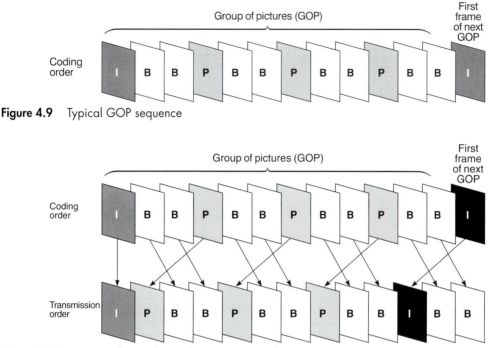

Figure 4.9   Typical GOP sequence

Figure 4.10   GOP coding order and transmission order

made of a B-frame. The secret is that, although the sequence is encoded as above, it is actually transmitted in a different order. There is a 'coding order' and a 'transmission order', and in Figure 4.10 the coding and transmission ordering difference is shown.

It can be seen that the first P-frame in the sequence is sent before the first pair of B-frames, as the B-frame information cannot be used before the P-frame to which it is linked has been decoded. Backward prediction requires that the future frames that are to be used for backward prediction be encoded and transmitted first, out of order. This picture 'shuffling' in the transmission adds delay to the overall codec process and therefore increases the latency, which as we have already discussed is particularly undesirable for live 'two-way' interviews in news broadcasts.

It also results in both the encoder and the decoder requiring increased amounts of memory ('buffers'). In the coder this is to store these frames after coding so that they are available for transmission as and when required, and in the decoder so that frames can be stored until they are required to reconstruct the coding sequence. This increases the complexity and cost of the equipment.

4.6.11   Motion prediction

The movement of objects over a period of time is represented in a frame structure by a part of the picture being in a different place from the previous picture, and in a different place again in the next picture. A frame is selected as a reference, and subsequent frames are predicted from the reference using a technique known as motion estimation. The process of video compression using motion estimation is also known as inter-frame coding. When using motion estimation, an assumption is made that the objects in the scene have only translational motion. This assumption holds as long as there is no camera pan, zoom, changes in luminance or rotational motion. However, for scene changes, inter-frame coding

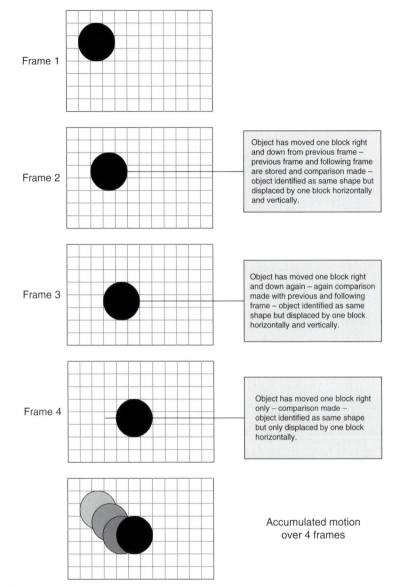

Frame 1

Frame 2

Object has moved one block right
and down from previous frame –
previous frame and following frame
are stored and comparison made –
object identified as same shape but
displaced by one block horizontally
and vertically.

Frame 3

Object has moved one block right
and down again – again comparison
made with previous and following
frame – object identified as same
shape but displaced by one block
horizontally and vertically.

Frame 4

Object has moved one block right
only – comparison made –
object identified as same shape
but only displaced by one block
horizontally.

Accumulated motion
over 4 frames

Figure 4.11 (a) Motion estimation

does not work well, because the temporal correlation between frames from different scenes is low. In these cases, a second compression technique is used, known as intra-frame coding. Intra-frame coding is outside the scope of this chapter.

Generally, an actual object does not change shape radically, if at all, from one frame to the next. It is simply the same object in a different position. In the context of the overall frame rate, the actual shift in position from one frame to the next is not very great, except for very fast-moving objects. Therefore, the block of data that describes that object can be 're-used' from one frame to the next by simply placing it in the new position, as shown in Figure 4.11a, which shows a much simplified sequence of a ball falling from left to right and coming to rest.

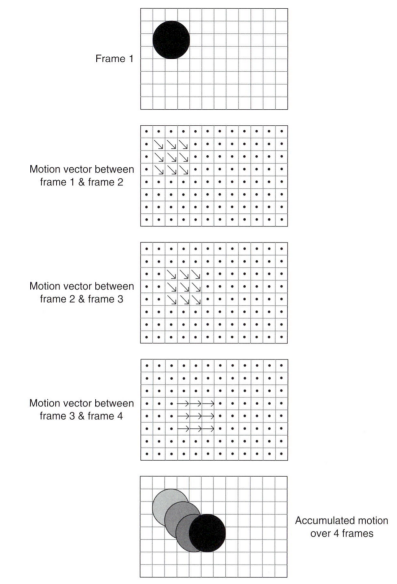

Figure 4.11   (b) Motion vectors

In the encoder a copy of each previous frame is 'held' (stored) while analyzing the current frame for the position of objects 'seen' in the previous frame, and also comparing it with the stored copy of the following frame – hence the encoder is always a number of frames behind in real time as it holds frames from different points in time to make comparison before sending the frames out in the normal correct order. By carrying out some intricate calculations, it is possible to estimate where the position of that object will be in the following frame to quite close accuracy, and to send only the co-ordinates of the new position of the object. This is called 'motion estimation' and this process achieves further compression.

In motion estimation, the offset between the two blocks of data is known as a 'motion vector', which indicates in which direction horizontally and vertically the macroblock must be brought from the next frame so that a match is made. Using our simplified ball sequence, the motion vectors are shown in Figure 4.11b. Motion estimation occurs in both B- and P-frames, and the macroblock structure is used as part of the estimation process for movement. A macroblock is made up of four luminance blocks, each 8 × 8 pixels in dimension (giving a total of 16 × 16 pixels), and again coded based on DCT. The choice of an 8 × 8 block size is a good compromise between the number of unique pieces of information coded and the amount of commonality between pixels within a block.

Each macroblock is compared to a macroblock in the reference frame using some error measure, and the best matching macroblock is selected. The search is conducted over a pre-determined search area. A vector denoting the displacement of the macroblock in the reference frame with respect to the macroblock in the current frame is determined. This vector is known as the 'motion vector'.

Motion estimation is not applied directly to the chrominance data, as it is assumed that the color motion estimation can use the same motion information as the luminance, i.e. the chrominance elements will move in the same manner as the luminance. The error between the current macroblock and the similar macroblock in the previous frame is encoded along with a motion vector for the macroblock. A sequence of macroblocks form a 'slice', and the coding of the slice is used to further reduce redundancy in frames by using differential compression coding within the frame.

The degree and complexity of the motion estimation can vary between different encoder models. Although a full exhaustive search over a wide area of the frame yields the best matching results in most cases, this performance imposes an extreme processing overhead in the encoder. Even if the search area for macroblock matching is limited to a fixed region size around the last known position of the macroblock, this can still very processing-intensive, and so there are a number of other techniques used to try and optimize the search matching process.

During reconstruction, the reference frame is used to predict the current frame using the motion vectors. This technique is known as 'motion compensation'. During motion compensation, the macroblock in the reference frame that is referenced to by the motion vector is copied into the reconstructed frame. Block matching at best can only attain an accuracy of one pixel, and so the other techniques also include sub-pixel interpolation for a better match, and in MPEG-2 the motion compensation target is to achieve a half-pixel resolution.

Motion estimation is the most computationally intensive process of the encoder, and is one of the key measures of its effectiveness.

4.6.12   Profiles and levels

The MPEG-2 standard details many different types of service, classified under 'profiles' and 'levels', which allow 'scaling' of the video. The profile defines the data complexity and the chrominance resolution (or bit-stream scalability), while the level defines the image resolution and the maximum bit-rate per profile: this is illustrated in Table 4.2, which shows the profiles and levels for both HDTV and SD (standard definition) TV.

Simple profile (SP)

The simple profile uses no B-frames, so there is only forward prediction, and consequently there is no re-ordering required for transmission. This profile is suitable for low-delay applications such as video-conferencing, giving a coding delay of less than 150 ms, and where coding is only performed on a 4:2:0 video signal. It is not commonly used in SNG applications.

Table 4.2 MPEG-2 levels: picture size, frame rate and bit-rate

Level	Max. frame width (pixels)	Max. frame height (lines)	Max. frame rate (Hz)	Max. bit rate (Mbps)
Low	352	288	30	4
Main	720	576	30	15
High-1440	1440	1152	60	60
High	1920	1152	60	80

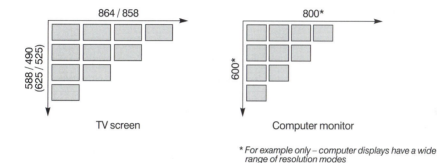

Figure 4.12 Pixel layout difference

Main profile (MP)

The main profile uses B-frames, and is the most widely used profile in both production operations as well as SNG. Although by using B-frames the picture quality is increased, coding delay is added to allow for the frame re-ordering. Main profile decoders will also decode MPEG-1 video, and most MPEG-2 decoders support MP@ML.

MP@ML refers to 720 × 486 pixel resolution video at 30 fps (NTSC) and 720 × 576 pixel resolution video at 25 fps (PAL), both at up to 15 Mbps. These pixel sample specifications are different from the ITU-601 standard shown in Appendix C because the pixel spacing in ITU-601 (a digital television standard only) is different between the vertical and horizontal planes, resulting in 'rectangular' pixels. In computer graphics, the practice has always been to create a symmetrical relationship and therefore equal resolution in both horizontal and vertical planes, giving 'square pixels'. Hence the sample rates in MPEG (which was originally aimed at the computer technologies) have been adjusted from the ITU-601 specification to give the same resolution in both planes. The difference between TV and computer display pixel structures is shown in Figure 4.12.

The coding can either be 4:2:0 MP@ML or 4:2:2 (the 4:2:2 profile is sometimes referred to as 422P@ML, or 4:2:2P), and 4:4:4 for high-quality applications (not SNG). The MPEG-2 macroblock structure used in 4:2:0, 4:2:2 and 4:4:4 is shown in Figure 4.13.

MPEG-2 coding can reduce the 168/166 Mbps uncompressed digital video data rates by a factor of up to around 25:1, using the techniques described, down to about 2–18 Mbps. The current generation of SNG encoders typically offer both 4:2:0 and 4:2:2 sampling. Originally it had been assumed that 4:2:2 sampling always gave inferior results to 4:2:0 for broadcast applications at bit-rates below 10–15 Mbps, particularly after evaluation by the EBU (European Broadcasting Union) and CBC (Canadian Broadcasting Corporation).[11,12] However, subsequent studies[13] indicated that 4:2:2 may always produce

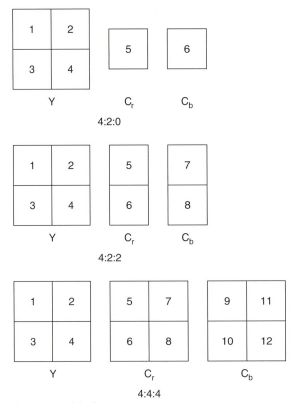

Figure 4.13 Color sampling: macroblock structure

better pictures, certainly down to 4 Mbps for 625-line systems and 2 Mbps for 525-line systems. At much lower bit-rates, the impairments introduced by the MPEG-2 coding and decoding process become increasingly objectionable, and it is generally accepted that MPEG-2 is virtually unusable below 2 Mbps. However, even in the face of these studies, SNG transmissions are still generally in 4:2:0 format.

Up until around 2002, MPEG-2 saw a steady improvement in its implementation in encoders by various manufacturers year on year, but developments have levelled off since then as focus has shifted to the development of MPEG-4.

4.6.13 Artifacts

When pushed to the limit, compression codec processes can produce visual defects, widely referred to as 'compression artifacts', mostly caused by some form of quantization error. These include a 'pixellation' effect commonly referred to as 'blockiness' or 'mosaicing', momentarily showing as rectangular areas of picture with distinct boundaries. The visible blocks may be 8×8 DCT blocks or misplaced macroblocks, perhaps due to the failure of motion prediction or because of transmission path problems. Other artifacts may be seen near the edges of objects, such as 'blurring' caused by reducing horizontal and/or vertical resolution. This is because an edge – which is a sharp transition – can generate frequencies outside the frequency range of the system. To counter this, a process called 'anti-aliasing' may be applied, which removes data at too high a frequency to be reproduced. If such data is left in a signal, it generates artifacts, but if anti-aliasing is applied too aggressively, this can also create artifacts.

Another artifact is 'mosquito noise', where quantizing step changes between scene changes cause errors, seen as a fine patterning of black dots in certain parts of the picture, usually around sharp edges of objects in a scene. However, one of the most frequently seen artifacts in a compressed video signal is chroma quantization error, often obvious on finely gradated areas of color, where there are seen to be distinct transitions (banding or contouring) from one shade to another in the same hue. This is caused by the limitations of the quantization of the chrominance signal.

4.6.14 High-Definition TV (HDTV)

Before we move on, we need to pause to consider the consequence of HDTV, which is becoming an increasingly important issue in SNG at time of writing (2007). Modern HDTV has the advantage of having being conceived in the 1990s as a digital standard from the beginning, and so there are no analog legacy issues to deal with.

There are a number of HDTV standards, but the six most common ones referred to are as follows:

- 720p/60
- 1080p/60
- 1080i/60
- 720p/50
- 1080p/50
- 1080i/50

The nomenclature is as follows. The first number is the number of active lines (i.e. vertical resolution), the 'p' is for progressive scan, and 'i' is for interlaced scan and the 50/60 figure refers to the number of fields per second, depending on the TV standard. Traditionally TV has used interlaced scanning for the reasons given earlier, but it is likely in the future that progressive scanning will become the norm for TV viewing.

Earlier we also referred to HDTV as having 1125 lines – this is the total number of lines in the picture – but only 1080 lines are deemed 'active' lines i.e. those with picture content. It is not within the scope of this book to discuss the relative merits of 720p versus 1080i – there is plenty of material available on the Internet. It seems that 1080i is the most favored standard, but whichever standard is used, there is a significant increase in bandwidth required.

High-Definition TV is also broadcast in a 'widescreen' format of 16:9. Traditional SDTV has a screen format ('aspect ratio') of 4:3 – the ratio of the width of the picture to its height (Figure 4.14). This means that the displayed picture is 4 units wide by 3 units high. (Note that 4:3 is the same as 12:9.)

The origins of the TV picture being this shape allegedly date back to the nineteenth century and the pioneer Thomas Edison when he was working on early cinematography. The cinema film industry used this aspect ratio for decades before they developed a variety of widescreen formats in the 1950s to compete with the rising popularity of television. The widescreen format in television is 16:9 – 16 units wide by 9 units high. The origin of the 16:9 format is that all the widescreen formats in use in the film industry in the 1980s when overlaid on top of each other fall within a rectangle with the ratio of 16:9 – hence it was decided that this should be the standard aspect ratio format for widescreen TV. The 16:9 format is not exclusively in the domain of HDTV – in some countries SDTV is also transmitted in widescreen 16:9 format.

Uncompressed HDTV requires a full transmission data rate of 1.485 Gbps – over 5 times the 270 Mbps data rate of SDI. Using MPEG-2, this can be reduced to the range 19–60 Mbps, depending on the quality required, and a compressed data rate of around 40 Mbps is typically defined as producing results of an acceptable quality. However, 40 Mbps, using QPSK modulation at 3/4 FEC, requires

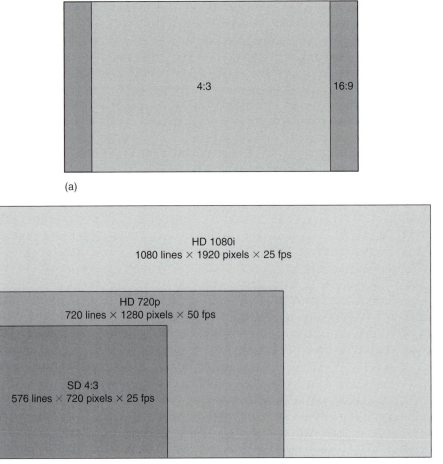

(a)

(b)

Figure 4.14 (a) Screen formats – 4:3 and 16:9 (b) Screen sizes comparison

satellite bandwidth of 39 MHz, which is a substantial (and expensive) amount of satellite capacity. Increasing the modulation scheme to 8-PSK, and running at 5/6 FEC, reduces the required bandwidth to 18 MHz, but will increase the power requirement to achieve the same degree of ruggedness as using QPSK. Remembering, of course, that 18 MHz is still double that of the 'conventional' SNG channel.

Advancing to transmitting HDTV is therefore a big step in terms of bandwidth usage. It also requires a different equipment set – the equipment changes that are necessary are:

- An MPEG-2 encoder that can run at up to 60 Mbps data rate
- A modulator that can also cope with high data rates, and also offer such enhancements as DVB-S2, and higher order modulation (8-PSK and higher)
- Higher power requirements (greater EIRP) – this will need to be met by using a larger HPA and/or antenna size

With HDTV well established in Japan, becoming established in North America, and soon to be established in Europe, as well as many other parts of the world, the use of HDTV satellite transmission for program contribution has been restricted to mostly sports and events (although one leading Japanese broadcaster has been newsgathering in HD for several years).

The future of HDTV use in SNG therefore undoubtedly lies in the use of new compression and modulation techniques, such as MPEG-4 AVC and DVB-S2, which we will examine shortly. These will moderate the excessive bandwidth demands using MPEG-2 and QPSK.

4.7   DVB and MPEG-2

In Chapter 3, we discussed the option of 'multiplexing' two program paths (or 'streams') in the digital domain by cascading two digital compression encoders together to provide a single digital data stream to the uplink chain. The MPEG standard defines the method of multiplexing and program-specific information (PSI) tables which enable the individual 'packetized elementary streams' (PES) to be transmitted and decoded correctly. The European DVB (Digital Video Broadcasting) standard has enabled this to be implemented in a transmission process for the consumer that can be used by manufacturers to produce equipment that will interoperate between manufacturers.

The DVB project was officially inaugurated in 1993, born out of the European Launching Group for Digital Video Broadcasting initiative. The project consists of a voluntary group of more than 200 organizations that have joined forces to develop standards for DVB. The MPEG-2 standard has been adopted as the DVB compression standard for broadcast distribution and transmission, and part of that standard covers the combining of program streams.

The DVB Project covers a range of transmission methods, including terrestrial cable and satellite. It has derived a number of standards that have been endorsed by both ETSI (European Technical Standards Institute) and then by the ITU.

4.7.1   DVB-S

The first specification was for the satellite delivery of DVB signals, entitled DVB-S,[14] ratified in 1994. This defined, for the first time, different tools for channel coding (see Chapter 2) which later on became important for all other transmission methods as well. Channel coding is used to describe the processes used for adaptation of the source signal to the transmission medium, and principally covers the compression, error correction and modulation processes.

The DVB-S specification enabled the start of digital DTH services via satellite in many parts of the world. Under this specification, a data rate of typically 38 Mbps can be accommodated within a satellite transponder channel bandwidth of 33 MHz. A typical satellite uses 18 such transponders and thus may deliver 684 Mbps to a small (60 cm diameter or less) satellite antenna for DTH services. As a DTH standard, a key feature of DVB is program security, so that only those who have paid for a service may receive it. As a result the specification has provision for conditional access (CA) using a 'common scrambling algorithm' (CSA). This is a powerful tool to make secure scrambling of multiplexed program channels ('transport streams', or TSs) or individual program channels ('packetized elementary streams' or PESs) possible.

MPEG does not specify the error-correction process, but in DVB-S it is specified, and follows the parameters included earlier in the chapter. Every transport stream packet is of a fixed length of 204 bytes and every packet has a 'header' of added which identifies the type of information carried in the packet, termed a Packet IDentifier (PID). All packets carrying the same program video and audio have the same PID, and it is this number that is used to be able to select the required channel from the multiplexed stream received at the decoder. The PID values are contained in the Program Map Table (PMT) packet

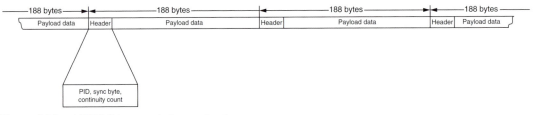

Figure 4.15 MPEG-2 transport stream structure

encoded as part of the transport stream, and these values (typically three- or four-digit numbers) are entered into the MPEG decoder. This is the same process as using a DVB receiver/decoder at home, where the PID value may have to be manually entered to select a particular program in a multiplex stream.

MPEG-2 transmissions are either transmitted as single channel per carrier (SCPC) or multiple channel per carrier (MCPC) feeds. An MPEG-2 encoder produces the final output data stream as a signal termed an ASI (Asynchronous Serial Interface) stream and this is a standard interface that can be directly fed to the modulator. A transport stream must come out at a specific aggregate data rate, and the TS components include the tables, elementary streams containing video and audio, and data associated with the programs.

However, at an individual program channel level, both SCPC and MCPC methods use the same system for building a data stream containing the video, audio and timing information. In SCPC, the combination of compressed video and audio forms a single transport stream and includes timing information to allow the audio and video to be synchronized together before modulation to DVB standard is carried out (Figure 4.15).

Although not as likely a problem as in the analog domain, it is considered desirable to add an energy dispersal signal to the transport stream (based on a pseudo-random 'noise' signal) to distribute any constant peaks of energy.

In MCPC, multiple PESs are multiplexed together into a larger stream and the service information (SI) stream gets added, resulting in the final MPEG-2/DVB multiplex transport stream that is uplinked to the transponder on the satellite.

Incidentally, it should be mentioned that it is not only 'native' MPEG-2 data that can be carried in an MPEG-2 stream – other data types can be carried. For example, Internet Protocol (IP) data can be carried, but first it has to be converted ('encapsulated') so that it can fit into the transport stream. In particular, 'null' packets, containing a dummy payload inserted to fill the intervals between information-bearing packets as part of the normal MPEG-2 stream, are often replaced with this other data. We will look at this further in Chapter 5.

As many of the MPEG-2 encoders used for SNG are derivatives of those used in program distribution, the ability to multiplex streams together is typically an integrated (optional) part of the encoder, or an external multiplexer is used. The ASI data stream output from the first encoder can be directly fed to the modulator, or to a second encoder or external multiplexer if several streams are to be multiplexed together (see Figure 3.1a).

The streams are combined at the uplink, and the downlink is able to de-multiplex the transport stream back into separate streams using the PID, the channel identifier containing all the navigation information required to identify and reconstruct a program stream.

A new standard – DVB-S2 – has recently been ratified by DVB, and this is of increasing importance for SNG. We will look at this later in the chapter after we have discussed MPEG-4/VC-1 where its significance will become apparent.

4.7.2 Scrambling

Scrambling (or encryption) is used on some SNG feeds where there is a fear that the material may be 'hijacked' by the unscrupulous, or where the material contained in the transmission has a high degree of exclusivity. The two standards designed for DSNG that are in common use are BISS (Basic Interoperable Scrambling System)[15] and BISS-E[16] (BISS – Encrypted), developed by the European Broadcasting Union (EBU) in 2000.

In BISS, the stream is scrambled by a fixed Control Word (CW), derived from a clear Session Word (SW) or key. The transmission is protected by a 12 digit 'session key' agreed by the transmitting and receiving parties prior to transmission. The key is entered into both the encoder and decoder, forming part of the encryption of the transport stream; thus only receivers with the correct key entered will decrypt the signal. It is not a very secure system, and so a second standard, BISS-E, was released by the EBU in 2002.

With BISS-E, the stream is scrambled by a fixed control word, derived from an Encrypted Session Word (ESW). The scrambling mechanism is defined in the DVB-CSA specification, and is commonly offered as an option on MPEG-2 encoders.

Mention also needs to be made of RAS (Remote Authorization System), a proprietary technique used by Tandberg Television in their MPEG-2 encoders, commonly used to encrypt DSNG feeds. As with BISS it uses a fixed control word to encrypt the data in the transport stream; however, it requires a Tandberg decoder to be used as well as a Tandberg encoder.

4.7.3 Interoperability

An important aspect of MPEG-2 and DVB is 'interoperability'. One of the aims of the DVB standardization process was to enable any signal processed by an encoder which is DVB-compliant to be decoded by a DVB-compliant decoder made by a manufacturer different to that of the encoder. There are so many variables in the process – symbol rate, video coding rate, video resolution and FEC rate – that this is not easy to achieve. We need to remember that although the MPEG-2 standard has certain fixed parameters, there is wide scope for manufacturers to use different algorithms to improve the quality of the video.

In SNG, there were several studies carried out to establish the level of interoperability between decoders manufactured for use in SNG applications. These studies were principally carried out by INTELSAT,[17] at the behest of WBU-ISOG (World Broadcasting Union – Inter-Union Satellite Operations Group). Other studies were also carried out by the EBU.[18]

A wide range of different manufacturers' encoders and decoders were tested, both in the laboratory and via satellite, in several of rounds of tests, and subsequently almost all the coders and decoders were fully interoperable within the test parameters. These interoperability tests resulted in the ISOG 'standard mode' for SDTV SNG operations:

Video encoding rate:	7.5 Mbps
Coding standard:	MPEG-2 MP@ML (4:2:0 sampling)
Audio data rate (stereo):	256 kbps
Audio sampling rate:	48 kHz
Transport stream (excluding RS encoding):	8.448 Mbps
Reed-Solomon code rate:	204/188
Inner FEC code rate:	3/4
Transmitted symbol rate:	6.1113 Msps

There is a slight variation to this, where the transport stream rate of 8.448 Msps is quoted including RS encoding; in which case, the resultant transmitted symbol rate is 5.632 Msps (6.113 multiplied by 188/204).

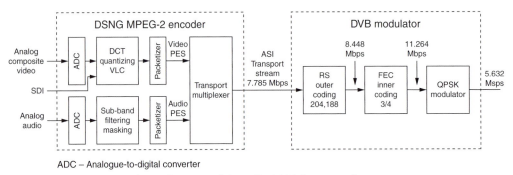

ADC – Analogue-to-digital converter

Figure 4.16 MPEG-2 encoder and DVB modulator (8.448 Mbps signal)

This can sometimes cause confusion in operational situations, and operators should always be clear as to whether RS encoding is included or not in symbol rate figures. It has been decided that in order to enable automated interoperability and the setting of the receiving parameters, this information should be signaled in the SI data stream of the transport stream.

At the time of writing, there is a second round testing of interoperability testing being undertaken by WBU-ISOG to ensure that MPEG-2 HDTV encoders will also be similarly interoperable.

A specification for DVB signals used for SNG (DVB-DSNG) was also issued by ETSI[19] in 1997, which formalized the parameters above, and also allowed for the option of using 8-PSK or 16-QAM instead of QPSK.

4.7.4 Future of MPEG-2

Over the least decade MPEG-2 performance has improved significantly, and broadcast quality encoders have improved in their efficiency by 50–75% as manufacturers have refined the algorithms and taken advantage of increased processing power in devices. While typical bit-rates of first generation MPEG-2 encoders were around 8 Mbps, current DTH transmissions of 2–3 Mbps typically give almost the same video and audio quality – and even in use in SNG, data rates are now often below 5 Mbps. Improvements have now peaked within the MPEG-2 specification, and opportunity for significant improvements in MPEG-2 performance are now very limited.

While MPEG-2 will continue to be widely used because of its widely installed user base, both within the context of SNG, as well as DTH, it is now at the end of its development, and so we will look at what is now likely to replace MPEG-2 by the end of the first decade of the twenty-first century.

4.8 MPEG-4

MPEG-4 was born out of a realization that the future would require compressed video and audio signals that could be streamed reliably over a wide range of data rates – from below 64 kbps for devices such as mobile phones to up to 4 Mbps for a standard definition broadcast video signal delivered over a broad-band connection. Over time, its ambitions have changed as the demand for HDTV grew, and it encompasses very low data rates for mobile phones to data rates up to 40 Mbps for high-definition broadcasts, and in the future will extend to over 1 Gbps. MPEG-4 AVC has shown significant efficiency gains over MPEG-2, an advantage that is compelling when bandwidth is limited or expensive. AVC effectively extends many MPEG-2 principles but is a big evolutionary step – an MPEG-4 AVC encoder is eight times more complex than an MPEG-2 encoder.

In addition it was planned as a standard for multimedia – encompassing video, audio, still objects, text and auxiliary data. The standard has had a lengthy gestation, with the focus shifting to object-oriented coding, interactive systems and video encoding improvements compared to MPEG-2. Started in 1993, it was not until 1997 that there was a formal draft, and it only became an ISO/IEC Recommendation in 1999, and was finalized in 2000.[20]

Frankly, perhaps because it was trying to be 'all things to all men', the initial version of MPEG-4 was not well received, particularly in the broadcast world. Like MPEG-2, it is not a single standard as such, but unlike MPEG-2 has now developed into a large and complex 'toolbox' of 23 different parts. The MPEG-4 standard defines a bewildering array of opportunities for processing multimedia material for a wide range of applications, from very low data rate delivery of material to cellphones at the bottom end of the scale to HDTV at the top end. Because of its highly complex nature, manufacturers can pick and choose which parts they wish to implement in their equipment to meet the application need. The critical amendment to the MPEG-4 standard to enable more advanced video coding techniques came in 2005 with publication of Part 10 to the MPEG-4 standard – MPEG–4 AVC.[21]

There is also the question of licensing. Both MPEG-2 and MPEG-4 technology requires a licence to be paid for by the manufacturer, administered by MPEG-LA, a one-stop technology platform patent licensing organization. With MPEG-2, this license cost is comparatively low, adding only a few US dollars to each encoder unit sold, and with no cost in participation fees to end-users (i.e. consumers). But at the time, with MPEG-4 there appeared to be much debate about a different approach to be taken to licensing, including participation fees to be paid by viewers. This uncertainty for the manufacturers about licensing costs caused the technology to be treated cautiously, particularly as it is a technology aimed predominantly at a very large mass consumer market.

As it turns out, currently MPEG-4 AVC license charges for encoder manufacturers are based on the number of units shipped a year. Currently up to 100 000 units sold per annum attract no royalty; between 100 000 and 5 million units per annum is charged at US$0.20 per unit, and beyond 5 million, US$0.10 per unit. There is a similar scale of fees for participant viewers of broadcasts. In addition there are terms proposed for free distribution over the Internet beyond 2010, and up until then it is free. There are also special provisions for free-to-air (FTA) television programs to be payable as a one off or annual fee. The licensing terms for MPEG-4 AVC have been principally aimed at distribution applications where licensees believe revenue is to be made, leaving contribution applications like SNG largely unaffected.

For these reasons, combined with the reality that early implementations of MPEG-4 were not particularly impressive in terms of picture quality, has meant that it has as yet failed to widely challenge MPEG-2 within the digital broadcasting world.

Not only that, but different variants of MPEG-4 are available under a bewildering array of different acronyms, not always equivalent.

Early MPEG-4
● MPEG-4
● MPEG-4 ASP (Advanced Simple Profile)

MPEG-4 Advanced Coding
● H.26L (an ITU descriptor), which in time became …
● H.264
● JVT (Joint Video Team)
● MPEG-4 Part 10/Chapter 10
● H.264 AVC (Advanced Video Coding)

In terms of traditional broadcasting, MPEG-4 ASP was of most interest before MPEG-4 AVC came along – it offered the best performance, and tantalizingly dangled the prospect of what MPEG-4 could be if more work was done. Then along came MPEG-4 AVC.

MPEG-4 AVC/MPEG-4 Part 10/H.264 is the latest version of MPEG-4, and yields the best results in terms of video and audio compression. From this point on we will focus on this version as it has been deployed in SNG, though many of the core principles are within the original MPEG-4 standard (Part 2).

4.8.1 MPEG-4 AVC principles

MPEG-2 was the basis on which MPEG-4 was constructed, and although there are some similarities, there are a greater number of differences. MPEG-2 has 11 parts to the standard – MPEG-4 has 21, including the all important Part 10, which relates to AVC.

The high degree of complexity in the MPEG-4 standard is such that we are only able to give an overview of the subject (if you thought MPEG-2 was complicated, MPEG-4 is another dimension altogether), and readers wishing to know more should refer to the Bibliography at the back of the book. What is important to note is that MPEG-4 AVC is claimed to achieve bit-rate savings of 50% over MPEG-2, and 30% over MPEG-4 ASP.

As with MPEG-2 (and MPEG-1), the MPEG-4 standard only defines the decoding process and the syntax and semantics of the data stream. The encoding process is not specified, only how a valid data stream must be produced. Again, as with MPEG-2, the standard can be thought of as a toolbox with a much bigger array of tools than are necessarily required for processing one particular type of content – the manufacturer chooses which tools (or parts of the standard) they wish to use to achieve the requirement of their encoder or decoder.

It should also be borne in mind that many of the principles used in video coding are applied to coding of audio, though we will focus on the video coding aspects. MPEG-4 is based on transmitting a number of layers of information simultaneously, so that if for some reason the decoder fails to receive the video information it can possibly reproduce the audio.

MPEG-2 is a process that treats the whole scene in a complete frame, but in MPEG-4, the whole scene is broken down into a number of discrete elements that are handled individually. Consider that in MPEG-4, a scene is treated as a visual concept rather than just as a signal, and there are sophisticated and highly computing power-intensive processes in train at both the encoding and the decoding ends to deconstruct, compress and then reconstruct the material. One of the benefits MPEG-4 offers by adopting this approach is to be able to assign more resolution to specific objects, i.e. a higher resolution applied to scrolling news captions used in a mobile television application than applied to the background studio, or a higher resolution applied to price labels on a low bandwidth shopping channel.

An MPEG-4 video stream can be divided into five hierarchical layers (see Figure 4.17). The lowest layer is the Video Object Plane (VOP) layer, which normally corresponds to a single frame of the video stream. One or more frames are grouped together to form the Group of Video Object Planes (GOV) objects.

Several GOPs are grouped together in the Video Object Layer (VOL). This layer contains information needed to display the video, such as the size of the video frames in pixels, the frame rate of the video and color information.

The two top layers, the Visual Object Sequence Layer and the Visual Object Layer, contain additional information about the type of the MPEG-4 objects, as well as the profile and level indicators of the encoded bit stream.

4.8.2 Video Objects, Video Object Plane and Video Object Layers

MPEG-4 is an object-orientated coding system. Because the video input to be coded by MPEG-4 is no longer considered simply as a rectangular region, it is assumed that each frame of the video sequence is divided into a number of arbitrarily shaped image areas or objects. It interprets a visual scene as a composition of these arbitrarily shaped image areas, or Video Objects (VOs), characterized by their shape, motion and texture.

In MPEG-4, a Video Session is a collection of one or more Video Objects each of which can consist of one or more layers and each layer consists of an ordered sequence of snapshots in time in the form of Video Object Planes (VOPs).

Each VO is coded individually and corresponds to an elementary bit-stream that can be separately accessed and manipulated, while composition information is sent in a separate stream. A VO can still be

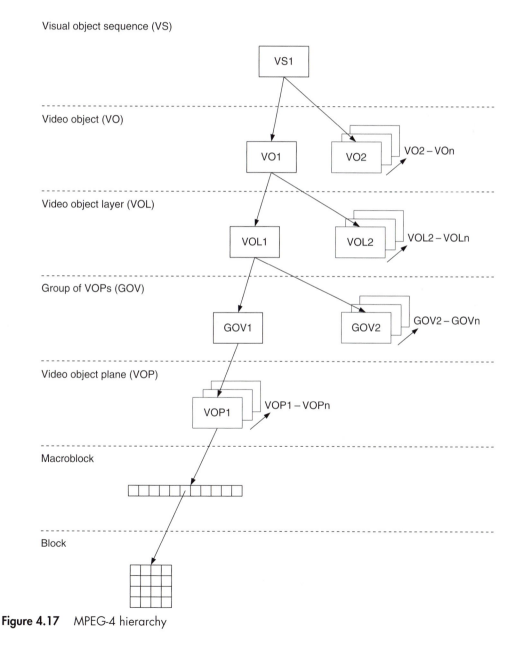

Figure 4.17   MPEG-4 hierarchy

a traditional MPEG-2 type sequence of rectangular frames formed by pixels – or alternatively it can correspond to a sequence of arbitrarily shaped sets of pixels with a significant meaning, given that this higher level information is somehow made available (e.g. by providing shape or transparency information). This latter case of arbitrary shape coding is of more use in computer generated imagery (CGI) or computer graphics – sometimes termed 'synthetic' video – than in naturalistic scenes ('natural' video) such as those found in the real world.

The same Video Object seen over a period of time translates into a Video Object Plane (VOP), belonging to a corresponding physical object in a scene. Thus each object within a video sequence is represented by a series of Video Object Planes (VOP), and the shape, texture and location of the objects can vary from frame to frame. The shape and texture information of each object is encoded and transmitted in separate VOPs within that scene.

A VOP is derived from any recognizable shape – from a face in the foreground, to a building in the background, a car in the mid-ground, or even captions that have been superimposed on the picture. All these are distinct elements that can be analyzed, and repeated on a frame-by-frame basis while they are present, even though their position and shape may change in some degree from one frame to the next.

The shape, motion and texture information of the VOPs belonging to the same VO is encoded and transmitted or coded into a separate VOL (Video Object Layer). In addition, relevant information needed to identify each of the VOLs – and how the various VOLs are composed at the receiver to reconstruct the entire original sequence is also included in the bit-stream. This allows the separate decoding of each VOP and the required flexible manipulation of the video sequence.

As with MPEG-2, MPEG-4 uses DCT (Discrete Cosine Transform) coding, but in a much less rigid and more flexible manner which depends on the picture content. Rather than just analyzing a picture block and generating a block of coefficients from differences with the so-called DC coefficient, MPEG-4 AVC can predict entire rows of coefficients in either the horizontal or vertical planes from a previous block. Basic MPEG-4 uses techniques of 'shape' and 'texture' coding to describe objects and their motion; MPEG-4 AVC uses further advanced techniques in coding shape and texture.

In MPEG-2 blocks of pixels were coded in the same manner irrespective of their significance within the frame, but in MPEG-4 each object is coded in the most efficient manner according to its content, and so there are multiple coding processes going on within any single frame that commonly has a number of objects.

4.8.3   Shape coding

Shape coding describes, as the name implies, the outline of the object, while texture coding describes the luminance and color detail (i.e. the image detail) of the object.

Shape coding is performed as a simple binary process, where each pixel is coded as a value of 1 or 0 depending on whether it is part of the object or not, and the resulting bitmap is termed a Binary Alpha Plane (BAP). Coding of the shape of an object is straightforward either side of the boundary of the object – if a pixel is within the object boundary, it has a value of 1, and if beyond the boundary, a value of 0. The difficulty lies on the boundary edge, where 'aliasing' can occur due to a sharp transition, and thus greyscale shapes result in a smoother and more natural looking edge transition compared to stark objects.

4.8.4   Texture coding

Texture coding – the description of the detail of the surface of an object – is applied to those areas that form part of the object. Rectangular objects within a scene are the easiest to code, if they can be broken down into rectangular sub-blocks of 16 pixels in either direction. Objects with a more complex shape are defined by the shape processing, and coding is carried out on the basis of 16 pixel blocks that fall entirely or partially within the object shape.

The capability for MPEG-4 AVC to handle scenes beyond natural video provides the basis for linking the video encoding aspects of the specification with the system elements, as defined in MPEG-4 Part 11, sometimes known as the system specification for Binary Information For Scenes (BIFS).

Texture and shape coding gives MPEG-4 a valuable tool to be able to allow the authoring of graphics material within the specification that is crucially not dependent upon a specific 'client' implementation. Like many aspects of MPEG-4, this complicated aspect of the specification has plenty of potential in mobile and IPTV (Internet Protocol delivered TV) systems. In computing, middleware refers to software agents acting as an intermediary between different application components; middleware that is independent of client devices is a powerful asset in a converged multimedia world. However, it remains to be seen whether this technically innovative aspect of the specification can gain a toehold and widespread adoption within the multimedia applications.

Note that the term 'middleware' is used to describe web servers, application servers, content management systems and similar tools that support the application development and delivery process. It is key to 'distributed processing' – the connection of multiple applications together to create a larger application over a network.

4.8.5 Motion compensation

In MPEG-4 a Group Of Video Object Planes (GOV) replaces the GOP (Group Of Pictures) structure of MPEG-2. The GOV groups together VOPs, and provides points in the stream where VOPs are encoded independently from each other, and can thus provide random access points into the stream to assist with editing and 'stream splicing'. Within a GOV, VOPs are coded in three ways (similar to MPEG-2) to achieve the best motion compensation.

Instead of I-, B- and P-frames used in MPEG-2, MPEG-4 AVC works with using I-, B- and P-VOPs for motion estimation. Consider an instant in time when a particular VOP is being analyzed – note that as we saw earlier in MPEG-2 encoding, the MPEG-4 encoder contains internal decoders as it performs iterative processes to derive frame data for processing.

- An Intra VOP (I-VOP) is encoded based purely on its content with no reference to any other VOP in the sequence
- A Predicted VOP (P-VOP) is generated based on estimation from a previously decoded VOP
- A Bi-directional VOP (B-VOP) is based on an estimation of the current VOP and neighboring I-VOPs and P-VOPS (not on other I-VOPs), which can be from a relatively wide range in the past (typically up to 5 I-VOPs previously)

With MPEG-2, motion prediction between frames was based on using a fixed block size (16×16 pixels), but MPEG-4 AVC uses an adaptive hierarchical scheme with a range of block sizes down to 4×4 pixels, enabling very precise segmentation of moving areas.

MPEG-4 AVC supports variable block sizes, including blocks that are not square. Blocks can be 16×16 pixels, 8×16 pixels, 16×8 pixels, 8×8 pixels, 4×8 pixels, 8×4 pixels or 4×4 pixels. The size, shape and orientation of each block is selected by the encoder in order to create groups of pixels with a high degree of similarity. Regions of a video frame that are very similar will tend to be coded with large blocks to minimize the number of block parameters coded. Regions of a frame with great detail will tend to be coded with smaller blocks in order to increase similarity and improve the accuracy of the coding.

In addition, quarter pixel interpolation significantly improves its ability to handle motion. It can also generate motion vector predictions from adjacent macroblocks, and then only sends those predicted differences, further reducing the amount of data sent.

4.8.6 Artifacts

What is striking with MPEG-4 is what happens when corruption of the data occurs. Rather than the picture breaking up into blocks, as in MPEG-2, one can observe the application of a de-blocking 'loop filter' that tries to minimize the picture artifacts. Some very strange effects, where the 'texture' of one object is mapped onto another object shape, have been observed in early MPEG-4 implementations. As the implementation of the standard improves, these effects will become less noticeable to the untrained viewer; meanwhile it should be recognized that MPEG-4 artifacts are different from MPEG-2.

4.8.7 Profiles

Within the whole of the MPEG-4 standard, profiles are also defined within the individual 'parts', so an implementation of a part is ordinarily not an implementation of an entire part. As we have glimpsed, MPEG-4 AVC is a highly versatile standard with a multitude of profiles and levels to suit specific applications a whole range, covering a whole gamut of applications from still objects to graphics to audio to visual (both standard and high definition). As we are primarily interested in the Visual part of MPEG-4 AVC, only those profiles are shown in Table 4.3.

Table 4.3 H.264 visual profiles

Tool	Profile						
	Baseline	Main	Extended	High	High 10	High 4:2:2	High 4:4:4
I Frame	X	X	X	X	X	X	X
P-Frame	X	X	X	X	X	X	X
B-Frame		X	X	X	X	X	X
Deblocking filter	X	X	X	X	X	X	X
CAVLC	X	X	X	X	X	X	X
CABAC		X		X	X	X	X
Interlaced		X	X	X	X	X	X
4:2:0 Chroma format	X	X	X	X	X	X	X
4:2:2 Chroma format						X	X
4:4:4 Chroma format							X
8 bit sample depth	X	X	X	X	X	X	X
9/10 bit sample depth					X	X	X
10/12 bit sample depth							X
8 × 8 Transform				X	X	X	X
Predictive lossless coding							X

Profiles define the following:

- tools from the standard that are used
- bit-rates
- image sizes
- numbers of objects

AVC Main Profile builds on Context Adaptive Variable Length Coding (CAVLC) with Context Adaptive Binary Arithmetic Coding (CABAC). CAVLC is used to encode transform coefficients; the CABAC method continually updates frequency statistics of the incoming data and adaptively adjusts the algorithm, improving compression performance. The CABAC option is complex to implement but yields remarkable efficiency capability.

In 2004 MPEG approved a number of important High Profile amendments, known as Fidelity Rate Extensions (FRExt). These extensions enhance efficiency and the scope of the standard by offering higher fidelity options, such as 4:2:2 coding, and greater sampling range to further extend the scope and value of MPEG-4 AVC.

4.9   Windows Media Video 9 and VC-1

While MPEG-4 is a large, sprawling and complex standard that can be used by manufacturers to implement hardware and software products to meet particular niche applications, Windows Media 9 is a complete software product which is currently only available from one vendor – Microsoft.

Microsoft were deeply involved in the development of the MPEG-4 standard (as were many other large and small companies), and so unsurprisingly its advanced codecs share many of the characteristics of MPEG-4 AVC – object and shape coding, DCT processing and so forth. The latest of these codecs, VC-1, completed the lengthy process of being ratified by the Society of Motion Picture and Television Engineers (SMPTE) as a standard[22] and has been implemented by Microsoft as Windows Media Video (WMV) 9 Advanced Profile, which supports both progressive and interlaced video content.

The VC-1 codec specification has so far been implemented by Microsoft in two versions. Firstly, there is a version of Windows Media Video 9 known as WMV3 that allows progressive encoding for PC displays. In WMV3, interlaced video content is de-interlaced to create a progressively scanned frame structure before encoding. The Windows Media Video 9 (WMV3) codec implements the Simple and Main modes of the VC-1 codec standard, providing high-quality video for streaming and down-loading.

The second version of VC-1 is WVC1, implemented to support the compression of interlaced content without first converting it to progressive scan, and allowing the delivery of Windows Media files over systems that were not Windows Media-based. WVC1 implements the advanced mode of the proposed VC-1 codec standard, offering support for interlaced content and is transport independent. With the previous version of the Windows Media Video 9 Series codec, Microsoft claimed users could deliver progressive content at data rates as low as one-third that of the MPEG-2 codec and still get the same quality as MPEG-2. According to Microsoft, Windows Media Video 9 Advanced Profile codec also offers this same improvement in encoding efficiency with interlaced content.

VC-1 allows delivery over MPEG-2 and RTP systems (see Chapter 5) to enable device manufacturers and content services to produce interoperable systems.

Profiles

Like MPEG-4, VC-1 has a range of profiles for different applications, though its structure is much simpler.

Profile	Level	Maximum bit rate	Resolution/frame rate	Application
Simple	Low	96 kbps	176 × 144/15 (QCIF)	Portable devices
	Medium	384 kbps	240 × 176/30	
			352 × 288/15 (CIF)	Low data rate devices
Main	Low	2 Mbps	320 × 240/24 (QVGA)	
	Medium	10 Mbps	720 × 480/30 (480p)	
			720 × 576/25 (576p)	SDTV
	High	20 Mbps	1920 × 1080/30 (1080p)	Low data rate HDTV
Advanced	L0	2 Mbps	352 × 288/30 (CIF)	
	L1	10 Mbps	720 × 480/30 (NTSC-SD)	
			720 × 576/25 (PAL-SD)	SDTV
	L2	20 Mbps	720 × 480/60 (480p)	
			1280 × 720/30 (720p)	HDTV
	L3	45 Mbps	1920 × 1080/24 (1080p)	
			1920 × 1080/30 (1080i)	
			1280 × 720/60 (720p)	
	L4	135 Mbps	1920 × 1080/60 (1080p)	
			2048 × 1536/24	

The significant point of VC-1 is that it is computationally less complex than MPEG-4, yet delivers similar subjective picture quality at comparable data rates.

4.10 DVB-S2

The world of SNG is now seeing the term 'DVB-S2' quoted in modulator specifications, and although this chapter has concentrated on compression, it is at this point that compression and advanced forms of modulation become intertwined. Whereas in Chapter 2, modulation could be treated as a separate entity, with DVB-S2, because of its derivation, it has to be considered in the context of compression and the MPEG data stream.

As we discussed earlier, DVB-S (and its derivative DVB-DSNG) has been the satellite transmission standard for digital distribution and contribution respectively. DVB-S was ratified by ETSI in 1994, and 11 years later its replacement arrived. The new standard DVB-S2[23] has been long awaited to meet the demands of providing new services, primarily focused on HDTV and interactive DTH services. Although the direct benefit to SNG is not apparent at first sight, there are improvements available – and in any case, it is likely that in the not too distant future, all modulators will implement DVB-S2 as standard. It is therefore important that we try and understand this new standard.

As we discussed in Chapter 2, the core of the existing DVB-S standard is based on using constant bit-rate QPSK modulation (although variations from this are permitted, as in DVB-DSNG), which while satisfying the requirements of digital satellite transmission through the 1990s and the beginning of this decade, is not up to meeting the now increasing demands from broadcasters and other content providers.

Figure 4.18   DVB-S2 modulator (Courtesy of Newtec)

What is required now is a modulation standard that can cope with differing content requirements in a single stream with increased capacity efficiency in the same bandwidth. So it is a further development of modulation techniques to save bandwidth.

While DVB-S defined only QPSK modulation, the DVB-S2 standard has five modulation schemes: BPSK, QPSK, 8-PSK, 16-APSK and 32-APSK (Amplitude and Phase-Shift Keying or Asymmetric Phase Shift Keying is similar to QAM in that it uses both phase and amplitude modulation). Higher order modulation has become easier to implement with improvements at the 'silicon' level been available and significantly increases the number of bits transmitted per hertz. This new standard provides a capacity increase of up to 30%, more robust reception and better spectral efficiency; the DVB Project has been quoted as saying that the specification is so good that it should not need to develop a DVB-S3 specification.

4.10.1   Low Density Parity Check Coding (LDPC)

The standard mandates the use of a technique called Low Density Parity Check coding (LDPC), a mathematically very complex coding system. During the evolution of DVB-S2 it was thought that Turbo Coding, which we discussed in Chapter 2, would be used to help achieve the improved error correction performance. However, the decision to use LDPC coding was based on laboratory performance testing of seven different coding schemes by the DVB-S2 technical committee, who concluded that LDPC was the superior technique.

The mathematician Gallagher first developed the theory of LDPC coding in the early 1960s, but only in the last decade (with developments in silicon technology) has a practical implementation for a different FEC modulation technique based on LDPC become feasible. Because it is so complex – similar to Turbo coding – we are not going to attempt to explain it here, and for the mathematically curious reader, there is any number of texts published on the theory. Suffice to say, with LDPC it is now practical to almost reach the theoretical coding efficiency limit defined by the Shannon theory – the Holy Grail of digital modulation efficiency.

4.10.2   Adaptive Coding and Modulation (ACM)

With DVB-S, each data block was treated the same in terms of modulation and error protection – QPSK modulation, the same FEC and Reed-Solomon coding rate. Once these parameters were set for a transmission, they could not be varied, and this was true for either an SCPC or MCPC carrier. Typically the link budget would be calculated (setting these values) for the most likely worst-case conditions – heavy rainfall, smallest receive antenna, etc.

With DVB-S2, each data block ('frame') in the multiplex stream can be switched both in terms of modulation (QPSK, 8-PSK, 16- APSK, 32-APSK), error correction (in the range 1/4 to 9/10) and bit-rate. Most significantly, this can be done all on an instantaneous basis – 'on-the-fly'. This is called Adaptive Coding and Modulation (ACM), and it has been designed for DTH broadcasting to provide the ability to change transmission parameters depending on reception conditions. For instance, if a single transport stream is serving areas with differing rainfall conditions, which will affect the satellite link quality, it would be possible to change the modulation parameters for the program delivered to an area suffering from a heavy rainstorm, compared to a program being delivered in the same stream to an area with no rain. Provision of a return channel (either terrestrially or by satellite) to feedback information on local conditions would be necessary to achieve this. This can be processed over a short time interval, allowing changes to services within the stream to ensure a consistent quality of service across the board.

Thus DVB-S2 provides the ability to apply differing error protection to data on a frame-by-frame basis. For example, a frame with QPSK 3/4 FEC rate targeted at small antennas could be transmitted, followed by a 32-APSK frame using 8/9 FEC rate for larger antennas, carrying over three times as much information using the same satellite resource. This allows the link to be optimized dynamically, without having to allocate extra link-budget margin to allow for worst-case conditions. Alternatively, the standard allows the mixing of different types of content – SDTV, HDTV, interactive services, etc. – with each service's transmission parameters (data rate, modulation, FEC, etc.) tailored just to its own requirement. This offers the benefit of significant savings in bandwidth.

As an analogy, if we think of a railway train with a locomotive pulling a number of wagons laden with gravel, each wagon containing the same amount and type of gravel – this is analogous to DVB-S. Each company that rents wagons has to carry the same load as the other companies, and they all pay the same even if they don't all need the same wagon capacity. In other words, the use of the bandwidth is equally distributed and the same error protection is applied across the entire stream.

DVB-S2 allows us to fill each wagon with different amounts of gravel and different grades of gravel, giving companies the ability to make the best use of their wagon according to the weight of the load carried in the wagons – the bandwidth usage and error protection level can be allocated on an individual need basis. Each wagon is marked with what it is carrying (analogous to the packet header information).

DVB-S2 supports single or multiple transport streams, and handles both MPEG-2 and common data formats such as IP and ATM (Asynchronous Transfer Mode). This allows non-MPEG-2 data to be transmitted natively, without the additional task of encapsulating it within the MPEG-2 transport stream (see Chapter 5). These new features not only further increase the efficiency of the satellite utilization by avoiding unnecessary framing layers, but they also reduce the need for expensive multiplexing and encapsulation equipment.

4.10.3 DVB-S2 and SNG

So the advantages for DTH and distribution are clear, but what about SNG—is there really any advantage there? Well, yes and no. Generally SNG uplinks are not combining multiple paths at very different data rates. At busy news events, some uplinks may transmit 2–6 streams ('paths') at usually very similar data rates. So varying FEC and modulation on-the-fly (ACM) for each path is of not much use for SNG. But DVB-S2 does offer the advantages of a more efficient coding, and combined with the improvements of MPEG-4 AVC or VC-1, the potential bandwidth savings are significant.

In a paper published by the EBU,[24] an example is given of a SNG uplink with a 90 cm antenna and 12 W HPA power, producing an uplink EIRP of 49 dBW, working into a 4 m receive antenna. Using DVB-S2, with QPSK at 2/3, 9.9 Mbps would be available in clear sky; 8.9 Mbps (QPSK 3/5) under typical conditions; and 3.68 Mbps (QPSK 1/4) under critical link conditions. This would offer a good picture quality using MPEG-2 coding, and excellent quality using MPEG-4 AVC coding.

With the same parameters, DVB-S using a QPSK 1/2 would require 5 dB more power to offer a constant bit-rate of 6.1 Mbps. So the advantages of DVB-S2 for SNG are clear, and it is likely that within a few years all satellite modulators used for SNG will be DVB-S2 capable.

4.11 Impact of DVB-S2 and MPEG-4/VC-1 on HDTV

DVB-S2 enables broadcasters to either enhance existing services or squeeze even more channels into the allocated bandwidth for the same spectrum cost. When it is used with MPEG-4 AVC, bandwidth savings of up to 50% are theoretically possible.

As an example, an uncompressed HDTV signal is 1.5 GBps; using MPEG-2 this can be reduced to 20–40 Mbps depending on the quality required; using MPEG-4 the signal can be compressed to 10–20 Mbps; then utilizing DVB-S2 modulation reduces this to approximately 7–15 Mbps. This is a theoretical calculation – the actual acceptable rates may vary from this depending on the subjective quality required of the source material.

The DVB-S2 standard means broadcasters can choose to either:

- increase throughput by 20–30% – more channels in the same space
- use the same bandwidth as previously but benefit from more robust reception
- or fit HD channels into bandwidth previously only capable of carrying SDTV

Typical current and future transponder usage is shown in Figure 4.19, and as can be seen, the efficiencies offered from the combination of both DVB-S2 and MPEG-4 AVC will make the availability of DTH HD channels much greater. For example, a 36 MHz transponder with DVB-S2 and QPSK could fit more than 6 channels of full-resolution HD, or with DVB-S2 and 8-PSK, more than 8 channels of full-resolution HD. However, in parts of the world there is a shortage of available spare spectrum, and there is an industry view that the demand for HD channels might not be able to be fully met due to lack of available bandwidth.

We mentioned earlier that using MPEG-2 for HDTV has led to an increase in the size of antennas and/or HPAs. The promise of MPEG-4 (or VC-1) and DVB-S2 is that the antennas and/or HPAs can revert to the usual size range as used for SDTV, as HDTV symbol rates fall to those for SDTV.

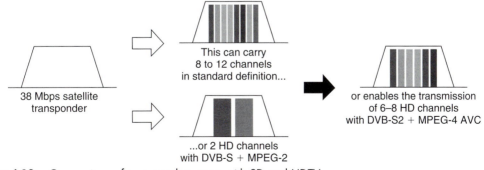

Figure 4.19 Comparison of transponder usage with SD and HDTV

4.12 Other compression standards

The reader will come across references to video compression techniques apart from MPEG and Windows Media Video, and the following is simply a brief explanation of the formats you may see mentioned.

4.12.1   H.261; H.263; H.263+

The coding standards for video-conferencing – H.261/263/263+ – used for some forms of SNG are covered further in Chapter 6 when we look at the use of Inmarsat. The H.261 standard[5] is very similar to the MPEG standard, but only I- and P-frames are used, resulting in less encoding and decoding latency delay. DCT is still used to reduce spatial redundancy, and forward motion prediction is used for motion compensation.

One feature that H.261 and H.263 have (unlike MPEG) is the ability to vary the frame rate within a video sequence. This is important in video-conferencing because an encoder must be able to both lower the frame rate to maintain reasonable visual quality and dynamically adjust to sudden changes in video content in real time.

4.12.2   QuickTime

This is a proprietary multimedia file format belonging to Apple Corp., and was originally introduced in 1991 for the Apple Mac OS. Now in its seventh generation, QuickTime 7 is available for both Mac OS X as well as Microsoft Windows. MPEG-4 compatibility was added to QuickTime 6 in 2002.

QuickTime 6 had limited support for MPEG-4 in that it could encode and decode Simple Profile (SP) but not Advanced Simple Profile (ASP) features like B-frames, making QuickTime-encoded MPEG-4 files suffer poorer performance compared to other full-featured encoders. QuickTime 7 decodes both MPEG-4 SP and ASP, though the encoder is still SP-only.

QuickTime 7's H.264 encoder conforms to the H.264 Main Profile, while the decoder supports Baseline, Extended and most of the Main Profile. High Profile features are not supported.

4.12.3   JPEG2000 and wavelet compression

Wavelet compression is a type of compression that has been increasingly advocated for video coding – in fact, it is one of the tools available for use within the MPEG-4 standard (for the compression of still images) – and forms the basis of the JPEG2000 compression standard.

Fundamentally, with Fourier analysis as used in MPEG, the complete signal within a certain time period is sampled, and then, using DCT, broken down to find the significant frequency components.

In wavelet signal analysis, the signal at a particular instant is repeatedly split into different frequency bands, and then a mathematical analysis is made of each of these bands. Once this analysis has been made, a progressive reduction in the number of components can be made, and so achieve compression of the signal.

Because the wavelet technique is better at resolving fine picture content (i.e. discontinuities, sharp edges, etc.) it is appropriate for high bit-rate applications such as post-production and archiving. While understanding wavelets from a mathematical perspective is complex, it is worth noting that the iterative nature of implementing the algorithm results in a compact hardware design that is well balanced in terms of encoder/decoder complexity. This, together with its capability to encode efficiently at high bit-rates, makes the wavelet approach good for post-production, archive and digital cinema applications – JPEG2000 has been developed with this application primarily in mind.

This is a hugely over-simplified description of wavelet compression, and as it is not currently relevant to SNG, we will draw a line under it here; though the reader may see reference to it on occasions when video compression is being discussed, particularly in relation to the use of wireless camera links.

4.13   Choosing an MPEG encoder for SNG

The choice as to which manufacturer's encoder is best suited for SNG is becomingly increasingly difficult, as the differences between the encoders for this type of application are diminishing. The choice will essentially center around the following key points (and in no particular order of significance).

Cost

The price of MPEG-2 products has dropped dramatically recently, and this is particularly important when considering the purchase of an encoder. As mentioned previously, MPEG-2 processing is asymmetric and this is reflected in the relative pricing of the encoders and decoders. At the time of writing, the list price of several encoder/modulators were below US$25 000, with a professional decoder (IRD) costing around 1/10 of the cost of an encoder. The costs of MPEG-4 AVC encoders (and professional decoders) are still relatively high, though they will inevitably fall over time.

Picture quality

This essentially comes down to a choice between whether the MPEG-2 encoder offers 4:2:2 or 4:2:0 sampling, and which 'chip-set' the encoder uses. A number of models offer both 4:2:2 and 4:2:0 sampling, which can be selected via the front panel, and 4:2:2 is used occasionally for SNG. At one time there was a significant price differential, but that has now all but disappeared.

There are two principal manufacturers of MPEG-2 chip-sets that are widely used (although not exclusively) – LSI (formerly C-Cube Microsystems Inc.) and Thomson Nextream. These chip-sets are based on ASIC (application-specific integrated circuit) technology, where an integrated circuit (IC) is tailored for a particular application. Some manufacturers offer encoders with either one of these chip-sets, or use what is known as a DSP chip set. A digital signal processor (DSP) chip is a specialized microprocessor designed specifically for digital signal processing, generally in real-time, and so a dedicated MPEG algorithm can be programmed into it. It is a lower cost than an ASIC solution, but often the performance is not as good. The choice between which is best is hotly contested, and the way the motion vector search function is implemented is often the most significant differentiating factor. MPEG-4 AVC encoders are currently only available in 4:2:0 as the processing power required for real time 4:2:2 color processing is very high, and chip-sets are as yet not available.

Latency

Particularly important for news operations with their high proportion of 'live' interactive interviewing and reporting is the degree of latency introduced by the encoder. This was a significant issue in the past, where there was a large disparity between some manufacturers' products, but the gap is closing. Bearing in mind the inherent satellite delay, it is important that the encoder has an 'interview' or low-latency mode, which sacrifices the amount of motion processing to achieve low delay for the typical news 'talking head' scenario – although not suitable for fast-moving sports action. Interview modes typically reduce the latency to under 100 ms. As mentioned previously, latency is still an issue with low bit-rate MPEG-4 AVC encoding.

(a)

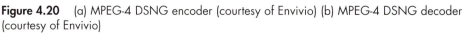

(b)

Figure 4.20 (a) MPEG-4 DSNG encoder (courtesy of Envivio) (b) MPEG-4 DSNG decoder (courtesy of Envivio)

Interoperability

It is essential for most SNG system operators to have equipment that offers the maximum degree of interoperability, as the type of decoder used at the downlink is often not known. Therefore, the end-user should carefully consider independent tests, such as those carried out by the EBU and other broadcasting organizations, as well as seeking assurances from the manufacturers.

Ease of use

A very important factor that distinguishes the suitability of an MPEG-2 encoder for use in the SNG field is how easy it is to operate. All encoders have an LCD screen on the front panel, with a control menu structure that is accessed by software-defined buttons at the bottom or side of the display. MPEG-2 encoders that have not been particularly well adapted from a fixed-distribution application will not offer easy access through the front panel menu structure to those controls which the SNG operator will need frequent and rapid access to. For instance, the following controls should be at or near the top level of the front panel menu:

- Video bit-rate and symbol rate
- Horizontal and vertical resolution
- Delay mode (normal/'interview' low-latency mode)

It should be noted that the measurement and interpretation of bit-rates and symbol rates is complex, usually necessitating the use of 'look-up' tables, and the encoder display needs to be viewed with caution when displaying the transmission parameters.

Figure 4.21   Front panel of MPEG-2 encoder/modulater (Scopus Technologies)

MPEG-2 encoders for SNG are available in compact sizes with the modulator installed inside to form a single modulator/encoder unit. Additionally, some essential controls will be available at or near the top level of the front panel menu:

● Carrier on/off
● IF Level control
● FEC selection/Modulation mode

Integrated multiplexer

An important consideration for SNG operators is the ability to uplink more than one program signal at a time. As has been previously discussed, one of the two methods for achieving this is in the digital domain by multiplexing MPEG-2 signals together into a single transport stream. An encoder that offers this facility integrated within the unit, so two or more MPEG-2 encoders can be 'cascaded', is plainly going to be more attractive to the end-user where size and weight of equipment is a constant issue.

These points are given as an outline guide – the end-user may very well have other points that they regard as important. Having examined the issues of video compression, we now need to look at how bandwidth is saved in the audio domain. All bar one of the standards so far described also have an audio specification, but we will be focusing on MPEG audio standards (which is Part 3 of all MPEG standards).

4.14   Audio compression

A number of digital audio compression systems aimed at dealing with both speech and music signals are 'perceptual' audio coders, rather than so-called 'waveform coders'. In a perceptual audio coder, the codec does not attempt to retain the input signal exactly after encoding and decoding; rather its goal is to ensure that the output signal sounds the same to a human listener. The primary psycho-acoustic effect that the perceptual audio coder uses is called 'auditory masking', where parts of a signal are not audible due to the function of the human auditory system. The parts of the signal that are masked are commonly called 'irrelevant', as opposed to parts of the signal that are removed by a source coder (lossless or lossy), which are termed 'redundant'.

4.14.1   Psycho-acoustics

Psycho-acoustics plays a key role by exploiting this reduction of 'irrelevance', i.e. compressing parts of the signal that are imperceptible to the human ear. The human ear hears frequencies between 20 Hz and 20 kHz, and the human voice typically produces sounds in the range 400 Hz–4 kHz, with the ear most sensitive in the range 2–4 kHz. The low frequencies are vowels and bass, while the high frequencies are consonants. The dynamic range (i.e. quietest to loudest sounds) of the human ear is about 96 dB (around four thousand million to one), with the threshold of pain at around 115 dBA and permanent damage at around 130 dBA. The dBA is a unit of measurement of sound pressure level, which is what the ear is sensitive to. It is therefore important to consider these frequency and dynamic ranges when determining the most suitable type of audio coding and compression to use for audio broadcast purposes.

4.14.2 Why compress?

It could be considered that audio does not need to be compressed as it uses relatively little bandwidth compared to video. CD audio, for instance, is not compressed, and has 44 100 samples per second (44.1 kHz sampling), with 16 bits per sample and 2 channels (stereo), which gives a data rate of 1.4 Mbps. It can also be argued (and is hotly by audiophiles!) that audio suffers when it is compressed. However, in early MPEG audio evaluation tests, expert listeners listened to audio in optimal listening conditions, with 16 bits per sample of stereo sampled at 48 kHz compressed by 6:1 to 256 kbps, and they could not distinguish between coded and original audio clips.

Therefore, in the context of transmission, it is both desirable and possible to compress the audio signal, with no discernible detrimental effect, to reduce the overall data rate of the program signal. There are several techniques for the real-time digitization and compression of audio signals, some having been defined as international standards, while some remain proprietary systems (e.g. Dolby AC-3 or Sony ATRAC). The status of Windows Media Video 9, as we have seen, lies between being proprietary and an international standard.

4.14.3 Sampling, quantization and modulation

The processes of sampling and quantization used in audio compression are, in principle, the same as in video compression. The audio signal has to be converted from analog to digital as the first stage of processing, and this is done in the same way as described earlier. Because of the higher 'resolution' required for audio due to the human psycho-acoustic characteristic, the audio is typically sampled with 16 bits per sample. In the psycho-acoustic model, the human ear appears to be more discerning than the human eye, which only requires a relatively limited dynamic range of dark to light. The typical sampling frequencies for audio are 32, 44.1 or 48 kHz (although there is a range of lower and higher sampling rates). After quantization the coded bit-stream has a range of rates typically from 32 to 384 kbps (although again this range is extended both lower and higher for certain applications).

There are a number of different quantization and modulation schemes, and firstly we will look at the waveform coding techniques before considering higher order perceptual coding.

PCM

Pulse code modulation (PCM) encoding is the simplest form of audio coding (digitization and compression), and is a waveform coding scheme. PCM encoding samples the amplitude of an audio signal at a given sampling frequency and quantizes these amplitudes against a discrete number of pre-determined levels. If these quantization levels are uniformly spaced then the encoding is said to be uniform PCM encoding.

However, if the quantization levels have been logarithmically spaced, thus enabling a larger range of values to be measured, then the coding is said to be μ-law or A-law, depending on the type of logarithmic transformation used. Because of the logarithmic nature of the transform, low-amplitude samples are encoded with greater accuracy than high-amplitude samples. The μ-law and A-law PCM encoding methods are formally specified in the ITU-T G.711 standard (see Chapter 6).

H.261/263

PCM encoding methods encode each audio sample independently from adjacent samples. However, usually adjacent samples are similar to each other and the value of a sample can be predicted with some accuracy using the value of adjacent samples. The adaptive differential pulse code modulation (ADPCM) waveform coding method computes the difference between each sample and its predicted value and encodes the difference (hence the term differential). Fewer bits are needed to encode the difference than the complete sample value and compression rates of typically 4:1 can be achieved.

The ITU-T G.722 standard is one of the most common ADPCM encoding methods used over both ISDN and satellite circuits. A coding delay of about 6ms makes it very suitable for live interviews and voice feeds over a satellite circuit. However, the audio bandwidth of 7.5 kHz is generally considered too narrow for music and so its use is limited to voice applications (see Chapter 6).

4.14.4 MPEG and perceptual coding

In order to achieve higher compression ratios and transmit a wider bandwidth of audio, MPEG audio compression uses the psycho-acoustic principles we outlined earlier, and in particular a technique known as 'masking'.

Imagine a musical ensemble comprising several different instruments and playing all at the same time. The human ear is not capable of hearing all of the components of the sound because some of the quieter sounds are hidden or masked by the louder sounds. If a recording was made of the music and the parts that we could not hear were removed, we would still hear the same sound but we would have recorded much less data. This is exactly the way in which MPEG audio compression works, by removing the parts of the sound that we could not hear in any case.

Imagine a strong tone with a frequency of 1000 Hz and a second tone nearby of 1100 Hz and 18 dB lower (a lot quieter) than the first. The human ear will not be able to hear the second tone because it is completely masked by the first 1000 Hz tone. If a third tone of 2000 Hz, also 18 dB less than the first, is introduced this will be heard because, the further away from a sound, the less the masking effect. In effect we can discard the second tone without affecting the sound heard by the human ear, thus reducing the amount of information that would need to be coded and recorded.

In MPEG processing, the frequency spectrum is divided into 32 sub-bands and calculates the masking effect of each sub-band on adjacent sub-bands. The MPEG coding also takes into account the sensitivity of the human ear to different frequencies. The ear is more sensitive to low frequencies than high frequencies and is most sensitive to frequencies in the range 2–4 kHz – the same range as the human voice. It would then make sense to have narrower sub-bands, thus giving more precision, in the lower frequencies and wider sub-bands in the higher-frequency range.

This psycho-acoustic model analyses the input signals within consecutive time blocks and determines for each block the frequency components of the input audio signal. Then it models the masking properties of the human auditory system and estimates the just noticeable noise level, sometimes called the 'threshold of masking'.

MPEG uses a set of 'bandpass' filters to confine quantization noise within each sub-band and dynamically allocates bits to each sub-band. If sub-band energy falls below the psycho-acoustic masking threshold, then that part of the signal receives zero bits; otherwise it is allocated just enough bits to keep the quantization noise in the sub-band just below the psycho-acoustic audible threshold. Masking not only occurs at different frequencies (frequency masking) but also before and after a loud sound (temporal masking). Pre-masking is only effective 2–5 ms before an event but post-masking can have an effect up to 100 ms after a sound event.

The MPEG decoder is much less complex, because it does not require a psycho-acoustic model: its only task is to reconstruct an audio signal from the coded spectral components.

4.14.5 MPEG audio standards

Both in MPEG-1 and in MPEG-2, three different layers are defined, each representing a group of coding algorithms; the layers are denoted Layer 1, Layer 2 and Layer 3. The different layers have been defined to give, as with MPEG video, a degree of scalability to cope with the wide range of applications that can make use of the standards. The complexity of the encoder and decoder, the encoder/decoder delay and the coding efficiency increase when going from Layer 1 via Layer 2 to Layer 3. This is summarized as follows.

Layer 1
Layer 1 has the lowest complexity and is specifically suitable for applications where the encoder complexity also plays an important role. The Layer 1 psycho-acoustic model uses only frequency masking, with 32 sub-bands each of 750 Hz. The audio data are divided into frames, each containing 384 samples, with 12 samples from each of the 32 filtered sub-bands. There is no temporal masking, i.e. taking into account the pattern of loud and quiet signals. It is a simple implementation, giving the lowest compression ratio (1:4), and is used in consumer audio systems. Its main advantage lies in the low cost of implementation.

Layer 2
In this layer, the psycho-acoustic model uses a more complex frequency characteristic. Layer 2 requires a more complex encoder and a slightly more complex decoder, and is directed towards 'one to many' applications, i.e. one encoder serves many decoders. Compared to Layer 1, Layer 2 is able to remove more of the signal redundancy and to apply the psycho-acoustic threshold more efficiently. Again there are 32 sub-bands, each of 750 Hz; but in addition, there are three temporal frames ('before', 'current' and 'next'), giving some temporal masking. Layer 2 gives greater compression (1:6–1:8) and is found in numerous consumer and professional applications. It is common for Layer 2 to be used for SNG applications.

Layer 3
This is a more complex MPEG 1/2 audio layer where the psycho-acoustic model uses improved band filtering to model human ear sensitivities (non-equal frequencies) and temporal masking effects; it also takes into account stereo redundancy and uses variable length coding. Layer 3 is directed towards lower bit-rate applications due to the additional redundancy and irrelevancy extraction from enhanced frequency resolution in its filtering. It gives the greatest level of compression (1:10 to 1:12) at the expense of complicated encoding and decoding, which increases the processing delay. Layer 3 is more commonly known as 'MP3' – music files stored in the MP3 format on computers and portable music players.

MPEG-1 audio coding provides both single-channel (mono) and two-channel (stereo or 'dual–mono') coding at 32, 44.1 and 48 kHz sampling rates. The pre-defined bit-rates range from 32 to 448 kbps for Layer 1, from 32 to 384 kbps for Layer 2, and from 32 to 320 kbps for Layer 3.

MPEG-2 audio coding provides extension to lower sampling frequencies, providing better sound quality at very low bit-rates. It extends to the lower sampling rates of 16, 22.05 and 24 kHz, for bit-rates from 32 to 256 kbps (Layer 1) and from 8 to 160 kbps (Layer 2 and Layer 3). It also provides for multi-channel sound. MPEG-2 audio supports up to five full bandwidth channels plus one low-frequency enhancement channel (such an ensemble of channels is referred to as '5.1'). This multi-channel extension is both forward- and backward-compatible with MPEG-1. Typical MPEG-2 transmissions use 48 kHz sampling, giving a frequency range of 40 Hz–22 kHz.

Advanced Audio Coding (AAC)

A further development in MPEG-2 (Part 7) introduced Advanced Audio Coding. AAC provides a very high-quality audio coding standard for 1–48 channels at sampling rates of 8–96 kHz, with multichannel, multilingual and multiprogram capabilities. AAC works at bit-rates from 8 kbps for a monophonic speech signal to over 160 kbps/channel for very high-quality coding that permits multiple encode/decode cycles. Three profiles of AAC provide varying levels of complexity and scalability – Main Profile, Low Complexity Profile and Scalable Sampling Rate Profile. An AAC bit-stream is not backward-compatible, i.e. it cannot be read and interpreted by an MPEG-1 audio decoder.

The MPEG-2 AAC standard provides very high audio quality at a rate of 64 kbps/channel for multichannel operation, with the capability of up to 48 main audio channels, 16 low-frequency effects channels, 16 overdub/multilingual channels and 16 data streams. Up to 16 programs can be described, each consisting of any number of the audio and data elements. AAC adheres to the same basic coding paradigm as MPEG-1/2 Layer 3, but has additional coding tools and improves on details. Some of the improvements implemented by AAC are a filter bank with a higher-frequency resolution, improved unpredictability (entropy) coding and better stereo coding. Two new coding tools are an optional backward prediction (used only in the Main Profile) and noise shaping in the time domain, which mainly improves quality of encoded speech at low bit-rates. As a result, AAC is approximately 30% more bit-rate efficient than MPEG-1 Layer 3.

The MPEG-4 AAC standard (Part 3) is a slightly modified version of MPEG-2 AAC, forming the basis of the MPEG-4 audio compression technology for data rates above 32 kbps per channel. Additional tools increase the effectiveness of AAC at lower bit-rates, and add scalability and error resilience characteristics. It has become popular for use on portable music players, particularly the Apple iPod.

4.14.6 MUSICAM and DAB

The ISO/IEC MPEG established in 1988 considered digital compression standards for audio as well as video material. Meanwhile, under the auspices of a technical body called Eureka – an international consortium of broadcasters, network operators, consumer electronic industries and research institutes – the digital audio broadcasting (DAB) standard was being developed to replace conventional broadcast radio technology (analog AM and FM). DAB is the most fundamental advance in radio technology since the introduction of FM stereo radio, as it gives listeners interference-free reception and high-quality sound, and the potential for enhanced text and information services.

This project was called Eureka 147, and one of the results of the project was a digital audio compression standard called MUSICAM (Masking pattern adapted Universal Sub-band Integrated Coding and Multiplexing). Meanwhile, another international group had devised a coding system called ASPEC (Adaptive Spectral Perceptual Entropy Coding). The International Standards Organisation (ISO) held a competition to select a world standard and MUSICAM, designed and manufactured by CCS (US), was judged to be the best overall system. Both the MUSICAM and ASPEC systems were submitted to ISO/MPEG, and ISO/MPEG subsequently took the best features of both systems to form the basis for MPEG audio Layers 1 and 2. Since the publication of the MPEG-1 audio standard, the original MUSICAM algorithm is not used anymore, although MPEG Layer 2 has sometimes generically (but not strictly correctly) referred to as MUSICAM.

4.15 Metadata

Finally, we should briefly mention 'metadata'. Metadata is defined as program content description information that is carried as an auxiliary data channel within the MPEG-2/MPEG-4 signal, and is classed as information relating to digital rights management (DRM). The overall concept is that metadata can carry a whole host of information about the program, including archive information, origin of material intellectual rights, etc. The level of information is almost boundless, and it is very much up to the end-user to define what information is carried with the signal. In the context of newsgathering, it has been suggested that metadata could be used to carry information relating to the material from the field which is often lost (who shot the pictures, where, when, etc.)

However, in the natural semi-chaos that often surrounds newsgathering in the field, it is not easy at the moment to see how this could practically be implemented. It would be possible to transfer the time, date and location information automatically by recording a signal from a GPS (Global Positioning System) receiver, for instance – provided the GPS receiver was integrated into the camcorder. Means to achieve the insertion of metadata in the field will be implemented as the pressure to improve archival information increases.

One of the great debates in the new digital broadcasting environment is how all the material that can be readily accessed in the medium of the video program server can be indexed and found again – but that's another story!

4.16   Conclusion

The impact and significance of digital compression technology should now be clear, and as was said at the beginning of the chapter, for the reader interested in the technical detail of these systems, there are a selection of papers and books available on the subject. Video compression is common in broadcasting generally, and SNG operations are solely in the compressed domain.

There are drawbacks to using digital compression, though these are of lesser importance in the realm of satellite newsgathering. The effect of compression on picture content varies widely depending on the content, and there is still no widely accepted scientific method of measuring picture quality – the human eye has been found to be the best guide, but it is a subjective evaluation. However, suffice to say that for most news organizations, the advantages of the cost of utilizing compression far outweigh what are considered esoteric concerns over issues of quality.

However, a secondary issue in video compression which is worth mentioning is the outcome of 'concatenation' through differing MPEG-2 systems. In a program path in a broadcasting environment, from SNG uplink to distribution to home that is increasingly in the digital domain, there is concern about the effects of a program signal being passed through a number of MPEG-2 processes. The signal can be coded, decoded and recoded a number of times, and each time a different DCT, quantization and GOP structure will be applied to the signal. This could potentially result in the finally delivered program signal being turned into a digital 'soup'-full of artifacts, lacking resolution, and with poor motion processing.

The refinement and improvement of MPEG-2 has reached its conclusion, though it is still the workhorse standard in the broadcast industry. The development of the advanced codecs of MPEG-4 AVC and VC-1 has sounded the death knell for MPEG-2, but the decline of MPEG-2 is not going to occur overnight. There is an enormous established user base of equipment – at both broadcaster and consumer ends of the market – that it will survive for some time yet.

MPEG-4 AVC as used in SNG is currently only available in 4:2:0, and is likely to become the replacement to MPEG-2 in the broadcast contribution sector in the next 5 years; while both MPEG-4 AVC and VC-1 will vie for supremacy in the distribution of program material to the home. The use of lower data rates than has been the custom in the past will become a feature of using new advanced compression systems.

References

1. ITU (1998) Recommendation ITU-R BT.601–5, Studio encoding parameters of digital television for standard 4:3 and wide-screen 16:9 aspect ratios.
2. ITU (1998) Recommendation ITU-R BT.656–4, Interfaces for digital component video signals in 525-line and 625-line television systems operating at the 4:2:2 level of Recommendation ITU-R BT.601 (Part A).
3. SMPTE 125M-1995, Component video signal 4:2:2 – bit-parallel digital interface.
4. SMPTE 259M-1993, 10-Bit 4:2:2 component and 4fsc NTSC component digital signals – serial digital interface.
5. ITU (1993) ITU-T Recommendation H.261 (3/93), Video codec for audiovisual services at p $\times$ 64 kbit/s.
6. ISO/IEC (1994) ISO/IEC Reference 10918, Digital compression and coding of continuous-tone still images.
7. ETSI (1992) ETS 300 174, Network aspects (NA): Digital coding of component television signals for contribution quality applications in the range 34–45 Mbps.
8. ISO/IEC (1993) ISO/IEC Reference 11172, Coding of moving pictures and associated audio for digital storage media at up to 1.5 Mbps.
9. ISO/IEC (1995) ISO/IEC Reference 13818, Generic coding of moving pictures and associated audio information.
10. ITU (1995) Recommendation ITU-T H.262 (7/95), Information technology – generic coding of moving pictures and associated audio information.
11. Caruso, A., Cheveau, L. and Flowers, B. (1998) *EBU Technical Review* 276, MPEG-2 4:2:2 profile – its use for contribution/collection and primary distribution.
12. Caruso, A., Cheveau, L. and Flowers, B. (1998) The Use of MPEG-2 4:2:2 Profile for Contribution and Primary Distribution, IBC 98, Amsterdam.
13. Cheveau, L. and Caruso, A. (1999) *EBU Technical Review* 279, Comparison between 4:2:2P and 4:2:0 for 525- and 625-line pictures.
14. ETSI (1994) EN 300 421: Digital broadcasting systems for television, sound and data services – framing structure, channel coding and modulation for 11/12 GHz satellite services.
15. EBU Tech 3290 Basic Interoperable Scrambling System (March 2000).
16. EBU Tech 3292 (rev.2) Basic Interoperable Scrambling System with Encrypted keys (August 2002).
17. INTELSAT (1996/1998) INTELSAT/ISOG interoperability tests.
18. EBU (1997) Digital satellite newsgathering using MPEG-2 MP@ML – EBU interoperability tests.
19. ETSI (1997) EN 301 210: Digital Video Broadcasting (DVB) –Framing structure, channel coding and modulation for Digital Satellite News Gathering (DSNG) and other contribution applications by satellite.
20. ISO/IEC (2000)14496: Information technology. Coding of audio–visual objects.
21. ISO/IEC (2000)14496-10: Information technology. Coding of audio–visual objects. Advanced Video Coding (AVC) file format.
22. SMPTE 421M-2006: VC-1 Compressed Video Bit-stream Format and Decoding Process.
23. ETSI (2004) EN 302 307: Digital Video Broadcasting (DVB); Second generation framing structure, channel coding and modulation systems for Broadcasting, Interactive Services, News Gathering and other broadband satellite applications.
24. Morello, A and Mignone, V. (2004) *EBU Technical Review* 300: DVB-S2 – ready for lift off.

5

Twenty-first century transport: SNG over IP

5.1 Introduction

In this chapter, we are going to cover a subject that will strike a chord with everyone who uses a computer and the Internet – and it is highly doubtful if that excludes any reader. In the last few years, we have seen the emergence of a new method of transporting video and audio signals across networks through the use of Transmission Control Protocol (TCP) and Internet Protocol (IP) – together referred to as TCP/IP – and the Ethernet Networking Protocol.

In networking, a 'protocol' is the term for a set of rules that allows the orderly exchange of information over a network, and many of them are defined by a body called the Internet Engineering Task Force (IETF). Protocols are to computers what language is to humans. Since this book is in English, to understand it you must be able to read English. Similarly, for two devices on a network to successfully communicate, they must both understand and use the same language – or protocols.

Interestingly, the birth of the Internet can be traced back to the launch of SPUTNIK in 1957, which we mentioned in Chapter 1. In 1958, US President Eisenhower was lobbied by the military and political establishment to initiate and fund the Advanced Research Projects Agency (ARPA) to draw together all the research being undertaken by the myriad of US military agencies at the time. Over the following years as ARPA developed, it encompassed a wider range of interests which included computing and control. By the early 1970s, ARPA had a comparatively small Intranet of 15 nodes across the US connected; and by the early 1980s, in association with a number of manufacturers and research laboratories, finally had a TCP/IP network interconnecting a significant part of US academic and military research facilities. From this, the Internet gradually emerged as a public network through the late 1980s and early 1990s.

This use of computer transmission technology has now extended to the world of SNG. The move toward compact SNG units has also seen a shift to the use of IP for providing connectivity for both MPEG-2 and MPEG-4 streams (or whichever other type of compression is used), as well as providing ancillary services on site at major news events, and thus an understanding of IP is now critical.

In simple terms, Internet Protocol (IP) works by sending packets of data across the Internet and Local Area Network (LAN) in a series of hops in a discontinuous stream, which are assembled at the destination. Data is sliced into packets which have addresses on the front for the destination. The packets are sent through a series of nodes (switches, routers, etc.) on a hop-by-hop basis. At each node, every packet is analyzed to decide which hop it should take next. This is decided on parameters completely unrelated to any importance that may be attached to this packet as part of the whole stream (a complete anathema to newsgatherers, who naturally regard their traffic packets as more important than anyone else's).

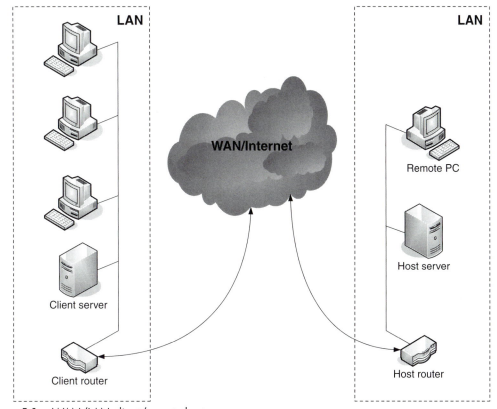

Figure 5.1 WAN/LAN client/remote host

Within the context of satellite newsgathering, IP generically refers to the means of exchanging data that is increasingly used both within and between broadcast centers over their Local Area Network (LAN) and Wide Area Network (WAN) – which includes the Internet (the global Ethernet network) – for video, audio, text and other data. The spread of computer technology within the broadcast center, combined with the mushrooming of the Internet, has resulted in some manufacturers of SNG equipment producing IP 'terminals' for use in the field. IP is also used as an ancillary service for providing network connection to a newsroom LAN and the newsroom production system, and can even be used to provide voice connectivity – VoIP (Voice over IP). As an example, IP has even become the backbone of some talkback systems used within remote OB trucks as well as studios.

Strictly speaking, IP is the addressing system of the Internet, as it defines the way packets of data (information messages) are routed across a network – whether via terrestrial, wireless or satellite; while Ethernet is the 'networking protocol', i.e. the way the data is packaged and transported.

The Internet is now a vast global system that it is essentially made up of a network of literally millions of 'routers' – devices which act as gateways and relays for data packets, deciding the best way of delivering the packets based on the rules programmed inside them, called 'routing tables'. These are interconnected with 'servers' – a server can be a simple PC, or it can be a sophisticated computer used for running server software applications.

The whole system is based on 'packet switching', where the route an individual packet takes from the point of departure to the destination is decided 'on-the-fly', and the fastest or least congested route from A to B is found for each packet.

This is unlike a telephone circuit, where there is a single dedicated connection established for the duration of the call and is not shared – this is based on a system called 'circuit switching'. This is like a train which travels along one railway track from A to B, with a string of carriages all traveling together on the same track.

With packet switching, routers along the way dynamically determine a path for each railway carriage or packet, re-ordering them to use any track or path available to get from A to B. Other packets from other sources run on these circuits as well, making the most use of each path, unlike circuit switched calls that occupy a single path to the exclusion of all others. So the train starts from the departure point as a complete train, but then gets split up along the way, but comes back together as a single train with all the carriages in the right order at the destination.

Thus a router determines the next network point to which a data packet should be forwarded to help it reach its destination. It is always connected to at least two networks and determines which way to send each data packet based on its current 'understanding' of the state of the networks it is connected to. Routers create or maintain a table of the available routes (the 'routing table') and use this information to determine the best route for a given data packet.

So for our purposes, we will use 'IP' to generically describe the technology for sending message signals using TCP/IP across Ethernet networks and the Internet.

IP has a number of benefits for SNG use, which can be summarized as follows:

- Relatively low cost as a consumer technology
- Agnostic in what is carried over a network – any traffic can be carried
- Conforms with the already powerful convergence between broadcast and computer technologies in the broadcast center

Because this will probably be the principal transport medium for SNG within a few years, its significance cannot be overstated. However as with many other topics covered in this book, there are a wide range of books dedicated to the subject, so we can only try to discuss basic principles and describe how it relates specifically to SNG.

5.2 Fundamentals

Obviously Ethernet and IP were developed for both private and public (i.e. the Internet) networks, and in order to understand its application to SNG, we will describe the basic structure.

The essential concept is that a stream of data packets is exchanged between a 'server' and a 'client' over an Ethernet network, and the connection could be across an office, a building, a city, a country or between continents (see Figure 5.1). A client can request data from the server, and vice versa, and all points within a network are generically termed 'hosts' or 'nodes', via designated points of presence (POP).

Much of the Internet is in fact connected by both satellite and optical fiber Ethernet networks that span the globe, and the connection within neighborhoods – colloquially known as 'the last mile' – is either over high-speed broadband connections via fiber optic (FTTH, Fiber To The Home) at 10–100 Mbps; cable (often referred to as DSL – Digital Subscriber Line) at up to 10 Mbps; or much slower dial-up telephone connection, at up to 56 kbps, or 64/128 kbps using ISDN.

The other method of connecting to a network is wirelessly, via several different types of technologies. 'Bluetooth' is a system currently capable of only 700 kbps and a theoretical range of up to 30 m, but destined to be capable of up to 2 Mbps in the second generation. Wireless connections via Bluetooth can be made to a GSM phone, and then a connection can be established over the mobile phone network either using GPRS or 3G connectivity. 'Wi-Fi' is capable of connecting a PC to a wireless router up to 100 m away at a theoretical speed of up to 108 Mbps, and is now a mature technology in its second generation. Finally, at the time of writing, 'WiMAX' is a new technology that is designed for a range of 3–50 km and with a connection speed of up to 72 Mbps.

In remote places, the connection may be via a small fixed satellite terminal called a VSAT (Very Small Aperture Terminal), and this is typically at connection speeds of up to 1 Mbps, although higher speeds are possible. Incidentally, an SNG uplink can be considered as a very rugged and portable type of VSAT (as long as it used in a bi-directional mode with a return path from the satellite and receive equipment). Inmarsat satellite phones can also provide connectivity to the IP network (Figure 5.2).

In order to simplify our discussion, Figure 5.3 shows a 'cake' with four different layers arranged in hierarchical fashion (there are in fact seven layers, but they are combined into four in this simplified version).

Cake layer 1: the Ethernet
At the bottom is the Ethernet, which is the physical data link, i.e. the mix of cable, fiber optic, wireless, satellite link and all the devices that connect these together that forms the transport medium – the physical highway.

Cake layer 2: IP
The next layer is the IP layer, which forms the key element of the network. It is all very well having a number of devices connected together, but if the devices cannot be addressed, it is useless as a network – so this provides the road numbering, destination naming and overall map of the highway system.

Cake layer 3: TCP
The third layer is the TCP (Transmission Control Protocol) layer, which is the fundamental transport mechanism for carrying data over Ethernet networks – the 'wheels' used on the highway system. As well as TCP/IP, later we will be looking at UDP (User Datagram Protocol) and RTP/SIP (Real-time Transfer Protocol/Session Initiation Protocol), which are important for video 'streaming'. It is important to note, however, that TCP/IP is not the only transport mechanism for packet data transmission – there are a number of other methods used on private networks such as ATM and Frame Relay – but it is the transport mechanism for the Internet and hence for many private networks as well.

Cake layer 4: Application
Finally, the top layer of the cake is the application layer – and these include applications such as HTTP (HyperText Transfer Protocol) – otherwise commonly known as the World Wide Web (WWW) – e-mail, TelNet (a simple control protocol) and the File Transfer Protocol (FTP). These are the uses of the highway.

5.2.1   Ethernet

Starting at the bottom layer, Ethernet is the standard communications protocol embedded in software and hardware devices, and by means of software, cable and other types of connections, network switch devices, data and resources (computers, printers, scanners, etc.), these can be shared among a number of users. A network typically has a large number of nodes, which may be multiple junctions or individual points, and within this data link layer every point has to have a physical address; e.g. the MAC (Media Access Control) address (in Ethernet) or a phone number (for a dial-up modem connection) (Figure 5.4).

Data from a PC is formed into packets or 'frames' conforming to the Ethernet Protocol, and each packet or 'datagram' consists of a 'header', which carries amongst other things the addressing of the data packet; the data itself, referred to as the 'payload' and finally the 'trailer', which carries error correction data.

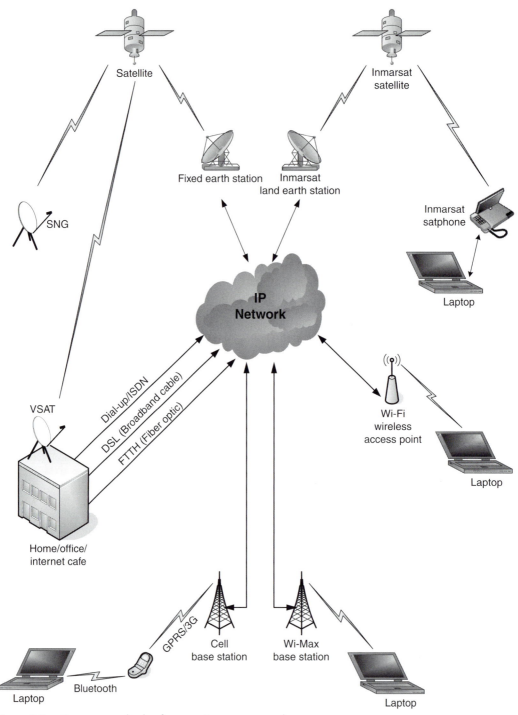

Figure 5.2 Common methods of connecting to a network

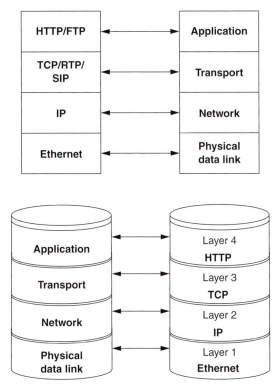

Figure 5.3   Network layer cake

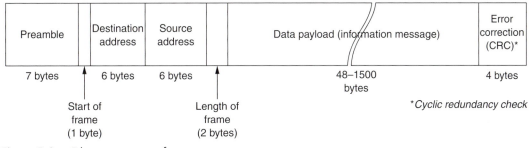

Figure 5.4   Ethernet transport frame

The header of a packet specifies the data type, packet number, total number of payload bytes, and the sender and receiver IP addresses. The addressing conforms to the IP standard, and the data is carried over the Ethernet network in accordance with the addressing contained within the frame. Millions of these frames from computer devices from all over a network merge and stream together, and the network switches instantaneously route the data packets to their destination by reading the addresses and following the routing tables that are loaded into each switch.

Notice that we refer here to network 'switches' – a switch is a generic term for any routing device, and this not only includes routers (which we have already covered) but also 'switches' and 'hubs'. Earlier in the chapter, we discussed the role of routers in directing traffic across the Internet. Hubs, switches and routers are all devices which allow the connection of one or more computers to other computers, networked devices or to other networks. Each has two or more input/output connections – termed 'ports' – into which one plugs in the cables to make the connection. Varying degrees of processing happen inside the device, and therein lies the difference.

Hubs are the simplest of these devices, where all the traffic that flows into one port is distributed across all the other ports. We will come back to the significance of ports later in the chapter. A hub is the least expensive, least intelligent and least complicated of the three. Its function is very simple – anything that comes in one port is distributed to all the other ports. Any packet entering any port is broadcast out of every port to each computer and thus hubs do not manage any of the traffic that comes through their ports. Since every packet is constantly being sent out through every port, this results in packet collisions, which greatly impedes the smooth flow of traffic. For years, hubs have been the low-cost method of interconnecting computers in small networks, but as the cost of switches has fallen, hubs are now used less and less.

A switch essentially does the same as a hub, but more efficiently. A switch isolates ports, meaning that every received packet is sent out only to the port on which the destination device may be found (assuming the proper port can be found; if it is not, then the switch will broadcast the packet to all ports except the port that request originated from). For example, if it sees traffic from PC 'A' coming in on port 1, it now knows that PC A is connected to that port, and that traffic to PC A needs only to be sent to that port and not to any other. The result of using a switch over a hub is that most of the network traffic only goes where it needs to, rather than to every port. Since the switch intelligently sends packets only where they need to go, the performance (speed) of the network is greatly increased.

A router is the most 'intelligent' and most complicated member of the family. Routers come in all shapes and sizes, from the small four-port broadband routers found in homes and small offices, to the large enterprise grade devices that steer traffic across the Internet itself. A simple way to think of a router is as a computer that can be programmed to learn, manipulate and route the data it is being asked to handle. For example, broadband routers include the ability to 'hide' computers behind a 'firewall', which involves slightly modifying the packets of network traffic as they traverse the device.

A firewall is a piece of hardware and/or software which prevents communications forbidden by a security policy, analogous to the function of firewalls in building construction. A firewall has the basic task of controlling traffic between different zones of 'trust'. Typical zones of trust can range from the Internet (a zone with no trust) to an internal network (a zone with high trust). The ultimate goal is to provide controlled connectivity between zones of differing trust levels through the enforcement of a security policy and connectivity model based on the least privilege principle.

All routers include some kind of user interface for configuring how the router will treat traffic. The very large routers include the equivalent of a high-level programming language to describe how they should operate, as well as the ability to communicate with other routers to describe or determine the best way to get network traffic from points A to B.

The physical Ethernet connection between the PC and the rest of the world in the first instance is via a NIC (Network Interface Card) installed inside the PC, usually via a type of cable called 'Cat 5' with an 'RJ-45' connector. This is commonly termed a '10/100 base-T' interface, as depending on the NIC and the router, connection speeds of 10 or 100 Mbps are possible. A new standard – Gigabit – offers up to 1 Gbps transfer speeds. Although we refer to a network 'card', on certain PC devices, e.g. laptops, it is typically integrated inside.

It is the NIC that converts the data to and from the Ethernet Protocol, and because it needs to be individually identified, every NIC has a factory-assigned unique 48-bit number termed a MAC (Media Access Control) address. It is important to note that a device MAC address is 'hard-wired' into a device – it does not change – but an IP address is both dynamic and relative as it can be changed. A MAC address is one of the few absolutes in the world of IP.

The Ethernet Protocol is blind to the transport medium used, and so it becomes largely irrelevant how the connection is made. What is important is how the data – or information – from the computer reaches its destination, and how information destined for that computer is routed to it. This is where IP and addressing come in.

5.2.2 IP

With the first layer in place, we can proceed to actually shape the network into something more than a collection of devices connected together. The network layer specifies the procedures for transmitting data across the network, including how to access the physical medium, such as the Ethernet (physical) layer. IP is also responsible for data addressing, transmission, and packet fragmentation and reassembly. An IP address is assigned to each node on a network, and is used to identify the location of that network and its 'sub-nets'. A sub-net is a range of logical addresses within the address range assigned to an organization.

It is important to grasp that IP works on the basis that every source, every destination and all the points in between have an address, just like your house. Without knowing the destination address or how to reach it, a message signal can be sent out over a network and will never arrive at its intended destination.

Any organization can have its own internal networks (Intranets) to connect to the Internet, though the addresses must conform to the Internet addressing format. As we have discussed, the Internet uses Transmission Control Protocol/Internet Protocol (TCP/IP) to transfer data, and every host connected on the Internet is assigned an IP address, sometimes just for the period of connection or 'session'.

All addresses used by routable protocols have a 'network' element, to route packets to the nearest router, and a 'host' portion, which indicates which host station the device is connected to on that routed segment.

5.2.3 Addressing

To understand IP addressing, we are going to build on our introduction to binary arithmetic covered in Chapters 2 and 4. You may recall that we said that in binary arithmetic, numbers are represented as '0' or '1', known as a 'bit'. Our normal counting system uses a base of 10, which we know as the decimal system (from the Latin *decima*, a tenth part), where we count in tens, hundreds, thousands, etc. In the decimal system, we multiply (or divide) by 10 each time we move a decimal place. This is shown in Table 5.1, where we show how, for example, the number 1 258 673 is made up.

In computer technology, using binary arithmetic which uses a base of 2, we multiply (or divide) by 2 each time we move a binary place. So, for example, the number 181 would be represented as 1011 0101, shown in Table 5.2.

Table 5.1 Decimal system

1 000 000	100 000	10 000	1000	100	10	1
1	2	5	8	6	7	3

Table 5.2 Binary system

128	64	32	16	8	4	2	1
1	0	1	1	0	1	0	1

Note that the binary number is shown as two groups of four bits – it is simply presented this way to make it easier for us to read (rather than as 10110101). Now add up the columns where there is a '1' (128 + 32 + 16 + 4 + 1) and you can see the answer is 181. The binary number 10110101 is much longer, and difficult for us to interpret, but simple for computers to calculate. Now it is no coincidence that we show this as an 8-bit number (although a binary number can be any number of bits), because the value of 8 has a special significance – an 8-bit number is called a 'byte'. The maximum binary number a byte can be is 1111 1111, or in decimal, 255 (= 128 + 64 + 32 + 16 + 8 + 4 + 2 + 1).

So a byte is a number in the range 0–255, and an IP address is made up of 4 bytes. This would be a 32-bit binary number if we expressed it in binary, so rather inconvenient to use. Instead the convention is to present an IP address as a block of decimal numbers (termed 'octets'), each separated by a period – termed 'dotted quad notation'. Hence the binary IP address in 32 bit form of 1100 0000 1010 1000 0000 1111 0000 0001 is expressed as 192.168.15.1 (4 octets) in decimal – much easier for human comprehension.

The current version of IP is referred to as 'IPv4', and under IPv4, the maximum range of addresses is from 0.0.0.0 to 255.255.255.255 – a total of 4 294 967 296 (2^{32}), or nearly 4.3 billion addresses. That is a considerable number of potential addresses for a computer or a router to keep track of, so traditionally there has been a further way of dividing addresses that makes it easier for processing.

Note that not just anyone can use addresses on the Internet – they are reserved for use by large entities, and are allocated by the Internet Assigned Numbers Authority (IANA).

The routing for an address is simplified by splitting IP address ranges into 'classes'. Those IP address ranges whose first byte is in the range 0–127 belong to networks called 'Class A' networks; there are 128 networks in this class each with 16 777 214 ($2^{24} - 2$) hosts. In Class A networks, the first 8 bits (1 byte) are the 'network prefix' and the last 24 bits (3 bytes) are the 'host' or 'node' allocation, i.e. these last 3 bytes can be allocated to the devices on the part of the network under your control (*network . local . local . local*).

Class B networks are those IP addresses whose first byte is in the range 128–192, and there are 16 384 networks in this class (i.e. 192 minus 128, multiplied by 256), each with 65 534 ($2^{16} - 2$) hosts. So we have 2 bytes for the network prefix and 2 bytes for the host allocation (*network . network . local . local*). This address range is reserved for medium-sized networks.

Class C networks are where the first byte is in the range 192–223, have a 3 byte network prefix and a 1 byte host allocation (*network . network . network . local*). There are 225 − 192 multiplied by 2^{24} networks in this range, each with 256 hosts. This is summarized in Table 5.3.

Classes D and E networks are where the first byte is in the range 224–254, and are either allocated for IP 'multicast' (Class D, which is allocated 224–240) or experimental (Class E). IP multicast is a service that allows material to be transmitted to many points on an Internet at one time – the Internet equivalent of broadcasting – and has been assigned addresses from within this range. This is of importance to us, as we shall see later.

Table 5.3 IP addressing

Class	Network bits (bytes)	Byte 1 address range	Sub-network mask	Sub-network mask (binary)	Networks/hosts (nodes) available
A	8 (1)	0–127	255.0.0.0	11111111 00000000 00000000 00000000	128/16 777 214
B	16 (2)	128–191	255.255.0.0	11111111 11111111 00000000 00000000	16 384/65 532
C	24 (3)	192–223	255.255.255.0	11111111 11111111 11111111 00000000	2 097 152/254

Note how neatly everything lines up on byte 'boundaries', and a way of isolating a block of bytes is called 'masking' – important in the use of 'sub-nets', which we will cover next. The Class C range of addresses is open for anyone to use, and not usually allocated on the Internet; this address range is used on the 'private' or local part of a network inside a building or within a small area.

Now, just to really confuse the reader, it should be pointed out that the above method of 'class' addressing is passing out of fashion as we move toward 'classless' addressing in IPv4, termed Classless Inter-Domain Routing (CIDR). So what was the point of explaining all of the above? Well, it is important that you have a grasp as to how addressing structures are made up, as there are still often references made to the 'class'-based address structure in many legacy systems and documents. We will not discuss CIDR here, as now the reader will have enough information to be able to read further elsewhere on IP addressing if desired.

We can see how IP addressing works using an analogy. Imagine the Internet is the postal network, and IP is the method of addressing just as we write a postal address. Think of an IP packet as an envelope (the header) containing information (the data payload) with an IP address on the front, and this IP address is the country, city, street and house number on the front of the envelope. Every TCP/IP-enabled device can be compared to a house mailbox, and every mailbox has an IP address.

5.2.4   Sub-nets

As we saw above, the application of the sub-network mask can define the range of IP addresses, and the use of 'sub-net' addressing greatly simplifies the information tables held in routers used to direct packets onwards to their destinations. The sub-net mask acts as a filter that is applied to a message's destination IP address. Its objective is to determine whether the local network is the destination network, or if the packet is to be delivered beyond the local network.

Returning to our postal analogy, let us suppose that we live in a small village, and the IP address range of our village is 201.50.25.0 to 201.50.25.255. This means that we have a Class C address, and our sub-net mask is 255.255.255.0 – the last octet of 0 shows that we have a theoretical range of up to 256 addresses available. So we have a range of 254 addresses for houses in the village. (Why not 256 addresses? – because two addresses are specially reserved; 0.0.0.0 is the 'network default address'; 255.255.255.255 is used for 'broadcast' service announcements on the network.)

Let us suppose we have a sophisticated postal system, which not only has the postman delivering letters to our house mailboxes, but also collecting from each one as well. When the postman comes to our house, he delivers some mail and collects two envelopes as well (data packets). One envelope has an address on the front which is 201.50.25.67 and the second envelope has the address 201.50.24.17.

Our postman takes these back to the post office in the village and examines the addresses by applying a mask of 255.255.255.0 to the address on Envelope 1. Instead of looking up each address, he simply applies a 'mask' over each of the addresses. This 'blanks' out the octets of the address that matches the octet sequence of the village address range. The last part of the octet sequence is a zero, so this means that if all the other octets are blanked, any number in the range 0–255 will be within the village's address range (Table 5.4a).

Hence the sub-net mask tells him that if the first three octets of the address on the envelope match the first three octets of the range allocated to the village, he can simply take Envelope 1 back out with him on his next delivery round in the village, and deliver it to the house which has the address of 67 (Table 5.4b).

Now he looks at Envelope 2, and makes the same comparison using his sub-net mask. Octets 1 and 2 match, but octet 3 is outside the range allowed by his sub-net mask – because of this, he doesn't even look at octet 4, but sends Envelope 2 onto the district postal sorting office, which deals with mail outside the village area.

So let us complete the postal analogy. The postal sorting office that sorts and forwards mail based on the address on the envelope is the router. If the address is on a postal round dealt with by that office

Table 5.4 (a) Checking 'Envelope 1'

Octet	Octet 1	Octet 2	Octet 3	Octet 4
Base IP range	201	50	25	0
Address	201	50	25	67
Sub-net mask	255	255	255	0
Decision	Same – ignore	Same – ignore	Same – ignore	Within range – local delivery

Table 5.4 (b) Checking 'Envelope 2'

Octet	Octet 1	Octet 2	Octet 3	Octet 4
Base IP range	201	50	25	0
Address	201	50	24	17
Sub-net mask	255	255	255	0
Decision	Same – ignore	Same – ignore	Different – not for the this area	–

(based on the sub-net mask), the envelope (data packet) is sent directly to the destination mailbox (network interface) via the postman (Ethernet). If the address is in another postal district, either in the same city or elsewhere, the envelope (data packet) is delivered by another postman (Ethernet) to the appropriate district and street post office (router), where the postal workers (routing software) sort and forward mail based on established post office sorting procedures (routing tables).

This has been a very brief overview of IP addressing, and is a subject that is of much greater depth than discussed here. However, it is important that the reader has some understanding of IP addressing, as generally it is the most common cause of despair in working with IP!

5.2.5 MAC addresses

IP addressing also depends on the MAC address of a device, which we referred to earlier. The MAC (Media Access Control) address is a theoretically unique identifier that is physically embedded inside a network card or network interface, and used to assign a globally unique address for the physical layer of the IP suite. MAC addresses take the form of xx-xx-xx-xx (Table 5.5).

In the original design of Ethernet, it was decided to give MAC addressing a 48-bit address structure, so there are potentially 2^{48} (or 281 474 976 710 656) possible MAC addresses. The addresses are shown in hexadecimal (2^{16}) format, which is a numbering system using a base of 16, written using 0–9 and A–F, as shown in Table 5.3. So an octet is now defined using two characters, and a MAC address is written with each octet separated by a dash or colon. An example of a MAC address would be 00-16-35-4A-6F-2B.

MAC address ranges are allocated by the IEEE (Institute for Electrical and Electronics Engineers) under the auspices of the ISO (International Standards Organization) on a company/organization basis, and the first three octets of a MAC address indicate which company or organization has that address range – in this example given above, Hewlett-Packard (HP).

Returning to our postal system analogy, until an envelope actually reaches its destination address, the recipient's name is generally irrelevant. Only the street address and zip code are important in getting the letter to your mailbox or to your door. Until someone calls out, 'Jonathan, you've got a letter!', neither

Table 5.5   Hexadecimal system

Decimal	Binary	Hexadecimal
0	0000	0
1	0001	1
2	0010	2
3	0011	3
4	0100	4
5	0101	5
6	0110	6
7	0111	7
8	1000	8
9	1001	9
10	1010	A
11	1011	B
12	1100	C
13	1101	D
14	1110	E
15	1111	F

I nor anyone else in the house will be worrying about how the envelope arrived. In other words, a MAC address is to a network interface what calling out 'Hey, Jonathan' is to the recipient of a letter inside your home. It identifies exactly to whom the letter (or data packet) is intended for.

MAC addresses are extremely important to a system's ability to function on a LAN because they are the only means by which a system can determine which packets to process from among the mix of TCP/IP traffic moving through the local network. MAC addresses have to be unique so that no two systems will attempt to process the same packets or maintain the same connections.

5.2.6   TCP

The transport layer uses the IP layer to carry data across a network, whether it is within a building or across the world over the Internet. This is why the term Transmission Control Protocol (TCP) is linked to IP as in TCP/IP.

The aim of the transport mechanism is to provide a reliable packet stream to ensure data arrives complete, undamaged and in the correct order. TCP tries to continuously measure how loaded the network is and adjusts its sending rate in order to avoid overloading the network. Furthermore, TCP will attempt to deliver all data in the correctly specified sequence. Part of the protocol is that packets are only sent after an acknowledgment has been returned from the receiving host or node confirming that the previous packet(s) have arrived.

TCP checks to make sure that no packets are lost by giving each packet a sequence number, which is also used to make sure that data is delivered to the TCP receiver at the other end in the correct order. The TCP receiving node at the far end sends back an acknowledgment for packets that have been successfully received.

However if an acknowledgment is not received within a practical 'round-trip time' (RTT), a timer at the originating TCP node will cause a timeout. The data is then assumed to have been lost and it will then be re-transmitted. TCP also checks that no bytes are damaged by using a checksum computed at the originating node for each block of data before it is sent, and then re-checked by the receiving node.

A checksum is a way of detecting errors by adding up all the bytes in the packet and transmitting the summed result at the end of the packet.

5.2.7 TCP & satellite delays

It is here that we come to a specific issue related to the use of TCP over satellite links and their inherent latency. If the acknowledgments arrive to late (or not at all), the TCP originating node assumes that packets have been lost due to congestion on the network, and adjusts its transmission speed downward accordingly in an attempt to minimize the loss by controlling the rate at which packets are sent.

Over a satellite link, the minimum RTT will be around 500 ms (2×250 ms), so the originating TCP node has to be adjusted to expect that there will be a minimum RTT of 500 ms, and probably significantly greater. Over a period of time, the traffic will run slower and slower, and may even 'time-out' completely.

There are a number of approaches to resolving this situation to try and improve at least the satellite-hop segment of the traffic path. The TCP can be carefully set up, but this requires some fine-tuning at each end of the link. It also assumes that there is both the time and the opportunity to do this.

Alternatively, a process of 'spoofing' may be introduced (sometimes called 'acceleration'), effectively fooling the TCP originating node into seeing acknowledgments from the receiving node. Such processes are proprietary and require the same manufacturer's equipment to be in place at each end of the link, which while acceptable within a 'closed' private network is not feasible in the more typical 'open' public networks which are used. There are many types of closed IP network systems that use these techniques, and are very successful in handling the majority of types of data traffic, but in SNG one does not necessarily control both ends of the link.

In the next section, we will examine the challenges of transmitting video and audio streams across a network, and the necessity of using different transport protocols – typically more than one at the same time – to achieve a more efficient and effective transmission of information.

5.2.8 Applications

Finally we come to the top of our 'cake', which concerns the content of the packets that are carried across the network. This traffic may be HTTP (HyperText Transfer Protocol) or the World Wide Web as it is more commonly referred to, or via File Transfer Protocol (FTP) for transmitting data files. We will look at these applications in more detail shortly.

5.2.9 Ports

At this point we need to return to the concept of 'ports'. In a network, a 'port' is a defined gateway for communicating between a program and another system or program, often passing through a hardware connection to a computer. The network port is usually numbered, and a standard network implementation like TCP, UDP or IP will attach a port number to data it sends in each packet header. The receiving application will guard and listen at the attached port number (gateway) to figure out which program to send data to on its system. A port may send/receive data one direction at a time ('simplex') or simultaneously in both directions ('duplex'). These software network ports may also connect internal programs on a single computer system. In TCP and UDP the combination of a port and an IP address is called a 'socket'.

The Internet Assigned Numbers Authority (IANA) administers the allocation of the 'standard' port numbering scheme. It is not obligatory to follow their rules, but like so many other recommendations issued by a number of bodies that administer the Internet, it is generally adhered to.

There is a widely published list of these port assignments, which can be found on the Internet. However, it should be noted that there is no commonly accepted standard UDP port number or range for RTP-based systems.

5.3   HTTP

The most common application used across public networks – the Internet – and the one that everyone is familiar with is HTTP (HyperText Transfer Protocol), and so by examining this we can become familiar with the concept of using an application (HTTP) to send and receive data across a network. In other words, using a web browser to access web pages remotely on a server on the far side of the Internet. It is useful to look at this for two reasons. Firstly, it is a use which ties together everything we've discussed in the chapter so far.

Secondly, and just as importantly, some SNG terminals now use an 'embedded' HTTP web server as part of their control system to allow the user to set up and control the uplink. This is becoming more and more important, as the web browser has become a ubiquitous GUI (Graphical User Interface) with which everyone has become familiar and requires no special training in using. It also allows the manufacturer to easily customize the 'front-end' of their control system by writing web pages in HTML (HyperText Markup Language) to make it as simple or as complicated as they wish, and conveniently make changes over the life of the product.

As an illustration, a web browser is installed on the local PC – e.g. Microsoft Internet Explorer (there are a number of other web browsers, but this is without question the most commonly used web browser) – and this communicates through a specific port on the PC (port 80) to the PC NIC and out onto the Internet, by whatever means of connectivity (dial-up modem, DSL, wireless, satellite link, etc.) and reaches the server which 'hosts' the desired website.

Web browsers work by using accessing web pages using a URL (Uniform Resource Locator). An example is www.google.com, the search engine Google, which strictly speaking, is written as http://www.google.com/. As we have seen, to access a destination on a network, you need an IP address, but because Google is a large organization, it doesn't just have one IP address, it has many, as it has tens of thousands of servers to service nearly 100 million users per month.

One of Google's server IP addresses is 64.233.161.104. A user can type that IP address into their web browser – and thus reach Google's domain 'home' page. But what they are far more likely to do is type 'www.google.com', and the PC would access a DNS (Domain Name Server), which is a like a telephone directory – it stores the IP addresses of websites. A DNS server is typically maintained or 'hosted' at the ISP (Internet Service Provider), and this is regularly receiving messages from across the Internet updating lists of major domains and associated IP addresses, as well as addresses of other domain name servers that may have links to the required site. Having 'resolved' the text web address into an IP address, the request for the page is passed on out across the Internet, through countless routers, to the destination server, and the web page information is returned to the web browser as HTML data and displayed on screen.

At the beginning of the chapter, we spoke of 'servers' and 'clients', and in this scenario, the local PC is the client and the remote destination web server is the host. It is described in this manner as the web server is giving information to the local PC – the web server is not getting any useful information from the PC apart from the simple page request – and is thus acting as a host for the information that the local PC – the client – requires. In fact, much of the common usage of the Internet is by this arrangement, and is why connections to the Internet are commonly asymmetric in nature – the 'uplink' connection, i.e. from the PC to the Internet, is much slower than the 'downlink' from the Internet to the PC. A common broadband connection might have downlink speed of 1 Mbps, but an uplink speed of perhaps only one-quarter, i.e. 256 kbps.

The typical flow of data accessing the Internet is very much less on the uplink – as it is mainly relatively small amounts of data being sent – whereas on the downlink side users are receiving large amounts of data to enable the fast display of often complex web pages and images. The scale of the downlink data flow becomes all the more significant when users are downloading music and video files, which are typically very large. The downlink connection speed for receiving live streaming video for full screen viewing at high quality requires download speeds of up to 10 Mbps.

This asymmetry is significant when we look later on at practical uses of Internet connections for newsgathering, for this asymmetric configuration is in direct inverse to the requirement to send live video and audio from a remote location.

It is also necessary to consider the issue of 'contention'. A public broadband connection is typically sharing a restricted amount of bandwidth between 20, 50 or 100 users, depending on the limitations of the service. In practice this means that at certain times of the day, the available bandwidth drops as the number of users sharing the overall data bandwidth increases. This leads us to the terms Committed Information Rate (CIR) and Burst Information Rate (BIR). On some networks – typically large private networks – routers may have a CIR assigned, which is the minimum guaranteed data rate. Often a BIR is also defined, which is the maximum data rate that the router has access to if there is the capacity available. These CIR and BIR parameters are important when considering the streaming of live video.

5.4   Transport of video & audio over IP

The initial application of IP in broadcasting was seen as a way of transmitting programs (or 'multicasting') over the Internet, and a number of organizations have attempted to stream video and audio streams as broadcasts, with varying degrees of success. The problem with the Internet in its current construct is that no packets have any priority, and any video decoder requires an almost uninterrupted stream of packets in order to reconstruct and maintain a constant video stream. The Internet is a busy highway, and other users are no respecters of a video stream trying to get through with its 'blue flashing light' on top – in fact, there is no blue flashing light available (otherwise termed Quality of Service, QoS) in IPv4. With IP, as each packet arrives at a node, it is treated as a fresh event, as the intermediate nodes do not keep track of what connections are actually flowing through them. This lack of information 'state' means that a special priority cannot be remembered and applied to a specific data packet flow as IP has no such way of assigning priority. Hence, all packets are equally important and treated accordingly – and that is the problem for newsgatherers where material is absolutely time-critical in 'live' working.

The development of a true IP broadcasting model depends on the next IP generation – IPv6 – that, amongst a whole host of new features, will have a QoS flag. One of the drivers for IPv6 has been the market for broadcast entertainment, with hundreds of TV channels and VOD (Video On Demand). Every TV will become an Internet appliance, and broadcasters require an Internet Protocol that supports large scale routing and addressing, and the minimum overhead to get the job done.

While the mechanism within TCP for re-transmitting packets is perfectly adequate for non-real-time applications, TCP is not a suitable protocol where it is critical that data packets arrive in the correct order and in a timely manner. There is no point in re-transmitting a lost packet since the receiving node will have already processed the missing packet as an error, having replaced the lost packet with an estimation of its contents, and will have moved on receiving subsequent packets.

Both video and voice/audio applications rely on packets arriving ideally as a continuous and smooth stream, or as a near a continuous stream as possible – any discontinuity results in 'jitter', causing the video or audio stream to have breaks or jumps within it.

MPEG video compression is extremely sensitive to timing jitter or any packet loss – it cannot tolerate a packet loss rate of more than 0.1% or 5–10 ms of packet jitter. In addition to timing concerns, certain packets contain critical information in the header. If this information is lost or received out of sequence, the decoder will be unable to properly decode the video stream for the entire GOP sequence – typically about a second, which is obviously very noticeable.

5.4.1 UDP

The User Datagram Protocol (UDP) is typically used for the real-time transmission of video and audio streams. UDP provides no guarantees for packet delivery and a UDP originating node does not track the state of UDP messages once sent out to the network. While any packet loss is uncompensated, there is no complication with waiting for acknowledgments before sending out the next packet.

UDP is commonly used for 'multicast' transmissions, which is the IP equivalent of a broadcast transmission. A 'unicast' is a single stream transmitted from an originating node to a single receiving node, which while perfectly suitable for point-to-point transmission, is unsuitable for broadcast-style transmission, i.e. one-to-many. This is because as each destination is added to the broadcast, the bandwidth increments accordingly. So a single multicast of 500 kbps to a single destination uses 500 kbps of capacity – but 10 simultaneous unicasts uses 5 Mbps (10 × 500 kbps) of capacity.

Thus a multicast delivers the stream over each link of the network only once, and then generates stream copies to each destination node as it branches out. With a multicast, whether the transmission is being received by one node or ten thousand nodes, the bandwidth used is the same – it is a stream to which clients can arbitrarily join or disconnect without any effect to the stream or the other participants. Referring back to earlier in the chapter, the reader may recall that multicast addresses are in the range 224.0.0.0 through 239.255.255.255.

Multicast transmissions are fraught with problems across the Internet, where there are likely to be a number of routers that may have difficulty handling multicast packets. But they are perfectly feasible in private networks that can be established in SNG applications.

5.4.2 RTP

UDP is too simple a tool to use on its own for multicasting video and audio, and so RTP (Real-time Transport Protocol) is used, along with SIP (Session Initiation Protocol). MPEG-4 encoders typically utilize RTP/SIP.

RTP is a protocol built on top of UDP for delivering audio and video over the Internet, formalized as a standard in 1996. Originally designed for multicasting, it is frequently used in streaming media systems as well as video-conferencing and voice communication systems, making it the technical foundation of VoIP (Voice over IP). (A note of caution about the term VoIP – in some circles it can mean Voice over IP, in others Video over IP!)

RTP is a derivative of UDP which provides end-to-end delivery services for real-time data such as video and audio, and in which a time-stamp and sequence number is added to the packet header. This extra information allows the receiving client to re-order out of sequence packets, discard duplicates and synchronize audio and video after an initial buffering period.

Applications typically run RTP on top of UDP to make use of its multiplexing and checksum services; both protocols contribute to the transport protocol functionality – we mentioned earlier that protocols for this type of application are used conjunctively. RTP may be used with other network or transport protocols supporting data transfer to multiple destinations using multicast distribution if provided by the underlying network. In itself RTP does not provide any mechanism to ensure timely delivery or QoS guarantees, but relies on lower-layer services to do so.

The sequence numbers included in RTP allow the receiving node to reconstruct the sender's packet sequence, but sequence numbers might also be used to determine the proper location of a packet, e.g. in video decoding, without necessarily decoding packets in sequence.

RTP really consists of two parts: the Real-time Transport Protocol (RTP), to carry data that has real-time properties; and the RTP Control Protocol (RTCP), to monitor the Quality of Service and to convey information about the participants in an ongoing session.

5.4.3 SIP & SAP

Essential to the use of RTP is SIP (Session Initiation Protocol), which is the signaling portion of a communication session. As TCP is bonded with IP as TCP/IP, RTP is usually associated as RTP/SIP.

SIP acts as a carrier for the Session Description Protocol (SDP), which describes the media content of the session, e.g. which IP ports to use, the codec being used, etc. In typical use, SIP sessions are simply packetized streams within the RTP stream, the carrier for the actual voice or video content itself. Within SIP, there is the Session Announcement Protocol (SAP) and the Session Description Protocol (SDP) that support the setup of multicast sessions. SDP defines the description of multimedia sessions, while SAP provides periodic multicast announcements of sessions about to start as well as those currently in progress. A session is announced by periodically multicasting a UDP announcement packet to a multicast address and port. The SAP announcements are originated from a different address to the RTP transmission, and one needs both addresses in order to be able to establish a connection to receive the multicast. The announcement rate for SAP is quite low, from tens of seconds to several minutes between repeated announcements of the same session. Thus a user starting a SAP receiving node may have to wait for a few minutes before seeing all the sessions announced.

SAP is generally used for sessions where participants are not known in advance. Where the participants are known in advance, then they are explicitly invited using SIP.

5.5 IP & MPEG

Interestingly, there are two ways that we use IP and MPEG together. Firstly, we can use spare capacity within the MPEG-2 stream to carry other data – typically IP data. Provided we have some kind of 'return path' to receive the acknowledgments as well as the return data, we can make use of this spare capacity.

Secondly, we can use the Ethernet to carry MPEG data as an IP stream, and this is particularly relevant to the use of MPEG-4 AVC and VC-1.

5.5.1 IP over MPEG

As mentioned in Chapter 4, an MPEG-2 transport stream (TS) must be transmitted at a specific aggregate data rate. Within the TS the useful components include the program tables, the program elementary streams containing video and audio, and data associated with the programs. One last component is used to bring the stream data rate up to the required value. These are null packets, 188 byte chunks of useless data inserted to fill the intervals between information-bearing packets. However, null packets are not predictable in number or incidence – they occur randomly, depending on the needs of the TS to maintain its nominal data rate.

When MPEG was first conceived, no one paid too much attention to the incidence of these packets, but over the years as more attention was focused on ways of making 'every byte count', it was seen that there could be ways of utilizing this 'opportunistic' data capacity. It cannot be used for principal data streams, because of their discontinuity, but they can be used for the carriage of non-critical data.

Figure 5.5 shows a sequence of six MPEG-2 frames over a time period. The dark gray areas in each frame indicate the null packets inserted to fill the frame to the required length – this also shows the capacity available for the insertion of opportunistic data that will not affect the transmission of the video/audio in the payload.

Using a protocol called Multi-Protocol Encapsulation (MPE), IP data packets can be inserted instead of the null packets, and we can then use the spare capacity to enable access to the newsroom computer system, the Internet, or even carry audio channels for IFB. Since we are adding data into the transport

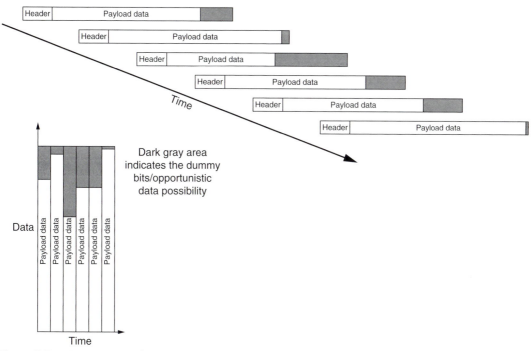

Figure 5.5 Opportunistic data insertion

stream, each destination IP address must be assigned to a particular PID. If there is a large amount of data, it is spread over a number of PIDs so as to reduce the load on the receiving nodes. A standard to assist in the use of this technique has been published by SMPTE.[1]

In the SNG environment, it would be an MPEG stream from the studio that would carry the outbound data from the newsroom computer system or the outgoing IFB channel. A complementary return channel from the SNG uplink needs to be provided, and this could be from:

- Within the MPEG stream from the SNG uplink (using its opportunistic data availability)
- Separate low data rate carrier over the satellite
- Inmarsat satphone
- GSM phone
- Phone landline

5.5.2 MPEG over IP

In Chapter 4, we described how MPEG data is formed into packets, and thus it becomes relatively easy to translate this data into a form suitable for IP transmission. In particular, MPEG-4 has been designed with IP transport in mind (and obviously VC-1 as well). Naturally, within an industry ruled by standards, a standard became a requirement to ensure interoperability of equipment. The DVB Project chose to not specifically address the issues of transporting of MPEG-2 over IP, but an organization called the Pro MPEG Forum has formulated a number of Codes of Practice (CoP) to facilitate standardized methods of transmitting and receiving TV signals over an IP network.

The Pro MPEG Forum was formed in 1998 as an association of broadcasters and equipment manu-facturers with interests in achieving interoperability of professional equipment for broadcasters and other professional end-users. Of particular interest is their Code of Practice 3 (CoP3)[2] which deals with the transmission of MPEG-2 transport streams over IP networks, and includes the important issue of error correction.

The packets within an MPEG transport stream have to be inserted into IP frames, and in an Ethernet network, there is a parameter termed the Maximum Transmission Unit (MTU). The default MTU value is 1500, i.e. there are 1500 packets within an IP frame. It is important to ensure that there is little or no fragmentation of the data – all the data to be sent in a certain time period should be contained in a single frame.

From Chapter 2, we can recall that MPEG-2 works with 188 bytes of payload data (204 bytes include the FEC data), and seven TS packets are the maximum an IP frame ($7 \times 188 = 1316$ bytes) can carry. Packet loss is measured by analyzing video packet flows and determining the presence of a continuity error event. Missing packets, out of sequence packets and duplicate packets are all counted as errors. Because each video transport stream packet carries a sequence number, continuity errors can be deter-mined with certainty at the decoder. Potentially, losing one IP frame results in the loss of seven MPEG-2 transport stream packets, causing decoding errors. Depending on the temporal or spatial components contained in the missing packets, a single packet error event may or may not be seen on the TV screen.

While using the maximum number of TS packets is undesirable due to the excessive impact (lost data) from losing a single IP packet, low packet usage causes a high overhead, so the value chosen is a compromise between these factors.

The CoP3 standard crucially looks at the issue of FEC, and recommends the use of a robust though complex two-dimensional error correction scheme using a 'column and row' format. MPEG streams can be protected either by using existing MPEG encryption (EBU-BISS) or by using an IP security encryption such as IPsec.

5.5.3   VPN

The transmission of data across the Internet suffers an increasingly significant drawback which not only applies to individuals, but also to companies, corporations and official bodies – the lack of privacy. Because data is transferred across any number of nodes owned and operated by third parties, it has the potential to be intercepted and monitored with disturbing ease and not necessarily by those third parties alone.

To try and minimize this risk, there is a technique to set up a 'private' connection through a 'tunnel' across and through the Internet whereby data can be passed with a reasonably high degree of security. This is a called a VPN (Virtual Private Network) connection, and the process is as follows.

A VPN works by using the shared public infrastructure while maintaining privacy through security procedures and tunneling protocols such as the Layer Two Tunneling Protocol (L2TP). In effect, the pro-tocols, by encrypting data at the sending end and decrypting it at the receiving end, send the data through a 'tunnel' that cannot be 'entered' by data that is not properly encrypted. An additional level of security involves encrypting not only the data, but also the originating and receiving network addresses.

News organizations can therefore use notoriously insecure public Internet access points – such as hotel and café Wi-fi hotspots – for their staff to send back reports from their own laptops that cannot be easily intercepted by anyone else. Putting in place such VPN systems is not a trivial task. Special soft-ware needs to be set up on laptops and routes into the organization's corporate IT structure have to be made, but where the material has a 'scoop' or commercial value, then the organization (such as a news agency that sells material to clients) may deem it commercially essential.

5.6   Video/audio transmission applications

We now come to look specifically at the use of IP for conveying a television signal, and particularly within the context of SNG. This also brings us incidentally to the use of the Internet for contributing video and audio back to a studio center, where the first part of the link may or may not be via a satellite. As we mentioned earlier in the chapter, the asymmetric configuration of typical Internet connections is in direct inverse to the requirement to send live video and audio from a remote location – we require a high upload speed, and do not really care about the downlink speed.

Not only that but the typical Internet connection is 'contended' – as we have discussed before, the sharing of the local Internet connection with a number of users usually varying according to the time of day. Many news organizations use broadband connections from remote bureaux to contribute live inserts, and currently one can often see that the broadcast pictures and sound have intermittent freezes and interruptions as the local Internet connection load varies, or possibly there are other variations across the Internet. Remember we said that there is currently no flashing blue light to ensure that video/audio traffic has a priority. So in our further discussion of the use of IP, what has to be weighed up are the undoubted economic savings of using the public Internet with the attendant risk to the 'live' program stream, against the high cost of providing dedicated private connectivity between the remote location and the studio.

5.6.1   Store & forward

A live video transmission of a quality conventionally acceptable for a news broadcast historically required a communications channel (terrestrial or satellite) with a capacity of at least 2 Mbps using compression standards that pre-dated MPEG-4 (MPEG-1, MPEG-2, H.2.61/H.263). However with MPEG-4 AVC, this channel requirement has dropped to 1 Mbps or below.

By encoding the high-quality video and audio in a process where it is digitized, compressed and then stored on a computer hard disk, the data can subsequently be transmitted via File Transfer Protocol. Once received at the studio, it can then be integrated into the news broadcast for transmission, and few viewers would notice the difference.

This is the essence of the store and forward video application, giving users the ability to transmit high-quality video at comparatively slow data rates. These data rates would normally be considered poor or unacceptable for TV transmission. Although the video material is not live, it need not be more than a few hours old, and the trade-off in terms of portability – the weight of a laptop PC in total compared to hundreds of kilos for a full SNG flyaway system – makes it a very attractive alternative.

The fundamental principle of the system is that video is played into a laptop equipped with a high-quality but relatively inexpensive video capture card, which digitizes the video and stores it as a AVI file on the hard disk of the PC – though an uncompressed AVI file may reach a file size of 2 GB for a 2 minute piece, depending on the resolution and the nature of the material. So the file is then compressed at a defined data rate, depending on the required end quality – and this is where the differences between many of the store and forward packages lie. The speed at which the AVI file can be compressed, and the size of the final compressed file, depends largely on the power of the laptop, and the efficiency of the compression algorithm. This completes the 'store' element.

The laptop can then be used as a desktop non-linear editor (NLE) with, again, high-quality but relatively inexpensive software editing package.

Now for the 'forward' part of the process; having produced a compressed file 10–30 MB in size for a 2 minute piece, the file is then transmitted back to the broadcaster/agency by FTP using whatever means are to hand. The laptop is connected to an IP connection either through a terrestrial link (dial-up, DSL, Wi-Fi) or a satellite IP terminal link established to a companion unit at the destination. When the

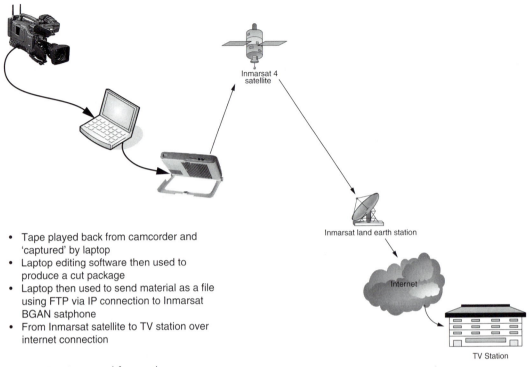

- Tape played back from camcorder and
  'captured' by laptop
- Laptop editing software then used to
  produce a cut package
- Laptop then used to send material as a file
  using FTP via IP connection to Inmarsat
  BGAN satphone
- From Inmarsat satellite to TV station over
  internet connection

Figure 5.6 Store and forward process

connection has been established, the video/audio data file is transferred over the link and saved as a file at the destination. Once the broadcaster/agency has received the file successfully, the material has now been 'stored' and 'forwarded'. The file can then be converted to real-time video and audio edited and/or played out (Figure 5.6).

The key to successful implementation of store and forward techniques is in the coding (digitization and compression) of the video. As we can surmise from Chapter 4, uncompressed digital video would create enormous data files of multi-gigabyte proportions. However, compression of the video during encoding reduces the file size to much more manageable proportions. In fact, compression ratios of between 25:1 and 100:1 are typical with the actual compression selection depending upon the desired video quality.

The length of the video and the sampling rate at which the video is digitized determines the size of the transmitted data file. The length of the video clip is determined largely on subject matter and editorial criteria, although it may be decided to keep it short in order to get the material back in time for the news broadcast. The amount of movement in each frame does not have a drastic effect on file size; the sampling rate largely determines the size of the file.

The transmission times are thus fundamentally determined by four factors:

- Video sequence length
- Video coding rate of the file (which can typically range from 512 kbps to 3 Mbps)
- Data channel transmission rate (64 kbps for Inmarsat GAN, and up to several hundred kbps for the BGAN service – see Chapter 6)
- Quality of the connection – noisy connections even at a 'high' connection speed are effectively quite slow because data packets have to be resent if they are not received error-free

The basic rule is that the longer the sequence length and the higher the coding rate of the file, the larger in size it will be and therefore the longer it will take to transmit.

The resultant pictures can sometimes have a 'filmic' look, reminiscent of 16 mm news cine film that was commonly seen up until the 1980s before the widespread use of ENG (electronic newsgathering), but on top-end feature pieces, if the correct sampling rate is chosen, the result is almost indistinguishable from a full broadcast-quality live feed.

The quality is often much improved if the shot scenes have high light levels, so that the pictures have few dark areas. In the conversion from a light signal to an electronic signal, dark areas of pictures create video noise in the camera and on the videotape. When the frames of pictures are digitized, the digital processing is unable to differentiate between noise and picture detail in dark areas. This causes ambiguity in the digitizing process, and the dark areas have resultant distracting artifacts as the coding process attempts to treat the random noise as rapidly changing detail. Digital video also contains detail components that the human eye cannot detect. By removing these components further data reduction can be achieved (see Chapter 4).

5.6.2 Video-conferencing over IP

In Chapter 6, we discuss the principles of video-conferencing as applied to ISDN telephone circuits, but it must be noted that the use of video-conferencing over broadband IP connections is rapidly increasing.

Video-conferencing (sometimes referred to as video tele-conferencing or VTC) was born in 1964 when AT&T demonstrated a system at the World Fair in New York, and offered a commercial service for businesses to communicate with each other over telephone circuits in the early 1970s with the Picturephone. Since then, it has developed to span a range from top-end high-quality multi-user systems using large plasma screens costing hundreds of thousands of dollars, down to the free applications offered by MSN, Yahoo and Skype for personal use based on simple webcams and tiny pictures sent over the Internet. High-grade video-conferencing is used for corporate communications as well as telemedicine, distance-learning, disaster management, and military command and control applications.

Through the 1990s, the ITU issued and revised the H.323 standard for packet-based multimedia applications, and this is commonly used in both Voice over IP (VoIP, Internet Telephony or IP Telephony) and IP-based video-conferencing. Some of the technology that has been developed for IP video-conferencing can and has been used for SNG-type applications – e.g. the 7E Communications TH-4 IP videophone.

5.6.3 VoIP & IFB

While packet switching can also be used for voice calls sent over digital networks, delay becomes critical. Packet switching as used for data is acceptable when accessing a web page or downloading a file, since small delays are hardly noticed. It would seem obvious that IP would be a good way of implementing IFB, and indeed there are a number of studio communication systems based on IP. But once such a system is extended out over a satellite circuit, then problems can start to arise.

This is because, as we have previously discussed, the human brain is particularly sensitive to voice, and so one notices even the tiniest delay. Hence circuit switching guarantees the best call quality because all the voice data packets are transmitted in order. Delays in packet switching for voice cause quality to deteriorate, as anyone who has tried using voice-over-Internet connections will have experienced.

This is not to say that IP cannot be used for delivering IFB to an SNG uplink – just that care has to be taken in how it is engineered and implemented.

5.7 IP & SNG

We have covered a substantial amount of the theory, so now is the time to look at some applications of using IP in SNG. This is still a developing area, and is being embraced enthusiastically by some newsgathering organizations, but more cautiously by others. Significantly, the application of IP to SNG is coming predominantly from the use of the Inmarsat BGAN system, described in Chapter 6.

The use of IP splits into hardware-based solutions and software-based applications. We will look at examples of each, starting with hardware.

5.7.1 Hardware solutions

The first example is an IP uplink terminal called the IPT Suitcase, manufactured by Swe-Dish Satellite Systems AB (Sweden), and widely used by a number of newsgathering organizations. The IPT was the first portable satellite IP terminal on the market, launched in 2000 and designed originally for military applications, and then produced in a version suitable for newsgathering. In its original form, it had an upper data transmission limit of 2 Mbps, but this has since been increased to 4 Mbps.

The Swe-Dish IPT is shown in Figure 3.15a/b and Figure 5.7, and it is classed as an ultra-portable terminal; a compact 39 kg unit, with a 0.9 × 0.66 m diameter elliptical antenna that segments into four pieces and dual-optic offset Gregorian feed assembly. The SSPA has an output power of 35 W, which with the antenna gives a maximum EIRP of 54 dBW.

While the IPT Suitcase is deployed into the field, at the base end it has to be matched with a specific modem/router which in turn is connected to the LAN at the broadcast center; or it can be connected to a WAN or the Internet. As we've seen, a link can be established between the receiving modem and the final destination, and hence data can be streamed between the units (remembering that it is a bi-directional link).

Incidentally, a version of this unit is also produced which offers the ability to transmit data at up to 10 Mbps using an external encoder and L-band modulator – this is not an IP device, but simply exploits the compact packaging of the antenna and power amplifier electronics.

Figure 5.7   Swe-Dish IPT unit in use (courtesy of Swe-Dish Satellite Systems)

The second example is the Norsat GlobeTrekker (Figure 5.8) which also falls into the category of an ultra-portable terminal. Offering a broadband IP connection speed of up to 4 Mbps, it is designed to be transported in two back-pack style cases, each of which weighs around 19 kg (40 lb). It has a segmented 1.0 m carbon fiber reflector, several different SSPA powers up to 15W and an Ethernet connection up to 50 m away from the terminal.

The user operation is designed for the non-technical, relying on a number of control inputs including a beacon detector, built-in spectrum analyzer, modem-carrier lock detector, DVB-S receiver, compass, GPS and inclinometer, all to achieve accurate antenna pointing.

5.7.2 Software solutions

Software solutions for newsgathering over IP are based on using a laptop (either Windows or Mac) and offer the opportunity of either streaming material 'live' or transferring video files. These transfers are not restricted to using satellite – one can also use dial-up, wireless, broadband or 3G cellphone connectivity. Four companies are particularly dominant in this area at the time of writing – Emblaze, Streambox, QuickLink and Livewire.

Emblaze VCON vPoint HD (Israel) is a low-cost COTS software package for personal video-conferencing, but the quality is so good that a number of global newsgatherers are using it for live shots. The vPoint HD software package is easily installed on a laptop and has a user interface that most find

Figure 5.8   Norsat GlobeTrekker (courtesy of Norsat)

very straightforward to navigate. The software can also receive a return video and audio feed from the studio to facilitate cueing; the studio simply requires the same software to be installed on a PC.

Streambox Portable Video Transport encoder is a software-based application (installed on a Windows or Mac laptop) using a proprietary compression system called ACT-L3 developed by Streambox Inc. (US). In the context of SNG, it is typically used with an Inmarsat BGAN terminal to enable editing and transmission of live video at full broadcast-quality resolution. At the studio end, a hardware Streambox decoder is required to decode the material ready for transmission to air.

QuickLink, developed by QuickLink (UK), is another software-based application using a proprietary compression system (VP7 developed by On2 Technologies) running on a laptop. At the studio end a dedicated server receives the transmitted files, or if required, QuickLink's own online file exchange server can be used. Any broadband connection can be used, including BGAN.

Finally, Livewire Digital (UK) offers a number of software applications designed for IP newsgathering in their M-Link family – principally the Voyager H.264 and IP Reporter H.264. The Voyager H.264 is designed to work with satellite (including Inmarsat BGAN), mobile, IP and ISDN connections, delivering either store and forward or live broadcast contributions. The IP Reporter H.264 is a lower-cost cutdown version of the Voyager system. As with QuickLink, Livewire offers a dedicated server system to receive material at the studio end.

5.8   Conclusion

Since the latter part of the 1990s, the spread of the use of the Internet and e-mail into newsrooms has steadily driven the development of IP techniques in newsgathering. With the fall in cost of video and audio editing software for PCs, many newsgathering organizations are sending edited reports from the field as compressed files, either as e-mail attachments or using FTP (File Transfer Protocol) via the Internet. This is particularly attractive from those parts of the world where traditional delivery of reports in quality via satellite would be difficult or prohibitively expensive. There is an added benefit in that these reports can be sent in a very secure manner so that the problems of censorship are not encountered, as they would be if the reports were sent by more open means. However, the Internet suffers problems dealing with live working because of path predictability and delay.

Hence a significant amount of newsgathering is now carried out over the Internet by a number of global newsgatherers using nothing more than a DVCam, a laptop, some software and a broadband connection – total cost less than US$8000. Sometimes, the broadband connection is a physical cable connection from a reporter's hotel room, apartment, Internet café or their local news bureau – at other times, it is directly provided by satellite, either Inmarsat BGAN terminal or an SNG uplink.

Its use within the conventional SNG uplink domain is as yet relatively limited for a number of reasons – some technical as we have seen in this chapter, and some related to manufacturers being relatively reluctant to move into a technology that either they may not feel very comfortable with or that they feel that their customers are not ready to use. Some broadcasters are also still wary of this technology. Hence our brief look in this chapter at the technology serves merely as an introduction to its inevitably wider use in SNG in the future, where its impact will be rapidly and increasingly felt over the next few years.

References

1. SMPTE 325M (1999) SMPTE Standard for Digital Television: Opportunistic Data Broadcast Flow Control.
2. Professional MPEG Forum – Code of Practice 3 (2004): Transmission of Professional MPEG-2 Transport Streams over IP Networks.

6

Have phone, will travel: Inmarsat services

6.1 Background

The use of satellite phones has become an integral part of newsgathering, not only for the broadcast market, but also for the newspaper industry. The term 'satellite phone' encompasses devices not only used for voice communications, but also for data. The name denotes a device which is essentially portable and offers 'dial-on-demand' access, with no pre-booking of satellite capacity as is generally found with conventional satellite communication systems. A number of systems are currently available – Inmarsat, Thuraya, Iridium and Globalstar – but some offer only voice communications, and Thuraya is a data only service.

The most widely used satellite phone system in electronic newsgathering is Inmarsat offering both voice and high-speed data services, and so this chapter will focus almost exclusively on this system.

The INMARSAT system was originally designed for maritime communication, but its use has expanded to other market sectors, including newsgathering. Within the last 25 years, the INMARSAT system has become a vital tool for global newsgathering, used not only for person-to-person voice communication for 'keeping in touch', but also for media material transfer applications as well. TV contribution using both 'store and forward' techniques as well as 'videophones' for live coverage, studio-quality audio for radio reports, and high-quality still pictures are sent from almost anywhere on the globe. This versatility, combined with increasingly compact equipment, has enabled INMARSAT to become a significant force in newsgathering, and every day it plays its part in delivering news stories into people's homes around the world.

The use of land mobile Inmarsat systems for SNG has been developing since the first portable satellite telephones became available. These MESs (mobile earth stations) were the satellite equivalent of the cellular telephone but offering near-global coverage. Broadcasters could use the satellite technology to send back reports by using a compact satellite telephone – the 'satphone' as it has became commonly known. Not only that, but the technology was developed further so that a high-speed data (HSD) 64 kbps circuit could be established over analog Inmarsat-A channels. With the right type of transportable terminal and a suitable ancillary equipment, a high-quality audio circuit could be established by a simple dial-up procedure, enabling news reports to be provided from almost anywhere in the world.

For a number of years, these satphones were used purely for radio SNG. A satphone could be used with a digital audio codec to produce near-studio-quality audio via an High Speed Data (HSD) 64 kbps dial-up connection on Inmarsat-A and -B systems. Further developments led to the transmission of high-quality video over an HSD circuit. In 1993, BT and INMARSAT were able to provide Reuters Television with near-live pictures of the Whitbread Round-the-World Yacht Race. They were 'near-live', because the pictures were actually stored on an on-board computer, compressed and then sent at a slow data rate, stored at the receiving end and then uncompressed and reconstituted into real-time video. The news market viewed this development with great interest, and many felt that the further development of this 'store and forward' type of system would be the key to future newsgathering techniques.

By 1994, compact new equipment designed specifically for newsgathering applications enabled the transmission of television news pictures, albeit not in real time. A handful of companies developed digital video compression units for television newsgathering that could transmit video and audio over HSD channels in store and forward mode.

The videophone was conceived in 1998 by the BBC and 7E Communications – a UK technology company deeply involved in INMARSAT technology – but it was not born until early 2000. Called the 'Talking Head', the videophone was designed to be used with a compact satellite phone – the Inmarsat M4 or GAN 'satphone' – to provide a compact two-box solution to live newsgathering.

There is now a new type of Inmarsat system that uses just a high-spec laptop PC and the Inmarsat terminal itself – Broadband Global Area Network (BGAN). The laptop has all the processing necessary to edit and file a story, or transmit the story live with the camera connected to the laptop directly via a Firewire (IEEE 1394) connection. The editing (video and audio) is carried through the use of one of a number of software applications available for both Microsoft Windows and Apple Mac laptop PCs, and cut packages can be sent by a variety of means, including satphones, Internet cafés, broadband wireless access – anywhere a relatively fast IP connection exists.

The Inmarsat system consists of a constellation of geostationary satellites providing a range of services for different markets – marine, aeronautical and land. There are a fleet of Inmarsat 2 and Inmarsat 3 series geostationary satellites that cover most of the Earth's surface and have a range of services with different capabilities. In addition, two Inmarsat 4 (I4) series satellites have been launched and have entered commercial service, eventually to replace the services carried by existing fleet of Inmarsat 3 satellites, as well as providing the BGAN service, which as we have said is of particular interest to newsgathering (Figures 6.1a and 6.1b).

However, all Inmarsat services offer the same common core feature: on-demand access, limited only by satellite capacity and coverage, using portable mobile terminals. In this chapter, we will examine the application of Inmarsat systems to newsgathering, and in doing so we will cover some basic aspects of ISDN and video-conferencing as well as features of the different Inmarsat services. So to begin with, let's look at the story behind the establishment of the original Inmarsat system.

6.2 History of INMARSAT

In 1973, the Assembly of the Inter-Governmental Maritime Consultative Organization (later to become the International Maritime Organization, or IMO) voted to convene a special conference. This conference was to discuss the possibilities of a truly global satellite communications system and try to achieve international agreement for such a system. There was a growing need for a system to meet both the demand for emergency distress communications and routine business communication between shipping lines and their vessels at sea. In 1975, the first of a number of conferences began the work which led to the INMARSAT Convention of 1976, and then to the establishment of International Maritime Satellite Organization – INMARSAT – in 1979.

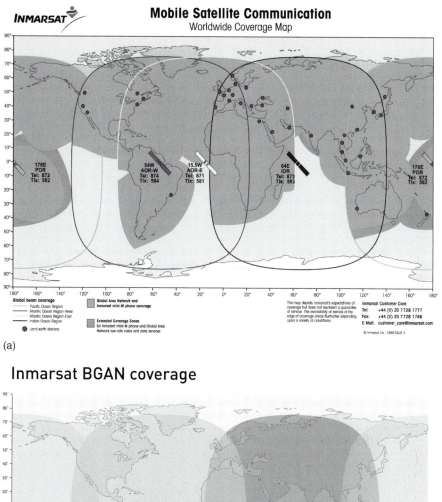

(a)

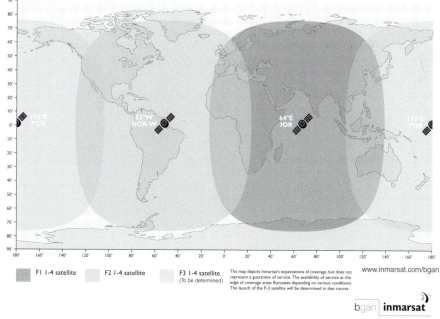

(b)

Figure 6.1 (a) INMARSAT coverage map – GAN/Mini-M (courtesy of Inmarsat) (b) INMARSAT coverage map – BGAN (courtesy of Inmarsat)

6.2.1 INMARSAT: the organization

The INMARSAT organization had 86 member countries, with its headquarters in London, and their satellite communications system came to be used in more than 160 countries.

Each member country (the Party) appointed a Signatory, typically the public telecommunications operator (PTO) in the country, who invested in INMARSAT and provided INMARSAT services to the end-user (the customer). In addition to the satellites, the INMARSAT system comprised of land earth stations (LESs) which were operated by Signatories and which provided the link between the satellites and the terrestrial telecom networks.

However, the INMARSAT system did not actually commence operations until 1982. INMARSAT began providing the world's first mobile-satellite communications system for the maritime market with the INMARSAT 'Standard-A system'. The INMARSAT satellite system originally consisted of two leased satellites from Marisat (operated by Comsat General), two MARECS satellites leased from the European Space Agency (ESA) and some capacity leased on an INTELSAT V series satellite.

The system grew quickly: in 1985 it was extended yet again to provide land mobile services, primarily for the truck and railway markets; by 1990 it had been further developed to provide aeronautical services. Over time a number of additional satellites have been brought into service. Coverage was centered on the three major ocean regions by using a fleet of satellites providing rapidly accessible links from virtually anywhere in the world. LESs were also established on all the continents to handle the traffic between the satellite and ground segment and connect to the international telephone network; at one time are now over 40 around the world.

The system operates with C-band links between the satellite and the LESs, and L-band links between the mobile terminals and the satellites. The earlier satellites used global beams, each covering approximately one-third of the Earth's surface, but the current satellites use both global (Inmarsat 2 series) and 'spot' beams (Inmarsat 3 and Inmarsat 4). Spot beams concentrate coverage in particular areas, primarily intended for the smaller, lower power mobile terminals, and allow re-use of the scarce frequency resource in the L-band allocated for Inmarsat.

In 1998, the INMARSAT Assembly agreed that INMARSAT would be privatized, and so INMARSAT became a private company in 1999, and a public company in 2005. There remains a separate intergovernmental body to ensure that INMARSAT continues to meets its public service 'lifeline' obligations, in particular the Global Maritime Distress and Safety System (GMDSS) which was established in 1992.

6.2.2 Inmarsat: the company

Inmarsat Global Ltd., with its headquarters in London, has terminals in use in more than 160 countries, and there are almost 300 000 mobile earth stations (MESs) – land terminals – in use, produced by a number of manufacturers around the world.

As of late 2006, Inmarsat operated a total of 10 satellites of three generations – three Inmarsat 2 satellites, five of the Inmarsat 3 series, and two of the latest Inmarsat 4 series (Figure 6.2). At that time there were (approximately) in excess of 5000 Inmarsat-A, 1000 Inmarsat-B, 30 000 Inmarsat-C, 100 000 Inmarsat-D+, 110 000 Inmarsat Mini-M, 10 000 RBGAN, 25 000 GAN and 8000 BGAN terminals in service.

Inmarsat services are provided by Land Earth Station Operators (LESOs) and Distribution Partners (DPs), representing the primary tier of distribution to the market, and have their own sales networks that market Inmarsat products and services.

LESOs are responsible for running the land earth station gateways that connect the end-user to the terrestrial data and voice networks via the Inmarsat satellites. The LESs – of which there are around

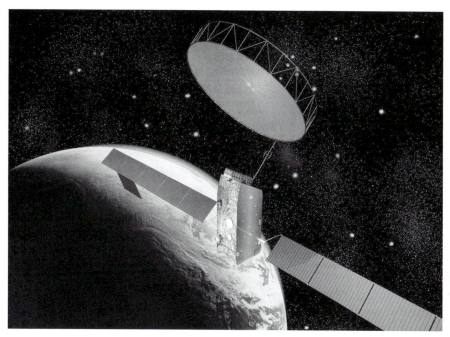

Figure 6.2 Inmarsat 4 (I4) satellite (courtesy of Inmarsat)

40 – are now operated by the LESOs; the major operators are:

- Telenor
- Stratos/Xantic
- France Telecom

While DPs are the primary distributors of BGAN services with their own sales networks, the advent of BGAN has seen Inmarsat take responsibility for running the gateways that connect the satellites to the terrestrial networks. DPs, therefore, are generally focused on sales and marketing rather than the physical delivery of the service. (Though some companies are both LESOs and DPs.)

Inmarsat sets the specifications for all terminals that are to access the network, and every manufacturer must fulfill Inmarsat's stringent-type approval procedures before its equipment can access the satellite system.

6.3 Types of Inmarsat systems

In the description of the different services below, we will concentrate on the use of the land mobile application. For convenience, we will use the term for the land mobile terminal (MES) used by all newsgatherers: the 'satellite phone' or 'satphone' – although as pointed out earlier, some of the terminal types do not support voice calls but only data. The following is a list of Inmarsat systems used for newsgathering – note that there are other Inmarsat systems not covered as either they never have been and/or are not currently used for newsgathering:

- Inmarsat-A
- Inmarsat-B

- Mini-M
- GAN
- BGAN

6.3.1 Inmarsat-A

The first system launched by INMARSAT was an analog system for the maritime market which is still used, though only by a relatively small number of terminals (less than 1000 at the end of 2006). The Inmarsat-A system was widely used in the early days of the application of INMARSAT for newsgathering, but its use in this regard disappeared with the introduction of the Inmarsat-B and then GAN services in the 1990s. The Inmarsat-A satphone for land use was quite bulky, around the size of a large suitcase. It typically weighed around 35 kg (77 lb) and had an antenna that was approximately 90 cm in diameter. Inmarsat-A uses analog modulation, though it can pass digital signals via a modem as with any analog public telephone circuit. It handles voice, telex, data and fax. A high-speed data (HSD) service is also available with data rates of either 56 or 64 kbps. It is now merely of historical interest, as the service is scheduled to cease at the end of 2007.

6.3.2 Inmarsat-B

This was the replacement service for Inmarsat-A, launched in 1992, using digital modulation. Inmarsat-B also has the added advantage that a satphone can have multiple 'identities'. This means that there are separate numbers for voice, fax and data, and that there can be several for each type. Typically, an Inmarsat-B satphone can have two voice numbers, two fax numbers, a low-speed data (9.6 kbps) number and an HSD number, though only one service can be used at any one time.

The satphones are around half the size and weight of those for the type-A system, although the antenna are approximately the same size (see Figure 6.3).

Figure 6.3 Inmarsat-B (courtesy of NSSL)

(a)

(b)

Figure 6.4 (a) Inmarsat Mini-M satphone (courtesy of NSSL) (b) Inmarsat Mini-M satphone in use (courtesy of NSSL)

Also largely of historical interest, as the use of Inmarsat-B for newsgathering has been replaced by the GAN service, it is still occasionally used in areas or situations where there is no coverage or where there may be congestion on either the GAN or BGAN services.

6.3.3 Inmarsat Mini-M

In 1993, a compact briefcase-sized digital terminal for the new Inmarsat-M system was launched just prior to Inmarsat-B, aimed at the business-traveler market on continental land masses. In 1996, an improved system called Mini-M was introduced and is still in use to this day. The Mini-M satphone is approximately the size of a laptop computer (see Figure 6.4). The satphone has the option of using a SIM card so that service is bought and access-controlled in the same way as GSM. The available services are voice, data and fax, but with no HSD service. The cost of both the satphones and call charges have fallen over the years falling – units currently cost under US$1500, and satellite costs vary between US$1.50 and US$2.50 per minute, depending on time of day.

From the point of view of keeping in touch in remote and hazardous areas, the Inmarsat Mini-M satphone has a distinct advantage for newsgatherers. It is available in vehicle-mounted versions from a few manufacturers, and this allows a small and relatively discreet auto-tracking antenna to be easily fitted to the roof of a car, with the handset and control unit inside the car. This has a great advantage in that the satphone is permanently rigged, and calls can therefore be made or received on the move, rather than having to stop and get out of a vehicle to set the satphone up before use.

6.3.4 GAN

This HSD service was introduced in late 1999, originally as a parallel service to Inmarsat-B, but now its successor. Although 'M4' (Multi-Media Mini-M) was the project title while the system was in development, it is marketed by INMARSAT as 'Global Area Network' (GAN) – but the term M4 is still sometimes used within the industry. The GAN satphones are the size of a laptop computer, weighing under 4 kg (10 lb), and offer voice services at 4.8 kbps (as Mini-M), and fax, file transfer and high-speed data at up to 56/64 kbps (as with Inmarsat-B) (see Figures 6.5a and 6.5b). As with Inmarsat-B, there can only be one channel working at any time, so for instance it is still not possible to have a voice call and a fax call running simultaneously.

The pricing of the satphones is US$5000 or less, and satellite time costs are between US$6 and US$8 per minute for HSD. It has been tailored for use by the oil and gas industries, resource exploration and broadcast users, because the units are very compact and marry up particularly well with compact videophones and store and forward units (dealt with later in this chapter). The units also offer a standard ISDN (S0) interface, enabling standard ISDN applications and hardware to be used with the HSD service.

The satphones feature a SIM card so that service is bought and access-controlled in the same way as GSM, and with the built-in lithium-ion battery, offers more than 100 hours of standby time. INMARSAT also offers a packet data service called MPDS (Mobile Packet Data Service) which provides a packet switched connection where users are charged for the amount of information sent and received rather than the time for which they are connected.

The coverage of Inmarsat GAN is, like Mini-M, primarily focused on continental landmasses (although, as with Mini-M, there is some coverage spillage into parts of the oceanic regions) (Figures 6.6a and 6.6b).

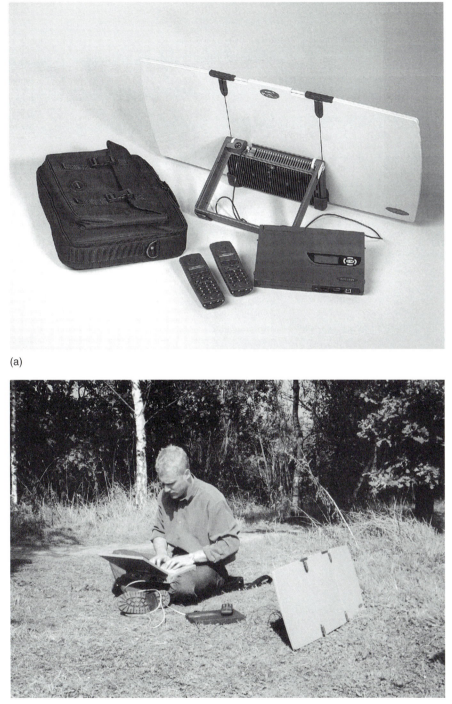

(a)

(b)

Figure 6.5   (a) Inmarsat GAN terminal (courtesy of Inmarsat) (b) Inmarsat GAN terminal in use (courtesy of NSSL)

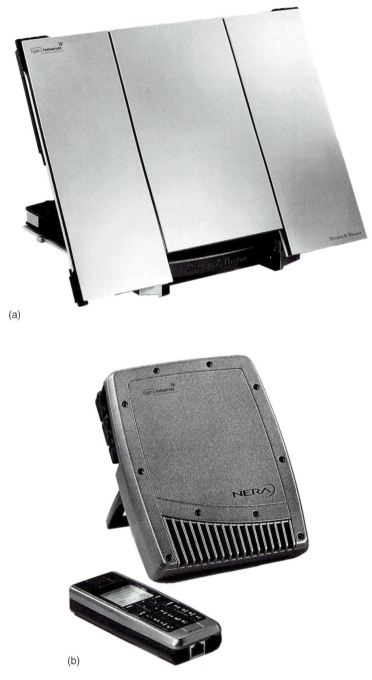

(a)

(b)

Figure 6.6 (a) Inmarsat BGAN – Thrane 700 (courtesy of Inmarsat) (b) Inmarsat BGAN – Nera WorldPro 1000 (courtesy of Inmarsat)

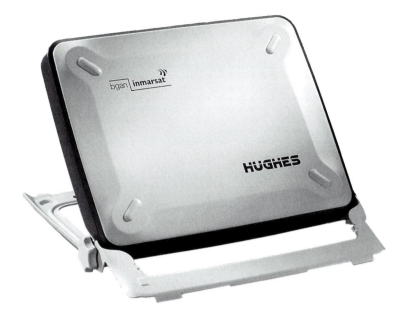

Figure 6.6   (c) Inmarsat BGAN – Hughes 9201 (courtesy of Inmarsat)

6.3.5 BGAN

The latest of the Inmarsat services to be introduced (and now its flagship offering) is the BGAN service, commercially launched in early 2006, and of significant interest to newsgatherers. Originally launched as a limited regional service in 2002, Regional Broadband Global Area Network (RBGAN) was an IP-based data only service which was originally delivered via the Thuraya satellite located at 44° E but subsequently migrated to the Inmarsat 4 satellite.

BGAN (Broadband Global Area Network) enables users to both access data applications at broadband speeds and make phone calls at the same time almost wherever they are in the world (see Figure 6.6c). The terminals are similar in size to the RBGAN units, and offer two types of service – a (shared) standard IP class and a (dedicated) streaming service.

The standard IP service offers access to corporate networks via a secure VPN connection at speeds up to 492 kbps. It enables the user to access e-mail and other office applications, browse the Internet and send large file attachments – which therefore allows the transmission of store and forward files.

For applications where quality of service is paramount, such as live video or video-conferencing, BGAN offers an 'on-demand' streaming IP service at speeds up to 256 kbps. The user selects the data rate depending on their requirement – and at least one manufacturer's BGAN terminal will support ISDN connections as well (though not simultaneously with a voice call); this is treated as a switched circuit service.

The user can make phone calls at the same time as accessing data applications via a standard desktop phone, custom handset or Bluetooth handset/headset, depending on the BGAN terminal.

The BGAN terminal is small, lightweight and weatherproof. It can be connected quickly and easily to a laptop or multiple laptops, with users choosing wired or wireless connections, including Bluetooth or

Figure 6.6 (d) Inmarsat BGAN terminal in use with videophone (courtesy of Inmarsat)

WLAN (WiFi), depending on their choice of terminal. There are a number of different terminals in the range with differing capabilities. All BGAN terminals feature a SIM card so that service is bought and access-controlled in the same way as GSM.

The smallest devices are designed to suit single users whose primary concern is portability. Larger terminals offer higher bandwidth and are particularly suitable for news teams who need to establish regular high bandwidth streaming connections to file live reports. All terminals are controlled from a laptop using a web-based interface accessing the BGAN LaunchPad software inside the BGAN terminal, common across all the terminals, and designed for ease of use and familiarity. The LaunchPad enables the users to customize the data connection options to match their application requirements, with the ability to pre-configure user settings for rapid set-up.

As with its predecessor RBGAN terminal, the BGAN system requires positional information from the terminal, and so the terminal has an integral GPS receiver which transmits its location back across the Inmarsat system for spot beam selection and billing purposes. Each satellite region is under the control of a Satellite Access Station (SAS), which controls and monitors the traffic based on the terminal-supplied GPS information.

6.4   Packet and circuit switching

In Chapter 5, we discussed the differences between packet and circuit switching, and it is important to reiterate the differences, as with the BGAN system, both methods of transport are available according to the service.

A telephone circuit is a single dedicated line established for the duration of the call – this is based on a concept called 'circuit switching'. This is like a railway train that travels along one track from A to B, with a string of carriages all trailing along together.

Packet switching is a system where the best (quickest) path for each railway carriage or packet is decided dynamically, re-ordered on-the-fly to use any track or path available to get from A to B. Other packets from other sources run on these circuits as well, making the most use of each path, unlike circuit switched calls that occupy a single path to the exclusion of all others. So the train starts from the departure point as a complete string of carriages, gets split up along the way, but comes back together as a single train with all the carriages in the right order at the destination.

However, while packet switching can also be used for voice calls sent over digital networks, delay becomes critical. Packet switching as used for data is acceptable when accessing a web page or downloading a file, since small delays are hardly noticed. But the human brain is particularly sensitive to voice, and so one notices even the tiniest delay. Hence circuit switching guarantees the best call quality because all the voice data packets are transmitted in order with no pause while packets are re-assembled in the correct sequence.

The important difference between the two systems in terms of delay is that while one provides a near instantaneous communication route, the other will probably experience some latency.

Specifically with BGAN, the significant difference in terms of cost between the two service classes is that the standard IP service (packet data) is charged differently to the streaming class (circuit switched) – standard IP on amount of data sent, streaming class on time spent with a call up on the network. To minimize costs on the streaming class service it is important to reduce the connected time, while on the standard IP service, the time connected is immaterial but the quantity of data transferred is critical.

6.5   ISDN

To understand the use of Inmarsat and the use of their non-IP-based HSD services, store and forward, and videophones, it is necessary to look at the basic principles of the integrated services digital network (ISDN) used for public dial-up data service in many countries around the world. We will firstly look at this in the way it is used in the typical application, i.e. in a building, which we will refer to as the 'subscriber's premises'. We can then move on to examine the cross-over into the Inmarsat system.

The ISDN standards are defined by the ISO (International Standards Organization). The standards for audio coding are set by the ITU (International Telecommunications Union), and for video coding by ISO, the IEC (International Electro-Technical Commission) and MPEG (Moving Pictures Experts Group). More details of these organizations may be found in Chapter 4 for ISO, IEC and MPEG, and Chapter 7 for the ITU.

The scope of the Inmarsat HSD 'channel' is between the Inmarsat user terminal – the satphone – and the terrestrial interface associated with the LES. From the terrestrial user's point, the Inmarsat HSD service is one of the digital networks that may be accessed via ISDN. Similarly, from the Inmarsat mobile user's point, ISDN is the usual HSD terrestrial network that is accessed via the Inmarsat LES. Hence the significance of examining ISDN in this context.

ISDN is the ITU-T (formerly CCITT) term for the digital public telecommunications network. It is offered in two packages: Basic Rate and Primary Rate. Alternatively, in the US there has traditionally been a digital data service called 'Switched 56' (referring to the 56 kbps data rate used); however, the US has now largely adopted the ISDN standard of 64 kbps as in Europe and many other parts of the world. The Inmarsat GAN service, which operates at 64 kbps, therefore naturally integrates with ISDN services.

6.5.1 Classes of ISDN service

Basic Rate ISDN (BRI) channel structures comprise two 64 kbps digital 'pipes' for user data, and one signaling data pipe, collectively termed '2B + D'. It aims to provide service for individual users and business applications such as computer local area network (LAN) data links or, for broadcast applications, high-quality audio feeds. It is provided as a dial-up service by the local telephone service provider and is charged for, like a normal telephone service, based on a standing (monthly or quarterly) charge and a usage charge per minute. The usage charge per channel is similar to normal telephone rates in most areas.

Primary Rate ISDN (PRI) provides up to 30×64 kbps (B) data channels and 1×64 kbps (D) signaling channel. It is aimed at high bandwidth business applications such as video-conferencing, company PBXs, and high-capacity on-demand LAN bridge/router links. Primary rate ISDN is the large data pipe and basic rate ISDN is the small data pipe. Because the GAN service operates at only 64 kbps it is normally used with the basic rate ISDN service in broadcast applications.

6.5.2 ISDN configuration

ISDN is normally implemented using existing two-wire, twisted-pair conductors from the local telephone exchange to the subscriber premises. This can be up to a maximum distance of 5.5 km from the exchange. At an ISDN subscriber's premises, the point at which the ISDN telephone line terminates is known as the 'U-interface', as shown in Figure 6.7. The ISDN connection is terminated at the U-interface by a network termination device known as 'NT1'. In the US the subscriber is responsible for providing the NT1; in the rest of the world it is provided as part of the ISDN service. Physically the NT1 is like an oversized telephone line-box and is normally permanently wall-mounted.

The ISDN subscriber interface at the NT1 is known as the 'T point' or 'T-interface'. It converts the data from the type used between the exchange and the socket to the type used in the subscriber's premises. If a second network termination device such as an ISDN switchboard is connected to the NT1 at the T-interface, then this is designated the 'NT2' and the ISDN subscriber interface is then the 'S point' or 'S-interface'. The physical and electrical characteristics of the S-interface and T-interface are identical and they are usually referred to as the 'S/T-interface' or 'S/T bus' (also 'S0-interface' or 'S0 bus'.) Physically the S/T-interface is an RJ-45 telephone connector. It is to the S/T-interface that the subscriber equipment is connected, and we will refer to the S/T node as the S0 node from here onwards in the text. In point-to-point applications, the S0 bus can connect equipment up to 1000 m apart. When used in a passive bus configuration (i.e. connecting up to eight physical terminals) it can span a distance of up to 500 m.

Interface conversion between the S0 bus and the serial communications interface on the subscriber data terminal equipment (DTE) is carried out using an ISDN terminal adapter (TA). The TA is typically packaged in a similar fashion to modems, i.e. either as a stand-alone unit or as a built-in PC card. A stand-alone TA is supplied configured with a serial communications interface such as RS.232, V.35 or X.21; the interface is normally specified by the subscriber according to the application. Nowadays most equipment capable of being used with ISDN can be supplied with an integral ISDN basic rate interface

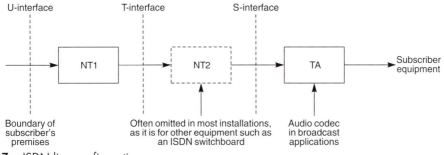

Figure 6.7 ISDN line configuration

(BRI). The DTE can be any type of data equipment such as a video-conferencing or videophone system, bridge/router or audio codec. The TA is also known as the data communications equipment (DCE).

Stand-alone TAs can be ordered with either a dual-channel 2B + D BRI or a simple single-channel B+ D BRI. As a GAN ISDN channel is equivalent to a single B-channel, it is preferable to use a single-channel TA with GAN ISDN applications. The single-channel TA will normally be less expensive than a full 2B+ D unit.

There are several differing implementations of ISDN worldwide. Protocol conversion between different ISDN standards is carried out transparently by the public telecom operator (PTO). However, ISDN BRIs differ with the various ISDN standards and so care must be taken to specify the correct country of use, and hence ISDN BRI, for the base station equipment. Fortunately, the DTE to be used with the GAN ISDN terminal uses a serial communications port (e.g. V.35, X.21, RS.232) and so is independent of any ISDN standard.

6.5.3 ISDN applications and GAN ISDN

Both the ISDN B-channel and the Inmarsat HSD channel support a 'clear' 64 kbps digital pipe with no restriction on the bit pattern to be transferred. The ISDN offers '2B + D'– two 64 kbps digital pipes and a signaling pipe. These are 'virtual' pipes, as in reality these data channels are all multiplexed together into a single data stream.

As the ISDN numbering system follows the same pattern as the normal telephone system, dialing is carried out in exactly the same manner as making a normal telephone call. The subscriber number is used with the same area codes as the telephone network and international codes are also the same.

ISDN calls to an Inmarsat satphone are made in exactly the same manner as a normal international ISDN call. Dial the international access code, followed by the Ocean Region code and finally the Inmarsat mobile number (IMN) of the ISDN port on the satphone. Note that in most countries the ISDN network will route automatically to a pre-defined LES, though in some cases the LES will not support the HSD service required.

The general format is:

    <<International access code + Ocean Region code + Inmarsat ISDN mobile number>>

The Ocean Region code is:

Atlantic Ocean Region – East	871
Pacific Ocean Region	872
Indian Ocean Region	873
Atlantic Ocean Region – West	874

For mobile-to-fixed dialing, the call is dialed as with any other international call as follows:

<<00 + destination country code + ISDN subscriber number>>

Many applications of the GAN satphone can be improved by increasing data capacity, and so two GAN terminals (from the same manufacturer) can be connected together to produce double the data speed – 128 kbps. This process is called 'bonding', and it is easily achieved with the use of a special cable. One manufacturer actually produces a dual-channel terminal that enables two simultaneous 64 kbps channels to achieve the 128 kbps data rate.

This technique of bonding terminals together is particularly useful for newsgathering applications using either 'live' or store and forward video, which we will cover later in the chapter.

6.6 Radio contribution applications

It was for radio news contribution that first saw the use of INMARSAT services in the late 1980s, and continues to this day.

The human ear hears frequencies between 20 Hz and 20 kHz, and is most sensitive in the range 2–4 kHz, while the human voice typically produces sounds in the range 400 Hz to 2 kHz. The low frequencies tend to be vowels, while the higher frequencies are consonants. These frequency ranges determine the most suitable type of audio coding and compression to use for audio broadcast purposes.

Uncompressed digital audio (as with video) can require a large amount of bandwidth to transmit. As has previously been outlined, several international standards and proprietary systems exist for the coding (digitization and compression) of audio signals in real time, all of which use different techniques to apply differing degrees of compression to the audio input – music or speech. The degree of compression applied determines the amount of bandwidth required for the coded audio data stream. The compression process also introduces a time delay that becomes greater as the degree of compression increases. Both of these factors – required bandwidth and coding delay – have to be taken into account in determining the most suitable coding algorithm for a particular application for use over the Inmarsat GAN HSD 64 kbps service. For video-conferencing, G.728 is the optimum coding standard because it allows for the maximum bandwidth in an Inmarsat HSD 64 kbps channel for video. However, where only audio is to be digitized and sent over the channel, G.722 is often used. Audio compression in general is described in more detail in Chapter 4, including MPEG audio.

Given that satellite propagation delays are of the order of 250 ms the need for greater audio bandwidth (i.e. greater compression) has to be balanced against a desire to keep any coding delays to a minimum. The following describes the three internationally recognized and commonly used coding standards, suitable for use over INMARSAT HSD services for audio applications.

6.6.1 Audio coding standards

G.711

The ITU-T standard G.711, which uses 64 kbps of bandwidth to provide 3 kHz telephone-quality audio, has very little coding delay and is generally used in telephony over ISDN. The shortest possible coding delay is highly desirable for satellite transmissions. However, the relatively narrow audio bandwidth of G.711 has limited use in broadcast applications and so generally a higher level of compression is required at the expense of greater coding delays.

G.722

The ITU-T G.722 standard, which also uses 64 kbps of bandwidth, is commonly used over both ISDN and satellite circuits for audio broadcast use, based on ADPCM (see Chapter 4). A coding delay of about 6 ms makes it very suitable for live interviews and voice feeds over a satellite circuit. However, the coding method is optimized for speech (the sound is split into two bands, the lower and higher frequencies, to make the coding more effective), and although the audio bandwidth of 7.5 kHz is generally considered perfectly acceptable for radio news items, it is unsuitable for transmission of music.

MPEG Layer 2

ISO/IEC MPEG Layer 2 is not widely used in radio news applications, although it is used in radio broadcasts of music. There are several different implementations of the MPEG Layer 2 standard, hence affecting the range of data rates available (see Chapter 4). However, the principal disadvantage in terms of newsgathering is the processing delay, making MPEG Layer 2 difficult to use for 'live' contributions which involve interaction with the studio. The actual delay is much greater than the theoretical delay figures. MPEG Layer 2 is often generically (but not strictly correctly) referred to as MUSICAM (see Chapter 4). MPEG Layer 1 is not widely used in broadcast applications.

apt-X

This coding 'standard' is a proprietary standard developed by Audio Processing Technology (APT) in the UK and though common it is not an international ITU standard. It uses ADPCM with a very low coding delay of less than 4 ms and, like G.722, delivers 7 kHz bandwidth in a 64 kbps HSD channel. However, because it is proprietary, it does not offer the universality of G.722.

6.6.2 Choice of coding standard

The advantages of G.722 for live radio newsgathering can now be appreciated, and it is likely to remain the favored coding system for the present. However, some organizations do prefer having the option of using MPEG Layer 2 (and Layer 1) and hence tend to use multi-standard codecs.

Typically, portable field-use audio codecs are fitted with a serial synchronous communications port such as RS.232, X.21 and V.35 which can be used for direct connection to the Inmarsat GAN satphone, although some may require interface converters. These interface converters are normally off-the-shelf items and can be ordered according to the type of interface conversion required.

On the terrestrial side, some studio audio codecs may also have an integral ISDN BRI, or one may be available as an option. However, many do not and will require connection to the NT1 using an ISDN TA with the corresponding serial synchronous communications interface (e.g. RS.232, X.21 or V.35).

G.722 audio codecs have no user-configurable settings and are connected directly to the Inmarsat GAN satphone. In general, there is a high level of compatibility between G.722 audio codecs of different manufacturers. Nevertheless, if any problems with the link are encountered the use of different makes of audio codecs has to be a prime suspect.

All audio codecs are duplex in operation (i.e. data can be sent simultaneously in both directions). Many MPEG Layer 2 audio codecs also incorporate the G.722 codec and are capable of symmetric and asymmetric dual-mode operation. This enables G.722 in both directions, MPEG Layer 2 in both directions, or MPEG Layer 2 in one direction and G.722 in the other direction. Asymmetric operation offers an advantage if the studio-to-remote path is in G.722, as delay is then minimized for 'live' contributions while offering maximum audio quality with MPEG Layer 2 in the remote-to-studio path. Care needs to be taken to ensure that the codecs at each end of the link are similarly configured.

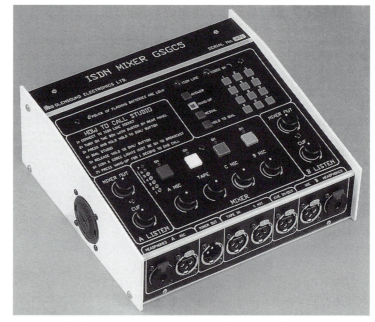

Figure 6.8   Glensound GSGC5 reporter unit (courtesy of Glensound Electronics)

Unlike G.722 audio codecs, there is not a high degree of compatibility between different makes of MPEG Layer 2 audio codecs because there are different implementations of the standard. If in doubt about the compatibility of two codecs, check them first on an ISDN circuit, as even the satellite delay can have an adverse effect. There are a wide variety of audio codecs that can be used with Inmarsat HSD; some are codecs alone, while others are combined terminal adapter and codec units (Figure 6.8).

6.7   Television contribution applications

6.7.1   Video-conferencing and the videophone

Video-conferencing is the technique for allowing two-way video, audio and data signals, currently at relatively low quality, to be used for live interaction over a communications circuit. There are a number of international standards for different levels of video-conferencing. There is a low-grade video-conferencing system, designed to be used with 28.8 kbps (V.34) modems over standard telephone circuits ('plain old telephone system', or POTS) to provide a 'videophone', utilizing the ITU-T H.324 standard[1] which was designed for this application. However, this standard does not produce anywhere near the quality required even for a breaking news story. Similarly, the use of 'webcams' does not constitute a means of achieving viable video transmission on the Internet for live news contribution, due to the unpredictable fluctuations in data rates which result in a discontinuous stream. We will therefore concentrate on video-conferencing standards designed for use over high-speed data circuits, typically either via ISDN or Inmarsat, and their application to the now ubiquitous videophone.

Video-conferencing is used either on a one-to-one basis or by groups of people who gather in a specific setting (often a conference room) to communicate with others. It may seem at first glance strange that we would consider use of video-conferencing techniques in the context of newsgathering. However, although not originally conceived for this purpose, video-conferencing used for newsgathering has increased over the last 6 years. This is due to two factors: quality and cost. As time passes, the quality of used video-conferencing at lower data rates is improving and the equipment cost is tumbling, as video-conferencing becomes an increasingly mass-market product. These shifts in quality and cost make video-conferencing very attractive, particularly for breaking stories or brief updates. The advantage that video-conferencing has over normal video is that for a 'live' update using a 'head and shoulders' shot, there is very little motion. Generally, with the human face in view, the lips will be the area of the picture that has the most movement, and hence very significant data compression is possible. Store and forward video units essentially use video-conferencing protocols for the 'live' mode of operation. In this section, we will focus on the video and audio aspects, ignoring the data and control details for the most part, as these are not relevant to newsgathering via Inmarsat.

Video-conferencing is normally achieved either as a dedicated system specifically designed for installation in a dedicated video-conferencing room or as PC hardware and software kits installed in desktop or laptop PCs. Either type will work with the GAN ISDN service. The international specification for video-conferencing over ISDN is ITU-T Recommendation H.320,[2] which is the basis for the family of standards which governs video-conferencing over narrow-band (64–1920 kbps) networks. The recommendation was designed primarily for ISDN and has become the *de facto* global video-conferencing standard.

6.7.2 Videophones

The videophone is essentially a video-conferencing unit adapted for field use. Certainly, the quality of transmission cannot match normal SNG equipment, but the videophone's key advantage is that it is both relatively easy to set up and carry around – but it is important to note that the videophone does not typically have a built-in camera.

The videophone unit used by many TV reporters weighs less than 5 kg and connects to a camera and one or two Inmarsat GAN satphones for live transmission of pictures. The whole system is carried in five laptop-size bags, can take an experienced operator less than 10 minutes to set up, and be powered via a vehicle cigarette lighter socket.

In the Iraq conflict in 2003, we saw widespread use of videophones by embedded reporters working with front line military units. But a particular incident in the Afghan conflict a few years earlier clearly illustrates the advantages and power of the videophone.

In November 2000 during the Afghanistan conflict, CNN senior correspondent Nic Robertson crossed into Taliban-controlled territory and within minutes he was reporting live on the air, bringing news to the world from Afghanistan. After gathering the news on the ground and interviewing a Taliban military commander, he did not want to wait. Because the Taliban had set up strict reporting restrictions, the CNN crew smuggled videophones past border guards, enabling them immediately to broadcast footage from their hotel balcony against the backdrop of Kabul. Although images from the videophone are lower quality than those from 'traditional' SNG uplinks, the videophone allowed CNN to broadcast scenes of the war almost a half-hour earlier than rival broadcasters who drove to an SNG uplink facility to send their reports.

While the images are not true broadcast quality, videophones have become popular with journalists traveling light. The videophone itself came to prominence in April 2001, when CNN used it to broadcast exclusive live footage of a US spy plane crew leaving Hainan Island in China after having been held hostage. Chinese security were then seen live on-air cutting the transmission as they realized what was happening.

Figure 6.9 (a) Talking Head 'videophone' reporter unit (courtesy of 7E Communications)

They may not have been the greatest pictures, but they were 'live'. The images were jerky because the reporter pointed the camera at the runway to capture the plane's tyres leaving the ground. Often called the Talking Head (named after the pioneering manufacturer's model), the videophone was designed to provide live pictures of a correspondent's moving head on a straight piece to camera mid-shot, not typically varying and moving TV footage.

The rapid development of high-quality, compact and low-cost domestic camcorders which produce excellent pictures at a fraction of the cost of broadcast TV cameras means the videophone can be used with a normal DVCAM camera (the pictures actually look poorer with a full broadcast-quality camera). Alternatively there is a high-grade type of webcam available as an option, which can be clipped to the top of the unit. The system typically consists of two units – the ruggedized field unit (the videophone) and a studio unit. The system can actually send video and audio in both directions at the same time, so a reporter can not only hear the studio but he/she can also see the studio output too. The system can either use one ISDN circuit to operate at 64 kbps or by using two terminals making two calls, operate at 128 kbps so giving higher quality. In addition, some models are produced in IP versions, aimed at use with Inmarsat BGAN terminals. The higher data rate allows the system to cope with more movement in the picture, or if desired improve the audio quality to studio standard (48 kbps rather than 16 kbps) *in lieu* of a smaller improvement in the picture quality.

Figure 6.9 (b) Talking Head videophone in use with BGAN (courtesy of Inmarsat)

So how is this equipment set up? At the receive end in the studio, one needs an ISDN line and the studio transceiver. In the field one of the following combinations is required:

- A single Inmarsat GAN satphone which provides an ISDN interface but is only capable of single-channel operation connection at 64 kbps
- Any two Inmarsat GAN satphones each of which can provide 64 kbps and a videophone which split the two channels of a 128 kbps ISDN-2 call across two single-channel ISDN connections, i.e. two satphones
- A single Inmarsat BGAN terminal for higher data rate transmissions

As we mentioned earlier, to provide a 128 kbps connection the two GAN satphones have to be bonded using a special interconnecting cable, or the 128 kbps terminal from one manufacturer can be used – in both cases a videophone can make 128 kbps calls. With an IP videophone and a BGAN terminal, streaming data rate of up to around 250 kbps is possible.

TV operates at 25 or 30 fps, and video-conferencing that operates at a true speed of 15 fps or greater is acceptable for most users. If operating at rates as low as 10 fps, picture jitter is noticeable, and a person speaking will show an apparent lack of continuity.

The videophone will, once the call is connected, typically take 5–10 seconds for each end of the link to synchronize and connect. If the call is established with an audio connection but no video is present then it is highly likely that one or both of the video-conferencing systems is in G.711 or G.722 audio mode. In this case it will be necessary to clear the call down, reconfigure one or both of the terminals (both should be configured for G.728) and re-dial the call. Alternatively, the video mode could be switched from CIF to QCIF to force a 'capability block' exchange, effectively resetting the system.

When using a Talking Head type of videophone, the following is advisable to improve the results:

● Make sure the satphone antenna is pointed in the right direction and the signal strength optimized to achieve the highest signal strength
● Try to use the camera on a tripod, and avoid jerky movements
● Keep background movement to a minimum by careful framing
● Keep the reporter correctly proportioned in the frame
● The reporter should avoid excessive body movement, and restrict their hand movement
● 'Mic up' the reporter correctly

Often trying to use a videophone without consideration of its limitations will lead to disappointing results – not for nothing is it called a Talking Head unit, and not a General Wide View unit!

6.7.3   Store and forward

An alternative to the use of the low-quality videophone is a store and forward system. It's important to note immediately that such systems don't operate in 'live' mode – they are intended for the transmission of material at higher quality at slower than real time. This means that every minute of material recorded will actually take several minutes to send. The principles of store and forward were covered in Chapter 5, and the same principles apply to their use on the Inmarsat system. The process generates a file for transmission, and the resultant data file is transmitted according to the ITU H.261 and G.722 protocols, which form part of the H.320 video-conferencing protocol as discussed in the next section. The H.320 protocol encompasses both H.261 for video and G.722 for audio.

Highly portable store and forward systems for use with Inmarsat satphones were originally developed in the mid-1990s weighing only about 12 kg (25 lb) and designed for use in rugged conditions. A common system first used for newsgathering in the field was the Toko VAST-p (no longer made). The VAST-p unit was in use with a number of newsgatherers (both broadcasters and news agencies) for a number of years, but has now been superseded by newer technological solutions (see Chapter 5).

Although in Chapter 5 we discussed the use of IP as the transport mechanism, the completed compressed file can also be sent via an Inmarsat ISDN connection to the studio for subsequent transmission. A number of manufacturers produce systems based on this type of technology. The video is typically either coded as a MPEG-2 or MPEG-4 file. Each of these coding standards is described in more detail in Chapter 4.

The data file can also be transmitted according to the ITU H.261 and G.722 protocols, which form part of the H.323 video-conferencing protocol as discussed in the next section. The H.323 protocol encompasses both H.261 for video and G.722 for audio. H.261 as a video coding standard was designed for coding rates between 40 kbps and 2 Mbps.

Sometimes MPEG-1 – the forerunner to MPEG-2 – is used. MPEG-1 is an ISO/IEC standard and defines a bit-stream for compressed video and audio optimized for encoding at 1.5 Mbps. However, the principles of operation of both MPEG-1 and H.261 are similar. With H.261, only the image elements that have changed need to be saved or transmitted because the other information exists in the previous frame or frames. In contrast, MPEG-1 (as with MPEG-2 and MPEG-4) looks forward as well as backwards when estimating motion. This means that although the coding delay is slightly longer, the quality and motion handling of MPEG-1 was considered superior.

However the use of MPEG-4 ASP and AVC for streaming applications is now overtaking the use of these older standards.

6.7.4   Compression formats

H.261

The H.261 standard was the first international digital compression standard, formalized in 1990, and it was from this that all subsequent international standards were based. It is designed for coding rates between 40 kbps and 2 Mbps, but only I- and P-frames are used, resulting in less encoding and decoding latency delay. DCT is still used to reduce spatial redundancy, and forward motion prediction is used for motion compensation. One feature that H.261 (and H.263) have (unlike MPEG) is the ability to vary the frame rate within a video sequence. This is important in video-conferencing because an encoder must be able to both lower the frame rate to maintain reasonable visual quality and dynamically adjust to sudden changes in video content in real time.

H.263/H.263+

The development and implementation of advanced compression algorithms H.263 and H.263+[3] (enhancements of H.261) offer a higher level of quality at low data rates that are acceptable for newsgathering. The H.263 algorithm outperforms H.261 by a factor of up to 3:1 in qualitative terms, and can transmit video data at rates much less than 64 kbps. It is certainly acceptable for breaking stories where there is no other way of getting reports back to the studio center, producing results at 64 kbps comparable to a 128 kbps ($2 \times$ BRI) circuit. A $2 \times$ BRI video-conference picture is certainly adequate for remote education, presentations, etc., and is also used for a breaking news stories. Rapidly changing scenes are still not very well handled, but as soon as movement within the picture diminishes, the sharpness, color and movement quality are impressive considering the limitations of the system. However, to achieve $2 \times$ BRI via INMARSAT requires two satphones to be bonded together. Therefore, the use of H.263 at 64 kbps, offering equivalent subjective quality, is certainly very attractive as it can be achieved with a single INMARSAT satphone.

A feature that H.261 and H.263 share is the ability to vary the frame rate within a video sequence. This is important for two reasons. Firstly, the bit-rate in a video-conference can be very low, so an encoder must be able to lower the frame rate to maintain reasonable visual quality. Secondly, the encoder must be able to dynamically adjust to sudden changes in video content in real time without warning. For example, at a scene change, the first compressed frame of the new scene tends to be large in terms of data because of the dissimilarity with the previous frame. With variable frame-rate encoding, the encoder can code the frame and then skip a few input frames to catch up before encoding the next frame.

Other standards specified within H.320 are H.221, H.230 and H.242, which are used respectively for framing, control and indication, and communications procedures.

H.320

H.320 is a suite of specifications which define how video-conferencing systems communicate over ISDN, defining video, audio and data standards. One of the important aspects to consider in respect of using an H.320 compliant system with the GAN ISDN service is that of the audio codec to be used. H.320 encompasses three audio compression standards.

These three audio compression algorithms are designed to handle a broad range of applications:

- ITU-T G.711[4] uses the whole of the 64 kbps of bandwidth to provide 3 kHz telephone-quality audio
- G.722[5] provides 7.5 kHz audio using 64 kbps of bandwidth
- G.728[6] provides 3 kHz audio using 16 kbps of bandwidth

However, as discussed earlier, G.711 and G.722 both require 64 kbps channels and are hence unsuitable for GAN ISDN video-conferencing applications, as they would each consume all of the available bandwidth. The greater the degree of compression applied, the greater the delay introduced into the transmission, i.e. G.728 will introduce the greatest delay and G.711 the least. It is for this reason that G.711 is the standard normally adopted for ISDN telephones. However, when using a narrow band 64 kbps service like GAN ISDN it is only possible to use G.728 because of the bandwidth limitations. An H.320 compatible video-conferencing system using GAN ISDN will use 16 kbps (G.728) for audio and 1.6 kbps for H.221 framing, leaving 46.4 kbps for video. On the other hand, G.722 is used for audio-only contributions, as we will see later in this chapter when we look at radio news contribution.

6.7.5 Picture resolutions

The ITU has defined a range of video formats by their resolution for use over telephony class circuits (Table 6.1), and they are based around what is described as CIF – Common Intermediate Format. These video formats are based on non-interlaced frames, i.e. progressive scanning.

The key component of H.320 is the H.261 video compression algorithm standard,[7] which uses two principal video resolutions from the ITU-T range: 352×288 CIF (common intermediate format) and 176×144 QCIF (quarter common intermediate format). QCIF is normally used for low bit-rate channels such as GAN ISDN and the frame rate can be up to a maximum of 30 frames per second (fps). On a 384 kbps channel, an H.320 video-conferencing system will achieve 30 fps at CIF and look comparable to a VHS picture.

Many Internet webcam style videophones are based on the 128×96 pixels SQCIF (subquarter common intermediate format) and QCIF resolutions. While this is an impressive accomplishment in the bandwidth available, it is not suitable for quality video-conferencing or, therefore, newsgathering.

On an Inmarsat GAN 64 kbps ISDN channel, the same system would achieve 10–15 fps at QCIF. The H.261 algorithm includes a mechanism that optimizes bandwidth usage by trading picture quality against motion so that a quickly changing picture will have a lower-quality than a relatively static picture.

Table 6.1 ITU-T coded video frame transmission formats

Abbreviation	Description	Pixel ratio (NTSC)	Pixel ratio (PAL)
SQCIF	Sub-quarter CIF	–	128×96
QCIF	Quarter CIF	176×120	176×144
FCIF	Full CIF	352×220	352×288
2CIF	Two times CIF	704×220	704×288
4CIF	Four times CIF	704×480	704×576
9CIF	Nine times CIF	1056×720	1056×864
16CIF	Sixteen times CIF	1408×960	1408×1152

Video-conferencing systems need to communicate at a resolution that can be handled given several factors. These factors include available line bandwidth, system processor capacity and the capacity of the software being employed. Another factor in video-conferencing is the frame rate of the session. The H.261/263 standard allows frame rates of 7.5, 10, 15 and 30 fps. Television operates at 25 or 30 fps and cinemas at 24 fps, and video-conferencing that operates at a true speed of 15 fps or greater looks acceptable for most users. If operating at rates as low as 10 fps, picture jitter is noticeable, and a person speaking will show an apparent lack of continuity.

Another major factor is the ability of the software and hardware to process the data both in compressing and decompressing the images. Since a great deal of compression is involved, and each frame must be processed, transmitted, stored and re-processed, then the slower the processor or the lower the efficiency of the system, the poorer the image and the slower the apparent frame rate. While a system may operate at a high frame rate, it may appear to be operating at a lower frame rate due to insufficient processing capacity. This will result in duplicate frames, or 'inferred' frames being used which can be identical to the last frame, rather than the actual data for that frame.

Dedicated video-conferencing systems were historically supplied with a synchronous serial communications port (usually X.21, V.35 or RS.232) which will enable direct connection to the GAN ISDN terminal. On the other hand, the latest video-conferencing systems are supplied either with an integral ISDN BRI or an Ethernet IP connection, and calls can be directly placed via the GAN satphone either by dialing the ISDN number or entering the IP address of the destination.

6.8   Satphone operation

The following explanations give an idea of the use of an Inmarsat terminal and the slight differences in operation between the Inmarsat GAN, BGAN and Mini-M satphones – currently the three Inmarsat systems commonly used by newsgatherers – and demonstrate how units of each type are typically assembled and operated. All three use an internal rechargeable battery as its primary power source, though there are cables supplied to enable powering from the local mains or connecting to a vehicle cigarette lighter socket or battery – any of these will charge the internal battery as well as power the terminal.

6.8.1   Inmarsat GAN

There is a limited range of brands of Inmarsat GAN satphones, and the Inmarsat GAN satphone typically consists of three parts – the antenna, the transceiver unit (usually integrated together but separable) and the DECT handset. DECT is a standard for wireless telephone handsets (Digital Enhanced Cordless Telephone), first developed in Europe but now used in over 100 countries worldwide.

Siting the satphone

The unit has a fold-out panel antenna, and the whole unit is pointed approximately toward the satellite. To operate successfully, the satphone needs to be able to 'see' one of the four Inmarsat satellites. When siting the antenna, a compass is used to check that there is a clear view toward the satellite – to the south if in the Northern Hemisphere, and to the north if in the Southern Hemisphere. The satphone can be used inside a building if the antenna is pointing out through a window – the window does not need to be open, but beware of metallized coatings on the glass used to prevent glare or offer privacy. The window obviously needs to offer a view of the sky in the right direction (Figure 6.10):

● Don't use a compass near the satphone while it is switched on, as the electromagnetic field from the satphone antenna can cause a false reading.

Figure 6.10   Siting an Inmarsat BGAN pointing out of a window (courtesy of Thrane & Thrane)

● Don't try and take a reading from a compass near vehicles (metal affects the reading), nor inside buildings, as many modern structures have an integral steel frame that will affect a compass reading. Tall buildings or trees close-by must not obstruct the view toward the satellite. For safety reasons, the antenna should not be pointed toward areas where people may pass or gather, and ensure that any cables don't create a trip hazard.

Operating

Switch the unit on, and enter the (usually required) PIN code. Within a few seconds after the satphone is switched on, the display should give various status indications, telling the user which LES is selected (usually the one last used).

To make a reliable HSD call the antenna must be pointing accurately at the chosen Ocean Region satellite. This is not the case for simple voice calls, which with a much lower data rate don't need such critical alignment. There is a chart supplied with the terminal that will give an estimate of the azimuth and the elevation of the antenna. The whole satphone may be rotated until the antenna points in the direction indicated by the compass. The terminal display gives an indication of signal strength often with a varying audio tone; you should refer to the manufacturer's manual for an explanation of the exact indication.

The unit typically has both an audible and visual display of signal strength, and as the unit is rotated slowly toward the satellite, the signal strength indication will increase. The elevation angle of the antenna also has to be adjusted to obtain optimum signal strength. Once the satellite is acquired, the display will indicate that it is ready to place a call. All commands are keyed into the DECT telephone handset, while operational controls are accessed from the handset with error messages and the progress of the call displayed on the terminal. Any additional units such as videophone, store and forward unit or audio codec will also need to be connected before an HSD call is made.

Why is the antenna pointing not as critical as for the larger SNG uplinks? The answer lies in the operating frequency of INMARSAT satphones. They all operate in L-band (around 1600 MHz), and therefore because the beamwidth is considerably wider, less pointing accuracy is required. Because the pointing is not so critical, it is possible to transmit videophone pictures from moving vehicles and ships.

Safety

The antenna produces significant levels of non-ionizing radiation and the manufacturers' recommendations for minimum clear distances in front of the antenna must be followed: 2 m is a typical 'safe zone'. Standing behind the antenna is perfectly safe, and it is advisable to mark out the safe zone with visual warning tape. However, all satphones effectively have an automatic transmission safety cut-out which operates within 5 seconds of an obstruction appearing in front of the antenna as the terminal loses connection with the satellite. This may not be the case when it is operating in voice-only mode, when care must be taken that no one stands in front of the antenna. Such is the resilience of the link for voice transmissions that the satphone may be able to maintain a connection even with a person standing in front of the antenna.

6.8.2 Inmarsat BGAN

Operation of a BGAN terminal is similar in principle, but varies in the way that the terminal is configured to go online. It relies on using the LaunchPad software application supplied with the terminal being loaded onto a laptop to enable control of the terminal and check its status during set-up.

Having unpacked the terminal and switched it on outside in a place where it can detect at least three GPS satellites, one must wait for the terminal to get a GPS 'fix'. Without this stage being achieved, it is impossible to get the terminal on the air. Once the terminal has a fix (indicated by a green LED on the side of the unit), then it is connected to the laptop (via either USB or Ethernet cable), and the LaunchPad application is run.

The terminal now has to be pointed as described previously toward the desired satellite in order to register onto the network. Having folded out the antenna, the LaunchPad application gives feedback on the GPS fix and the received signal strength with the satellite. As the unit is rotated slowly toward the satellite, the signal strength indication will increase.

Once the optimum signal is achieved, the user then clicks on the 'Register Now' button on the LaunchPad screen, and within a few seconds an established link will be made and indicated and the terminal will open a standard IP connection whose status will be shown on the LaunchPad screen. Choice of the type of service and the operating parameters may then be set (Figure 6.11).

6.8.3 Inmarsat Mini-M

The operation of the Inmarsat Mini-M satphone is simpler and very similar to that of the GAN. The satphone comes in a small case and the antenna is integral to the case. It is simply a matter of flipping the antenna up, pointing it approximately in the direction of the satellite, and optimizing the position in azimuth and elevation to get the strongest signal strength. Once this has been done, the handset can be used to dial the call directly (see Figure 6.12). Because the RF power from the Mini-M satphones is much lower, there need only be a 1 m area kept clear in front of the satphone.

6.9 Impact of INMARSAT services on newsgathering

6.9.1 Radio

Only Inmarsat-A and -B satphones could be used for radio newsgathering contributions up until the mid-1990s (though not for television newsgathering), but their use was limited to a degree by the size of

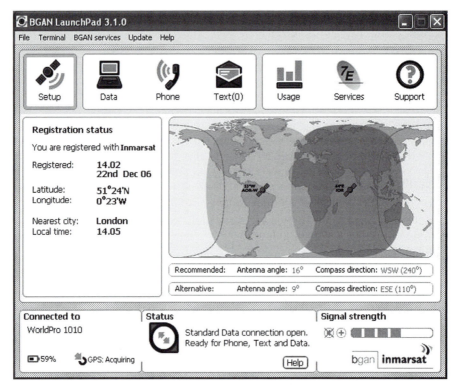

Figure 6.11   Screenshot of LaunchPad application (courtesy of 7E Communications)

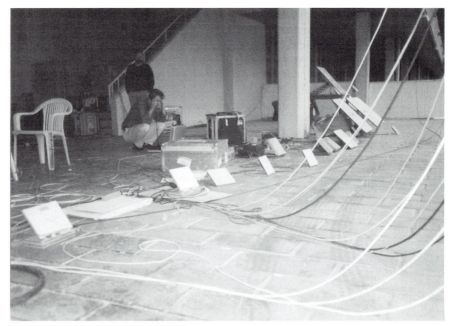

Figure 6.12   Media satphone 'farm' in Baghdad (photo courtesy of Paul Szeless)

the units. The development of the briefcase-size Inmarsat-M in 1993, and then the even more compact Mini-M in 1996, meant that radio news reports could be filed from many places where the heavier and more bulky (and conspicuous) Inmarsat-A and -B terminals could not be used. In recognition of the fact that these smaller units were designed for a larger mass business-traveler market, INMARSAT actively sought wider approval for the importation and use of these systems in countries that had previously been resistant to such use. Gone was the need in many countries for special permissions for to use these satphones and pay high fees for importation licences. Partly these controls had been for political control, partly due to protectionism. The public telephone operators (PTOs) of these countries were protective of revenues from lucrative international call traffic through their own national telephone systems.

6.9.2 Television

By 1994 compact new equipment designed specifically for newsgathering enabled the transmission of television news pictures, albeit not in real time. The transmission of newspaper stills pictures had been possible for many years via analog channels. Several manufacturers developed digital video compression units for television newsgathering that could transmit video and audio over HSD channels in 'store and forward' mode. The broadcast news market felt that the further development of this store and forward type of system would be a key to future newsgathering techniques. Store and forward units have been and still are used by the major global newsgatherers, including the US, Japanese and European networks, as well as the principal international television news agencies.

After 2000, when 7E Communications (UK) launched their Talking Head reporter unit – the first videophone designed for newsgathering use – a trend was started where having live low bit-rate video became an essential part of coverage of many dramatic breaking news stories.

The significant impact of both videophone and store and forward units is the ability to transmit news pictures from places where:

● There is no infrastructure for television transmissions
● Local politics or the overall logistics prevent the deployment of conventional SNG flyaways
● The news story has not developed to the point where it is considered cost-effective to deploy a full SNG flyaway

6.10 Trans-border issues

Although technically it is possible to use Inmarsat satellite communications virtually anywhere in the world, some countries either do not permit its use, or if they do, make it prohibitively expensive to do so (see Chapter 7). Inmarsat is continually encouraging those countries to remove or reduce the regulatory barriers that restrict or prevent the use of its equipment within their borders.

Some countries prohibit any use of mobile-satellite communications equipment, while others permit it only in particular circumstances, such as for disaster relief or emergencies, or in limited geographical areas. High licence fees, taxes and customs duties are all factors intended to put off many potential users – in some countries the annual licence fee can be thousands of US dollars. Additional type-approval of Inmarsat equipment is sometimes demanded, even though the equipment has already been type-approved and meets internationally recognized standards. Often these regulatory barriers exist because the country does not have a policy or regulatory framework covering mobile-satellite services or because they fear bypass of their terrestrial network (even in areas where there is no network to bypass). Some countries are concerned that mobile-satellite earth stations may be used for criminal activity. Another reason for regulatory barriers is concern about interference to other telecommunications equipment, but spectrum sharing studies show that this is not an issue.

In 1997, the International Telecommunications Union (ITU) hosted a meeting of 88 administrations, satellite system operators, manufacturers and service providers which agreed a Memorandum of Understanding (MoU), the aim of which was to facilitate the free movement of Global Mobile Personal Communications by Satellite (GMPCS) terminals. This was finally implemented by the ITU in 1998[8]. Anyone considering taking an Inmarsat terminal to a different country is advised to contact the telecommunications licensing authority in the country they plan to visit, to get up-to-date information on any conditions attached to use of the terminal in the visited country.

Failure to secure the appropriate approvals is likely at the very least to result in confiscation of the equipment at the point of entry to the country or even, in some countries, arrest on the grounds of suspected espionage. Trans-border issues are discussed further in Chapter 7.

6.11 Conclusions

The use of Inmarsat for newsgathering is now ubiquitous, and with the Inmarsat GAN and BGAN systems, combined with the compact videophones and store and forward laptop systems, more newsgatherers have been able to afford entry into this area of technology. At the time of writing, data has overtaken voice as the principal use for Inmarsat services, accounting for 75% of the company's traffic and 55% of its revenue, growing at 15% per year. The use of Inmarsat services for delivering radio news contribution is well established, and the ability of Inmarsat GAN satphones to easily interface with off-the-shelf ISDN products and applications has enhanced its use for audio newsgathering as well, of course, expanding its use for video. Inevitably the use of IP (on dedicated streaming connections) will overtake ISDN in the future.

BGAN offers a new and easy way to achieve reasonable IP connection speeds from the most inhospitable destinations, and there is little doubt that Inmarsat will remain unchallenged for the foreseeable future as the principal means for rapid newsgathering from remote and difficult locations.

References

1. ITU (1998) ITU-T Recommendation H.324 (2/98), Terminal for low bit-rate multimedia communication.
2. ITU (1997) ITU-T Recommendation H.320 (7/97), Narrow-band visual telephone systems and terminal equipment.
3. ITU (1998) ITU-T Recommendation H.263 (2/98), Video coding for low bit-rate communication.
4. ITU (1988) ITU-T Recommendation G.711 (11/88), Pulse code modulation (PCM) of voice frequencies.
5. ITU (1988) ITU-T Recommendation G.722 (11/88), 7 kHz audio coding within 64 kbit/s.
6. ITU (1992) ITU-T Recommendation G.728 (9/92), Coding of speech at 16 kbit/s using low-delay code excited linear prediction.
7. ITU (1993) ITU-T Recommendation H.261 (3/93), Video codec for audiovisual services at p × 64 kbit/s.
8. ITU (1998) Ninth Plenary Meeting, Resolution 1116, Implementation of the GMPCS-MoU arrangements.

7

Across the spectrum: regulation and standards

The technical practicalities of satellite newsgathering are difficult enough to master. To understand the administrative, regulatory and commercial aspects can be just as challenging, and so in this chapter, we will look at these issues and put them into context. Be warned, however, that to understand this aspect of telecommunications requires a good memory for abbreviations and acronyms!

Operating SNG uplinks virtually anywhere in the world requires some degree of administrative process to be undertaken, and any operation has to take place within the international regulation of spectrum. These individual national administrative procedures are used to regulate SNG uplinks both in terms of political and technical controls. The constant push to provide the latest news is the driver behind allowing satellite newsgathering greater freedom, particularly into places where it is not wanted and even viewed with mistrust and fear. Broadcasting and telecommunications are often considered matters of national security and social policy in many countries, and in some countries the concept of foreign newsgatherers bringing in their own transmitting equipment is a question of sovereignty. The issues of obtaining permissions and licences in different countries will be examined later, along with the impact of impending new international agreements.

To operate an SNG uplink system anywhere in the world, there are normally three areas of administration that have to be covered:

- Permission has to be granted to the uplink operator, on either a temporary or permanent basis, to operate the uplink in the country and area where it is to be operated.
- The SNG uplink operator has to obtain authority, usually by way of registration, with satellite system operators who may be providing the space segment to be used, to access that space segment with the uplink equipment.
- Space segment has to be secured by way of a satellite transponder/channel booking.

Looking at all these issues, we will see how and where they interact – and to begin with, we will look at how the electromagnetic (or frequency) spectrum is regulated as a resource. To appreciate fully the administrative context within which satellite newsgathering operates, we need to understand the regulatory aspects of spectrum. There are a bewildering number of organizations and bodies involved in the setting of standards, regulation and administration of the spectrum. Amongst all of these, we need to understand where the process of satellite newsgathering overlaps with international and national regulation.

7.1 Spectrum

There is a constant pressure for the resources of bandwidth and power by telecommunications services providers seeking to deliver IP data, telephony and video services, particularly in the sectors of the

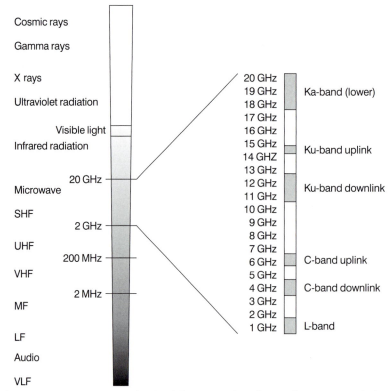

Figure 7.1 Electromagnetic spectrum: the SNG frequency bands are shown expanded

frequency spectrum used for satellite communications. The desire to deliver more services to more people has never been greater nor technologically more feasible, and to meet this pressure there is a need to be ever more efficient in the allocation and use of spectrum. The drive to provide these services comes from the obvious opportunities for commercial gain, spurred on by a desire to provide increasingly sophisticated means of communicating.

In telecommunications, the electromagnetic spectrum resource is commonly referred to as 'RF' – the abbreviation for radio frequency. In this context, 'radio' does not refer to radio media, such as radio stations and their broadcasts, but is used in the scientific sense, as defined in a dictionary as 'rays' or 'radiation'. This can be confusing for non-scientists, but is in fact the original definition of 'radio'. It has also been historically referred to as 'airwaves' or as the 'ether', and a specific frequency in the spectrum can be referred to as a 'wavelength'. But all these terms refer to aspects of electromagnetic spectrum.

The known electromagnetic spectrum ranges from nothing to gamma radiation, with visible light just over half way up the spectrum, as shown in Figure 7.1 (the commercial satellite frequency bands of interest for SNG are shown expanded). Electromagnetic spectrum can be viewed as a natural element, such as water or air, but only available in a relatively controlled amount to be useful. It can be imagined that without international agreement and regulation of usage there would be chaos. Each country could use whatever spectrum and transmitter power level they pleased, but as a natural resource and no respecter of man's political boundaries, the airwaves would be crowded with transmissions interfering with each other. Anyone who has tried to listen to short-wave or medium-wave radio at night will hear this type of interference as atmospheric conditions alter at night to 'throw' the signals further afield.

There is also a significant amount of interference from outer space affecting many parts of the frequency spectrum.

The international regulation of the spectrum deals in fact with 'normal' conditions, and cannot fully take account of random atmospheric effects caused by the onset of night or abnormal weather conditions, which can particularly affect the lower end of the spectrum as used for most radio transmissions.

There are a number of regional and global standards-setting organizations, which are linked either directly or voluntarily. There is, however, a single global body that oversees all aspects of the use of spectrum – the International Telecommunications Union (ITU). It encompasses all administration of spectrum, and it is worth spending a little time examining this organization.

7.2 The ITU

The International Telecommunications Union (ITU) is concerned with international co-operation in the use of telecommunications and the radio frequency spectrum, and with promoting and facilitating the development, expansion and operation of telecommunications networks in developing countries. It is the leading world body for the co-ordination and development of technical and operating standards for telecommunications and radiocommunications (including satellite) services.

The ITU, founded in Paris in 1865 as the International Telegraph Union, changed its name to the International Telecommunication Union in 1934, and became a specialized agency of the United Nations in 1947. It is an intergovernmental organization (IGO), currently (2006) made up of 191 member states and 643 members (scientific and industrial companies, public and private operators, broadcasters and regional and international organizations), within which the public and private sectors co-operate for the development of all telecommunications for the common good. Through agreement it creates and defines international regulations and treaties governing all terrestrial and space uses of the frequency spectrum as well as the use of the geostationary satellite orbit. Within this framework, countries adopt their national telecommunications legislation. It also has a particular mission to promote and facilitate the development, expansion and operation of telecommunications networks in developing countries. However, it is important to realize that the ITU does not have the power to impose regulations – it is not a supranational power – and its strength lies through achieving agreement between member countries.

The ITU is therefore the ruling world body for the co-ordination and development of technical and operating standards for telecommunications, including satellite services. However, it should be noted that the ITU has no powers of enforcement, and relies on the consensual co-operation of all its members to achieve its objectives.

7.2.1 A short history of spectrum administration

The invention and subsequent patenting of wireless telegraphy (the first type of radio communication) by Guglielmo Marconi in 1896 saw the utilization of this new technology primarily for maritime purposes. The beginning of spectrum administration was prompted from an international dispute involving the Marconi Company.

Guglielmo Marconi formed a company to commercially exploit his invention in the maritime market – which was clearly the major area of development. In 1901, Marconi signed an exclusive contract with the insurers Lloyd's of London to provide Marconi operators and Marconi equipment on board insured ships to track their progress, and Marconi established a presence in all the major seaports of the world. Meanwhile, since competitors from America and Germany had appeared, the Marconi Company established its most controversial policy, known as the 'non-intercommunication rule'. Marconi operators on ship or shore could only communicate with other Marconi operators. Clients using other apparatus were excluded from the Marconi network; only in the event of a serious emergency was this rule to be suspended.

In March 1902, the German Kaiser's brother, Prince Henry of Germany, was returning home to Germany after a highly publicized visit to the United States. He was sailing aboard the German liner *Deutschland*, which was equipped with wireless equipment made by a German competitor to Marconi – Slaby-Arco. None of the Marconi stations on either side of the Atlantic would communicate with the ship because of its rival apparatus. Prince Henry, who tried to send wireless messages to both the US and Germany, was outraged.

Following this incident, Germany demanded that an international conference be called to discuss wireless telegraph ('radiotelegraph') communications and the monopoly that the Marconi Company held over maritime communications. A month before this first international wireless conference in Berlin in 1903, Telefunken was formed by two competing German firms, Slaby-Arco and Braun-Siemens-Halske, to present a united German front against Marconi, encouraged by the German government. Although the conference was supposed to address a number of wide-ranging issues, the only real issue was the Marconi Company's refusal to communicate with other systems. All the countries at the conference, with the exception of Italy and Great Britain, favored compelling Marconi to communicate with all ships because they opposed his *de facto* monopolization of the airwaves.

The emerging problems surrounding the financing and regulation of the new technology, and the sanctity of each country's territorial airwaves, were embodied in the Marconi-German confrontation. The issue over whether a private company should gain dominance over a natural resource such as the airwaves and dictate their use was overriding. Germany, France, Spain and Austria had all assumed control of wireless in their own countries under governmental control because of its military significance. While Marconi was involved in commercial exploitation, the governments of these countries saw huge strategic value in the airwaves.

However, the issue was not resolved at this first conference, but in 1906 the International Radiotelegraph Conference was held in Berlin and the International Radiotelegraph Convention was signed. The annex to this Convention contained the first regulations governing wireless telegraphy – the Conference required any public shore station to communicate with any wireless-equipped ship, so defeating the monopoly of the Marconi Company, and included the adoption of the 'SOS' distress signal. These and other regulations, which have since been amended and revised by numerous World Radio Conferences held over the years, formed the basis of the Radio Regulations (RR).

In 1924, the Comité Consultatif International des Communications Téléphoniques á Grande Distance (International Telephone Consultative Committee – Consultatif International des Fils a Grande Distance acronym CCIF) was set up ('F' stands for 'fils', a French colloquialism for cable). The Comité Consultatif International des Communications Telegraphes á Grande Distance (the International Telegraph Consultative Committee, acronym CCIT) was set up in the following year. Then, in 1927, the Comité Consultatif International des Communications Radio á Grande Distance (the International Radio Consultative Committee, acronym CCIR) was also established, and these committees were jointly made responsible for all technical studies in telecommunications. The International Consultative Committees (CCIs) thus became involved in the preparation of the Union's regulatory conferences at which international agreements governing all types of telecommunications were concluded. (In 1956, the CCIF and the CCIT merged to form Comité Consultatif International des Communications Téléphoniques á Grande Distance, acronym CCITT.)

In 1927, the ITU allocated frequency bands to the various radio services existing at the time (fixed, maritime and aeronautical mobile, broadcasting, amateur and experimental). This was to ensure greater efficiency of operation, particularly in view of the increase in the number of services using frequencies and the technical requirements of each service.

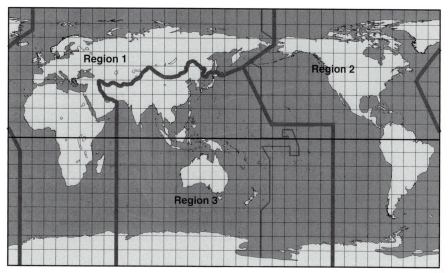

Figure 7.2 ITU regions (courtesy of ITU)

In 1947, after the Second World War, the ITU held a conference with the aim of developing and modernizing the organization. Under an agreement with the United Nations, it became a specialized agency of the United Nations in October 1947, and the conference decided that the headquarters of the organization should be transferred in 1948 from Bern to Geneva. The International Frequency Registration Board (IFRB) was set up to manage the frequency spectrum, which was becoming increasingly complicated and congested, and the Table of Frequency Allocations originally introduced in 1912 became mandatory. This Table allocates to each service using radio spectrum specific frequency bands with a view to avoiding interference between stations, such as in communications between aircraft and control centers, ships at sea and coast stations, radio stations, or spacecraft and earth-based stations. As mentioned at the beginning of the chapter, freedom from interference is one of the primary reasons for international co-ordination on spectrum usage.

The Frequency Allocation Table forms Article 8 of the ITU Radio Regulations, which is several hundred pages long, and is the most frequently referred to document of the ITU. It divides the world into three administrative regions: Europe, Africa and Northern Asia (Region 1); the Americas (Region 2) and Southern Asia and Australasia (Region 3) (Figure 7.2). Each region has individual allocations of frequencies for some services, and common allocations for others. Frequencies are allocated for primary and secondary usage, so that some parts of the frequency bands are allocated on an exclusive basis to some services and shared for other services. National administrations are not bound to allow usage of frequencies as allocated in the Frequency Allocation Table in their country, as local priorities may dictate otherwise. On the other hand, national administrations in general do not permit usage of a particular frequency band for a purpose other than that defined for that region in the Frequency Allocation Table.

The inauguration of the space age in 1957 with the launch of the first artificial satellite, SPUTNIK 1, by the former USSR posed new demands on the ITU. In 1959, to meet the challenges of the space age, the CCIR set up a Study Group responsible for studying space radiocommunication, and in 1963 an Extraordinary Administrative Conference for Space Communications was held to allocate frequencies to the various space services. The first telecommunications satellite, 'TELSTAR 1', had been launched and put into orbit in 1962 and the ITU subsequently administered space communication uses of spectrum.

7.2.2 The role of the ITU

As well as administering frequency allocations for satellite use, the ITU also acts as the global co-ordinating body for the allocation of orbital slot positions for satellites. The ITU allocates sectors of the geostationary arc nominally to countries in the region below each arc sector. There are of course certain areas of the geostationary arc which give excellent continental and transcontinental coverage, and these are highly sought after by satellite operators as they offer significant commercial advantages.

National administrations, in co-operation with the ITU, require operators of potential satellites to lodge an application for a particular orbital slot in the geostationary arc with the relevant national administration. The national administration then co-ordinates the application with the ITU, checking for potential conflicting demands with adjacent national administrations, and thus the ITU, as well as allocating the arc sectors, also acts as a global 'clearing house' for individual orbital slot allocations. These applications are made years in advance of the actual placing of the satellite in position, and many organizations place applications and hold allocations for orbital slots that may never be used – otherwise known as 'paper' satellites. In an environment where there is an ever-increasing demand for slot allocations, there is great pressure to reduce the number of 'paper' satellites.

7.2.3 The structure of the ITU

The ITU Council governs ITU affairs between each of the ITU Plenipotentiary Conferences, which are held every 4 years. The ITU Council is composed of 46 Members of the Union elected by the Plenipotentiary Conference, representing all five regions of the world (Americas, Western Europe, Eastern Europe and Northern Asia, Africa, Asia and Australasia). The Member Governments are party to the Constitution and Convention, which are the basic parts of the ITU treaty. Only the ITU's Plenipotentiary Conference can alter these basic treaties, which are augmented by the International Telecommunication Regulations and the ITU Radio Regulations (ITU-RR).

The ITU structure is based on three sectors:

- The radiocommunication sector (ITU-R) provides the forum for treaty-level agreements on international use of radio frequencies and for broadcasting, radiocommunication and satellite transmission standards. The regular summit conference for this sector is the World Administrative Radiocommunication Conference (WARC).
- The telecommunication standardization sector (ITU-T) establishes global agreements on standards ('Recommendations') for telecommunications. The regular summit conference for this sector is the World Telecommunication Standardization Conference (WTSC).
- The telecommunication development sector (ITU-D) provides technical assistance to developing countries within a new strategic planning framework. The regular summit conference for this sector is the World Telecommunication Development Conference (WTDC).

Of these, only the WARC is at treaty level and can devise and amend the Radio Regulations. Broadcasters, telecommunications carriers and other elements of the communications industry have a close interest in the work of the ITU, and many participate in the ITU sectional work in Study Groups. Each year, there are as around 80 ITU meetings, including the specialized Study Groups. The WARC is the relevant body which has direct control over the frequencies used for satellite newsgathering around the world.

7.2.4 Radio frequency standards

As previously mentioned, in 1927 the International Radio Consultative Committee (CCIR) was established by the ITU, one of three Consultative Committees. The CCIR undertook tests and measurements in the various fields of telecommunications, and contributed to the drawing up of international standards. It was also in 1927 that the ITU allocated frequency bands to the various radio services existing at the time (fixed, maritime and aeronautical mobile, broadcasting, amateur and experimental). The primary aim was to ensure greater efficiency of operation in view of the increase in the number of services using frequencies and the technical requirements of each service.

The CCIR was originally the standard-setting section of the ITU, and regulating the use of frequencies is an essential aspect of the work of ITU. To carry out this work, it was decided to separate the standards-setting activities of the CCIR from its management of the radio frequency spectrum in terrestrial and space radiocommunications. The standards-setting functions have been merged with those of the former International Consultative Telegraph and Telephone Committee (CCITT) to form the telecommunication standardization sector, ITU-T. The management of the radio frequency spectrum, along with the regulatory activities formerly carried out by the International Frequency Registration Board (IFRB), was integrated into the new radiocommunication sector, ITU-R.

The role of ITU-R is to ensure the efficient and economical use of the radio spectrum, including the geostationary satellite orbit, and carry out studies from which recommendations are made. Areas covered include:

- Spectrum utilization and monitoring
- Interservice sharing and compatibility
- Science services
- Radio wave propagation
- Fixed-Satellite Service (FSS)
- Fixed services
- Mobile-Satellite Service (MSS)
- Sound broadcasting
- Television broadcasting

Of particular interest in ITU-R is the Study Group known as Working Party 4 (WP 4), which deals with fixed-satellite services, and the subgroup WP 4B. WP 4B undertakes studies specifically relating to satellite newsgathering, and in particular has issued nine recommendations for SNG, the most significant including Recommendations ITU-R SNG.722–1 'Uniform technical standards (analog) for satellite newsgathering (SNG)' and the subsequent ITU-R SNG.1007 'Uniform technical standard (digital) for satellite newsgathering (SNG)'.

In 2005, the ITU passed its most recent and important recommendation for SNG, the ITU Recommendation SNG.1710 (04/05) 'Satellite newsgathering carriers universal access procedures' – generally referred to as the UAP. The significance of this document is that it sets out for the first time a standard method for SNG uplink operators to access satellite space segment and satisfy the co-ordination requirements of satellite operators (see Appendix G). It was jointly drafted by the industry bodies WBU-ISOG, SUIRG (Satellite Users Interference Reduction Group) and a number of satellite operators for presentation to the ITU. We will look further at WBU-ISOG in Chapter 8.

7.2.5 WARC

Under the control of the ITU, the World Administrative Radiocommunication Conferences are held every 2 years, lasting four weeks, along with a Radiocommunications Assembly. The main function of WARC is to review and revise as necessary the Radio Regulations, on the basis of an agenda adopted by the ITU Council following consultation of the membership of Member Administrations.

The general scope of this agenda is established 4 years in advance and the ITU Council establishes the final agenda usually 2 years before each conference. The agenda usually focuses on a particular aspect of spectrum management and specific services, though there is normally a WARC to consider the entire frequency spectrum every 20 years. WARC may also recommend to the ITU Council items for inclusion in the agenda of a future conference and give its views on forthcoming agendas for at least a 4-year cycle of WARC.

After WARC-92, the 'Administrative' part of the title was dropped, to become the World Radiocommunications Conference (WRC), following the decision to extend participation to allow observers from non-governmental organizations (NGOs) to attend. However, only Member Administrations have voting powers.

The WRCs are attended by experts and administrators from each member country to rule by international agreement on the allocation of all radio frequencies in the range from 9 kHz to 400 GHz, and to define RF power levels for each service in each region. The WRC are open to all ITU Member Administrations and to the United Nations, international organizations, regional telecommunication organizations, intergovernmental organizations (IGOs) operating satellite systems, the specialized agencies of the United Nations and the International Atomic Energy Agency (IAEA). In addition, system operators authorized by their country to participate in the work of the sector are allowed to participate.

The deliberations of WRC are long and weighty, and its reports are highly technical and not light reading. The radiocommunication agencies of each country adopt the relevant WRC agreements into national regulations for their own administration, although there may be regional amendments.

WRC-03

The most recent WRC was held between June 9 to July 4, 2003 in Geneva, Switzerland, and, not surprisingly, it considered a number of satellite-related services over the four weeks of the Conference. Over 2200 delegates, the largest number ever, from 138 ITU Member States attended, and the delegates considered some 2500 proposals, and over 900 numbered documents relating to 50 Agenda items. The output of the Conference consisted of 527 pages of new and revised text of the Radio Regulations.

The wide range of satellite services regulated by the WRC includes Meteorological, Radio Navigation, and Radio Astronomy among many others, as well as FSS, MSS and Broadcast-Satellite Service (BSS). MSS includes Land Mobile, Aeronautical Mobile and Maritime Mobile Services; satellite newsgathering services are encompassed within FSS and MSS.

The significance of the ITU and its organization is in establishing the overall regulatory framework within which SNG operates, and development of SNG depends to a degree on the decisions of the ITU.

The ITU is a regionally orientated organization, and it is clear that regional variations are allowed for and encouraged to meet the particular needs of that region. Europe has for a number of decades sought to establish its own regulatory framework as part of the overall principle of achieving a unified European approach. Several organizations have been established.

7.3 CEPT

The Conference Europeane des Administrations des Postes et des Telecommunications (CEPT) was founded in 1959 as an official body for developing postal and telecommunications services between European administrations, and making recommendations to improve these services. It formulates and recommends telecommunications standards for member countries, which although not obligatory, are in general adopted by all members. The European Radiocommunications Committee (ERC), governed by the CEPT, administers spectrum matters for Europe through the European Radiocommunications

Office (ERO) in Denmark, which is staffed by experts in the field of frequency management. The ERO is focused on undertaking studies looking ahead to demands for frequency management in Europe.

7.4   ETSI

The European Technical Standards Institute (ETSI) is a non-profit-making organization set up in 1988 on the joint initiative of the EU and the CEPT to produce telecommunications standards for telecommunications across the European Union and beyond. Its aim is also to facilitate the 'single market' for telecommunications within Europe by harmonizing separate technical standards to form a set of harmonized European standards.

ETSI plays a major role in developing a wide range of standards and other technical documentation as Europe's contribution to worldwide standardization in telecommunications, broadcasting and information technology. ETSI's prime objective is to support global harmonization by providing a forum in which all the key players can contribute actively. Based in Sophia Antipolis (France), ETSI is an open forum that has around 650 members from 59 countries representing national administrations, telecommunication network operators, manufacturers, broadcasters, service providers and users. Its members, who are responsible for approving its objectives, therefore determine the Institute's work program. As a result, ETSI's activities are maintained in close alignment with the market needs expressed by its members.

Any European organization proving an interest in promoting European telecommunications standards has the right to join ETSI and thus to directly influence the standards-making process. ETSI produces voluntary standards – some of these may then be adopted by the EU as the technical basis for Directives or Regulations – and because those who subsequently implement these voluntary standards have a hand in defining them, the standards are practical rather than abstract.

The relationship between the standards and the Directives of the EU is often very close. Standards are formulated which may later become a 'technical basis for regulation' (TBR) and eventually may be converted into a 'common technical regulation' (CTR) of the EU. The time-scale for these standards to become CTRs is measured in years rather than months, and some national administrations may adopt these standards in advance of them becoming a common EU standard.

Throughout all of these, however, is the focus on developing harmonized European standards. Since April 2001, many existing TBRs referenced in the CTRs have been converted to ENs (European Norm). ETSI conforms to the worldwide standardization process whenever possible and the work is coordinated with the activities of international standardization bodies, mainly the ITU-T and the ITU-R.

ETSI consists of a General Assembly, a Board, a Technical Organization and a Secretariat. The Technical Organization produces and approves technical standards. It encompasses ETSI Projects (EPs), Technical Committees (TCs) and Special Committees. More than 3500 experts are working for ETSI in over 200 groups.

There is a very wide range of standards produced by ETSI covering telecommunications, but of particular interest for satellite newsgathering is CTR-030 (formerly ETS 300 327 and then TBR-030) and ETS 300 673, as they relate to 'type-approval'.

7.5   Type-approval

Type-approval of an uplink system may be required in a country before a licence can be granted. This may be an international standard, as in Europe, or a national standard, such as that in the US.

Type-approval is also used in a slightly different sense. As will be seen later, satellite system operators require registration of an SNG system before access is permitted to their system. In particular, the performance of the antenna is of great interest as it is the single most important component that has an effect on interference with adjacent signals on a satellite. To facilitate registration for the end-users, many antenna manufacturers have obtained 'type-approval' of their antenna products with satellite system operators and national authorities (see Chapter 8).

7.5.1 CTR-030 (ETS 300 327)

TBR-030 was originally published by ETSI as standard ETS 300 327 in 1994, issued as TBR-030 in 1997, and adopted by the EU as CTR-030 in September 1998. This standard was formulated to establish minimum performance specifications for the operation of SNG uplinks in Europe. It is limited to:

- Systems working in the Ku FSS bands
- Systems having attended operation, i.e. operator constantly with the uplink
- Systems that have an antenna size of less than 5 m
- Systems that can operate to satellites with 3° spacing in the geostationary arc

In common with ITU regulations, the standard is aimed to minimize the risk of interference, and defines parameters that the system has to meet in terms of off-axis power radiation, transmit polarization and mechanical performance to maintain pointing accuracy.

There is also another ETSI standard – ETS 300 673 – originally issued in 1997 and revised in 1999, which deals with the electromagnetic compatibility (EMC) required of satellite earth stations, including SNG uplinks. It is a common requirement for licensing in European countries that SNG uplinks meet both these standards. Proof of a system meeting both CTR-030 and ETS 300 673 may be demonstrated by having obtained German type-approval from the former Bundesamt für Zulassungen in der Telekommunikation (BZT).

The BZT was privatized in early 1998 as part of the overall privatization of state-controlled German telecommunications and is now CETECOM GmbH. 'BZT approval' (as it is still commonly referred to) or CETECOM approval is recognized in most other European countries that currently have no type-approval system of their own.

7.5.2 FCC

In the US, the Federal Communications Commission (FCC) is the regulatory body for radio spectrum. In 1927, the Federal Radio Communications (FRC) was formed to allocate radio spectrum. The Federal Communications Commission was formed in 1934 by combining the functions of the FRC and interstate regulation for common carriers.

The FCC sets the standards that all radio transmission equipment must conform to, including SNG uplinks. All SNG uplinks have to be registered and licensed with the FCC prior to use in the US, and there are technical criteria that must be met before the uplink can be granted a licence. These are set out in Title 47 (Telecommunications) of the Code of Federal Regulations (CFR), Part 25 (Satellite Communications).

The FCC, in accordance with ITU recommendation, requires that the antenna meet the requirement to be able to operate to satellites at only 2° spacing in the geostationary arc. This is defined in terms of antenna transmission sidelobe peaks, which automatically sets a lower limit to the antenna size (due to the physics relating to beamwidth). This means that in the US, it is not accepted that it is possible to use an SNG antenna smaller than 1.2 m.

On the other hand, Eutelsat, the principal European regional satellite operator, also demands compliance to 2° spacing for operation onto their capacity, but will allow antennas as small as 0.9 m provided that compliance to 2° spacing can be proven. The 2° criterion is often referred to by engineers as the '29−25 log θ' characteristic (pronounced '29−25 log theta'), and this technical characteristic is described more fully in Chapter 2. The reason for the demand for 2° spacing is that, in the 1980s, it was anticipated that the number of satellites was going to steadily increase and there was going to be a need to move satellites closer together to increase capacity. Therefore the old CCIR requirement of '32−25 log θ', which effectively defined 3° spacing, was modified by a number of satellite operators and some national administrations, including the FCC in 1983.

Most SNG antennas registered in the US are 'type-approved' by the antenna manufacturers to FCC requirements in terms of transmit beam patterns (i.e. compliance to the 29−25 log θ characteristic). The registration application requires the type-approved patterns (i.e. design patterns) for the particular model of antenna to be submitted, along with other information including maximum uplink power and modulation schemes to be used in the system, as well as administrative information. If the antenna is not type-approved by the FCC, then range test patterns of the specific antenna requiring registration have to be submitted.

The FCC also requires a practical test of the SNG uplink to be completed within 1 year of the initial registration to demonstrate compliance. This test can either be carried out on an antenna test range or more usually on satellite, and the results are then submitted to the FCC. The licence is then finalized if the uplink tests are satisfactory.

The registration application also requires an RF hazard study to be submitted. This deals with the potential hazard from non-ionizing radiation, and this issue is discussed fully in Chapter 9. In essence, the study has to demonstrate that the operation of the uplink will not cause any significant hazard to either the public or the uplink operator. In practice the hazard study should normally show that a hazard does exist in most regions of the transmit path, and in doing this shows the FCC that the licensee is aware of the hazard and that the antenna will be used in such a way as to not endanger the general public. In the hazard study it should also explain what measures have been implemented to limit the hazardous exposures.

The FCC process is somewhat bureaucratic, but provided all the steps are carried through in the correct order and manner, then registration is a relatively straightforward process.

7.6 National control and trans-border issues

The movement of mobile-satellite transmission equipment around the world is often fraught with difficulties. Some countries prohibit any use of mobile-satellite communications equipment totally, while others permit it only in particular circumstances, such as for disaster relief or emergencies, or in limited geographical areas. High licence fees, taxes and customs duties cause significant difficulties for newsgatherers; in some countries additional type-approval is sometimes demanded, even though the equipment has been type-approved elsewhere or meets internationally recognized standards, as a further hindrance.

Often these regulatory barriers exist because the country does not have a policy or regulatory framework covering mobile-satellite telecommunications or because they fear 'bypass' of their terrestrial network (even in regions where there is no network to bypass), so reducing their telecommunications revenues.

7.6.1 The control of SNG

The national administrations dealing with telecommunications, even in these days of increasing privatization, are still in general under government direction, and they control access to satellite capacity by SNG uplinks to varying degrees. The level of control varies from countries where the use of SNG uplinks cannot even be contemplated, to countries where there is a highly regulated control system for allowing access to space segment by SNG uplinks through licensing and frequency clearance. The latter is often used as a way of generating a lucrative income stream.

Cross-border issues are probably the largest remaining problem in the free movement of satellite newsgathering. Newsgatherers usually want to take their own facilities into a foreign country for some or all of the following reasons:

- The use of their own SNG uplink may be more cost-effective than using the local telecommunication facilities
- There may be a feeling that greater editorial freedom is available by having their own facility
- The story being covered may involve areas of a country that do not have any local telecommunications structure to support the rapid transmission of reports

The technology allowing easy movement of SNG uplinks has advanced at a far more rapid rate than political and regulatory recognition in a significant number of countries. Although many national administrations allow satellite newsgathering operations by their own nationals within their borders, many still forbid foreign operators from entering their country. However, changes in global agreements should lead to the easing of restrictions with respect to allowing foreign newsgatherers to transport their own equipment into other countries.

In particular, INMARSAT has worked hard to ease the restrictions on trans-border use of some types equipment needed as part of its system (see Chapter 6). To this end, in 1997 the ITU ratified a Recommendation[1] that at least encouraged national administrations to allow the passage across their borders and the use of INMARSAT satphones for satellite newsgathering for radio. Furthermore, the ITU has implemented a Memorandum of Understanding on the use of equipment for Global Mobile Personal Communication by Satellite (GMPCS),[2] and maintains a list of GMPCS-MoU signatories including administrations, and a registry for type-approval letters, all available on the ITU website (www.itu.int).

7.6.2 World Trade Organization

In the aftermath of the Second World War, three international bodies were set up by the UN in 1948 to promote agreements on international economic development and trade. These three organizations were the World Bank, the International Monetary Fund (IMF) and the International Trade Organization (ITO). Although the other two have survived, the ITO never flourished and instead the General Agreement on Tariffs and Trade (GATT) was established. The aim of GATT was to encourage free trade between nations by reducing tariffs, subsidies, quotas and regulations that discriminate against imported products.

In 1995, after over 7 years of negotiation in the so-called 'Uruguay Round' of discussions of the members of GATT, a new body called the World Trade Organization (WTO) was created to administer all world trade agreements. In the same year, the General Agreement on Trade and Services (GATS) was agreed, and the WTO was henceforth charged with administering both GATT and GATS. There are 132 member nations who are signatories to the WTO.

The GATS covers virtually all services including those involved with broadcasting such as audio-visual and telecommunication services. Agreement was reached in the WTO negotiations within the Group on Basic Telecoms (GBT) in 1997.

The successful agreement comprises commitments by about 70 countries with regard to market access and rules concerning fair market practices. As a result of this Memorandum of Understanding (MoU), basic telecommunications services are covered by the GATS, ensuring that market access is transparent and available on terms and conditions that are reasonable and non-discriminatory. The purpose is to lower customs duties on information technology and telecommunications equipment, including mobile-satellite earth stations, in the context of the Information Technology Agreement, agreed by WTO ministers in 1996.

A further round of talks took place in Doha (Qatar) in November 2001 resulting in some far-reaching decisions on the future development of the WTO including helping developing countries implement the existing WTO agreements.

Many countries use the UN Central Product Classification (CPC) as the basis for determining their commitment under GATS. However, the CPC is not updated at the same rate as technology advances, and it is constantly out of date. Some countries deem broadcasting to be an audio-visual service, while in other countries it is deemed a telecommunications service. Different aspects of broadcasting can be split into either of these service definitions. However, by 2005, only 26 WTO Members had made commitments or offers in audio-visual services (leaving 122 WTO Members who have made no commitment and no offer at all in this sector).

The WTO agreement covers the provision of telecommunications services involving simple transmission such as voice and fax, and data transmission including the supply of international and domestic services on a facilities basis and through resale.

Countries have committed to varying degrees of market access through allowing market entry for new carriers and resellers and through foreign investment in existing carriers and resellers. The stress is on the phrase 'varying degrees' so far as satellite newsgathering is concerned. The free movement of SNG uplink systems is thought to potentially fall under this agreement, although many countries may deem it an audio-visual service. Some have undertaken significant market liberalization while others have made commitments based on their existing regulatory regimes. Nevertheless, WTO agreements represent important steps toward a worldwide liberal telecommunications market.

The important point for our purposes is that the WTO MoU on Telecommunications has increased freedom of movement for SNG uplinks across national borders over the last 5 years, and one can only hope that this will continue.

7.6.3 National controls

There are two main reasons for reluctance by national governments to allow free movement of SNG uplinks across national borders. Firstly, there is the fear of the power of unbounded dissemination of information that the use of satellite newsgathering can bring, and many countries have been very slow to react to the rapid changes in technology.

Many governments are suspicious of the motives of newsgatherers who wish to operate uplinks, fearing open criticism of their political regimes which their own population may see or hear coming back via broadcasts from abroad. So they forbid any news organizations using satellite newsgathering within their borders as a matter of political control. They may not even allow their own broadcasters to use this equipment, and certainly would not allow foreign newsgathering agencies to bring in their own SNG equipment.

Some allow foreign SNG uplinks to operate but insist on government supervision during transmissions, including 'screening' tapes before they can be fed. The ease with which foreign broadcasters are able to comment on policies and actions is a direct reflection of the fear that exists relating to the power of the operation of an SNG uplink.

It may be that a government has no legislation to cope with licensing the use of SNG uplinks, though increasingly this is changing in many countries. Governments may allow the use of satellite newsgathering by their own national entities, which may be either a single monopoly supplier or a limited and controlled number of providers.

Secondly, some national administrations bar the use of foreign SNG uplinks because of the anticipated loss of income via their own broadcast and telecommunication facilities. A 'licence' or access fee may be levied if SNG equipment is to be allowed into a country, which is estimated to equate to this anticipated loss of revenue. Some foreign newsgatherers may pay this simply to obtain the flexibility that having their own facility can give them, or they may decide not to bring in their own uplinks and use the facilities available within the country.

In general, there are two levels or types of access granted to SNG uplink operators, depending on the degree of advancement of telecommunication administration in a country. These categories are loosely 'permissions' and licences. The point at which a 'permission' can be termed a licence is a little blurred. There is a further control, called frequency co-ordination, which is related to purely technical considerations of potential interference by the SNG uplink.

7.6.4   Permissions

Where a country has no system of licensing for SNG uplinks, a formal 'permission' issued by the government of the country is the administrative route by which foreign newsgatherers obtain clearance to take uplinks into a country, usually on a temporary basis. Often this 'permission' is granted on a political basis, after reference by the national telecommunication administration or the Ministry of Information (which are sometimes one and the same) to the political leadership of the country. The permission is granted depending on a political calculation weighing up whether granting access may work to the advantage of the leadership. Therefore very often permission may be granted on one occasion and refused on another. Permission may be granted for a foreign satellite uplink if it is to cover an international sporting event taking place in the country in question, but refused if it is to cover a news event of political interest. As previously mentioned, the fact that their own population may see or hear material detrimental to the political leadership coming back via broadcasts from abroad – courtesy of CNN International, or BBC World Service, for example – can be a significant fear.

There may also be a financial price associated with that permission. This may be related in some way to the perceived loss of revenue (which can, in reality, be a significant loss of foreign revenue) because a foreign broadcaster uses their own facility rather than that country's TV station and satellite earth station. Sometimes this fee can run to thousands of dollars, to the extent that it directly equates to the equivalent use of a country's facilities. On these occasions, the only benefit that newsgatherers obtain is the known quality and convenience of their own facility.

Incidentally, it is often the case that where a permission has to be obtained with a national administration which is apprehensive or obstructive to the idea of a foreign operator sending in their own uplink, local contact on the ground is by far the best way of moving matters forward. This is often a cultural issue, where the 'western' practice of making demands by telephone or fax are seen as being insulting, and 'pressing the flesh' over cups of iced tea or coffee is far more likely to produce results. Financial inducements to officials are common in many cultures and do not hold the same negative connotation as in western culture, and western newsgatherers must be prepared to surrender to this practice if they want to get their equipment in.

7.6.5   Licences

The approximate differentiation between permissions and licences is the legislative structure underpinning telecommunications that exists within a country. In countries with a statutory system regulating the use of telecommunications, including satellite newsgathering, a structure is usually in place for the issuing of licences, subject to certain provisions or restrictions. Licences can be granted on a per occasion basis or even on an annual or regularly renewable basis. Typically SNG uplink operators in their native country are granted permission to operate under the terms of a licence.

Obtaining a licence may involve a number of steps. It may involve simply filling out a form giving details of the technical parameters of the uplink. It may require details of any satellite system registrations the uplink already has, or a declaration as to whether it is going to be connected to a telecommunications network or operate as a stand-alone uplink – which is typically the case for satellite newsgathering. It may involve also submitting what are referred to as 'range patterns'. These are frequency test patterns of the performance of the antenna measured on a test range, and define the performance of the antenna, and in particular prove its 'sidelobe' performance, i.e. its directional performance. This is particularly important as it shows the integrity of the antenna, particularly demonstrating that it will not cause interference.

Upon approval of the technical parameters, and payment of the necessary fee, the licence is issued for the specified period. There may be a further fee for renewal or if alteration to the licence is required due to changed parameters of the uplink system.

Some countries do not require so much technical information or proof that the antenna meets a particular standard. They simply require the uplink to be registered with them and the requisite fees to be paid.

The following are some examples of licences available for SNG uplinks in a few countries around the world – note that SNG uplinks fall into a class defined by the ITU as Transportable Earth Station (TES). Licensing agencies typically require the TES to be type-approved:

- In the UK, the Office of Communications (Ofcom) grant SNG licences on annual basis at a typical cost of £1400 per annum – the actual fee depending on bandwidth and uplink power used.
- In Germany, licences are granted for a 10-year period (€100), with an annual fee (€30) by the Federal Network Agency (Bundesnetzagentur).
- In France, the Autorité de Régulation des Communications électroniques et des Postes (ARCEP) permits operation in the band 14.0–14.25 GHz as licence-exempt. Operation in the 14.25–14.5 GHz band is difficult, as frequency co-ordination has to be carried out to avoid interference with terrestrial microwave links.
- In Japan, the Ministry of Posts and Telecommunications (MPT) will only allow Japanese nationals to apply for licences. Additionally, no SNG uplink can operated for or by a foreign government or its representative. However, the Space Communications Corporation (SCC) of Japan, a private satellite company which owns and operates the SUPERBIRD series of satellites in the Pacific Ocean Region, has been enabled to sub-license foreign operators under their own licence for SNG uplinks.
- In Hong Kong, the Office of the Telecommunications Authority (OTA) will issue a Self-Provided External Telecommunication System (SPETS) Licence to operate an SNG uplink to foreign operators, upon payment of a fee, subject to certain conditions being met.
- In the US, an uplink is registered and licensed with the FCC subject to it meeting the required technical standards. Following approval, the registration is valid for the life of that system, and no payment is required beyond minimal initial filing and legal fees. (Incidentally, as in Japan, no SNG uplink is permitted to operate if acting on behalf of a foreign government or its agent.) Foreign operators may be able to facilitate the process if they have an ally amongst one of the US networks who will be able to help them with their application. (However, it has to be recognized that with the large SNG hire market in the US, the need for any foreign operator to bring their own uplink in is questionable.)

In Europe, the EU has a Memorandum of Understanding (MoU) in place on the mutual recognition of satellite communication licences signed in 1992 by France and Germany, and in 1993 by the Netherlands and the UK. It offered the possibility of an arrangement to achieve 'one-stop shopping' for licences for SNG uplinks across Europe. For over a decade various efforts were made at European level to achieve agreement for SNG licensing, but unfortunately, never came to fruition as trying to obtain detailed agreement between over 25 different administrations across Europe proved to be an impossible task; in 2005 the project was abandoned. This was a bitter disappointment to the European SNG community.

7.6.6   *Frequency constraints and clearance*

As we discussed earlier in the chapter, within the ITU, frequency bands are often shared between different services, and in the three ITU regions of the world the primary and secondary uses of each frequency band are defined. However, as we saw, the ITU does not have an absolute right to enforce these designations, and individual country administrations have the scope to re-define the use of these bands, provided they do not interfere with neighboring countries' use of the same bands. Hence there is a complex interplay of both national and international frequency co-ordination, and natural geographical groups of countries – e.g. Europe, the Middle East, South-East Asia – work together to ensure that their use of the frequency bands meet their own needs without causing a problem with their neighbors.

So far as the frequency bands that many satellite services use, they are most often shared with terrestrial microwave networks, scientific services (e.g. radio astronomy) or military usage. The purpose of the frequency clearance is normally to ensure that the uplink transmissions will not interfere with any other transmission. The most likely services that can be interfered with are terrestrial point-to-point microwave links operating at or near the same frequency, where the transmission beam from the uplink may cut through or be very near to the point-to-point terrestrial microwave link path.

Additionally, some administrations define 'exclusion zones' around sites which are considered sensitive to SNG transmissions – these include military bases, airports and sites connected with national security.

In some countries, frequency clearance is required for each individual transmission of the SNG uplink – this is in addition to having a licence, and the licence may be withdrawn if it is discovered that frequency clearance has not been obtained.

Hence, national frequency co-ordination is a common requirement in both Ku- and C-bands – this is where the frequency of operation of the SNG uplink at the desired location is checked against other users of the frequency in the area, such as terrestrial microwave frequency links. As an example, if we look at the Ku-band, it is split into three sub-bands: 13.75–14.0, 14.0–14.25 and 14.25–14.5 GHz:

- 13.75–14.0 GHz: Up until very recently, this band has been closed to small antenna (and hence SNG) operation in many parts of the world. It is a band that is also used for some military radar systems and a small part is reserved for earth-to-space communications for the International Space Station. However, it has been used in the Middle East for SNG for a number of years, and is starting to be used in some parts of Europe. Historically there has been a minimum antenna size limit of 4.5 m for working in this band, but in WRC-03 the ability for more administrations to relax this limit was recommended, and now 1.2 m is a common minimum antenna size specified by many administrations in this band.
- 14.0–14.25 GHz: This band is defined in many parts of the world as the 'exclusive' or primary usage band for FSS, which thus have exclusive access to this band. Hence it has not become populated with terrestrial microwave links, and in many countries the regulatory touch is either very light or even in a few non-existent.
- 14.25–14.5 GHz: This band is shared with terrestrial microwave links in many developed parts of the world, and FSS usage is defined as secondary. Therefore frequency co-ordination is commonly required.

The parameters typically required for frequency clearance are the transmit frequency of the uplink, its location, the satellite to which it is going to work, its orbital position, the ITU emission code and the times of the transmission. The ITU emission code is an internationally recognized alphanumeric code that defines the transmission characteristics of the signal, as shown in Appendix E.

The national authority will either send back an acknowledgment authorizing the transmission or in some countries no reply can be interpreted as consent. Frequency clearances are compulsory in C-band in most developed countries, and may take weeks or months to obtain due to the high likelihood of inter-ference with terrestrial point-to-point microwave links commonly operating in this band, which may necessitate international co-ordination.

It should be noted that many countries do not require any frequency clearance at all in the Ku-band (e.g. the US), so that this is one less piece of administration for the SNG uplink operator to be con-cerned about.

7.7 Conclusion

It can be clearly seen in this chapter that the 'legitimate' use of SNG uplinks involves varying degrees of administration in different countries. Although these processes can be seen as irksome in the face of meeting the challenge trying to cover 'breaking' news, or even sustaining basic news coverage, it is essential in the long term for the ordered and controlled use of a scarce natural resource.

The level of administration and the financial costs associated with operating an SNG uplink in many countries is likely to increase in an effort by national administrations to control the demand for spectrum. However, on the positive side, the continuing decrease in the bandwidth and power demands of digital SNG uplinks is likely to make these types of system more attractive to national administrations. The political control of the use of SNG uplinks is likely to remain a continuing problem, though there are signs of easing of restrictions in a number of countries that have previously taken a rigid stance in oppos-ing the use of such equipment. It is hoped that this is in part through the efforts of the WTO to open up the market. Restrictive regulations usually impede only the country's own socioeconomic and political development as, in addition to socioeconomic benefits, a liberalized telecommunications environment will help generate new revenues in the country. However, for almost every sovereign state, telecommuni-cations and access to radio spectrum is invariably as much a political issue as a technical one.

References

1. ITU (1995) Recommendation ITU-R SNG.1152, Use of digital transmission techniques for satellite newsgath-ering (SNG) (sound).
2. ITU (1998) *Ninth Plenary Meeting*, Resolution 1116, Implementation of the GMPCS-MoU Arrangements.

8

Fitting the pieces together: satellites, systems and operations

8.1 Introduction

Having looked at the regulatory and administrative environment in which satellite newsgathering exists, we can now move on to examine some of the principal global and regional satellite systems, focusing on those that allow access for SNG, and how these can be accessed by SNG uplinks. It is not intended to detail every satellite that is in orbit, for that information changes quite often, preferring to describe what is in orbit at time of writing. It is best to consult the satellite operators directly, all of whom publish details of their current fleets on their websites (see Appendix J). It is also important to note that information given here for any satellite system is only current as at the time of writing (nor have we listed every satellite that organizations featured have launched over the years), and will probably have changed by the time you read this.

Overall, there are a few global systems, and many regional systems. As well as carrying SNG traffic, these systems also carry services such as:

- Direct-to-home (DTH)/direct broadcasting services (DBS) for radio and TV
- Backbone video/audio distribution services
- Telephony and data, including Internet connectivity
- Private data networks for financial institutions, corporations and a wide variety of other businesses including retail outlets

Many satellites are in orbit to provide only these other services (although there are some that cater for SNG as well as other services). The range of services is wide, and the demand in all these areas is growing, feeding a multi-billion US dollar global industry. With almost US$53 billion in revenue in 2005, satellite operators constitute a dynamic business, made even more challenging by consolidation and new entrants, globalization and the search for added value in service provision. This in turn is applying pressure on spectrum, and the result of this is that the number of geostationary satellites is increasing, with virtually all the satellite system operators expanding their fleets. There are also an increasing number of mergers and strategic alliances being formed to try to dominate as much of the market as possible; recent examples include Intelsat's acquisition of PanAmSat and SES's acquisition of New Skies Satellites (NSS). Table 8.1 shows the principal global and regional satellite systems that allow access for SNG uplinks.

It is also worth noting that some companies both operate their own satellites and also buy lease capacity on a long-term basis on other satellite systems, usually in order to provide as diverse an offering of services and wide area of coverage as possible. These organizations tend to be smaller in size, without the resources to economically provide this added range. They may be in the process of expanding, and sub-leasing capacity from another operator is a stepping stone to fully developing their services. For other operators, it may be a way of offering some degree of service in an area that is only going to have a limited demand for them.

Table 8.1 Principal global and regional satellite operators

Satellite system	HQ	Coverage areas	Number of satellites*
Apstar	Hong Kong	Asia	5
Arabsat	Saudi Arabia	Middle East, North Africa, Europe	5
Asiasat	Hong Kong	Asia	3
Eutelsat	France	Europe, Middle East, Russia	19
Hellsat	Greece	Europe, Middle East, Russia	1
Hispasat	Spain	Europe and Americas	5
Intelsat	US	Global	51
JSAT	Japan	Pacific/North America	9
Loral Skynet/SatMex	US	Europe, Americas, Asia Pacific	9
Nahuelsat	Argentina	South America	1
Optus	Australia	Australasia and Pacific	5
Palapa	Indonesia	Far East	1
RSSC	Russia	Asia and Europe	9
SES Americom/New Skies/Sirius	Luxembourg	Global	41
Superbird	Japan	Far East	4
Telenor	Norway	Scandinavia and Europe	2
Telesat	Canada	North America	8
Thaicom	Thailand	Asia, Australasia, Europe, Africa	2
Turksat	Turkey	Europe, Turkey, Central Asia	3

*In orbit in December 2006, excluding planned launches.
Note: Not all satellites offer access to SNG services.

All satellite system operators, whatever their size, are aiming to provide as much of a 'one-stop shop' for their customers as they can, whether it be purely regional service or where trans-global connectivity is required – including where appropriate fiber circuit connectivity. Satellite operators are also trying to offer as high a reliability as possible because of the commercial value of the traffic carried.

8.2 In the beginning, there was INTELSAT . . .

We will begin with INTELSAT, which was the first satellite system available for trans-global commercial use. It was also the first system that allowed international access for satellite newsgathering. As the first global commercial satellite system, it held a commanding position in the global market for decades, but came under intense pressure from the competition of other satellite systems for most services in the last 20 years.

INTELSAT's satellites allowed over 200 member and non-member nations alike access to global interconnection. The organization's primary focus was the provision of international 'fixed' (e.g. telephone and broadcast) public telecommunications services, but it grew to provide a range of products including Internet and corporate network services. INTELSAT was the first provider of television transmission links between continents. Since its creation, there has been rapid growth in traffic, improvements in quality, and reductions in the cost of global telecommunications services.

The early history of INTELSAT was closely bound up with US dominance in satellite communications. In 1961, soon after his inauguration, President John F. Kennedy promoted the development of the US space programme as an intrinsic part of US foreign policy, including the establishment of a commercial satellite telecommunications programme. This was in response to the rapid development of the space programme of the USSR, who astonished the world by launching the first space satellite, SPUTNIK, in October 1957, closely followed by SPUTNIK 2 a month later. The US launched a number of experimental satellites in what was to become an intense race to beat the Russians; but Kennedy effectively propelled the 'space race' forward as a key strategy of US foreign policy from 1961.

In 1962, the US Congress passed the Communications Satellite Act, which called for the construction of a commercial, communal satellite system that would contribute to world peace and understanding. The Act called for the establishment of a US commercial communications organization. A private company was then established and in 1963 incorporated as COMSAT. In 1964, COMSAT entered into temporary agreements with 10 other countries to establish an international telecommunications consortium to provide global satellite coverage and connectivity, forming the International Telecommunications Satellite Organisation (INTELSAT).

The two initial agreements were only temporary because several of the other member nations feared US domination through COMSAT. The 11 initial Signatories did not finally reach full agreement on all aspects of the new organization until negotiations were completed in 1971, and in 1973 INTELSAT officially became a legal entity. In the meantime, however, INTELSAT launched a number of satellites to establish and develop the system.

INTELSAT's activities were governed by two separate but interrelated agreements mentioned. The first, the INTELSAT Agreement, was completed by Member Nations (the Parties) and set forth the prime objective of the organization as well as its structure, rules and procedures. The second, the INTELSAT Operating Agreement, set forth the rights and obligations of INTELSAT Signatories and investors.

The Assembly of Parties met every 2 years to consider issues of general policy and long-term objectives of special interest to governments. INTELSAT's operations were governed by its Meeting of Signatories – the investors in the INTELSAT system – and managed by its Board of Governors, which had principal responsibility for the design, development, operation and maintenance of the INTELSAT system. Signatories were designated by the member governments and included many national telecommunications agencies and companies, some of which were still owned in part by national governments. The national PTT was usually the representative for each country in operational terms, and national administrations were also represented at meetings. Signatories were responsible for financing INTELSAT, with each Signatory owning a share in the organization and contributing capital in proportion to its use of the satellite system. Capital contributions supported INTELSAT's operations, as well as the direct and indirect costs of designing, developing and operating the system. Signatories received a return on capital based on the success of INTELSAT operations.

The first satellite in the INTELSAT system was the INTELSAT I (EARLY BIRD) satellite, launched into geostationary orbit over the Atlantic Ocean in 1965. It was primarily used for telephony traffic, but was occasionally used for television transmissions including President Lyndon B. Johnson's address to the UN, the Pope's visit to New York and a concert by The Beatles.

The INTELSAT II satellites were launched in 1966/1967, and INTELSAT III satellites covered all three major ocean regions – Atlantic, Pacific and Indian – by 1969, which established the first true global coverage by a commercial geosynchronous communications satellite system. The INTELSAT IV series of satellites were launched through the 1970s. With each generation of spacecraft the sophistication increased, with more accurate pointing towards the Earth's surface, higher power and improved coverage. The constellation of satellites that was established provided 'lifeline' communications and other commercial routes for international telecommunication services.

INTELSAT followed on with the INTELSAT V, INTELSAT VI, INTELSAT VII, INTELSAT VIII and INTELSAT IX series before the transition to privatization.

8.2.1   Privatization of INTELSAT

INTELSAT was created as an intergovernmental organization designed to bring satellite services – such as international telephone calls and relay of television signals internationally – to countries around the world. As an operator of an international network of satellites, INTELSAT was capitalized and controlled primarily by the designated signatories of the governments that entered into the agreement to form INTELSAT. During the 1990s, there was considerable criticism from new commercial satellite companies on the difficulty of competing against an organization with the advantages that came from INTELSAT's intergovernmental status.

Due to its intergovernmental nature, INTELSAT benefited from many privileges that privately owned companies did not enjoy. At about the same time, decision-makers within INTELSAT began to believe that its intergovernmental structure resulted in a slow decision-making process that did not enable INTELSAT to be sufficiently nimble in the increasingly dynamic global communications marketplace. In order to meet these challenges, and because of pressure from the WTO and other commercial imperatives, the monolithic (and often bureaucratic) INTELSAT had to change.

Private corporations take strategic commercial decisions rapidly, whereas an international treaty organization such as INTELSAT had to secure agreement with over 140 parties in what tends to be (necessarily) an extremely cumbersome (and therefore slow) process. It could literally take years to respond to major commercial challenges in the market, and commercial decisions may directly conflict with individual national administration interests, to the potential detriment of the whole organization. As previously pointed out, bureaucracy is an inevitable result where the first priority of an organization is seeking to be fair to all 143 parties.

In its move toward its privatization, in 1998 INTELSAT began a process of restructuring. The governing bodies of INTELSAT recognized the potential conflict of interest between treaty obligations and the requirement to ensure the commercial survival of their system. To achieve privatization, the Assembly decided to establish a spin-off company, New Skies Satellites N.V. (NSS), which was incorporated in the Netherlands in April 1998. INTELSAT officially transferred five operational satellites, plus a sixth which was under construction, to New Skies Satellites N.V. in late 1998 (New Skies subsequently become wholly privatized in 2004).

At the same time, a serious threat to the privatization of INTELSAT emerged due to opposition in the US legislature. Because INTELSAT is based in Washington DC, and the US was one of the powerful parties behind the establishment of INTELSAT, the privatization attracted interest from the US government. It supported the privatization in general, but naturally considered that it had a significant 'stakeholder' interest in the future of INTELSAT. This interest in the privatization of INTELSAT caused the US government to seek to dictate the terms and the timetable for the privatization process.

In 2000, the US Congress passed the Open-market Reorganization for the Betterment of International Telecommunications Act (ORBIT Act) to help promote a more competitive global satellite communication services market. Subsequently the INTELSAT privatization process began in 2001, and was completed in April 2005, when the US Federal Communications Commission (FCC) finally approved the US$5 billion sale of INTELSAT's satellite system to private investors.

8.2.2   The acquisition of PanAmSat

Up until 2006, Intelsat was in direct competition with the private satellite operator PanAmSat, but then took it over for a purchase price of US$3.2 billion. PanAmSat was at the time the world's third largest commercial satellite system, with 25 satellites in orbit. Originally the first privately owned international satellite operator, it merged with the Hughes Communications 'Galaxy' domestic US satellite system in

1996, to form a global fleet to challenge the then INTELSAT. Hughes was the majority shareholder, and it brought a fleet of 11 domestic satellites to the merger, combining with the four international satellites operated by PanAmSat at the time.

The Pan American Satellite Corporation (PanAmSat) was founded in 1984 by the late René Anselmo, a multi-billionaire businessman who had worked for a number of years in the Spanish-speaking television industry, establishing the Spanish International Network. He was acutely aware of the monopoly power of INTELSAT in providing international satellite telecommunication services and wanted to create a commercial challenge to this monopoly. Anselmo's aim was to launch the world's first privately owned international satellite, with a particular focus on providing services between Ibero-America and Spain.

Consequently his company PanAmSat launched PAS-1 in 1988, and positioned it over the Atlantic Ocean, making it the first private-sector international satellite service operator. CNN became its first customer the following year, using PAS-1 for distributing its programming to Latin America. In 1991, PanAmSat announced plans to become a fully global service operator with the construction and launch of another three satellites, which were all in place by 1995. Alongside the normal broadcast distribution and business television that trans-global satellite systems rely on for the backbone of their business, PanAmSat made a positive effort to become established in the SNG market by offering Ku-band capacity specifically targeted at satellite newsgathering.

The history of Hughes Galaxy goes back a little further. In 1979 Hughes Communications Inc. (HCI) was created with five employees. The parent company was Hughes Electronics Corporation, a subsidiary of General Motors Corporation. The objective of the company was to foster a commercial market for satellite communications technology that previously had been reserved almost exclusively for scientific and military purposes.

HCI introduced many pioneering concepts into the US domestic satellite market, such as transponder leasing, cable TV-dedicated satellites, in-orbit spare satellites and digital compression technology for DTH services in the US and Latin America. HCI pioneered the concept of marketing satellites dedicated exclusively to cable programming when it launched its first commercial spacecraft, Galaxy I, in 1983. Home Box Office (HBO) became the first Galaxy I customer, signing a contract for six transponders.

By 1984, Galaxy II and III had been launched to expand the fleet, and Hughes Galaxy had become a significant player in the US domestic satellite (domsat) market. In 1985 HCI entered its first international joint venture with the formation of the Japan Communications Satellite Company (JCSAT) – the first private telecommunications firm to operate in Japan.

In 1989, HCI acquired four of the Western Union 'Westar' satellites to become the largest commercial C-band satellite operator in the US. The Westar satellites were renamed as the 'Galaxy' fleet of satellites. In 1990 HCI acquired the SBS series satellites from the Satellite Transponder Leasing Corporation (STLC), a subsidiary of IBM. In 1993 HCI sold its share in JCSAT, enabling JCSAT's merger with a newly licensed satellite competitor in Japan called Japan Satellite Systems. In 1996, Hughes Electronics announced the proposed merger of its Hughes Communications Galaxy business with PanAmSat to form a new publicly held company operating under the PanAmSat name. In 2004, PanAmSat was bought by a consortium of private investors for $4.3 billion, and was then subsequently sold to INTELSAT in July 2006.

Following the takeover of PanAmSat, Intelsat operates a fleet of 51 satellites at the time of writing, making it the largest satellite operator in the world by far.

8.3 SES

The second largest satellite operator at the time of writing is SES, with a fleet of 41 satellites, is based in Betzdorf, Luxembourg. Société Européenne des Satellites (SES) was established in 1985 as Europe's first private satellite operator, with their first satellite Astra 1A being launched in 1988. SES Astra, as it became known, pioneered direct-to-home (DTH) satellite broadcasting in Europe and rapidly established itself as Europe's leading DTH satellite system. It currently operates three satellites at 28.2°E and six satellites at 19.2°E serving the European DTH market by reaching 47 million households (2006).

In the late 1990s, SES Astra decided to move from being a regional European operator to a more global player. In 1999, it acquired a one-third stake in AsiaSat, followed in 2000 by acquiring a 50% share of Nordic Satellite AB, operator of the Sirius satellites, and a 20% stake in Embratel, operator of the Brasilsat satellite series.

However, the acquisition that really pushed into the major league was the acquisition of GE Americom in 2001, and establishing a new group name of SES Global with SES Astra and SES Americom as subsidiary companies. ('Global' was dropped in early 2007.)

GE Americom had its roots in the GTE Satellite Corporation, which was formed in 1972 to provide an earth station network for telecommunications within the US. By 1975, it had formed a partnership with AT&T to further develop its system, and by 1980 it had commissioned the construction of its own GSTAR series of Ku-band satellites. In 1983, GTE SPACENET was formed with the acquisition of the Southern Pacific Satellite Company, which had also commissioned the construction and launch of its own SPACENET series of satellites. Seven GSTAR and SPACENET satellites were launched into orbit between 1984 and 1990. By the time GTE SPACENET had been acquired by GE Americom in 1994 it had become the largest volume provider of US domsat space segment. At the time of acquisition by SES Global in 2001, GE Americom operated 11 satellites providing coverage of North America, with the GE-1E satellite covering Europe. In South America, GE Americom was a partner in the Argentinean-based NahuelSat satellite system, and so SES Global acquired this interest but subsequently disposed of it in 2005.

The latest significant acquisition has been that of New Skies, the original spin-off from INTELSAT, which was completed in 2006 for a purchase price of US$1.2 billion. With the creation of SES New Skies, and interests in the other various regional operators, SES Global now offers access to a fleet of 44 satellites. Until the Intelsat takeover of PanAmSat it was the world's largest satellite operator, but has now replaced PanAmSat as the original primary global competitor to Intelsat.

Unlike Intelsat, which following the PanAmSat takeover, declared that it was one company with a single commercial operation, SES is a complex mix of wholly owned subsidiaries and part shares of other satellite operators.

8.4 Regional satellite systems

Having looked in some detail at the global satellite systems, it is worth having a brief look at the regional systems to gain an overview of the development of satellite communications in various parts of the world.

8.4.1 North America

Since the early development of satellite communications largely occurred in the US, the growth of US domsat and some of the companies involved is of considerable interest. These companies spurred on the commercial development of satellite and spacecraft technology, which has in turn benefited the rest of the world. As well as Hughes, other companies such as AT&T, Western Union (who owned the Westar satellites mentioned above), GTE Corporation and Loral, have all played a part in establishing the multi-billion dollar US domsat (domestic satellite) market.

The nature of the US market is such that companies have often been merged and then further merged again, forming an almost bewildering variety of alliances and changes of name. The following is a brief summary of the principal features of the North American market, and all the systems discussed below cater for SNG use as well as programme distribution.

Telesat

Telesat is Canada's primary satellite system and was formed in 1969. It launched Anik A1 in 1972, and was the world's first commercial domsat in geostationary orbit. Telesat currently operates three Anik F series satellites, and four Nimiq series DBS (Direct Broadcast Satellite) satellites for direct-to-home programming. Canadian broadcasters obviously also have access to the US-based domsat systems.

In late 2006, Loral Skynet bought Telesat from its then owner BCE (Canada) at a price of US$2.8 billion, and at the time of writing plans are in hand to merge the satellite fleets of the two companies and operate under the Telesat name.

Loral Skynet is part of Loral Space & Communications and a US satellite operator that operates the Telstar satellite fleet. Initially part of AT&T Communications, the Skynet division was one of the pioneers in the development of the US domsat system.

The launch of Telstar 1 in July 1962 was AT&T's first venture into satellite technology. Telstar 1 was a joint experimental operation between AT&T's Bell Laboratories, which designed and built the satellite, and NASA, which launched it into an elliptical orbit. The Telstar satellite experiments demonstrated the feasibility of transmitting multiple simultaneous telephone calls, data and video signals across the Atlantic – though the satellite only covered the Atlantic Ocean for a maximum of 102 minutes/day – and Telstar lasted for 6 months before it expired. AT&T continued to provide satellite services during the 1970s through a joint venture with GTE, leasing four COMSTAR satellites from the COMSAT Corporation and providing voice communications to the US from seven earth stations.

The COMSTAR satellites reached the end of their life during the 1980s, and AT&T Skynet re-established the Telstar series, offering services to the broadcasting market. The first of the Telstar 3 series of satellites was launched in 1983, with Telstar 303 still in service in 1998. AT&T Skynet was acquired by Loral Space & Communications in 1997 to become Loral Skynet.

Loral Skynet continued the Telstar series, but after some financial difficulties it sold its North American Telstar fleet (Telstar 4–8 and 13) in 2004 to Intelsat for US$1 billion, now currently owning three Telstar satellites (Telstar 11, 12 and 18) and operating Telstar 10 (Apstar 2R under lease). In addition, following the privatization of Mexico's satellite system in 1997, Loral acquired a controlling interest in Satellites Mexicanos (SatMex) and now manages the SatMex fleet of four satellites.

8.4.2 European regional satellite systems

The European market is smaller than the North American market, with SES Astra and EUTELSAT being the primary operators for the region (though SES Astra does not provide any access for SNG). Hispasat operates the 'Hispasat' series and Telenor operates the 'Thor' series. These companies are important providers for SNG capacity within Europe. However, without doubt the principal SNG space segment provider is Eutelsat.

EUTELSAT

The European Telecommunications Satellite Organisation (EUTELSAT) was founded in 1977 by the CEPT to develop a European regional satellite system for satellite telephony distribution. Membership criteria for countries was that they were a European sovereign state, and a member of the ITU. EUTELSAT was formally established as an organization in 1985, and as an inter-governmental entity, had a bureaucratic structure not dissimilar to that of INTELSAT.

In association with the European Space Agency (ESA), EUTELSAT launched the OTS-2 (Orbital Test Satellite) in 1978 to experiment with and develop the use of Ku-band communications over Europe

(OTS-1 was lost on launch in 1977). EUTELSAT 1 Flight 1 was launched in 1983, followed by a further three satellites in the EUTELSAT 1 series and six satellites in the EUTELSAT 2 series.

But just as with INTELSAT, by the late 1990s EUTELSAT was beginning to feel the burden of being an inter-governmental organization was restricting its development. Customers had to principally buy capacity through the Signatories, and this caused potential conflicts of interest between the Signatories role as shareholders and as distributors of EUTELSAT'S services, respectively. In 2000 the European Commission approved restructuring proposals which would transfer EUTELSAT assets to a privatized entity, Eutelsat S.A. based in Paris in July 2001. Initially it consisted of 48 shareholders – the then current Eutelsat Signatories – but over the years as many state PTTs themselves became privatized, they disposed of their shareholdings. In late 2005, Eutelsat shares were offered out in an IPO (Initial Public Offering) and it subsequently became a fully privatized company, operating over 20 satellites at the time of the IPO.

At the time of writing, Eutelsat operates a fleet of 19 satellites of its own and leases capacity on four other satellites.

8.4.3 Other regional systems

In the Middle East/Africa region, the principal providers are Arabsat and Turksat. In the Asia/Pacific region, the principal providers are AsiaSat, Apstar, JSAT and RSSC. In South America, the principal operators are SatMex, Brasilsat (a partner of SES) and Nahuelsat.

The market is changing so rapidly that it is difficult to cover adequately even the current situation in a book. Therefore, for the latest information see the reference to source materials in Appendix J. Within any region, space segment for SNG is always available from either a regional or global satellite operator.

8.5 Earth Station type-approval and registration

We have previously discussed the requirement for SNG uplinks to be pre-registered with satellite operators; and there is a further process by which SNG antenna manufacturers can obtain 'type-approval' for their products, which aids the process of registration of an uplink by an SNG operator.

8.5.1 Type-approval

The production by a manufacturer of a 'type-approved' antenna or system means that the manufacturer's equipment meets the satellite operator's stringent performance requirements and that each unit of a particular model closely reproduces the performance of every other unit of this model. This consistency of performance is the result of advanced manufacturing and assembly technology which makes it possible to very accurately duplicate performance in production.

Manufacturers frequently seek type-approval for particular models of their antennas from the major satellite operators (normally Intelsat and Eutelsat, though Intelsat discontinued its type approval process at the beginning of 2007). This is a process whereby a number of sample test results, taken at random from a small production batch of antennas, are submitted to the satellite operator. This, combined with some additional testing undertaken on the operator's satellites, is taken by the satellite operator as being representative of the antenna. Assuming the results are satisfactory, then the particular model of antenna is granted 'type-approval'. This smoothes the path for obtaining uplink registration, which saves time for all.

There are typically two types of type-approval applicable to SNG uplinks that apply to antennas and pre-approved systems, respectively:

1. *Type-approved antenna models*: This approval is for the antenna and 'feed' system only. Transmission and frequency stability testing will be required after the antenna and feed have been integrated with the transmission equipment. The satellite operator will test samples of the manufacturer's production of the antenna and, subject to the necessary performance criteria being met consistently across the test batch, will issue type-approval certification that a particular model of antenna meets the necessary technical standards. A number of antenna manufacturers' models will have already been type-approved by the satellite operators, who encourage the use of type-approved antennas because it is mutually beneficial to the satellite operator and the SNG uplink operator, allowing them to begin service more rapidly.

2. *Type-approved SNG uplinks*: This is the most all-encompassing type of approval because it is for the entire uplink system. Using type-approved equipment eliminates the need for verification testing of each individual SNG uplink, and thus no further verification testing is necessary prior to the uplink being brought into service.

Where there is no manufacturer's type-approval on either the antenna or the transmission system, type-approval has to be obtained on a case-by-case basis where the individual antenna and system is tested by either the manufacturer or the end-user. In the case of an antenna not being type-approved by the satellite operator, 'range' test patterns of the specific antenna have to be submitted. This is a complicated process and it is always best for the SNG uplink operator to either use type-approved models of equipment, or ensure that the type-approval has been obtained from the vendor of the system upon delivery to the customer.

8.5.2 Registration

Uplink registration is a process whereby a satellite operator approves and then assigns a unique earth station code to an uplink planning to use their system. It is normally conducted by completing a form giving technical parameters of the uplink as well as details of ownership and contact details.

Satellite operators demand that transmitting earth stations wishing to operate onto their capacity fulfil certain stringent performance criteria, and publish these requirements as technical standards accordingly. The purpose of these standards is to define the minimum technical and operational requirements under which approval to access leased space segment capacity may be granted to an applicant by the satellite operator. For instance, Intelsat class SNG uplinks as Standard G earth stations, and the technical standards that Standard G earth stations must meet are contained in Intelsat Earth Station Standard (IESS) 601.[1] Eutelsat classes SNG uplinks as Standard L earth stations, and the specification is contained in Eutelsat's EESS 400.[2]

Typically, the satellite operator will require an 'on-satellite' test as the final part of the registration procedure, where the SNG uplink undertakes a number of tests on a satellite in the satellite operator's fleet, which is monitored at the satellite operator's network operations center (NOC) or a designated ground earth station.

8.6 The use of capacity

We can now turn to examining the different ways of accessing satellites, and look at the different types of satellite capacity available, the difficult process of determining which is the best capacity for an application and how satellite capacity is typically accessed. SNG uplinks can be used across all types of capacity but we will look at occasional use (OU) capacity in particular.

The price structure of capacity, whether it is occasional, long- or short-term lease, pre-emptible or not, is determined on at least the following four parameters:

- period required
- bandwidth
- power
- geographical coverage

Satellite capacity can be bought for periods from 10 minutes to 15 years, and this encompasses the range of services from occasional to long-term full-time lease.

Bandwidth can be bought from 100 kHz to 150 MHz. For analog video, the smallest bandwidth channel is 17 MHz and the largest is 36 MHz, with 27 MHz being a typical channel size. For digital video, the data rate of the channel is usually between 3 and 40 Mbps, with typically 5–7 Mbps for video distribution to cable head-ends, 3–8 Mbps for news contributions and 20–40 Mbps for sports and events contributions, either in SD or HD.

Audio carried as a separate digital channel can have a data rate as low as 64 kbps for a mono speech signal and 128 kbps for a stereo speech signal or better quality mono signal; but for a high-quality music circuit, the data rate is typically up to 2 Mbps.

There is also the issue of the power required from the satellite, as this is a factor which is one of the key parameters in determining the life of a satellite. If a large amount of transmitted power is required from the satellite to the ground, this will affect the pricing. Similarly (and this is particularly relevant to SNG), if the satellite channel has to have increased gain in the receive stage (to be more 'sensitive'), this will also affect the pricing. Adjustments to the power either in transmit or receive are referred to as 'gain-steps', and any alteration to the nominal gain-step of a transponder to accommodate a customer's requirements will have a reciprocal effect on all the other channels in the transponder. These effects need to be calculated by the satellite operator and the impact on other customers assessed and minimized.

Satellite operators produce 'link budgets' (see Chapter 2 and Appendix B) to assess the parameters required on the satellite for a given set of parameters for the uplink and the downlink, and this is also used as a basis for the financial calculation of the charge for the space capacity.

Finally, capacity is also priced according to the 'beam coverage' required. There are different beam patterns depending on the frequency band, and the precise geographical coverage is defined by the pattern chosen.

In the Ku-band, there are 'spotbeams' and 'widebeams' (also called 'broad beams', 'superbeams' or in Europe 'Eurobeams'); while in the C-band there are 'global', 'hemi-' and 'zone' beams. Ku-band spotbeams and C-band zone beams are often 'shaped' to cover landmasses rather than oceans, as obviously the landmass is where signals need to be concentrated. Sometimes island groups are included if there are significant population numbers present to be served.

Spotbeams offer the highest concentrated power coverage in the Ku-band, either in terms of the uplink or the downlink, and therefore command the highest prices. A spotbeam will usually cover an area approximately 3000 km (2000 miles) in diameter, though this can vary from satellite to satellite, and is determined by the design of the antennas of the satellite. Sometimes two spotbeams may be combined to provide a larger service area, as in the US where 'CONUS' is sometimes used to describe the coverage of a particular transponder where it covers both the eastern and western halves of the US (CONUS being an acronym for CONtiguous US). On some US domestic satellites ('domsats'), beams are referred to as half-Conus; e.g. as in 'west-half CONUS'.

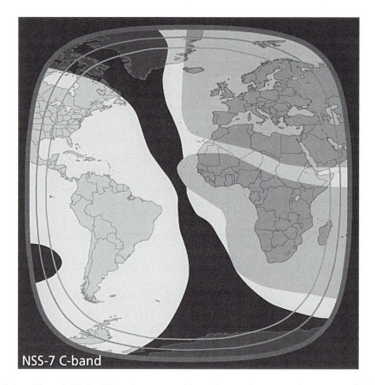

NSS-7 C-band

Figure 8.1   (a) New Skies NSS-7 C-band zone and hemi-beam footprints (courtesy of SES New Skies)

Ku-band widebeams offer broader coverage, perhaps 8000 km (5000 miles) in diameter, but are only available at lower power levels because the power is spread over a wider area.

In the C-band, a global beam describes a wide area low-power beam that covers a significant amount of the Earth's surface – although plainly it is impossible for a beam to literally cover the whole of the globe. In fact, a global beam symmetrically covers just less than half the hemisphere, with the center of the beam often centered on the Equator.

A hemi-beam is a C-band beam that covers approximately half the area of a global beam, and might typically cover a continent or straddle parts of two continents to provide inter-continental connectivity, and is therefore 'shaped'. It is a higher power beam than the global beam because the power is more focused onto a specific area.

Finally, zone beams can be thought of as being the C-band equivalent of the Ku-band widebeam, with high gain covering a reduced area.

Each satellite has a defined area of coverage, both for the uplink and the downlink, and the satellite operator defines these in planning a service from a satellite before it has even been launched. The coverage is published by the satellite operator in the form of 'footprints', which show the geographical coverage of each of the uplink and downlink beams from the satellite; Figure 8.1 shows a typical footprint map.

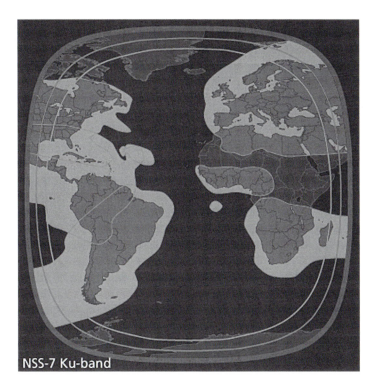

NSS-7 Ku-band

Figure 8.1 (b) New Skies NSS-7 Ku-band zone and spot-beam footprints (courtesy of SES New Skies)

8.7 Types of capacity

Satellite capacity is broadly divided into 'distribution' and 'contribution'. Distribution capacity is used to deliver signals to cable 'head-ends' and transmitters for terrestrial distribution, and for direct-to-home (DTH) satellite delivery. Contribution capacity provides routes for transmitting material from point to point (generally) for inclusion in distributed programmes after (usually) some post-production processes.

There are several different types of satellite capacity that can be accessed by SNG uplinks, and satellite system operators broadly class these as follows:

- dedicated/non-dedicated
- pre-emptible/non pre-emptible
- long-/short-term leasing
- occasional use
- inclined orbit

The type of capacity determines, in a number of ways, the method of working for an SNG uplink (this is true whether it is a truck or flyaway system). An uplink can access capacity which covers a number of the above types; for instance, it could have a booking for 'occasional', 'dedicated' capacity, which might be in 'inclined orbit'.

8.7.1 Dedicated and non-dedicated capacity

The term used for capacity on a satellite that has been specifically set aside for a particular purpose is 'dedicated'. So for instance, on a typical inter-continental satellite, there is dedicated capacity allocated individually for services such as business data, video (multilateral video distribution, DTH and SNG), audio and radio services, public telephony, paging and messaging, and Internet, amongst others.

The reason why there is a separation of capacity for dedicated uses is that this allows the satellite operator to optimize the technical parameters of a transponder (or group of transponders) providing a particular service. For example, a satellite operator may concentrate DTH services on one particular satellite, so that consumers can have their satellite dishes pointed at a single satellite only for a wide range of channels. For instance, by the end of 2006, Eutelsat maintained that over 120 million satellite and cable TV households received programming from Eutelsat's four Hot Bird satellites at 13°E and Eurobird 1 at 28.5°E.

The characteristic for digital transmission tends towards lower power services but great in number, and therefore if they are grouped together, the technical performance can be optimized for a large number of similar signals. It is usually preferable to keep large-power analog signals grouped together, and away from lower power digital signals.

Similarly, SNG places particular demands on the satellite operator. SNG signals tend to be made up of a number of relatively short-duration signals of differing power levels, with transmissions starting and ending in an apparently random sequence. Therefore, it too tends to be grouped onto a particular transponder or group of transponders on a satellite. This allows the perturbations of transmissions frequently beginning and ending from possibly interfering with other services. The delicate power–bandwidth balance of a transponder can be upset by a pattern of transmissions separated by no activity, and therefore it is preferable to keep such transmissions away from continuous services.

There is an increasing amount of capacity allocated for SNG purposes, which is kept available for 'ad-hoc' or 'occasional use' (OU) traffic. Often the capacity allocated to occasional SNG traffic is capacity not normally required for any other purpose except for 'restoration' – a service we will look at later.

Non-dedicated capacity is spare capacity that can be used for SNG or any other temporary use on occasions if it is available. Every satellite operator always has some spare capacity available to accommodate in-service failures on satellites, and if the circumstances are right, this capacity may be made available for SNG. For instance, if an important news story breaks in a particular area, satellite operators may be prepared to offer capacity not committed to some other service for SNG, provided that the acceptance of SNG traffic does not cause problems with adjacent services. It has even been known for a satellite operator to 'shuffle' services around to create suitable capacity for SNG, if they perceive that there may be a significant financial advantage (due to demand) in offering SNG short-term capacity on a major news story.

Capacity may also change from 'dedicated' to 'non-dedicated' at various times. This may be a transponder, or a part-transponder, that is vacant between the ending of one long-term lease (also called a 'full-time' lease) and the beginning of the next.

8.7.2 Pre-emptible or not?

Capacity is also classed as being either 'pre-emptible' or 'non pre-emptible'. These terms refer to the level of guarantee of service.

Pre-emptible service is where, under certain conditions (and these can vary according to the conditions of the lease), service can be interrupted or discontinued. The pricing of the lease reflects this potential loss of service, and the reason for offering capacity is that it may suit both the satellite operator and the customer to take a lease on this basis. For instance, it may allow the satellite operator to offer capacity that is normally reserved for 'restoration' service or capacity that is currently available but cannot be absolutely guaranteed for either commercial or technical reasons to be available over the whole term of the lease. For the customer, it can be a lower cost alternative to purchasing guaranteed service, perhaps because the service being bought is either not essential to their business or where it fulfils an interim solution until capacity that is more reliable becomes available. So it is a mutually beneficial arrangement, and such capacity tends to be offered over shorter periods than non pre-emptible services. Short-term leases are typically on pre-emptible capacity, and customers can generally expect little or no notice of termination of service if the capacity is required for 'restoration' service.

Non pre-emptible capacity is, as the term suggests, the provision of a service that is generally absolutely guaranteed. In case of failure, either due to spacecraft or transponder faults interrupting service, the satellite operator is absolutely bound to provide equivalent alternative service within a strictly defined time-scale as defined in the contract with the satellite operator. Failure to do so can result in severe financial penalties being placed on the satellite operator. There is a very high premium attached to such a service, and large multi-national corporations that provide telecommunication, financial or other such high value, high dependency services are typical customers for this type of service. In the world of video and audio services, it is bought primarily for essential distribution services, although some large broadcast networks buy some of this high-cost capacity for key contribution routes.

Some satellite operators offer different degrees of non pre-emptibility, with associated pricing advantages.

8.7.3 Leases

Leased capacity is where full-time capacity has been purchased for a period of time on a particular satellite, generally for a period of at least a year. Short-term leases are available but leasing is more generally considered as a long-term option.

The advantages of leasing are as follows:

- Price fixed under contract: like all long-term trading of a commodity, this could be both an advantage and a disadvantage
- Guarantee of dedicated capacity: a competitive advantage
- Contingency for failure may be built-in – 'restoration' service

Leases are bought and sold on the basis of four principal factors:

- Length of lease
- Bandwidth/data rate
- Coverage
- Level of service guaranteed

Leases are deemed as long term where they are of a duration of at least a year, while short-term leases provide the capacity over days, weeks or months.

8.7.4 Long-term leases

Satellite operators may offer leases on different terms and conditions, so for the purposes of illustration we will examine in outline how Intelsat have historically offered long-term leased capacity.

Long-term leases are generally available on 1-, 2-, 3-, 5-, 7- and 10-year terms, and because of the size of the investment, the taking up of a lease is usually planned well in advance of the commencement date. A lease booked in advance is termed a 'reservation' and is offered as one of two types:

1. *Guaranteed reservation (GR)*: Where a reservation will be accepted up to 1 year in advance on currently operational satellite capacity, and up to 3 years in advance for planned satellite capacity.
2. *First right of refusal (FRR)*: Where INTELSAT will offer first refusal on specific capacity (subject to a fee being paid in advance). If INTELSAT receives a guaranteed reservation for capacity held under a first right of refusal, the FRR holder could choose either to upgrade the reservation to GR or relinquish the capacity. FRR reservations can be made up to 3 years in advance for operational capacity or 5 years for planned capacity.

Once a long-term lease has been entered into, it can be extended once at any time during the lease term at the prevailing lease rate, and there is a minimum length of extension of 1 month. However, there are penalties:

- If the lease is a pre-emptible service and is canceled during the term, there is a penalty payment equivalent to the first 2 years' service and 25% payable on the remaining term of the lease.
- If the lease is on non pre-emptible capacity and is canceled, then full payment on the entire lease is due.

There are other special discounts available on other types of leased capacity and on renewal of an existing non pre-emptible lease.

8.7.5 Short-term leases

As previously mentioned, these are available for short periods and the same pricing formulae are applied, taking into account bandwidth, power and coverage required. Short-term leases are particularly popular where a major news or sporting event is taking place in an area where interested broadcasters and newsgatherers do not already have leased capacity available. A number of satellite operators made capacity especially available for the 'handover' of Hong Kong in 1997, the second Gulf war in 2003, the FIFA Football World Cup competitions, the Sydney and Athens Olympics in 2000 and 2004, respectively, as well as numerous lesser events in between.

To give an idea of scale of cost, a short-term lease for a single 9 MHz digital channel (which can carry an 8 Mbps signal) would cost in the order of US$15 000 per week in 2006. For a longer term, a 5-year non pre-emptible lease on a 36 MHz Ku-band spotbeam providing European/Middle Eastern coverage would cost approximately US$3.85 million per annum (US$19.25 million over the 5-year term).

Particularly on major breaking news stories, satellite operators will go to the lengths of 'steering' satellite beams to provide coverage in areas where coverage is not normally available. Satellites have also been brought into service that have only just been launched, and are still in their pre-service test phase (which every satellite goes through), or satellites that are in-orbit spares have been moved temporarily to a different orbital position.

Short-term leases offered on this type of capacity are usually offered for periods of 1–4 weeks, and can be highly lucrative for satellite operators as the major US and European newsgatherers scramble to secure capacity for their SNG uplinks to operate on. Newsgatherers from the Far East are able to route through the US to cover these events.

Short-term leases are charged at a higher pro-rata rate than long-term leases, and can provide a useful source of business on satellite capacity that becomes available between long-term leases. Some satellite operators keep a certain amount of capacity available for short-term leasing because of the high returns that can be gained.

8.7.6 Occasional capacity

Occasional use (ad hoc) capacity is scarce in some areas of the world and relatively plentiful in others. For most newsgatherers, the availability of occasional 'on-demand' capacity is critical. Even though a news-gathering organization may have leased capacity, a story can break in an area out of the geographical serv-ice area of their leased capacity, or create such a demand for feeds that extra capacity needs to be bought in. Smaller newsgatherers may depend totally on being able to access occasional capacity, whether they are global or regional newsgatherers, and this is an important market for satellite operators.

However, whenever there is a big news story in a poorly served area, it is often a struggle for satellite operators to meet the demand. This is certainly true of Ku-band, although the situation is improving in some areas of the world where previously there had been little or no Ku-band capacity, e.g. Southern Africa and the Far East.

The relative cost of occasional capacity is high in comparison to leased capacity, but it is reasonable when considering the extra work that a satellite operator has to undertake to meet occasional use serv-ice requests.

To offer occasional service, a satellite operator will have to:

- offer a 24-hour, 365-day per annum booking operation, with multi-lingual staff
- provide responsive technical back-up to rapidly troubleshoot capacity problems
- make available capacity on transponders at short-notice, allowing for constant fluctuation of transmissions
- operate a sophisticated billing process

Such an operation tends to be relatively labor and resource intensive, with time-critical systems in place, and that in turn makes for an expensive operation. Bookings are usually of a minimum 10-minute duration, extendible in 1- or 5-minute increments. It is not unusual for a booking to be placed at less than 15 minutes notice.

There are high cancellation charges, which are factored depending on how much notice is given before the booking is canceled. Virtually all satellite operators will demand 100% payment with less than 24 hours notice of cancellation, with varying penalty charges depending on the length of notice given up to 14 or 28 days. However, discounts are given for regular periodic bookings or for a commit-ment to use a given number of hours of capacity in a month/year. Some satellite operators offer discount thresholds as the accumulated total of bought occasional capacity increases through a year.

8.7.7 Inclined orbit

As described in Chapter 2, satellites of interest for newsgathering purposes are in a geostationary orbit, but the process of sustaining a perfectly maintained geostationary orbit cannot be continued indefinitely. Station-keeping maneuvers consume energy on board the satellite that cannot be replenished, as the thruster motors that correct the position and attitude of the satellite consume liquid fuel rather than elec-trical power. At a certain point in the life of a satellite, a decision is taken to abandon North–South station-keeping maneuvers, as they are not critical to sustaining the correct orbit. East–West station-keeping is considered important, as satellites can be spaced as close as 2° and if this axis of station-keeping is not maintained satellites may move in too close together. A significant proportion of fuel is used to sustain

North–South station-keeping, so the serviceable life of the satellite can be considerably extended if these maneuvers are abandoned.

When North–South station-keeping is abandoned, the satellite is said to be in 'inclined orbit' – this state is more fully described in Chapter 2. Essentially as the satellite is 'observed' from the Earth's surface, it no longer appears to be stationary in relation to that point on the Earth's surface, and requires tracking by both the SNG uplink as well as the downlink earth station. When there is insufficient fuel to even sustain East–West station-keeping, the satellite is deemed to be finally terminated, and is moved out to the 'graveyard' orbit (see Chapter 2).

What has this to do with the commercial issues of selling space segment? Capacity that is completely station-kept (i.e. stable) commands a higher premium than capacity deemed to be in inclined orbit. The disadvantage of inclined orbit capacity is that both the uplink and the downlink have constantly to track the path of inclination. At the downlink, this is commonly performed by auto-tracking equipment, which not only gradually moves the antenna to keep the satellite on-beam but also 'learns' the daily cycle so that it is able to predict the direction to move the antenna. In terms of SNG uplink, this tracking usually has to be performed manually, and although this cycle can also be learnt by the uplink operator, it is often beneficial to make use of daily computer predictions to aid the uplink operator.

Hence this capacity is available at lower cost on satellites which are in the final phase of their operational life. Typically capacity is available at discounts of 50% or more of the stable orbit cost, and is obviously very attractive if the disadvantages can be accommodated. In fact, inclined orbit capacity is attractive for SNG, as the majority of transmissions are point-to-point and therefore the characteristics of an inclined-orbit satellite can be coped with.

With the range of types of capacity, it is a constant juggling act for satellite operators to maximize the usage of as much of their capacity as possible, with the right mix of capacity usage to be able to cope with the occasional satellite anomaly or failure. It may be thought that it is desirable for a satellite operator to have as much capacity on non pre-emptible use as possible, but in fact, it is essential to have capacity that can be 'pre-empted' so that anomalies can be accommodated. Which brings us on to 'restoration' service, which we have mentioned several times in this chapter.

8.7.8   Restoration

'Restoration' is the term used by satellite operators to describe the process of providing alternative capacity for use by a particular service due to either a temporary or permanent in-flight failure. As can be imagined, the provision of a satellite service on a permanent lease basis can become a commercial and business lifeline upon which a large or small company depends. For instance, the loss of a high-capacity data feed from the regional headquarters of a large financial institution such as a bank or an insurance company to its head office, which may carry all the transactions and financial information for the previous 24 hours, could be catastrophic for the institution. It pays for the reliability of the service, and if service is lost, it expects back-up service to be provided within minutes or certainly within hours.

The provision of a service with 99.99% reliability commands a very large premium from the satellite provider, and in return, when service is lost for whatever reason, the satellite operator has to be able to provide an alternative quickly. Therefore, satellite operators always keep some capacity available for such an occurrence, and have extensive contingency plans to cope with in-orbit failures. In the event of a serious failure, the satellite operator will try to use whatever capacity it has available on its own satellites, and if necessary will utilize capacity from another satellite service operator until the problem can be solved. Any significant problem is termed by satellite operators as an 'anomaly'.

It has to be said that the majority of failures occur on launch, which by its very nature is the time of greatest risk in the life of a satellite. Such failures are usually caused by some problem with the launch vehicle, and each year there are always a number of failures. These affect not only commercial geostationary satellites, but also scientific and military satellites destined for both geostationary and non-geostationary orbits. Almost every year, one organization will suffer an unfortunate number of failures. For instance, in 1998, PanAmSat had a particularly bad year, suffering the total loss of Galaxy IV (terminal failure after 5 years) and Galaxy X (lost on launch 1 minute 20 seconds after leaving the pad), and also anomalies on PAS-4, PAS-5, PAS-8, Galaxy VII and Galaxy VIII-i. Other organizations suffered as well, of course, and in other years others have suffered as badly as PanAmSat did in 1998.

Let's look at two examples of major in-orbit failures which are worth examining as each instance shows how satellite operators are able to respond to such crises.

INTELSAT 605

At 15:13 GMT on 11 September 1997, the INTELSAT 605 satellite, located at 335.5°E, suffered an anomaly which could potentially cause a major disruption to traffic on the satellite. The central telemetry unit (CTU) had failed – this is the central on-board system feeding back confirmation signals confirming that ground control instructions have been acted on. Note that this was the back-up CTU unit: all mission-critical components on-board a satellite are duplicated, and the original CTU had failed in 1992, forcing INTELSAT engineers to use the back-up unit (for 5 years, though, before this anomaly).

The result of this failure was that the satellite was not responding to interrogation from the ground. However, INTELSAT was able to observe that transponder control instructions sent to the satellite were having an effect, and that the transponders all seemed to be working normally. What they could not be sure of was for how long this situation would last. Tests continued over the following hours, and INTELSAT engineers were able to verify operation by observing slight changes in the 'beacon' signal transmitted from the satellite, indicating that instructions were being executed. (The beacon signal serves a number of functions – not only does it act as a distinctive frequency marker for the satellite, making it easier for earth stations to identify the satellite, but also certain basic 'health' monitoring signals from the satellite are modulated onto it.)

INTELSAT's contingency plan for this eventuality on the satellite was to 'preempt' all traffic on INTELSAT 601 at 332.5°E, move it from this orbit position to INTELSAT 605's position at 335.5°E (3° of movement), and resume the traffic, which included a significant number of PSTN (Public Switched Telephone Network) services. However, INTELSAT 601 carried a significant amount of video traffic and INTELSAT was conscious of the loss that would be suffered by fixed ground stations that accessed video services at the 332.5°E slot. Since INTELSAT 605 appeared to be operating normally for the moment, INTELSAT decided to formulate a different plan that would not cause such a major disruption to video services at 332.5°E.

The enormity and complexity of the undertaking, and the ability of INTELSAT staff to plan the relocation of hundreds of carriers and leases within about four or so hours was amazing. The actual transitions took several weeks to accomplish because the satellites were so heavily loaded. This included the utilization of occasional-use TV capacity at 335.5°E and 325.5°E as bridging capacity until all carriers and leases could be relocated. The principal activity was completed in phases over about 6 weeks without a hitch.

This alternative plan depended firstly on the success of the planned launch of INTELSAT 803 on 23 September (12 days after the anomaly occurred), and secondly the successful launch of INTELSAT 804 in December 1998. The INTELSAT Board of Governors approved this plan on the afternoon after the anomaly (12 September). What was to occur over the following weeks and months was a carefully orchestrated set of maneuvers involving six satellites (shown in Figure 8.2), finally completed in May 1998.

Why such a complicated set of maneuvers over such an extended period? Fundamentally, the problem lay in the careful transfer of PSTN traffic in a large number of phases, mirrored by re-alignment of

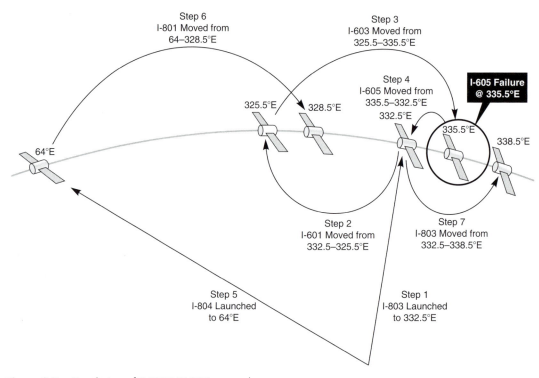

Figure 8.2 Resolution of INTELSAT-605 anomaly

ground earth stations. To do this effectively, the global beams normally allocated for use for video services had to be used for PSTN traffic, and video services were suspended while these alignments were occurring.

It should be noted that INTELSAT VIII series satellites were not suitable for PSTN services due to differences in beam design from the INTELSAT VI series, and therefore could not be used as a long-term replacement for any INTELSAT VI series service.

The result was that INTELSAT was able to maintain all its existing services (though it did delay the implementation of a number of new services intended for the new satellites until they were finally parked in their original orbit positions). INTELSAT – and their customers – were fortunate in three ways. Firstly, INTELSAT 605 did not suffer a total failure, only the monitoring was affected. Secondly, the launch of INTELSAT 803 had been planned for only 12 days after the anomaly occurred, and the launch was successful and on time. Thirdly, INTELSAT was able to gain the co-operation of two separate groups of customers – the PSTN services and the video services – to maintain as high a level of service as possible to both groups. There was disruption for both groups of customers, and INTELSAT had to be very imaginative in its deployment planning. However, this incident is just one example of how a satellite provider can cope with a potentially very damaging anomaly.

Telstar 401

A far more serious anomaly occurred with Telstar 401, an AT&T satellite serving North America at orbital slot 97°W. On Saturday January 11, 1997, at 11:15 GMT, the AT&T ground control station in Pennsylvania, US lost all contact and control of Telstar 401. The satellite was still relatively young – coming into service in early 1994 – and total loss of contact with a satellite is extremely unusual.

For the next 6 days, AT&T engineers tried to re-establish contact, but the satellite was finally declared permanently lost on Friday 17 January 1998.

The services of 40 transponders were suddenly lost (24×36 MHz C-band, 16×54 MHz Ku-band) and amongst the services carried were ABC, PBS (Public Broadcasting Service) and other US network TV feeds. Some of these feeds had contracts that guaranteed capacity and these services were immediately transferred to Telstar 401-R with no discernible interruption to service. Other customers who did not have such contracts had to wait until AT&T could find alternative capacity. Some traffic was also moved to SBS-6, an HCI satellite. Telstar 401 also carried a considerable amount of SNG traffic within North America, and the ripples of this loss spread out for some time afterwards. With such a catastrophic loss, it was extremely difficult to respond in the way that INTELSAT was able to later in the same year with INTELSAT 605, where the organization suffered a controllable anomaly.

AT&T and Lockheed Martin (the satellite manufacturer) spent some time trying to analyze what occurred, as such a loss was very unusual so early in a mission. The cause of the loss was finally attributed to a severe magnetic storm, which had been detected approaching the Earth 5 days earlier and which reached the Earth in the early hours of 11 January.

Unfortunately for AT&T, this occurred during the transition of the AT&T Skynet system (of which Telstar 401 was a valuable part) to Loral Space & Communications (see Chapter 6), and this seriously devalued AT&T Skynet, as the satellite was valued somewhere in excess of US$130 million.

It is a fact that in the last few years the number of failures either on launch or in orbit has been on the increase, and there is a view in the industry that standards of construction of both launch vehicles and satellites has deteriorated, and hence resulted in these failures. It is not clear why this may have happened, and to try to analyze it here would be pure speculation, but insurance premiums have been increasing as a direct result of these failures. The setting of insurance premiums in any business is a statistical analysis process, and the statistics on losses in the satellite industry have been on a downturn.

8.7.9 Leases and newsgathering

Plainly one of the biggest factors when considering leasing is cost. As we have seen, it will cost several millions of US dollars per annum to lease a transponder on a satellite that will give guaranteed capacity over even a limited geographical area. For even a large corporation, this considerable investment has to show a guaranteed return. Leased capacity for purely newsgathering is unlikely to show this return, as few news organizations can find enough raw news to gather to fill even a single channel on a satellite transponder for 24 hours a day, 365 days a year. The capacity will have to be used for other purposes such as sports traffic or providing connectivity between studio centers. Additionally, non-broadcast data traffic (transmission plans allowing) – intra-company telephony, Internet/Intranet access – can be used to improve the usage of the capacity. Sub-leasing of capacity to other users including newsgatherers may be considered if editorial competitive advantage is not lost.

In these days when every news operation is under severe financial pressures, long-term leased capacity can be both liberating and restricting. It is liberating in that there is the ability to get material back from anywhere within the footprint of the lease and this relieves the burden of finding capacity to cover a news story, which may in itself be creating such a demand that occasional capacity becomes scarce and/or expensive. On the other hand, it can be restrictive for it can indirectly apply subtle editorial pressure in deciding whether to cover a story out of the footprint of the transponder if it means buying occasional capacity. This is considered a form of 'double-spend' as additional capacity is being bought in at a higher price, while capacity already paid for is lying 'idle'.

There is also the pressure that the leased capacity is costing money constantly, and every minute and every hour it is not being used for any traffic, money is being spent 'unnecessarily'.

The taking up of a long-term lease involves a difficult decision process unless the level of traffic is guaranteed. There has to be a careful calculation and a degree of gambling in trying to weigh up whether the traffic levels are sufficient to tip the balance in favour of the expenditure on a lease. Careful statistical analysis of past, current and predicted traffic levels has to be carried out for the calculation. For many users it is a very complex decision, and if there is a choice to be made the different deals available from each satellite system can make direct comparisons even more tortuous.

Transponder loadings need balancing, and the inclusion of any ancillary traffic (such as data) also has to be taken into account. Some users – the US networks are an example – have transatlantic leases with US downlink beams and spotbeams on Europe for the uplink, which for special events can be steered to cover a different part of the Western Hemisphere. This is not always possible if the lease is a half-transponder, as the satellite operator has to take into account the users on the other half of the transponder. However, being able to steer the capacity in this way is a very cost-effective way of utilizing capacity. A significant amount of the traffic for the US networks is from Europe (usually London) into the US (usually New York), and so London forms a European 'gateway'. For example, if the transponder can be steered away from centring on Europe to cover a story in Africa, then the London traffic can be booked on occasional capacity – if the 'big story' is not generating much traffic from London it may not be a significant issue.

This ability to steer beams is, as previously mentioned, not a decision that is taken lightly, and requires close liaison and co-operation with the satellite operator. But this scenario is becoming more common, and latest generation spacecraft currently being launched have more of this type of flexibility designed in, including greater transponder switching ability as well as steering of beams. Satellite operators have adapted to a market that is demanding more of this flexibility.

Leased capacity allows the use of both fixed earth stations at foreign bureaus as well as SNG uplinks to readily access guaranteed paths into the contribution hub – the master control room (MCR) at the network headquarters.

It is usually a half- or full transponder (typically 36 MHz or 72 MHz, respectively). If it is a half-transponder, then any changes have to be negotiated with the occupant of the other half of the transponder. This is because what occurs in one-half of the transponder has an effect (possibly detrimental) to the occupant of the other half of the transponder. Therefore, power limits have to be calculated and set to achieve the correct power sharing arrangement. If one side 'saturates' its side of the transponder, then this will affect the other occupant, possibly causing interference. This is certainly the case where large power analog signals are involved, but less of a problem in the digital domain where lower powers are used.

The satellite operator has to carefully balance up the requirements of each occupant of a transponder, and then each transponder as part of the whole payload of the spacecraft. Operators want to maximize the capacity and revenue while minimizing prime electrical power consumption, which will impact the overall level of service of the satellite. Digital carriers ease the situation, as they are more spectrally efficient and operate at lower power levels.

Sometimes deals can be struck which allow a user to buy capacity in addition to the long-term leased capacity at a discounted rate and even on a different satellite belonging to the satellite operator.

Leased capacity also gives operational freedom in terms of how earth stations – fixed or SNG uplinks – can operate on that capacity. Once the satellite operator is assured that the user is competent, a good deal of freedom is allowed the user on how they power up and down on the transponder, provided it accords with the transmission plan submitted to the satellite operator. The satellite operator control center often leaves the management of a leased segment of the transponder very much up to the lessee, and they can power up ('come up') and power down ('come down') at will. So long as the other occupants of the transponder and the satellite itself are not subject to interference from the uplink, then the long-term lease-holder can enjoy far greater freedom than the occasional user.

8.7.10   C-/Ku-band 'cross-strapping'

Unrelated to the commercial basis on which the capacity is being bought, some satellite operators offer a facility called 'cross-strapping'. This is where the uplink transmits in one frequency band and the satellite receives and 'cross-straps' (frequency translates) this signal to a different frequency band to the downlink. It is also particularly useful in parts of the world where there is extensive C-band coverage, but the customer wants to receive the signal in the Ku-band. A satellite can receive a transmission from an uplink in the C-band, the signal undergoes an on-board frequency-shifting process to Ku-band and is then transmitted to the downlink. This process is controlled from the satellite operator's TT&C (tracking, telemetry and control) ground station.

8.8   Uplink operations

In this section, we will methodically progress through all the necessary steps to carry out a successful SNG transmission. Some of these steps are a once-only process, others are repeated on every transmission.

8.8.1   *Practical steps in registering an SNG uplink with a satellite system*

It was mentioned earlier that almost all satellite systems require registration of an SNG uplink before bookings can be accepted. The purpose is to ensure that the SNG system operates within the prescribed parameters of the satellite system, and will not cause any interference or disruption to any other service on a satellite.

The procedure for this is in some ways similar to obtaining an operating licence for a particular country. Technical details (and sometimes range patterns) are required, and the satellite system operator will require an 'on-satellite' test to be carried out. The satellite system operator will nominate a test time, and the uplink initiates a transmission under the co-ordination of the satellite system control center. Such tests last typically 30 minutes, as the satellite system operator makes various checks as the power level from the uplink is gradually increased, and then various checks on performance are made at full power. The main point of these tests is to verify that the uplink cannot cause interference with other traffic on a satellite, and to confirm the integrity of the system. Once the tests have been completed, the satellite system operator issues a registration number for the uplink which is normally the registration mark for that system for life.

Intelsat and Eutelsat have historically had a reciprocity agreement that allowed an uplink registered on one system to be registered on the other system with the minimum amount of paperwork and usually without any tests. This is because the technical requirements of both satellite systems are very similar, and it is not in the interests of either Intelsat or Eutelsat to make customers undertake virtually identical test procedures. The regulations and tests are there to protect their systems, but SNG systems sold by reputable manufacturers will meet these requirements unless the uplink antenna is faulty or out-of-specification due to some damage. Other reciprocity agreements exist between some of the smaller satellite systems. Some satellite systems will accept prior registration with Intelsat or Eutelsat as adequate proof of uplink system integrity and allow operation on their system without any further tests, or they may require the SNG system to be tested individually on their system.

The registration number given by Intelsat or Eutelsat becomes, in general, the primary identifying mark for that system, and any changes made to the system need to be notified to the satellite system operator. Other registration identifiers for other satellite systems may be given, but the Intelsat system registration is the most widely recognized globally.

Sometimes a minimum antenna diameter for the SNG uplink may be specified for certain satellites that are located close together because of potential interference from 'sidelobes' of the uplinked signal.

For instance, Intelsat currently has satellites located at 60°E, 62°E, 64°E and 66°E, and Intelsat has imposed a minimum antenna size of 2.4 m at C-band and 1.2 m at Ku-band in order that the integrity of the 2° spacing can be maintained. There are SNG systems with 2.2–3.7 m antennas for use in C-band, and Intelsat will consider SNG access to this capacity using smaller antennas on a case-by-case basis. Occasionally other satellite operators impose other such restrictions.

8.8.2   Operating an SNG uplink

As an aside, we have not discussed what qualifications or training a person operating an SNG uplink needs to have. Amazingly, considering the potential damage that an uplink can cause both to the satellite and to people in the vicinity of the SNG uplink (as we shall see in Chapter 9), there is no qualification required to operate a satellite uplink in many countries. A few countries may require an individual to hold a general radio operator's licence, but in most other countries no qualifications or minimum statutory training is required – the exception being Japan, where SNG operators must undertake training before being issued with an operator's license by the Japanese Ministry of Internal Affairs and Communications. In the US, job advertisements for SNG operators sometimes request preference for an FCC general class licence or SBE certification (Society of Broadcast Engineers). The FCC requires a trained operator to be in attendance on the uplink; but what is 'trained'? Most satellite operators demand that the uplink has to be under control, but do not specify the level of skill required. But in general, neither national administrations nor satellite systems operators demand that operators should have undertaken specific satellite operations training or reached a defined level of competence before being allowed to switch an uplink into transmit.

The emphasis is, and always has been, on the equipment meeting very stringent technical requirements, but no parallel requirements for the operators. Consequently, the majority of training is 'on the job', and the company operating the uplink allows an individual to operate an uplink when they are satisfied that the operator is competent. There are only a few specific training courses in SNG uplink operations (listed in Appendix J).

8.8.3   Placing a booking for occasional space segment

Having obtained satellite system registration for the uplink, deployed the uplink to the location of the story with skilled operators (!), and secured whatever licence or permission is required to operate, the process of securing satellite capacity (assuming a dedicated lease is not already in place) should have already begun.

To find and book occasional capacity segment there is a process that has to be followed, step by step. In many parts of the world, finding and booking space segment is like shopping around for any other commonly traded commodity, particularly where there is a thriving competitive market to provide space segment.

Before seeking capacity, the operator will need to obtain a suitable licence or permission from the national administration of the country of operation. Having obtained this, or at least begun the process, there are a number of basic parameters that need to be established:

- The location where the uplink is going to operate
- The registration identity of the SNG uplink for the relevant satellite systems
- Certain basic technical parameters of the SNG uplink, such as power, antenna size/gain, Ku- or C-band
- The date and times for transmission
- The downlink parameters, including if it is self-provided, or whether downlink facilities are also required (most satellite operators can also supply downlink and connectivity to the studio center)

A typical service order is shown in Appendix F. As previously mentioned, capacity is normally bought on the basis of a minimum booking of 10 minutes of transmission, with extra time being bought in 1- or 5-minute increments. Often a 5-minute allowance is given prior to the transmission for technical line-up, provided there is time available on that particular channel/transponder.

For digital SNG transmissions, where it is common for a data rate of 8 Mbps or lower to be used, the transponder can be sub-divided into a number of channels, typically 4.5 and 9 MHz. This is true for both Ku- and C-band transponders. As a very rough rule of thumb, in 2006 occasional use capacity cost typically US$7.50 per minute for 9 MHz, and US$4.50 for a 4.5 MHz slot.

Certainly in the US and Europe, the process of purchasing capacity is essentially very simple. Armed with the required information, as above, it is a matter of telephoning service providers, whether they be system operators or satellite segment brokers, and placing the enquiry. In highly developed markets, the whole process of seeking offers and deciding as to which suits best in terms of either price or service can be achieved in under an hour, virtually around the clock.

Before finally committing to using the capacity, there will probably be a requirement to provide the national radiocommunications administration with the details of the transmission for frequency clearance or as a condition of the terms of the licence or permission.

8.8.4 Locating an uplink

The uplink plainly has to be located where the story is, and the logistical and safety considerations involved in the decision where to place the uplink are covered in Chapter 9. Because of the wide range of uplinks available – both trucks and flyaways – it is not possible in this chapter to give detailed instructions on how to set up an uplink, and the uplink operator must rely on manufacturers' training courses and instruction manuals. Figure 8.3 shows an example of an uplink being rigged up.

Figure 8.3 Rigging the uplink (courtesy of Paul Szeless)

Figure 8.4 Flyaway on USS Enterprise

Hopefully it has become clear from earlier discussion in Chapter 2 that both satellite uplinks and down-links have to be accurately positioned and pointed at the satellite. For SNG uplinks, essentially transient in terms of their location, this is an important consideration in deciding where an uplink can be placed.

The uplink has to be stable and, therefore, whether mounted on a vehicle or as a flyaway sitting on the ground or the roof of a building, it must not be in a position where it could be knocked or blown off alignment. If the uplink is to be used on a ship, then it will require some form of additional stabilization such as a 'gyro-stabilized' platform, even if the ship is in dock. Ships move slightly even when tied up in harbor, and therefore it cannot be assumed that an uplink will work sitting on the deck of a ship in harbor. Gyro-stabilized platforms are relatively large, complex structures, and are not appropriate for temporary uplink transmissions. Even INMARSAT system antennas when mounted on vessels have to be a gyro-stabilized, despite the wide angle of the beam from the antenna.

Having said that, the BBC did achieve a 'first' in 1998 when it achieved 'live' news transmissions from a flyaway on a battleship while on 'active-service'. In the spring of 1998, the British aircraft carrier HMS *Invincible* was patrolling the Persian Gulf during the tense situation with Iraq, and the BBC were invited by the UK Ministry of Defence to provide a UK 'pool' transmission facility on-board *Invincible* for UK broadcasters. The BBC achieved this by using a 90 cm digital SNG flyaway, placed on the flight deck of the carrier. Several days of experimentation (in between flight operations) with the enthusiastic co-operation of the ship's crew followed. It was found that if the ship made a particular heading into the wind at a certain speed (around 15 knots), thus minimizing the pitch and roll of the ship, and by manually tracking the flyaway antenna to maintain correct pointing at the satellite, successful transmissions could be made. Of course, the size of the ship (20 000 ton) and the relative calmness of the Gulf (which is a shallow sea), allied to the good weather conditions and the wide beamwidth of the small antenna (1.2°), were all vital factors that enabled this operation to be completely successful (not forgetting the highly skilled uplink engineers). This type of operation from ships has since been repeated on many occasions by other organizations (Figure 8.4).

Figure 8.5   Crane jib obstructing uplink signal (courtesy of Jack Raup)

Having found a stable position, the uplink has to be sited where it has a look-angle that gives it a clear 'get-away' to the satellite. This means that it has to be sited so that there are no obstructions such as buildings, trees or passing high-sided vehicles that can block the transmission path to the satellite. In urban areas, in particular, this can be quite difficult, as even a roof-mounted antenna on a truck can be obscured by a moderately tall building close by. It is of particular concern where the uplink may be located on streets running on an East–West parallel which may obstruct the path to a satellite to the North or South (depending on the hemisphere). If the satellite is on a particular low elevation angle (typically below 20°) this will increase difficulties in built-up areas.

Figure 8.5 illustrates an incident that occurred in Vienna, Austria, when the uplink truck's signal was partially blocked as the jib of crane on a nearby construction site swung across and then stopped. The downlink could still receive the signal, but at reduced power. Such incidents are not uncommon, and SNG operators need to bear the possibility of the unexpected in mind.

Setting up the uplink

When aligning a satellite uplink the operator must not just 'spray' signals around while searching for the satellite. Before beginning to rig the uplink, the operator should have a table of the satellites that can be 'seen' from the location. This list must include the azimuth and elevation figures for the satellites, and particularly important is having the magnetic azimuth figures for the satellites so that the antenna can be accurately pointed using a compass and a clinometer (a device for measuring the elevation angle of the antenna). Knowing the range of satellites to the east and west of the desired satellite will assist in determining which satellite the antenna is pointing at.

Also useful is an up-to-date copy of a satellite channel listings magazine so that any DTH satellites can be clearly identified from the programmes they are carrying, assuming of course that there is a suitable satellite receiver available. Another very useful source of information of traffic on specific satellites is LyngSat (www.lyngsat.com).

Whether the uplink is truck mounted or a flyaway, the uplink needs to be placed in a level position, or if not exactly level, the amount in degrees of elevation that the uplink is displaced needs to be known – this can then be added or subtracted from the absolute elevation position required.

As we have described previously, the feedhorn of the antenna can also connected to the satellite receiver, via the LNB (Low Noise Block downconverter), so that the uplink operator is able to view signals received from the satellite.

Connecting the spectrum analyzer into the system to monitor the output of the LNB, and ensuring the antenna is set to the appropriate polarization (horizontal or vertical), the operator can look for the desired satellite. This can be done by pointing the antenna to the azimuth and elevation angle predicted for the satellite, and then make minute adjustments in elevation and azimuth to find the satellite. Appendix D describes how to use the spectrum analyzer to find the satellite, and the technique for identifying and optimizing antenna alignment using a beacon signal from the satellite.

So to summarize, to set up an uplink, it is recommended that the operator has the following in addition to the basic uplink transmission equipment:

- compass and clinometer (to check azimuth and elevation angles of satellites from location)
- satellite position table
- spectrum analyzer
- satellite programme listings (to identify TV programmes transmitted on DTH satellites)
- domestic satellite receiver (easier to use to identify DTH programmes than a professional IRD)

8.8.5   Co-ordination and line-up procedures

Each time an uplink is to undertake a transmission, there is always contact via a co-ordination telephone line, which can be a land-line, cellular or satellite phone (see Figure 8.6). Co-ordination describes the process by which the 'line-up', start of transmission and end of transmission are discussed and agreed by telephone between the two points. This will occur either between the uplink and the final destination of the transmission (such as the destination downlink control center, as usually occurs with long-term leases and some short-term leases) or between the uplink and the satellite operator's control center (for occasional transmissions). Booking information is checked and confirmed, as well as the technical parameters. If there are any problems at either point during the transmission, this is dealt with via the co-ordination line. The number of the co-ordination line must be known to the control center, and must be kept clear of other traffic during the transmission in case of a problem that the control center needs to alert the uplink operator about.

The satellite operator's control center is usually in its home country, though they may have more than one. For example, Intelsat's Carrier Management Center (CMC) is in Atlanta, USA, and Eutelsat's Satellite Control Centre (CSC) is in Paris, France.

Line-up is the term used for the initial establishment of the signal from the uplink, and it is the period during which the signal is checked for technical compliance by the reception point. Normally, after no longer than 5 minutes, line-up is terminated by the commencement of the transmission. When the transmission is terminated, the end time (known as the 'good night') is agreed by the uplink and the satellite operator's control center. This is particularly important for occasional transmissions where the chargeable period has to be accurately agreed and recorded for billing purposes.

Figure 8.6 'Lining-up' with the satellite control center (courtesy of Simon Atkinson)

Once the uplink is rigged and aligned to the correct satellite (commonly referred to as being 'panned-up'), a typical sequence for an occasional booking is as follows (the time of the start of transmission is often referred to as 'TX'):

- **TX – 10 minutes**: Uplink calls satellite operator control center. On identifying its uplink registration, the booking details are confirmed, including uplink frequency and polarization.
- **TX – 5 minutes**: Line-up usually begins. With clearance from control center, the uplink starts to transmit ('brings up') an unmodulated ('clean') carrier at about −30 to −20 dB below 'nominal' power. Control center checks the carrier is at the correct frequency, polarization and will then request the operator to increase the power to nominal level to check there are no 'out-of-band' harmonics (intermodulation products, or IPs).
- **TX – 3 minutes**: With the carrier still at low level, the control center instructs modulation to be switched on. The modulating signal will normally be a video test pattern with an identifying caption from the uplink, though the satellite operator control center may not be able to decode the digital modulation. Once control center agrees the modulated signal looks correct, power is raised to the power level specified by the control center. Control center finally checks the signal and agrees transmission can commence.
- **TX**: Chargeable period commences. Test signal is removed and programme signal now switched to transmission.
- **TX + *n* minutes**: End of transmission. Uplink 'brings down' signal and agrees end time of transmission with control center – often called the 'good night'.

In an attempt to regularize this whole procedure, in 2004 the satellite industry co-operated on drawing up a standardized set of instructions for SNG uplink operators, known as the Universal Access Procedures (see Appendix G). The ITU subsequently adopted it as a draft Recommendation and it is hoped that it will become a firm ITU Recommendation. The UAP gives a definitive step-by-step guide to operators as to how they should conduct the line-up, and was drawn up to both regularize the procedure amongst all the satellite operators and reduce the incidents of interference, which we will look at shortly.

8.8.6 Over-runs

During the transmission, the uplink operator may need to extend the booking; for instance, if the 'live' slot has been moved in the news programme running order, or the tape has arrived at the last minute and there is more material to be fed than had been anticipated. A last-minute booking extension is termed an 'over-run'. Although it will be in the interests of the satellite operator's control center to grant an over-run (as it is increased income), it may not be possible if there is another booking on the same channel immediately after the booked time. Obtaining an over-run may not be possible if the uplink is unable to contact the satellite operator control center before the end of the booked time – the control centers can be quite busy and not always able to answer all phone calls. However, it is strictly forbidden by all satellite operators for any uplink operator to continue to transmit beyond the end of the booked time unless prior authorization has been obtained.

8.9 Multi- and unilateral operations

When a satellite transmission is from point-to-point, it is described as a 'unilateral' transmission. This is the typical SNG transmission from an uplink in the field back to a single destination such as a broadcaster's studio. Where a transmission is from one origin to a number of destinations simultaneously, this is called a 'multilateral' transmission. In the television news environment, examples of multilaterals are the daily news exchanges between members of broadcasting unions, e.g. Eurovison (EBU) and Asiavision (ABU), where news material shot by one member is offered up for sharing with other members – a type of news co-operative.

Another type of multilateral is where an uplink is providing 'pool' material to a number of clients. A 'pool' is where a group of newsgatherers agree to share the pictures on a story for common use, and a pool may be set up for a number of reasons. A number of broadcasters and news agencies have standing arrangements to share material with each other, and some similar arrangements exist between individual broadcasters. The purpose is usually either to save cost or because access to a particular news event has been granted on the basis that material will only be shot by one camera crew and pooled with all other interested parties.

8.10 The WBU Inter-Union Satellite Operations Group

In the world of international SNG, one organization has been active over the years in seeking better resolution to issues in the satellite industry, and we mentioned them in Chapter 4 in relation to MPEG-2 inter-operability tests. The World Broadcasting Union Inter-Union Satellite Operations Group (WBU-ISOG) is an industry lobby group, made up of broadcasters from the eight broadcasting unions of the world, which seeks to influence satellite operators and the satellite technology industry, particularly in the area of SNG.

In 1985, the North American National Broadcasters Association (NANBA – but now NABA after dropping the 'National' in their title) instigated a series of meetings with INTELSAT and the North American Signatories to discuss areas of common interest. These initial discussions set the tone for the establishment of a permanent structure for dealing with the system-wide operational problems.

Table 8.2   World Broadcasting Union (WBU) members

Broadcasting Union	Abbreviation	Headquarters
Arab States Broadcasting Union	ASBU	Tunisia
Asia-Pacific Broadcasting Union	ABU	Malaysia
Associacion Internacional de Radiodiffusion	AIR	Uruguay
Caribbean Broadcasting Union	CBU	Barbados
European Broadcasting Union	EBU	Switzerland
North American National Broadcasters Association	NABA	Canada
Organizacion de la Television Iberoamericana	OTI	Mexico
African Union of Broadcasting	AUB	Senegal

In 1986, the eight broadcasting unions of the world, under the umbrella of the WBU, created the Inter-Union Satellite Operations Group (ISOG). Its members are drawn from the editorial and operational membership of the broadcasting unions (see Table 8.2). Their directive was to maximize satellite resources for radio and television broadcasters by making satellite systems sensitive and responsive to operational needs, and to ensure the streamlining of processes. SNG has always been a particular focus of the group and will continue to be so.

Since 1986, the ISOG has usually hosted meetings twice a year. One meeting is generally held in the Americas and the other in another region of the world. Local regulatory bodies and broadcasters are encouraged to attend these meetings so that they may keep up to date with the latest developments and with each other's ever-changing requirements. A different venue is chosen for each meeting, allowing the group to focus on different regional concerns from meeting to meeting. While overall attendance remains fairly constant at about 200, the geographical mix of delegates changes with the venue. The purpose of the ISOG meetings is to provide a forum for broadcasters and satellite service operators to exchange information, outline requirements and resolve common problems.

An area in which ISOG has been particularly active in the last decade, in association with Intelsat, is in establishing digital SNG standards for services and testing different manufacturers' MPEG-2 compression equipment for interoperability. This has led to a valuable focus on the importance of interoperability to ensure that no matter where a signal is originated, on whichever MPEG-2 compression equipment, it can be received anywhere else with different MPEG-2 compression equipment. The current focus of WBU-ISOG is in interoperability tests between different MPEG-2 HD encoders and decoders.

8.11   Interference

The issue of satellite interference is one that is increasingly discussed in the satellite industry, as with the ever growing increase in the use of satellite communications generally, there is an increase in the amount of interference caused. It affects DTH TV transmissions as well as contribution feeds, and also causes problems with commercial and governmental use of satellites. Over 4000 incidents are reported each year, according to the Satellite Users Interference Reduction Group (SUIRG), an industry lobby group made up of satellite operators, equipment manufacturers and industry groups. For both satellite operators and users, interference can cost time and money, and it is important that every SNG uplink operator is aware of the issue. SNG uplinks do cause interference from time to time, though it is not thought in general to be a disproportionate contributor to the whole problem.

Interference to transmissions has a number of causes, the principal being:

- Misalignment and/or faults of uplink transmission equipment
- Human error in operation of uplink transmission equipment, including SNG uplinks
- Interference from adjacent satellites
- Terrestrial interference to satellite downlink stations
- Deliberate 'jamming' of transmissions for political reasons

For an SNG uplink, it can mean that either it is possibly causing interference to other users of the satellite, or that its signal is being interfered with. Common causes are:

- Transmitting toward the wrong satellite
- Transmitting on the wrong frequency/polarization
- Transmitting at the incorrect time i.e. not the booked time
- Cross-polarization errors
- Equipment faults e.g. generation of IPs (intermodulation products)

However, the specific cause of a large proportion of interference incidents are unknown, and the industry battles every year to try and isolate and identify the reasons. When an interference issue occurs, it is often possible for the satellite operator to identify the location of the interferer. The majority of commercial satellite operators utilize Communication System Monitoring (CSM) equipment at their control centers which, as well as detecting unauthorized carriers in vacant capacity, can also detect a interfering transmitting carrier 'underneath' (i.e. same frequency and polarization) a legitimate carrier, causing interference to the legitimate carrier. If the interference occurs on a regular basis, with the use of adjacent satellites that can also pick up vestiges of the interfering carrier, it is possible for the interferer's location to be identified down to an approximately $10 \times 30\,\mathrm{km}$ elliptical area. Once the approximate area of the interferer has been identified, then actions to identify the interferer are carried out locally. Often competing satellite operators work co-operatively to identify nuisance carriers, such is the disquiet within the industry about this increasing problem.

Aimed at reducing the possibility of incidents of interference from SNG uplinks, the UAP (Universal Access Procedure) mentioned earlier was drawn up by WBU-ISOG for the guidance of SNG operators, and was subsequently endorsed by a number of organizations including SUIRG, CASBAA (Cable & Satellite Broadcasters Association of Asia), SIA (Satellite Industry Association) and the WTA (World Teleport Association).

In addition, the industry has been working for some years toward the standardization of an identifier being inserted into the MPEG transport stream in the encoder, which would contain details of the encoder manufacturer, serial number, uplink operator, contact phone number, and – ideally – GPS information so that the exact location of the uplink is available to the satellite operator. Then in the case of interference, the satellite operator could decode the stream using their CSM equipment and identify the uplink causing the problem. This project is still underway, but a number of major MPEG encoder manufacturers are already implementing this facility in their new equipment. The problem, of course, is what can be done about older equipment, and how to keep the information programmed into the encoder up to date, as equipment is traded between users.

Within the SNG community, more attention needs to be paid to this problem, and higher levels of training would help toward this.

8.12   Conclusion

Two of the organizations dealt with in this chapter – INTELSAT and EUTELSAT – which had originally been established as non-governmental organizations (NGOs) are now privatized. The privatization
of INTELSAT (and INMARSAT – see Chapter 6) was partly pushed by the WTO to remove national
monopolies operated by national signatories of the respective organizations. This in turn reflects the
commercial pressure on the global telecommunications market, which has also seen the privatization
through the 1990s of a number of national telecommunications providers (PTTs). The steady transition
of the control of spectrum from state control to licensed agencies is a feature seen in Europe, and this
change goes hand in hand with a more commercial attitude to the use of spectrum. There is no doubt
that this change is slowly spread to other parts of the world, helped by the developments in the WTO
GATS initiative in telecommunication.

The processes examined in this chapter, and others, should give the reader a reasonable understanding of the way satellite systems are used for SNG, and the steps necessary for an uplink operator to verify that their system is compliant with the satellite system operator, and why these steps are necessary.
The regulatory issues in each country vary widely, but only in rare situations (such as war) will an
uplink operator be able to avoid dealing with national administrations at some level or other.

As the use of SNG increases around the world, so the procedures become less arduous compared to,
say, 20 years ago in the late 1980s, when the use of SNG was still relatively new to satellite system operators such as INTELSAT, and completely foreign to a large number of governments. The impact of coverage of globally significant events by CNN, BBC and others has made many more individuals and
organizations, and most importantly, governments, aware of the existence of SNG and its place in a
global information environment.

References

1. INTELSAT (2005) Intelsat Earth Station Standards (IESS) 601 Issue 12: Standard G – Performance characteristics for earth stations accessing the Intelsat space segment for international and domestic services not covered
   by other earth station standards.
2. EUTELSAT EESS 400 issue 12 Rev. 0 (2006) – Standard L – Minimum Technical and Operational
   Requirements for Earth Stations transmitting to Leased Capacity in the EUTELSAT Space Segment.

9

Get there, be safe: safety and logistics

9.1 Introduction

The operation of SNG uplinks inevitably brings both the operator and occasionally the public into contact with a number of potential hazards. In this chapter, we will examine the range of hazards and the measures that can be taken to minimize the risks. There is health and safety legislation in many countries covering these hazards, so for illustrative purposes we will look at how these are addressed by safety agencies in the UK and in the US.

In the UK, the primary safety agency is the Health and Safety Executive (HSE), and in the US, the Occupational Safety and Health Administration (OSHA). These two safety agencies have adopted best practice in formulating their safety policies, and both of these primary safety agencies defer to specialist agencies where there are specific hazards of a highly technical nature.

Secondly, we will look at the various issues of planning and logistics when deploying SNG uplinks, both domestically and internationally. This will involve looking at the use of road transport, the transportation of SNG systems on aircraft, and the influence of time pressures on achieving a safe, speedy and cost-effective deployment. We will also look at the intertwined issues of safety and logistics when operating in hostile environments, particularly natural disasters and war zones.

9.2 Safety

The most important consideration when operating an SNG uplink is safety, and there is a saying in the business, 'no story is worth a life'. To consider the impact on the operation it is necessary to identify the specific risks. As we are going to spend some time looking at risks and hazards, it is perhaps worth reminding ourselves of the definition of 'risk' and 'hazard', as occasionally there is confusion in their usage.

A 'hazard' is anything that can cause harm; e.g., electricity is a hazard associated with SNG equipment. 'Risk' is the chance, whether high or low, that somebody will be harmed by the hazard; e.g. how much of a chance is there that someone will be electrocuted in either operating or being close to an SNG uplink. It is important that the hazards and risks are clearly identified for two reasons. Firstly, a human injury or life may depend on the correct action being taken, and secondly, the owner and/or operator of the SNG equipment may be liable to prosecution for failing to identify the hazards and take suitable steps to minimize the risks.

9.2.1 Outline of hazards

There are two levels of potential hazard encountered when operating SNG uplinks – for our purposes, we will classify them as primary and secondary. The primary hazards are:

- Non-ionizing radiation (NIR)
- Electrical hazards
- Manual handling issues

The secondary potential hazards are:

- Driving of vehicles
- Operating in hostile environments, including areas where natural disasters have occurred and war zones

9.2.2 Non-ionizing radiation

The mere mention of the word 'radiation' usually imbues people with fear, and one of the first lessons anyone has to learn when being involved with the use of SNG uplinks is the hazard of radiation – but it is non-ionizing radiation (NIR), which is significantly different to ionizing radiation. So to dispel some myths, let us be clear about the differences between ionizing and non-ionizing radiation.

Ionizing radiation is that emitted by X-rays, gamma rays, neutrons and alpha particles that has sufficient energy to knock electrons out of atoms and thus ionize them. When this radiation passes through the tissues of a living body, in amounts above a safe level, then there is sufficient energy to permanently alter cell structures and damage DNA. This in turn can have dramatic and potentially catastrophic effects on living tissue, including, of course, human beings. However, used in controlled doses, ionizing radiation is widely used as a medical diagnostic and treatment tool, and provided the doses are within acceptable limits and there are adequate precautions to minimize the risk, there is little to fear from such use.

However, this is not the type of radiation associated with microwave transmitting equipment. Non-ionizing radiation is described as a series of energy waves composed of oscillating electric and magnetic fields traveling at the speed of light. All radio transmitting equipment (which of course includes Inmarsat satphones and SNG uplinks) emits some degree of NIR. In the following discussion on NIR, the term SNG uplink can be taken to include Inmarsat satphones.

The whole issue of the safety of exposure to NIR has risen to prominence most notably in the last decade in one area of widespread public concern – the use of mobile phones. There is a continuing public debate in a number of countries about the potentially adverse biological effects of using mobile phones, but there is still no conclusive scientific evidence at the time of writing demonstrating that the use of mobile phones – even prolonged use – has any abnormal biological effect on human beings.

The definition of NIR is any electromagnetic radiation that does not carry enough energy to completely remove an electron from an atom or molecule in a living organism. This encompasses the spectrum of ultraviolet radiation, light, infrared radiation and radio frequency radiation (including radio waves and microwaves). It is of much lower energy than ionizing radiation and hence unable to remove electrons from atoms. When this type of radiation passes through the tissues of the body it does not have sufficient energy to ionize biologically important atoms, and therefore to alter cell structures or damage DNA. However, it does have thermal effects, and frequencies in the range 30–300 MHz have the greatest effect as the human body can more easily absorb them. At frequencies above this range, the body absorption is less, but may still be significant if the power levels are high enough.

The primary health risk of NIR is considered to be the thermal effect. The absorption of RF energy in the body varies with frequency. Microwave frequencies produce a skin effect – you can literally sense your skin starting to feel warm if you are exposed to high power levels at microwave frequencies. After all, this is the principle on which microwave ovens operate, and you can cook human tissue just as easily as animal tissue with this type of power. RF radiation may penetrate the body and be absorbed in deep body organs without the skin effect which warns an individual of danger. This is called deep burning, and there are certain parts of the human body that are particularly vulnerable to these deep heating effects, e.g. the eyes and, additionally in males, the testicles, because of the relative lack of available blood flow to dissipate the excessive heat load.

Burns from contact with metal implants, spectacles, etc. have also been known to occur. In general, power levels around microwave transmitting equipment need to be below a certain level to minimize the risk to people. The general public need to be kept away from the most dangerous parts of this equipment, especially the antenna, which is designed to focus all this energy in a particular direction, i.e. toward the satellite.

The biological effects can be expressed in terms of the rate of energy absorption per unit mass of tissue, and this is often referred to as the specific energy absorption rate (SAR). The SAR, measured in W/kg, is generally used in the frequency range 100 kHz to 10 GHz and may be either expressed as 'whole body' or specified for specific areas of the body – e.g. the limbs or trunk. It is accepted that exposure to NIR that induces even a body temperature rise of 1–2°C can cause the (temporary) adverse effects of heat exhaustion and heat stroke. The safety limits can also be expressed as power density levels, in W/m^2 (or mW/cm^2), usually for frequencies above 10 GHz.

The study of the effects of NIR is highly complex and a significant body of research has turned up other non-thermal effects. All the internationally recognized standards have so far based their exposure limits solely on preventing thermal problems, though research continues.

9.2.3   NIR Hazards with SNG equipment

The most hazardous area when operating SNG uplinks is in front of the antenna. This is a particular problem with SNG flyaways and transportable INMARSAT satphones as they are often placed on the ground, or operated so that the beam is at a height through which people may walk. It is less of an issue with SNG trucks, where the antenna is mounted either on the roof or at least high up on the vehicle structure, and hence out of harm's way.

It is not necessarily a lower risk with a smaller rather than a larger antenna, as the potential hazard is directly related to the output power delivered from the antenna, which is related to the size of the HPA as well as the antenna. However, it is recognized that, as an SNG antenna is directional, the area of risk can be clearly defined (see Figure 9.1). This makes the task of reducing the risk to manageable proportions much more viable, even in a public area. However, the amount of power is effectively focused into a high-power beam and a significant level can be measured even a considerable distance away from the antenna in the direction of the satellite. Incidentally, this potentially creates a secondary risk relating to aircraft, as we shall see later.

There are two areas in the path of the antenna where NIR can be measured: the 'near-field' and the 'far-field' zones. The definition of these zones is complex, but broadly is defined by the number of wavelengths between the transmitter and the point in question. Engineers who wish to examine and calculate these should refer to Appendix I. For the rest of this chapter, the limits quoted and measures taken in relation to NIR apply in general to the area around the SNG uplink.

SNG antennas are directional, and therefore the likelihood of significant human exposure to NIR is considerably reduced. The power densities in areas where people may be typically exposed are substantially less

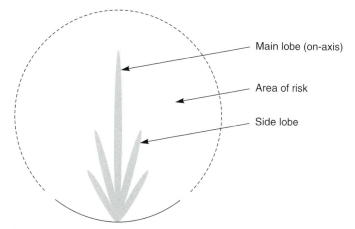

Main lobe (on-axis)

Area of risk

Side lobe

Figure 9.1 Parabolic antenna radiation pattern

than 'on-axis' power densities, as the antenna radiation pattern should produce rapidly diminishing power density the further off-axis the measurement is taken.

Nevertheless, the potential for exposure must take into account the following:

- The direction (azimuth and elevation) the SNG antenna is pointing
- Its height above ground
- The operational procedures followed to minimize the risks

When calculating and applying the limits, consideration needs to be taken of the potential time of exposure. The limits set by both US and UK safety agencies are given within a limited time frame of exposure; but in practice, it is wise to apply these limits as if they relate to an instantaneous exposure. By doing so, any uplink operator is going to be erring on the side of safety.

The International Non-Ionizing Radiation Committee (INIRC), which was set up by the International Radiation Protection Association (IRPA) in 1977, defines international standards. The INIRC has promoted research in this area and in association with the World Health Organization (WHO) has published a number of health and safety documents covering the full spectrum of NIR. The national standards that follow have been developed from this international body of knowledge.

9.2.4 *The position in the US*

The standards-setting body in the US originally active in this area was the American National Standards Institute (ANSI) which first issued guidelines in 1982, but the work has now been taken on by the Institute of Electrical and Electronics Engineers (IEEE) in the US.

The Federal Communications Commission (FCC) first issued guidelines relating to human exposure to RF emissions in 1985, and these were subsequently updated in 1996[1] and are concerned with RF emissions in the range 300 kHz to 100 GHz.

The FCC defines maximum permissible exposure (MPE) limits, based on exposure limits recommended by the US National Council on Radiation Protection and Measurements (NCRP). Over the whole range of frequencies, the exposure limits were developed by the IEEE and adopted by the American National Standards Institute (ANSI) to replace the 1982 ANSI guidelines. There are two limits: one set for members of the general public ('general population') and the other for workers involved in operating and maintaining RF transmitting equipment ('occupational'), as shown in Figure 9.2.

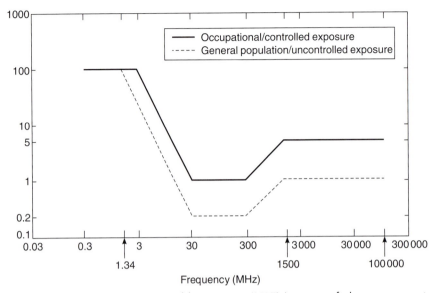

Figure 9.2 FCC limits for maximum permissible exposure (MPE) (in terms of plane-wave equivalent power density)

The MPE for general population exposure for the frequency range 1.5–100 GHz, which encompasses all SNG frequencies, is 1 mW/cm^2, averaged over a 30-minute period. The FCC deems that general population (i.e. uncontrolled) exposures apply where the general public may be exposed, or where workers may not be fully aware of the potential for exposure or cannot exercise control over their exposure.

The MPE for occupational exposure, which allows a higher exposure limit for the same frequency range, is 5 mW/cm^2, averaged over a 6-minute period. Occupational (i.e. controlled) limits apply where workers are exposed, provided they are fully aware of the potential for exposure and can exercise control over the degree of their exposure. Occupational exposure limits are also relevant in situations when an individual is passing through a location where occupational/controlled limits apply, provided they are made aware of the potential for exposure.

As discussed in Chapter 7, the FCC requires an RF hazard study to be submitted with a registration application for an SNG uplink, and this is based on calculations defined by the FCC.[1]

9.2.5   The position in the UK

In the UK, the National Radiological Protection Board (NRPB), part of the UK Health Protection Agency (HPA), is responsible for research and advising best practice in the area of radiation hazards, including NIR. It was established in 1970, and published recommendations in 1993 on NIR exposure levels, but the current recommendations were revised in 2004 as a precautionary measure in response to concerns about the risk from mobile phones.

Up until 2004, the NRPB made no distinction in exposure levels between the general public and workers involved in RF transmission, but under the new recommendations, it follows ICNIRP 1998 recommendations to set two levels (as in the US) for general public and occupational exposure.

It also does not define absolute limits, but sets 'investigation levels', below which adverse biological effects are not likely to occur. Exceeding these investigation levels does not automatically infer biological damage will occur, but that further biological investigation may be necessary and is recommended.

Table 9.1 NRPB (UK) limits on NIR (f is in GHz)

Population	Frequency band	SAR	Time period of exposure averaged over	Applies to
Occupational	10 MHz to 10 GHz	0.4 W/kg SAR averaged over the whole body	6 minutes	INMARSAT terminals (C-band SNG prohibited in UK)
	10–300 GHz	50 mW/cm^2	$68/f^{1.05}$ minutes (approximately 4 minutes at 14 GHz)	Ku-band uplinks
General Public	10 MHz to 10 GHz	0.08 W/kg SAR averaged over the whole body	6 minutes	INMARSAT terminals (C-band SNG prohibited in UK)
	10–300 GHz	10 mW/cm^2	$68/f^{1.05}$ minutes (approximately 4 minutes at 14 GHz)	Ku-band uplinks

It also uses different methods of measurement depending on the frequency band concerned. Within the frequency bands of interest to us, it has an exposure level for 10 MHz to 10 GHz, and a different level above 10 GHz. To further complicate matters, the limit for the 100 kHz to 10 GHz band has a limit expressed in SAR (W/kg) over one time period, while for the upper band it is expressed in power density (W/m^2 or mW/cm^2) over two different time periods, depending on the frequency. There is no easy way to measure SAR directly, though equivalent measurements can be made (Table 9.1).

The NRPB limits are more complicated than the FCC MPEs, and in practice, there is not a great deal of difference between the two limits so far as the SNG operator is concerned in terms of their own safety. Unlike in the US, there is no requirement for an RF hazard study to be submitted to the UK Office of Communications (Ofcom) on applying for a licence for an SNG uplink.

9.2.6 Practical steps to minimize risks

Having examined the recommended maximum limits, we need to see the practical steps that can be taken to minimize the risk to both operator and general public. Assuming that the antenna and HPA equipment are in an area to which either the uplink operator or a member of the public has access, i.e. it is not mounted on a vehicle roof, then there are relatively simple measures that can be taken which will give reasonable protection.

In order of importance, they are:

- Rigging an uplink in an area of restricted access
- Cordoning-off of a 'safety zone' and using warning signage (see Figure 9.3)
- Checking measurements around the perimeter of the safety zone
- Restricting access
- Supervising and checking during transmissions

Figure 9.3   Safe area cordon around an SNG antenna

Obviously, the risk of exposure, particularly for members of the general public, can be greatly minimized if the uplink can be rigged in a position which has secure access while also meeting the requirements of the operation. This is not always possible, but if it can be achieved then the risk of exposure is limited to the uplink operator. Unfortunately time and logistics, as we shall see later, can conspire against achieving this aim, particularly in a breaking news story situation.

The idea of the safety zone is to protect anyone from entering an area where there is a risk of exposure over any part of his or her body. In essence this means that there must be no risk of dangerous exposure from head height down to the ground, assuming 2 m as head height (see Figure 9.4), which gives an approximate indication of the area that people need to be excluded from. A zone should be cordoned off around the front and side areas of the antenna. The limit of this safety zone depends on three factors: the angle of elevation of the antenna, the operating frequency band (C or Ku) of the uplink, and the maximum output power capable of being delivered from the antenna. Generally, the nearer the equator the uplink operating location is, and therefore the greater the elevation angle, the smaller the safety zone need be, as there is a reducing likelihood of NIR 'spillage' from the antenna.

There are two methods of determining this area: either by theoretical calculation or by practical measurements with an NIR field strength meter. These meters are available from a number of manufacturers in a variety of different forms, from personal protection 'badges' with an audible and visual alarm, up to laboratory-grade precision measurement meters. Personal protection products are available at a relatively moderate cost, considering the degree of protection they can offer.

Of the two methods of assessing the safe zone for operation, practical measurement is perhaps the safest and easiest in a fast-developing operational environment. Having set the elevation angle of the antenna, a generous distance should be allowed and cordoned off – up to 10 m if possible. Once a satellite uplink is transmitting, the operator can then check that at the perimeter of this safety zone the exposure level is below the limit defined. If the level is below the limit, the operator can then move in slowly toward the antenna in a scanning arc path, checking the reading on the field strength meter, until the operator is near to the maximum level of exposure. This defines the minimum limit of the safety zone,

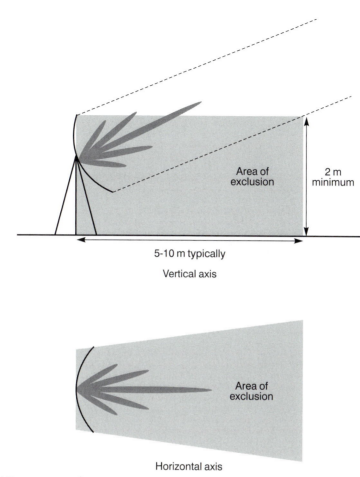

Figure 9.4 SNG antenna exclusion zone

and ideally the zone should be set slightly further out from the point of near-maximum exposure, remembering that there should be no risk of exposure from ground level to 2 m. Obviously, if a flyaway is sited on a rooftop, pointing out over the side of the building, then there is little likelihood of anyone being able to stray in front of the antenna.

It should noted at this point that we have so far concentrated on the risk of exposure from the antenna. However, there is also a risk of NIR leaking from the waveguide and its connection between the output flange of the HPA and the input flange of the antenna feed. This is particularly true of flexible wave-guides, which although flexible, deteriorate over time with the flexing of the waveguide from rigging and de-rigging the flyaway equipment. The waveguide should be regularly inspected for physical signs of wear, cuts or burn marks ('hotspots'), which are an early indication of impending failure (these marks may be noticed as a series of evenly spaced transverse marks along the length of the waveguide). Once the uplink is rigged, and before the first transmission, the HPA should be run up to full power into a 'dummy'

Figure 9.5   International pictogram for NIR (black on a yellow background)

load. The flanges and the waveguide should then be carefully checked with the field strength meter. It is a wise precaution to carry a spare length of waveguide, for obvious reasons. Leakage from flanges may be due to incorrect tightening of the flange screws or damage due to corrosion or mishandling to the faces of the flanges – either of which would prevent a snug fit.

The operator should keep an eye on any movements of people near the perimeter and try to be vigilant in ensuring that nobody attempts to stray inside the safety zone perimeter. Signs warning of a risk should also be placed at the perimeter, and international pictogram signs are available that depict the hazard (Figure 9.5).

At regular intervals throughout an operation, the zone perimeter, the waveguides and flange joints should be checked to ensure that the operation continues to be safe, both for the operator and the general public.

9.2.7 Operations near or in sensitive zones, including aircraft flight paths

We mentioned earlier that a potential hazard existed thus creating a risk relating to aircraft flight paths. In the UK the civil aviation governing body, the Civil Aviation Authority (CAA), considers that the high-energy beam from an SNG antenna operating in the Ku-band could cause a serious malfunction in an aircraft's instrumentation if it is in close proximity. This is considered to apply if an aircraft, on approach or take-off, was to fly through the beam from an uplink that is only a few kilometers away. It is a requirement of the UK Office of Communications (Ofcom),[2] therefore, that if an uplink is being operated within 20 km of an airport with ILS (instrument landing systems), the operator has to inform the airport. Confirmation that this requirement has been met must be shown on the frequency clearance application made to Ofcom. In addition, there is a 'cone of protection' that the uplink signal must not infringe on both the approach and take-off flight paths of the airport.[3] Other countries have a more relaxed attitude the subject.

9.2.8 Military installations

In the UK and many other countries, operation near or at military installations is restricted, although special clearance may be obtained. This may be justified on the grounds of either potential electromagnetic interference with military communications or munitions, or security. However, other countries (e.g. the US) do not restrict operations beyond the perimeter of the installation. Incidentally, in deploying SNG to military installations it is paramount that a full dialog takes place between SNG technicians and military

Figure 9.6 Dangers of rigging an uplink near live munitions

technicians to determine that there will be no effect from the SNG uplink transmissions on military communications or weapons systems.

Figure 9.6 illustrates this point quite graphically. As can be seen from the photograph, an SNG uplink has been rigged on the deck of an aircraft carrier, and there are missiles close by (indicated by arrow). After consultation with the ship's munitions officer, it was decided not to attempt any transmissions, just in case the strong field from the antenna and/or the associated equipment triggered the firing circuitry in the missiles. These were not the only munitions nearby, and there was no other convenient point to move the uplink to.

There are strong electromagnetic fields from military systems and it is not unusual for this to have an effect on the camera rather than the SNG uplink. Radar in particular (as it produces very large but short pulses of RF) can affect the pictures, resulting in 'black line flashing' on digital cameras and strange disturbances in broad bands in the color and composition of the picture.

That concludes our consideration of the hazard of NIR. However, before leaving this aspect of SNG safety, it is perhaps worth relating a story, which although possibly apocryphal, illustrates the importance of vigilance in restricting access.

In the winter of 1989/1990, at the fall of the Berlin Wall, there were a large number of uplinks operating on the ground in Berlin covering the story. It was winter, bitterly cold, and many of the flyaway uplinks were being operated with almost all the uplink equipment (and the operators) enclosed in a tent, with just the antenna protruding out through the tent flaps. One of the US network uplinks was in transmission, with the operators huddled inside the tent behind the antenna, when a call came from the US on the co-ordination phone that the signal had suddenly been lost. The operators checked their signal monitoring equipment and were very puzzled, as everything seemed fine. Finally, one of the technicians happened to venture out into the cold, to find a passer-by warming their hands cupped around the end of the feed arm, blocking the signal to the antenna reflector! Of course, if this story is true, then the 'passer-by' must have known something about NIR, and it would have been a stupid prank. But, more importantly, it perhaps illustrates the importance of always trying to operate this type of equipment with your wits about you, as it is a potentially dangerous piece of equipment if not treated with respect (Figure 9.7).

Figure 9.7   The unfortunate US network antenna in Berlin

9.2.9 *Electrical hazards*

As with any electrical equipment, electrical power has to be supplied to make the equipment function. It would be preferable if this power could be provided from low-power batteries, hence minimizing hazards associated with electrical power. Unfortunately, the demand for 'primary' supply power for an SNG uplink and all the associated equipment is quite high, even for a small system. Typically, an SNG uplink requires at least 3 kW, and large SNG systems require at least 6 kW. This can only be derived from AC power sources, and therefore there are hazards in operating SNG equipment related not only to the integrity of the power source itself, but also to the condition of the equipment.

The rugged life the equipment endures also has to be borne in mind, as well as the exposure to widely varying weather conditions, which over time can cause a deterioration in the electrical integrity of the equipment itself unless it is regularly checked by competent technicians. SNG uplinks can be operated in desert conditions, with temperatures reaching over 40° C; in tropical conditions, with relative humidity over 90%; or in Arctic conditions, with temperatures as low as −40° C. The equipment is expected to be able to perform consistently in all these conditions, and this can take its toll on the electrical integrity of the equipment over time.

There is an added hazard in that the amplifying element typically used in most SNG HPAs – the 'traveling wave tube' (TWT) – requires a very high voltage supply, which although generated internally in the HPA power supply unit (PSU), nevertheless is a potential hazard. Some of the monitoring equipment also has high voltage supplies, so all the equipment in a system is vulnerable.

Regular care of the equipment, as well as respect in its use, is vital to minimize the risks. But care also has to be taken in sourcing the supply of primary power. Generally, the uplink operator can either obtain power from a local supply, or more likely, transport a generator (usually petrol) along with the system. With a truck-based operation using vehicles built for the purpose, this is relatively straightforward and very professional and safe power systems are installed in these vehicles. They usually incorporate various safety features to ensure minimal risk to people and equipment.

With a flyaway operation, the situations are usually much more difficult. It is common to transport a system with its own generator, as one never knows if there is an adequate power supply at the destination – if there is one at all. Having arrived at the location, assuming the local supply is not reliable or safe enough (often the case in areas where flyaways are typically deployed), the generator has to be placed in a convenient position. Some thought also has to be given to refueling arrangements (including the safe storage of fuel) as well as the safe routing of cable runs from the generator to the uplink equipment.

Finally, it is worth considering the use of a residual current device (RCD) in the supply to the uplink equipment. An RCD is a device that monitors the power supply, constantly checking for a fault. It measures the amount of current flowing in the live and neutral (line and ground) wires, and if there is a difference, then a fault may be present and the supply is broken to protect the personnel and the equipment (see Chapter 3). The assumption is that there is some current flowing out of the circuit and that it may be flowing through a person. It does not act as an over-current circuit breaker or fuse, which protects the circuit from drawing too much current beyond the capacity of the cable and the equipment, but is an additional safety device.

The advantage of the RCD is that it does not require a good earth connection, or any earth connection at all for that matter, to operate. It will protect people even when using the most basic electrical source, and is compact and cheap. Also, the risk from 'nuisance tripping' is now very low, compared to early models.

9.2.10   Manual handling

The issue of manual handling in the workplace – which is about minimizing the risk of musculoskeletal disorders – is pertinent when looking at the operation of flyaway SNG uplinks in particular. As discussed in Chapter 3, flyaway systems are typically made up of a large number of boxes, and some of these cases are particularly heavy – up to 40 kg (88 lb). Although back injuries through lifting awkward or heavy cases do not account for work-related deaths, they do contribute to a significant amount of human suffering, loss of productivity, and economic burden on compensation systems. Back disorders are one of the leading causes of disability for people in their working years, and SNG operators quite commonly suffer some degree of discomfort from back pain caused by lifting during their work.

Back problems can either be caused by a single traumatic incident or more often through a gradual process of repetitive strain over a period. Because of the slow and progressive onset of this internal injury, the condition is often ignored until the symptoms become acute, often resulting in disabling injury. Acute back injuries can be the immediate result of improper lifting techniques and/or lifting loads that are too heavy for the back to support. While the acute injury may seem to be caused by a single well-defined incident, the real cause is often a combined interaction of strain coupled with years of weakening of the muscles, ligaments, vertebrae and disks in the back, either singly or in combination.

Typical actions that occur when handling the SNG systems and can lead to back injury are:

- heavy lifting
- poor posture
- reaching, twisting or bending while lifting
- lifting with forceful movement
- poor footing

These are further exacerbated if the operator has not been trained in correct body mechanics – how one lifts, pushes, pulls or carries objects. Additionally, poor physical condition results in losing the strength and endurance to perform physical tasks without strain.

Working on news stories almost invariably involves very long hours, varying from periods of relative inactivity interspersed with bursts of intense activity, to periods of sustained intense activity, all of which cause fatigue. Often meals are missed, sleep patterns disrupted and dehydration can occur due to the pattern of work. If working in a different country, the operator may have to cope with changes in diet, drinking water and perhaps effects from working across a different time zone. Commonly, operators talk of

Figure 9.8 Standard flyway equipment rigged on the roof of a locally acquired vehicle in Jerusalem (courtesy of Steve Williams)

'landing on the ground, feet running', as their work begins immediately the moment they disembark from the aircraft. They will be directly involved in getting a very large amount of equipment through customs and loaded into vehicles, then quickly moving to the location and setting up the equipment as rapidly as possible. It is the nature of the business that an operation is expected to be up and running within hours of arrival, as the story is probably 'moving' and material is required for news broadcasts as quickly as possible. Once the uplink is working, of course, the work continues as the transmissions get underway.

But what does this have to do with back injury? Quite simply, it is all too easy to forget about the weight of what you are lifting if all the pressure is on you to get those cases moved into position as quickly as possible. Local porters may be available, but invariably one gets involved in moving cases as well. If you are feeling tired due to jet-lag or just generally unwell because of the change in environment, combined with the pressure by producers to get the uplink working as quickly as possible, it is hardly surprising that injuries can occur. Very experienced operators, of course, have various methods of minimizing the effects of all these factors, but nonetheless back injuries are suffered by even the most experienced.

We have dealt with the primary safety issues and can now turn to the secondary potential hazards as identified at the beginning of the chapter.

9.2.11 Driving of vehicles

The two principal methods of transportation for SNG equipment are by air and by road; the flexibility of both these methods is vital for newsgathering. In countries with a well-developed road system, the use of vehicles for domestic SNG is often the most effective and cost-efficient method to cover news. Even if a system is transported by air, a truck is used to carry the equipment on the final leg of the journey to the location. Obviously, in metropolitan areas, road travel is the only option.

SNG operators are therefore regularly required to drive vehicles carrying SNG systems. This can be a dedicated SNG vehicle or a general-purpose load-carrying van or truck, either of which can generally range in weight from 2 to 12 tonnes (4500–26 000 lb). The driving of larger vehicles in this range is in itself a safety issue.

When driving these vehicles, both the physical dimensions of the vehicles (equipped SNG trucks are sometimes quite high even with the antenna stowed) and the handling characteristics of the vehicle need to be taken into account. High centers of gravity and extended braking distances are common characteristics.

In a number of countries, including those in Europe and North America, there are driving regulations that apply to some sizes of vehicles in this range. The regulations are designed to regulate the way that vehicles are operated with safety uppermost in mind.

Europe

Within the member states of the European Union, there are rules that apply to many vehicles in the weight range commonly used for SNG relating to:

- categories of drivers' licences relating to maximum gross vehicle weights
- the number of hours spent driving and total hours worked by the driver
- record-keeping
- speed limits

Drivers' licences generally fall into three categories with regard to the maximum gross vehicle weights (GVW) that can be driven. These categories are:

- under 3500 kg
- 3500–7500 kg
- over 7500 kg

There are also some age limits attached to these categories. In the range 3500–7500 kg, it is necessary to have a light goods vehicle endorsement (C1 class) on a standard driving licence, while to drive vehicles above 7500 kg it is necessary for a heavy goods vehicle (HGV) licence to be held.

Within the EU, there is free movement of traffic as far as vehicles from other member European states are concerned, with no customs procedures, duties or tolls. However, each country has national regulations for driving, called National Rules, and in addition, there is an EU-wide set of regulations, termed European Community (EC) Rules. Both sets of rules apply to commercial vehicles over 3500 kg, with additional restrictions for vehicles over 7500 kg. Below 3500 kg most vehicles (including SNG vehicles) are treated as cars and are therefore not subject to either National or EC Rules.

Within any country, commercial vehicles can normally be operated under one set of rules or the other, but not a mixture of both. Where vehicles are engaged in some specific non-commercial activities, including broadcasting (into which category SNG vehicles are usually classed), then they are said to be 'exempt' from certain parts of National and EC Rules where the SNG vehicle has permanently installed 'fixed-plant' equipment. Where load-carrying vehicles happen to be transporting boxed SNG equipment, then they are not usually classed as exempt and are subject to all the rules that normal commercial vehicles operate under.

For vehicles over 3500 kg, under either sets of rules, there are restrictions on the maximum number of hours of driving each day, the number of hours of work in a day and in the week, the timing of rest breaks, and the minimum periods of rest. A driver is not permitted to drive for more than 4 hours without at least 45 minutes break time, and there is a maximum of 10 hours driving in an 11-hour duty period. There are also weekly rest requirements which limit the maximum number of hours for both driving and working.

In addition, some form of record-keeping of hours is required even for exempt vehicles, usually by the use of a tachograph. Exempt vehicles may use a driver's logbook instead of a tachograph if so desired.

For all vehicles above 3500 kg, there are specific speed limits according to the type of road, with a maximum of 100 kph (60 mph) on autoroutes. In some countries, particular speed limits apply to vehicles over 2800 kg. All countries of the EU excluding the UK and Eire ban vehicles over 7500 kg from driving through built-up areas on Sundays and public holidays, but this does not affect typical SNG vehicles as they are exempt.

North America

As in the nation states of Europe, each of the states in the US has their own state rules, although unlike the EU, there is not an over-arching set of rules which can be adopted instead of state rules. However, all states are required to set minimum standards based on federal law, administered by the US DOT (Department of Transportation). There is no distinction as found in Europe between broadcasting (and therefore SNG) vehicles and other commercial vehicles.

There are various weight classes, which differ somewhat to those found in the EU. The gross vehicle weight (GVW) thresholds are at 10 000 and 26 000 lb (4500 and 11 800 kg, respectively). Above 26 000 lb, a commercial driver's licence (CDL) is required. There are rules on drivers' hours relating to driving commercial vehicles requiring a CDL, and these are broadly similar to EU Rules, with a maximum of 11 hours driving in a 14-hour duty period, separated by a 10-hour period. However, a CDL is not necessarily required for SNG trucks in most states as the majority are below 26 000 lb, allowing drivers with standard licences to drive such vehicles.

Most states deem any vehicle over 10 000 lb as 'goods carrying' and therefore a commercial motor vehicle (CMV), and although a CDL is not required, drivers need to have regular medical certification and the use of a driver's logbook is a statutory requirement. If an SNG truck weighs in over 10 001 lb the driver is required to have a medical card and is also required to log their hours, to a maximum of 11 hours of driving in a 14-hour period. However, if the SNG truck driver is operating within 100 miles of their base and not driving out-of-state, then they are exempt from these rules.

Nevertheless, some TV stations still require their SNG operators to have a CDL even if they are driving a truck weighing less than 26 000 lb as they are operating commercially, and if they travel interstate, it saves any argument if another state requires a CDL for a particular vehicle size. In addition, if a CDL is held, a driver's medical certificate is required irrespective of the weight of the vehicle being driven.

In Canada, the requirement for a different type of licence for trucks applies to vehicles with a GVW of greater than 4500 kg.

Australia

Each state has its own driving regulations, but these are now integrated into a common National Driver Licensing Scheme. There are no particular restrictions below 4500 kg, but above this limit a commercial driver's licence is required. There are different licence categories for 4500–8000 kg and over 8000 kg. As with the EU and the US, there are restrictions on the number of hours that can be driven in the day/week, and log books are also required to be kept.

9.2.12   *Time pressure and fatigue*

Without doubt, however, no matter which country the SNG truck is being driven in, the greatest hazard the SNG operator faces is time pressure. Particularly on a breaking story, there is an inherent pressure on the operator to get to the location as quickly as possible to get on-air. This pressure may or may not be directly applied – but it is always there. SNG truck operators need to exercise considerable self-discipline in order that this pressure does not affect their driving. Stress and fatigue are the two most likely causes of a vehicle accident; both of which are common when working in newsgathering.

Even when not driving, the effects of time pressure combined with tiredness will impact upon an SNG operator's judgement, and will inevitably lead to mistakes being made – which may result in an accident of some type. This type of hazard tends to be under-stated and is taken to be 'part of the job', but nevertheless it should be treated seriously and measures taken to ensure that anyone working in the field is not put under undue stress.

9.3 Logistics

9.3.1 Background

Logistics is historically a military science, though it has now extended into a wide range of commercial activities all over the world. In this section, we will look at how logistics play a part in newsgathering, primarily in the international arena, though we will spend some time looking at domestic markets.

Logistics in the context of SNG can be defined as the science of moving equipment and personnel from A to B in the quickest time at the lowest cost. It is probably the key strategy for success in satellite newsgathering, rising above how technologically advanced the equipment is, or how skilled the operators are. There is no merit in having highly skilled staff with the very latest technology if they are not where the story is. Yet the challenge of moving often quite large volumes of equipment even to relatively accessible areas of the world in the shortest time can frustrate even the most experienced newsgatherers. To do this cost-effectively is an additional pressure on all news operations.

As has previously been said, the two principal methods of transportation of SNG equipment are by air and by road, each having advantages in particular areas and offering the flexibility vital for newsgathering. That is not to imply that the use of other modes of transport is not an option. Other methods, such as by sea or rail (or even pack mule!), have been used but are more suited to operations where there has been a fair degree of pre-planning or where these methods of transportation offer particular logistical advantages.

It cannot be denied, however, that for international newsgathering, air transport offers the greatest flexibility. Various factors have to be weighed up before choosing a particular method of routing both equipment and personnel to a location – and they do not necessarily travel by the same method on pre-planned operations. When covering stories in hostile environments such as war zones, there may not be any choice to be exercised if, e.g., facilities for the press are being provided by organizations such as the UN.

9.3.2 Critical factors

There are five fundamental factors to be considered when deploying an SNG uplink to a news story. These are:

- The location
- How quickly
- The costs
- The availability of transportation
- The availability of space segment

Although they can be classified neatly into these five areas, there is a complex inter-reaction that means they have to be considered in parallel, rather than in sequence as this list might suggest at first glance.

These are also not necessarily the only issues, but they are the ones that have to be considered on all deployments. It would be neat to be able to represent these as a logical flow diagram, but unfortunately the processes involved do not fit into an ordered, sequential model. Instead, Figure 9.9 shows a 'cloud' diagram which although not an exhaustive model indicates these processes and their inter-relationship.

The following discussion therefore will attempt to deal with all five of these factors. It is not possible to consider them one by one in isolation, because of the inter-relationship that exists in the decision-making process.

Getting to the location is, however, the first factor to be considered. For a local story, the answer is probably perfectly obvious, and an SNG truck can be sent. The story can be on the air within the hour and no thought to the process is necessary by the newsroom dispatcher. The location becomes an issue when it is more remote from the broadcasting center or news agency headquarters; though in recent years, SNG trucks have been driven across continents to reach a remote story location, where previously flyaways would have been flown in. This was seen in the war in Kosovo, possibly the first time SNG units were driven to a war.

It is an inevitable truism that many of the world's worst disasters, which involve the natural forces of weather and the earth, tend to occur in regions which are often the most remote and therefore relatively inaccessible. As we have all seen on the television screen (due to the power of SNG), very large numbers of people are often killed or injured in these disasters, and the emergency services and relief agencies struggle to access these areas.

The news media, and television in particular, are also in a race to bring the story of the events to the wider world, and are hot on the heels of the relief services, obviously using the same methods of access. The earthquake disaster in Turkey in August 1999 provided an illustration of this, for even though

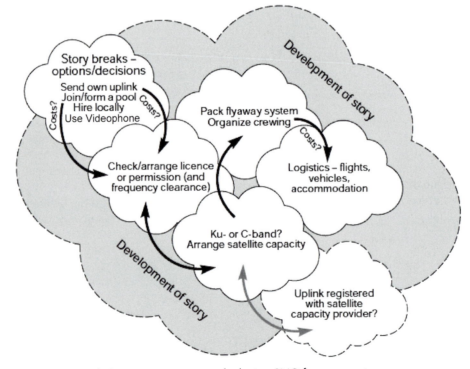

Figure 9.9 Operational planning processes on deploying SNG for a news story

Turkey is a developed country, the scramble to get there when the news broke was chaotic – though fortunately, on this story, the international airport in Istanbul was not affected by the disaster.

Tragic events have occurred in relatively developed regions, but where the particular location is in an inaccessible part of the region, frustrating even highly developed emergency services in their efforts to get to the scene. For example, huge areas of North America are relatively remote, and when there have been significant disasters in these remote areas, it has taken a considerable time for the emergency services to arrive and start their work. Even where the location is in a very highly developed region, the scale of the disaster can completely overwhelm a country's resources. An example of this was the huge earthquake in Kobe, Japan, in 1995, where within a few minutes, 6000 people were killed, 30 000 injured, and over 100 000 buildings were destroyed – and the whole infrastructure of the region was destroyed.

A more recent example of a developed country struggling to cope with the breakdown of infrastructure following a natural disaster was in the Southern US with Hurricane Katrina in 2005. SNG trucks from all over the US flocked to the area to cover the unfolding physical and humanitarian disaster, and then faced their own problems of obtaining water, fuel, food and shelter while also facing the hazards of disease from the flood waters and the collapse of sewage systems.

In general for any newsgathering team to cover these types of event, the problems of the location can dictate how the story is covered. Many of the large news networks have been forced to pool their SNG resources, as the problems of access, transportation, cost and local politics may conspire against them each having their own facilities on the ground. Often these 'pools' are organized on a national or regional basis; for instance, the US networks may form a pool serving US interests, the Japanese networks form a pool for their interests, and the EBU may provide facilities for its members. At other times, where strategic alliances exist between certain newsgatherers, joint operations may be established.

Assuming the location is in another country or continent, the choices facing the newsgatherer in terms of getting the equipment and personnel to the location of the story fall into the category of deciding how to get there by air. The equipment can either be sent on a scheduled flight, either as excess baggage or as freight, or on a specially chartered flight.

The decision to be made on these three options (charter, excess baggage or freight) is further affected by the factors of time and cost.

9.3.3 Chartering

The fastest and probably the most expensive way of getting to a story is usually on an aircraft chartered especially for the assignment. It probably seems amazing that with the number of scheduled aircraft and the route capacity covered in the statistics mentioned earlier, that there are places in the world that cannot be quickly and easily reached by scheduled flights. However, there are locations that cannot be reached within the desired time-scale except by charter.

There is also a potential problem that although a flight may be available at the right time with the required number of seats for the newsgathering team, there is not the aircraft hold capacity to take an SNG flyaway, which can take a significant amount of baggage space. Then a decision has to be made as to whether to wait for the availability of a flight that meets all the required criteria, or seek an alternative in using a special charter (Figure 9.10).

But on the other hand, this may not be so expensive if the story is significant enough that other press organizations are willing to share the cost for space on the flight. This may, in fact, turn out to be the cheapest option for all parties if the aircraft is large enough to get everyone (reporters, producers, technicians) and their equipment on board – and that includes camera and editing equipment as well as the SNG uplink. Typically for a large party of press with a number of organizations involved, chartering an aircraft the size of, say, a Boeing 737 may be the most cost-effective way of traveling out to the story. This has happened on a number of major stories.

Figure 9.10 Charter plane from Nairobi into Kigali being loaded with SNG flyaway system (courtesy of Paul Szeless)

9.3.4 Excess baggage

For stories of lesser significance, the fastest method, after chartering, is to travel on a scheduled flight with the equipment carried as excess baggage. Bearing in mind that the typical weight of a SNG fly-away and all associated equipment can approach 1 tonne and that for most of the world, excess baggage rates are typically 1–1.5% of the one-way full price economy class or first class passenger fare per kilogram on long-haul flights, the bill could run into tens of thousands of dollars. This is for just a one-way trip, and will probably exceed the cost of the airline seats for the news team by a significant factor. However, in the US many carriers operate a 'per piece' policy on excess baggage, and this reduces the cost; while many large newsgathering organizations have negotiated special bulk rate deals with a number of carriers, and rates can drop significantly if such a deal is in place.

For example, typical excess baggage costs (at time of writing) for shipping an SNG system from London to Nairobi are US$27/kg, and for a journey from London to Delhi, US$40/kg. Assuming a system shipping weight of 800 kg, this equates to US$21 600 for London to Nairobi, and US$32 000 for London to Delhi – and team air fares are on top of this!

In addition, the issue of weight limits on individual pieces of checked baggage need to be borne in mind – one major international British carrier has instituted an absolute limit of 23 kg per item flying from London, although some arrangements could be made 24 hours in advance or at time of booking beyond that – not very convenient for rapidly deploying for a breaking news story. This has caused concern to a number of major global newsgatherers who have their SNG operations currently based out of London.

Finally, getting an SNG system onto an aircraft as excess baggage is always subject to whether there is enough space in the hold for such a huge volume, along with regular passenger baggage.

9.3.5 Freighting

The third option is to airfreight the equipment. This is possible where the operation can be pre-planned to cover a known event (such as an international conference or national elections). It also an option at the end of a major news story where the equipment can be brought back at a more leisurely pace. Although significant cost savings can be achieved by moving equipment by this method, the drawbacks are:

- The time taken for the whole process – this can be considerably longer than just the actual travel time
- The inaccessibility of the equipment while it is in transit

The process of freighting equipment is more involved because of the customs procedures at the point of departure and at the destination. It is essential to use a freight-handler, who will locate shipping agents and find and book the freight capacity on a flight which will meet as closely as possible the required date for arrival and, crucially, the date of clearance through customs at the destination, before passing the equipment to the embarkation shipping agent.

The equipment has to be delivered to a shipping agent with full documentation that lists each piece of equipment and includes the following information:

- A description of the item and its serial number
- The country of origin/manufacture
- The value

The shipping agent at the point of embarkation will need to know the flight details and arrange for the equipment to be checked by customs. The shipment will be issued an air waybill with a unique number, which is an identifier that will be used to track the shipment through its journey. The shipper will arrange for a shipping agent to handle the equipment at the destination. Once the equipment has been cleared by customs, it is ready for loading onto the flight.

On arrival at the destination, the equipment similarly has to be handled by the destination shipping agent, who will arrange for clearance through customs. The time taken at each end to process the shipment can be between 2 and 4 days, and it should be remembered that in many countries there may be national holidays on which no customs activity for freight occurs. So it may take 7–10 days to airfreight equipment to a destination, even though it may only be on a flight of less than 24 hours, i.e. it takes considerably longer than the actual travel time. This is of course a significant factor to take into account, for this is 'dead' time for the equipment. Once it has embarked on this route, it is virtually irretrievable if it is suddenly required for another story.

The advantage of course is the costs, which are likely to be a fraction of excess baggage costs – typically less than 10–20%. Using the previous journey examples, typical freight costs for an SNG system from London to Nairobi, US$4 per kg, and for a journey from London to Delhi are US$5. Assuming a shipping weight of 800 kg (and with excess baggage costs in brackets for comparison), this equates to US$3200 for London to Nairobi (US$ 21 600) and US$4000 for London to Delhi (US$32 000) – again one-way.

Although the speed of processing at each end officially cannot be accelerated, a competent and skilled shipping agent will often have contacts to be able to get the equipment 'cleared' from customs and available for collection in faster than average time. Local knowledge and contacts are vital qualities for such a shipping agent.

9.3.6 Carriage of systems on aircraft

No matter how the equipment is going to be transported, it has to be packaged correctly for travel, and the issue of the packaging of flyaway systems was discussed in Chapter 3. The industry body that deals with international civil aviation is the International Air Transport Association (IATA). It establishes the regulations and standards for safe international air transport, and its membership is made up of all the international air carriers. One of the areas it regulates is how and what goods are carried, and SNG flyaway systems are treated no differently to any other type of cargo. The flyaway flight cases have to be within certain dimensions, as covered by the IATA rules on the dimensions of packaging cases, and of course have to be rugged enough to withstand the rigors of international air transport.

One of the items typically carried as part of an SNG flyaway system is a petrol generator for powering the system. Unfortunately, it is a difficult piece of equipment to transport by air, as it is classed as 'dangerous goods'.

9.3.7   Dangerous goods

IATA has regulations that cover the carriage of all hazardous goods.[3] This includes internal combustion engines fitted in machinery, under which category petrol generators are classified (a petrol generator is essentially a petrol engine driving a small electrical generator).

In the packing and transportation of generators of this type, the regulations require that the fuel tank and the fuel system be completely drained. In practice, most carriers require more than this, in that it is expected that there is no aroma of fuel vapor at all. This means that either a brand-new, unused generator has to be shipped, or that the fuel system has to be completely flushed and deodorized so that no smell of petrol can be detected. Failure to comply with this requirement will result in the generator not being loaded onto the aircraft. If the generator is packed into a packing case, then a special label as prescribed by IATA must be affixed to the crate showing the contents. Some carriers place further restrictions under their own rules.

In practice, many carriers are not keen to carry petrol-engined generators, even if all the above precautions have been taken. If there is the slightest smell of petrol vapor they will not permit them to be loaded onto the aircraft. It is possible to obtain generators that have no built-in fuel tank, and can be fuelled from jerry cans directly instead, but they are not as commonly available.

Diesel does not have the same degree of flammability as petrol, and so there are not the same restrictions. The drawback is that it is desirable that the generator is 'quietened' in its design, so that when it is running it cannot be heard in the background of a live report. The only diesel generators that are quietened are bigger than required (10 kW or larger) and very heavy (over 250 kg).

Liquefied petroleum gas (LPG) powered generators are just as difficult to transport by air as petrol-engined generators.

Of course, there is the option to try to hire or buy locally on arrival, but this leaves too much to chance. The availability of generators, particularly in a disaster zone or a hostile environment, is likely to be poor and much time could be wasted trying to source a generator while stories wait to be transmitted.

The generator is not the most obvious component in a flyaway system, yet it is so essential to most overseas SNG flyaway operations to provide flexibility. It is also the one item that has been left behind on the airport tarmac on more occasions than most newsgathering teams care to remember.

9.3.8   Use of road transport

SNG systems can be transported both locally, regionally, nationally and internationally by road. For local stories, the vehicle-based SNG systems – usually a purpose-built SNG truck – are, as has already been said, the obvious choice. Flyaway systems can be transported by road, and even if the majority of the journey has been by air, often have to be transported by road for the local connections at the beginning and end of the journey. There is little more to be said on this mode of transportation that has not already been covered in Chapter 3 or earlier in this chapter when discussing safety issues.

Figure 9.11   Transporting an uplink by road into Rwanda (courtesy of Paul Szeless)

9.4   Operating in hostile environments

9.4.1   Background

A 'hostile' environment in terms of newsgathering can range from a civil riot to an international war. Operating SNG uplinks in these environments brings a new set of problems in terms of safety and logistics. Obviously, the greatest challenge is in operating in war zones – be it a civil war, such as in Bosnia, or an international conflict as in the Persian Gulf region. In addition, areas where a terrible natural disaster has occurred offer a slightly different set of challenges.

These situations are the areas where the greatest problems occur with respect to both safety and logistics in deploying SNG systems, and these aspects are so intertwined that we have to deal with them as one. It is also the area of newsgathering where satellite transmissions from the field have had the greatest impact in shaping news bulletins and so in turn our view of these significant events. The following discussion relates to the situation where it has been decided to send a newsgathering team that includes an SNG uplink to cover a story in a war zone, as this reveals the range of decisions that have to be made. Lesser stories, or smaller scale situations, will still require some difficult decisions, but neither the number nor to the degree that covering a war demands.

9.4.2   Decisions... decisions...

SNG systems are typically deployed into these areas with consideration of a larger set of factors than considered earlier. As outlined above, the logistical (e.g. personnel and equipment) and technical (e.g. availability of space segment) criteria must be met, and in addition all the decisions relating to the dangers and consequent protective measures need to be taken. The following issues are involved:

● How to get the personnel and the SNG uplink to the location, weighing up cost and time considerations?
● Is a pool arrangement valid?

Figure 9.12   Uplink in sandbags in Baghdad in First Gulf War (courtesy of Paul Szeless)

- Assessing the level of risk to personnel and the availability of personal protection equipment if required.
- Insurance with respect to special risks?
- How to get the personnel and the SNG uplink into the zone of military operations?
- Will the uplink be 'embedded'?
- Where to site the SNG uplink for minimum risk and maximum usefulness?
- How to move the SNG uplink around if necessary?
- How to get the personnel (and hopefully the equipment) out to safety in a hurry?

As was said earlier, these are parallel processes, so Figure 9.13 shows how these interrelate in a summary overview.

9.4.3   *The immediate response*

For newsgathering in hazardous or difficult and remote locations, the first major problem faced is getting into the area with a means of reporting 'live' as quickly as possible. The first 24 hours for any newsgatherer in this situation can be the most difficult, while they attempt to 'ramp up' their own resources or hire in resources form the nearest available supplier in the region. The demand for coverage from even the most difficult and remote location is intense, particularly as there will be fierce competition from the other major newsgatherers to secure facilities for coverage. Some newsgathering organizations have prepared for this eventuality by signing up to arrangements with local providers in various regions around the world. The option of using videophones or some other Internet-based delivery system is also an obvious one. For many it is very often a race as to who gets to book the nearest SNG uplink facilities, and this can be intense. In the pressure of the breaking of the story, no one can afford to spend too much time haggling over prices, as speed of reaction is just as important to the independent operator as to the client newsgatherer. Standard 'rate cards' tend to go out of the window in these circumstances, and it becomes a matter of the highest bidder who can secure the facilities by being the fastest on the phone or the fax machine.

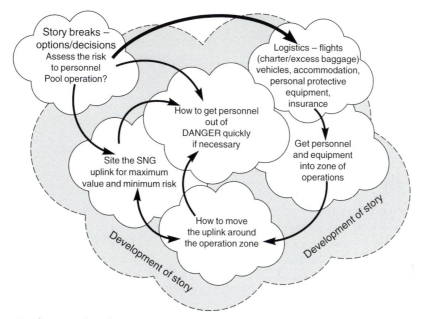

Figure 9.13 Deploying to hostile environments

We then enter the next stage, where having somehow responded to provide coverage in the first 24 hours, the story develops and grows larger and more resources need to be organized and brought to the location – be they hired or the newsgatherer's own facilities. In the succeeding days, more and more in the way of resources tends to be poured into the story, and it can become a logistical and financial nightmare to track what equipment has been sent where, and then to identify and control costs. Covering events on major scale is very expensive: it was reported that, at its peak, CNN were spending an additional US$150 000 a day on the Kosovo situation.

9.4.4   Risk to personnel

As was said earlier in the chapter, 'no story is worth a life', and that has to be the overriding consideration when deploying any newsgathering team to cover a story in a hostile environment. Taken to the extreme, the story may not be covered, so it is a matter of the inherent risks being minimized as much as is possible. There are some situations where unfortunately the risks are too high, as it has been obvious that during the 1990s the media themselves became targets in some conflicts (e.g. in Chechnya, Kosovo and, most recently, in East Timor). This is a new phenomenon, as in conflicts in previous decades the presence of the media was generally tolerated. That can no longer be assumed, and is an added factor when trying to assess the risks a newsgathering team will face.

The typical newsgathering team – usually a minimum of reporter, producer, cameraman, video editor and sound technician, as well as the uplink operators – should all ideally be equipped to deal with such situations, and strategies worked out to deal with the various possible scenarios.

This may imply that the planning involved in covering a war or civil disturbance is formulaic, but that is not the case. Nor is there necessarily much time to debate and prepare as much as would be ideal. It is a matter of ensuring that certain steps are taken to ensure, as much as possible, the safety of the team. Circumstances permitting, this may include picking team members who have had previous experience of working in war zones, and ideally who have had relevant survival training. At the very least, the planning will include the engaging of a local 'fixer' – a local civilian contact who can keep abreast of the situation, possibly cultivating military, police and other contacts, and act as translator to the newsgathering team in the field. Any source that can be used to develop a body of intelligence about the situation, including reports from other press coverage, all adds to the quality of the planning process, which may also involve discussion with other 'friendly' newsgatherers involved in covering the same story to share hazard assessments.

The hazards faced by the team obviously vary from situation to situation. The reporter, producer, cameraman and sound technician will be working a lot of the time at the 'front line', while the video editor and uplink operators will probably be in a situation further away, at the 'base' position. Alternatively, the base position may also be liable to attack, and the whole team equally vulnerable.

Many newsgathering teams were trained to be able to defend themselves for NBC attacks (nuclear, biological and chemical) in the Persian Gulf conflicts, and traveled to such areas with appropriate personal protection equipment. Other training that some media personnel have undertaken includes battlefield first aid, how to deal with hostage situations (where they are the hostages), anti-ambush techniques and survival training. Flak jackets and helmets, as well as other personal protective equipment, are basic tools nowadays for the well-traveled newsgathering team, and the well-prepared newsgathering team has usually had some degree of paramilitary training in personal protection. There are a number of specialist companies that have sprung up since the 1990s, often run by ex-military special forces personnel. These companies have developed short, intensive training programmes for media personnel who are to be deployed into war zones or other types of hostile environment (Figure 9.14).

Other equipment that is commonly used includes hand-held GPS navigation aids and typically the compact Inmarsat Mini-M and Iridium satphones. It should be noted that GPS units are position-reporting equipment, and in some conflicts a hostile military force may consider this as espionage equipment if a newsgathering team is caught with such equipment in their possession.

Each member of the team should accept the assignment knowing the risks, and ideally a full risk assessment will have been completed to protect personnel. As the overall objective is journalistic, the producer or the reporter will obviously lead the team, but every member of the team has their part to play, and they will be working together in an intense and frightening environment for days or weeks. The whole team is also under considerable pressure to 'make it' on time in terms of transmissions. Reports are often only prepared shortly before the transmission time, as there is always a feeling of having to work 'up to the wire' for the transmission to contain the very latest information and situation report.

9.4.5 Getting into the war zone

Having made the decision to try to cover the story, the next problem to be solved is how to get into the conflict zone. Normally, as soon as a country is approaching a war footing, scheduled airline flights are canceled and civilian airports are closed. It may still be possible to get in by chartered aircraft, although chartering fees are likely to be increased due to the high risks of aircraft either being attacked or impounded on landing. It is also possible that the situation is so volatile that although there seemed no obstacle on landing, and having dropped off the newsgathering team, by the time the aircraft is ready to take off, the situation has deteriorated preventing departure.

In recent conflicts, newsgatherers have on occasion been able to 'hitch a ride' with aircraft involved in UN peacekeeping activities in the conflict. This can be difficult, as it may be a matter of waiting until an aircraft is available with enough payload to carry all the equipment.

As discussed in Chapter 1, particularly since the Gulf conflict in 1990, it has become generally accepted that the electronic media serve a role in publicizing the events in a conflict, and contribute to the overall political process – although whether positively or negatively is a matter of opinion and

Figure 9.14 Operating an uplink under fire: Sarajevo TV station (courtesy of Paul Szeless)

Figure 9.15 (a) Uplinks on the border the night before the UN advance from Macedonia into Kosova (1999) (courtesy of Simon Atkinson)

debate. All conflicts have some degree of news reporting from inside the conflict zone and media will always find a way in. Nevertheless, it is unlikely that any newsgathering organization will wish to send a conventional style of SNG flyaway uplink into a conflict zone where the team has to be able to move quickly and at short notice. Dragging over a tonne of equipment around flies in the face of this, but as discussed in Chapter 5, there are other compact SNG systems which can still enable newsgatherers to deliver timely news reports.

An interesting facet of the coverage of the conflict in Kosovo is that the deployment of SNG trucks into an area of major international conflict was seen for the first time (in addition to the use of flyaways). Due to the fact that the Balkans are part of Europe, with countries having developed infrastructures on all sides, a significant number of newsgatherers and independent operators were able to get trucks in either overland via Romania, Bulgaria, Hungary and Greece, or by ferry across the Adriatic from Italy. Many of the trucks waited in Albania, Macedonia and Montenegro until the NATO forces were ready to move in, providing coverage of the story, and some were at the vanguard of the push into Kosovo with NATO forces as the Serbian army and militia left (see Figure 9.15a). A few trucks were damaged, either by Kosovan Serbs (for revenge) or by Serbia on the grounds of no permission to operate having been given (mostly NATO nationality operators). Others were impounded by Macedonia on the way out as the story died down, on the grounds of customs violations. (Several newsgatherers also had flyaway systems damaged or lost in Serbia – either damaged inadvertently in the NATO attacks or again impounded by the authorities.)

This development in the deployment of SNG trucks was a sign of the rapid expansion of the number available in Europe: trucks came from the UK, the Netherlands, Germany, Austria, Turkey and Italy, among others. A few of the 'SNG trucks' were no more than vehicles with SNG flyaway systems hurriedly and temporarily rigged-up in the back, with the enterprising help of local carpenters! The conflict was also notable for the way the number of independent SNG hire companies took systems in (in addition to the major newsgathering organizations), with the development of a dynamic market for providing uplink facilities and open touting for business (some of it on the Internet). This again had not been seen before in a major conflict.

However, it has to be realized that the availability of SNG trucks in the Balkans was unusual, and unlikely to be repeated often. It was simply a reflection that a major conflict had occurred in Europe, which has in general very good road connections, and is not a trend that is likely to be repeated until a conflict occurs in another relatively developed area of the world.

9.4.6   Embedding

As mentioned in Chapter 1, by the time of the Second Gulf War in 2003, the US and UK governments were determined to take advantage of controlled media exposure by 'embedding' news crews to assist them in their publicity campaigns.

The embedding of reporters – and compact SNG units which accompany them – is a double-edged sword, both from a safety and an editorial point of view. Putting aside the editorial debate of the difficulty of objective reporting within military discipline in this context, the safety of news crews can be enhanced by being able to travel within the protection of a military convoy, and hence benefit protection to the same degree as if they are military personnel themselves.

On the other hand, being part of a military unit will inevitably cause them to be put in harms way, and care needs to be taken to ensure that only those who can adapt to a military life-style should be put into this situation. Additionally, it should be remembered that according to the Geneva Convention, journalists accredited by an accompanying military force are considered part of the military entourage and must be treated as prisoners of war in the event of capture.

From the perspective of using SNG uplinks in this situation, there are number of factors to consider. Is the SNG terminal going to travel with the reporter, or be based further back? Are 'satcom-on-the-move' (SOTM) uplink set-ups going to be used within a moving convoy, or will SNG uplinks only be operated while the convoy makes its stops? Is an Inmarsat or Ku-band system going to be used?

Looking back at the Second Gulf War in 2003, we can look at some differing approaches. A number of newsgathering organizations chose to use Inmarsat terminals with auto-tracking antennas mounted on a US High Mobility Multi-purpose Wheeled Vehicle (HMMWV or Humvee) or SUV to enable them to be able to transmit back pictures while on the move. Others used ultra-compact SNG systems mounted onto Humvees or SUVs that could only be operated when the convoy halted for a period.

Perhaps the most ingenious set-up was used by NBC with an SOTM vehicle. Their correspondent David Bloom had conceived the idea of using a gyro-mounted camera (absorbing most of the shocks and bumps en route to produce stable pictures) on a refurbished heavily armored M88 tank recovery vehicle. This vehicle transmitted live video and audio via a digital microwave link back to a Ford F450 crew-cab truck several miles further down the US Army third Infantry Division convoy. The Ford truck was equipped with an MTN gyro-stabilized 1.2 m VSAT antenna, in a radome, transmitting at 2 Mbps up to Loral's Telstar 12 satellite, and downlinked directly in New York. This whole set-up was dubbed the 'Bloomobile' and enabled David Bloom to send live reports in superior quality to his newsgathering competitors while traveling at up to 80 kmph (50 mph) in the convoy (Figures 9.15b and 9.15c).

Without doubt this was a technological triumph over the opposition, and Bloom's reports were widely watched with a degree of awe around the world. Tragically, David Bloom was subsequently killed in the conflict – ironically not from a bullet, grenade, mortar shell or accident to the Bloomobile, but from DVT (Deep Vein Thrombosis), caused by spending weeks crouched, sleeping and riding in his creation. Everything possible in the circumstances had been done to protect Bloom and his crew from the obvious hazards, but Bloom had been suffering leg cramps. He was examined by an Army doctor weeks previously to his death and diagnosed as possibly suffering from this condition – but chose to ride on anyway, assuaging the condition with aspirin. Later it also emerged that he had an inherited blood coagulant disorder that increased the risk of DVT.

This story demonstrates that no matter how good the planning is carried out to protect personnel in these situations, little can be done to cover for the unexpected. It also demonstrates the risk of personnel so buoyed up by the professional mission they are undertaking that they can dismiss issues which in ordinary life they would have paid more attention to.

9.4.7 Locating the uplink

Having taken an SNG uplink into a war zone, it needs to be in as safe a position as possible which still allows relative ease of access to the news of interest. It may be in a hotel, at a government facility or even in a private house rented for the operation. In some situations, all the newsgathering operations are gathered together in one place while in others they are scattered around. From the newsgatherer's point of view, the advantage of the media being together is that they are able to help each other out (as long as it does not interfere with editorial competitiveness), and it also facilitates the sharing of material where such arrangements exist. What determines where the media gather can vary from government dictat to wherever happens to be a natural congregating point.

For instance, during the Iraq crises from 1997 to 1999, the foreign media in Iraq were required by the government to be grouped together at the Ministry of Information in Baghdad, and they were all required to stay at the nearby Al-Rashid Hotel. During the conflict in Bosnia, most of the media in Sarajevo were grouped at the local TV station, not because of any dictat, but because that was a natural congregation point. In the Gulf crisis of 1990, the main center of media activity was in Dharhan in Saudi Arabia as that was where the Saudi government had allowed the UN headquarters to be established.

The uplink is often located on a rooftop or balcony of a building, and it is usually rigged so that in case of attack it can be remotely controlled from inside the building, enabling live transmissions to continue. Inmarsat satphones are also similarly rigged so that communications can be maintained at all times. The advantage of this arrangement has been seen in the Iraqi crises in particular, where live reports from Baghdad have been sustained during air attacks from American and British aircraft. Of

(b)

(c)

Figure 9.15 (b) The 'Bloomobile' used by David Bloom (NBC) in Iraq 2003 (courtesy of Maritime Telecommunications Network [MTN] and NBC) (c) Inside the radome of the 'Bloomobile' under construction, showing 1.2 m Ku-band gyro-stabilized antenna (photo courtesy of MTN and NBC)

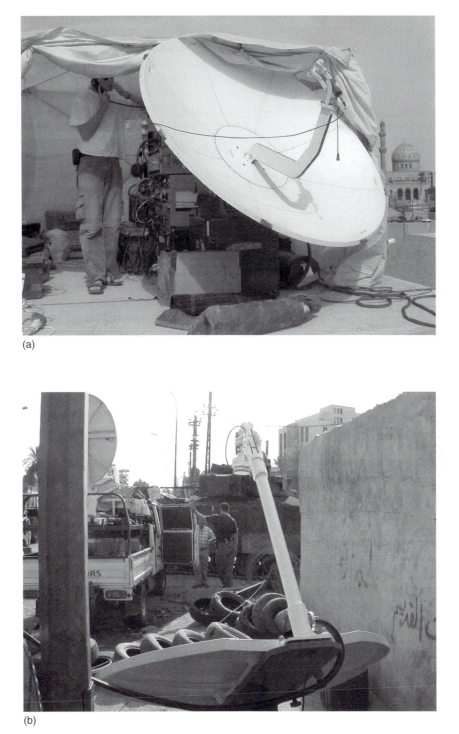

(a)

(b)

Figure 9.16 (a) Operating in Baghdad, 2003 (courtesy of Jack Raup) (b) Operating in Baghdad, 2004 (courtesy of Jack Raup)

course, the fact that western media are gathered in particular locations means that these locations are not targeted.

The decision as to where to site the SNG uplink for minimum risk and maximum usefulness is regularly reviewed during an operation (at times daily), to take account of changing military and editorial circumstances. Plans on how to move the SNG uplink around have to be devised, and we will come onto this next.

9.4.8 Moving the SNG uplink around

During the course of a conflict, it is sometimes necessary to be able to move the SNG uplink to other locations within the zone. This will inevitably be by road, and usually involve at least two sturdy four-wheel drive vehicles. The use of the word 'road' here is meant in its loosest sense, as wars tend to destroy road systems, and therefore four-wheel drive vehicles are an absolute necessity. It may also be prudent to use armor-plated vehicles if there is a serious risk of the team coming under fire, and the vehicles can be brought in. This will obviously give a greater degree of protection to the reporter and camera crew as they move around, as well as offering a way of moving the SNG uplink if required. The degree of armor protection can vary from 'semi' to 'full', with the available payload on the vehicle decreasing (rapidly!) as the level of protection is increased, and this will also affect the power and speed of the vehicle. There may also be importation or exportation issues relating to (essentially) military equipment.

It is worth noting here that the mere possession of such vehicles can also make the newsgathering team subject to attack. This is either because they can be mistaken for legitimate targets or because, particularly in a civil war, one or both sides is likely to be short of arms and military equipment and desirous of any such attractive transport available for the taking. The fact that the vehicle is being operated by a news organization is of no consequence, as the following story illustrates.

During the Bosnian conflict, an independent news facilities company bought a full military specification armored personnel carrier (APC), and they were contracted by one of the US networks for deployment to Bosnia, keen to gain a competitive edge. After having (at great expense) equipped it with a lot of equipment, including a flyaway SNG system, they showed it off with great pride to other newsgatherers at a publicity event in London. The team could thus move around in safety and venture into zones that other newsgatherers could not. Unfortunately, once deployed into Bosnia the vehicle broke down, was abandoned by the team while they went to get help, and while they were gone the APC was appropriated by some local guerrillas. It was never returned to its rightful owners (who wince even now when it is mentioned).

Other newsgatherers have also used heavily armored vehicles – the BBC famously had one called 'Miss Piggy', named after the *Muppet Show* character, as 'she' was rather large and cumbersome (Figures 9.18a). These vehicles have typically been based on four-wheel drive Land Rovers and Toyotas, and have not therefore been quite as attractive to local connoisseurs of military vehicles as an APC.

In 1999 in Kososvo, the use of armored vehicles became de rigueur but they were in short supply, and the prices of these vehicles were typically up to US$100,000. With the increasing death toll of journalists and cameramen in these types of conflict, every organization now realizes the importance of these vehicles – unlike in the early 1990s when those who made use of them were considered 'wimps'.

Some organizations have recently had discreetly armored SNG vehicles built (Figure 9.18b), which ostensibly look like a standard vehicle but actually have heavy duty armored protection underneath, in the sides, and doors, complete with armored glass. These are most likely to give maximum protection to the occupants while not drawing undue hostile attention.

Figure 9.17   Traveling light with an uplink in Macedonia (courtesy of Simon Atkinson)

Figure 9.18   (a) Armored vehicles at the UN HQ in Sarajevo (courtesy of Martin Cheshire)

It is also worth mentioning here of the risks of the 'herd' mentality. It is all to easy in the fierce competition of newsgathering to follow other organization(s) lead into an area without fully taking into account the risks – 'following the herd'. Each news team must make their own independent assessment of the safety of a venture, and not assume that because another organization has judged it safe, that it is indeed safe.

Figure 9.19   (a) Uplink operating in Bande Aceh, Indonesia during Indonesian tsunami aftermath 2004 (courtesy of Leo Tucker-Brown)

● Provision of food and water supplies
● Provision of fuel
● Security
● Exit strategy
● Traumatic stress.

As with war zones, there are challenges in getting into the area in the event of a natural disaster, either because there is scarce capacity for media to get in (as happened with the Indonesian tsunami) or local government agencies try to prevent access (as happened during Hurricane Katrina's aftermath). Communications with personnel on their way in and while they are there usually becomes completely dominated by the use of satphones (Inmarsat or Iridium).

Having got into an area, news crews then face a desperate situation, accompanied by the threat of disease, untrustworthy local food and water supplies, and the possibility of encountering hundreds or even thousands of corpses. These situations tend to bring the risk of water-borne diseases, ranging from diarrhoea at the mildest end to dysentery, hepatitis, polio and typhoid at the severe end of the disease spectrum. Immunizing personnel before they go into these areas is not always possible, and even immunization does not guarantee invulnerability to catching something very unpleasant. The combination of water and heat also brings the additional possibility of mosquito-borne diseases such as malaria, dengue fever, West Nile virus, encephalitis and yellow fever – to mention but a few. The provision of water-purifying tablets and taking the precaution of not even bathing in untreated water are vital to minimize the risk of illness.

Figure 9.19   (b) Uplink operating in Thailand during Indonesian tsunami aftermath 2004 (courtesy of Swe-Dish Satellite Systems)

Importing supplies of water and food to sustain personnel, along with fuel to keep vehicles and generators running, is always a severe logistical challenge. Accompanying this is the need to provide security for personnel, who become the targets of the desperate and the unscrupulous as they are seen to have what others don't have. Just as with extraction out of a war zone has to be planned for, so the same applies in a natural disaster, as personnel inevitably fall ill, are injured, or simply require to be rotated out of the zone for rest and recuperation.

Finally, perhaps more than in situations of war zones where often casualties and the dead are seen to be 'enemy' losses, news crews have to face seeing significant numbers of the dead and the dying, many of them the very youngest or the very eldest in the affected community, and all innocent victims of a dreadful tragedy. This can impose a tremendous mental stress on those in the field covering the situation, which can even extend back to those in the newsroom who also view raw unedited footage of the most appalling scenes.

Natural disasters can happen anywhere from underdeveloped regions to the most developed parts of the world, as was seen with Hurricane Katrina, where it seemed astounding that one of the world's most advanced countries seemed to be hit as badly as an underdeveloped country.

9.5 Conclusion

It can be seen that operating SNG uplinks has a number of factors to be considered that go beyond the merely technical and that have a direct impact on the safety of people (uplink operators, colleagues and the public) in a number of different dimensions. The influence of time pressure on covering news events can push the significance of some of these factors into the background unless there is a commitment not to ignore them.

International travel with the typical volume of SNG flyaway equipment escalates the stakes, and deploying to a hostile environment pushes the decision-making processes to a very high level of pressure, both in terms of safety and costs. In the fiercely competitive news environment, everyone in the field wants to be first and 'live' – but really above all, they need to be first, alive.

References

1. FCC (1997) *Office of Engineering and Technology (OET) Bulletin 65 Edition 97-01*: Evaluating Compliance with FCC Guidelines for Human Exposure to Radiofrequency Electromagnetic Fields.
2. NRPB (2004): *Advice on Limiting Exposure to Electromagnetic Fields* (0–300 GHz).
3. IATA (2007, 48th edition; updated annually) *Dangerous Goods Regulations*.

10

On the horizon

10.1 Finale

So we have arrived at the final chapter, and we'll spend a while looking at how gathering news by satellite (or otherwise) is developing. While the title of this chapter infers we are looking at future developments, we also cover some developments that have already occurred and are ongoing, but that will have an impact on the way SNG may be used in the future. The topics covered are disparate, and so some developments touched on in this chapter may seem at first glance as not necessarily having a great impact on conventional SNG – but that would be complacent. Any technology that offers the opportunity of gathering news more cheaply, more effectively and more easily (although possibly at lower quality) is always worth considering. Unfortunately for the reader, these developments are occurring so quickly that by the time this chapter is read, some of them may no longer be significant.

As it should now be apparent to every professional working in any aspect of newsgathering, the requirement to deliver ever higher volumes of news material within a time-frame and location ever closer to the event is irresistible – even if it means material is delivered at a level of quality lower than would have been accepted 15, 10 or even 5 years ago.

10.2 Cellphones and third generation wireless services

10.2.1 Background

Through the 1990s, mobile telephony grew faster than anybody could have predicted with the introduction of the digital Global System for Mobile Communications (GSM) in 1992, and is the world's most successful wireless communications standard. It has more than 1 billion subscribers in over 210 countries (2006), and it attracts 20 million new users every month. It took approximately 12 years to reach the first 1 billion GSM subscriptions in 2004, but only 2½ years to hit the next billion GSM subscriptions. GSM cellphones are cheap to buy and cheap to operate, and the reliability of services is very high.

For newsgathering, the GSM cellphone has become as much a tool of the trade as the camera, the notepad and the laptop PC. It enjoys usage across continents, from sophisticated metropolitan areas in the developed world to less-developed areas, where mass usage has leapt from the traditional landline telephone to the digital GSM network in one bound – or even where the first public telephone system has been GSM.

Journalists carry cellphones everywhere and expect them to work anywhere, which, despite the different variations on the GSM system across the globe, is easy with multi-band cellphones.

The development of the 'third generation mobile system' (3G), the first generation being analog and the second digital, has led to very sophisticated handsets. First generation cellular systems had one frequency channel assigned to one user for as long as they needed it. Second generation systems use TDMA (Time Division Multiplex Access), and third generation systems use W-CDMA (Wideband Code Division Multiplex Access). 3G is an enhanced digital system that provides universal personal communications to anyone, anywhere, enabling wireless Internet access, video-conferencing and other broadband applications – including newsgathering.

In Europe, the 3G system developed under the regulatory framework of ETSI is called the Universal Mobile Telecommunication System (UMTS). Similarly, the ITU formulated the IMT-2000 (International Mobile Telecommunications) in parallel, which is a group of systems that will allow users to roam worldwide with the same handset, with UMTS as part of this group. UMTS supports up to 11 Mbps data rates in theory, although currently users in deployed networks can expect a performance in the downlink connection at up to 384 kbps with some handsets, and 3.6 Mbps for other handsets. UMTS networks have been rolled out to a number of countries since 2003 and generally operate in, or adjacent to, existing GSM frequency bands. UMTS-only handsets are incompatible with GSM, so 3G networks typically provide dual UMTS/GSM handsets.

Meanwhile, IMT-2000 ensures that 3G systems are globally compatible and provide uniform communications. An important aspect of UMTS is the sequential upgrade path from current GSM systems, and the incremental increase in data capacity is of particular interest. The first significant development was called High-Speed Circuit Switched Data (HSCSD). The next step forward was General Packet Radio Services (GPRS). This provides data rates up to 115 kbps on GSM phones, and is packet-based allowing permanent connection. It is the predominant method of data connection for GSM phones.

After GPRS, a further development was Enhanced Data rates for GSM Evolution (EDGE). This changes the modulation method for GSM data transfer but leaves the rest of the system unchanged. Largely ignored in many parts of the world as 3G overtook it, it is used in North America.

10.2.2 Application in newsgathering

Apart from the obvious use of the cellphone as a ubiquitous newsgathering voice communication tool, there are two other areas where cellphones impact on newsgathering.

The first is as tool for what has been described as 'citizen journalism', where both still and moving pictures have been taken by members of the public and subsequently been used on news broadcasts. The most recent events which highlighted this use of cellphone technology were Hurricane Katrina and the London terrorist bombings in 2005. The development of both GSM and 3G services to transmit data at ever higher rates, combined with the integration of relatively high-resolution cameras into phones and offering a picture quality that was not even achievable on digital cameras 5 years ago, has enabled pictures to be sent from locations to give an immediacy that would otherwise been unachievable – the same *raison d'être* behind SNG. The use of MPEG-4 compression on these phones has made the acceptance of the video material sent inevitable.

Secondly, newsgatherers have been involved with cellphone network operators to use the advances in this technology – particularly 3G – to provide their own reporters with a tool to present more polished coverage from difficult locations. Specially adapted cellphones have been provided by some cellphone network operators to broadcasters in a symbiotic relationship – the network operators to drive forward their business into niche B2B (business-to-business) markets, and the broadcasters to make use of smaller, lighter and cheaper tools to service their news broadcasts.

So does this pose a threat to SNG? The answer is, as it stands, 'no', as just as the videophone and INMARSAT GAN filled a gap below SNG, so 3G cellphones fill a gap below the videophone (see Figure 10.1).

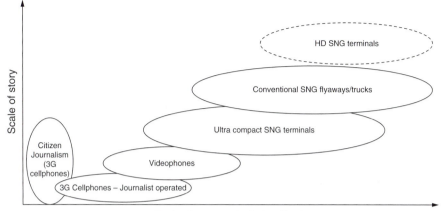

Figure 10.1 Newsgathering technology hierarchy

10.2.3 Future cellphone developments

We are currently at the roll-out of 3G services, so the next development is 4G (fourth generation). There is no set definition as to what 4G is; however, the features that are predicted for 4G can be summarized as follows.

4G will be a fully IP-based integrated system of systems and network of networks achieved after the convergence of wired and wireless networks as well as computer, consumer electronics, communication technology and several other convergences. It will be capable of providing speeds of up to 1 Gbps in both indoor and outdoor environments with end-to-end QoS and high security, offering any kind of services anytime, anywhere, at affordable cost and one billing.

The WWRF (Wireless World Research Forum), an influential global industry forum co-ordinating research and development in wireless technologies, defines 4G as a network that operates on Internet technology, combines it with other applications and technologies such as Wi-Fi and WiMAX, and runs at speeds ranging from 100 Mbps (in cellphone networks) to 1 Gbps (in local Wi-Fi networks). 4 G is not just one defined technology or standard, but rather a collection of technologies and protocols to enable the highest throughput, lowest cost wireless network possible.

For newsgathering, this sounds like the Holy Grail – but as with all promises of seemingly amazing technological development, it must be treated with a degree of prudence.

10.3 The future of the transmission medium

10.3.1 The Internet and its challenge to SNG

The term 'SNG' implies by its very name that satellites are the principal transmission medium, but this is not necessarily the case. As we approach the end of the first decade of the twenty-first century, a multiplicity of telecommunication routings in addition to satellite are available – terrestrial wireless and microwave links, 'local-loop' through local telephone companies, intra- and transcontinental fiber – and some of these both challenge and complement the traditional satellite territory of the last 50 years.

Some newsgathering organizations have already grasped this, and in the last few years have embarked upon a program called DNG (Digital Newsgathering). This uses the tools we have already covered in Chapters 5 and 6 of the laptop PC, low cost software, and broadband connections provided from fixed locations such as bureaux, hotels, Internet cafés and public access points. The aim is to:

● reduce dependence on (expensive) SNG uplinks
● reduce costs
● increase flexibility
● increase amount of material and diversity of stories for a range of outlets

The further development of the Internet will further drive the use of this method of newsgathering, and it has had an impact on the use of SNG. A number of global newsgatherers have in recent years deliberately pursued a policy of reducing SNG deployment in favor of jumping on the back of the large-scale roll-out of broadband connectivity around the world. This has often been in some incongruous locations such as Afghanistan and other poorer Asian countries where the local demand for Internet connectivity has seen broadband (along with mobile phone networks) put in place either hand-in hand with – or even faster than – conventional telephone landline networks.

Many of these newsgathering organizations are seeking to increase the breadth and amount of material they can produce in order to service not just a TV channel or two, but also delivery of stories to audiences via the web and 3G mobile phones. This has to be done often with a budget that has not increased in proportion to the number of outlets. So it is hardly surprising that the use of the expensive resource of an SNG uplink is being used with more caution.

10.3.2 Compression

In 2005, as the broadcast engineering world was still adjusting to the newly emerged H.264 (MPEG-4 AVC) standard, mention was heard of a new standard that was being planned for sometime after 2011. The ITU have H.265 scheduled within its 2005–2008 work plan, and consideration of what it might entail has already begun.

A spokesman for the respected research organization, the Fraunhofer Institute (the largest organization for applied research in Europe), said in 2006 that while the researchers were looking hard at various promising developments including wavelet compression, it was likely that an H.265 standard would emerge in 5 or 6 years, spurred on by improved processing power at both the broadcaster's encoder and the home set-top box. The aim of H.265 is to improve on H.264 by up to 50%. To put this in context, remember H.264 promises to achieve bit-rate savings of 50% over MPEG-2, and 30% over MPEG-4 ASP.

However, it was also questioned how much extra image quality – and thus processing power – viewers actually needed. While broadcasters were seeking realism in transmitted images, the usual challenges of rendering complex fine detail found in pictures – (grass, hair, sand, clouds and water) would remain. But with the accelerating take-up by consumers of large flat panel displays, the artifacts found in current compression algorithms are often all too apparent.

As before, the drive for further advanced compression is being driven by perceived consumer demand, and this will inevitably spin-off, as before, into developments in the contribution (and therefore) SNG market.

10.3.3 Lower the bit-rate ...

The issue of the acceptability of lower bit-rates was widely debated in the latter part of the 1990s. However, with the introduction of the use of videophones, and the acceptance of pictures from consumer cellphones, these discussions now seem faintly archaic. What is key is the use of the best compression system for the data rate available.

However, the extensive use of video and audio processing in studio and transmission centers, including transition through computer-based server architectures, means that even for news one has to be careful in trying to preserve the technical integrity of the material. In Chapter 4, reference was made to the issue of concatenation of digital signals through multiple processes, and although MPEG-2 algorithms are constantly being improved and refined, using very low bit-rates at the start of the chain is not going to make matters any easier – quite the contrary.

It has already been observed that the standard use of 4:2:0 MPEG-2 signals for SNG is sometimes replaced by the higher quality 4:2:2 processes in order that quality can be maintained. This has forced the use of 4:2:2 coding even for news feeds because of the fragility of 4:2:0 signals through video server manipulation. Experience has already shown how multiple encode/decode/re-encode processes have affected output, and as more broadcasts are transmitted digitally to audiences – either via satellite DTH or digital terrestrial television (DTT) services – any defects in the chain are more obvious even to the untrained eye and ear. In a sense, the use of servers determine that the quality of the contribution process be kept as high as possible.

Current strategies in designing news production systems focus on the use of automation and hence reducing the staffing levels previously required to produce news bulletins. All the costs of the contribution process (staff and resources) are also subject to this downward pressure. Even though lower bit-rates mean less bandwidth and power, and hence fewer dollars, the drive to reduce costs to achieve 'more for less' may not be as productive if lower quality becomes too objectionable to the viewer.

10.3.4   Impact of HDTV

HDTV is now a feature of the broadcasting landscape in many parts of the world, and although the amount of newsgathering performed in HD as a native format for SNG is currently minimal, the inevitable increase in its use will proceed with the roll-out of the use of MPEG-4 AVC/VC-1 and DVB-S2 in SNG. Several manufacturers have launched HD SNG encoders in preparation for the take-up, and undoubtedly this will come. It is, however, unlikely that we will move away from conventional size SNG systems for HD SNG in the foreseeable future.

10.3.5   The use of Ka-band for SNG

While newsgatherers will continue for the present to use C- and Ku-band for SNG uplinks, the development of the Ka-band (see Appendix A) for broadband Internet applications has prompted the question amongst the technically minded as to whether there is any advantage in using this type of capacity for newsgathering. The pure physics tend to suggest not. It may offer the potential of 60 cm or smaller antennas, but there is an issue of how rugged the error correction has to be because of the propagation limitations of this band. The Ka-band is more susceptible to the effects of rain fade and this would necessitate an increase in uplink power to compensate.

A number of satellite operators designed and equipped some of their satellites with Ka-band capacity in the latter part of the 1990s in anticipation of a diminishing availability of Ku-band capacity. For a number of reasons, partly caused by the economic downturn in the telecommunications industry generally in the late 1990s and early part of this decade, this decreased availability at Ku-band broadly did not occur. Hence many satellites have Ka-band payloads either lying idle or little used, and have so far to date lost money for the satellite operators.

Of course, a number of satellite operators offer broadband Internet access via Ka-band satellite in some regions – WildBlue in North America currently being a case in point. But such publicly offered services suffer the problem that we have already identified – asymmetric upload/download speeds which are contrary to the requirements of sending contributions to a studio center.

Overall there currently seems little advantage, but a number of disadvantages, in a move to the use of SNG in the Ka-band. Satellite coverage is not widespread, the power amplifiers are still more expensive than Ku-band equivalents, and the constraints of weather potentially limit the usefulness of such a system.

10.3.6 Satcom on the move

An interesting development has been a growing interest in what is known as SOTM (satcom on the move). While this has been possible for a number of years with some of the Inmarsat systems, there is a growing interest in its possibilities in the Ku-band with the development of more compact terminals and higher power satellites. The clearest manifestation of this came in the Second Gulf War in 2003 and the use NBC made of a modified marine VSAT system (the Bloomobile), referred to in the previous chapter. A number of very expensive systems have been developed for military applications; and there is undoubtedly an interest among a number of the major newsgatherers to have the capability to not only be on the front line to report events as they unfold, but also travel alongside it and not be tied to regular stops for transmissions.

However, there is only an interest if this can be achieved in a cost-effective manner, as these types of gyroscopically based systems are relatively expensive in order to perform at speeds of up to 80 kmph (50 mph). An SNG manufacturer that can achieve the same result at lower cost with equipment that is not dedicated for only that purpose will find a market ready to receive it – the question is if that market is large enough to offset the costs associated with developing and manufacturing such equipment.

10.4 Challenges to traditional working practices

The way in which SNG has traditionally been used, and the whole mechanics of the newsgathering process, is being changed in a bid to reduce costs. This has resulted in a number of existing practices being challenged and alternative (cheaper) processes being implemented. In this section, the principal issues are briefly examined.

10.4.1 De-skilling the SNG process

One method to reduce cost and increase productivity that emerged through the 1990s was 'multi-skilling' or 'multi-tasking'. Much of newsgathering management has seen that this offers the potential to reduce the most expensive part of the newsgathering process – employment of people. The concept is that equipment (and this includes everything in the acquisition process from the camcorder and audio recorder, to editing equipment and the SNG uplink) becomes easier to operate as it becomes more 'intelligent' and 'intuitive'. Therefore, the number of people in the field can be reduced, and in particularly the traditional craft-skilled technicians (cameramen, sound recordists, uplink operators) can be reduced in number or eliminated, thereby driving down costs.

Crudely, the theory is that one person, who is trained primarily as a journalist, can arrive at the scene of a news event, find out the facts of the story, present and shoot a report using a digital camcorder (and edit the report on the ground if it is not being sent back 'live'), and then transmit the story back using a very compact satellite link. If the story can be covered in such a sequential way, and the time-scale allows, then this is possible under these circumstances – perhaps.

Unfortunately, the nature of most news stories is that such a process could fail at or near the very beginning. As a way of covering smaller news stories, with less of a time imperative, it has without doubt frequently been successful. But on a big story many journalists often have to produce 'output' for a number of outlets almost simultaneously (this applies to those working for large networks or as freelance 'stringers'), and the pressures to simply keep up with the editorial demands makes meeting the technical demands incompatible.

Ironically, the logical culmination of this concept was seen in the late 1980s on US television. There was an entertainment show called *Saturday Night Live* on NBC, and it featured some comedy sketches of spoof news reports called *Weekend Update* from the field. These featured the comedian Al Franken as 'the one man mobile uplink', playing a reporter with a small antenna fixed to his helmet, a satellite uplink transmitter on his back and a camera mounted on his Steadicam harness. Al Franken was supposed to be able to report items as well as operate all the equipment, and for those involved in the newsgathering industry, it presents an eerie fantasy of what many television news editors then, now, and in the future would like to see.

So the question has to be posed: are journalists able and willing to operate a lot of equipment in the field themselves as well as doing their own 'real job'? There are some journalists in the field – typically freelance 'stringers' – who are able to offer this type of service within certain limitations. Certainly, a number of the global newsgatherers have succeeded in making this work, particularly with journalists who have adapted easily to the technology.

10.4.2 'Send the flyaway!': or not

With the development of Internet delivery that we have discussed in previous chapters, for many stories it is clear that this method of newsgathering will suffice. But at other times – if the story is big enough to begin with, or slowly builds in scale – there will be a point at which the newsgathering organization will need to consider escalating the technical resources on location.

Many of the global and regional newsgatherers have found that as countries have developed, there are an increasing number of local SNG services available for hire. As described in Chapter 8, the problems of shifting SNG uplink flyaway systems around the world are often significant, both in terms of the amount of work involved and in the costs. The concept of shipping the '30 box/1000 kg' flyaway around the globe has become rarer as there are more SNG service providers across the globe, hence there is less need to ship systems around the world. Some major broadcasters – whose principal objective can be seen as news dissemination rather than newsgathering – have chosen not to provide their own facilities and look to 'outsource' from local service providers. We have described the 'comfort factor' that many organizations feel by having their own people and facilities, which supersedes considerations of cost on very large stories. It is also arguable as to whether it is appropriate for broadcasters in particular to try and 'play all the positions on the field', or concentrate on their core strengths of journalism and editorial expertise, leaving the provision of the technical facilities to independent service providers.

The development of the SNG uplink hire market in a number of regions of the world has come on apace, so that local hire is often a viable alternative to newsgatherers sending their own SNG uplink systems. It is certainly the case that in some countries the number of local SNG service providers is so great that it is questionable for any organization to want to take in their own uplink equipment. A classic example is the US, where the SNG uplink hire market is of such size and is so competitive that it makes it highly uneconomic for newsgathering organizations from outside North America to go to the effort and expense of shipping their own systems there. Added to this are the hurdles in obtaining a temporary uplink licence from the FCC.

However, the local SNG market cannot always be relied upon, even if there are a number of operators offering service. On a number of occasions, in the hours after a natural disaster, it has been impossible for foreign newsgatherers to contact the local providers by voice or by fax because of the major disruption to telecommunications, which has put the local mobile and landline telephone networks out of action. Similarly the use of e-mail to try to contact the operators can prove futile. Foreign broadcasters (and news agencies), in the absence of being able to guarantee local hire, will therefore be reliant on being able to send their own systems to cover such major stories.

For the time being, it seems likely that those broadcasters who already have their own flyaway systems will continue to operate them on stories that they consider their use essential, while smaller broadcasters will perhaps not need to invest in systems as the availability of both truck-based and flyaway SNG uplinks for hire increases and costs are driven down.

10.4.3   Do we send a truck or a laptop?

This rhetorical question is somewhat tongue-in-cheek, but does indicate that many stories are covered by compact equipment – particularly as it offers considerable cost savings. The development of the laptop 'store and forward' and 'live video' systems described in Chapters 5 and 6, often combined with the use of Inmarsat GAN and BGAN satphones, has now made it practical for a journalist to travel with two attaché-sized cases; one containing the laptop store and forward/live video unit, and the other the satphone – and the journalist is truly self-sufficient without technical help on-hand. There is of course the issue of quality, but as we have already discussed, nothing is ruled out on the grounds of quality if it gets the breaking 'live' update back.

So what SNG platforms are we likely to see in the future? In so far as the use of trucks, of particular interest on both sides of the Atlantic is the direction in which the construction of SNG vehicles is going. The development of newsgathering using SNG vehicles appears to be polarizing into a choice between a small vehicle, up to 4500 kg (10 000 lb) GVW, or a larger vehicle that has the capability of handling more complex news productions and HDTV, based on vehicles in the 7500–10 000 kg (16 500–22 000 lb) range. The industry is effectively deciding whether anything is required in the middle – customer requirements seem to gravitate toward one extreme or the other.

Other tasks now drive the size of the vehicle more than the uplink capability itself, such as handling multi-camera operations, field editing facilities and serving multiple outlets simultaneously through multi-path working. For the SNG vehicle constructors, this is proving to be a challenge as almost invariably every customer wants the smallest vehicle in physical size while fitting in the maximum amount of equipment and functionality.

There also seems to be a need to allow for scaling of facilities, with systems needing to be modular in approach and design. This is so that the vehicle can be fitted with enough equipment for the immediate news response requirement, yet be able to be easily upgraded to cope with a higher level of production activity by just 'sliding in' the extra equipment. Many have noticed that production demands often require an SNG vehicle or flyaway that effectively becomes an integrated location production facility, coping with the scaling of a news 'story' into a news 'event'.

Particularly in the US, which has come late to DSNG, small SNG vehicles are replacing traditional terrestrial microwave ENG vehicles in some markets. Using direct (or near) line-of-sight communication, terrestrial microwave links have been the traditional means of covering domestic news stories for many local stations in the US for 20 years (and in Europe for almost as long). There is an extensive existing ENG infrastructure of receiver sites in every major town and city, as well as transmitters fitted to every ENG vehicle.

Coincidentally, due principally to the spectrum demands for the development of IMT-2000 and UMTS, the existing ENG infrastructure has to be replaced. In the US, the Federal Communications Commission (FCC) has mandated that television broadcasters who operate ENG links in the 1990–2110 MHz spectrum band must replace and/or upgrade their 2 GHz transmission facilities by September 2007 to operate within

2025–2110 MHz. This relocation also involves migrating equipment from analog to digital to operate in the new channel plan and retuning equipment to the new frequencies.

In Europe, where DSNG caught on much earlier than in the US, there has already been a large-scale move away from terrestrial ENG. Europe too faces the same pressure to vacate the traditional 2 GHz ENG band, widely used around the world.

10.5   Political considerations

With all this technological innovation and inherent editorial freedom, what are the implications for sovereign states? This is the issue of sovereignty and control of information by governments, already covered with reference to SNG in Chapter 7.

We have a situation where reporters can use equipment so compact and discrete in use that it can be brought in and used undetected. Many countries have strict censorship rules for religious and/or political reasons, yet governments are increasingly in the position that whereas previously they have been able to easily regulate the use of conventional SNG flyaway systems, they are unable to regulate use of the new tools – equipment which is increasingly either compact professional equipment or 'consumer' items, and therefore hard to distinguish in usage.

For instance, during the lengthy civil war in Sri Lanka in early 1999, the Sri Lankan government approved the use of Iridium satphones in Sri Lanka so long as there was no service offered in guerrilla-held areas. The defence ministry opposed the extension of the use of Iridium satphones (or those of any other system) to the zone where Tamil Tiger guerrillas were fighting government forces. The Tamil Tigers were already known to operate Inmarsat satphones to communicate with their offices abroad. Iridium agreed that Sri Lanka's embattled north and eastern territories would be excluded from their system because of national security considerations. However, despite similar requests from the government to Inmarsat, the technology used by Inmarsat cannot restrict coverage to a particular region.

It is often extremely difficult to meet this type of request, on technical grounds, but this is symptomatic of the problems faced by commercial telecommunication companies when dealing with many governments. The WTO GMPCS MoU (see Chapter 6) is intended to facilitate the free movement of GMPCS equipment, but it will still be years before this is achieved on a fully global scale.

With individual nation's censorship rules becoming virtually impossible to enforce, the development in technology has now forced sovereign control of foreign media to become a thing of the past. Independent access to the Internet using a satellite terminal, bypassing a country's Internet censorship mechanisms, is now so easily achieved that such governments are relatively helpless in the face of the technology.

10.6   Outlook

So what is the future of satellite newsgathering? We have touched on a number of technological developments and changes in working practices that directly impact the process of newsgathering and therefore ultimately what is seen on the television screen, the PC, or heard on the radio. The speed of development is so fast that by the time this book is read, some of the projected changes will have either occurred or possibly fallen by the wayside.

For the journalists in the field, there is an ever-increasing demand to 'go live', to be in the midst of the story rather than just reporting from the edges, and for those who work for networks with multiple outlets to the consumer, to produce the maximum amount of output for every dollar spent. Unfortunately, in many cases journalists are becoming simply 'content providers', and the investment in satellite technology is there to feed this drive. More facilities are being demanded in the field on the major stories; while at the other end of the scale, domestic camera equipment is being thrust into the hands of journalists who are individually expected to provide what a team of three or four people would have produced just over a decade ago.

Even in the middle of a war zone, there is the desire to give the audience the feeling of 'being there', and this requires the use of wireless cameras, short-hop microwave and laser links, and ever-more mobile SNG uplinks, to combine instant mobility with guaranteed 'live' transmissions. Just being at the nearest hotel reporting the story is now seen as mundane.

The one clear advantage that SNG has over any other method is that with only the addition of a power source (generator or vehicle battery), an SNG uplink is completely self-sufficient in an environment where there is no network, electricity, infrastructure or order. The smaller and more lightweight that SNG uplink is, the sooner it will be in at the heart of the story and sending back pictures.

So for the foreseeable future, satellites will continue to play a vital role in delivering news to audiences from remote locations. Hopefully the subjects covered in this book will have given you some insight into the very wide range of issues that face the satellite newsgatherer, whether it is for coverage of local, national, international or global news.

Appendix A
Frequency bands of operation

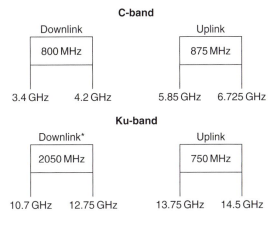

C-band

Downlink | Uplink
800 MHz | 875 MHz

3.4 GHz   4.2 GHz   5.85 GHz   6.725 GHz

Ku-band

Downlink* | Uplink
2050 MHz | 750 MHz

10.7 GHz   12.75 GHz   13.75 GHz   14.5 GHz

* Includes bands used for DTH services as well as mobile uplinks

C-band	3–7 GHz
Ku-band	10–18 GHz
Ka-band	18–40 GHz
L-band	1.0–2.0 GHz
(X-band	7–9 GHz, for interest only, mostly used for military operation)

There are a number of different definitions for frequency bands, depending on whether for commercial, military or space use – the above are those broadly accepted for commercial satellite usage. C-band is divided into a number of sub-bands (with ranges in GHz), as follows:

Standard C-band
    Uplink frequency   5.925–6.425
    Downlink frequency   3.7–4.2
Extended C-band
    Uplink frequency   5.85–6.425
    Downlink frequency   3.625–4.2
Super-extended C-band
    Uplink frequency   5.85–6.725
    Downlink frequency   3.4–4.2

Ku-band is divided into a number of sub-bands (with ranges in GHz), as follows:

Uplink frequency
Standard Ku-band	14.0–14.5
Extended Ku-band	13.75–14.0

Downlink frequency
Lower Ku-band	10.95–11.7
Middle Ku-band	11.7–12.2
Upper Ku-band	12.25–12.75

DBS band (with ranges in GHz)
Uplink frequency	17.3–18.4
Downlink frequency	11.7–12.2

Ka-band (with ranges in GHz)
Uplink frequency	28.35–28.6
	29.25–30.0
Downlink frequency	18.3–18.8
	19.7–20.2

Appendix B

Sample link budget

Scenario: A major news event has occurred at Buckingham Palace in London, and an SNG uplink is going to be set-up to provide live coverage. The uplink is working onto a Eutelsat satellite, and the digital 8 Mbps TV signal is going to be downlinked at a number of locations, including a teleport in London.

We need to calculate the link budget for a digital transmission, as well as calculating positional information for setting up the uplink.

The link budget shown is of the simplified type – full link budgets have to take into account many more parameters than we have included, but the basic principles are illustrated here.

Note: Many of the trigonometric calculations have to be performed with values in radians rather than degrees.

Uplink position and pointing

Firstly, we need to calculate certain parameters related to the position of the uplink relative to the satellite being used.

Longitude of uplink: Latitude of uplink:

$$LO_{es} = 0°8'18'' \quad LA_{es} = 51° 29'56''$$

Converting from degrees and minutes to decimal form:

$$LO_{es} = 0.14° \quad LA_{es} = 51.5°$$

Satellite being used is Eutelsat W1 at 10°E, satellite longitude (LO_{sat}) = 10°

We need to calculate the difference in longitude between the uplink and the satellite (uplink at 0.14° West compared to satellite at 10° East – we're only interested in the size of angular difference at this stage and need not worry about the sign):

$$(LO_{es} - LO_{sat}) = LO_{diff} = 10.14°$$

Let E = an angle that describes the relative longitudinal difference to the uplink latitude.

$$
\begin{aligned}
\cos E &= (\cos LO_{diff} \cos LA_{es}) \\
&= (\cos 10.14° \cos 51.5°) \\
&= (0.9844)(0.6225) \\
&= 0.6128 \\
E &= \arccos (0.6128) \\
&= \mathbf{52.2°}
\end{aligned}
$$

This is of no direct significance – it is an intermediate calculation that we require for computing the angle of elevation (EL_{es}) of the uplink, and slant path length (S) from the uplink to the satellite.

Azimuth angle to satellite (AZ$_{es}$)

The equation varies according to the part of the hemispheric quadrant in which the uplink is located compared to the satellite:

- If uplink is West and North of satellite position over the Equator, true azimuth = 180 − Az
- If uplink is East and North of satellite position over the Equator, true azimuth = 180 + Az
- If uplink is West and South of satellite position over the Equator, true azimuth = 360 − Az
- If uplink is East and South of satellite position over the Equator, true azimuth = Az

This uplink is West and North of the position of the Eutelsat W1 satellite, so true azimuth = 180 − Az:

$$
\begin{aligned}
AZ_{es} &= 180 - \arctan\left(\frac{\tan LO_{diff}}{\sin LA_{es}}\right) \\
&= 180 - \arctan\left(\frac{\tan 10.14}{\sin 51.5}\right) \\
&= 180 - \arctan\left(\frac{0.1788}{0.7826}\right) \\
&= 180 - \arctan(0.2285) \\
&= 180 - 12.87 \\
&= \mathbf{167.13°}
\end{aligned}
$$

This is the bearing in degrees ETN (East True North), i.e. measured clockwise from True North looking down on the uplink. Note that magnetic variation between True to Magnetic North at this part of the UK is +4°, and this must be allowed for and the compass reading taken accordingly.

Elevation angle to satellite

$$
\begin{aligned}
EL_{es} &= \arctan\left(\frac{\cos E - 0.1513}{\sin E}\right) \\
&= \arctan\left(\frac{0.6128 - 0.1513}{\sin 52.2}\right) \\
&= \arctan\left(\frac{0.4616}{0.79}\right) \\
&= \arctan(0.5842) \\
&= \mathbf{30.3°}
\end{aligned}
$$

Polarization skew

Having got the azimuth and elevation figures for the antenna, we need also to calculate the skew angle Θ:

$$
\begin{aligned}
\theta &= 90° - \arctan\left(\frac{\tan LA_{es}}{\sin LO_{diff}}\right) \\
&= 90° - \arctan\left(\frac{\tan 51.5°}{\sin 10.14°}\right) \\
&= 90° - \arctan\left(\frac{1.257}{0.176}\right) \\
&= 90° - \arctan(7.14) \\
&= 90° - 82° \\
&= \mathbf{+8°}
\end{aligned}
$$

The antenna has to be adjusted by $+8°$ in skew; however, this is a theoretical calculation which has to be adjusted in operation as it does not take into account exactly where the satellite is located in its orbit. It is adjusted in the field by examining received signals from the satellite on a spectrum analyser.

Slant range

Slant range path length from uplink to satellite (S) is given by:

$$
\begin{aligned}
S &= 35758\sqrt{1 + 0.4199(1 - \cos E)} \\
&= 35758\sqrt{1 + 0.4199(1 - 0.6128)} \\
&= 35758\sqrt{1.163} \\
&= 35758(1.078) \\
&= \mathbf{38\ 555\ km}
\end{aligned}
$$

Antenna gain

The uplink frequency (f) is $14.25\,\text{GHz} = 14.25 \times 10^9\,\text{Hz}$
Speed of light (c) $= 2.99793 \times 10^8\,\text{m/s}$

$$
\begin{aligned}
\text{Wavelength } (\lambda) &= \frac{c}{f} \\
&= \frac{2.99793 \times 10^8}{14.25 \times 10^9} \\
&= \mathbf{0.02104\ m}
\end{aligned}
$$

Antenna diameter (D) $= 1.5\,\text{m}$
Antenna efficiency (η) $= 0.6$

Antenna gain

$$G^{ANT} = 20 \log_{10} \left(\sqrt{\eta}\, \frac{\pi D}{\lambda} \right)$$
$$= 20 \log_{10} \left(\sqrt{0.6}\, \frac{\pi 1.5}{0.02104} \right)$$
$$= 20 \log_{10}(173.5)$$
$$= \mathbf{44.8\,dBi}$$

HPA power

HPA maximum output $(P^W) = 175\,\text{W}$
$$= 22.43\,\text{dBW}$$
Waveguide losses $(W^{loss}) = 0.75\,\text{dB}$

Uplink EIRP

The maximum EIRP capability of the uplink is given by:

$$P^{eirp} = P^{HPA} + G^{ANT} - W^{loss}$$
$$= 22.43 + 44.8 - 0.75\,\text{dBW}$$
$$= \mathbf{66.48\,dBW}$$

Free space attenuation (FSA)

$$FSA = 20 \log_{10} \left(\frac{4\pi S}{\lambda} \right)$$
$$= 20 \log_{10} \left(\frac{4\pi 38555 \times 10^3}{0.02104} \right)$$
$$= 20 \log_{10} \left(\frac{4.8449 \times 10^8}{2.104 \times 10^{-2}} \right)$$
$$= 20 \log_{10} (2.303 \times 10^{10})$$
$$= \mathbf{207.25\,dB}$$

We now have all the basic parameters on uplink position to calculate the link budget. This is very much a theoretical calculation, as to aid understanding, we are not going to take into account every parameter that will have an effect on the link budget.

Uplink power to the satellite

London lies on the +4 dB/K G/T satellite's receive antenna's gain advantage contour, and Eutelsat has specified that an IPFD of −87 dBW/m² is required on the −0.5 dB/K uplink reference contour at this location to achieve saturation of the transponder. (This can vary from transponder to transponder and this information needs to be sought from the satellite operator).

The IPFD at the satellite to cause saturation from its +4 dB/K contour is given by:

$$\text{Saturated IPFD} = -87 - (4 + 0.5)\ \text{dBW/m}^2$$
$$= -87 - 4.5$$
$$= -91.5\ \text{dBW/m}^2$$

However, an IBO of 12 dB is required to achieve a more linear operation of the transponder, which is necessary for digital carrier operation to prevent interference between the multiple carriers which would normally share a transponder.

$$\text{Required IPFD} = -91.5 - 12$$
$$= \mathbf{-103.5\ dBW/m^2}$$
$$\text{Spreading loss } (L_{spread}) = +10\log_{10}(4\pi S^2)\ \text{dB(m}^2)$$

where S (slant range) is in *metres* (rather than in kilometres as we have shown):

$$L_{spread} = +10\log_{10}[4\pi(38555 \times 10^3)^2]$$
$$= \mathbf{+162.72\ dB(m^2)}$$

We also need to consider some loss attributable to 'pointing' error of the antenna and the slight movement of the satellite within its station-kept box. Most of the pointing loss is not because one cannot point a dish accurately at a satellite – it is because the satellite is not always in the same place, as it moves within the station-kept box. So we will estimate L_{point} as being 0.5 dB. The atmosphere will introduce some loss (L_{atmos}), which we will estimate as 0.6 dB. (As this is a simplified link budget, we will consider all other losses as negligible.)

Uplink EIRP required ($EIRP^{up}$) = IPFD + spreading loss + atmospheric loss + pointing loss

$$= \text{IPFD} + L_{spread} + L_{atmos} + L_{point}$$
$$= -103.5 + 162.72 + 0.6 + 0.5$$
$$= \mathbf{+60.32\ dBW}$$

This is approximately 6 dB below the maximum EIRP that the uplink can produce, and this is a good margin to have in hand – it means the HPA will be running at around 37 W, so it will be backed-off to a very linear part of its gain characteristic, and there will be plenty of margin for rain-fade or any other unpredicted atmospheric attenuation.

Digital signal parameters

We are going to uplink an 8.448 Mbps signal. For the digital link budget we need to know how much of this is carrying useful information, the so-called Information Rate (*IR*). In this case, the 8.448 Mbps includes a Reed–Solomon error-protection code which limits the usable information carried to 188/204ths of the total. So that $IR = 7.785$ Mbps.

The overall FEC rate in a system with concatenated coding such as the Reed–Solomon code mentioned above, followed by the convolutional coding used in the satellite modem, is the product of the two coding rates. In our example, we have an RS code of (204,188) followed by 3/4 convolutional coding, therefore the overall FEC rate is:

$$FEC = \frac{3}{4} \times \frac{188}{204} = 0.6912$$

The Symbol Rate (SR) is:

$$
\begin{aligned}
SR &= \frac{0.5 \times IR}{FEC} \\
&= \frac{0.5 \times (7.785 \times 10^6)}{0.6912} \\
&= \textbf{5.632 Mbps}
\end{aligned}
$$

We shall assume that the noise bandwidth of the digital signal is a bandwidth equal to the symbol rate, i.e. 5.632 MHz.

We need to calculate the noise power in the bandwidth of the uplink signal, which is:

$$
\begin{aligned}
B^{power} &= 10 \log_{10} \left(0.5 \times \frac{IR}{FEC} \right) \text{(dB)} = 10 \log_{10} NBW \text{ (dB)} \\
&= 10 \log_{10} \left(0.5 \times \frac{7.785 \times 10^6}{0.69} \right) \\
&= \textbf{67.5 dB}
\end{aligned}
$$

Uplink carrier-to-noise ratio

So, including uplink losses, the uplink C/N is:

$$
\begin{aligned}
\left(\frac{C}{N} \right)_{up} &= EIRP^{up} - L_{up-total} + \left(\frac{G}{T} \right)_{sat-up} - k - B^{power} \text{ (dB)} \\
&= 60.32 - 208.35 + 6 - (-228.6) - 67.51 \\
&= \textbf{19.06 dB}
\end{aligned}
$$

Downlink carrier-to-noise ratio

The downlink we are going to use is also in London, just 6.4 km away from the uplink, so the same azimuth, elevation and slant range figures can be used as the difference in distance is so small. On the downlink, we will assume for convenience that atmospheric losses are the same – in practice, they would be somewhat smaller due to the lower frequency of the downlink. The downlink antenna is 9 m in diameter, with a G/T of + 36 dB/K, and London lies within the 48 dBW EIRP saturated receive contour of the widebeam from Eutelsat W1. However, the pointing loss at the downlink antenna is likely to be smaller, because of the use of an automated tracking system which is essential for big dishes. So let us assume the pointing loss is now 0.3 dB, and as the downlink frequency is 11.5 GHz, the FSA has now changed to 205.4 dB, and thus:

$$L_{down\text{-}tot} = \text{FSA} + L_{down\text{-}point} + L_{atmos}$$
$$= 205.4 + 0.3 + 0.6$$
$$= \mathbf{206.3\,dB}$$

However, as we mentioned earlier, an IBO of 12 dB is required to achieve a more linear operation of the transponder, and this happens on the nominated transponder to result in an OBO of 7 dB, which has to be subtracted from the saturated EIRP of the satellite:

$$\left(\frac{C}{N}\right)_{down} = EIRP_{sat} - OBO - L_{down\text{-}tot} + \left(\frac{G}{T}\right)_{downlink} - k - B^{power} \text{ (dB)}$$
$$= 48 - 7 - 206.3 + 36 - (-228.6) - 67.5$$
$$= \mathbf{31.8\ dB}$$

Overall carrier-to-noise ratio

The overall C/N *as expressed in power ratios* the complete link path is:

$$\left(\frac{C}{N}\right)_{overall} = \cfrac{1}{\cfrac{1}{\left(\dfrac{C}{N}\right)_{up}} + \cfrac{1}{\left(\dfrac{C}{N}\right)_{down}}}$$

In dB's, the expression looks like:

$$\left(\frac{C}{N}\right)_{overall} = -10\log_{10}\left(10^{-\frac{\left(\frac{C}{N}\right)_{up}}{10}} + 10^{-\frac{\left(\frac{C}{N}\right)_{down}}{10}}\right) \text{ (dB)}$$

So substituting the figures we have derived:

$$\left(\frac{C}{N}\right)_{overall} = -10\log_{10}\left(10^{-\frac{19.06}{10}} + 10^{-\frac{31.8}{10}}\right)$$
$$= -10\log_{10}(10^{-1.906} + 10^{-3.18})$$
$$= \mathbf{18.33\ dB}$$

Looking at the uplink and downlink C/N ratios, it can be seen that the lower (worse) figure is on the uplink, and therefore this link is 'uplink limited' – no matter what improvements are made on the downlink, the overall quality is mainly unaffected.

Overall E_b/N_0 ratio

The overall E_b/N_0 is:

$$\left(\frac{E_b}{N_0}\right)_{overall} = \left(\frac{C}{N}\right)_{overall} + 10\log_{10} NBW - 10\log_{10} IR$$
$$= 18.83 + 10\log_{10}(5.632 \times 10^6) - 10\log_{10}(7.785 \times 10^6)$$
$$= \mathbf{17.42\ dB}$$

This figure only takes nominal account of interference from other carriers within the transponder, and none at all from cross-polar interference (XPI), which can have a more drastic effect on a digital link than an analog link. It should be noted that this could reduce this figure by as much as 5–6 dB.

In the real world, a link budget has to be carried by the satellite operator, who can take into account all the potential interference parameters on the satellite. However, from the calculations, this is a very acceptable quality link, acceptable for both 'news' and 'non-news' events (an E_b/N_0 of 10 dB or greater received at the downlink is considered 'good quality').

We haven't as yet dealt with the impact of rain on the link budget. The reason to plan for high C/N ratios is to have enough margin to cope with rain-fading. This link has about 7.5 dB difference between the calculated E_b/N_0 and the desired target of 10 dB which means that it should meet the desired performance reliably even in heavy rain conditions. In many real-world cases (particularly SNG), one has to accept less margin and carry a greater risk of failure.

Note that the strong concatenated error-protection codes used for this link exhibit a very rapid failure at an E_b/N_0 value of about 5–6 dB depending on equipment performance. During a rain-fade, the link will typically change from perfect reception to complete failure over a very narrow range of value of E_b/N_0. (This differs from an analog link where, even during severe rain-fades, a watchable if far from perfect picture can still be received.)

Hopefully the link budgets shown here have given the reader some idea of the influence of the various basic parameters that are accounted for in link budgets. The calculations are very tedious, and some satellite operators make software tools available from their website (e.g. Intelsat's LST application) to carry out these calculations. There are a number of commercially available satellite link budget programs as well, some of which are mentioned in Appendix J.

Appendix C
Digital video

ITU-R BT.601

	25 Hz	30 Hz
Frame rate	25	30
Field rate	50	60
Line scanning rate	15 625	15 750
Lines per frame	625	525
Luminance samples per line	864	858
Chrominance samples per line	432	429

Luminance sampling frequency = line scan rate × luminance samples per line:

For 625/50 standard TV signals: 525/60 standard TV signals:
$$=15\,625\,000 \times 864$$ $$=15\,750\,000 \times 858$$
$$=13.5\,\text{MHz}$$ $$=13.5\,\text{MHz}$$

Chrominance sampling frequency = line scan rate × chrominance samples:

For 625/50 standard TV signals: For 525/60 standard TV signals:
$$= 15\,625\,000 \times 432$$ $$= 15\,750\,000 \times 429$$
$$= 6.75\,\text{MHz}$$ $$= 6.75\,\text{MHz}$$

Therefore, for both standards, the total (composite) sampling frequency
$$= 13.5 + 6.75 + 6.75 = 27\,\text{MHz}$$

Data rate is number of samples × sampling frequency:
8 bits $= 8 \times 27\,\text{MHz} = 216\,\text{Mbps}$
10 bits $= 10 \times 27\,\text{MHz} = 270\,\text{Mbps}$

Active video

Additionally, in both 525- and 625-line pictures, not all the lines contain 'active' picture information. Due to the use of interlace in TV, in 525/60 systems there are an average of 19½ lines per field (39 lines per frame) of primarily synchronization information for the television display (24½ lines per field, 49 lines per frame, in 625/50). These can be replaced in a digital system with a simpler timing signal. The number of active picture lines is therefore 486 lines in 525/60 and 576 in 625/50 systems, and for both systems, 720 samples per line for luminance and 360 samples per line for chrominance.

With 4:2:2, there are 8 luminance bits, and 8 bits for each chrominance sample which occurs at every other luminance sampling point in the horizontal plane, i.e. half the luminance sampling rate (but the same number of samples in the vertical plane); therefore the uncompressed bit-rates are:

$$\text{bit-rate} = Y^{\text{sample}} + C_b^{\text{sample}} + C_r^{\text{sample}}$$

For 525/60:

= (720 pixels × 480 pixels × 8 bits × 30 fps) + (720 pixels × 240 pixels × 8 bits × 30 fps) + (720 pixels × 240 pixels × 8 bits × 30 fps)

= **165.888 Mbps**

= (720 pixels × 486 pixels × 8 bits × 30 fps) + (720 pixels × 244 pixels × 8 bits × 30 fps) + (720 pixels × 244 pixels × 8 bits × 30 fps)

= **167.962 Mbps**

For 625/50:

= (720 pixels × 576 pixels × 8 bits × 25 fps) + (720 pixels × 288 pixels × 8 bits × 25 fps) + (720 pixels × 288 pixels × 8 bits × 25 fps)

= **165.888 Mbps**

For 4:2:0, there are 8 luminance bits, and 4 bits for each chrominance sample which occurs at every other luminance sampling point in the horizontal plane and in between each luminance sample in the vertical plane; therefore the uncompressed bit-rates are:

For 525/60:

= (720 pixels × 480 pixels × 8 bits × 30 fps) + (360 pixels × 240 pixels × 8 bits × 30 fps) + (360 pixels × 240 pixels × 8 bits × 30 fps)

= **124.416 Mbps**

For 625/50:

= (720 pixels × 576 pixels × 8 bits × 25 fps) + (360 pixels × 288 pixels × 8 bits × 25 fps) + (360 pixels × 288 pixels × 8 bits × 25 fps)

= **124.416 Mbps**

Appendix D

Spectrum analyzer operation and its use to locate satellites

Connection of the spectrum analyzer

As we have described previously, the feedhorn/OMT of the antenna is also connected to a satellite receiver, via the LNB (Low Noise Block downconverter), so that the uplink operator is able to view signals received from the satellite.

By connecting the spectrum analyzer into the system at the output of the LNB, pointing the antenna toward the satellite arc, and then making careful adjustments in elevation and azimuth the operator can find the desired satellite. In the following description, we are assuming Ku-band frequency and linear polarization.

Before we begin, it is important to note that great care must be taken to ensure that there is no DC voltage present on the cable connected to the input of the spectrum analyzer. Many models of spectrum analyzer will be damaged if a DC voltage is fed into the signal input.

Operation of the spectrum analyzer

For manual operation an SNG uplink, the use of a spectrum analyzer is vital in order to find and identify signals (or 'traffic') being transmitted by a satellite. Fundamentally, it is a radio receiver which can repeatedly and automatically tune across a selected band of frequency spectrum, displaying the amplitude (voltage) of signals present in that band on a visual display, thus providing a plot or trace of signal amplitude against frequency.

When a signal is fed into the analyzer and as the analyzer rapidly and repeatedly tunes (scans) across a specified frequency range, the display sweeps from left to right across the screen and individual signals are displayed as a voltage signal. Although there are spectrum analyzers available that can directly work at Ku- or C-band frequencies, it is common to use one that covers the L-band range (typically up to around 2–3 GHz). Therefore we will assume that the operator is setting up and using an L-band range spectrum analyzer (and was the type used in the figures).

Apart from display settings, there are three key settings to be made before being able to analyze a satellite signal:

1. Center frequency
2. Frequency Span
3. Reference amplitude

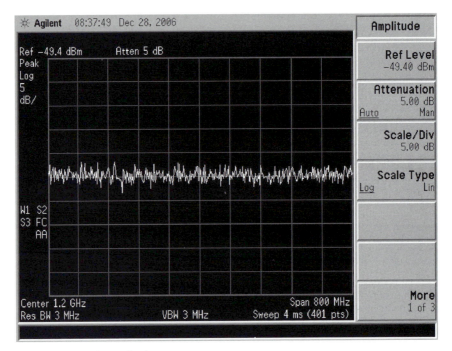

Figure D.1   Spectrum analyzer display

The display

The display has a 'graticule' which typically has 10 major horizontal and 10 major vertical divisions (Figure D.1). The horizontal axis of the analyzer is linearly calibrated in frequency, with the higher frequency at the right hand side of the display. The vertical axis is calibrated in amplitude. Although there is normally the possibility of selecting a linear or logarithmic scale, for locating and measuring satellite signals, the logarithmic scale should be selected. This is because it enables signals over a much wider range to be seen on the spectrum analyzer.

To start with, typically a value of 5 dB per division is used. This scale is normally calibrated in dBm (decibels relative to 1 mW) and therefore it is possible to see absolute power levels as well as comparing the difference in level between two signals. As the desired signals are found, the operator can choose to increase the displayed signal by changing the amplitude to 3 dB per division.

Setting frequency parameters

To set the frequency parameters of a spectrum analyzer, there are two selections that need to be made that are independent of each other. The first selection is the 'center frequency'. As the name suggests, this sets the frequency of the center of the scale to the chosen value. It is normally where the signal to be monitored would be found. In this way the principal signal and the area in frequency above and below can be monitored.

For the purposes of the description here, let us assume that the center frequency is set to 1300 MHz (1.3 GHz) – this frequency is often used as this will enable the operator to see most if not all of the LNB output frequency band, whether it is a low- or high-band LNB.

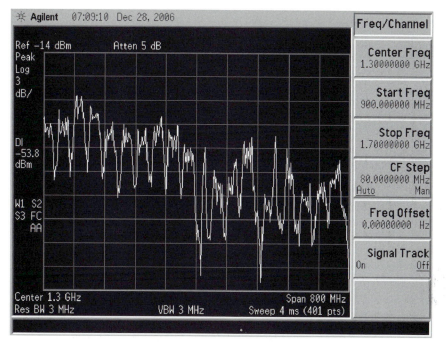

Figure D.2   View of DTH satellite channels received with frequency parameters set

The second selection that is made on the analyzer is the 'span', or the extent of the region either side of the center frequency that is to be viewed. Depending on the model, the span may be set as a given frequency per division, or as the total span that is seen on the calibrated part of the screen, i.e. within the maximum extent of the graticule. Another option that is typically available is to set the 'start' and 'stop' frequencies of the scan. This is another way of expressing the span, as the difference between the start and stop frequencies is equal to the span (if the span is set, then the start and stop frequencies are automatically set).

For our purposes, the span should be set to 800 MHz – the display will then display signals in the band 900 MHz at the lower end to 1700 MHz (1.7 GHz) at the upper end (Figure D.2).

Amplitude

The third important parameter to set is the amplitude, and in particular, the 'reference level'. This is the level at which the input signal is measured and displayed preferably on the center of the vertical axis of the display, and for satellite signals (depending on their strength) can range from -20 to -70 dB. This is directly related to both the size of the antenna (and hence it receives gain) and the gain of the LNB (typically 60 dB).

For our purposes, the reference amplitude level should be set to -30 dB to begin with.

Other controls

There are many other controls on a spectrum analyzer. Most of these fall into one of two categories. The first is associated with the gain or attenuation of sections within the spectrum analyzer. If sections are overloaded, then spurious signals may be generated within the instrument. The other controls concern the filter bandwidths within the instrument.

The spectrum analyzer operates by scanning across the set frequency span from the low to the high end of the required range. The speed at which it does this is important.

The faster it scans the range the faster the measurement can be made. However the rate of scan of the spectrum analyzer is limited by two other elements within the instrument. These elements are the filter that is used in the IF, and the video filter may also be used to average the reading. These filters must have time to respond otherwise signals will be missed and the measurements rendered useless.

Nevertheless it is still essential to keep the scan rate as high as is reasonably feasible to ensure that fast changing signals (such as might be seen as the antenna is moved) and measurements are made as quickly as possible. Often the filter scan rate and the filter bandwidths are linked to ensure the optimum combination is chosen.

Filter bandwidths

The other controls concern the filter bandwidths within the instrument. There are generally two types, namely the IF and video filters.

The IF filter basic provides the resolution of the spectrum analyzer in terms of the frequency. Choosing a narrow filter bandwidth will enable signals to be seen that are close together. However by the very fact that they are narrow band these filters do not respond to changes as quickly as wider band ones. Accordingly a slower scan rate must be chosen when using them.

The video filters enable a form of averaging to be applied to the signal. This has the effect of reducing the variations caused by noise and this can help average the signal and thereby reveal signals that may not otherwise be seen. Note however that using video filtering also limits the speed at which the spectrum analyzer can scan (Figure D.3).

When aligning an antenna, as fast a scan speed as possible is desirable, otherwise a satellite's signals might not be seen as the antenna is moved.

Understanding the LNB

An LNB consists fundamentally of two stages – a low noise amplifier and a block downconverter.

The LNB produces an L-band signal from the Ku- (or C-) band signal transmitted from the satellite, and this is accomplished by frequency shifting the transmit frequency down (after amplification) by using a 'local oscillator' within the device. The frequency of this local oscillator (LO) is an important parameter to know as it is used in setting the L-band spectrum analyzer to display the signal. It is a well-known phenomena in electronic engineering that by 'mixing' or 'heterodyning' two signals at different frequencies (the word *heterodyne* is derived from the Greek *hetero* meaning 'different' and *dyne* meaning 'power').

An electromagnetic carrier wave which is carrying a signal by means of amplitude modulation or frequency modulation can transfer that signal to a carrier of different frequency by 'heterodyning'. A heterodyne receiver 'beats' or heterodynes a frequency from a local oscillator (LO) within the block-downconverter with all the incoming signals.

This is accomplished by mixing the original modulated carrier with a pure sine wave of another frequency. The mixing of each two frequencies results in the creation of two new frequencies, one the sum

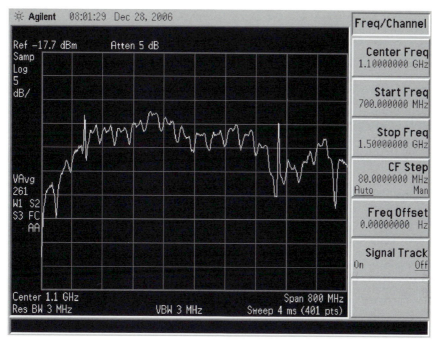

Figure D.3   Display of DTH satellite with video averaging applied

of the two frequencies mixed (creating a signal at much higher frequency), and the other the difference (creating a signal at much lower frequency). Either the higher or the lower (typically) can be chosen as the IF – in an LNB, the lower is used at the output.

Finding the satellite using the spectrum analyzer

The operator, having connected the spectrum analyzer, now adjusts the antenna's azimuth and elevation to the position to find the desired satellite. As this is done, and the antenna is panned across the satellite arc in the sky, the operator should see many satellite signals appear and disappear from the spectrum analyzer display. There are three ways to find and identify the desired satellite:

1. Find the satellite beacon
2. Identify a known program on the satellite using the spectrum analyzer and an IRD
3. The reference method

'Finding the beacon' method

Having pointed the antenna in the correct direction to find the desired satellite, as shown in Figure D.4, the spectrum analyzer can be set more precisely to find a particular signal. As we have discussed, some satellites also transmit a beacon signal. If a beacon signal is present, then it may be possible (but only with a

actually adjust the polarization so that the beacon signal is minimized or 'nulled out' on the spectrum analyzer display.

Noting this angle of polarization, and knowing the polarity of the beacon signal, the operator is then able to use this to reference the optimum polarization for transmission (as specified by the satellite operator). This will depend on the TX polarization referenced to the RX polarization of the beacon.

If the required TX polarization is opposite (i.e. 90° from the RX polarization), then nulling out the beacon is the same as the TX polarization, and therefore sets the TX polarization.

If the required TX polarization is the same as the beacon RX polarization, then nulling out the beacon is the same as 90° from the TX polarization, and adding or subtracting 90° to the polarization position will put the antenna at the correct polarization – or certainly close enough to be finally adjusted when line-up with the satellite operator is carried out.

'Identifying a known program' method

If there is no beacon signal transmitted, or the beacon signal is on both polarizations, then another method is to find a known TV program being transmitted from the satellite (this can be found referring to www.lyngsat.com). Figure D.6a shows a number of DTH multiplexes on the satellite as we found in Figure D.4, and in Figure D.6b the operator can zoom in to see a single whole multiplex, with a center frequency of 11.116 GHz (again the LNB LO is 10 GHz). Optimize the antenna for transmission by adjusting the azimuth and elevation, and adjusting the polarization to get the best signal strength on the IRD (which may be measured in level or C/N ratio).

Set the IRD to the same frequency, and once it has locked on to the signal, then select the known channel. If the known channel is found, then the operator is on the correct satellite. Optimize azimuth and elevation, and set the antenna for the correct TX polarization.

'Reference satellite' method

Thirdly, the operator can use the 'reference satellite' method. Find a DTH satellite (which transmits very strong signals), and then using a satellite table, calculate the differential in terms of azimuth and elevation to find the satellite required. For example, in Europe and the Middle East, the Hot Bird DTH satellites at 13° East (there are several co-located in the same orbital slot) are a very clear and easy to find 'marker'. The operator can then find the satellite required by calculating the differential figures from the DTH satellite and adjusting the antenna accordingly.

As an example, for a location in Paris shown on the satellite table, let us suppose the uplink operator needs to align the uplink for a transmission on Eutelsat Atlantic Bird 1 (AB1).

If the antenna is aligned to Hot Bird, Figure D.7 shows the typical plot on the spectrum analyzer display. Noting the actual azimuth and elevation readings of the antenna pointing at the 'reference' satellite, the operator can now re-align the antenna to AB1, and if all is well, will be able to find it relatively easily. As before, iterative adjustments to the azimuth, elevation and polarization will be required to correctly align the antenna.

No matter which method is used, finally, the operator should call the satellite operator's control center, and double check that the satellite signal carriers seen at various frequencies confirm with what the satellite is transmitting.

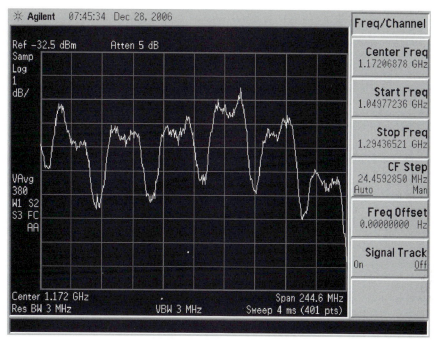

(a)

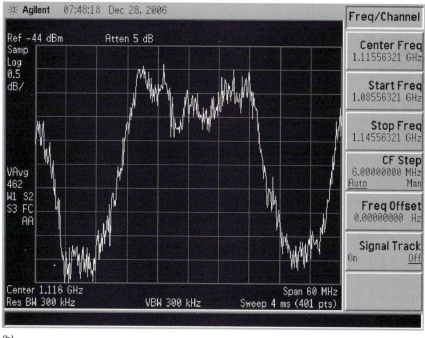

(b)

Figure D.6 (a) TV multiplexes (b) Desired DTH multiplex – 60MHz span with video averaging

Table D.1 Reference satellite method

	Satellite			
	Name	Longitudinal Position	Az (M)	Elevation
Desired	Atlantic Bird 1	12.5°W	194.6°	32.1°
Reference (DTH)	Hot Bird	13°E	166.9°	33.0°
Differential			27.7	0.9
Adjustment to find desired			Move antenna WEST by 28°	Move antenna DOWN by 1°

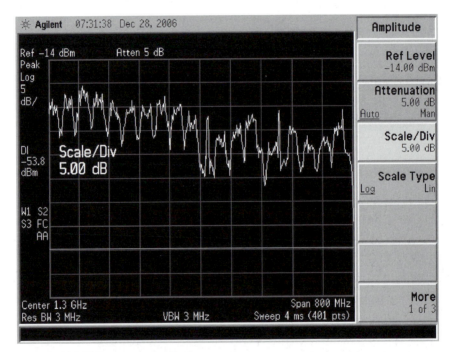

Figure D.7 Hot Bird 13° East spectrum display

Once the uplink is transmitting, and assuming the uplink is within the downlink of the satellite, a typical 8 Mbps QPSK signal will look as Figure D.8.

If the satellite cannot be found, then it may be for one or more of the following reasons:

- Mis-reading of the compass and/or inclinometer, and pointing in the wrong part of the sky
- Miscalculated its position if using the reference satellite method
- Spectrum analyzer incorrectly set up
- LNB is not the correct one for the band being checked
- LNB is faulty or not being supplied with a DC voltage
- Information being used is out-of-date

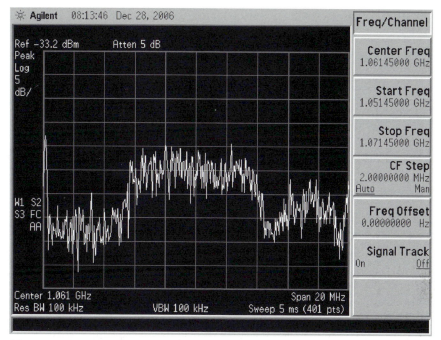

(a)

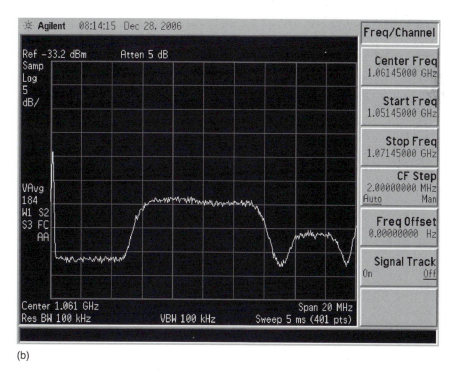

(b)

Figure D.8 (a) Typical 8 Mbps QPSK signal (b) Typical 8 Mbps QPSK signal with video averaging

So to summarize, to set up an uplink, the operator needs the following equipment in addition to the actual uplink transmission equipment:

- compass
- clinometer
- satellite position table
- spectrum analyzer
- satellite programme listings
- satellite receiver/IRD

LNB stability

We mentioned earlier that to use the 'beacon' method, the LNB had to be of a high-stability type. Domestic LNBs, and low-cost full band professional LNBs, use a local oscillator based on a DRO (Dielectric Resonant Oscillator) that have a frequency stability of 1–2 MHz, i.e. the amount the LO can drift up and down in frequency. This is perfectly acceptable for locking on to signals of at least 2–3 MHz in bandwidth, such as large SCPC signals and DTH multiplexes, but will not be able to resolve signals narrower in bandwidth than this.

Beacons are, as we have seen, of narrow bandwidth and low level, and to be able to resolve a signal to this degree requires an LNB which has a frequency stability of at least ±50 kHz, and more typically ±25 kHz. This type of LNB has a local oscillator based on a PLL (Phased Lock Loop) design and are inherently very stable.

Appendix E

ITU emission codes for the classification of transmissions

The ITU has formulated an internationally recognized code for electromagnetic emissions, which are frequently used on all types of applications for SNG transmissions, including when applying for a telecommunications licence or permission to operate. Transmissions are designated according to their bandwidth and signal classification.

The basic characteristics are as follows:

- First symbol: type of modulation of the main carrier
- Second symbol: nature of signal(s) modulating the main carrier
- Third symbol: type of information to be transmitted

The following two characters are optional:

- Fourth symbol: details of signal(s)
- Fifth symbol: nature of multiplexing

Necessary bandwidth

The full designation of a transmission and the necessary bandwidth, indicated in four characters, is added just before the classification symbols. The letter occupies the position of the decimal point and represents the unit of bandwidth.

- Between 0.001 and 999 Hz shall be expressed in Hz (letter H): 0.1 Hz = H100; 400 Hz = 400H
- Between 1.00 and 999 kHz shall be expressed in kHz (letter K): 6 kHz = 06K0; 12.5 kHz = 12K5
- Between 1.00 and 999 MHz shall be expressed in MHz (letter M): 8 MHz = 08M0; 30 MHz = 30M0
- Between 1.00 and 999 GHz shall be expressed in GHz (letter G): 5.95 GHz = 5G95; 14.25 GHz = 14G0

Format of code

Number	Number	Letter	Number	Modulation	Signal	Information	Details	Multiplexing
[	BANDWIDTH	]						

Examples

Digital SNG transmission with no comms carrier: 06M0G1WWN

- 06M0 describes the signal occupying a 6 MHz bandwidth
- G describes phase modulation (QPSK)
- 1 describes that the signal carries a single channel containing quantized or digital information without the use of a modulating sub-carrier
- W describes that the signal has a combination of video and sound components
- W describes that the signal is complex, with a combination of several elements
- N defines no multiplexing

Digital SNG transmission with comms carrier: 08M0G7WWN

- 08M0 describes the signal occupying an 8 MHz bandwidth
- G describes phase modulation (QPSK)
- 7 describes that the signal carries two or more channels containing digital information (this signal has a main program carrier and a comms carrier)
- W describes that the signal has a combination of video and sound components
- W describes that the signal is complex, with a combination of several elements
- N defines no multiplexing

First symbol: modulation of the main carrier

N   Unmodulated carrier
A   Amplitude-modulated – Double sideband
H   Amplitude-modulated – Single sideband, full carrier
R   Amplitude-modulated – Single sideband, reduced or variable level carrier
J   Amplitude-modulated – Single sideband, suppressed carrier
B   Amplitude-modulated – Independent sidebands
C   Amplitude-modulated – Vestigial sideband
F   Frequency modulation
G   Phase modulation
D   Transmission in which the main carrier is amplitude- and angle-modulated either simultaneously or in a pre-established sequence
P   Sequence of unmodulated pulses
K   Pulse amplitude modulation
L   Pulse modulated in width/duration
M   Pulse modulated in position/phase
Q   Pulse modulation in which the carrier is angle-modulated during the period of the pulse
V   Pulse modulation which is a combination of the foregoing or is produced by other means
W   Pulse modulation – combinations of amplitude, angle and pulse modulation
X   Cases not otherwise covered

Second symbol: nature of signal(s) modulating the main carrier

0   No modulating signal
1   A single channel containing quantized or digital information without the use of a modulating sub-carrier

2   A single channel containing quantized or digital information with the use of a modulating sub-carrier

3   A single channel containing analog information

7   Two or more channels containing quantized or digital information

8   Two or more channels containing analog information

9   Composite system with one or more channels containing quantized or digital information, together with one or more channels containing analog information

X   Cases not otherwise covered

Third symbol: type of information to be transmitted

N   No information transmitted

A   Telegraphy – for aural reception

B   Telegraphy – for automatic reception

C   Facsimile

D   Data transmission, telemetry, remote command

E   Telephony (including sound broadcasting)

F   Television (video)

W   Combination of the above

X   Cases not otherwise covered

Fourth symbol: details of signal(s)

A   Two-condition code with elements of differing numbers and/or durations

B   Two-condition code with elements of the same number and duration without error-correction

C   Two-condition code with elements of the same number and duration with error-correction

D   Four-condition code in which each condition represents a signal element (or one or more bits)

E   Multi-condition code in which each condition represents a signal element (of one or more bits)

F   Multi-condition code in which each condition or combination of conditions represents a character

G   Sound of broadcasting quality (monophonic)

H   Sound of broadcasting quality (stereophonic or quadraphonic)

J   Sound of commercial quality

K   Sound of commercial quality with the use of frequency inversion or band-splitting

L   Sound of commercial quality with separate frequency-modulated signals to control the level of demodulated signal

M   Monochrome

N   Color

W   Combination of the above

X   Cases not otherwise covered

Fifth symbol: nature of multiplexing

N   None

C   Code-division multiplex

F   Frequency-division multiplex

T   Time-division multiplex

W   Combination of frequency-division multiplex and time-division multiplex

X   Other types of multiplexing

For further information, see *ITU-R Radio Regulations*, Appendix S1 – Classification of emissions and necessary bandwidths.

Appendix F

Sample satellite booking form (occasional use capacity)

DATE: October 8, 2006   **FROM:**   News-TV, LONDON

CONTACT: S. Cole   **TEL:**   + 44 207 123 4004   **FAX:** + 44 207 123 4005

TO: Eutelsat Bookings, Paris

REQUEST ☑ **AMENDMENT** ☐ **CANCELLATION** ☐

OUR BOOKING REFERENCE: SNG 4789/99

A. **(Date)**   October 15, 2006

B. **(Times) Start:**   22:00   **End:**   22:15   **(UTC)**

C. **(Satellite):** W1 10 degrees East

D. **(Uplink Location):**   Baghdad, Iraq   **(Uplink Registration):**   UKI-3003

E. **(Uplink Contact Telephone):** + 44 7750 5544223

F. **(Downlink Location):**   London, UK

G. **(Transmission Parameters) Symbol Rate:** 5.632   **(Msps)**   **FEC Rate:**   3/4

H. **(Comments):**

Please send invoices to: Accounts Department, SNG-TV, PO Box 123, LONDON, UK

Appendix G

Universal Access Procedures

FDMA services

Definitions

FDMA = Frequency-Division Multiple Access – the mode of operation where several carriers with different frequencies are loaded onto a single transponder – differentiated from TDMA services which follow their own access procedures

ESO = Earth Station Operator

LOC = Space segment Lessee Operating or control Center (either a Broadcasting organization, a Union or Consortium or Broadcasters, a Telecom Operator or any other third party)

SOOC = Satellite Operator's management/Operations Center

TES = Transportable Earth Station (a fixed earth station that is not permanently dedicated to an orbital slot, should be treated the same way)

FES = Fixed Earth Station that is dedicated to an orbital slot (and most of the time with fixed settings for specific carriers).

Purpose

This document defines the procedures all ESO must follow in order to access satellites. This document also describes the criteria for obtaining line-up exemptions in specific cases.

Customer access requirements

All ESO who receive authorization (either directly from the satellite provider or through a third party LOC) to transmit to a satellite must contact the Satellite Operator's Operations Center (SOOC) of that satellite provider prior to access so that the initial uplink can be verified, monitored, and documented by an SOOC controller. However, before calling the SOOC, the ESO should always first call the LOC to verify authorization and check for schedule changes.

English is the universally accepted language. All uplink ESO should be able to communicate and follow instructions given to them in English. Other languages may be used at the discretion of the satellie operator but must be agreed upon with the LOC as a matter of principle.

Before the satellite access, the uplink operator must call the Ops Center in order to check the following:

- Exchange of earth station identification/registration code and phone numbers for emergency contacts; confirmation of expected transmission time (due to possible overruns of previous transmissions); satellite, transponder and uplink/downlink frequency slot allocations

During the satellite access, the SOOC controller must check the following:

- earth station registration code
- confirmation of correct transmission time (to be in line with the LOC check above)
- satellite, transponder and frequency slot allocations
- uplink polarization
- cross-polarization isolation
- carrier power level, signal quality, etc.

During the access procedure, the ESO will be required to:

- transmit signals of differing power levels (both modulated and unmodulated)
- peak the transmit antenna
- rotate/adjust the transmit antenna polarizers
- the ESO must call the SOOC with enough time to allow the controller to complete the entire access procedure, including cross-pol verification. Failure to do this may result in access delays

The ESO must also inform the SOOC before making any online equipment modifications in real time or before ending a transmission on occasional use capacities (i.e. a *goodnight*).

Copies of the *Uplink Operator's Checklist* and *Uplink Operator's Procedure* are attached to this policy document.

Access line-up verification exemption

The SOOC may grant access line-up verification exemption, by way of example:

- When one or several FES for full or part-time access to a satellite is used
- Between successive uplinks from a TES from the same site, for part-time access to a satellite, provided the TES had not been depointed (i.e. event lasting several days)

This exemption enables the LOC controller to manage third-party accesses without performing cross-pol measurements or adjustments.

Guidelines for exemptions and special authorizations

All exemptions and special authorizations are granted, and remain in effect, at the sole discretion of the SOOC. When an exemption or authorization is granted, the SOOC shall send written confirmation to the LOC confirming the exemption or authorization and detailing any specific conditions. A copy of all such confirmations shall be kept on file in the SOOC.

An exemption or authorization may be revoked at any time if interference or other problems occur that can be linked to an ESO antenna, service or space segment management. Although confirmed in writing, all revocations are effective as soon as the customer is notified by phone, fax, e-mail or other means. A copy of all revocation letters shall be kept on file in the SOOC.

Attachment 1: Uplink operator's checklist

1. **BEFORE** calling the satellite operator (SOOC), make sure the following table has been completed by cross-checking the space segment allocations with the LOC:

Contact Information:

Earth station registration code for operator concerned:

Your name: _____

The uplink company: _____

Uplink phone number: _____

Dedicated to technical conversations: _____

Your assigned satellite/transponder/slot: _____

Type of Call: □ Access □ Interference report □ Goodnight

Special Cases: □ New full-time service □ Cross-pol exempt antenna

Assigned Frequencies: Uplink: Downlink: Bandwidth:

Type of Ad Hoc Customer: □ Third-party resale □ Ad hoc

Access Information:

Actual Downlink EIRP: **Target Downlink EIRP:** **Transmit EIRP:**

Cross-pol isolation (Leave blank; use this space to record the controller's reading): _____

To

Scheduled access time (UTC): _____

UTC

Actual access time (Leave blank; use to record actual access time): _____

Signal Quality (Leave blank; use to record the controller's readings as applicable):

C/N: FEC: Symb/s: BER: CER:

---

2. When you are ready with this information, **BEFORE** calling the satellite provider, make sure your equipment is ready.
   - The transmitter is in standby mode at maximum attenuation. For earth stations performing multiple uplinks through a single uplink chain, please ensure that the modulator is at maximum attenuation.
   - All uplink equipment is warmed, stable and tuned to the correct frequency with proper sub-carriers, if applicable.
   - The antenna is properly pointed, optimized and set for the correct polarization. For optimum performance, antenna pointing should be performed during the center of box period for the spacecraft (this information can be provided by the SOOC/LOC).
   - The waveguide switches are configured properly.
   - ATIS is enabled (US domestic analog transmissions only).

3. Follow the Uplink Procedure (Attachment 2).

Attachment 2:   Uplink operator's procedure

1. Before making the call to the SOOC, use the Uplink Checklist (see Attachment 1) to check transmission equipment and to gather necessary information for the access, by cross-checking with the LOC about 10 minutes before the scheduled access time. If necessary, the LOC will then direct you to the SOOC as per 2 hereunder.
2. Contact the SOOC at least 5 minutes before the scheduled access time and provide the SOOC with the information you gathered on the Uplink Checklist (see Attachment 1).
3. When directed, provide the lowest possible power, unmodulated carrier. Tell the controller you have done this as you throw the switch.
   IMPORTANT: During the access procedure, **DO NOT** change power, frequency, polarization or antenna aiming without specific direction to do so from the SOOC controller, or the LOC by delegation. If you are instructed to cease transmission, you must comply **IMMEDIATELY** without discussion.
4. Wait for further instruction while the controller checks the cross-pol and frequency of the carrier.
5. At the direction and discretion of the SOOC, modulate and increase power to nominal levels, which will be confirmed by the SOOC. After power levels have been set, verify downlink.
6. Wait for further instructions while your transmission is checked.
7. The transmission should commence only when the SOOC has given confirmation that the carrier specifications are correct.
8. The controller will verify your phone number that should be available throughout the transmission/event in case a problem in relation with your uplink has to be solved. The controller will remind you to call the SOOC again just before the end of the transmission (goodnight call for occasional use space segments).
9. It is mandatory to contact the LOC for goodnighting in all circumstances.

Appendix H

Sample information typically required for a request for permission to operate in a foreign country

The amount of information required by a country can vary widely, and the list given below is likely to be the most that might have to be provided. Because of the sometimes sensitive nature of the issuing of permissions, if in doubt, it is probably best to provide as much information as possible. This should then reassure any authorizing entity that the applicant is not trying to subvert the government or in any way interfere in the politics of the country.

General details

- The reason for the importation of the uplink
- The dates when the equipment will enter the country and depart, and the ports of entry and departure
- Where the uplink will be operate: the town, city or region
- The types of transmissions; for example, to cover transmissions of news material of a named event
- *Named contacts in the country during operation: this is optional information*

Technical information

- The satellite system registration number of the uplink
- The satellite(s) to be used for transmissions
- The ITU emission code
- A description of the types of transmission: analog or digital
- The serial number of the uplink: as an uplink can be made up of a number of components, it is best to quote the serial numbers of the principal components, including the antenna and HPA
- The maximum EIRP of the uplink
- The international technical standard to which the uplink complies, e.g ITU-R S.465 (formerly CCIR Rec. 465)

Additional information

Sometimes the authorizing entity in the country of operation may require a letter from the satellite system operator confirming that the uplink will be permitted access to the space segment.

Request the contact and address to which any fees have to be paid. These may have to be paid in advance of the authorization being given to temporarily import the uplink, or at time of entry into the country.

Appendix I
Formulae for calculating non-ionizing radiation levels

Non-ionizing radiation is measured in a number of ways, but in practice for microwave equipment, the safety limits are often expressed as power density levels, in W/m^2 or mW/cm^2 as these can be easily measured.

The near-field region is the region in general proximity to an antenna in which the electric (E) and magnetic (H) fields do not have a substantially plane-wave character, but vary considerably from point to point. In other words, as the signals are not necessarily in phase at any single point, the sum of the signals do not add up in-phase.

The far-field region is that region of the field of an antenna where the angular field distribution is essentially independent of the distance from the antenna. In this region (the free space region), the field has a predominantly plane-wave character, i.e. a locally uniform distribution of E and H field strengths in planes transverse to the direction of propagation. The signals are essentially in-phase and therefore add up at any particular point.

Calculations can be made to predict power density levels around antennae. These equations have to a certain extent been developed empirically and are generally accurate in the far-field of an antenna but will over-predict power density in the near-field, where they could be used for making a 'worst-case' prediction. This is because the power density decreases inversely with the square of the distance ($1/D^2$).

$$S_{ff} = \frac{PG}{4\pi R^2} \tag{1}$$

where:
S_{ff} = far-field power density (W/m)
P = power input to the antenna (W)
G = antenna power gain (relative to an isotropic radiator)
R = distance from the surface of the antenna (m)

It should be noted that the antenna power gain G in Equation (1) is the numeric gain. Therefore, when the power gain is expressed in logarithmic terms (dB), the power figure in dB has to be converted:

$$G = 10^{dB/10} \tag{2}$$

For example, a typical SNG flyaway antenna, 1.9 m in diameter, has a logarithmic power gain of 45 dB, which is equal to a numeric gain of 31 623. If the antenna gain is not known, it can be calculated from the following equation (using actual or estimated value for aperture efficiency):

$$G = \frac{4\pi\eta A}{\lambda^2} \tag{3}$$

where:

η = aperture efficiency (typically 0.55–0.75)
G = antenna power gain (relative to an isotropic radiator)
λ = wavelength
A = antenna area

$$A = \pi r^2 \qquad (4)$$

where r = radius of antenna

In the near-field zone of the antenna, the power density reaches a maximum before it begins to decrease with distance. It can be calculated thus:

$$R_{nf} = \frac{D^2}{4\lambda} \qquad (5)$$

where:

R_{nf} = extent of near-field
D = antenna diameter (cm)
λ = wavelength (cm)

The maximum power density of the near-field antenna on-axis zone is:

$$S_{nf} = \frac{16\eta P}{\pi D^2} \qquad (6)$$

where:

S_{nf} = maximum near-field power density (W/m)
η = aperture efficiency (typically 0.55–0.75)
P = power input to the antenna (W)
D = antenna diameter (m)

In the far-field region, power is distributed in a series of maxima and minima as a function of the off-axis angle (defined by the antenna axis, the center of the antenna and the specific point of interest). For constant phase, or uniform illumination over the aperture, the main beam will be the location of the greatest of these maxima. The on-axis power densities calculated from the above formulae represent the maximum exposure levels that the system can produce. Off-axis power densities will be considerably less.

For off-axis calculations in the near-field it can be assumed that, if the point of interest is at least one 'antenna diameter' distance from the center of the main beam, the power density at that point would be at least a factor of 100 (20 dB) less than the value calculated for the equivalent distance in the main beam. For practical estimation of RF fields in the off-axis vicinity of aperture antennas, use of the antenna radiation pattern envelope can be useful.

Use of the gain obtained from the antenna radiation pattern envelope in simple far-field calculations will generally be adequate for estimating RF field levels in the surrounding environment, since the apparent aperture of the antenna is typically very small compared to its frontal area.

Appendix J
Useful contacts

The following is a directory of useful contacts. It is by no means an exhaustive list, but is intended as offering points from which the reader can further explore. The author infers no particular endorsement of any of the companies listed, and cannot be held in any way responsible for the quality of the services or products provided. All the companies and organizations listed have varying degrees of involvement in the SNG market. The information was correct at time of compilation (2007).

Satellite system operators

The following is a list of satellite system operators who cater for the SNG market:

Apstar
Asia Pacific Telecommunication Satellites Company Ltd., 22 Dai Kwai Street,
Tai Po Industrial Estate, Tai Po, New Territories, Hong Kong
Tel.: +852 26002100 Fax: +852 25220419/29181716
Website: www.apstar.com

Arabsat
Arabsat, PO Box 1038, Riyadh 11431, Saudi Arabia
Tel.: +966 1 4820000 Fax: +966 1 4887999
Website: www.arabsat.com

AsiaSat
Asia Satellite Telecommunications Company Ltd., 17/F, The Lee Gardens,
33 Hysan Avenue, Causeway Bay, Hong Kong
Tel.: +852 2500 0888 Fax: +852 2500 0895
Website: www.asiasat.com.hk

Eutelsat
Eutelsat S.A., 70 rue Balard, F-75502 Paris Cedex 15, France
Tel.: +33 1 5398 4747 Fax: +33 1 5398 3700
Website: www.eutelsat.com

Hellas Sat
Hellas Sat S.A. 99 Kifissias Avenue, Maroussi, GR-151 24, Athens, Greece
Tel.: +30 210 6100 600 Fax: +30 210 6111 545
Website: www.hellas-sat.net

Hispasat

Hispasat S.A., C/ Gobelas, Urbanizatión La Florida 41, Madrid ES-28023, Spain
Tel.: +34 91 710 2540 Fax: +34 91 307 6295
Website: www.hispasat.es

Inmarsat

Inmarsat Ltd, 99 City Road, London EC1Y 1AX, UK
Tel.: +44 20 7728 1000/1177 Fax: +44 20 7728 1044/1142
Website: www.inmarsat.com

Intelsat

Intelsat Ltd, 3400 International Drive, Washington, DC, 20008, USA
Tel.: +1 202 944 6800 Fax: +1 202 944 7898
Website: www.intelsat.com

Insat

Indian Space Research Organization, New BEL Road, Bangalore 560 094, India
Tel.: +91 80 341 5275 Fax: +91 80 341 2253
Website: www.isro.org

Loral Skynet

500 Hills Drive, PO Box 7018 Bedminster, NJ 07921, USA
Tel.: +1 908 470 2300 Fax: +1 301 258 3222
Website: www.loralskynet.com

JSAT

Japan Satellite Systems Inc., Toranomon 17 Mori Bldg. 5F, 1–26–5 Toranomon, Minato-ku, Tokyo 105-0001, Japan
Tel.: +81 3 5511 7777/8 Fax: +81 3 3597 0601
Website: www.jsat.net

Nahuelsat

Nahuelsat, Bouchard 680, 12th Floor, Buenos Aires, 1106, Argentina
Tel.: +54 11 5811 2600 Fax: +54 11 5811 2688
Website: www.nahuelsat.com.ar

Optus

Optus Satellite Marketing & Engineering Group, 495 Victoria Ave, Level 12, Chatswood, NSW 2067, Australia
Tel.: +61 2 9027 0085 Fax: +61 2 9027 0090
Website: www.optus.com.au

RSCC

Russian Satellite Communications12/5 str. 7, Kursovoy pereulok, Moscow RU-119034, Russia
Tel.: +7 495 7300 445 Fax: +7 495 7300 383
Website: www.rscc.ru

SatMex

SatMex Satelites Mexicanos, Blvd. M. Avila Camacho 40, Col. Lomas de Chapultepec, Mexico D.F., 11000, Mexico
Tel.: +52 (0)55 5201 0898 Fax: +52 (0)55 5201 0892
Website: www.satmex.com.mx

SES Americom

SES Americom, Four Research Way, Princeton, NJ 08540-6684 USA

Tel.: +1 609 987 4000 Fax: +1 609 987 4517

Website: www.ses-americom.com

SES New Skies

SES News Skies B.V, Rooseveltplantsoen 4, The Hague, The Netherlands NL-2517 KR

Tel.: +31 70 306 4100 Fax: +31 70 306 4101

Website: www.ses-newskies.com

Superbird

Space Communications Corp., 2–8, Higashi-shinagawa 2-chrome, Shinagawa-ku Tokyo 140-0002, Japan

Tel.: +81 3 5462 1350 Fax: +81 3 5462 0520

Website: www.superbird.co.jp

Telesat

Telesat Canada, 1601 Telesat Court, Gloucester K1B 5P4, Ontario, Canada

Tel.: +1 613 748 0123 Fax: +1 613 748 8712

Website: www.telesat.ca

Thor

Telenor Space Systems Division, Snaroyveien 30, M3B, Fornebu, N-1331, Norway

Tel.: +47 67 89 00 00 Fax: +47 67 89 36 55

Website: www.telenorsbc.com

Thaicom

Shin Satellite Public Company Ltd., 41/103 Rattanathibet Road, Nonthaburi 11000, Thailand

Tel.: +662 591 0736 Fax: +662 591 0705

Website: www.thaicom.net

Turksat

Turksat Satellite Communication and Cable TV Operation AS, Konya Yolu 40. Km., Golbasi, Turkey

Tel.: +90 312 615 3000 Fax: +90 312 499 5115

Website: www.turksat.com.tr

Standards organizations

CETECOM

CETECOM ICT Services GmbH, Untertuerkheimer Strasse 6-10, 66117 Saarbruecken, Germany

Tel.: +49 6 81 5 980 Fax: +49 6 81 5 98 90 75

Website: www.cetecom.com

ETSI

European Technical Standards Institute, 650 route des Lucioles, 06921 Sophia Antipolis Cedex, France

Tel.: +33 4 92 94 42 00 Fax: +33 4 93 65 47 16

Website: www.etsi.org

FCC – Office of Engineering and Technology
Federal Communications Commission, Office of Engineering and Technology,
445 12th Street SW, Washington, DC 20554, USA
Tel.: +1 202 418 2470 Fax: +1 202 418 1944
Website: www.fcc.gov/oet

US Government Regulations (including FCC documents)
Website: www.regulations.gov

IEEE
Institute of Electrical and Electronic Engineers, Inc., 445 Hoes Lane, Piscataway,
NJ 08854-4141, USA
Tel.: +1 732 981 0060 Fax: +1 732 981 1721
Website: www.ieee.org

ITU
International Telecommunications Union, Place des Nations,
Geneva 20, CH-1211, Switzerland
Tel.: +41 22 730 51 11 Fax: +41 22 733 7256
Website: www.itu.int

SMPTE
Society of Motion Picture and Television Engineers, 3 barker Avenue, White Plains,
NY 10601, USA
Tel.: +1 914 761 1100 Fax: +1 914 761 3115
Website: www.smpte.org

Safety: organizations

ICNIRP
International Commission for Non-Ionizing Radiation Protection Committee;
Scientific Secretary – G. Ziegelberger, ICNIRP c/o BfS, Ingolstaedter Landstr. 1,
85764 Oberschleissheim, Germany
Tel.: +49 1888 333 2156 Fax: +49 1888 333 2155
Website: www.icnirp.de

NRPB (Health Protection Agency – Radiation Division)
Health Protection Agency, Center for Radiation, Chemical and Environmental Hazards, Radiation
Protection Division, Chilton, Didcot, Oxfordshire, OX11 0RQ, UK
Tel.: +44 1235 831600 Fax: +44 1235 833891
Website: www.hpa.org.uk/radiation/

OSHA
US Department of Labor, Occupational Safety and Health Administration (OSHA), 200 Constitution
Avenue NW, Washington, DC 20210, USA
Website: www.osha.gov

Safety: equipment

Non-ionizing radiation protection meters

Narda

Narda Safety Test Solutions, 435 Moreland Road, Hauppauge, NY 11788, USA

Tel.: +1 631 231 1700 Fax: +1 631 231 1711

Website: www.narda-sts.com

SNG antenna manufacturers

Advent

Advent Communications Ltd., Nashleigh Hill, Chesham, Bucks HP5 3HE, UK

Tel.: +44 1494 774400 Fax: +44 1494 791127

Website: www.adventcomms.com

Andrew

Andrew Corporation, Worldwide Headquarters, 3 Westbrook Corporate Center, Suite 900, Westchester, IL 60154 USA

Tel.: +1 708 236 6600 Fax: +1 708 349 5444

Website: www.andrew.com

AvL

AvL Technologies, 130 Roberts Street, Asheville, NC 28810, USA

Tel.: +1 828 250 9950 Fax: +1 828 250 9938

Website: www.avltech.com

ERA

ERA Technology Ltd., Cleeve Road, Leatherhead, Surrey KT22 7SA, UK

Tel.: +44 1372 367000 Fax: +44 1372 367099

Website: www.era.co.uk

GigaSat

GigaSat Ltd., Tring Business Centre, Icknield Way, Tring, Hertfordshire, HP23 4JX, UK

Tel.: +44 1442 892000 Fax: +44 1442 892010

Website: www.gigasat.com

Holkirk

Holkirk Communications Ltd., Unit 17 Pulloxhill Business Park, Greenfield Road, Pulloxhill, Bedfordshire, MK45 5EU, UK

Tel.: +44 1525 721118 Fax: +44 1525 719734

Website: www.holkirk.com

IGP

IGP BV, Gooimeer 1c, 1411DC Naarden, The Netherlands

Tel.: +31 35 699 0 333 Fax: +31 35 699 0 345

Website: www.igp.net

ND SatCom

ND SatCom AG, Graf-von-Soden-Strasse, 88090 Immenstaad, Germany

Tel.: +49 7545 939 0 Fax: +49 7545 939 8780

Website: www.ndsatcom.com

Patriot

Patriot Antenna Systems Inc., 704 North Clark Street, Albion, MI 49224, USA
Tel.: +1 517 629 5990 Fax: +1 517 629 6690
Website: www.sepatriot.com

Sat-Comm

Sat-Comm Ltd., 15 Chiswick Avenue, Mildenhall, Suffolk, IP28 7PU, UK
Tel.: +44 1638 515000 Fax: +44 1638 515055
Website: www.sat-comm.com

SISLink

SISLink, Whitehall Avenue, Kingston, Milton Keynes, MK10 0AD, UK
Tel.: +44 1908 86 5500 Fax: +44 1908 86 5501
Website: www.sislink.tv

SWE-DISH

SWE-DISH Satellite Systems AB, Torggatan 15, 3rd floor, Solna, Sweden
Tel.: +46 8 728 50 00 Fax: +46 8 728 50 50
Website: www.swe-dish.com

Vertex

General Dynamics/Tripoint Global SATCOM Technologies, PO Box 850, 1500 Prodelin Drive, Newton, NC 28658, USA
Tel.: +1 828 464 4141 Fax: +1 828 464 4147
Website: www.tripointglobal.com

SNG systems manufacturers/SNG system integrators

Advent

Advent Communications Ltd., Nashleigh Hill, Chesham, Bucks HP5 3HE, UK
Tel.: +44 1494 774400 Fax: +44 1494 791127
Website: www.adventcomms.com

Bickford

Bickford Broadcast Vehicles, 4001 A Westfax Drive, Chantilly, VA 20151, USA
Tel.: +1 703 818 1008 Fax: +1 703 818 9090
Website: www.bickfordbroadcast.com

CommSystems

CommSystems Inc.,6440 Lusk Blvd., D-100, San Diego, CA 92121, USA
Tel.: +1 858 824 0056 Fax: +1 858 824 0057
Website: www.comm-systems.com

Dawson

Dawcom Ltd., Unit 1–2, Tything Park, Arden Forest Industrial Estate, Alcester, Warwicks B49 6ES, UK
Tel.: +44 1789 765 850 Fax: +44 1789 765 855
Website: www.dawson-dynamic.com

Eclips

Eclips nv., Mercelislaan 8, B-2275 Lille, Belgium
Tel.: +32 3 3117795 Fax: +32 3 3091053
Website: www.eclips.be

E-N-G

E-N-G Mobile Systems, 2245 Via De Mercados, Concord, CA 94520, USA
Tel.: +1 925 798 4060 Fax: +1 925 798 0152
Website: www.e-n-g.com

Extel

Extel Engineering, Paraná 275, 3° Of. 6 (C1017AAE) Buenos Aires, Argentina
Tel.: +54 11 4371 2371 Fax: +54 11 4371 3454
Website: www.extel.com

Frontline

Frontline Communications Corp., 12770 44th Street North, Clearwater, FL 33762, USA
Tel.: +1 727 573 0400 Fax: +1 727 571 3295
Website: www.frontlinecomm.com

Gerling

Gerling & Associates Inc., 138 Stelzer Court, Sunbury OH 43074, USA
Tel.: +1 740 965 2888 Fax: +1 740 965 2898
Website: www.gerlinggroup.com

GigaSat

GigaSat Limited, Tring Business Centre, Icknield Way, Tring, Hertfordshire, HP23 4JX, UK
Tel.: +44 1442 892000 Fax: +44 1442 892010
Website: www.gigasat.com

Holkirk

Holkirk Communications Ltd., Unit 17 Pulloxhill Business Park, Greenfield Road, Pulloxhill, Bedfordshire, MK45 5EU, UK
Tel.: +44 1525 721118 Fax: +44 1525 719734
Website: www.holkirk.com

IGP

IGP BV, Gooimeer 1c, 1411DC Naarden, The Netherlands
Tel.: +31 35 699 0 333 Fax: +31 35 699 0 345
Website: www.igp.net

Instec

Beijing Instec Video Tech Co. Ltd., Area C, Tower B, China International Science and Technology Convention Center, No. 12 Yumin Road, Chao Yang District, Beijing City 100029, China
Tel.: +86 10 82252961 Fax: +86 10 82252968

Megahertz

Megahertz Broadcast Systems Ltd., Unit 39 Lancaster Way Business Park, Witchford, Ely, CB6 3NW, UK
Tel.: +44 1353 645 000 Fax: +44 1353 658 919
Website: www.megahertz.co.uk

ND SatCom

ND SatCom AG, Graf-von-Soden-Strasse, 88090 Immenstaad, Germany
Tel.: +49 7545 939 0 Fax: +49 7545 939 8780
Website: www.ndsatcom.com

Norsat

Norsat International Inc., 110-4020 Viking Way, Richmond, British Columbia, Canada V6V 2N2
Tel.: +1 604 821 2800 Fax: +1 604 821 2801
Website: www.norsat.com

Sat-Comm

Sat-Comm Ltd., 15 Chiswick Avenue, Mildenhall, Suffolk, IP28 7PU, UK
Tel.: +44 1638 515000 Fax: +44 1638 515055
Website: www.sat-comm.com

Shook

Shook Mobile Technology, 7451 FM 3009, Schertz, Texas 78154, USA
Tel.: +1 210 651 5700 Fax: +1 210 651 5220
Website: www.shook-usa.com

SISLink

SISLink, Whitehall Avenue, Kingston, Milton Keynes, MK10 0AD, UK
Tel.: +44 1908 865500 Fax: +44 1908 865501
Website: www.sislink.tv

SWE-DISH

SWE-DISH Satellite Systems AB, Torggatan 15, 3rd floor, Solna, Sweden
Tel.: +46 8 728 50 00 Fax: +46 8 728 50 50
Website: www.swe-dish.com

TEC

Television Engineering Corporation, 2647 Rock Hill Industrial Court,
St. Louis, MO 63144, USA
Tel.: +1 314 961 2800 Fax: +1 314 961 2808
Website: www.tvengineering.com

Wolf Coach

L3 Communications Wolf Coach, 7 B Street, Auburn, MA 01501, USA
Tel.: +1 508 791 1950 Fax: +1 508 799 2384
Website: www.wolfcoach.com

SNG compression equipment manufacturers

Envivio

Envivio Inc., 400 Oyster Point Boulevard, Suite 325, South San Francisco,
CA 94080, USA
Tel.: +1 650 243 2700 Fax: +1 650 243 2750
Website: www.envivio.com

Harmonic

Harmonic Inc., 549 Baltic Way, Sunnyvale, CA 94089, USA
Tel.: +1 408 542 2500 Fax: +1 408 542 2511
Website: www.harmonic.com

Link Research

Link Research Ltd., Century House, 2 Century Court, Tolpits Lane, Watford, Hertfordshire,
WD18 9RS, UK
Tel.: +44 1923 474060 Fax: +44 1923 474093
Website: www.linkres.co.uk

Radyne

Radyne Inc., 3138 East Elwood Street, Phoenix, Arizona 85034, USA
Tel.: +1 602 437 9620 Fax: +1 602 437 4811
Website: www.radn.com

Tandberg

Tandberg Television Ltd., Strategic Park Comines Way, Hedge End,
Southampton, Hants S030 4DA, UK
Tel.: +44 2380 484000 Fax: +44 2380 484003
Website: www.tandbergtv.com

Scopus

Scopus Video Networks Ltd., 10 Ha'amal St., Park Afek Rosh Ha'ayin, 48092, Israel
Tel.: +972 3 900 7777 Fax: +972 3 900 7888
Website: www.scopus.net

Modulator/upconverter/downconverter manufacturers

Advent

Advent Communications Ltd., Nashleigh Hill, Chesham, Bucks HP5 3HE, UK
Tel.: +44 1494 774400 Fax: +44 1494 791127
Website: www.adventcomms.com

Comtech EF Data

Comtech EF Data Corp., 2114 West 7th St, Tempe, AZ 85281, USA
Tel.: +1 480 333 2200 Fax: +1 480 333 2540
Website: www.comtechefdata.com

Newtec

Newtec Productions N.V., Laarstraat 5, B9100 St-Niklaas, Belgium
Tel.: +32 3 780 6500 Fax: +32 3 780 6549
Website: www.newtec.be

Peak

Peak Communications Ltd., Kirklees House, 22 West Park Street,
Brighouse, West Yorkshire, HD6 1DU, UK
Tel.: +44 1484 714200 Fax: +44 1484 714229
Website: www.peakcom.co.uk

Rohde & Schwarz

Rohde & Schwarz GmbH & Co., KG, Muehldorfstrasse 15, 81671 Muenchen, Germany
Tel.: +49 89 4129 0 Fax: +49 89 4129 12164
Website: www.rohde-schwarz.com

Willtek

Willtek Communications GmbH, Gutenbergstr. 2-4, 85737 Ismaning, Germany
Tel.: +49 89 996 41 0 Fax: +49 89 996 41 160
Website: www.willtek.com

Inmarsat satphone manufacturers

Glocom

Glocom Inc., 20010 Century Blvd, Germantown, MD 20874, USA
Tel.: +1 301 916 2100 Fax: +1 301 916 9438
Website: www.glocom-us.com

Hughes

Hughes Network Systems LLC, 11717 Exploration Lane, Germantown, MD 20876, USA
Tel.: +1 301 428 5500 Fax: +1 301 428 1868
Website: www.hns.com

MTI

Mobile Telesystems Inc., 205 Perry Parkway, Suite 14, Gaithersburg, MD 20877, USA
Tel.: +1 301 963 5970 Fax: +1 301 963 4674
Website: www.mti-usa.com

Thrane & Thrane/Nera

Thrane & Thrane A/S, Lundtoftegardsvej 93D DK 2800 Kgs. Lyngby, Denmark
Tel.: +45 39 55 88 00 Fax: +45 39 55 88 88
Website: www.thrane.com

Wideye

Addvalue Technologies Ltd., 190 Changi Road, #02-02 Singapore 419974
Website: www.wideye.com.sg

Inmarsat and IP newsgathering application specialists

7E

7E Communications Ltd., Signal House, 127 Molesey Avenue, West Molesey, Surrey, KT8 2FF, UK
Tel.: +44 20 8487 3200 Fax: +44 20 8487 3210
Website: www.7e.com

Comrex

Comrex Corporation, 19 Pine Road, Devens, MA 01434, USA
Tel.: +1 978 784 1776 Fax: +1 978 784 1717
Website: www.comrex.com

Emblaze

Emblaze VCON., Beit Rakefet, 1 Emblaze Square, Industrial Area, Ra'anana 43662,
PO Box 2220, Israel
Tel: +972 9 762 7800 Fax: +972 9 762 7801
Website: www.vcon.com

Glensound

Glensound Electronics Ltd., 6 Brooks Place, Maidstone, Kent ME14 1HE, UK
Tel.: +44 1622 753662 Fax: +44 1622 762330
Website: www.glensound.co.uk

Livewire

Livewire Digital Ltd., Units 14 & 15, First Quarter, Blenheim Road, Epsom, Surrey KT19 9QN, UK
Tel.: +44 1372 731400 Fax: +44 1372 731420
Website: www.livewire.co.uk

QuickLink

Quicklink Video Distribution Services Ltd., Summerfield House, 9 Monks Hill,
Worlebury, Bristol, BS22 9RQ, UK
Tel.: +44 1934 440001
Website: www.quicklink.tv

Streambox

Streambox Inc., 1848 Westlake Avenue N, Seattle, WA 98109, USA
Tel.: +1 206 956 0544 Fax: +1 206 956 0570
Website: www.streambox.com

Miscellaneous products

Cabling systems

Belden

Belden Inc., 7701 Forsyth Boulevard, Suite 800, St. Louis, MO 63105, USA
Tel.: +1 314 854 8000 Fax: +1 314 854 8001
Website: www.belden.com
(Multi-core cable systems suited for ENG/SNG)

Camplex

Concept W Corp., 3302 West 6th Avenue, Suite C, Emporia, KS 66801, USA
Tel.: +1 620 342 7743 Fax: +1 620 342 7405
Website: www.camplex.com
(Video/audio multiplexers for cabling)

Telecast Fiber

Telecast Fiber Inc., 102 Grove Street, Worcester, MA 01605, USA
Tel.: +1 508 754 4858 Fax: +1 508 752 1520
Website: www.telecast-fiber.com
(ENG/SNG Fibre Optic Systems)

Flight cases

EDAK

EDAK AG, Rheinauerweg 17, Dachsen 8447, Switzerland
Tel.: +41 52 647 2111 Fax: +41 52 647 2230
Website: www.edak.com

Hardigg

Hardigg Industries Inc., 147 North Main Street, South Deerfield, MA 01373–0201, USA
Tel.: +1 413 665 2163 Fax: +1 413 665 4801
Website: www.hardigg.com

Zero

Zero Manufacturing Inc., 500 West 200 North, North Salt Lake, Utah 84054, USA
Tel.: +1 801 298 5900 Fax: +1 801 299 7389
Website: www.zerocases.com

Satellite link software

Satmaster Pro

Arrowe Technical Services, 58 Forest Road, Heswall, Wirral CH60 5SW, UK
Tel.: +44 151 342 4846 Fax: +44 151 342 5142
Website: www.arrowe.com
(Uplink pointing & link budget software)

AcuSat

Blue Ravine Software, PO Box 6477, Folsom, CA 95763–6477, USA
Website: www.acusat.com
(Uplink pointing calculation software)

SATfinder

Satnews Publishers, 800 Siesta Way, Sonoma, CA 95476, USA
Tel.: +1 707 939 9306 Fax: +1 707 939 9235
Website: www.satnews.com
(Satellite database and link budget software)

SNG Training Courses

SlingPath

BeaconSeek Ltd.
Tel.: +44 1582 842717 Fax: +44 1582 849013
Website: www.slingpath.com
(Online courses and practical training for SNG operations available all the year round)

BBC

BBC Training & Development, Wood Norton, Evesham, Worcs, WR11 4YB, UK
Tel.: +44 870 122 0216 Fax: +44 870 122 0145
Website: www.bbctraining.co.uk
(Courses run several times a year)

NAB

National Association of Broadcasters, 1771 N Street, NW Washington, DC 20036, USA
Tel.: +1 202 429 5300 Fax: +1 202 775 3520
Website: www.nab.org
(Course run once a year)

Trade exhibitions

The following trade shows feature SNG equipment.

NAB

National Association of Broadcasters Annual Convention & Exhibition, Las Vegas, USA
National Association of Broadcasters, 1771 N Street, NW Washington, DC 20036, USA
Tel.: +1 202 429 5300 Fax: +1 202 775 3520
Website: www.nab.org
(Held annually in April in Las Vegas, USA)

IBC

International Broadcasting Convention, RAI Centre, Amsterdam, The Netherlands
International Broadcasting Convention (IBC), Aldwych House, 81 Aldwych, London WC2B 4EL, UK
Tel.: +44 20 76117500 Fax: +44 20 76117530
Website: www.ibc.org
(Held annually in September in Amsterdam, The Netherlands)

CABSAT

Dubai International Convention and Exhibition Centre, Sheik Zayed Road, Convention Gate,
P.O. Box 9292, Dubai, UAE
Tel: +971 4 3321000 Fax: +971 4 3312173
Website: www.cabsat.com
(Held annually in Spring in Dubai)

BroadcastAsia

Singapore Exhibition Services, 47 Scotts Road, 11th Floor Goldbell Towers, Singapore 228 233
Tel: +65 6738 6776 Fax: +65 6732 6776
Website: www.broadcast-asia.com
(Held annually in June in Singapore)

Inter BEE

(Held annually in November in Japan)
Website: www.jesa.or.jp

Satellite <year>

Satellite Convention & Exhibition, Washington, DC, USA
Access Intelligence Satellite Group, 4 Choke Cherry Road, Second Floor, Rockville, MD 20850
Tel: +1 301 354 2000
Website: www.satellite <year>.com
(Held annually in Spring in Washington, DC, USA)

Information sources

Publishers – Print

Broadcast Engineering
Prism Business Media, 9800 Metcalf Avenue, Overland Park, KS 66212, USA
Website: www.broadcastengineering.com
(Publishers of Broadcast Engineering)

Inmarsat – see previous entry
(Publishes *Via Inmarsat* – specialist magazine on Inmarsat-related subjects)
Email: via.inmarsat@inmarsat.org

Access Intelligence Satellite Group
Access Intelligence Satellite Group, 4 Choke Cherry Road, 2nd Floor, Rockville,
MD 20850, USA
Website: www.satellitetoday.com
(Publishers of *Satellite News*, *Via Satellite*, *Satellite Industry Directory* and organizers of the Satellite
<year> trade show)

Publishers – Electronic

Line Of Sight
Website: www.beaconseek.com
(SNG newsletter published three times per year – free subscription)

Mobile Satellite Users Association (MSUA)
Website: www.msua.org
(Weekly electronic newsletter – free subscription)

Satnews Weekly
Website: www.satnews.com
(Weekly electronic newsletter – free subscription)

SpaceDaily Express
Website: www.spacedaily.com
(Daily digest of space and satellite news – free subscription)

The Satellite Encyclopedia
Website: www.tbs-satellite.com
(Publishers of satellite systems information on the web and by e-mail newsletter,
both on subscription)

Industry bodies

WBU-ISOG
WBU Inter-Union Satellite Operations Group
Website: www.nabanet.com/wbuarea/committees/isog.asp

SUIRG
Satellite Users Interference Reduction Group
Website: www.suirg.org

Useful websites

www.etsi.org – ETSI
www.itu.int – ITU
www.lyngsat.com – Lyngsat: listing of commercial satellite in orbit and programmes carried
www.regulations.gov – US Government Regulations (including FCC documents)
www.tvz.tv – Daily updates on deployments of SNG uplinks at news events

Glossary of terms

16-QAM Sixteen-state quadrature amplitude modulation.

16-APSK Sixteen-state amplitude/asymmetric phase shift keying.

29 – 25 log$_{10}$ Mathematical characteristic describing performance of an SNG uplink antenna to meet the 2° satellite spacing requirement.

2B+D Basic rate ISDN, with 2×64 kbps bearers and a 16 kbps data channel.

32-APSK Thirty-two-state amplitude and phase-shift keying or asymmetric phase-shift keying.

3G Third generation digital cellular mobile telephony system.

4:2:0 Describes a picture where the chrominance is sampled at half the rate relative to luminance, in both the horizontal and vertical planes.

4:2:2 Describes a picture where the chrominance is sampled at half the rate relative to luminance in the horizontal plane, but at the same rate as luminance in the vertical plane.

4:4:4 Describes a picture where the chrominance and luminance are sampled at the same rate in both the horizontal and vertical planes: effectively chrominance is given the same bandwidth as the luminance.

601 See ITU-R BT.601.

64-QAM Sixty-four-state quadrature amplitude modulation.

8-PSK Eight-phase-shift key modulation.

A Ampere (or amp): measurement of electrical current.

AAC Advanced Audio Coding.

ABC American Broadcasting Company: US network formed in 1945 from the Blue Network Company, which was originally NBC's Blue Network.

AC Alternating current: type of electrical current.

AC-3 See Dolby AC-3.

ACATS Advisory Committee on Advanced Television Service.

Access The general term for the ability of a telecommunications user to make use of a network.

Acceleration The process of an uplink station continuously transmitting TCP/IP data packets over a satellite link without waiting for the receiving station to send an acknowledgement, to minimize latency.

ACM Adaptive Coding and Modulation.

ACT-L3 Proprietary video/audio compression system developed by Streambox Inc. (US).

ACTS Advanced Communication Technologies and Services (EU project).

Ad-hoc capacity Capacity available for bookings on a temporary basis; see Occasional use; capacity.

ADC Analog-to-digital conversion: process of converting analog signals to a digital representation. DAC represents the reverse translation.

ADPCM Adaptive differential pulse code modulation.

Algorithm Refers to the computational code used to compress or decompress a signal.

AM Amplitude modulation.

Amplifier Device used to increase the power of an electronic signal.

Amplitude modulation Process where a baseband message signal modulates (alters) the amplitude and frequency of a high-frequency carrier signal, which is at a nominally fixed frequency, so that the carrier signal varies in amplitude.

Analog Signal which can take on a continuous range of values between a minimum and a maximum value; method of transmitting information by continuously variable quantities, as opposed to digital transmission, which is characterized by discrete 'bits' of information in numerical steps.

ANIK Canadian domestic satellite system.

ANSI American National Standards Institute (US).

Antenna Device for transmitting and receiving radio waves; in SNG, the directional parabolic antenna used for satellite transmissions.

AOR Atlantic Ocean Region: describes coverage area of a satellite.

APC Armoured Personnel Carrier.

Aperture Cross-sectional area of a parabolic antenna.

Apogee The point in a satellite's orbit when it is furthest away from the Earth.

A-pol INTELSAT circular polarization definition.

APSK Asymmetric Phase-Shift Keying; Amplitude and Phase-Shift Keying

APT Audio Processing Technology.

ARCEP Autorité de Régulation des Communications électroniques et des Postes.

ARPA Advanced Research Projects Agency.

Artifacts Imperfections in a digital signal caused by the compression process.

ASBU Arab States Broadcasting Union.

ASI Asynchronous serial interface; DVB compliant signal stream.

ASIC Application Specific Integrated Circuit.

ASP Advanced Simple Profile (MPEG-4).

ASPEC Adaptive Spectral Perceptual Entropy Coding.

AT&T American Telephone and Telegraph (US).

ATLANTIC Advanced Television at Low bit-rate And Networked Transmission over Integrated Communication systems (EU ACTS project).

ATM Asynchronous transfer mode: division of digital signals into small packets and transmitted in small-, fixed-size data 'cells'.

Atmospheric losses Losses caused by the travel of the signal through the atmosphere – encountered on both the uplink and the downlink.

ATRAC Adaptive Transform Acoustic Coding.

ATSC Advanced Television Systems Committee.

Attenuation Loss in power of electromagnetic signals between transmission and reception points.

Attitude control Orientation of the satellite in relationship to the Earth and the Sun.

ATV Advanced TV.

Audio sub-carrier An extra carrier typically between 5 and 8 MHz carrying audio information on top of a video carrier.

Automatic frequency control AFC: circuit which automatically controls the frequency of a signal.

Automatic gain control AGC: circuit which automatically controls the gain of an amplifier so that the output signal level is virtually constant for varying input signal levels.

Availability The percentage of time over a year that a satellite link will be received successfully. Not particularly applicable to SNG uplinks.

AVC Advanced Video Coding – part of MPEG-4 standard.

AVI Audio–Visual Interleave; multimedia file format.

Azimuth Angle of rotation (horizontal) that a parabolic antenna must be rotated through to point to a specific satellite in a geosynchronous orbit; the compass bearing of the satellite in the horizontal plane from a point on the Earth's surface.

Backhaul Contribution circuit: traditionally a terrestrial communications path linking an earth station to a local switching network; now also refers to satellite contribution paths.

Back-off Process of reducing the input and output power levels of a traveling wave tube to obtain more linear operation and hence minimize the risk of distortion. Expressed in dB.

Bandpass filter Active or passive circuit which allows signals within the desired frequency band to pass but prevents signals outside this pass band from getting through.

Bandwidth Measure of spectrum (frequency) use or capacity; the amount of information that can be passed at a given time over a certain span of frequency.

BAP Binary Alpha Plane (MPEG-4).

Baseband Basic direct output signal obtained directly from a camera or videotape recorder or other video source.

Basic rate ISDN ISDN service of 2×64 kbps bearers and a 16 kbps data control channel. Also referred to as 2B+D.

Baud Rate of data transmission based on the number of symbols transmitted per second; see Symbol.

BBC British Broadcasting Corporation: UK network formed in 1927 from the British Broadcasting Company established in 1922.

Beacon Low-power carrier transmitted by a satellite which provides the satellite operations control center on the ground with a means of monitoring telemetry data and tracking the satellite.

Beam Signal from uplink or satellite.

Beamwidth Angle or conical shape of the beam the antenna projects.

Bearer Generic term for a carrier signal.

BER Bit error rate: a measurement of the quality of a data link.

B-frame Bidirectional compressed frame, encoded as a combination of forward and backward motion prediction information. B-frame can only be encoded after processing the requisite previous and future frames. It can be considered as the average of two P-frames – one that has already been encoded and sent (i.e. in the past) and one that has been encoded but not yet sent (i.e. in the future) – used as predictors for the current input frame to be processed.

BGAN Broadband Global Area Network (Inmarsat).

BIFS Binary Information for Scenes (MPEG-4).

Binary See Digital.

BIR Burst Information Rate.

Bird Colloquial term for satellite.

BISS Basic Interoperable Scrambling System (EBU standard).

BISS-E Basic Interoperable Scrambling System – Encrypted (EBU standard).

Bit Single digital unit of information.

Bit error rate See BER: the fraction of a sequence of message bits that are in error. A bit error rate of 10^{-6} means that there is an average of one error per million bits.

Bit-rate Speed of a digital transmission, measured in bits per second.

Bit-stream Continuous stream of data bits transmitted over a communication channel with no separators between the character group.

Block A group of pixels in a compression process.

Block-downconverter Device used to convert the C- or Ku-band signal down to L-band.

Blockiness Picture degradation where the macroblocks are seen.

Bonding Method of combining a number (*n*) of discrete data channels of data bandwidth *d* to provide the user with a single combined data channel of $n \times d$.

Boresight Main focus of an antenna; the direction of maximum gain of an antenna.

Box Area in which the satellite has to be maintained while in station-kept geostationary orbit; see Station-kept box.

B-pol INTELSAT circular polarization definition.

bps Bits per second.

BPSK Binary phase-shift key: modulation technique.

BRI Basic rate ISDN; Basic Rate Interface (for ISDN).

Broadband Referring to a bandwidth greater than the baseband signal; a single path that has multiple independent carriers multiplexed onto it; a large-bandwidth digital 'pipe'.

Broadbeam See Widebeam.

BSS Broadcast-Satellite Service: ITU service designation.

BUC Block upconverter.

Buffer Digital memory store on the input and output of a compression device.

BW Bandwidth.

Byte Block of 8 bits.

BZT Bundesamt für Zulassungen in der Telekommunikation: former German national standards body, now privatized as CETECOM GmbH.

C/N See Carrier-to-noise ratio.

CA Conditional Access (MPEG-2).

CABAC Context Adaptive Binary Arithmetic Coding (MPEG-4).

Cable television System which receives transmissions from program sources and distributes them to users (usually homes) via fiber-optic or cable, usually for a fee.

Capacity Satellite bandwidth or channel.

Carnet Customs document used for international transportation of goods.

Carrier; carrier frequency Continuous (usually high-frequency) electromagnetic wave which can be modulated by a baseband signal to carry information; main frequency on which a voice, data or video signal is sent.

Carrier-to-noise ratio C/N: the ratio of the received carrier power and the noise power in a given bandwidth, expressed in dB.

CASBAA Cable and Satellite Broadcasters Association of Asia.

Cascading Concatenating connection of devices.

CAVLC Context Adaptive Variable Length Coding (MPEG-4).

C-band Frequencies in the 4–6 GHz range, used both for terrestrial microwave links and satellite links.

CBR Constant Bit Rate.

CBS Columbia Broadcasting System: US network formed in 1928 by William Paley from the struggling United Independent Broadcasters company.

CCIF ITU International Telephone Consultative Committee – Consultatif International des Fils a Grande Distance.

CCIR ITU International Radio Consultative Committee – Comité Consultatif International des Communications Radio á Grande Distance.

CCIR-601 Recommendation developed by the CCIR for the digitization of color video signals; now ITU-R BT.601.

CCITT ITU International Telegraph Consultative Committee – Comité Consultatif International des Communications Telegraphes á Grande Distance; part of the ITU established in 1956 when the CCIF and the CCIT merged.

CDL Commercial driver's license (US).

CDMA Code division multiple access: refers to a multiple-access scheme where the transmission process uses spread-spectrum modulations and orthogonal codes to avoid the signals interfering with one another.

CENELEC Comite Europeen de Normalisation Electrotechnique (European Committee for Electrotechnical Standardisation).

Center frequency Frequency of the center of a channel on a satellite transponder.

CEPT Conference Europeane des Administrations des Postes et des Telecommunications.

CES Coast earth station: historical alternative term for LES in Inmarsat system.

CETECOM CETECOM GmbH: successor to BZT; privatized German telecommunications standards entity.

CFR Code of Federal Regulations (US).

CGI Computer Generated Imagery.

Chain Transmission path; usually in an SNG uplink referring to the equipment that makes up the transmission channel.

Channel Specific frequency range in which a signal is transmitted in a satellite transponder.

Check-bits Data bits added for error detection.

Checksum Way of detecting errors by adding up all the bytes in the packet and transmitting the summed result within the packet.

Chip-set Set of integrated circuit devices which form the heart of a compression encoder.

Chrominance Color signal.

CIF Common intermediate format: developed so that computerized video images could be shared from one computer to another. An image that is digitized to CIF format has a resolution of 352×288 or 352×240, which is essentially one-half of CCIR-601.

CIR Committed Information Rate.

Circular polarization Geometric plane in which the electromagnetic signals are transmitted. Circular polarization can be either clockwise (left-hand circular polarization, or LHCP) or counterclockwise (right-hand circular polarization, or RHCP).

Clarke Belt; Clarke Orbit Geostationary orbit; named in honor of Arthur C. Clarke.

Clean carrier Unmodulated carrier signal.

Cleanfeed Studio audio output transmitted to the remote site so that the reporter is able to conduct a two-way dialog with the studio presenter. Also called IFB, mix-minus, return sound or return audio.

Cliff-edge effect Describes the fact that digital signals suffer from achieving either perfect results or nothing: as a digital signal passes a particular threshold, the signal fails catastrophically with no warning.

Clock Term for electronic timing signal or circuit.

CMV Commercial Motor Vehicle (US).

CMC Carrier Management Center: master control operation for Intelsat.

CNN Cable News Network: US network.

Coax Coaxial cable, used for carrying signals at frequencies from video baseband up to IF.

Codec COder/DECoder: a device which converts an analog signal into or from a digital signal.

Codeword Descriptor of a block of data.

Coding delay See Latency.

Coding order Order in which a group of pictures is coded in a digital compression process.

Coefficient Mathematical term for a number with a particular algebraic significance.

Co-located Where a number of satellites share the same geostationary orbital assignment.

Color difference Signals representing the difference in brightness between the luminance and the relative color signal.

Color sub-carrier Sub-carrier that is added to the main video signal to convey the color information.

Common carrier Regulated telecommunications company which will carry signals for a fee; common carriers include telephone companies as well as owners of communications satellites.

Companding COMpressing/exPANDING: a noise-reduction technique that applies compression at the transmitter and complementary expansion at the receiver.

Component video Video presented as three separate signals: luminance (Y) and two color difference signals (Cb and Cr), with line and field timing synchronization pulses.

Composite video TV signal with multiplexed luminance and chrominance signals with line and field timing synchronization pulses.

Compression Process of removing redundant data to minimize the use of bandwidth, ideally without visibly or audibly degrading the program.

COMSAT Communications Satellite Corporation, original US Signatory to INTELSAT.

CONUS CONtiguous US: description of arrangement of satellite coverage beams to cover the whole of the US except Hawaii and Alaska.

Convolutional code Type of error correction code used in digital coding.

CoP; CoP 3 Codes of Practice (Pro MPEG Forum); Code of Practice 3 (Pro MPEG Forum).

COTS Commercial Off The Shelf; referring to technology that is freely available in the commercial market, and is not bespoke.

CPC Central product classification (UN).

Cross-modulation Form of signal distortion in which modulation from one or more RF carrier(s) is imposed on another carrier.

Cross-polar discrimination XPD: measurement of immunity from interference from signals on the opposite polarization; describes the ratio of (wanted) signals on the desired polarization compared to the (unwanted) signals on the opposite polarization.

Cross-polar interference XPI: interference from signals in the same transponder (IPs) or adjacent transponders, and signals at similar frequencies but on the opposite polarization – related to XPD.

Cross-strapping Process on-board a satellite where an uplinked signal in one frequency band is converted to a different frequency band for the downlink, e.g. C-band uplink to Ku-band downlink.

Cross-talk Unwanted leakage of signal from one channel to another.

CRT Cathode Ray Tube.

CSA Common Scrambling Algorithm (DVB).

CSC Center for Satellite Control, Eutelsat, Paris.

CSM Communication System Monitoring – used by satellite operators to monitor satellite traffic.

CTR Common Technical Regulation (EU).

CTR-030 EU standard defining operation of SNG systems in Europe; formerly TBR-030 and ETS 300 327.

CTU Central telemetry unit: central satellite on-board system, feeding back confirmation signals confirming that ground control instructions have been acted on.

CW Control Word – used in BISS.

D1 Generic but incorrect reference to full resolution digital video – see ITU-R BT.601.

DAB Digital audio broadcasting.

DAMA Demand-assigned multiple access: highly efficient means of instantaneously assigning channels in a transponder according to immediate traffic demands.

Data communication Transfer of digital data by electronic or electrical means.

dB Decibel: logarithmic unit of measurement of electronic signals.

dBA Measure of sound pressure level.

Encryption Process of encoding or scrambling television signals so that unintended audiences are unable to view the signal.

Energy dispersal ED: in digital systems, pseudo-random signal added to reduce energy peaks.

ENG Electronic NewsGathering.

Entropy The random or unpredictable information content of a signal: 'unpredictability'.

Entropy coding Process where values are looked up in a fixed table of 'variable length codes', where the most probable (frequent) occurrence of coefficient values is given a relatively short 'code word' and the least probable (infrequent) occurrence is given a relatively long one.

EOL End of life – of a satellite.

Ephemeris data Data regularly published by satellite operators describing cyclical influences of gravity from the Sun and the Moon, as well as solar radiation. These all affect the positioning of the satellite.

ERC European Radiocommunications Committee: governed by the CEPT. Administers spectrum for Europe.

ERO European Radiocommunications Office: agency of the ERC. A planning agency for pan-European frequency management.

Error correction Process where bits are added in the modulation of a digital signal to correct for errors in transmission.

ESA European Space Agency.

ESOG EUTELSAT System Operations Guide.

ESW Encrypted Session Word (BISS).

ETS European telecommunication standard (ETSI).

ETS 300 327 European technical standard for SNG, now superseded; see CTR-030.

ETSI European Technical Standards Institute: established in 1988 on the joint initiative of the EU and the CEPT to produce technical standards for telecommunications across the EU.

Eureka International consortium of broadcasters, network operators, consumer electronic industries and research institutes that developed digital audio standards; included the Eureka 147 project which devised MUSICAM.

Eurobeam European widebeam.

EUTELSAT European Telecommunications Satellite Organization – now a privatized company.

Exciter Generic term for the combination of a modulator and upconverter, which provides the drive signal to the input of an HPA.

Fade margin The difference between the calculated or actual performance of a link and the threshold of operation; see Threshold margin.

Far-field Zone of non-ionizing radiation.

FCC Federal Communications Commission (US): national telecommunications regulatory body.

FCIF Full CIF – see CIF.

FDMA Frequency division multiple access: refers to the use of multiple carriers within the same transponder where each uplink has been assigned a frequency slot and bandwidth, usually employed in conjunction with frequency modulation.

FEC Forward error correction: data correction signal added at the uplink to enhance concealment of errors that occur on the passage of the signal via the satellite to the downlink.

Feed Generic term for the feedhorn, or the feedhorn and the antenna; a generic term for a transmission.

Feeder link Backbone Earth–satellite links in contribution and distribution networks.

Feedhorn In SNG, the assembly on the end of the arm extending out from the antenna from which signals are transmitted into the focus of the antenna.

FET Field-Effect Transistor – semiconductor device commonly used in Solid-State Power Amplifiers.

Fiber-optic Transmission process using mono-frequency sources of light modulated with a signal or group of signals transmitted through a glass fiber.

Field Partial scan of a frame; there are two fields in a single TV frame.

Figure of merit G/T: a measure of the performance of a downlink station expressed in units of dB/K, depending on the receive antenna and low-noise amplifier combination G (in dBi), and the amount of receiving system noise T expressed as a temperature in Kelvin (K). The higher the G/T number, the better the system.

Figure-of-eight orbit See Inclined orbit.

Firewall Hardware and/or software which prevents communications under a security policy in an IP network.

Firewire IEEE 1394: data transfer standard for consumer and semi-professional audio–visual devices.

Flange power The output power of the HPA delivered to the output port for delivery to the uplink antenna.

Flight-case Electronics transit case built for ruggedness, typically made from aluminum alloy or polypropylene, with internal shockproofing, to withstand the rigors of shipping by air.

Flux-gate compass Electronic compass.

Flyaway Transportable earth station used for SNG which can be broken down and transported in cases to location.

FM Frequency modulation.

Focal point Area toward which the antenna reflector directs a signal for transmission, or where the signal is concentrated for reception.

Footprint Arrangement of satellite coverage beams to cover a particular area; a map of the signal strength of a satellite transponder showing the EIRP contours of equal signal strengths as they cover the Earth's surface.

Forward error correction FEC: inner convolutional coding that adds unique codes to the digital signal at the source so errors can be detected and corrected at the destination.

fps Frames per second.

Frame A single TV picture is referred to as a 'frame' and there are two 'fields' in every frame.

Frequency The number of times that an electromagnetic wave goes through a complete cycle in 1 second. One cycle per second is referred to as 1 Hertz (Hz) and is the basic measurement of frequency.

Frequency band Specific span of electromagnetic spectrum.

Frequency co-ordination Process to analyze and eliminate frequency interference between different satellite systems or between terrestrial microwave systems and satellites.

Frequency modulation Process whereby a carrier signal is shifted up and down in frequency ('deviates') from its 'at rest' (center) frequency in direct relationship to the amplitude of the baseband signal.

FRExt Fidelity Rate Extensions (MPEG-4).

FRR First right of refusal: method of reserving satellite capacity before that capacity is available.

FSA; FSL Free space attenuation; free space loss: the ionospheric and atmospheric attenuation of the signal.

FSS Fixed-Satellite Service: ITU designation.

FTA Free to Air.

FTP File Transfer Protocol (Internet).

FTTH Fiber to the Home.

G.711 ITU-T specification for audio data coding using 64 kbps of bandwidth to provide 3 kHz telephone quality audio.

G.722 ITU-T specification for audio data coding using 64 kbps of bandwidth to provide 7.5 kHz audio over a 64 kbps circuit.

G.728 ITU-T specification for audio data coding using 16 kbps of bandwidth to provide 3 kHz audio of bandwidth.

G/T See Figure of merit.

Gain Measure of amplification expressed in dB.

Gain step The gain setting of a transponder, which can be varied in discrete steps from the TT&C ground station according to operational requirements.

Galactic noise Thermal noise (interference) from space.

GAN Global Area Network (Inmarsat) – alternatively called M4.

GATS General Agreement on Trade and Services (UN).

GATT General Agreement on Tariffs and Trade (UN).

GB Gigabyte: equivalent to one thousand million (1×10^9) bytes of information, measure of capacity.

Gb Gigabit: equivalent to one thousand million (1×10^9) bits of information, measure of speed.

GBT Group on Basic Telecoms (WTO).

GEO Geostationary Earth Orbit.

Geostationary Earth Orbit GEO: describes a special geosynchronous orbit which is symmetrical above the Equator such that the satellite appears to remain stationary relative to a location on the surface of the Earth.

Geosynchronous orbit Describes a circular orbit around the Earth, with an average distance from the center of the Earth of about 42 000 km (26 000 miles) in which the satellite orbit has a period equal to the rotation period of the Earth.

Get-away The path toward the desired satellite from the uplink or downlink to obtain a clear look angle.

GFI; GFCI Ground fault interrupt; ground fault circuit interrupter.

GHz Gigahertz: unit of frequency equal to one thousand million cycles per second, or 1×10^9 Hz (1 000 000 000 Hz).

Glitch Imperfections in a digital signal.

Global beam C-band satellite antenna pattern which effectively covers one-third of the globe, typically aimed at the center of the Atlantic, Pacific and Indian Oceans.

GMDSS Global Maritime Distress and Safety System: operated by Inmarsat as a life-saving service.

GMPCS Global Mobile Personal Communication by Satellite (ITU).

GMT Greenwich Mean Time: same as UTC.

Good-night Verbal confirmation between uplink and satellite control center at the end of a transmission.

GOP Group of pictures.

GOV Group of video object planes.

GPRS General packet radio services: wireless packet-data service; part of the third generation of digital cellular telephony (3G).

GPS Global Positioning System: satellite-based navigation system.

GR Guaranteed reservation: where a reservation will be accepted up to 1 year in advance on currently operational satellite capacity, and up to 3 years in advance for planned satellite capacity (INTELSAT).

Graveyard orbit Satellite orbital position at which at the end of operational life, satellites are recommended to be finally placed (245–435 km beyond the geostationary arc), thus this space junk can then be monitored to reduce the risk of debris damaging any active spacecraft.

Ground station Generic term for satellite communications earth station.

Group of pictures (GOP) Digital picture compression sequence that contains a combination of I-, B- and P-frames.

GSM Global System for Mobile Communications: digital cellular telephony standard.

GTO Geostationary transfer orbit: see Transfer orbit.

Guard-band; guard-channel Separation of signals in a transponder to minimize the risk of interference with each other.

GUI Graphical User Interface.

GVW Gross Vehicle Weight.

H.221 Framing protocol used as part of H.320 (ITU-T standard).

H.230 Control and indication protocol used as part of H.320 (ITU-T standard).

H.242 Communications procedure protocol used as part of H.320 (ITU-T standard).

H.261 Audio compression algorithm standard (ITU-T standard).

H.262 MPEG-2 (ITU-T standard).

H.263+ Further refinement of H.320 to improve performance (ITU-T standard).

H.264 MPEG-4 Advanced Video Coding (AVC).

H.320 Specification for video-conferencing over ISDN (ITU-T standard).

Half-transponder Method of transmitting two TV signals within a single satellite transponder through the reduction of each TV signal's deviation and power level.

HD; HDTV High Definition Television: television system with approximately twice the horizontal and twice the vertical resolution of current 525-line and 625-line systems, with component color coding, picture aspect ratio of 16:9 and a frame rate of at least 24 Hz.

HD-MAC High Definition Multiplexed Analog Components – obsolete European analog HDTV standard.

HD High Definition video.

Headend Control center located at the antenna site of a cable television system, for processing of received signals for transmission to the cable system subscribers.

Hemi-beam C-band beam that typically covers a continent, or straddles parts of two continents to provide intercontinental connectivity.

Hertz Hz: term for the basic measure of an electromagnetic wave completing a full oscillation from its positive to its negative pole and back again in what is known as a cycle; thus 1 Hz is equal to one cycle per second.

HGV Heavy goods vehicle (UK).

Hop A single Earth–satellite–Earth path.

Horizontal blanking interval Contains the horizontal timing and synchronization information for the television display.

Horn See Feedhorn.

Hot-spot Burn points on a waveguide or feed assembly.

HPA High-power amplifier; Health Protection Agency (UK).

HSCSD High-speed circuit switched data: digital cellular data standard.

HSD High-speed data.

HSE Health and Safety Executive: UK safety agency.

HT High tension: refers to voltages over a thousand volts, often found in HPAs.

HTML Hyper Text Markup Language (Internet).

HTTP Hyper Text Transfer Protocol (Internet).

Humvee HMMWV: High Mobility Multi-Purpose Wheeled Vehicle.

Hz Unit of frequency, where 1 Hz describes one cycle per second; 1 kHz = 1000 Hz (1×10^3 Hz); 1 MHz = 1 000 000 Hz (1×10^6 Hz); 1 GHz = 1 000 000 000 Hz (1×10^9 Hz).

IAEA International Atomic Energy Agency.

IANA Internet Assigned Numbers Authority (Internet).

IATA International Air Transport Association: international civil aviation industry body.

IBO Input back-off: see Back-off.

IBS Intelsat Business Services: describes specific data service of Intelsat.

IC Integrated Circuit.

ICNIRP International Commission on Non-Ionizing Radiation Protection.

IDR Intermediate data rate: refers to Intelsat's general data services.

IDR framing See Overhead framing.

IEC International Electrotechnical Commission (European).

IEEE Institute of Electrical and Electronics Engineers (US).

IEEE-1394 See Firewire.

IESS An INTELSAT earth station standard.

IESS-306 An INTELSAT earth station standard for the modulation of analog TV frequency-modulated carriers.

IESS-308 An INTELSAT earth station standard for the modulation of QPSK-modulated digital carriers.

IESS-309 An INTELSAT earth station standard for phase requirements for higher-order modulation and error correction schemes.

IESS-310 An INTELSAT earth station standard for phase requirements for higher-order modulation and error correction schemes.

IETF Internet Engineering Task Force (Internet).

IF Intermediate frequency signal, between stages in an uplink or downlink transmission chain – typically at frequencies of 70 MHz, or in the L-band (at around 1000 MHz or 1 GHz).

IFB Interruptible foldback or interruptible feedback: allows a producer, director, etc. to communicate with the reporter during a 'live' remote transmission.

I-frame Intra-compressed frame: only has compression applied within (intra) the frame, and has no dependence on any frames before or after.

IFRB International Frequency Registration Board: part of the ITU.

IGO Intergovernmental organization.

IMF International Monetary Fund.

IMN Inmarsat mobile number.

IMO International Maritime Organization: founder of INMARSAT.

IMT-2000 International mobile telecommunications for the second millenium: ITU equivalent to European UMTS.

Inclination Angle between the orbital plane of a satellite and the equatorial plane of the Earth.

Inclined orbit Satellite status near the end of its operational life, when North–South station-keeping maneuvers are largely abandoned; this type of capacity is often used for SNG.

Information rate Fundamental video data rate.

INIRC International Non-Ionizing Radiation Committee.

Injection orbit See Transfer orbit.

In-line fed prime focus Antenna where the feedhorn is directly in front of the vertex of the antenna.

INMARSAT International Maritime Satellite Organization: operated a network of satellites for international transmissions for all types of international mobile services including maritime, aeronautical and land mobile – now privatized as Inmarsat.

Inner code Error correction code; see Forward error correction.

Input back-off IBO: where the input signal to the HPA is reduced so that the TWT is operating on the linear part of its power transfer curve; expressed in dB.

INTELSAT International Telecommunications Satellite Organization, now privatized as Intelsat.

Interface The point at which two pieces of equipment may be connected together; an electrical standard defining input and/or output parameters of a piece of equipment.

Interference Energy which interferes with the reception of desired signals.

Interlace In a television frame of two TV fields, where each TV field is offset by a line, and each pair of TV fields is sent in an alternate sequence of odd- and even-numbered lines in the field.

Interleaving Where consecutive bits are interleaved amongst other bits in the bit-stream over a certain period of time to improve ruggedness of data.

Intermodulation products IP: spurious signals generated typically in the HPA which cause interference to other adjacent signals.

Interoperability The ability of one manufacturer's equipment (e.g. an MPEG-2 encoder), compliant to an agreed standard, to operate in harmony with the same type of equipment from another manufacturer.

Interview mode Low-latency mode (typically less than 250 ms) on an MPEG-2 encoder.

Intra-frame coding Form of compression of looking for spectral and spatial redundancy inside each frame without reference to any other frame, and sending such frames in a continuous sequence.

Inverse DCT Reverse process to DCT coding.

Inverter Electrical powering device that produces 110/240 V from a 12/24 V source, e.g. a vehicle battery.

Ionizing radiation Electromagnetic radiation of X-rays, gamma radiation, neutrons and alpha particles, that can have sufficient energy to permanently alter cell structures.

IOR Indian Ocean Region: describes coverage area of a satellite.

IOT In Orbit Test.

IP Intermodulation product (RF); Internet protocol (Internet).

IPFD Input power flux density: a measure of the required illumination of the satellite by the uplink.

IPO Initial Public Offering.

IPsec IP Security (Internet).

IPTV Internet Protocol Television.

IRD Integrated receiver decoder: an integrated MPEG-2 digital receiver which combines a downconverter, a demodulator and a compression decoder.

IRPA International Radiation Protection Association.

ISDB-S Integrated Services Digital Broadcasting Satellite (Japan).

ISDN Integrated services digital network: ITU-T term for integrated transmission of voice, video and data on the digital public telecommunications network.

ISDN-2 See 2B + D.

ISO International Standards Organization.

ISOG see WBU-ISOG.

Isotropic antenna A hypothetical omni-directional point-source antenna that radiates equal electromagnetic power in all directions – the gain of an isotropic antenna is 0 dBi – that serves as an engineering reference for the measurement of antenna gain.

ISP Internet Service Provider.

IT Information Technology.

ITN Independent Television News (UK).

ITO International Trade Organization.

ITU International Telecommunications Union: undertakes global administration of spectrum. Founded in 1865 as the International Telegraph Union, it changed its name to the International Telecommunication Union in 1934.

ITU-D ITU development sector: provides technical assistance to developing countries.

ITU-R ITU radiocommunication sector: establishes global agreements on standards for international use of radio frequencies, broadcasting, radiocommunication and satellite transmission standards.

ITU-R BT.601 Formerly CCIR-601; recommendation developed for the digitization of color video signals.

ITU-T ITU telecommunication sector: establishes global agreements on standards for telecommunications.

I-VOP Intra-VOP (MPEG-4).

JPEG ISO Joint Picture Expert Group standard for the compression of still pictures that shrinks the amount of data necessary to represent digital images from 2:1 to 30:1, depending on image type.

JPEG2000 Wavelet-based compression system.

JVT Joint Video Team (MPEG-4).

K See Kelvin.

Ka-band Frequency range from 18 to 31 GHz; in satellite communications, the frequency band 17.75–19.50 GHz is used for transmission.

kbps Kilobits per second (1000 bits per second).

Kelvin K: the temperature measurement scale used in the scientific community, where 0 K represents absolute zero and corresponds to -273 degrees Celsius (-459 degrees Fahrenheit); thermal noise in an electronic system is measured in Kelvin.

kHz Kilohertz: Hz $\times 10^3$ (1000 Hz).

Kilohertz See kHz.

kmh Kilometers per hour.

Ku-band Frequency range from 10 to 18 GHz; in satellite communications, the frequency band 13.75–14.50 GHz for transmission and 10.7–12.75 GHz for reception.

kVA Kilovolt amperes: measurement of absolute maximum electrical power into an electrical load, which is in reality usually reduced due to the electrical characteristics of the load.

L2TP Layer 2 Tunneling Protocol (Ethernet).

LAN Local area network (Ethernet).

Latency Delay through a compression process.

Launcher Generic term for the feedhorn; vehicle – typically a rocket – used to carry a satellite into orbit.

Layer MPEG group of audio coding algorithms.

L-band In SNG terms, the frequency band 1.0–2.0 GHz.

LCD Liquid Crystal Display.

LDPC see Low-Density Parity Check.

Leasing The rental of satellite capacity for a fixed term, typically 1 week to 5 years.

Left-hand circular polarization See Circular polarization.

LEO Low-Earth Orbit: below 5000 km.

LES Land earth station (fixed); ground station, usually Inmarsat.

LESO Land Earth Station Operators (Inmarsat).

Level In MPEG, the level defines the image resolution and luminance sampling rate, the number of video and audio layers supported for scaleable profiles, and the maximum bit-rate per profile.

LHCP See Circular polarization.

Licence Formal authority permitting radio transmissions, usually incurring a fee.

Linear polarization Geometric plane in which the electromagnetic signals are transmitted. Linear polarization is divided into vertical (Y) and horizontal (X) polarization.

Linearizer Part of an HPA design that effectively compensates for the non-linearity near the top of the power transfer characteristic.

Line-up Period of time before the beginning of a transmission when operational technical parameters are checked and confirmed with satellite control center.

Link budget Calculation to ascertain the performance of a complete satellite link system.

Lip-synch error Where the audio is out of synchronism with the video – commonly seen on compressed transmissions due to system errors.

Live shot Short-live transmission, typically for a brief news update.

Live stand-up See Stand-up.

LNA Low-noise amplifier.

LNB See Low-noise block-downconverter.

LO Local oscillator, low-noise block-downconverter.

Look angle Azimuth and elevation angles that an uplink or downlink has to be orientated along to point toward the desired satellite.

Loopback; Lookback Ability at the uplink to receive its own signal downlinked from the satellite for verification.

Lossless Compression process that creates a perfect copy of the original signal when it is decompressed at the end of the signal chain.

Lossy Compression process that relies on the fact that the human eye and ear can tolerate some loss of information yet still perceive that a picture or sound is of good or adequate quality.

Low-Density Parity Check LDPC: high-order error correction scheme (DVB-S2).

Low-noise amplifier LNA: pre-amplifier between the antenna and the earth station receiver, located as near the antenna as possible for maximum effectiveness, usually attached directly to the antenna receive port. The LNA is especially designed to contribute the least amount of thermal noise to the received signal.

Low-noise block-downconverter LNB: combination of a low-noise amplifier and downconverter built into one device attached to the feed; it amplifies the weak signal from the satellite and frequency shifts it down from Ku-band (or C-band) to L-band, as required at the input to the satellite receiver.

LPG Liquefied petroleum gas.

LSI Large-Scale Integration.

Luminance Brightness of a video picture.

M4 Multi-Media Mini-M (Inmarsat): formally known as Global Area Network.

MAC Media Access Control (Ethernet).

Macroblock Number of 8×8 pixels luminance blocks, used as part of motion prediction in the digital compression process.

Magnetic North Direction toward which a compass needle will ordinarily point when influenced by the magnetic field of the Earth.

MARECS Maritime European Communications Satellite.

Margin Amount of signal in dB by which the satellite system exceeds the minimum threshold required for operation.

Mask Antenna radiation performance pattern with respect to a particular specification, e.g. to meet 2° spacing of satellites.

Matrix Switching router that can connect any input source to any output destination.

MB Megabyte: 1 million bytes per second (1×10^6 bytes per second).

Mbaud Megabaud: 1 million symbols per second (1×10^6 symbols per second).

Mbps Megabits per second: 1 million bits per second (1×10^6 bits per second).

MCB Miniature Circuit Breaker.

MCPC Multiple channels per carrier.

MCR Master control room.

MEO Medium Earth orbit: 10 000–20 000 km above the Earth.

MES Mobile earth station.

Metadata Program content description information that is carried as an auxiliary data channel within a digital signal.

MHz Megahertz: unit of frequency equal to 1 million cycles per second or 1×10^6 Hz (1 000 000 Hz).

Microwave Refers to frequencies typically in the range of 2–30 GHz.

Mix-minus The transmission to the remote location of the output of the studio *minus* the contribution from the remote location; see Cleanfeed.

Modem MODulator/DEModulator: device that transmits and receives data.

Modulation; modulator Process of manipulating the frequency or amplitude of a carrier in relation to a signal; device which combines a 'message' signal with a high-frequency carrier signal for transmission.

Modulation rate Modulated symbol rate.

Motion JPEG Method of using JPEG coding techniques to compress and transmit television pictures.

Motion prediction; estimation Process of calculating the position of an object from one frame to the next and sending only the co-ordinates of the block of data that describes that object from one frame to the next by simply placing it in the new position.

Motion vector The difference co-ordinates of the block of data that describes an object that has moved in position between one frame to the next.

MoU Memorandum of understanding: interorganizational or intergovernmental agreement establishing fundamental principles and understandings.

Mount Mechanical assembly upon which the SNG antenna is mounted, complete with all necessary mechanical adjustment controls.

MP Main profile – MPEG.

MP3 Moving Picture Experts Group Layer-3 Audio (audio file format/extension).

MPDS Mobile Packet Data Service (Inmarsat).

MPE Multi-Protocol Encapsulation; Maximum Permissible Exposure.

MPEG Motion Pictures Expert Group.

MPEG-1 Video compression standard for non-interlaced, computer-type data streams. Typical MPEG-1 video compression goes up to 100:1 for images composed of 352 pixels (picture elements) $\times$ 288 lines at a refresh rate of up to 30 frames per second.

MPEG-2 Standard covering the compression of data (coding and encoding) for digital television, derived from MPEG-1 and defined for interlaced broadcast TV. It provides improved picture quality, higher resolution and additional features such as scaleability.

MPEG-2 MP@HL MPEG-2 main profile at high level: the higher bit-rate system adopted to provide high definition television in wide-screen format.

MPEG-4 Compression system developed as a successor to MPEG-2.

MPEG-LA MPEG Licensing Authority – organization for co-ordinating licence fees for MPEG.

MPV Multi-Purpose Vehicle.

ms Millisecond: one thousandth of a second (1×10^{-3})

MSD Medium-speed data: usually for INMARSAT purposes; equivalent to a data rate of 9.6 kbps.

MSps Mega-symbols per second: measurement of data rate – 1 000 000 symbols per second (1×10^6 symbols per second).

MSS Mobile-Satellite Service: ITU designation.

MTU Maximum Transmission Unit (Ethernet).

Multilateral Transmission from one origin to a number of destinations simultaneously.

Multiple channels per carrier MCPC: where multiple program signals are combined onto one carrier signal and uplinked.

Multiplexer Combines a number of separate signals into one signal for simultaneous transmission over a single circuit.

MUSE Multiple Sub-Nyquist Encoding.

MUSICAM Masking pattern adapted Universal Sub-band Integrated Coding And Multiplexing: digital audio compression standard.

NAB National Association of Broadcasters.

NABA North American Broadcasters Association – a trade association based in Canada.

NASA National Aeronautical Space Administration (US).

NBC National Broadcasting Company: US network formed in 1926 by RCA; nuclear, biological, chemical: describes a method of protection used in warfare.

NCRP National Council on Radiation Protection.

Near-field Zone of non-ionizing radiation.

Newsgathering Journalistic and technical process of gathering news for broadcast.

NGO Non-governmental organization.

NHK Nippon Hoso Kyokai (Japan Broadcasting Corporation).

NIC Network Interface Card (Ethernet).

NIR Non-Ionizing Radiation.

NLE Non-Linear Editor/Editing.

NOC Network Operations Center.

Noise Unwanted and unmodulated energy that is always present to some extent within any signal; interference or unwanted signals.

Noise figure Figure of merit of a device, such as an LNA or receiver, expressed in dB, which compares the device with a perfect one.

Noise floor Level of constant residual noise in a system.

Non pre-emptible Satellite capacity that is guaranteed and cannot be pre-empted for restoration or other operational reasons.

Non-dedicated Satellite capacity that is not dedicated for any particular purpose, e.g. telephony, Internet, DTH.

Non-ionizing radiation Electromagnetic radiation encompassing the spectrum of ultraviolet radiation, light, infrared radiation and radio frequency radiation, with low energy, insufficient to permanently alter cell structures.

NRPB National Radiological Protection Board (UK).

NSS New Skies Satellites N.V.: privatized part of INTELSAT.

NT1 Network termination device – ISDN.

NT2 Point at which a second network termination device such as an ISDN switchboard is connected to the NT1 at the T-interface.

NTSC National Television Systems Committee: generic term for US analog color television system used in North America and Japan, based upon 60 fields per second and 525 lines.

OB Outside broadcast.

Oblate Describes the shape of the Earth, which is not perfectly circular but slightly flattened in the Polar regions.

OBO Output back-off.

Occasional capacity; Occasional use Capacity available for ad-hoc bookings.

Occupied bandwidth Absolute bandwidth occupied by the signal within a transponder or allocated channel.

OET Office of Engineering and Technology, FCC (US).

Ofcom Office of Communications (UK): national radiocommunications regulatory body.

Offset prime focus Type of parabolic antenna where the focus of the antenna is displaced: instead of being at the center of the parabola (the 'vertex') the focus is shifted up.

OHF See Overhead framing.

OMT Orthogonal mode transducer.

On-axis In line with the main beam of an antenna.

Orbital period Time taken for a satellite to go through one complete orbit.

Orthogonal mode transducer OMT: multi-port microwave device that allows the transmission of signals on one polarization while receiving signals on the opposite polarization.

OS Operating System.

Oscilloscope Electronic instrument for viewing and measuring electrical and electronic signals.

OSHA Occupational Safety and Health Administration: US national safety agency.

OTS Orbital Test Satellite: early UK satellite program of the 1970s.

OU Occasional Use – ad-hoc satellite capacity.

Outage Failure of satellite link.

Outer code Adds a number of parity (check) bits to blocks of data.

Output back-off OBO: the amount of the output signal of an HPA is reduced as a result of input back-off being applied. Expressed in dB.

Overhead framing Additional data signal added to the data stream from the encoder to carry auxiliary information data – used in wider telecommunications applications. Often generically referred to as IDR framing.

Over-run Last-minute satellite booking extension.

Packet switching Data transmission method that divides messages into standard-sized packets for greater efficiency of routing and transport through a network.

PAL Phase alternate line: the European CCIR analog TV standard based upon 50 fields per second and 625 lines.

Panning-up Process of accurately aligning satellite uplink antenna to the satellite.

Paper satellites Orbital allocation applications made well in advance of the actual placing of a satellite in position; many organizations hold allocations for orbital slots that may never be used, as a 'spoiling' tactic.

Parabolic antenna Antenna with a reflector described mathematically as a parabola; essentially an electromagnetic wave lens which focuses the radio frequency energy into a narrow beam.

Path Transmission chain of equipment.

Payload Load carrying capacity; on a rocket launch vehicle, the satellite is the payload. On a satellite, the payload is the transponders that carry the traffic.

PBS Public Broadcasting Service.

PBX; PABX Private Branch Exchange; Private Automatic Branch Exchange.

PCM Pulse code modulation.

PDA Personal Digital Assistant.

PDU Power distribution unit.

Perceptual coding A coding technique which takes advantage of the imperfections of the human visual and auditory senses.

Perigee The point of a satellite's orbit where it is closest to the Earth's surface.

Permission Agreement from a national government for SNG transmissions.

PES Packetized elementary stream.

Petal Segment of a flyaway antenna.

PFD Power flux density: a measure of the satellites illumination of the Earth's surface.

P-frame Predicted compressed frame: calculated by applying motion prediction to a previous frame and deriving a difference signal (intercoding).

Phase noise Phase interference in the wanted digital signal which can cause the digital signal to fail to be demodulated correctly.

Phase stability Characteristic that is important in digital transmission components – lack of phase stability can cause the digital signal to fail to be demodulated correctly.

Phase-combiner Multi-port microwave device which ensures that the individual outputs from two HPAs are combined together so that the outputs are added inphase.

Phase-locked loop PLL: type of electronic circuit used to demodulate satellite signals. Used in professional grade LNB.

PID Packet Identifier: identifies parts of a specific program signal (MPEG-2).

Piece-to-camera Where a reporter gives a news report face to camera.

PIN Personal Identification Number.

Pipe Generic term for a data circuit.

Pixel Smallest element that is discernible (quantified and sampled) in a picture.

Pixellation Aberration of a digitally coded television picture where the individual digitally coded samples can be seen.

PLL See Phase-locked loop.

PMT Program Map Table: carries the program information of an MPEG-2 transport stream.

Pointing loss Loss due to misalignment of boresight of antenna toward satellite, and movement of satellite within its station-kept 'box'.

Polarization Geometric plane in which the electromagnetic signals are transmitted.

Polarization rotator Device that can be manually or automatically adjusted to select one of two orthogonal polarizations on an antenna.

Polarization skew An uplink or downlink waveguide is rotated to compensate for the angular difference between the antenna position on the Earth's surface and the satellite position above the Equator.

Pool Grouping of newsgathering entities, usually for a limited period, to pool resources to cover a news event.

POP Point of presence (terrestrial networks).

POR Pacific Ocean Region: describes coverage area of a satellite.

POTS Plain Old Telephone Service.

Power balancing The operational adjustment of two signal powers to minimize the production of intermodulation products; the adjustment of carriers to minimize small signal suppression.

Power density Density of radiated power from an antenna, measured in W/m^2 (mW/cm^2).

Power meter A measurement instrument which can be connected directly to the sample port of the HPA to give a constant readout of the power being produced from the HPA.

pp Peak-to-peak.

Precipitation loss Loss due to rain attenuating the signal, particularly in the Ku-band, and further dispersing the signal as it passes through the drops of water.

Precipitation zone To aid in calculating the effect of precipitation loss, the world is divided into precipitation zones or rain climatic zones, each of which has a numerical value defined by the ITU, used in the calculation of a link budget.

Pre-emphasis Type of frequency-dependent level boosting/cutting or filtering.

Pre-emptible Satellite service that may be interrupted or displaced by another, higher-priority service, typically (but not exclusively) during a satellite contingency situation.

PRI Primary rate ISDN.

Primary rate ISDN PRI: primary rate ISDN provides 30×64 kbps (B) data channels and 1×64 kbps (D) signaling channel.

Profile Profiles define the color space resolution in MPEG compression and also the scaleability of the bit-stream; the combination of a profile and a level produces an architecture which defines the ability of a decoder to handle a particular bit-stream.

Progressive scan Alternative to interlaced scanning, where each line is scanned in sequence in the frame.

PSI Program Specific Information (MPEG-2).

PSK Phase-shift key modulation: digital phase modulation.

PSTN Public Switched Telephone Network.

PSU Power supply unit.

Psycho-acoustic; psycho-visual Description of the models of the brain's perception of vision and sound.

PTC Piece-to-camera.

PTO Public telecommunications operator; power take-off: where a generator may be driven through a vehicle's road engine and transmission system while the vehicle is at rest.

PTT Post, telephone and telegraph administration: national telecommunications agencies directly or indirectly controlled by governments, in charge of telecommunications services in most countries of the world.

Pulse code modulation PCM: time division modulation technique in which analog signals are sampled and quantized at periodic intervals into digital signals – typically represented by a coded arrangement of 8 bits.

P-VOP Predicted VOP (MPEG-4).

QAM Quadrature amplitude modulation: modulation technique.

QCIF Quarter common interchange format: 176×144 pixels.

QoS Quality of Service.

QPSK Quadrature phase-shift key: modulation technique.

Quantization The process that assigns a specific number of bits (resolution) to each frequency coefficient after DCT coding.

Rain climatic zone See Precipitation zone.

Rain outage Loss of signal due to absorption and increased sky-noise temperature caused by heavy rainfall.

RAS Remote Authorization System (MPEG-2).

RBGAN Regional Broadband Global Area Network (Inmarsat).

RCA Radio Corporation of America.

RCCB Residual current circuit breaker.

RCD Residual current device: a device that measures the difference in current flowing between the supply wires; if a difference exists then a fault is assumed and the supply is rapidly disconnected.

Receiver Rx: device which enables a particular satellite signal to be separated from all others being received by an earth station, and converts the received signal into video and audio.

Redundancy Protection against failure of either a part or the whole of the system that would thus make the entire system inoperable. In an SNG uplink that is redundant, there are two transmitters and two modulators.

Reed-Solomon code Type of outer convolutional error correction code; for each given number of symbols forming a block, an additional parity check block of data is added to make up a complete block of data.

Resolution Sharpness of the picture.

Restoration The action of a satellite system operator to sustain defined service level in the event of satellite failure or anomaly.

Return audio; reverse audio See Cleanfeed.

RF; RF bandwidth Radio frequency: refers to radio transmissions or relating to that part of the electromagnetic spectrum used for radio transmissions.

RHCP Right-hand circular polarization.

RJ Registered Jack.

RJ-45 Registered Jack-45 (8 wire connector used in networking).

Router Network device that determines the optimal path along which network traffic should be forwarded.

Routing matrix See Switching matrix.

RR Radio Regulations: instruments of the ITU.

RS Reed-Solomon code.

RS.232 Common serial data interface.

RTCP Real-Time Transport Control Protocol.

RTP Real-Time Protocol (Ethernet).

RTT Round Trip Time.

RU Nineteen-inch rack-height unit; See U.

RX Receive; receiver.

S-point See S-interface.

S/N Signal-to-noise ratio – typically expressed in dB.

S/T bus; S/T-interface See S0 bus/interface.

S0 bus; S0-interface Converts the ISDN data from the format used between the exchange and the socket to the type used in the subscriber's premises.

Sample port Monitoring point for measuring RF signal.

Sampling Instantaneous measurement of the picture at a particular point in time; the value of the signal at that instant is typically converted to a binary number.

Sampling frequency (rate) Rate at which samples are taken.

SAP Session Announcement Protocol (Ethernet).

SAR Specific energy absorption rate: the biological effects of non-ionizing radiation expressed in terms of the rate of energy absorption per unit mass of tissue.

SAS Satellite Access Station (Inmarsat BGAN).

Satellite link Microwave link between a transmitting earth station and receiving earth station through a satellite.

Satellite newsgathering SNG: the means by which news is gathered for television and radio broadcast using satellite communications.

Satellite system operator Organization which operates and controls one or more satellite spacecraft.

Satellite, artificial Electronic communications relay station orbiting the Earth.

Satellite, geostationary An electronic communications relay station orbiting 35 785 km (22 237 miles) above the Equator, moving in a fixed orbit at the same speed and direction as the Earth, i.e. approximately 11 000 kph (7000 mph).

Satphone Generic term for satellite telephone, usually used on the Inmarsat system.

Saturated flux density SFD: the power required to achieve saturation of a single channel on a satellite.

Saturation Where a high-power amplifier is driven into the non-linear part of its power transfer characteristic, such that an increase in input power results in little or no increase in output power.

SBE Society of Broadcast Engineers.

Scintillation Rapid fluctuation in amplitude and phase caused by the signal traveling a longer path through the atmosphere and ionosphere.

Scope See Oscilloscope.

SCPC Single channel per carrier.

Screening Process of checking material for political content by censor before transmission.

SD; SDTV Standard definition; Standard definition television.

SDI Serial digital interface.

SDP Session Description Protocol (Ethernet).

SECAM SEquentiel Coleur A Memoire: analog color television broadcast standard of France, Russia and a number of other French-speaking nations (typically former colonies) which, though based on 50 fields per second and 625 lines, is incompatible with PAL.

Sensitivity Ability of an electronic device (typically a receiver) to detect and process very small signals satisfactorily.

Serial digital video Digital video transmitted serially, typically at a data rate of 270 Mbps.

Shannon theory Information theory showing that signals will always have some degree of predictability; data compression commonly uses the principle of statistical analysis of a signal to predict changes.

SHF Super High Frequency.

Shore power Power from an external source.

SI Service Information (MPEG-2).

SIA Satellite Industry Association.

Side-chain An auxiliary transmission path on an SNG uplink.

Sidelobes A parabolic antenna does not produce a completely perfect radiation pattern, which would be a single focused beam, but has a main 'lobe' (centered on the boresight) and a number of 'sidelobes' radiating out from the antenna.

Sidereal cycle The Earth rotates once in every 23 hours, 56 minutes and 4.1 seconds, rather than exactly 24 hours – equivalent to one sidereal day.

SIF Source Input Format; Standard interchange format: format for exchanging video images of 240 lines $\times$ 352 pixels for NTSC, and 288 lines $\times$ 352 pixels for PAL and SECAM.

Signal-to-noise ratio S/N: ratio of the signal power and noise power in analog systems; a video S/N of 54–56 dB is considered to be of full broadcast quality.

Signatory National administration or organization which forms part of the establishment of an international treaty organization such as ITU.

SIM Subscriber Identity Module.

Simplex Transmission in one direction only between sending and receiving station.

Single channel per carrier SCPC: a transmission of single program signal on one carrier.

S-interface The ISDN subscriber interface where the connection to the ISDN network is through another network termination device such as an ISDN switchboard.

SIP Session Initiation Protocol (Ethernet).

Skew An adjustment that compensates for slight variance in angle within the same sense of polarity.

Sky To point the satellite antenna upwards away from the satellite arc.

Slant range The length of the path between a satellite and the ground earth station.

Slice Sequence of macroblocks across the picture in a digital compression process.

Slot, orbital Longitudinal position in the geosynchronous arc at which a communications satellite is located – allocated by the ITU.

Small signal suppression Suppression effect seen on a relatively low-power carrier signal when a low-power carrier and a high-power carrier share the same transponder on a satellite.

SMPTE Society of Motion Picture and Television Engineers (US). (Also humorously referred to as the Society of Many People Talking Endlessly.)

SMPTE-125M US standard for 4:2:2 component video signals – equivalent to CCIR-601.

SMPTE-259M US standard for 270 Mbps serial digital video.

SNG Satellite newsgathering.

Sniffer port See Sample port.

Snow Form of noise seen on analog pictures caused by a weak signal from the satellite, characterized by alternate dark and light dots appearing randomly on the picture tube.

Solar eclipse Event when the Earth moves between the satellite and the Sun, preventing the satellite from receiving energy from the Sun to provide solar power.

Solar noise Description of the electromagnetic 'noise' generated from the Sun.

Solar outage Event during the equinoxes when the satellite is on that part of its orbit where it is between the Sun and the Earth, causing a downlink receiving antenna pointed at a satellite to become 'blinded' as the Sun passes behind the satellite.

Solid-state power amplifier SSPA: a high-power amplifier using solid-state electronics as the amplifying element, as opposed to a vacuum tube device.

SOTM Satcom on the Move.

Sound-in-sync SIS: audio signal carried as a digitized signal in the sync (line timing) pulses of the analog TV video signal – European standard.

SP Simple Profile (MPEG).

Space segment Generic term for the part of the transmission system that is in the sky.

Spatial redundancy The similarity between pixel values in an area of the picture which can be exploited to save the amount of information transmitted: more often than not, two neighboring pixels will have very nearly the same luminance and chrominance values.

Spectral redundancy The similarity between frequency values in an area of the picture which can be exploited to save the amount of information transmitted.

Spectrum The full range of electromagnetic radio frequencies.

Spectrum analyser A radio signal measurement instrument with the ability to repeatedly and automatically tune across a band of electromagnetic spectrum, showing the amplitude of signals present in that band on a display screen.

Spike A voltage or energy surge; irregularities in the power supply waveform.

Spill-over Satellite signal that falls on locations outside the beam pattern's defined edge of coverage.

Splitter Passive device (one with no active electronic components) which distributes a signal into two or more paths.

Spoofing See Acceleration.

Spotbeam High-power satellite signal with a focused antenna pattern that covers only a small region.

Spreading loss As a signal is transmitted by an antenna, the signal spreads out to cover a very wide area and gets weaker as it travels further away from the antenna.

Spurious radiation Any radiation outside a defined frequency band; potential source of interference.

SQCIF Sub-quarter common intermediate format: 128 × 96 pixels.

SSOG Satellite Systems Operations Guide – INTELSAT.

SSPA Solid-state power amplifier.

Stand-up Position where a reporter gives a news report; generic term for a short news report from the field.

Station-keeping Small orbital adjustments regularly made to maintain the satellite's orbital position within its allocated 'box' on the geostationary arc.

Station-kept box The space in which the satellite is maintained while in station-kept geostationary orbit.

Store and forward Process by which high-quality video is digitized and compressed at the high bit-rate, stored, and later transmitted in non-real time through a low data rate circuit, e.g. INMARSAT.

Sub-carrier An additional signal to carry additional information piggybacked onto a main signal, and which is applied at a frequency above the highest frequency of the main carrier.

Subnet Range of logical addresses within the address range assigned to an organization.

Sub-sampling Processing of chrominance components to remove spectral redundancy.

Sub-satellite point Point on the Equator directly beneath the satellite; if a line was drawn from the center of the Earth to the satellite, the point at which the line passes through the Earth's surface.

SUIRG Satellite Users Interference Reduction Group.

Sun-out See Solar outage.

Superbeam See Widebeam.

SUV Sports Utility Vehicle.

SW Session Word (EBU-BISS).

Switched-56 56 kbps digital telephony data service in the US; now superseded by ISDN.

Switching matrix Router that can connect different source inputs to different destination outputs; also called a routing matrix.

Symbol; symbol rate Used in connection with the transmitted data, where a defined number of bits represents a 'symbol' – a unit of information. One symbol per second is termed a 'baud'.

Synchronization Process of achieving the same timing relationship at the transmitter and the receiver in order that information can be correctly conveyed.

System noise Unwanted signals and artifacts generated within a receive system, typically expressed as a power figure to balance against the signal power.

T-point See T-interface.

TA ISDN terminal adapter: provides interface conversion between the S0 bus and the serial communications interface on the subscriber data terminal equipment (DTE).

Tachograph Device fitted to a vehicle (typically a goods vehicle) which records vehicle activity over a 24-hour period onto a circular chart. Used for statutory reasons.

Talkback Bidirectional circuit to allow studio-remote conversations, instructions and information to be exchanged, between the remote location and the control room of the studio.

Talking-head Colloquial term for a single head shot of a reporter.

Tape feed Video or audio tape transmission.

TBR Technical basis for regulation (ETSI).

TBR-030 Precursor to CTR-030.

TCP Transmission Control Protocol.

TCP/IP Transmission Control Protocol/Internet Protocol.

TDMA Time division multiple access: refers to a form of multiple access where a single carrier is shared by many users so that signals from earth stations reaching the satellite consecutively are processed in time segments without overlapping.

Teleport Fixed earth station; typically has a large number of satellite antennas.

Telstar Early US satellite.

Temporal redundancy Similarity in pixel values between one frame of a picture and the next frame, which can be exploited to save the amount of information transmitted; redundancy in the data from one frame to the next can be removed.

TES Transportable earth station: mobile microwave radio transmitter used in satellite communications, includes SNG systems.

TFT Thin Film Transistor – used in flat panel displays.

Threshold Point at which a signal will fail to be correctly demodulated: a digital receive system will fail abruptly with either a 'frozen' or black picture when the input signal fails to achieve threshold; an analog system will suffer increasing degradation to the point of failure the further below threshold the signal level drops.

Thruster Small booster rocket motor typically found on a satellite, used to maintain correct station keeping.

T-interface ISDN subscriber interface at the NT1.

Tonne One thousand kilograms.

TR Technical Report (ETSI).

Tracking, Telemetry and Control (or Command) Management of in-orbit satellite primary systems from the ground; sometimes referred to as tracking, telemetry and command.

Transfer orbit Transitional orbit by which a satellite is moved from the parking orbit into geostationary orbit.

Transmission order Order in which the group of pictures is transmitted.

Transmission rate Aggregate data rate – including RS, convolutional encoding and the information rate.

Transmitter Electronic device consisting of oscillator, modulator and other circuits which produce an electromagnetic signal for radiation into the atmosphere by an antenna.

Transponder Combination receiver, frequency converter and transmitter package, physically on-board the satellite.

Transport stream Multiplex of program channels in a DVB system.

Traveling wave tube TWT: powerful microwave amplifying vacuum tube used in a high-power amplifier, commonly employed in SNG systems as well as on satellites.

True North Theoretical North Pole: geographical designation of North Pole at 90°N latitude, 0° longitude.

Truncation noise On an analog uplink, if the receiver IF filter bandwidth is too narrow, high-order 'sidebands' of the vision signal, corresponding to areas of highest deviation, are severely attenuated.

TS Transport stream.

TT&C See Tracking, telemetry and control (or command).

Turbo Code Higher-order error correction scheme considered for DVB-S2 standard.

Turnaround Act of downlinking a satellite signal, altering it and instantaneously uplinking it again; often used to provide a multi-hop path around the globe, or to change the signal from Ku-band to C-band.

Turnkey System or installation provided complete and ready for operation by a manufacturer or supplier.

TVRO Television receive only: description of a small receive-only facility, using a small antenna; in SNG often used for off-air check or cueing purposes.

TVSC TV Service Centre: Intelsat satellite booking center.

Tweeking Engineering slang for adjustment to optimize performance.

Two-way Studio–remote interview in a news broadcasts.

TWT Traveling wave tube.

TWTA Traveling wave tube amplifier.

TX Transmit; Transmission; Relative time reference to the start of a transmission.

Type-approval Official process of obtaining technical approval for an earth station to be used with a particular satellite system.

U Rack-height unit: a unit of measurement of height for equipment racks, where $1\,U = 1.75$ in. (44.5 mm); also referred to as RU.

UAP Universal Access Procedures.

UDP User Datagram Protocol (Ethernet).

U-interface The point at which the ISDN telephone line terminates at a subscriber's premises.

UMTS Universal Mobile Telecommunication System: ETSI system.

Unilateral Transmission from one origin to one destination only.

Upconverter Earth station equipment to convert from IF to RF frequency: transforms the modulated IF signal from the modulator up to the desired transmit frequency by a process of frequency shifting or conversion.

Uplink Earth station used to transmit signals to a satellite; the transmit earth station-to-satellite connection.

UPS Uninterruptible Power Supply.

URL Uniform Resource Locator (Internet).

USB Universal Serial Bus.

UTC Universal time co-ordinated: measurement of time, locked to an atomic clock reference, particularly used in space science and engineering; regard as same as Greenwich Mean Time.

V Volt: measurement of electrical potential difference.

V.35 Protocol used for communications between a network access device and a packet-data network (ITU-T standard).

VA Volt amperes: a measurement of power.

VAC Volts, alternating current.

Variable length coding Process where further efficiencies are used to reduce the amount of data transmitted while maintaining the level of information.

VAST-p Video and audio storage and transmission – portable: store and forward video unit for newsgathering manufactured by TOKO in the 1990s, now obsolete.

VBI Vertical blanking interval.

VBR Variable Bit Rate.

VC Video-conferencing.

VC-1 SMPTE standard for Microsoft Windows Media 9.

VDC Volts, direct current.

Vertex Geometric center of the parabola on an antenna.

Vertical blanking interval Contains the vertical timing and synchronization information for the television display.

Video-conferencing The process of visually and aurally linking two or more groups across a telecommunications network for (typically) business meeting purposes.

Viterbi Decoding algorithm for FEC.

VLC Variable length coding.

VO Video objects (MPEG-4).

VOD Video on demand.

VoIP Voice Over Internet Protocol.

VOL Video object layer (MPEG-4).

VOP Video object plane (MPEG-4).

VP7; VP6 Proprietary compression algorithm developed by On2 Technologies.

VPC Variable phase combiner: particular type of phase combiner which has a variable adjustment to match the phase of the two inputs.

VSAT Very small aperture terminal: refers to small-fixed earth stations, usually with antennas up to 2.4 m, used in a 'star' or 'mesh' network for business communications.

VSWR Voltage standing wave ratio: measurement of mismatch in a cable, waveguide or antenna system.

VTC Video Tele Conferencing.

VTR Videotape Recorder.

W Watt: measurement of power.

WAN Wide Area Network.

WARC World Administrative Radiocommunication Conference, see WRC.

Waveguide Metallic microwave conductor, typically rectangular in shape, used to connect microwave signals with antennas; generic term for the feedhorn assembly; the connecting piece (or pieces) between the output of the HPA and the feed arm of the uplink antenna.

Waveguide loss Loss due to waveguides introducing some attenuation to the signal.

WBU World Broadcasting Union.

WBU-ISOG Broadcasting industry lobby group of the WBU, which seeks to influence particularly in the areas of SNG and contribution circuits.

W-CDMA Wideband Code Division Multiplex Access

WHO World Health Organization.

Wideband Large-frequency bandwidth: see Broadband.

Widebeam Ku-band satellite antenna pattern offering broader coverage, up to 8000 km (5000 miles) in diameter, but only available at lower power levels because the power is spread over a wider area.

WiMAX Worldwide Interoperability for Microwave Access – based on IEEE 802.16 standard (Internet).

WLAN Wireless LAN (Internet).

WMV-9 Windows Media Video 9 – video/audio compression scheme to rival MPEG-4 AVC – see VC-1.

WP 4B ITU Study Group which undertakes studies specifically relating to satellite newsgathering.

WP Working Party (ITU).

WRC World Administrative Radiocommunication Conference: regular summit conference for the ITU-R. After 1992, renamed World Radiocommunications Conference.

WTA World Teleport Association.

WTDC World Telecommunication Development Conference: the regular summit conference for the ITU-D.

WTO World Trade Organization (UN).

WTSC World Telecommunication Standardization Conference: regular summit conference for the ITU-T.

WWW World Wide Web (Internet).

X polarization Vertical polarization – the linear geometric plane in which the electromagnetic signals are transmitted.

X.21 Serial communications interface standard (ITU-T standard).

X.25 Data packet-switching standard (ITU-T standard).

XPD Cross-polar discrimination.

XPI Cross-polar interference.

Y polarization Horizontal polarization – the linear geometric plane in which the electromagnetic signals are transmitted.

Zone beam C-band equivalent of Ku-band widebeam, with high gain covering a smaller area.

Bibliography

General interest: Newsgathering

Arnett, P. (1994) *Live From The Battlefield*. Bloomsbury Press.
Bell, M. (1996) *In Harm's Way*. Penguin Books.
Gall, S. (1994) *News From The Front*. Heinemann.
Simpson, J. (1999) *Strange Places, Questionable People*. Pan.

Satellite communications engineering

Evans, B. (ed.) (1999) *Satellite Communication Systems*. Inspec/IEE.
Gordon, G.D. and Morgan, W.L. (1993) *Principles of Communication Satellites*. John Wiley.
Maral, G. and Bousquet, M. (2002) *Satellite Communications Systems: Systems, Techniques and Technology*. John Wiley.
Morgan, W. and Gordon, G. (1989) *Communications Satellite Handbook*. John Wiley.
Pratt, T. and Bostian, C. (2003) *Satellite Communications*. Wiley.

Digital compression

Richardson, I.E.G. (2003) *H.264 and MPEG-4*. Wiley.
Symes, P. (2004) *Digital Video Compression*. McGraw Hill.
Watkinson, J. (2004) *The MPEG Handbook*. Focal Press.

Papers

Knee, M. (2006) *MPEG Video*; Snell & Wilcox; www.snellwilcox.com.
Morello, A. and Mignone, V. (2004) *DVB-S2 – Ready for Lift Off* EBU Technical Review 300; www.ebu.org.
Strachan, D. (1996) *SMPTE Tutorial: Video Compression, SMPTE*; www.smpte.org.
Tudor, P.N. (BBC) (1995) MPEG-2 video compression. *IEE Electronics and Communications Engineering Journal*, December, 257–264; www.bbc.co.uk/rd.

Index